SAVAGE MESSIAH

SAVAGE MESSIAH

LAURA GRACE FORD

VERSO
London • New York

This new and updated edition first published
by Verso 2019
First published by Verso 2011
© Laura Grace Ford 2011, 2019
Introduction © Mark Fisher 2011, 2019
Preface © Greil Marcus 2019

1 3 5 7 9 10 8 6 4 2

Verso
UK: 6 Meard Street, London W1F 0EG
US: 20 Jay Street, Suite 1010, Brooklyn, NY 11201
www.versobooks.com

Verso is the imprint of New Left Books

ISBN-13: 978-1-78663-785-7

British Library Cataloguing in Publication Data
A catalogue record for this book is available from the
British Library

Library of Congress Cataloging-in-Publication Data
A catalog record for this book is available from the
Library of Congress

Typeset by MJ Gavan, Truro, Cornwall
Printed and bound by CPI Group (UK) Ltd,
Croydon, CR0 4YY

PREFACE

From 2006 through 2009, Laura Grace Ford produced the
issues of the fanzine collected here. Altogether (and
it is altogether, with Ford's work perhaps finding a
truer home between these covers than as haphazardly
distributed, thrown away, or picked up and then read
and then discarded again) hundreds of pages of text,
maps, flat drawings of vague faces, and cumulatively
riveting photos of architectural detritus – roads,
graffiti, housing blocks, filthy courtyards, store-
fronts, overgrown building sites, almost all of them
utterly depopulated – chronicling a long walk through
the back alleys and abandoned patches of a London
remade through Thatcherist and New Labour gentrification and the evictions and new constructions of the
then-looming 2012 Olympics. Read straight through,
Ford's work is the most convincing follow-through
there is on the project of poetic urban-renewal
inaugurated by the situationists Guy Debord, Ivan
Chtcheglov, and Michèle Bernstein. In the early '50s,
they and a few other young layabouts began an explo-
ration of Paris as a city that ran according to its
own backward-forward-spinning clock, where an all-
night drift down the streets might so scramble time
that 1848 would exert a stronger spiritual gravity
than 1954. 'All cities are geological; you cannot
take three steps without encountering ghosts bearing
all the prestige of their legends', Chtcheglov wrote

in 1953 in 'Formulary for a New Urbanism', under the name Gilles Ivain. That could be his challenge; Ford proceeded as if she'd heard it.

   In places she echoes Ed Ruscha's 1966 photographic mapping of *Every Building on the Sunset Strip*; Nan Goldin's *The Ballad of Sexual Dependency*, her slide-show of bohemian sex and death in the 1980s; and the cityscape in Andrea Arnold's 2006 film *Red Road*, where, in a decaying Glasgow, foxes dart around the bases of apartment buildings that are corroding from the inside. On any given page, Thomas De Quincey, from his 1821 *Confessions of an English Opium-Eater*, might be holding Ford's hand: 'I could almost have believed, at times, that I must be the first discoverer of some of these *terrae incognitae*, and doubted whether they had yet been laid down in the modern charts of London.'

   Number by number, *Savage Messiah* is a delirious, doomstruck celebration of squats, riots, vandalism, isolation, alcohol, and sex with strangers, all on the terrain of a half-historical, half-imaginary city that the people who Ford follows, herself at the center, can at times believe they built themselves, and can tear down as they choose. The past is a shadow, an angel, a demon: most of what Ford recounts seems to be taking place in the '70s or the '80s or the '90s, with the first decade of the twenty-first century a kind of slag-heap of time – of boredom, enervation, despair, and hate – that people are trying to burrow out from under. '1973, 1974, 1981, 1990, 2013', she chants on one page. 'Always a return. A Mirror touch. A different way out.' 'Queen's Crescent is the nexus of knife crime, a flashing matrix of Sheffield steel', Ford writes in *Savage Messiah* #6, in lines that could be from the first draft of the Clash's 'This Is England', their shattering last gasp from 1985, '...suspended', Ford goes on, years now signifying no specific time but a sense of time passing, 'somewhere between 1968 and 1981, and I sense my darling there, on the corner of Bassett St and Allcroft Road. I'm searching the brickwork with dusty fingertips for the first Sex Pistols graffiti of 1976. He was here then, and possibly now, we drift in circles around each other' – and answering herself on the facing page: 'In the fabric of the architecture you can always uncover traces and palimpsests, the poly-temporality of the city. As I lay my palm flat against the wall I grasp past texts never fully erasing the traces of earlier inscriptions.'

'We move within a *closed* landscape whose land-marks constantly draw us toward the past', Chtcheglov wrote, as if answering Ford in advance. 'Certain *shifting* angles, certain *receding* perspectives, allow us to glimpse original conceptions of space, but this vision remains fragmentary. It must be sought in the magical locales of fairy tales and surrealist writings: castles, endless walls, little forgotten bars, mammoth caverns, casino mirrors.' Chtcheglov is tracing Ford's method: as she walks past endless walls, they are covered with casino mirrors. Everything appears, with the most squalid glamorized by the passion of the walker's gaze. And in this sense, Ford joins other familiars (not the celebrated flâneur, but someone much more careful, storing details in a notebook or in the memory): the surrealist Louis Aragon in 1926, traversing the Passage de l'Opéra in *Paris Peasant*, or Walter Ben-jamin in Berlin, taking two years, from 1924 to 1926, to explore the length of a single, half-imagined one-way street in his *Einbahnstrasse*.

Benjamin was looking for what he called 'the revolutionary energies that appear in the "out-moded"' – the way the impulse toward utopia can embed itself in the design of a doorknob, the way a discarded bicycle part can speak, and tell the listener, Aragon or Benjamin or Chtcheglov or Ford as he or she walks by, 'I'm not satisfied.'

On Ford's long walk, the aura of a mystical quest hovers over even the most sordid incidents, the ugliest photos of belongings piled up at the foot of an apartment block. John Legend's 'Ordinary People' is on the jukebox: 'And all the guilt I harboured, all the shame, the walk around Highbury with so much hanging in the balance, tyranny of choice and the crashing cruelty of desire, it was all locked into that one anodyne song.' It is all here in this unlocked book.

Greil Marcus
2019

INTRODUCTION

'Always Yearning for the Time That Just Eluded Us'

'I regard my work as diaristic; the city can be read as a palimpsest, of layers of erasure and overwriting,' Laura Grace Ford has said. 'The need to document the transient and ephemeral nature of the city is becoming increasingly urgent as the process of enclosure and privatisation continues apace.' The city in question is of course London, and *Savage Messiah* offers a samizdat counter-history of the capital during the period of neoliberal domination. If *Savage Messiah* is 'diaristic', it is also much more than a memoir. The stories of Ford's own life necessarily bleed into the stories of others, and it is impossible to see the joins. 'This decaying fabric, this unknowable terrain has become my biography, the euphoria then the anguish, layers of memories colliding, splintering and reconfiguring.' The perspective Ford adopts, the voices she speaks in – and which speak through her – are those of the officially defeated: the punks, squatters, ravers, football hooligans and militants left behind by a history which has ruthlessly Photoshopped them out of its finance-friendly SimCity. *Savage Messiah* uncovers another city, a city in the process of being buried,

and takes us on a tour of its landmarks: The Isle of
Dogs ... The Elephant ... Westway ... Lea Bridge ...
North Acton ... Canary Wharf ... Dalston ... King's
Cross ... Hackney Wick ...

   In one of many echoes of punk culture, Ford calls
Savage Messiah a 'zine'. She began producing it in
2005, eight years into a New Labour government that
had consolidated rather than overturned Thatcherism.
The context is bleak. London is a conquered city;
it belongs to the enemy. 'The translucent edifices
of Starbucks and Costa Coffee line these shimmering promenades, "young professionals" sit outside
gently conversing in sympathetic tones.' The dom-
inant mood is one of restoration and reaction, but
it calls itself modernisation, and it calls its
divisive and exclusionary work – making London safe
for the super-rich – *regeneration*. The struggle over
space is also a struggle over time and who controls it. Resist neoliberal modernisation and (so we
are told) you consign yourself to the past. *Savage
Messiah*'s London is overshadowed by the looming
megalith of 'London 2012', which over the course of
the last decade has subsumed more and more of the
city into its banal science fiction telos, as the
Olympic Delivery Authority transformed whole areas
of East London into a temporary photo opportunity
for global capitalism. Where once there were 'fridge
mountains and abandoned factories' out of Tarkovsky
and Ballard, a semi-wilderness in the heart of the
city, now a much blander desert grows: spaces for
wandering are eliminated, making way for shopping
malls and soon-to-be-abandoned Olympic stadia. 'When
I was writing the zines,' Ford remembers, 'I was
drifting through a London haunted by traces and
remnants of rave, anarcho-punk scenes and hybrid
subcultures at a time when all these incongruous
urban regeneration schemes were happening. The

idea that I was moving through a spectral city was
really strong, it was as if everything prosaic and
dull about the New Labour version of the city was
being resisted by these ghosts of brutalist architecture, of '90s convoy culture, rave scenes, '80s
political movements and a virulent black economy of
scavengers, peddlers and shoplifters. I think the
book could be seen in the context of the aftermath
of an era, where residues and traces of euphoric
moments haunt a melancholy landscape.'

All of these traces are to be eliminated from the
Restoration London that will be celebrated at London
2012. With their lovingly reproduced junk-strata,
overgrowing vegetation and derelict spaces, *Savage
Messiah*'s images offer a direct riposte to the slick
digital images which the Olympic Delivery Authority
has pasted up in the now heavily policed, restricted
and surveilled Lee Valley. Blair's Cool Britannia
provides the template for an anodyne vision of London
designed by the 'creative industries'. Everything
comes back as an advertising campaign. It isn't just
that the alternatives are written over, or out, it
is that they return as their own simulacra. A familiar story. Take the Westway, West London's formerly
deplored dual carriageway, once a cursed space to
be mythologised by Ballard, punks and Chris Petit,
now just another edgy film set:

> This liminal territory, cast in a negative light in
> the 70s was recuperated by MTV and boring media types
> in the 90s. The Westway became the backdrop for Goril-
> laz imbecility, bland drum & bass record sleeves and
> photo shoots in corporate skate parks.
>
> Cool Britannia. Old joke.
>
> 'Space' becomes the over arching commodity. Notting
> Hill. New Age cranks peddling expensive junk. Homeo-
> pathy and boutiques, angel cards and crystal healing.

Media and high finance on the one hand, faux-mysticism
and superstition on the other: all the strategies of
the hopeless and those who exploit them in Restoration
London ... Space is indeed the commodity here. A
trend that started thirty years ago, and intensified
as council housing was sold off and not replaced,
culminated in the insane super-inflation of property
prices in the first years of the twenty-first century.
If you want a simple explanation for the growth in
cultural conservatism, for London's seizure by the
forces of Restoration, you need look no further than
this. As Jon Savage points out in *England's Dreaming*,
the London of punk was still a bombed-out city, full
of chasms, caverns, spaces that could be temporarily
occupied and squatted. Once those spaces are enclosed,
practically all of the city's energy is put into
paying the mortgage or the rent. There's no time
to experiment, to journey without already knowing
where you will end up. Your aims and objectives
have to be stated up front. 'Free time' becomes
convalescence. You turn to what reassures you, what
will most refresh you for the working day: the old
familiar tunes (or what sound like them). London
becomes a city of pinched-face drones plugged into
iPods.

Savage Messiah rediscovers the city as a site for
drift and daydreams, a labyrinth of side streets and
spaces resistant to the process of gentrification
and 'development' set to culminate in the miserable hyper-spectacle of 2012. The struggle here is
not only over the (historical) direction of time
but over different uses of time. Capital demands
that we always look busy, even if there's no work
to do. If neoliberalism's magical voluntarism is to
be believed, there are always opportunities to be
chased or created; any time not spent hustling and
hassling is time wasted. The whole city is forced
into a gigantic simulation of activity, a fantacism

of productivism in which nothing much is actually produced, an economy made out of hot air and bland delirium. *Savage Messiah* is about another kind of delirium: the releasing of the pressure to be yourself, the slow unravelling of biopolitical identity, a depersonalised journey out to the erotic city that exists alongside the business city. The eroticism here is not primarily to do with sexuality, although it sometimes includes it: it is an art of collective enjoyment, in which a world beyond work can – however briefly – be glimpsed and grasped. Fugitive time, lost afternoons, conversations that dilate and drift like smoke, walks that have no particular direction and go on for hours, free parties in old industrial spaces, still reverberating days later. The movement between anonymity and encounter can be very quick in the city. Suddenly, you are off the street and into someone's life-space. Sometimes, it's easier to talk to people you don't know. There are fleeting intimacies before we melt back into the crowd, but the city has its own systems of recall: a block of flats or a street you haven't focused on for a long time will remind you of people you met only once, years ago. Will you ever see them again?

I got invited up for a cup of tea in one of those Tecton flats on the Harrow road, one of the old men from the day centre I work in. I took him up Kilburn High Road shopping and watered the fuchsias on his balcony. We talked about the Blitz and hospitals mostly. He used to be a scientist and wrote shopping lists on brown envelopes dated and filed in a stack of biscuit tins.

I miss him.

I miss them all.

Savage Messiah deploys anachronism as a weapon. At first sight, at first touch – and tactility is crucial

to the experience: the zine doesn't feel the same
when it's JPEGed on screen – *Savage Messiah* seems
like something familiar. The form itself, the mix
of photographs, typeface-text and drawings, the use
of scissors and glue rather than digital cut and
paste; all of this make *Savage Messiah* seem out of
time, which is not to say out of date. There were
deliberate echoes of the para-art found on punk
and postpunk record sleeves and fanzines from the
1970s and 1980s. Most insistently, I'm reminded of
Gee Vaucher, who produced the paradoxically photo-
realistically delirious record covers and posters for
anarcho-punk collective Crass. 'I think with the look
of the zine I was trying to restore radical politics
to an aesthetic that had been rendered anodyne by
advertising campaigns, Shoreditch club nights etc.,'
Ford says. 'That anarcho-punk look was everywhere
but totally emptied of its radical critique. It
seemed important to go back to that moment of the
late '70s and early '80s to a point where there was
social upheaval, where there were riots and strikes,
exciting cultural scenes and ruptures in the fabric
of everyday life.' The return to the postpunk moment
is the route to an alternative present. Yet this is
a return only to a certain ensemble of styles and
methods – nothing quite like *Savage Messiah* actually
existed back then.

Savage Messiah is a gigantic, unfinished collage,
which – like the city – is constantly reconfiguring itself. Macro- and micro-narratives proliferate
tuberously; spidery slogans recur; figures migrate
through various versions of London, sometimes
trapped inside the drearily glossy spaces imagined by
advertising and regeneration propaganda, sometimes
free to drift. She deploys collage in much the same
way William Burroughs used it: as a weapon in time-
war. The cut-up can dislocate established narratives,
break habits, allow new associations to coalesce. In

Savage Messiah, the seamless, already-established capitalist reality of London dissolves into a riot of potentials.

  Savage Messiah is written for those who could not be regenerated, even if they wanted to be. They are the unregenerated, a lost generation, 'always yearning for the time that just eluded us': those who were born too late for punk but whose expectations were raised by its incendiary afterglow; those who watched the Miner's Strike with partisan adolescent eyes but who were too young to really participate in the militancy; those who experienced the future-rush euphoria of rave as their birthright, never dreaming that it could burn out like fried synapses; those, in short, who simply did not find the 'reality' imposed by the conquering forces of neoliberalism liveable. It's adapt or die, and there are many different forms of death available to those who can't pick up the business buzz or muster the requisite enthusiasm for the creative industries. Six million ways to die, choose one: drugs, depression, destitution. So many forms of catatonic collapse. In earlier times, 'deviants, psychotics and the mentally collapsed' inspired militant-poets, situationists, rave-dreamers. Now they are incarcerated in hospitals, or languishing in the gutter.

  No Pedestrian Access To Shopping Centre

Still, the mood of *Savage Messiah* is far from hopeless. It's not about caving in, it's about different strategies for surviving the deep midwinter of Restoration London. People living on next to nothing, no longer living the dream, but not giving up either: 'Five years since the last party but he held his plot, scavenging for food like a Ballardian crash victim.' You can go into suspended animation, knowing that the time is not yet right, but waiting

with cold reptile patience until it is. Or you can
flee dystopian London without ever leaving the city,
avoiding the central business district, finding
friendly passages through the occupied territory,
picking your way through the city via cafes, comrade's
flats, public parks. *Savage Messiah* is an inventory
of such routes, such passages through 'territories
of commerce and control'.

The zines are saturated in music culture. First of
all, there are the names of groups: Infa Riot and
Blitz. Fragments of Abba, Heaven 17 on the radio.
Japan, Rudimentary Peni, Einsturzende Neubauten,
Throbbing Gristle, Spiral Tribe. Whether the groups
are sublime or sub-charity shop undesirable, these
litanies have an evocative power that is quietly
lacerating. Gig posters from thirty years ago – Mob,
Poison Girls, Conflict – call up older versions of
you, half-forgotten haircuts, long-lost longings,
stirring again. But the role of music culture goes
much deeper in *Savage Messiah*. The way the zine is
put together owes as much to the rogue dance and
drug cultures that mutated from rave as to punk fanzines; its montage methodology has as much in common
with the DJ mix as with any precursor in visual
culture. *Savage Messiah* is also about the relationship between music and place: the zine is also a
testament to the way in which the sensitive membranes
of the city are reshaped by music.

This sombre place is haunted by the sounds of lost acid
house parties and the distant reverberations of 1986.
Test Department . 303. 808. Traces of industrial noise.

The roundhouse was easy to get into, and the depot
itself, disused for years is lit up with tags and dubs.

You can hear these deserted places, feel the tendrils
creeping across the abandoned caverns, the derelict
bunkers and broken terraces. Midsummer, blistering

heat under the concrete, Armagideon Time(s), a hidden
garden, to be found, and lost again.

Superficially, the obvious tag for *Savage Messiah*
would be psychogeography, but the label makes Ford
chafe. 'I think a lot of what is called psychogeography now is just middle-class men acting like
colonial explorers, showing us their discoveries and
guarding their plot. I have spent the last twenty
years walking around London and living here in a
precarious fashion, I've had about fifty addresses.
I think my understanding and negotiation of the city
is very different to theirs.' Rather than subsuming
Savage Messiah under the increasingly played-out
discourses of psychogeography, I believe it is better
understood as an example of a cultural coalescence
that started to become visible (and audible) at
the moment when Ford began to produce the zine:
hauntology. Towards the middle of the last decade,
Simon Reynolds and I started to use the concept
that Derrida coined in *Specters of Marx* to label
a series of – predominantly but not exclusively –
musical artists whose work expressed a sense of
broken time. The specters here were not so much
ghosts from an actual past; they were instead the
traces of futures that had never arrived but which
once seemed inevitable. The most striking sonic
parallel for *Savage Messiah* is the London audio-poet
Burial. Like *Savage Messiah*, Burial's music invokes
a sense of London after the rave: the long comedown
of night bus journeys, the keening pain of being
yourself again now that the collective ecstasy has
faded. This is London seen through the rheumy eyes
of ravers fifteen years on: the former warehouse
spaces where raves or free parties were held have
now disappeared behind redevelopment facades; the
old gang are married off, drug casualties or worse.
'The London I conjure up ... is imbued with a sense

of mourning,' Ford says. 'These are the liminal zones where the free party rave scene once illuminated the bleak swathes of marshland and industrial estates.' So many dreams of collectivity have died in neoliberal London. The brutalist tower blocks that feature on so many pages of *Savage Messiah* recall the abandoned promises of what Owen Hatherley has called militant modernism – a new kind of human being was supposed to live here, but that all had to be cleared away so that the restoration could begin.

Haunting is about a staining of place with particularly intense moments of time, and, like David Peace, with whom her work shares a number of affinities, Ford is alive to the poetry of dates. 1979, 1981, 2013: these years recur throughout *Savage Messiah*, moments of transition and threshold, moments when a whole alternative time-track opens. 2013 has a post-apocalyptic quality (in addition to being the year after the London Olympics, 2012 is also, according to some, the year that the Mayans predicted for the end of the world). But 2013 could also be Year Zero: the reversal of 1979, the time when all the cheated hopes and missed chances are finally realised. *Savage Messiah* invites us to see the contours of another world in the gaps and cracks of an occupied London:

> Perhaps it is here that the space can be opened up to forge a collective resistance to this neo liberal expansion, to the endless proliferation of banalities and the homogenising effects of globalization. Here in the burnt out shopping arcades, the boarded up precincts, the lost citadels of consumerism one might find the truth, new territories might be opened, there might be a rupturing of this collective amnesia.

Mark Fisher
2011

SAVAGE MESSIAH

SAVAGE MESSIAH

#1

UNCENSORED

7½P

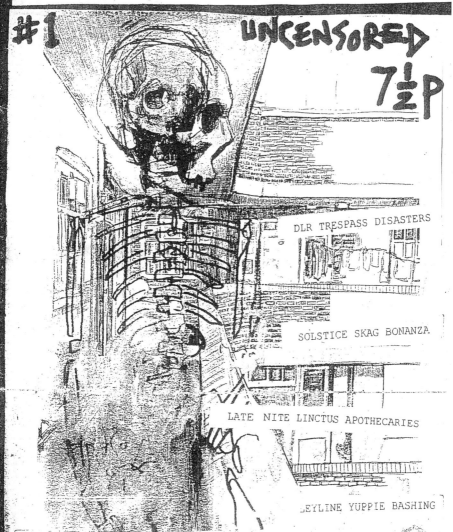

DLR TRESPASS DISASTERS

SOLSTICE SKAG BONANZA

LATE NITE LINCTUS APOTHECARIES

LEYLINE YUPPIE BASHING

WELCOME TO THE ISLE OF DOGS

ANARCHITECTURE WEEK JUNE 05

LAURA OLDFIELD FORD

2

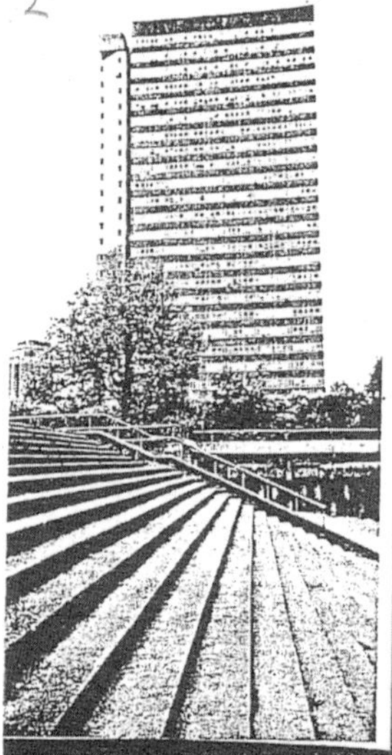

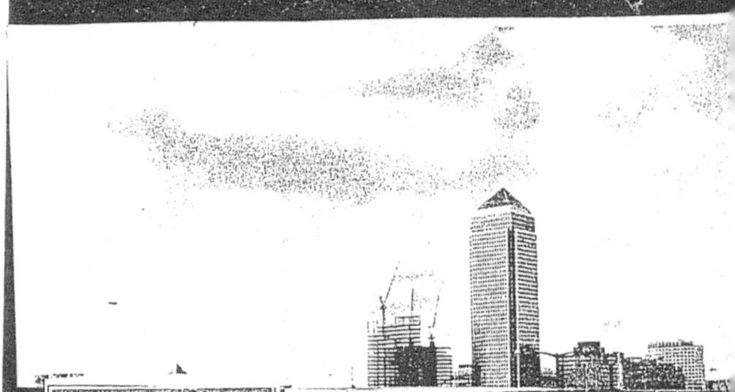

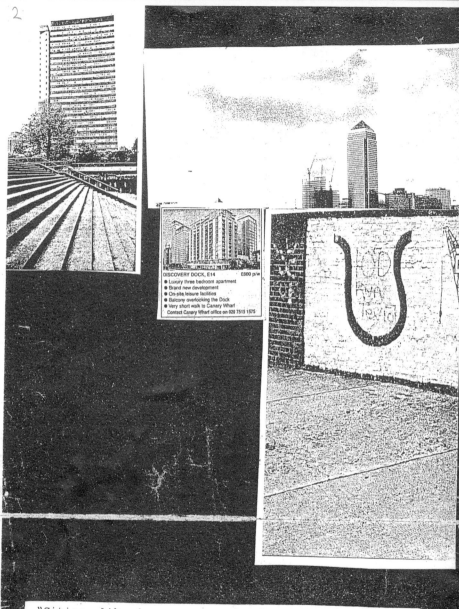

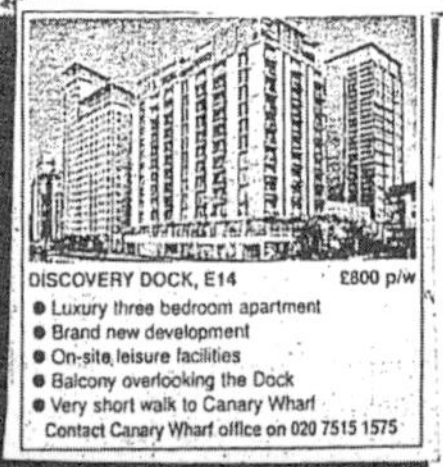
DISCOVERY DOCK, E14
£800 p/w
Luxury three bedroom apartment
Brand new development
On-site leisure facilities
Balcony overlooking the Dock
Very short walk to Canary Wharf
Contact Canary Wharf office on 020 7515 1575

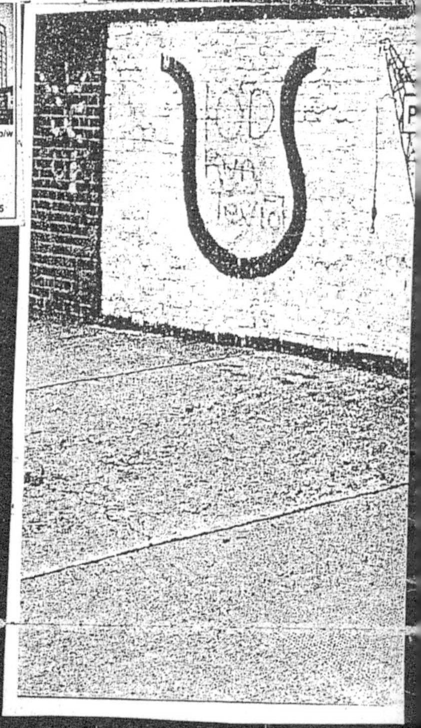

"Cities, like dreams, are made of desires and fears even if the thread of their discourse is secret, their rules are absurd, their perspectives deceitful and everything conceals something else."
Italo Calvino Invisible Cities.

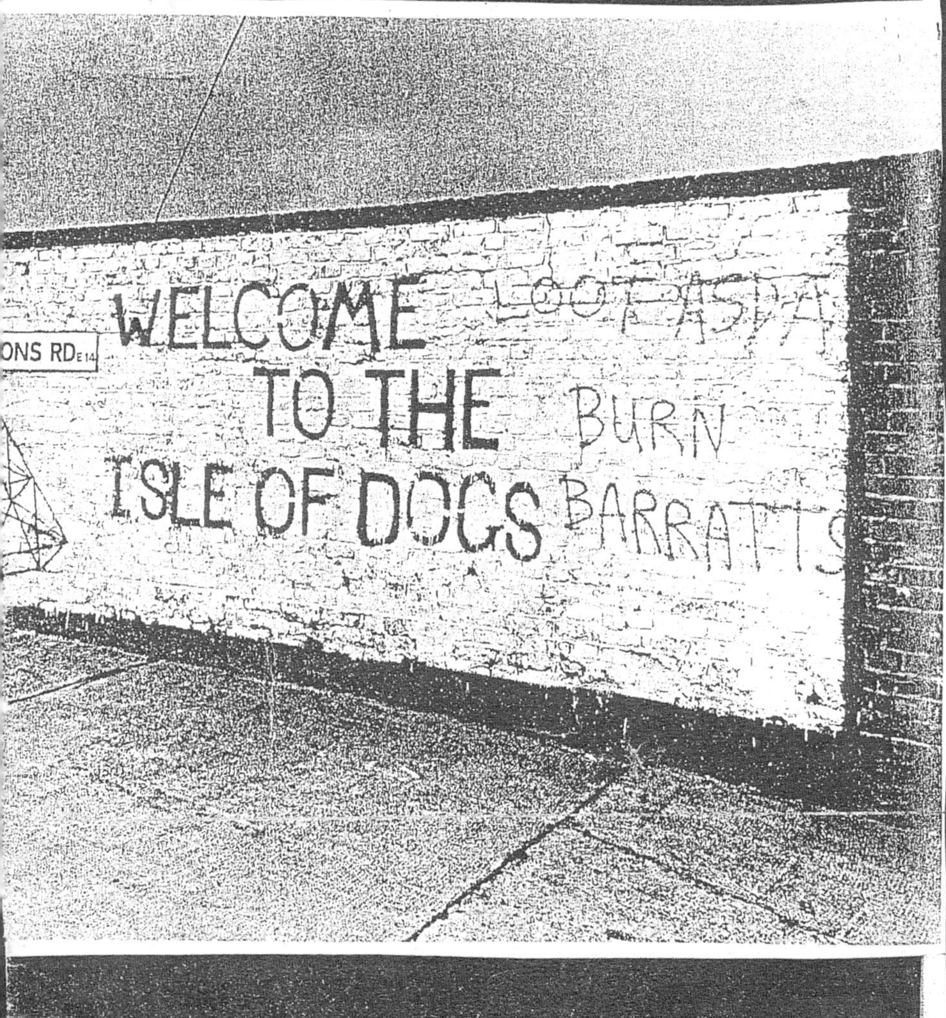
ONS RD E14
WELCOME
TO THE
ISLE OF DOGS
BURN
BARRATTS

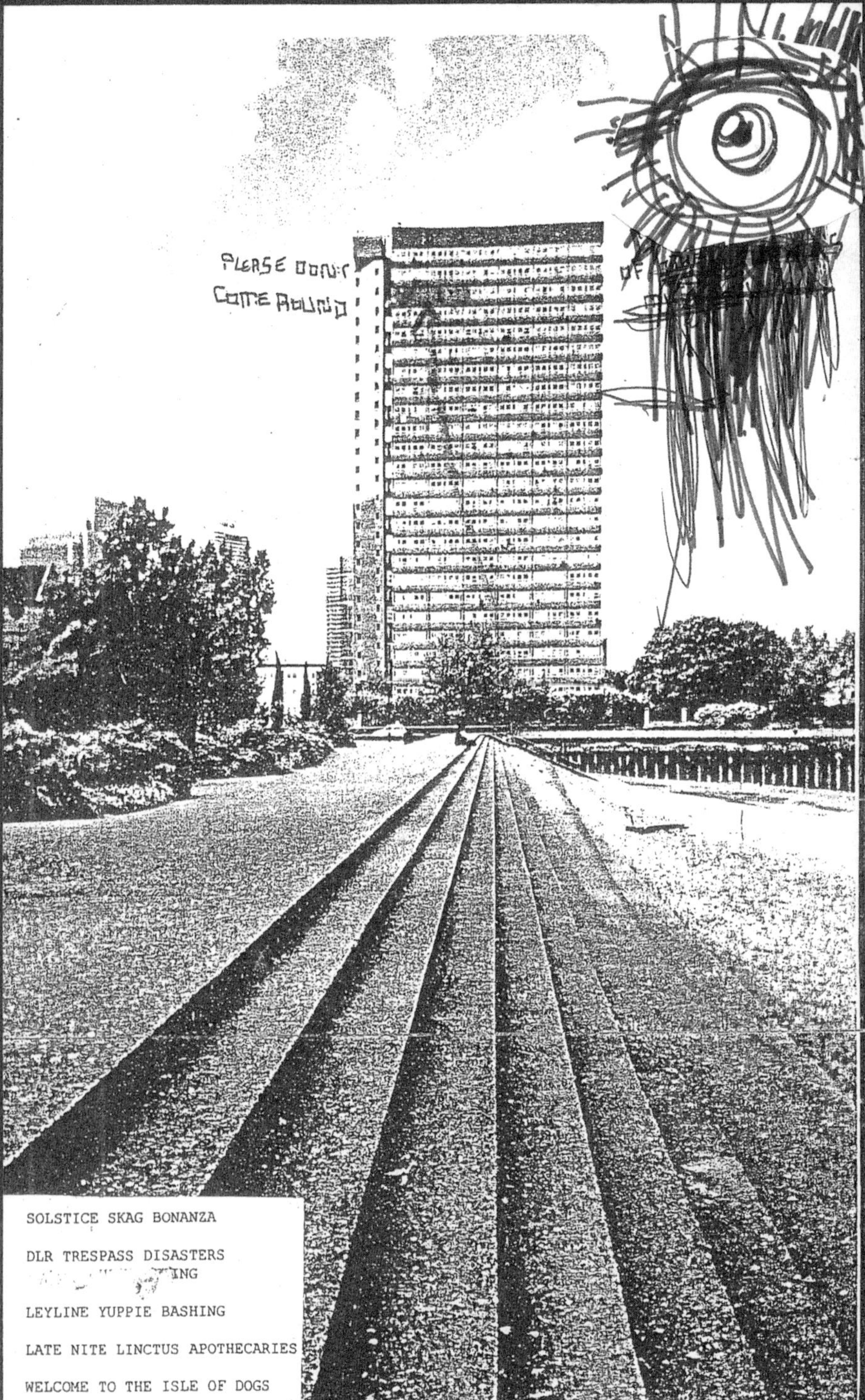
PLEASE DON'T
COME ROUND
SOLSTICE SKAG BONANZA
DLR TRESPASS DISASTERS
ING
LEYLINE YUPPIE BASHING
LATE NITE LINCTUS APOTHECARIES
WELCOME TO THE ISLE OF DOGS
7777777777777777777777777777777

ILL RANTING

~~WE HATE HUMANS~~

WE HATE HUMANS.

Panic in the streets.
Jesus Christ they've done it.
Room of maps, circles drawn in red felt tip.
Cascades.
Pound shop with baubles, tinsel, shrieking santas. We break in.
To a lower room. Fall through trap doors, palletes leading down a grey corridor
to another shop.

Pylons melted. Grey blankets dragging bundles of clothes, binliners.
Ultra violet light.
Radio news.
There's something coming.

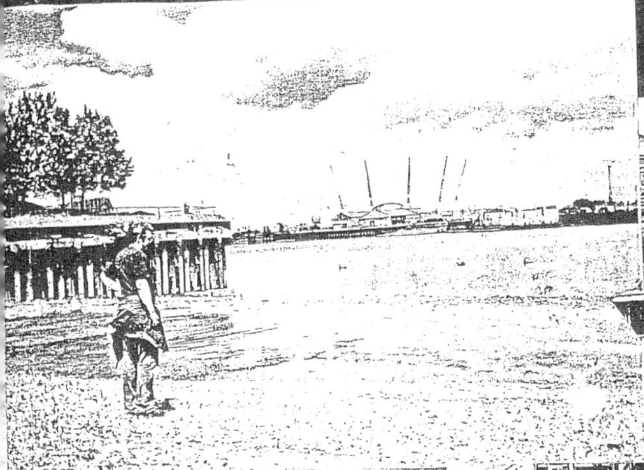

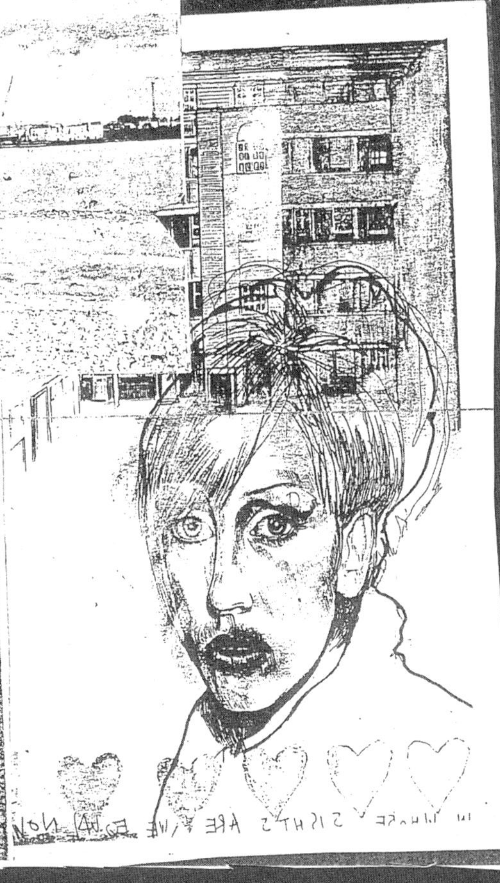

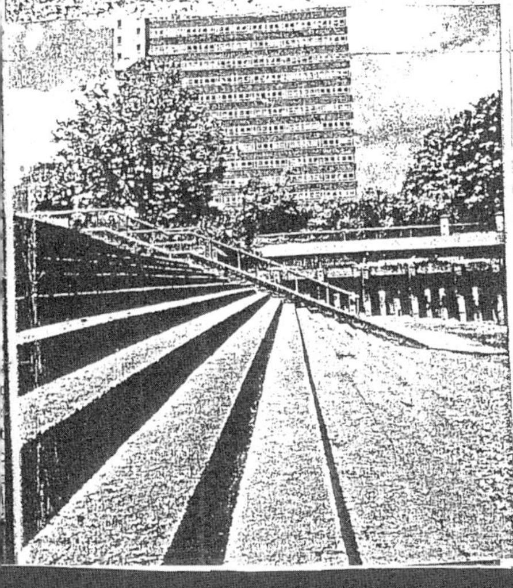

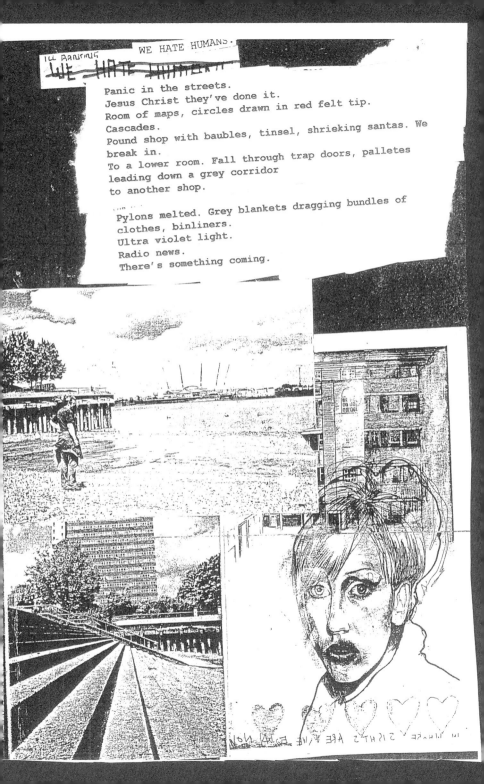

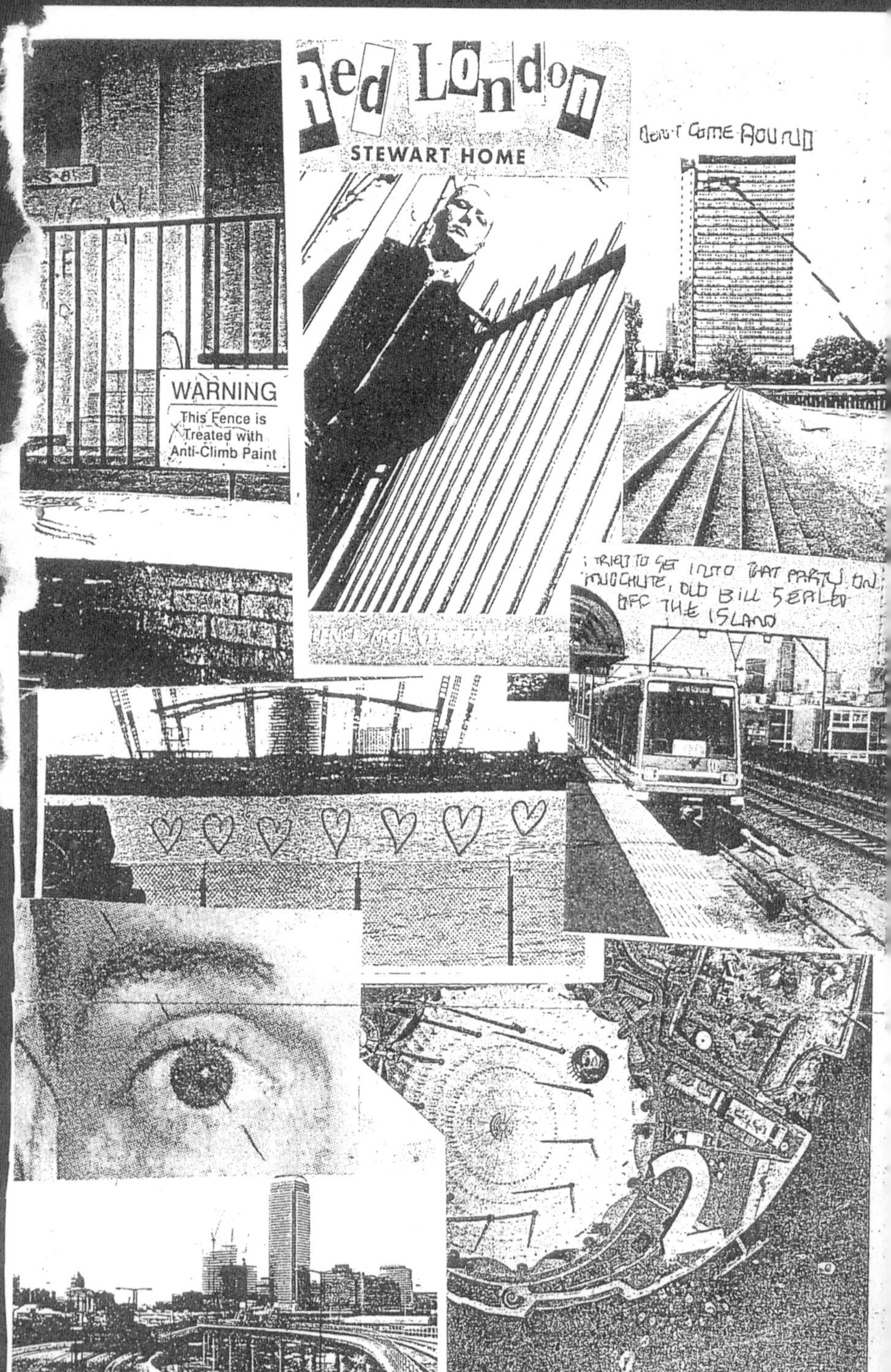

Red London
STEWART HOME
DON'T COME AROUND
WARNING
This Fence is
Treated with
Anti-Climb Paint
I TRIED TO GET INTO THAT PARTY ON
MUDCHUTE, OLD BILL SEALED
OFF THE ISLAND
…oubled Millennium Dome will be sponsored by 02 and transformed

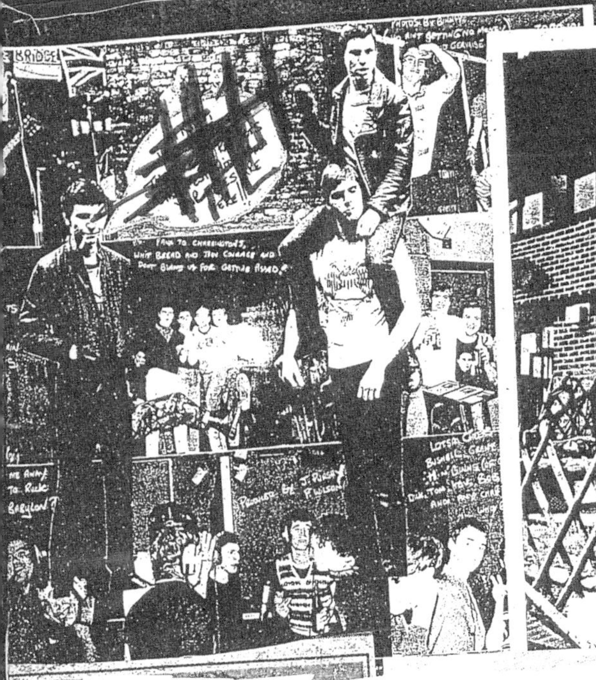

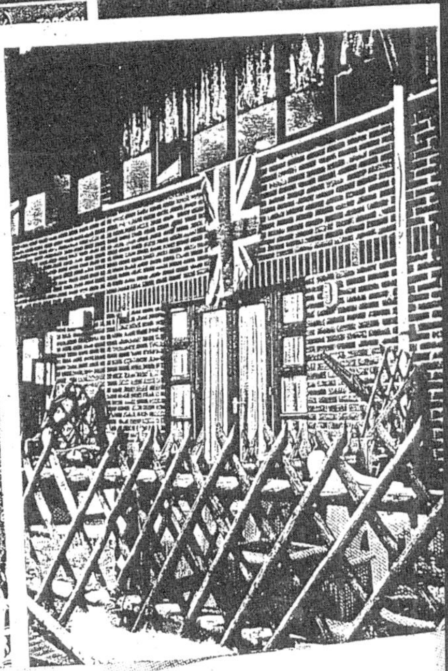

Walkways,
dusty mazes of loss and paranoia.
The Island. Leaching into silt lagoons, seeping and shifting.
E14.
The Samuda estate.
Kelson house. Fugitives hidden in upper chambers.
spatial disparities
walkways ghosting the dead docks.

After Broadwater the abolition of walkways intensifies. 1985 riots. Tottenham. Battle of Beanfield. Wapping and Warrington. Networks of connecting corridors with their potential for attack and surveillance. Elevated pavements feared by authorities, projectiles hurled, debris shattered on concrete floors.

Residues of contempt for 60s estates, blocking of access, gates and barriers…
police hatred, malarial swamp of souped up monkeys, criminal sub class.

We stand on a nameless beach, waiting for revenge. A flight of ceremonial steps leads to the foyer of Kelson House. Ghosts of miners, printers , travellers, seething hatred of Thatcher. Sultry July night. Wapping Highway. 1986 . Drawn by the lantern glow of that rose interior, cigarette smoke, glazed tiles, burnt sienna.

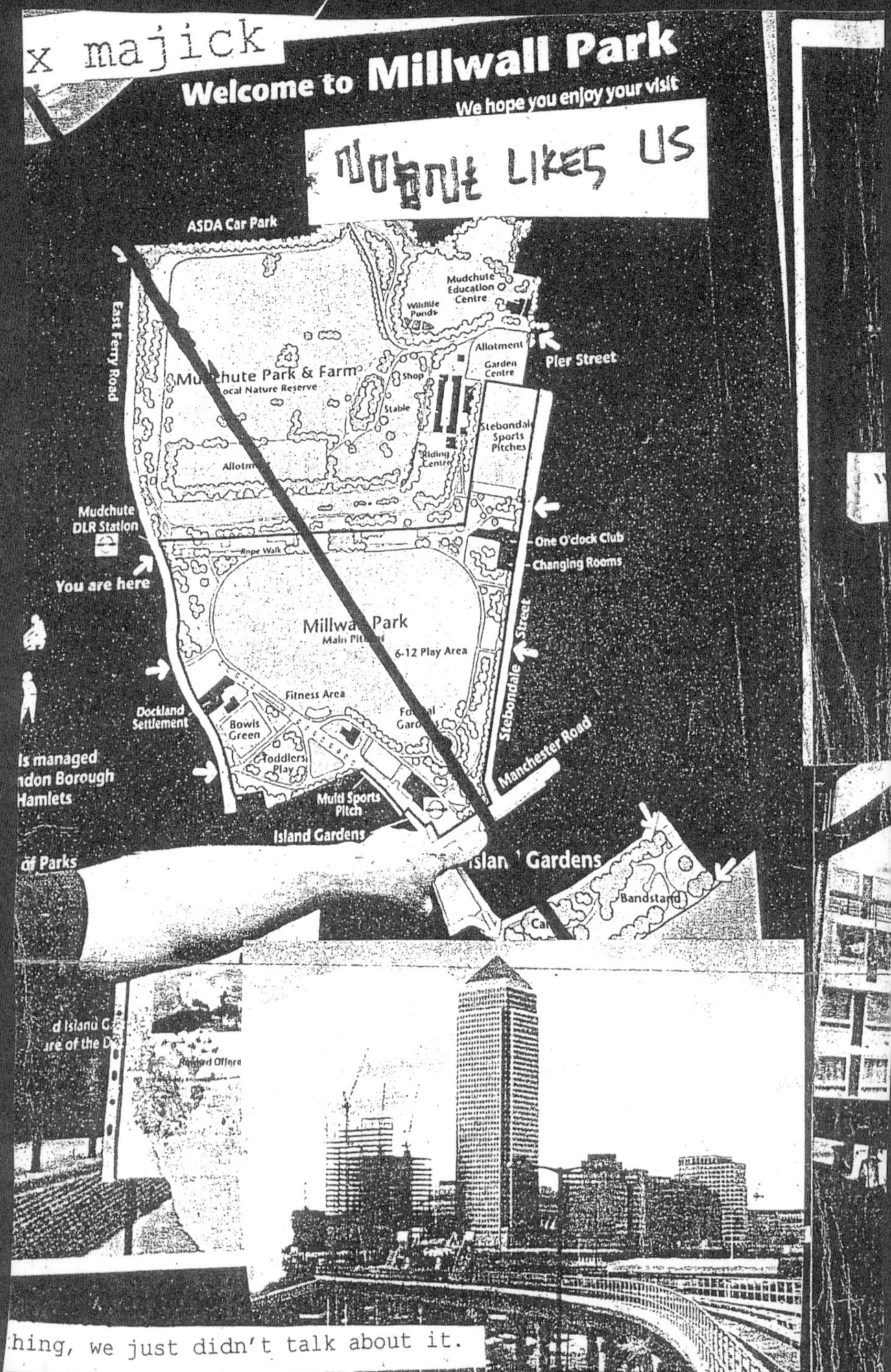

x majick

Welcome to **Millwall Park**

We hope you enjoy your visit

NOBODY LIKES US

ASDA Car Park

East Ferry Road

Mudchute Park & Farm
Local Nature Reserve

Mudchute
Education
Centre

Wildlife
Ponds

Allotment
Garden
Centre

Pier Street

Shop

Stable

Stebondale
Sports
Pitches

Riding
Centre

Allotment

Mudchute
DLR Station

You are here

Rope Walk

One O'clock Club

Changing Rooms

Millwall Park
Main Pitches

6-12 Play Area

Stebondale Street

Manchester Road

Dockland
Settlement

Fitness Area

Bowls
Green

Formal
Gardens

Toddlers
Play

Is managed
ndon Borough
Hamlets

Muld Sports
Pitch

Island Gardens

of Parks

Island Gardens

Bandstand

d Island G
are of the D

Reward Offers

hing, we just didn't talk about it.

Circle a gated enclave, a confusion of padlocks and
blank windows. Infantile 80s pastiche, grotesqueries of
riverside developments.. across the water the skulking
Dome.
Find traces of anti LDDC graff.
Bricks thrown at TNT lorries.

NO ONE LIKES US WE DON'T CARE.
Canary wharf, arrogant totem. That and a cluster of cap doffing
comforters. You look away and it's like mushrooms in a field,
they're suddenly there, springing up from nothing.
Masonic henge conjuring medieval Italy. Height and prestige,
riches stashed on the top floor. Enclosed courtyards.
Proto gated communities.
Canary wharf PLC, jealous controllers. No development allowed
higher than Tower One.
Canary Wharf symbolised a failure of 80s values, Olympia and
York, receivership and swathes of redundant computer terminals.
Now Blair takes Thatcher's project onto new and more audacious
levels.

Anxiety levels high before 9-11. There were checkpoints here
already. IRA had a go. Twice. The Tower and the South Quay.
1996, ring of steel around the complex, 100 million pounds
worth of damage.

Canary Wharf is built on Poplar Gut, it all sinks back to the
marshes.

Punk rock blaring from Reef House on the Samuda estate. Cockney
Rejects, window rattling volume. Sitting down to smoke amidst
the detritus of a light blocked living room.
//Solstice skag bonanza/
Round the headland, looping now, blocks emerging from woodland,
hazy in violet light. Filtered through an amethyst lens, Maze
Hill and Greenwich shimmering across the river.
Grand vistas unfolding. Greenwich Hospital. Palace of
Placentia.
Balmy summer night. Drinking in a beer garden beneath St
Alfege's , lilac shadows, orange street glow.
Honeysuckle, jasmine and rose.
Fire of London.

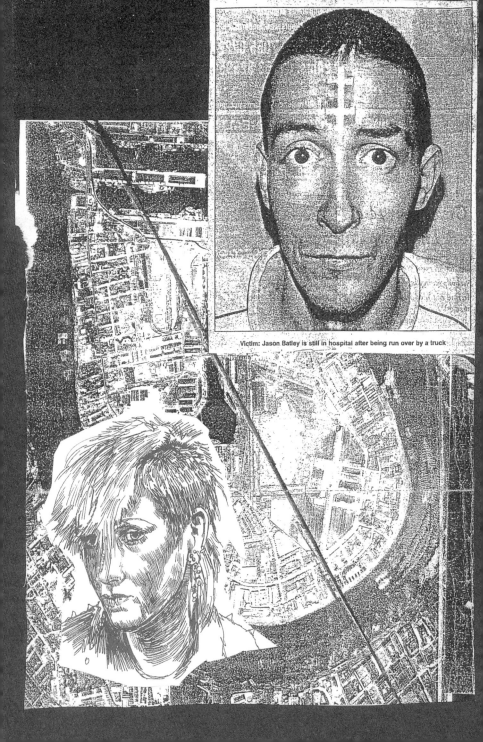

Victim: Jason Batley is still in hospital after being run over by a truck

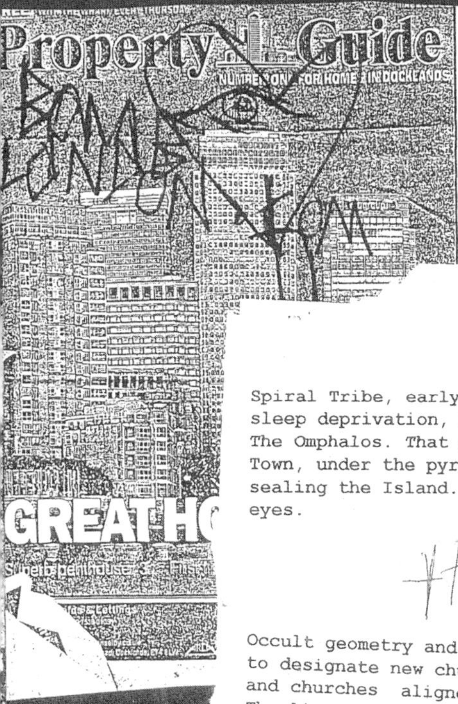
Property Guide
GREAT HO

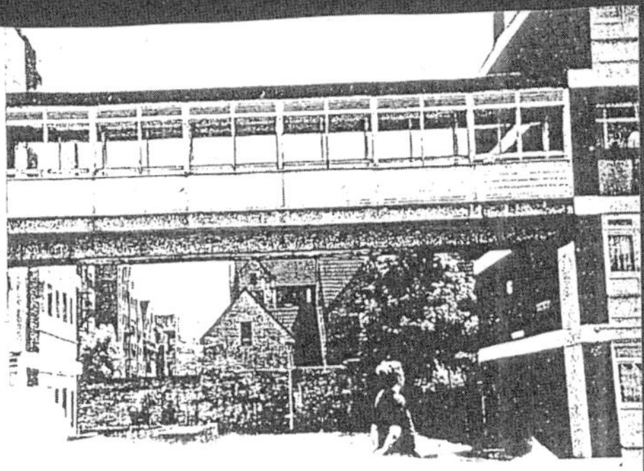

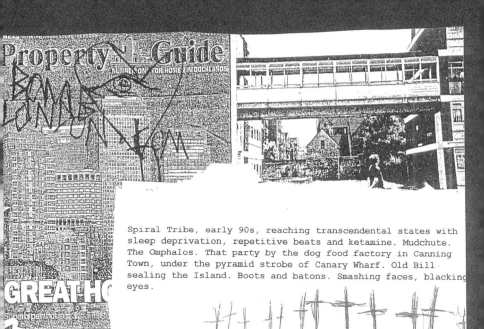

Spiral Tribe, early 90s, reaching transcendental states with sleep deprivation, repetitive beats and ketamine. Mudchute. The Omphalos. That party by the dog food factory in Canning Town, under the pyramid strobe of Canary Wharf. Old Bill sealing the Island. Boots and batons. Smashing faces, blacking eyes.

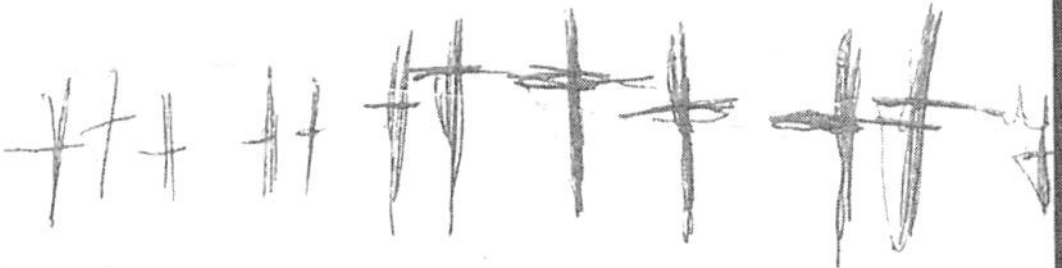

Occult geometry and architectural control. A commission set up to designate new churches. Wren and Hawksmoor. Naval College and churches aligned.
The line cuts through subatomic research at Queen Mary's College and the experimental malice of Throbbing Gristle in Martello street.
Island closed.

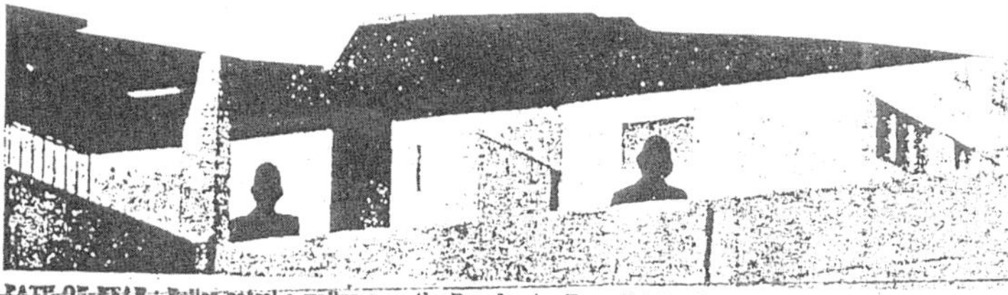

PATH OF FEAR: Police patrol a walkway on the Broadwater Farm Estate where the Tottenham riots erupted.

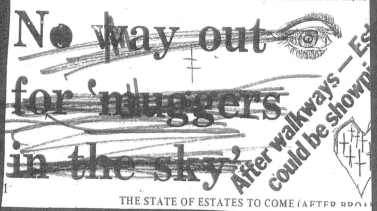

No way out for 'muggers in the sky'

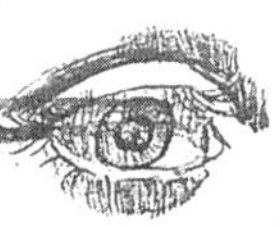

After walkways — Es…
could be showi…

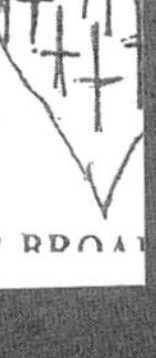

THE STATE OF ESTATES TO COME (AFTER BROA…

Pass the river portal, a silverfish edifice that tugs you
shivering under the murky Thames.
 Ferry House pub.
 An explosion of expletives. Dark beer stains,, cigarette
smoke unfurling. This is ENGLAND. Nexus of empire.
Bacchinelean revel, blood spattered walls and smashed glass.

Millwall Park. WE HATE HUMANS! The Den not here now, shoved
down Bermondsey, but the anger and hate remains, spat into
the fabric like fossilised webs.

Adrenalin   ,sharp intoxication, vodka and coke. Wapping
gentrification /industrial struggle,, explosions of Class hate
. Millwall crews rampaging,   constructions of menace,, steel
fencing , video cameras and barbed wire.

Isle of Dogs delivers conflict, we will not leave this
Island!'.' HItler couldn't get me out of Poplar,' incentive
schemes won't work ..
14 grand and a transfer to a Northern sink estate.

Got to be joking.
Heaps of bricks and stones.
NO MORE NEW HOMES FOR THE RICH!!
THE SAMUDA ESTATE, Wood Henge, an emblem of no future, of bio
degradable sinking into the dirt. 1985, solstice exclusion
zones , tactics from Orgreave shift to Wiltshire . Police road
blocks, fractured skulls and vehicles destroyed.

YUPPIES OUT!!!
 What they want for the Island is one big gated community, iri
scanning and ID cards to get in. You can't even walk down the
Thames without yuppie flats bundling out onto the landings/
PRIVATE PROPERTY KEEP OUT.

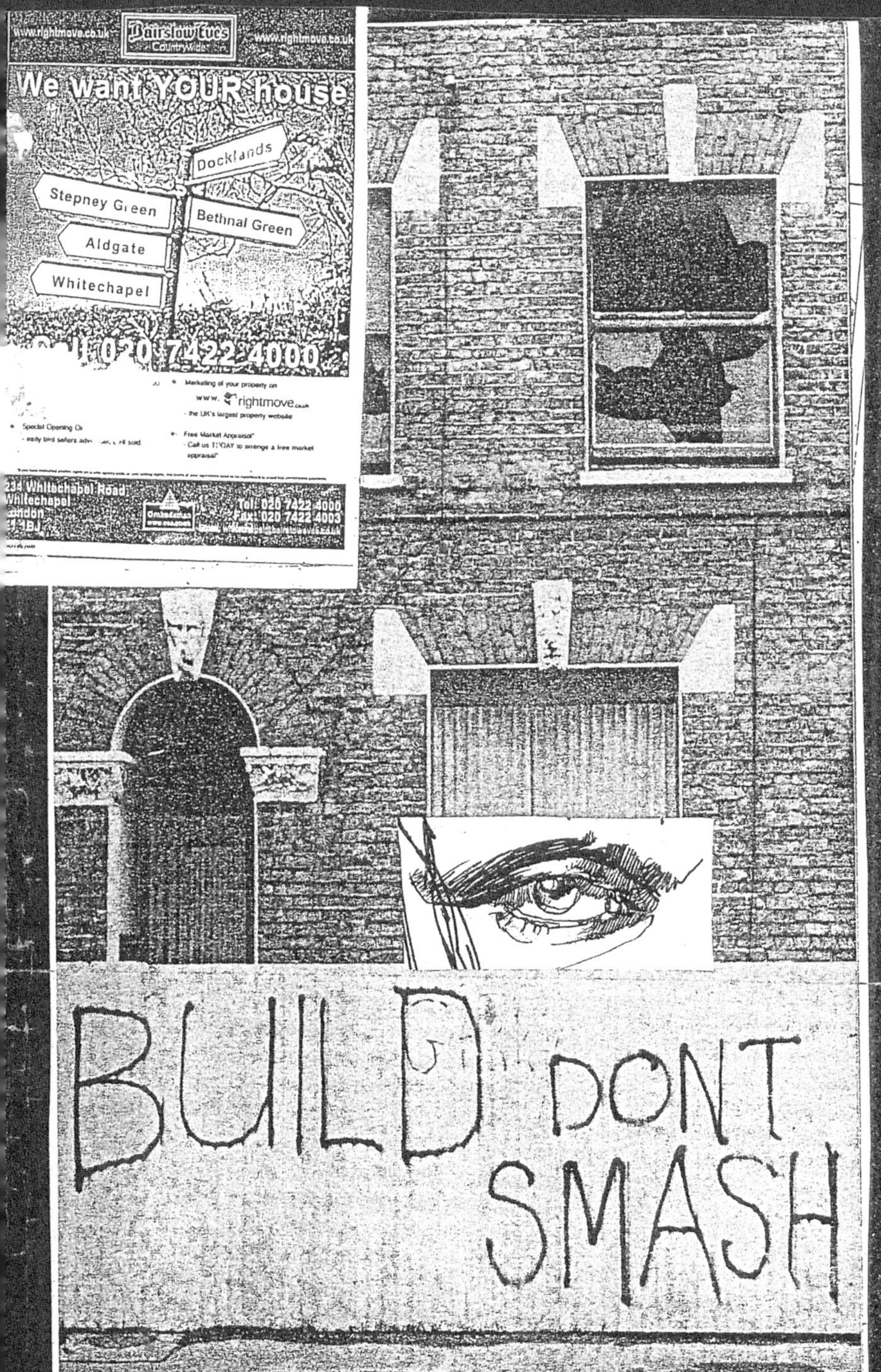

www.rightmove.co.uk
Bairstow Eves
CountryWide
www.rightmove.co.uk
We want YOUR house
Docklands
Stepney Green
Bethnal Green
Aldgate
Whitechapel
020 7422 4000
Marketing of your property on
www.rightmove.co.uk
the UK's largest property website
Free Market Appraisal
Tel: 020 7422 4000
Fax: 020 7422 4003
BUILD
DONT
SMASH

Cubitt Town. Eerie drum and bass emanating from an estate built in 1936 .

Photek, 'Hidden Camera'.

Canary Wharf, ghoulish needle, Thatcher's Britain, gleaming obelisks overseeing dilapidated streets.
Rigging and spars, landbridges and dungeons.
A confusion of space,

Daniel Asher Alexander and the jails of Dartmoor and Maidstone. Money and power, the air thick with a heady confection of cinnamon, tobacco and rotting wood.
De Quincey. Warm opiates. Verlaine and Rimbaud intoxicated by glyphs.

Dizziness, inner ear malfunction, swaying like I'm out at sea. Drawn in chamber after chamber, worlds and vistas unfolding like a computer game. Staggering through, level after level, clambering on with no thought to what lies above or below. I am drawn by curiosity and desire, to play the game for the sake of playing.

No 777 Commercial road. Masonic planning. Limehouse. Pale
authority of St Anne's, chalky pyramids replicating in the
shadows.
Sacrifice. The Accursed share. Back the Bid . Social
cleansing.

The Star of the East. Ghosts of opium dens. Pennyfields, the
Chinese quarter, Fan-Tan and Pak a Pu gambling shops, men with
Mandarin moustaches marking ledgers with camel hair brushes.
  Pogrommed out .,,
· burnt out of area in a vortex of moral panic and fear of
the white slave trade.
The last small streets to escape the Blitz and the wreckers
ball become fragments hidden in a maze of LCC blocks. East
India Dock road,, dark dilapidation,, blackened nets. Amoy
place,, corrugated alley of breezeblocks and bins.; Cherry
blossom and low rise maisonettes in Ming street.
And now the regeneration projects of Sylhet are where dreams
of the future are being made. Turmeric and cumin scent the
air.
 Backwards and forwards, other realms, a psychotic envelope of
human suffering and desire. Shadows green under orange street
lamps, the phosphorescent aura of a spectral tower.

 Post apocalyptic phantoms of stadia, overgrown velodromes,
the dome laid to waste under a convolvulus matrix. London
2013. Apotheosis of Thatcher's project, neo liberal
expansion, exurbia and the Thames Gateway. Hazily estuarial,
new towns not yet named, the reaches of Thurrock become an
invocation of America with Drive thru Macdonalds , luminous
clowns and an Ikea.
Blue eyes steely, a constructivist angle and a motorway bridge
set scene for encounters, bouts of malice and ultra violence.
My skin is bruised, purple and yellow, livid tattoos. He
lurches out of the Spar on Manchester road, post brawl tremor.
Once he was part of the Treatment, now he's on largactil and
only comes out once a day to buy tomato soup.

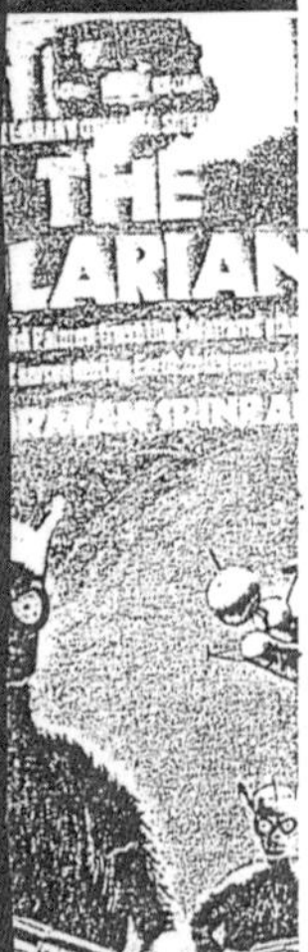
THE
LARIAN

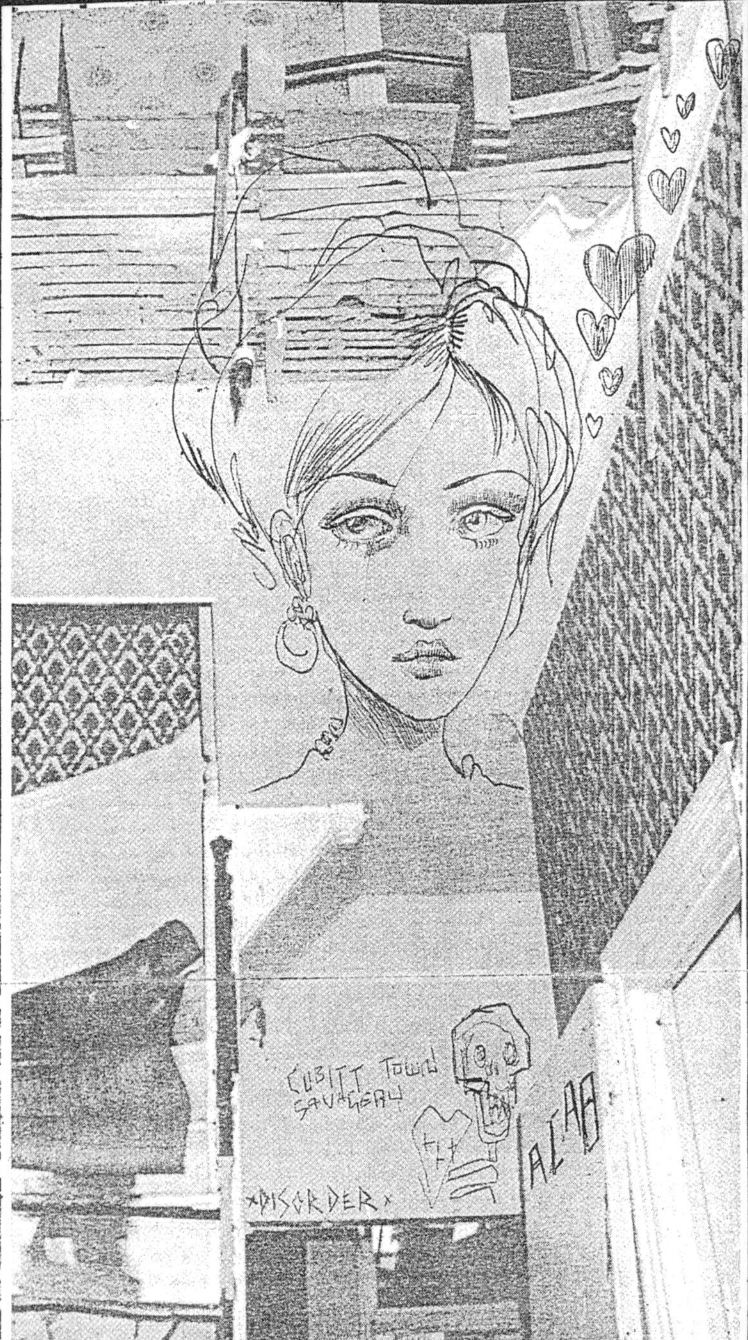
CUBITT TOWN SAVAGERY
xDISORDERx

SOLSTICE SKAG BONANZA
77777777777777777777777777

~~A tale of blissed out debauchery and sex majick~~
~~pixies~~ ~~floor of a tower block~~
~~A ch~~

An

ce encounter on Commercial road, I think I've seen
your face before.
. We go up to the top floor and sit at your table,
there are pills and powders all arranged in patterns,
And biscuits and raisins,

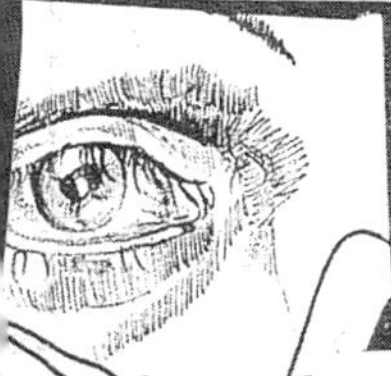

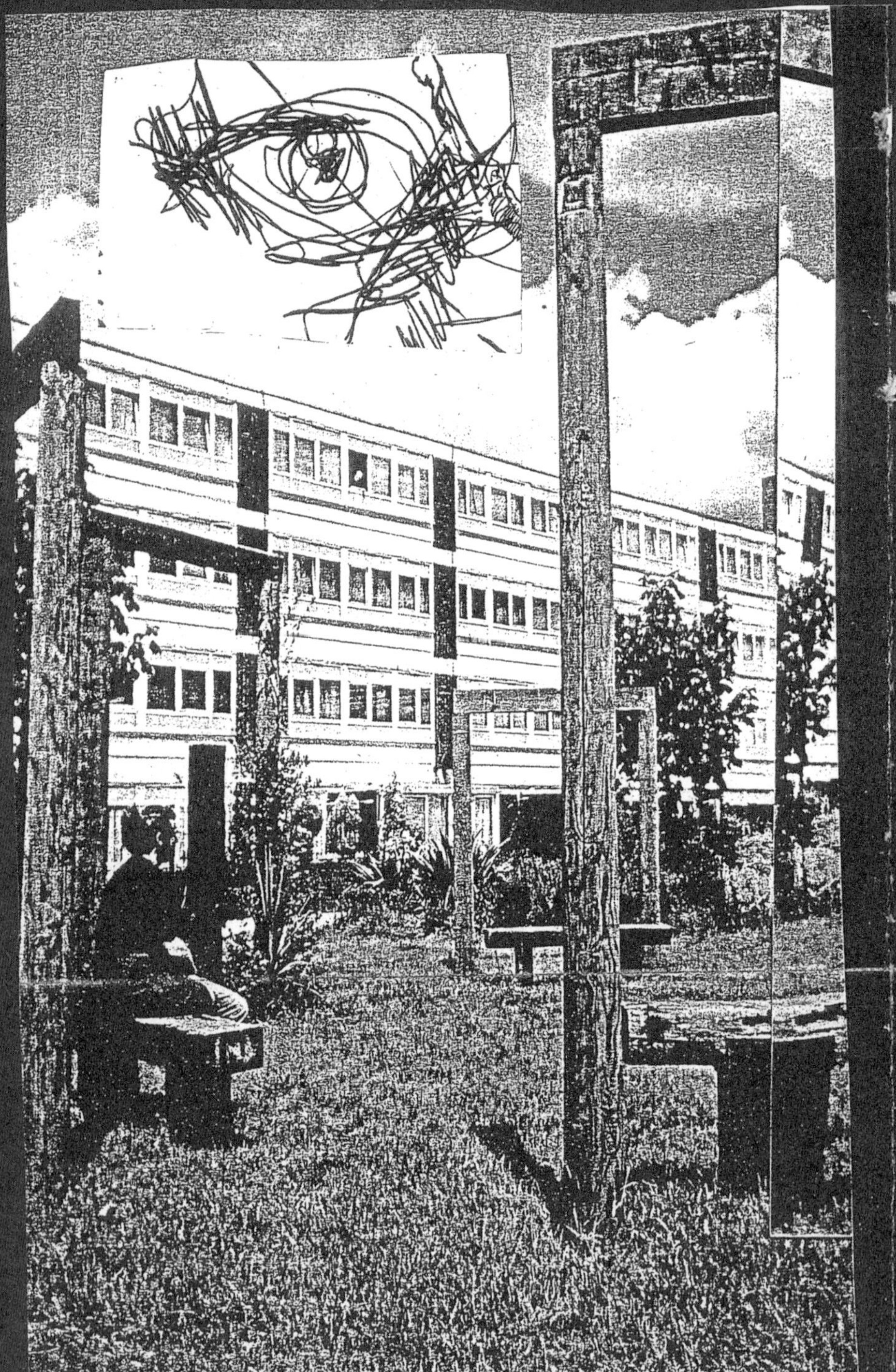

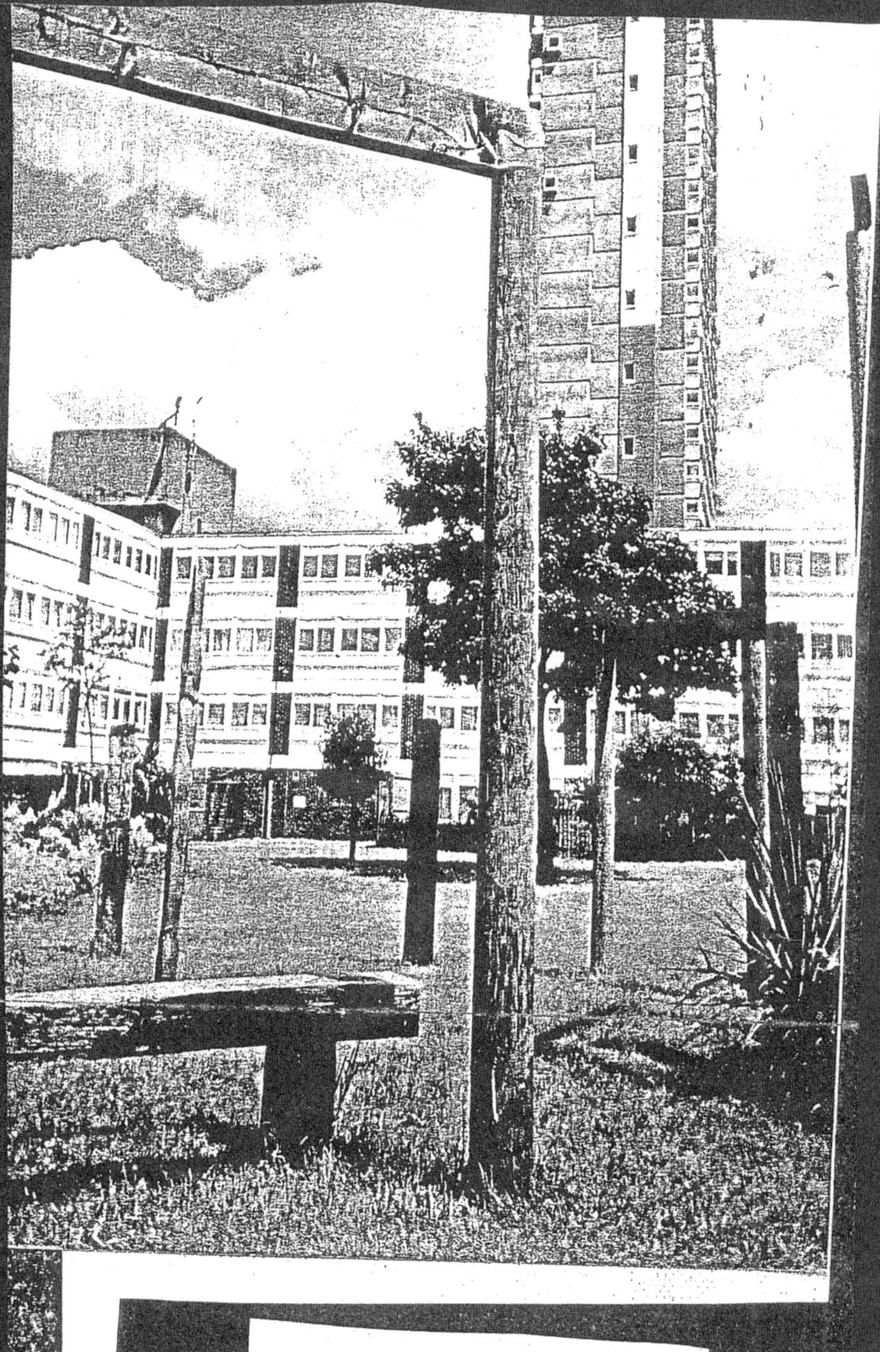

SOLSTICE SKAG BONANZA

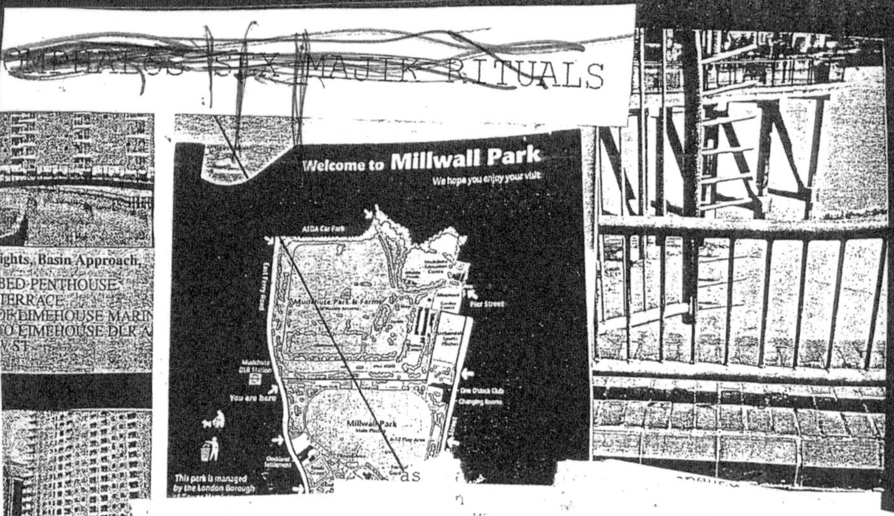
SIX MAJIK RITUALS
Welcome to Millwall Park
We hope you enjoy your visit
Millwall Park
You are here
Pier Street
ASDA Car Park
Mudchute Park & Farm
ights, Basin Approach,
BED PENTHOUSE
TERRACE

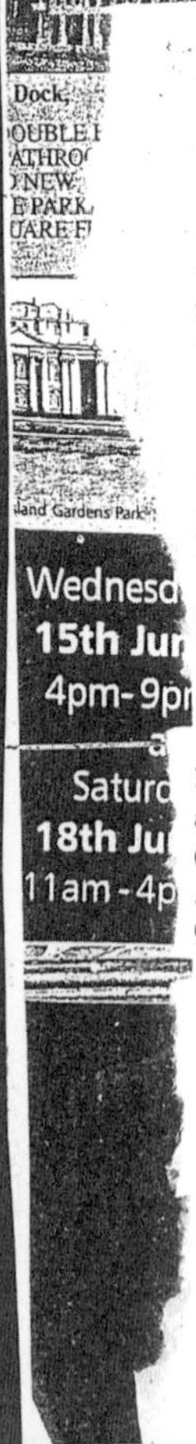
Wednesd
15th Ju
4pm-9p
Saturd
18th Ju
11am-4p

29th July 1995, Deptford free festival, Fordham Park.

This street was nearly demolished. We opened a place, it didn't last long, now we're down the other end of the terrace.
I'm sprawling, staring at the wallpaper, feeling the metal coils of the mattress jabbing through the threadbare fuzz into my back. Layers of 70s geometric orange are torn away to reveal yellowing 50s chintz, mouldering roses with Disorder and UK Subs written over the top in marker pen.
Spotty Ulster punk, outstretched arms.
Another attempt to crush the demons, keep out the fear. Dust and cobwebs in the exposed rafters. Hammer drill pounding behind the eyes but I have to move before he wakes.
Just over from Belfast, he's modelled himself on Sid Vicious, black glue hair and skinny white frame. They were downstairs off their heads on glue lurching about, manically ranting for a few seconds then collapsing back to the floor.

It's a hot July day. The garden is cracked cement with bindweed and poppies. Sham 69 on a battered tape recorder.
Orange settee, two mildewed patio chairs and a swivel chair arranged in a circle.
The sky is turquoise

> Creep downstairs and confront myself in the hall mirror. Peroxide hair a tangled mess, mascara smeared under eyes, trying to avoid the missing floorboards.

Some of the New Cross crew are in the boozer over the road waiting for us with a sound system.
The landlord hates us but not enough to refuse our money. There's signs up about travellers and George crosses all over the bar. They serve us and give water to the dog in a Fosters ashtray. One pint later I go to the Ladies and look in the mirror. I do my make up, fierce kohl and gold eye shadow. Knock back vodka and orange from a plastic bottle. Look better now.

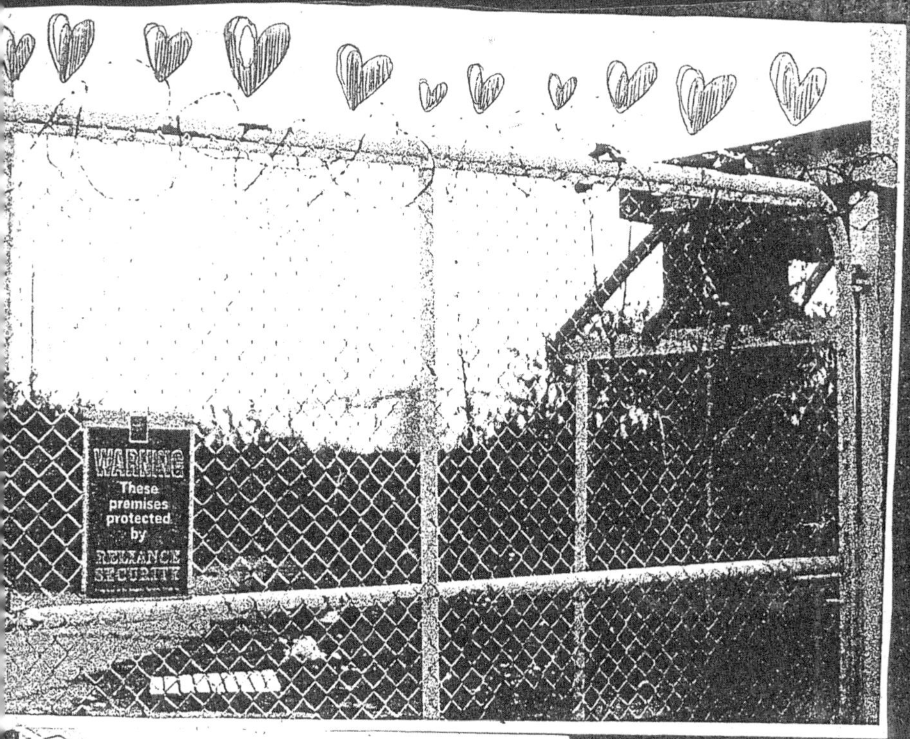
WARNING
These premises protected by
RELIANCE SECURITY

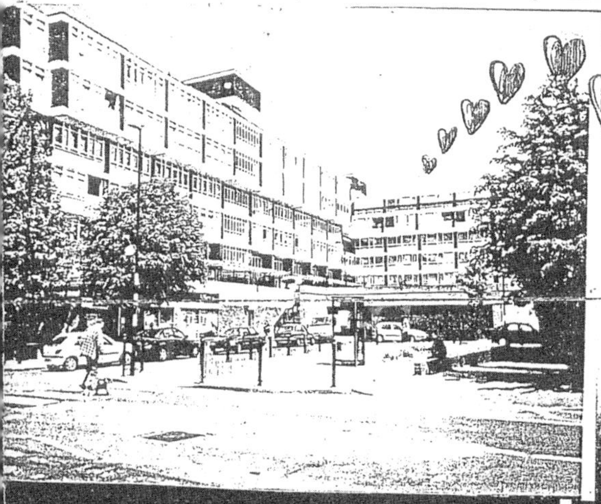

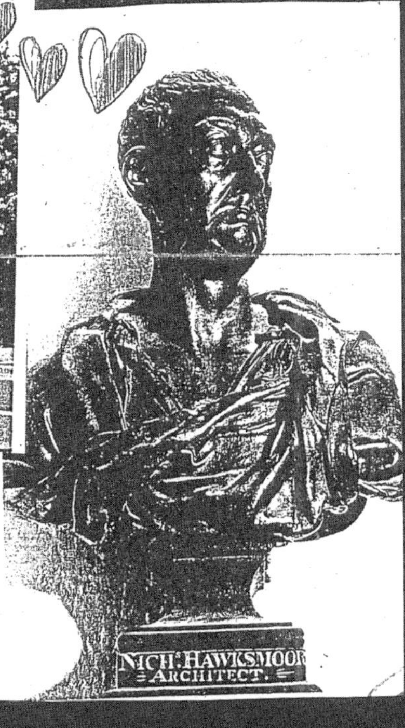
NICH: HAWKSMOOR
ARCHITECT.

Back in the street I feel good, soft edges and a warm glow,
everything shimmering pink and gold. The Ulster punks come
staggering out of the squat and join us on the pavement
outside. The Sid clone hands me a tiny envelope. I make space
and let him sit down. Two pints later and we're bundling into a
van. I share the wrap of whizz with some green haired bloke in
a sub humans t shirt. Leaving the Island we lift off, X Ray
Spex, looping and shrieking, feeling invincible.
BURN THE YUPPIE FLATS.

Not enough rioting now, last lot of crew just released from
Brixton for the Poll Tax, three years for knocking a coppers
helmet off, two years for trying to scale the gates at Downing
street. Should've knocked his fucking head off.

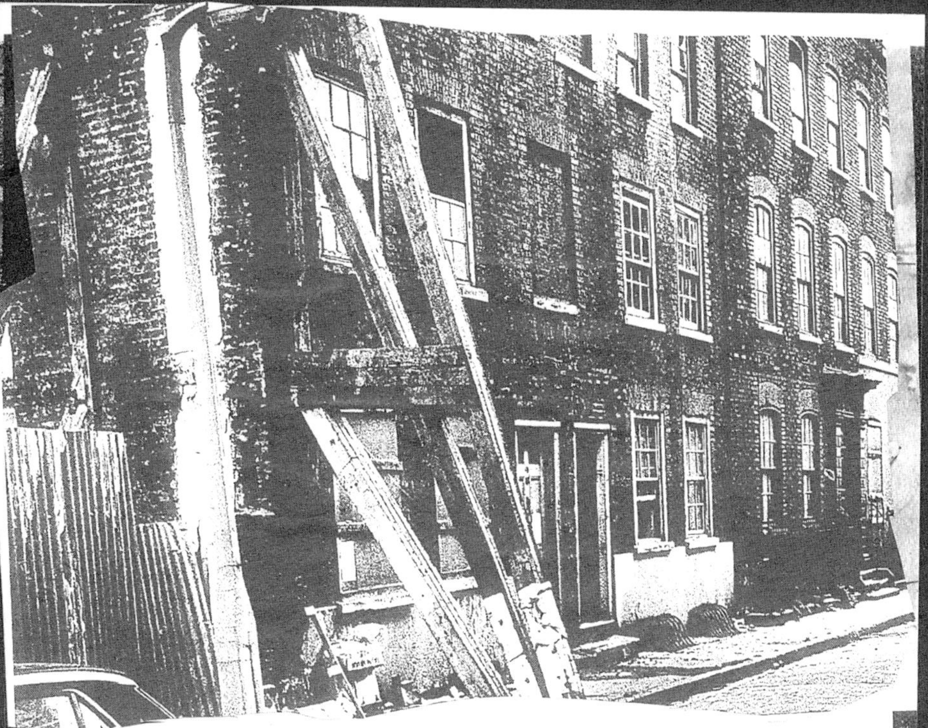

PUT FUCKIN COCK SPARRER ON!!!

Out the van, fall headlong into a bloke I've seen before with black hair and royal blue eyes. He tried calling my old house in Leeds, I was never there to speak to him. He left numbers, we were both on the move, itinerants, impossible to keep track of. A heated encounter, one night,, eyes flashing violet. Behind the Dew drop Inn, face ground to the wall, mouthful of brick dust, his palm pressed hard , a black ace on pale skin/

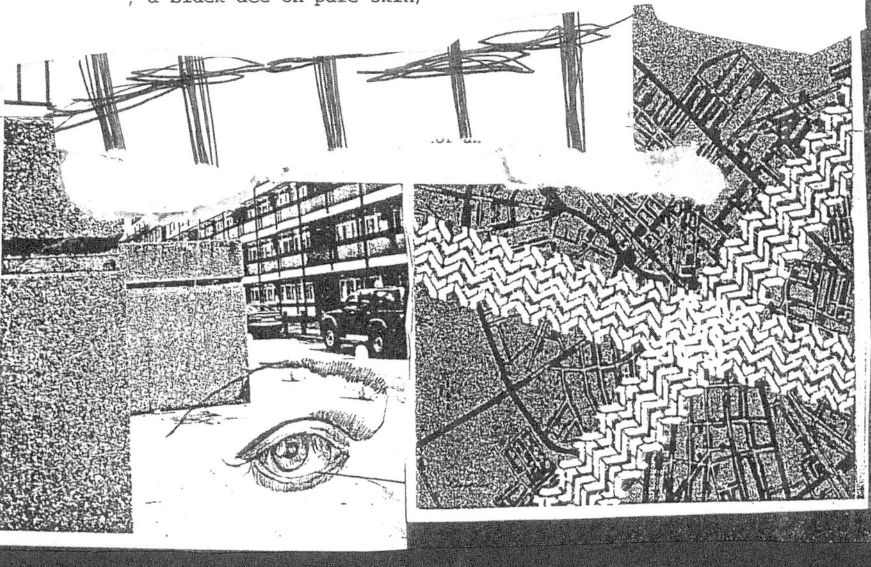

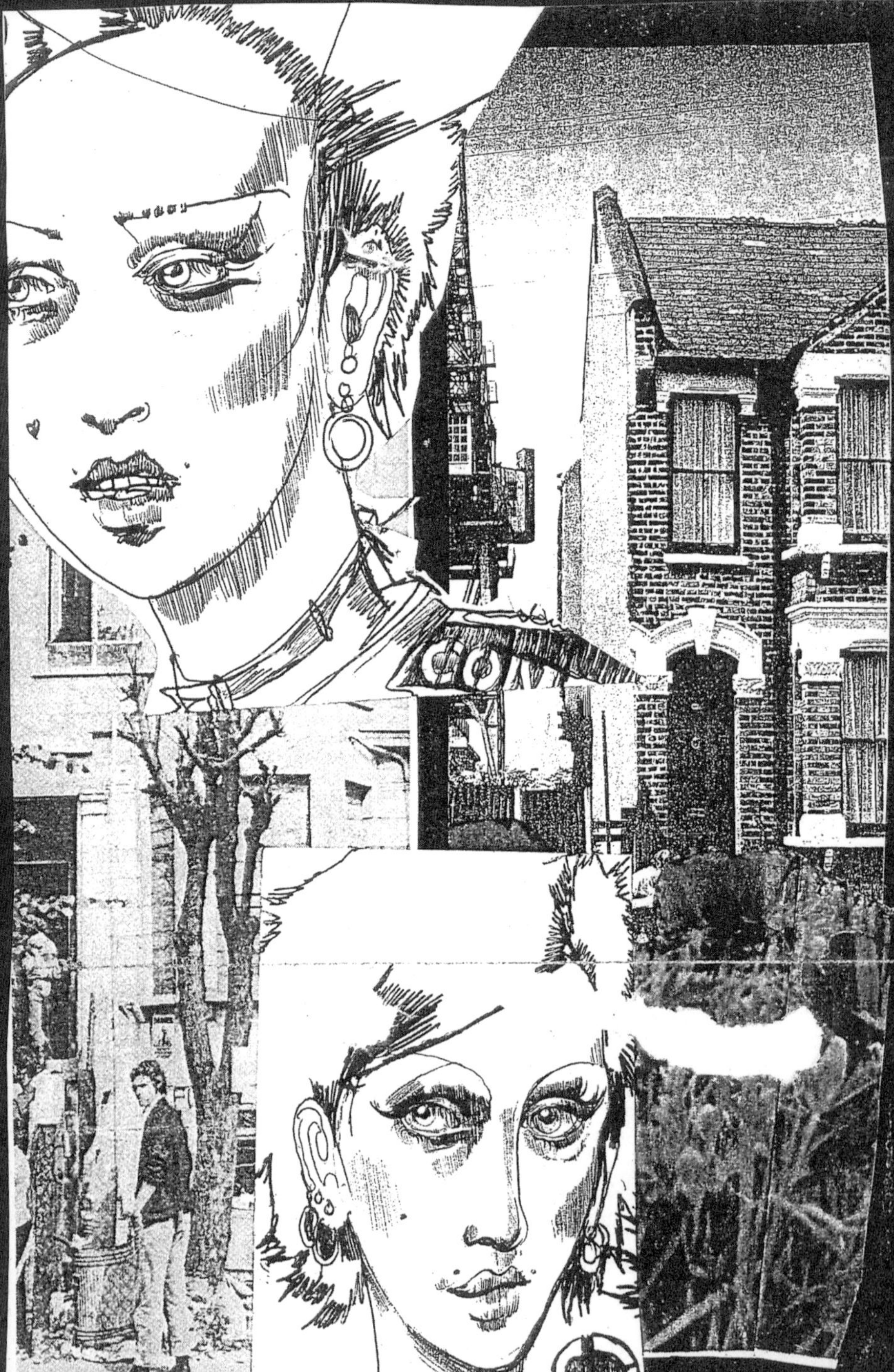

a multitude of blanked out memories from a bed in council-run drying out yard, the drugs I'm on in here seems to make all my memories flow seamlessly clean and bright, there are a million little episodes played out high speed so this is the first fragment of the first one.When I finish the story it isn't the end just the end of that moment,then ther'll be another rush and it's another episode.

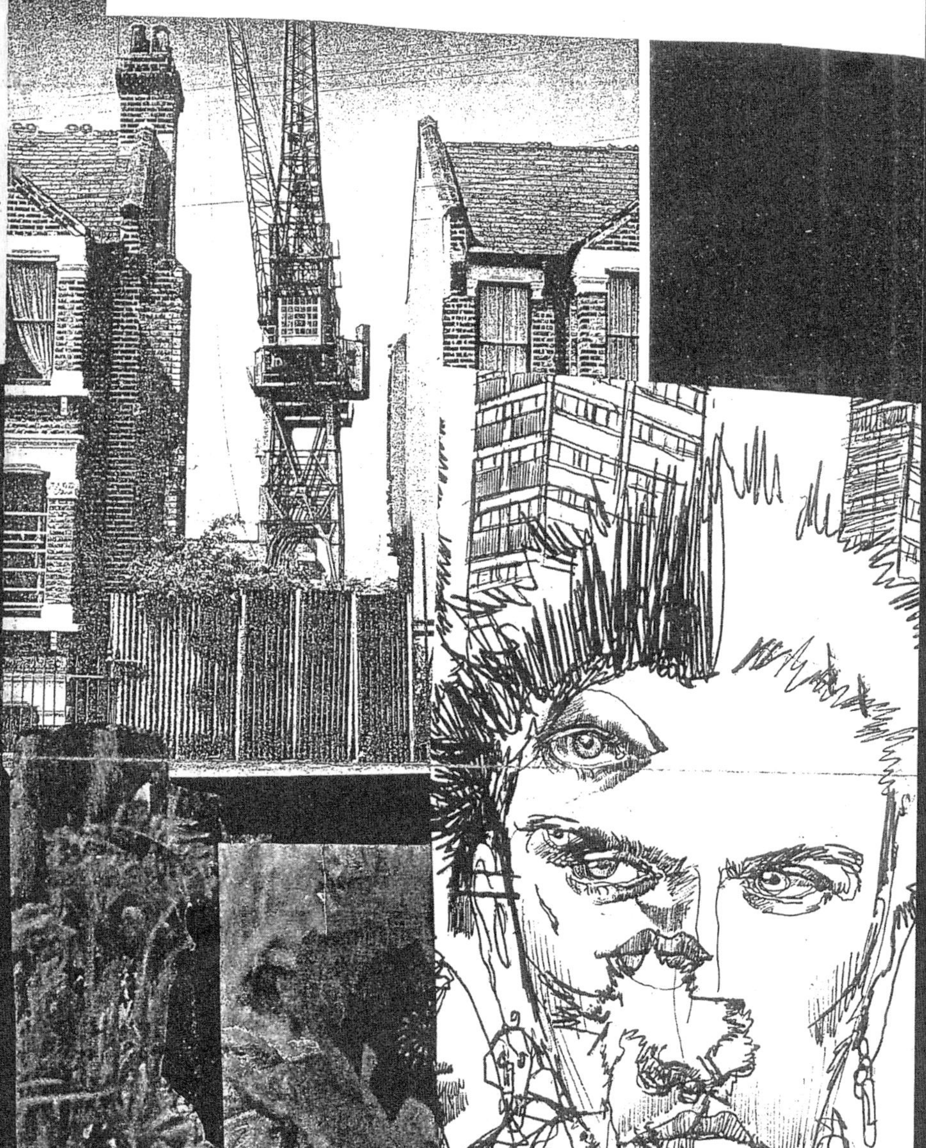

60s Mosaic entropy.
8888888888888888888

Weaving in and out, falling back against soft walls. Warm
night, orange curtains shimmering in tattered strips. Little
tiles, yellow and purple, making patterns all round the lifts
like arcade games or little faces laughing. This floor, the
23rd, my paradise.

Falak al aflak.

 One night I stood on the balcony and the sky was red. All the
sky and even the buildings seemed on fire, everything dying
and everything raging one last time.

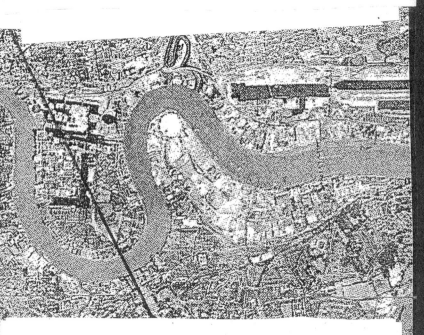

I lay back and my body felt light and beautiful. I was lifted
up, slowly by gentle hands, my whole body tingling, a euphoric
levitation.
    I lived on the 23rd floor , never beyond E14, watching the
river looping round, sometimes white gold or slate grey and
mercury. The Island, small from up here, you could hold out
your hand and let it settle in your palm then blow it like a
dandelion clock and it would always land like it was meant to
be, with all the roads and houses back in the same place.

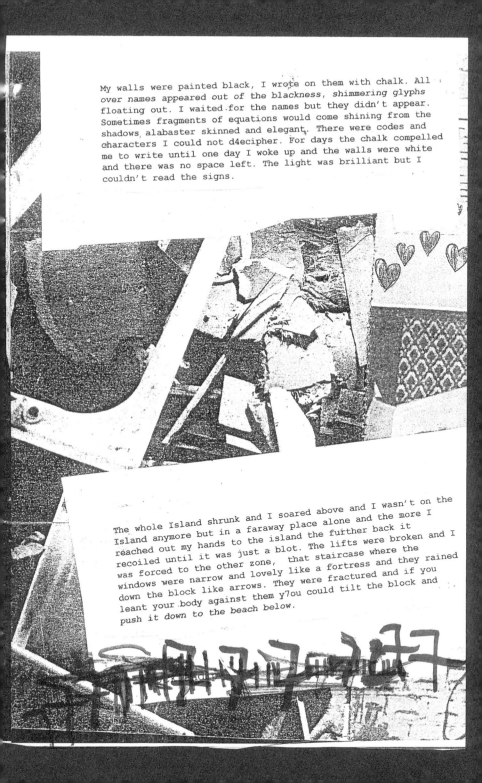

My walls were painted black, I wrote on them with chalk. All over names appeared out of the *blackness, shimmering glyphs* floating out. I waited for the names but they didn't appear. Sometimes fragments of equations would come shining from the shadows, alabaster skinned and elegant. There were codes and characters I could not d4ecipher. For days the chalk compelled me to write until one day I woke up and the walls were white and there was no space left. The light was brilliant but I couldn't read the signs.

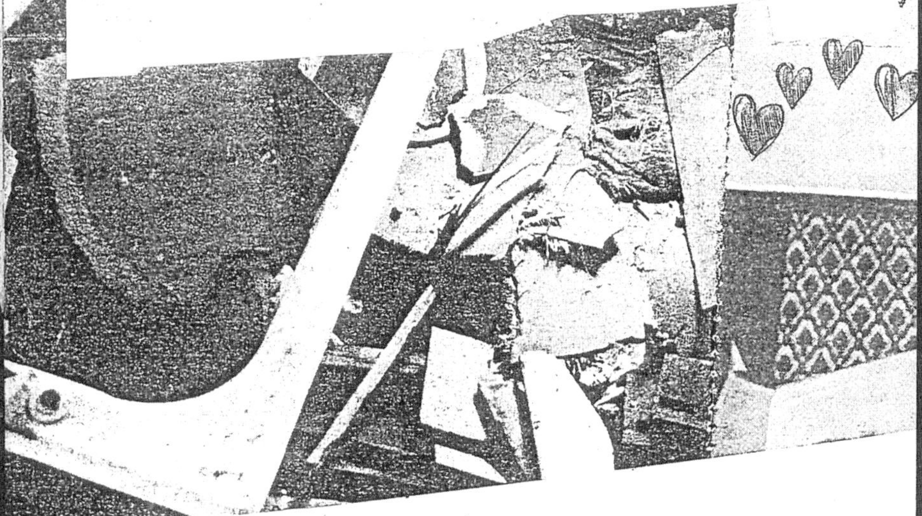

The whole Island shrunk and I soared above and I wasn't on the Island anymore but in a faraway place alone and the more I reached out my hands to the island the further back it recoiled until it was just a blot. The lifts were broken and I was forced to the other zone, that staircase where the windows were narrow and lovely like a fortress and they rained down the block like arrows. They were fractured and if you leant your body against them y7ou could tilt the block and *push it down to the beach below.*

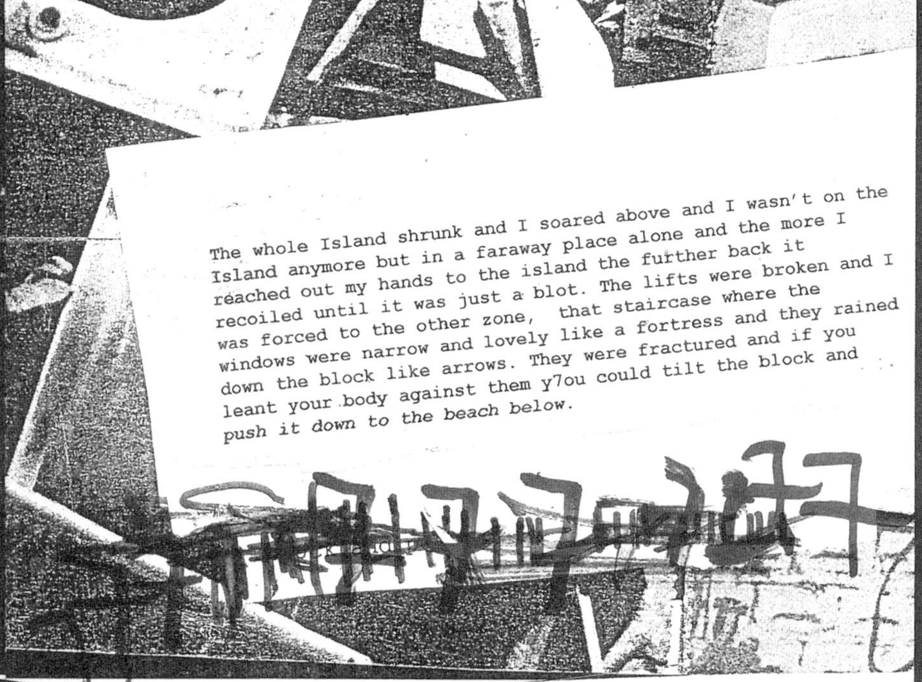

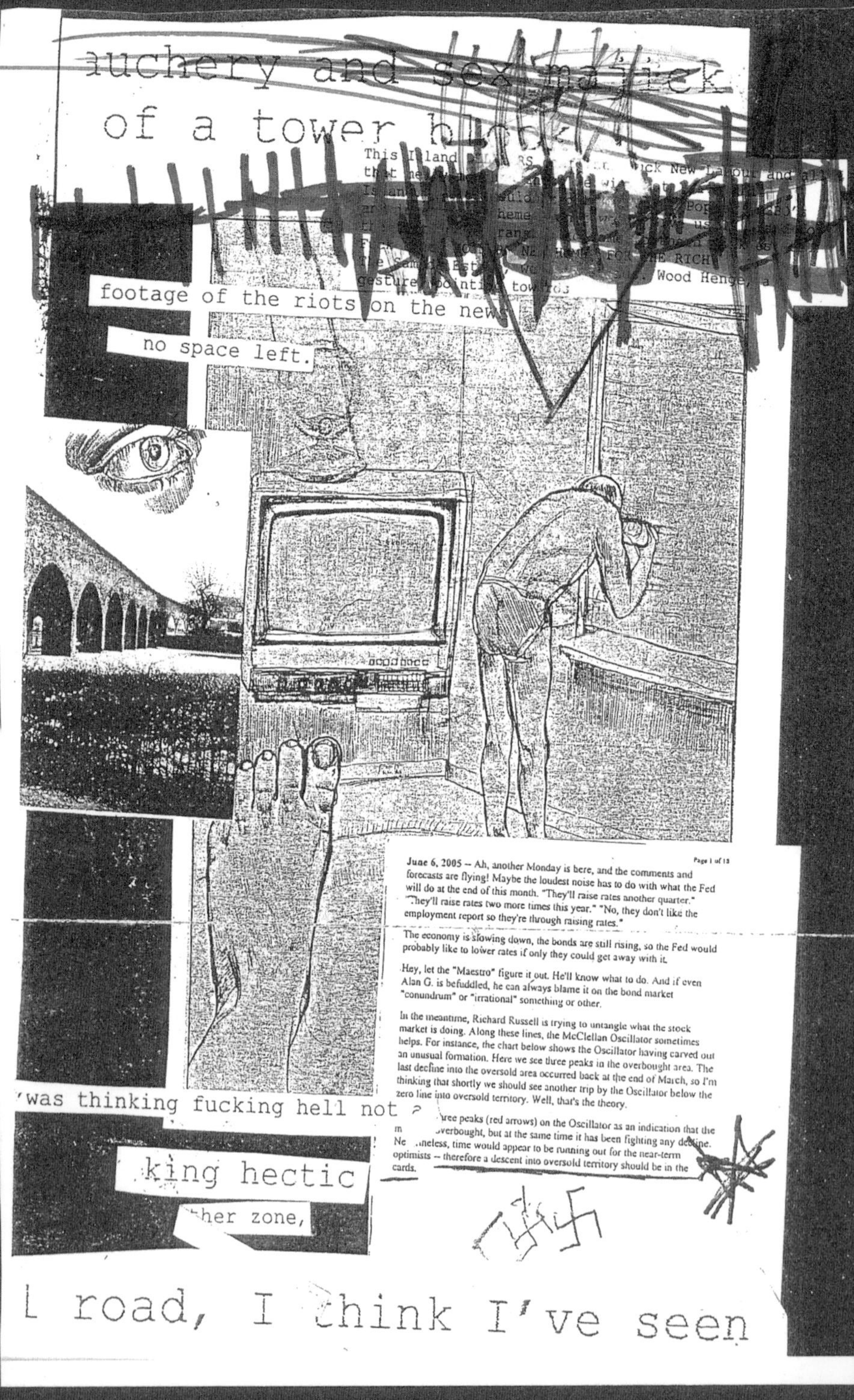
auchery and sex magick
of a tower bl
This Island
Wood Henge, a
gesture
footage of the riots on the news
no space left.
June 6, 2005 -- Ah, another Monday is here, and the comments and forecasts are flying! Maybe the loudest noise has to do with what the Fed will do at the end of this month. "They'll raise rates another quarter." "They'll raise rates two more times this year." "No, they don't like the employment report so they're through raising rates."
Page 1 of 13
The economy is slowing down, the bonds are still rising, so the Fed would probably like to lower rates if only they could get away with it.
Hey, let the "Maestro" figure it out. He'll know what to do. And if even Alan G. is befuddled, he can always blame it on the bond market "conundrum" or "irrational" something or other.
In the meantime, Richard Russell is trying to untangle what the stock market is doing. Along these lines, the McClellan Oscillator sometimes helps. For instance, the chart below shows the Oscillator having carved out an unusual formation. Here we see three peaks in the overbought area. The last decline into the oversold area occurred back at the end of March, so I'm thinking that shortly we should see another trip by the Oscillator below the zero line into oversold territory. Well, that's the theory.
ree peaks (red arrows) on the Oscillator as an indication that the
m overbought, but at the same time it has been fighting any decline.
Ne neless, time would appear to be running out for the near-term optimists -- therefore a descent into oversold territory should be in the cards.
was thinking fucking hell not a
king hectic
ther zone,
l road, I think I've seen

zers,   and went rucking with the filth

ney were fractured and if

23rd floor of a tower block.

? No future. Don't stay on the Island unless y
...lord it. you haven't got what it takes. One
...scanned
...private owned
bundling out onto the landing. PRIVATE PROPERTY
OUT

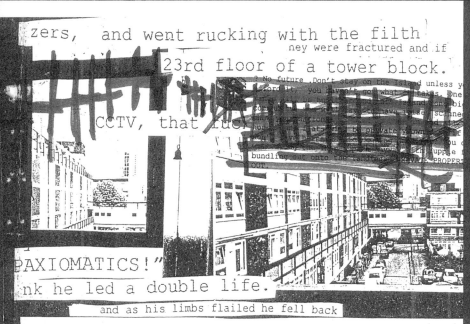

CCTV, that fuck

PAXIOMATICS!"

nk he led a double life.

and as his limbs flailed he fell back

A tale of blissed out debau
rituals on the 23rd floor o

My walls were painted black, I wrote on them

SKAG

RITUALS

MILLWALL HATE KREW

LONDON 2006... A WAVE OF TERRORIST ATTACKS HAVE SWEPT THE CAPITAL. THE CITY STREETS SWARM WITH ROVING GANGS OF NAZI 'VIGILANTES' SMASHING HEADS AND BURNING BUILDINGS.....

ENGLAND FIGHT BACK

THE PUBLIC DEMAND IMMEDIATE INTRODUCTION OF COMPULSORY ID CARDS AND QUEUE WILLINGLY.

HUGE SWATHES OF THE CITY ARE DEPOPULATED AS THE RICH FLEE TO THEIR NATIVE HOME COUNTIES

THOSE WHO REMAIN STAY LOCKED IN THEIR HOMES TOO SCARED TO GO OUT...

FEVERISHLY MONITORING THEIR NEIGHBOURS....

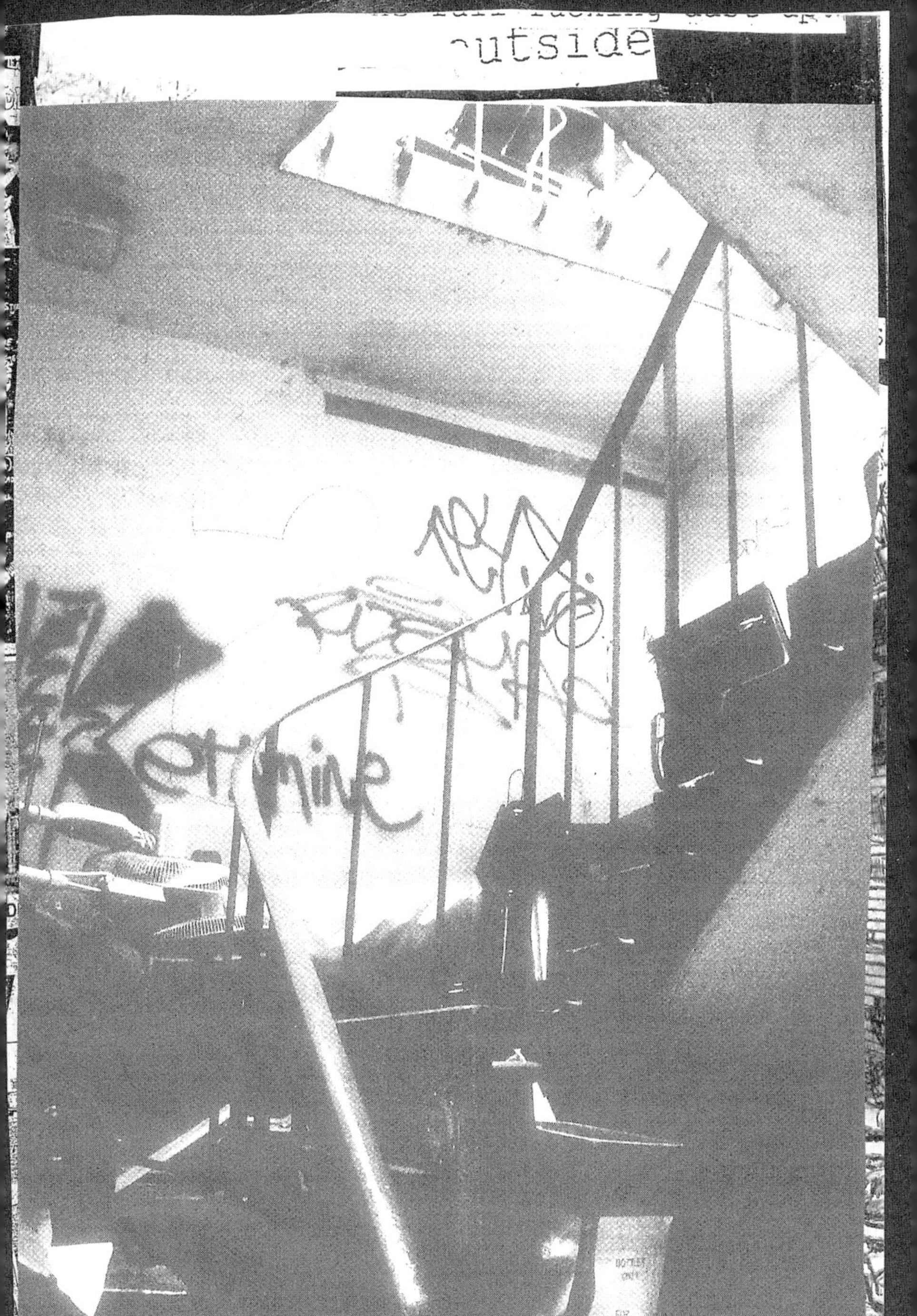
utside

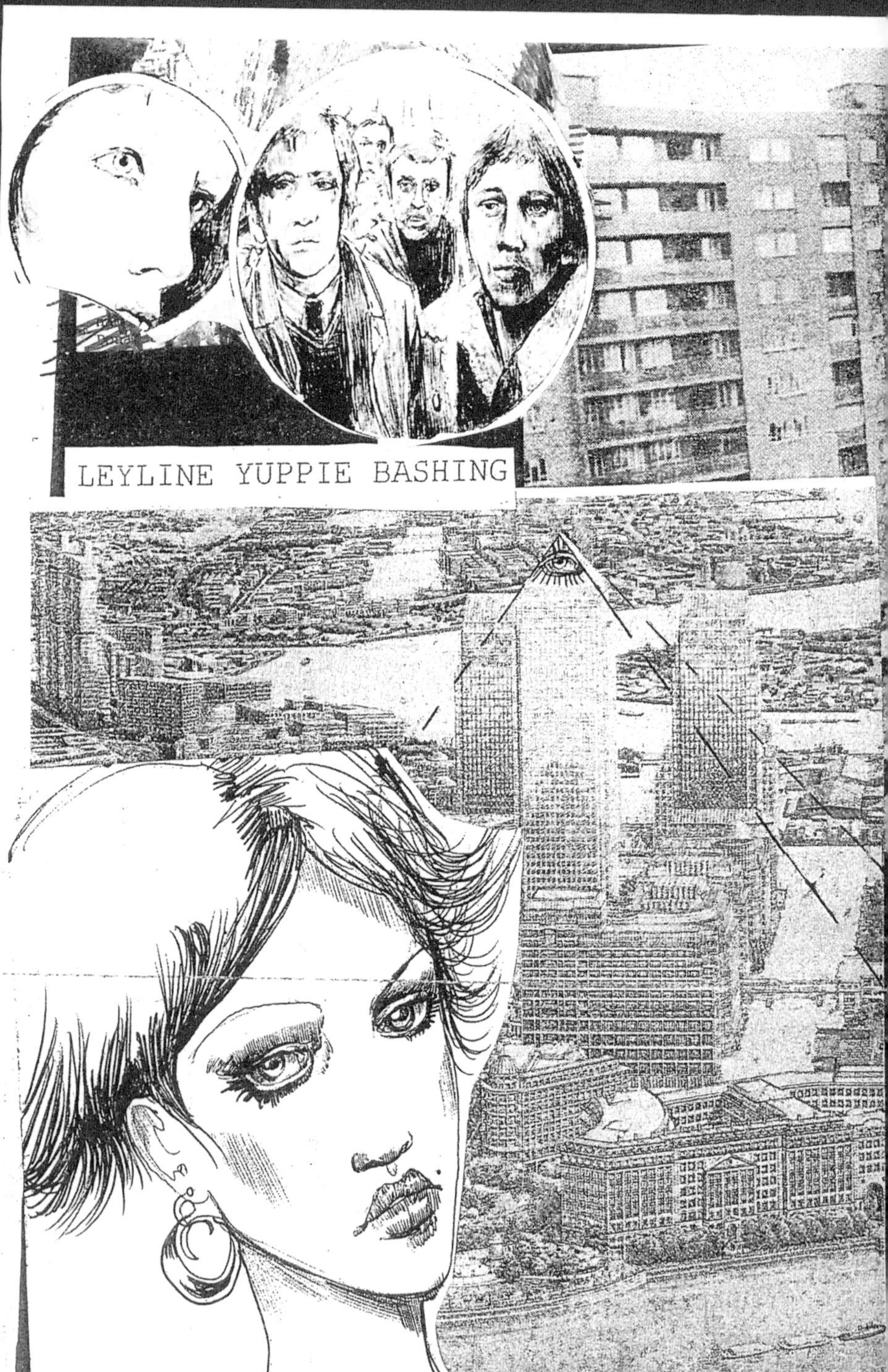
LEYLINE YUPPIE BASHING

MILLWALL HATE KREW

Mark was a copper but he never told his 'mates' in the Den that. When he was on the piss in Bermondsey boozers he said he worked as a contractor on the Isle of Sheppey. One time it all got really hectic and kicked off outside the Den. It went up and Mark was leading us in, he was aggravating it big time, he suddenly came to life.

It went up massive, there were loads of old bill injured, knocked off horses and given proper kickings. Me and him slipped into a side street by the railway arches and I told him to get out of the area and he dumped his jacket and scarf in the bin and jumped on a bus up the old Kent road.

We thought that was it but we hadn't bargained on the CCTV, that fucked it right up, suddenly there;s footage of the riots on Sky Tv and close ups of his face with a white circle on it calling him the ring leader. It was a bit grainy but you could tell it was him.

They were really after him and we thought it's just a matter of time, someone's bound to grass us up, we were just waitng for the knock at the door. They must have played that bit of film a hundred times with the grass line number flashing up all over the screen. I was thinking fucking hell not again cos I'd only been out of Belmarsh a year but Mark I didn't know nothing about where he came from, whether he had previous or nothing we'd never talked about it and then we all thought about how none of us knew him and that was after he just disappeared and we never heard nothing else on the news about the ring leader of the riot.

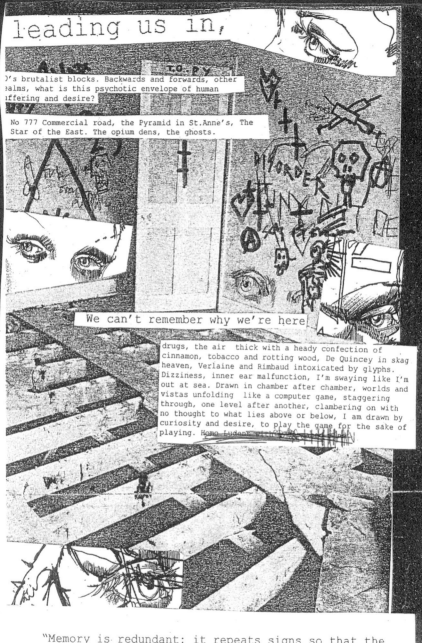

leading us in,

)'s brutalist blocks. Backwards and forwards, other ealms, what is this psychotic envelope of human iffering and desire?

No 777 Commercial road, the Pyramid in St.Anne's, The Star of the East. The opium dens, the ghosts.

We can't remember why we're here

drugs, the air thick with a heady confection of cinnamon, tobacco and rotting wood, De Quincey in skag heaven, Verlaine and Rimbaud intoxicated by glyphs. Dizziness, inner ear malfunction, I'm swaying like I'm out at sea. Drawn in chamber after chamber, worlds and vistas unfolding like a computer game, staggering through, one level after another, clambering on with no thought to what lies above or below, I am drawn by curiosity and desire, to play the game for the sake of playing. Homo Ludent

"Memory is redundant: it repeats signs so that the city can begin to exist."
Italo Calvino Invisible Cities

INFO @PAKI·TV
WWW·paki tv

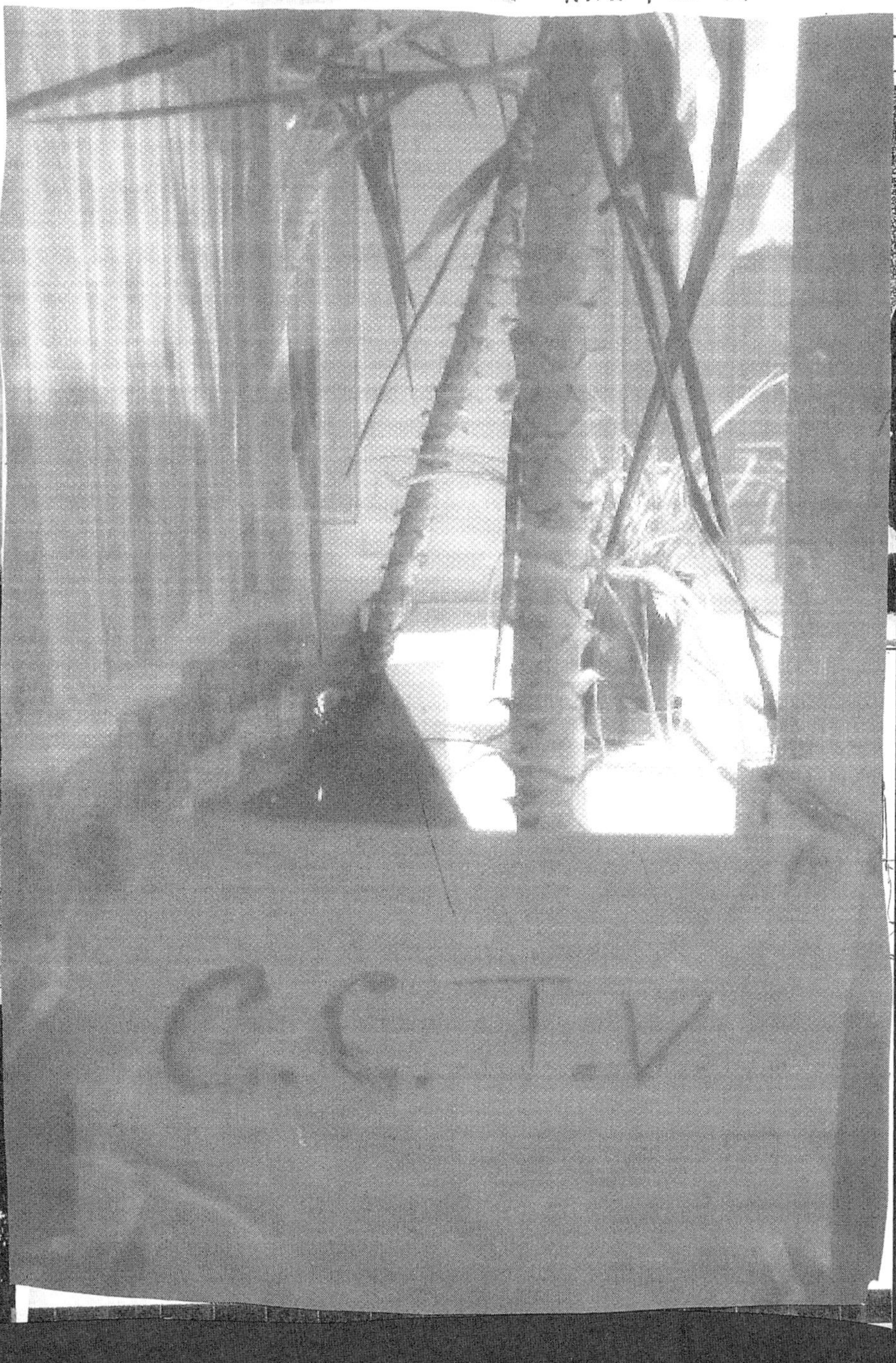

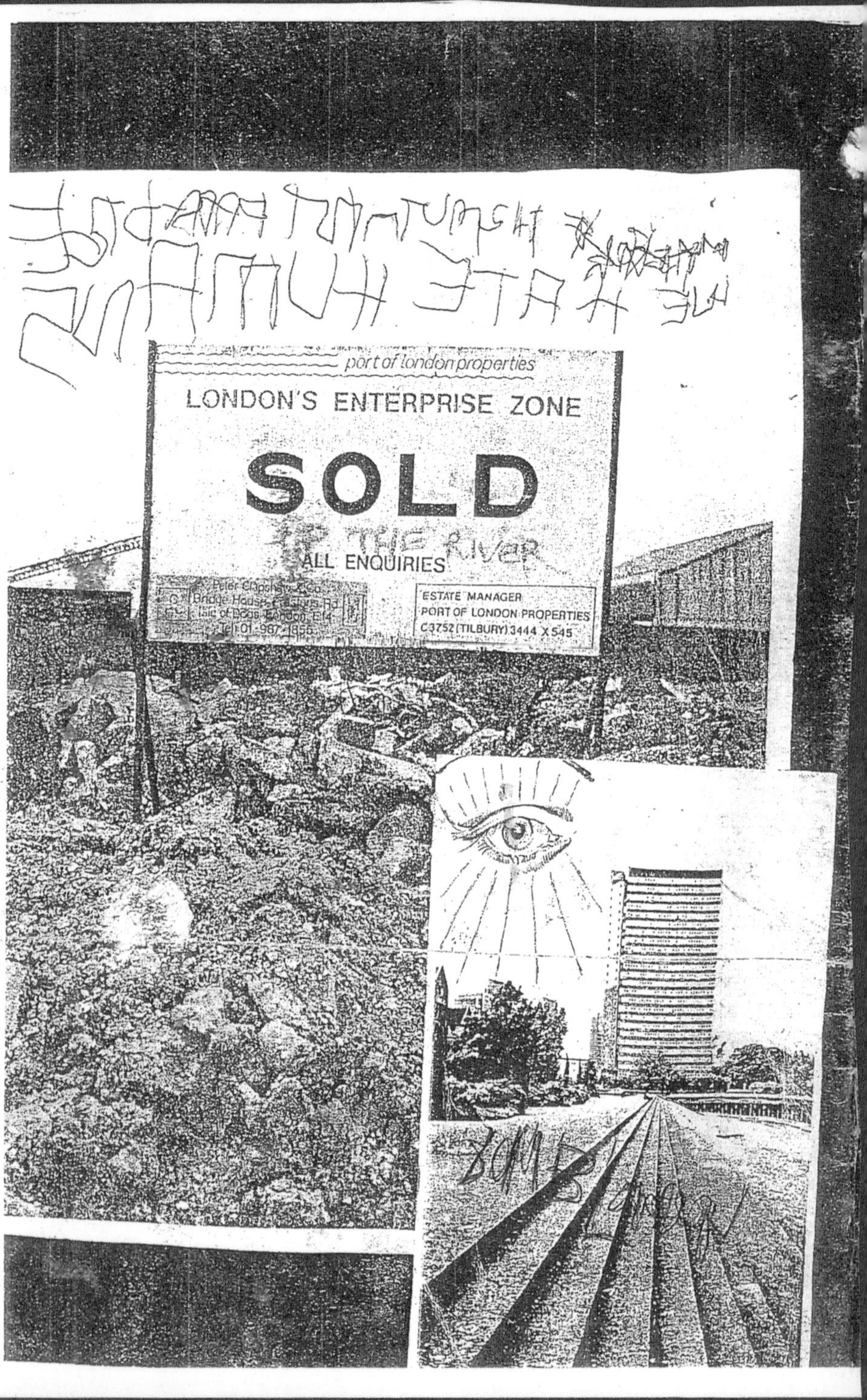
port of london properties
LONDON'S ENTERPRISE ZONE
SOLD
THE River
ALL ENQUIRIES
Tel 01-987-1855
ESTATE MANAGER
PORT OF LONDON PROPERTIES
C3752 (TILBURY) 3444 X 545

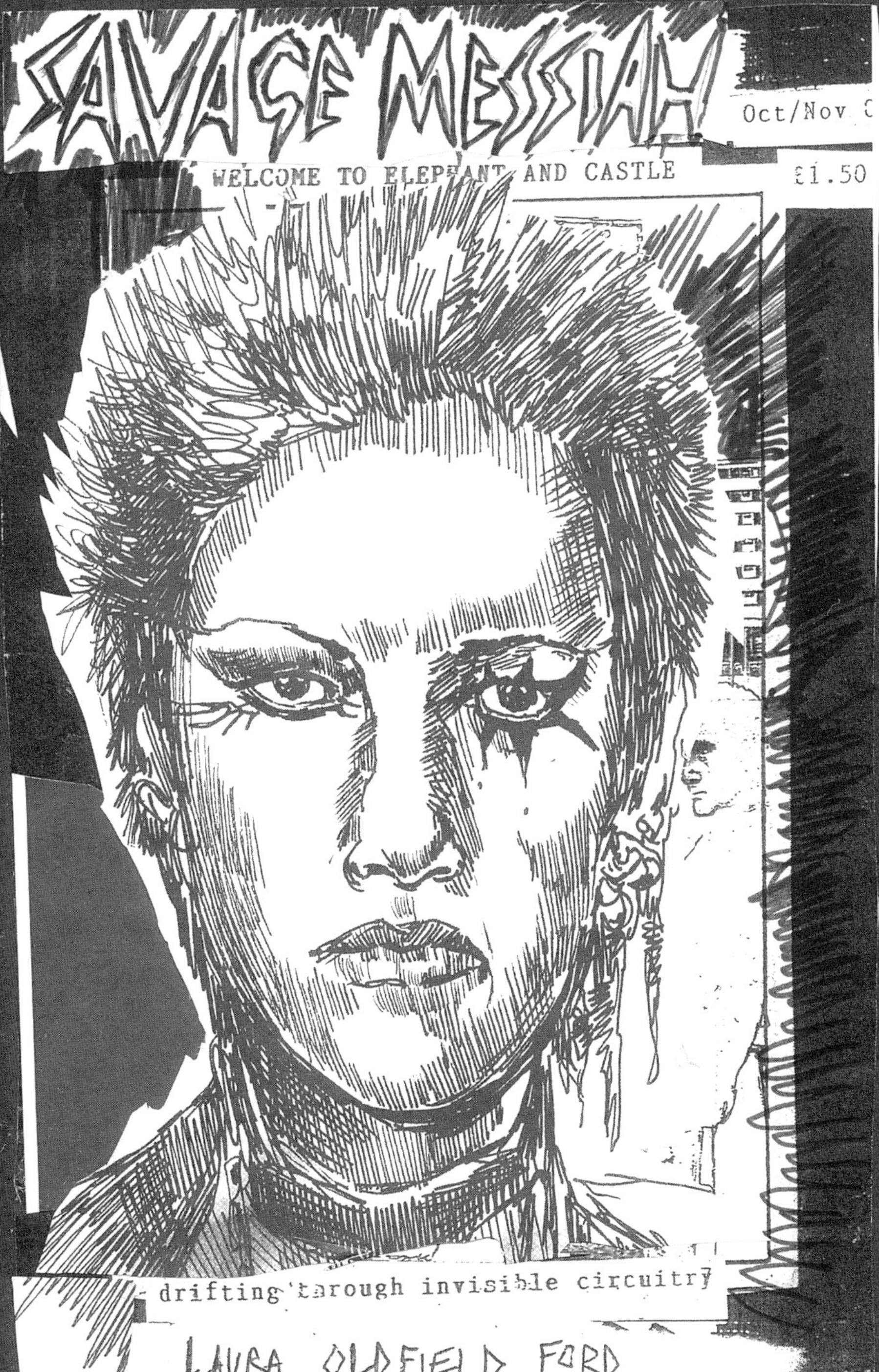
SAVAGE MESSIAH
Oct/Nov
WELCOME TO ELEPHANT AND CASTLE
£1.50
drifting through invisible circuitry
LAURA OLDFIELD FORD

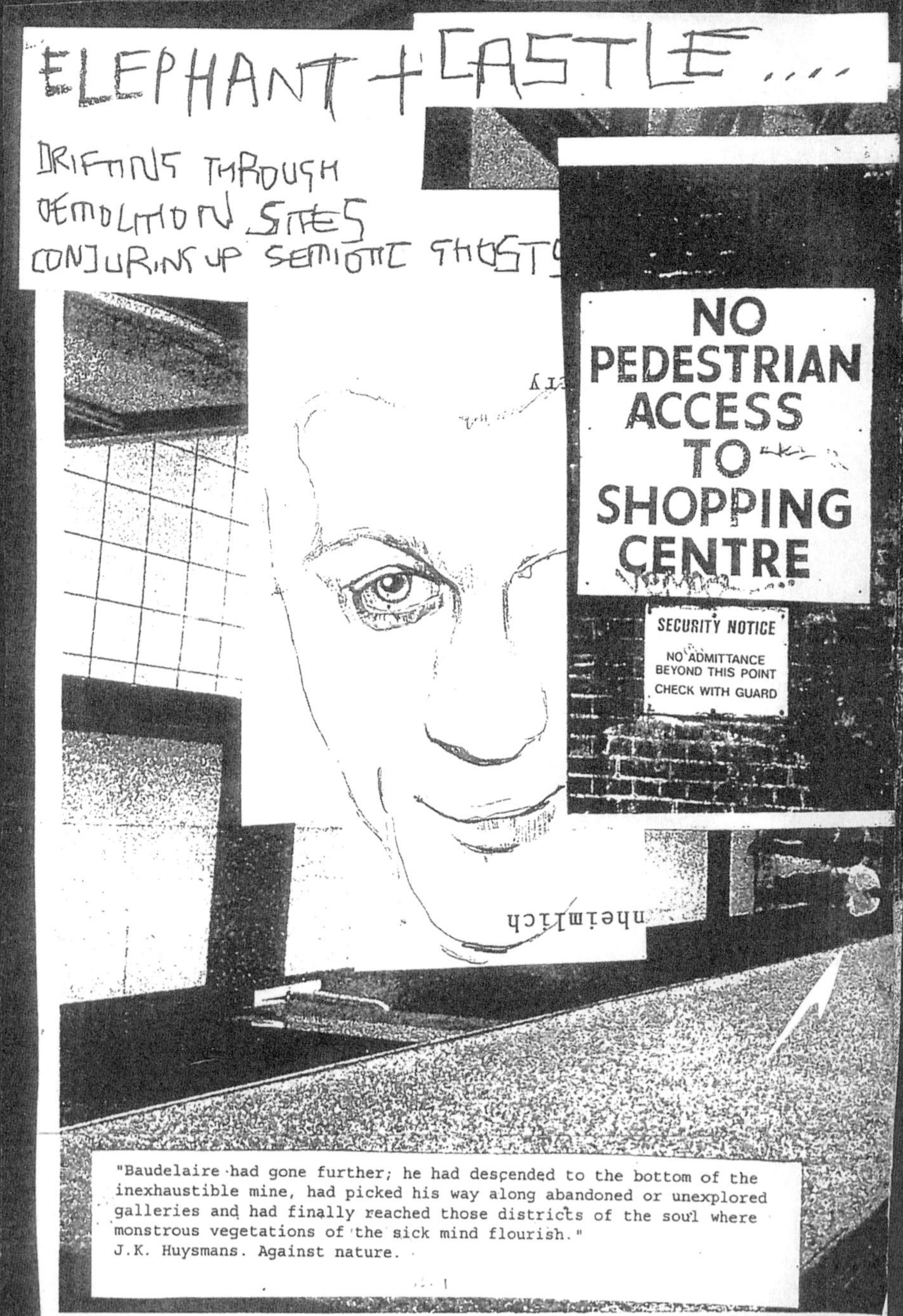
ELEPHANT + CASTLE....
DRIFTING THROUGH
DEMOLITION SITES
CONJURING UP SEMIOTIC GHOSTS
NO PEDESTRIAN ACCESS TO SHOPPING CENTRE
SECURITY NOTICE
NO ADMITTANCE BEYOND THIS POINT
CHECK WITH GUARD
"Baudelaire had gone further; he had descended to the bottom of the inexhaustible mine, had picked his way along abandoned or unexplored galleries and had finally reached those districts of the soul where monstrous vegetations of the sick mind flourish."
J.K. Huysmans. Against nature.

is

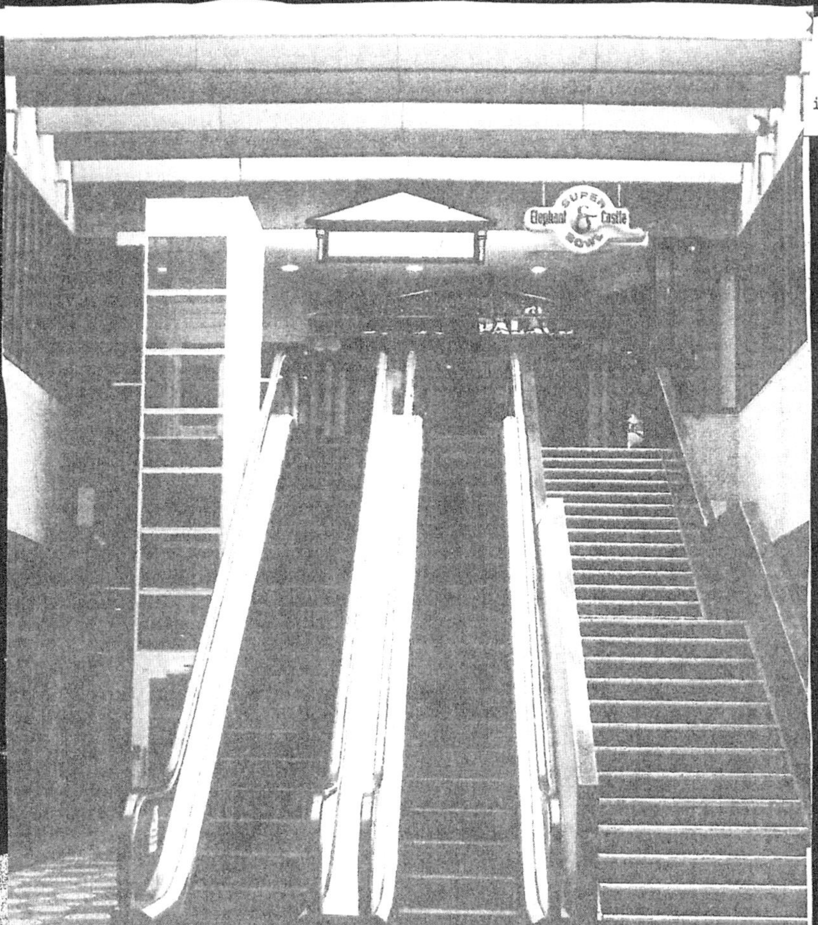
Elephant SUPER & Castle BOWL

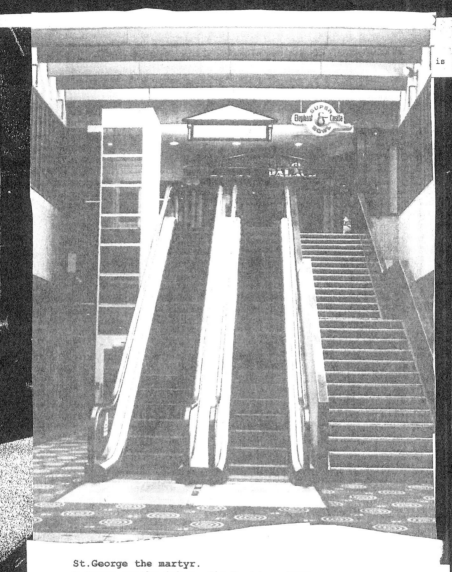

St.George the martyr.
A tramp cracks jokes. Jim Davidson 1981.
Beyond the tobacconists and apothecaries of Tabard Street the damp construction of another yuppiedrome. Scaffolding spines and the bright faces of imagined tenants.
Ghosts of Marshalsea, marker pen scrawls across the hoardings. "DEBTORS PRISON OPEN SOON".

August 2001. Aylesbury Estate. The end of a three month bender , cascading episodes of heat and destruction. I remember needing to escape the sultry claustrophobia of the flat, to walk out of that block and leave that whole life behind me. Trinity Street and Merrick square. Drifting through shady Regency enclaves I sensed escape routes emerging in the blackness.

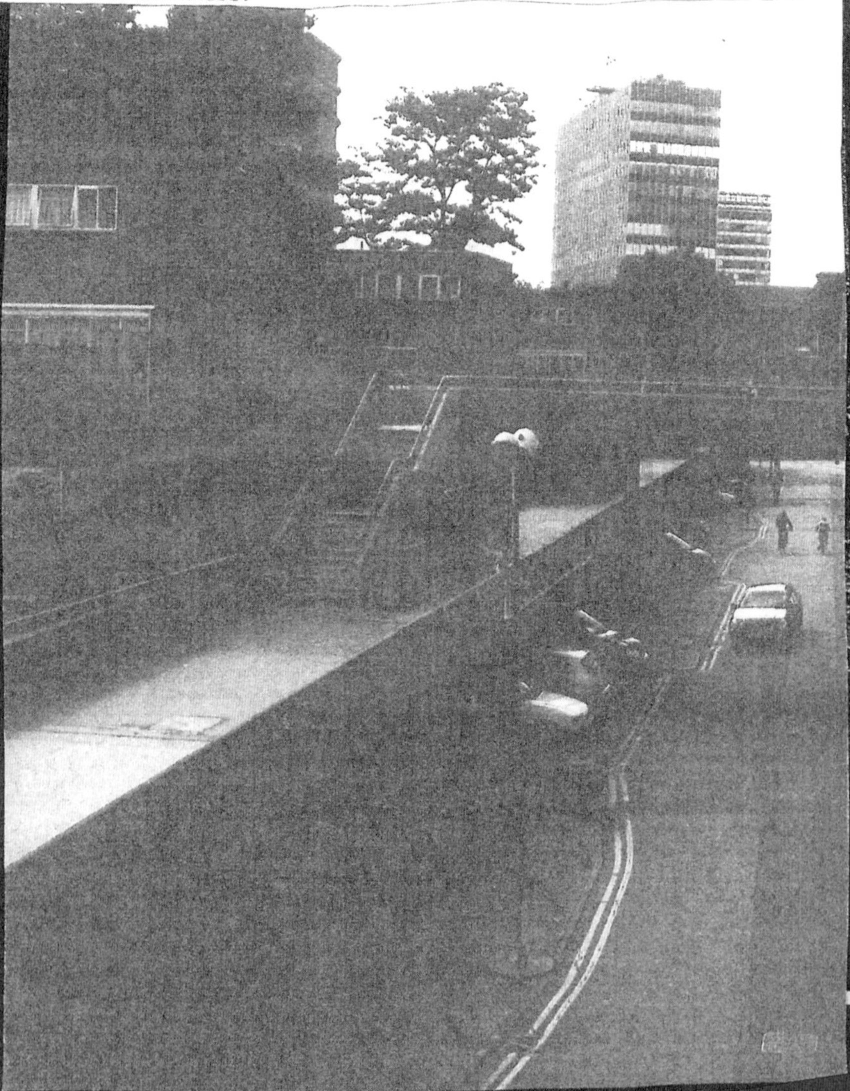

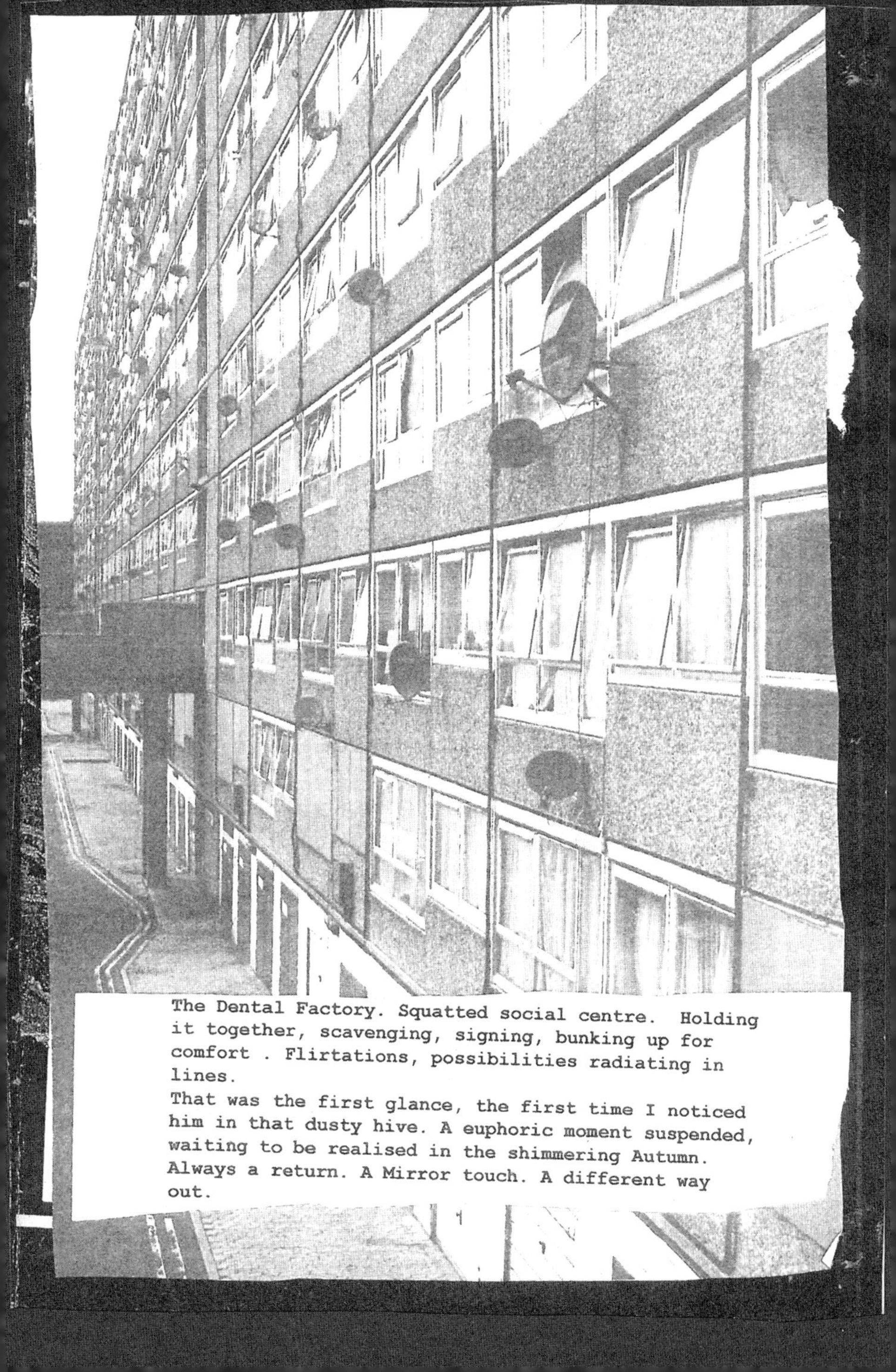

The Dental Factory. Squatted social centre. Holding it together, scavenging, signing, bunking up for comfort . Flirtations, possibilities radiating in lines.

That was the first glance, the first time I noticed him in that dusty hive. A euphoric moment suspended, waiting to be realised in the shimmering Autumn. Always a return. A Mirror touch. A different way out.

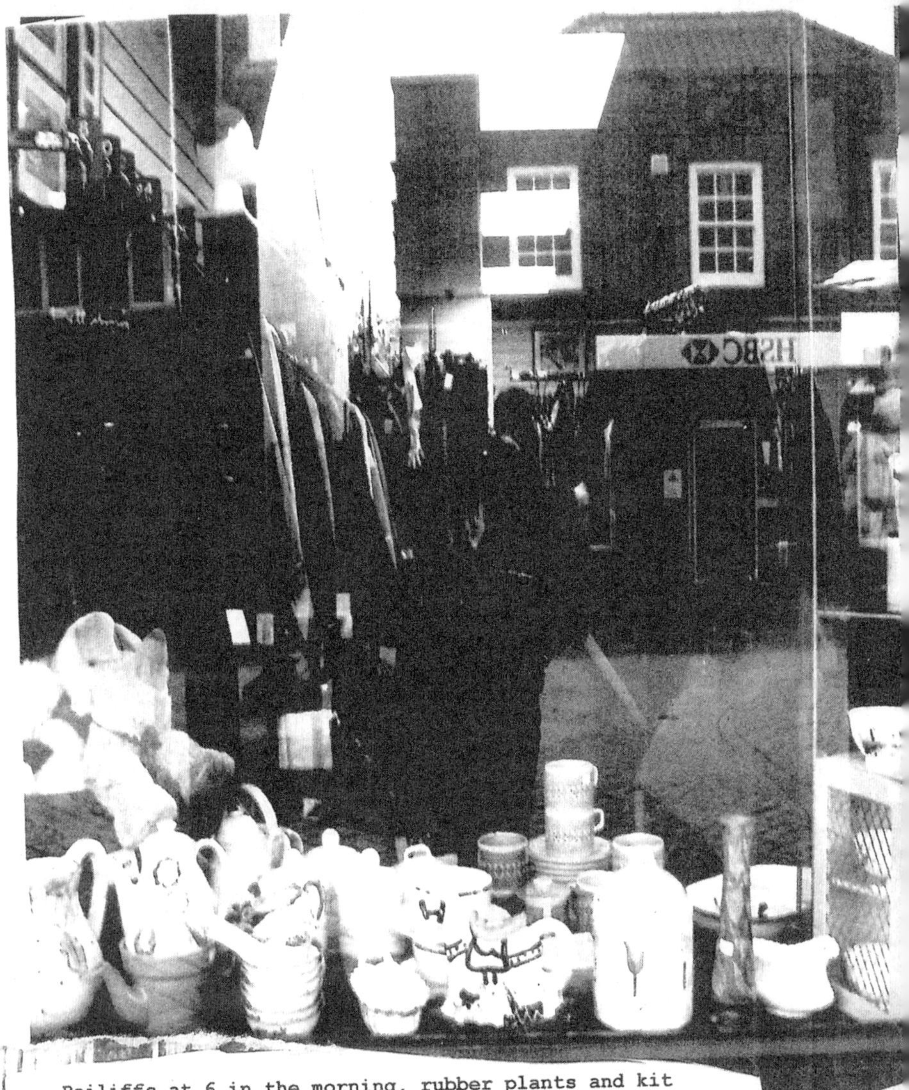
HSBC

Bailiffs at 6 in the morning, rubber plants and kit bags scattered across the pavement. Belway Homes. Craters of dirt, faux Georgian new builds on that contested site. JBW . Hired thugs. Denture moulds hurled from first floor windows.

52 Beckett House, Austin Osman Spare's Alaphabet of Desire carved on powdery walls. Erasure and repetition, the ego at the brink of dissolution. "We are what we desire. Desire nothing and there is nothing you shall not realise'. Dense showers of sigils oscillate and shimmer in the abandoned council flat.

England.
Black Horse Court. George crosses and wooden scaffolds, fences built on communal lawns.
50s Estate pub. A fragment of PIL's Death Disco sparkles for a moment before dissipating in a wall of fruit machines. 777, acid greens and glowing oranges. Treasure Island, Rainbow Riches ,Cashino.

I sense the River Neckinger beneath the paving slabs, the queasy toxicity shifting to St.Saviours dock. The Devils Necktie. A chalked eye glowers up. Bricklayers arms, a tangle of flyovers and concrete islands. The Old Kent road lifts in a confusion non Euclidean space.

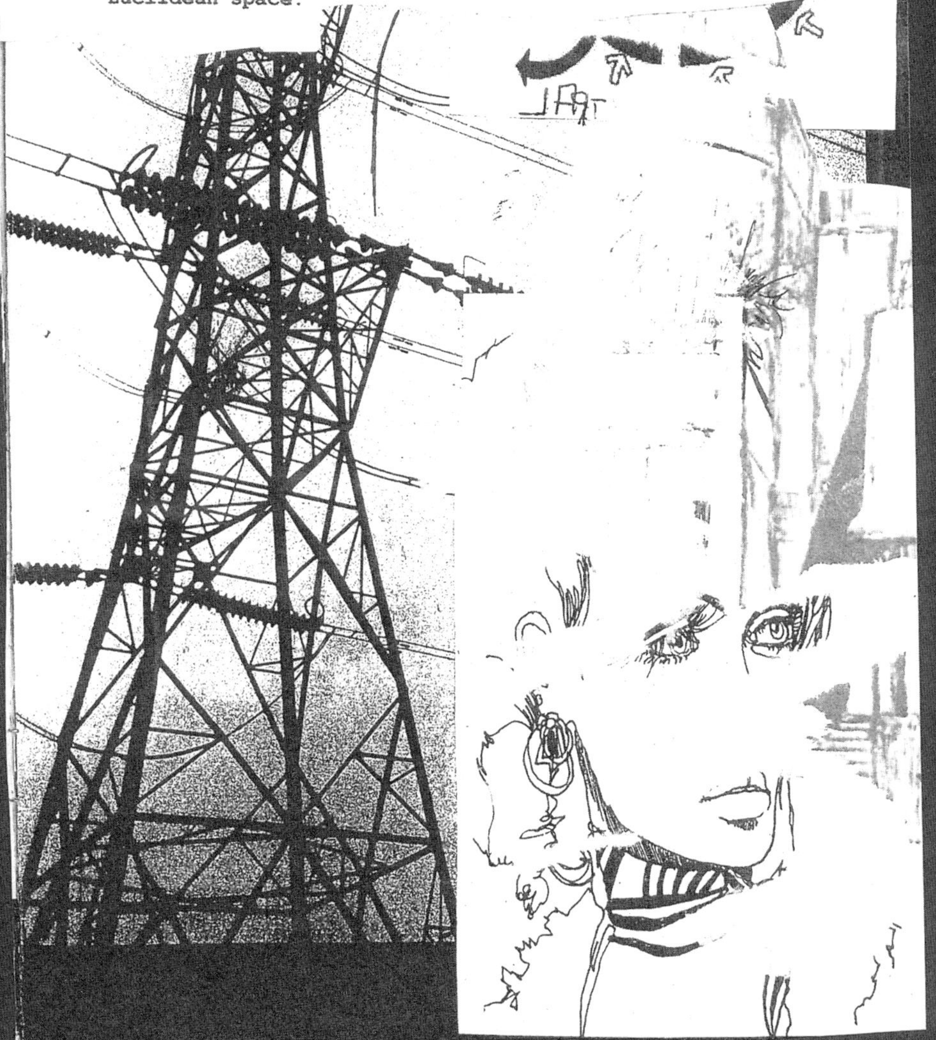

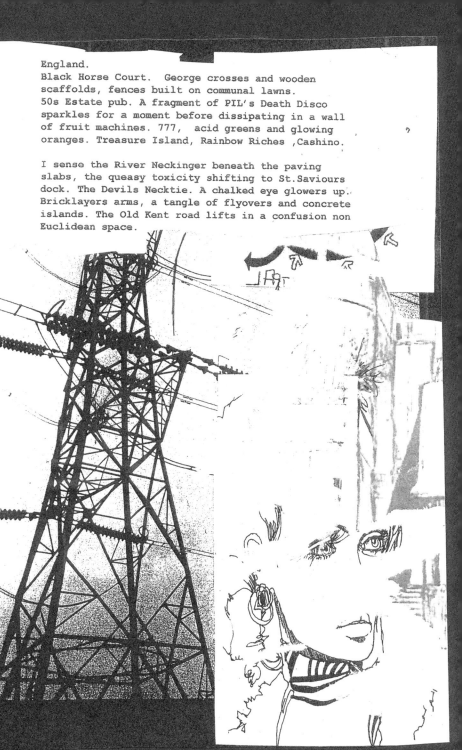

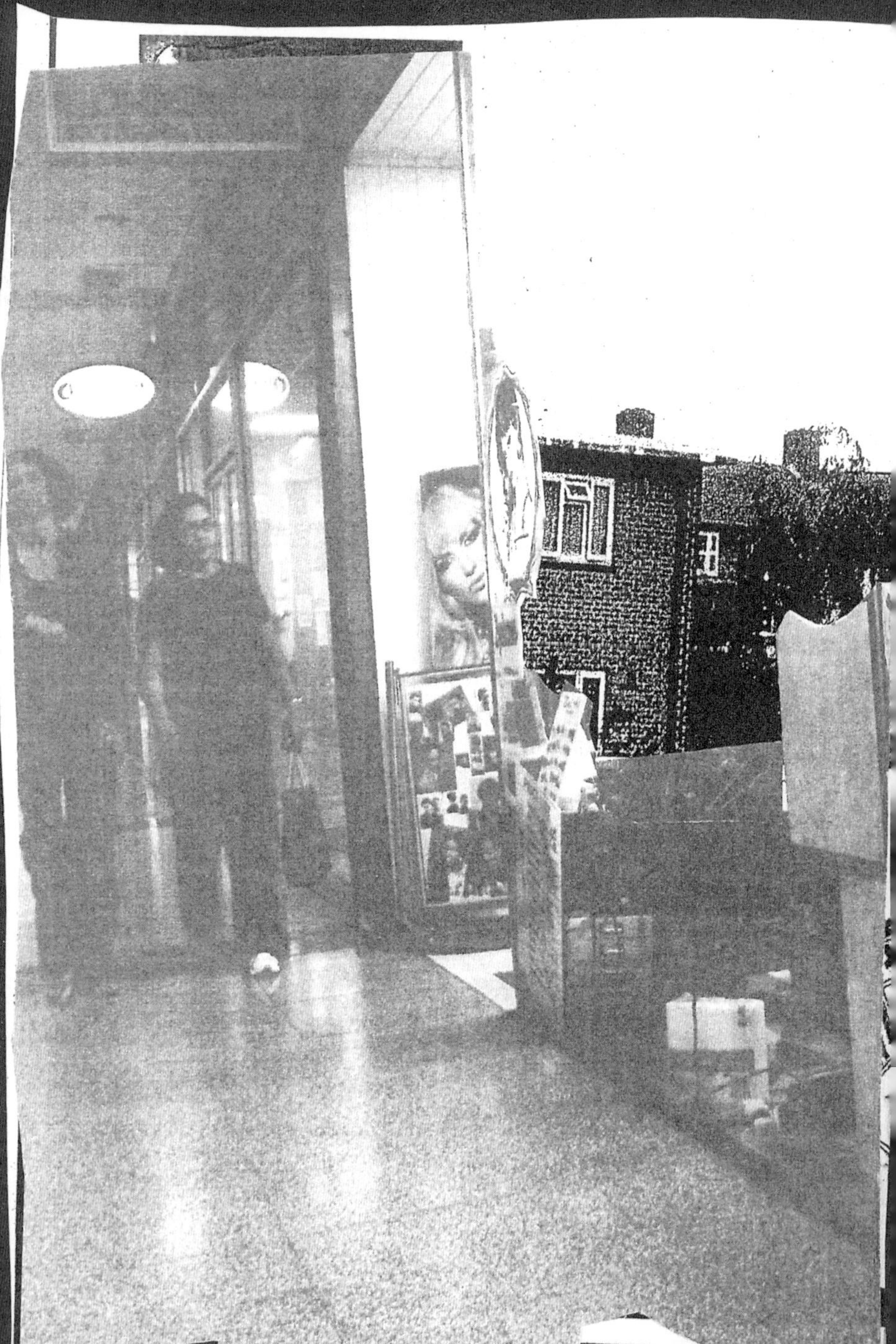

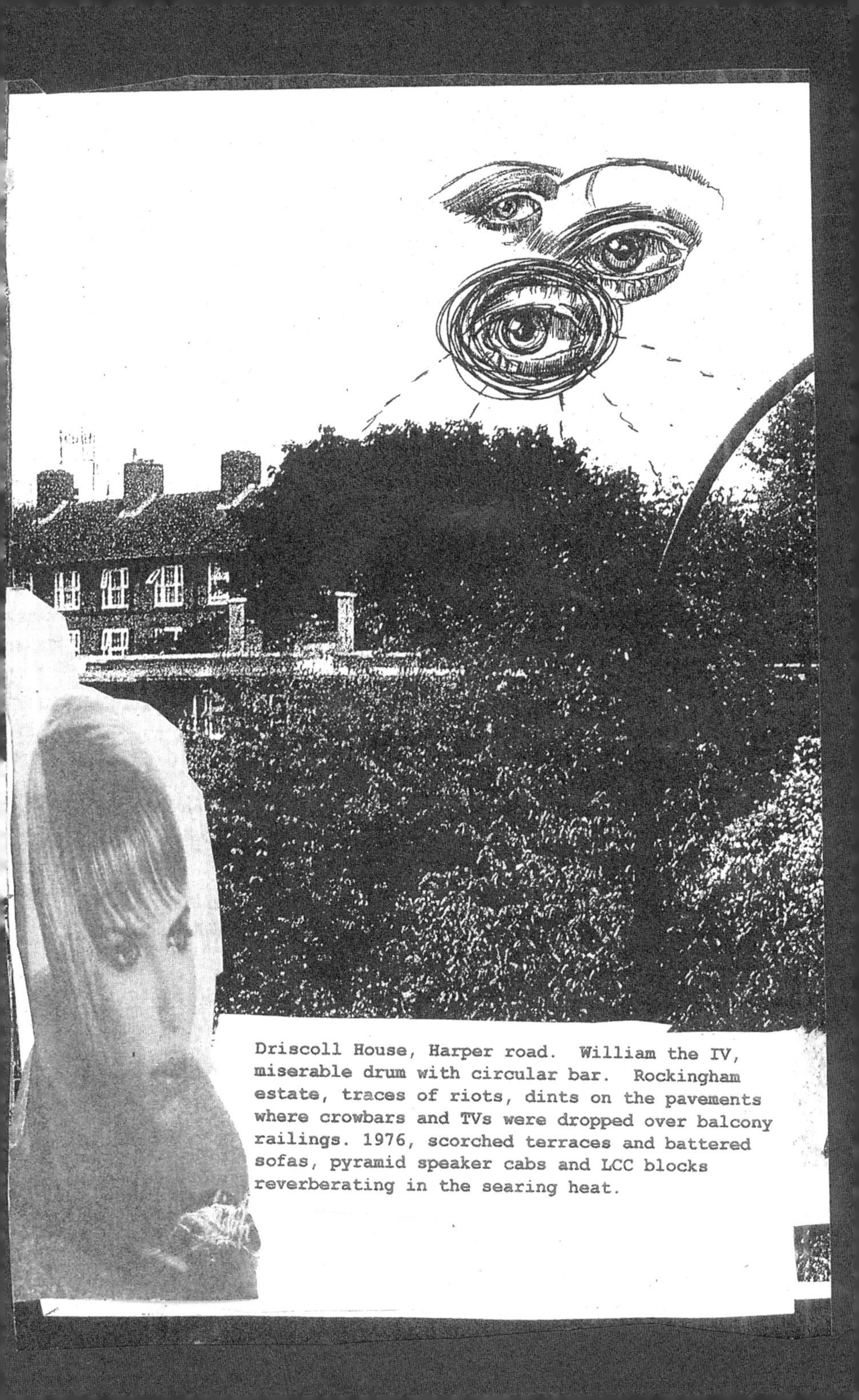

Driscoll House, Harper road. William the IV, miserable drum with circular bar. Rockingham estate, traces of riots, dints on the pavements where crowbars and TVs were dropped over balcony railings. 1976, scorched terraces and battered sofas, pyramid speaker cabs and LCC blocks reverberating in the searing heat.

May 2001. A macabre play of semiotic markers conjuring the phantom of an imagined England. NF hyperactivity . Bermondsey, that knotwork of bombsites and dank maisonettes, ghost of Surrey canal pulling us deep into hostile terrain. Festering hatred in rotten pubs, eggs thrown from seventh floor flats. Squads and spotters,, eyes darting with suspicion and territorial assertion. A pointless escapade round Southwark Park road, cracking ribs to prise open police cordons. Drinking plans laid to waste as we ride caged up in the back of a meat wagon to Stokey nick. Thrown out at 4a.m, flats raided in a series of petulant Section 18s.

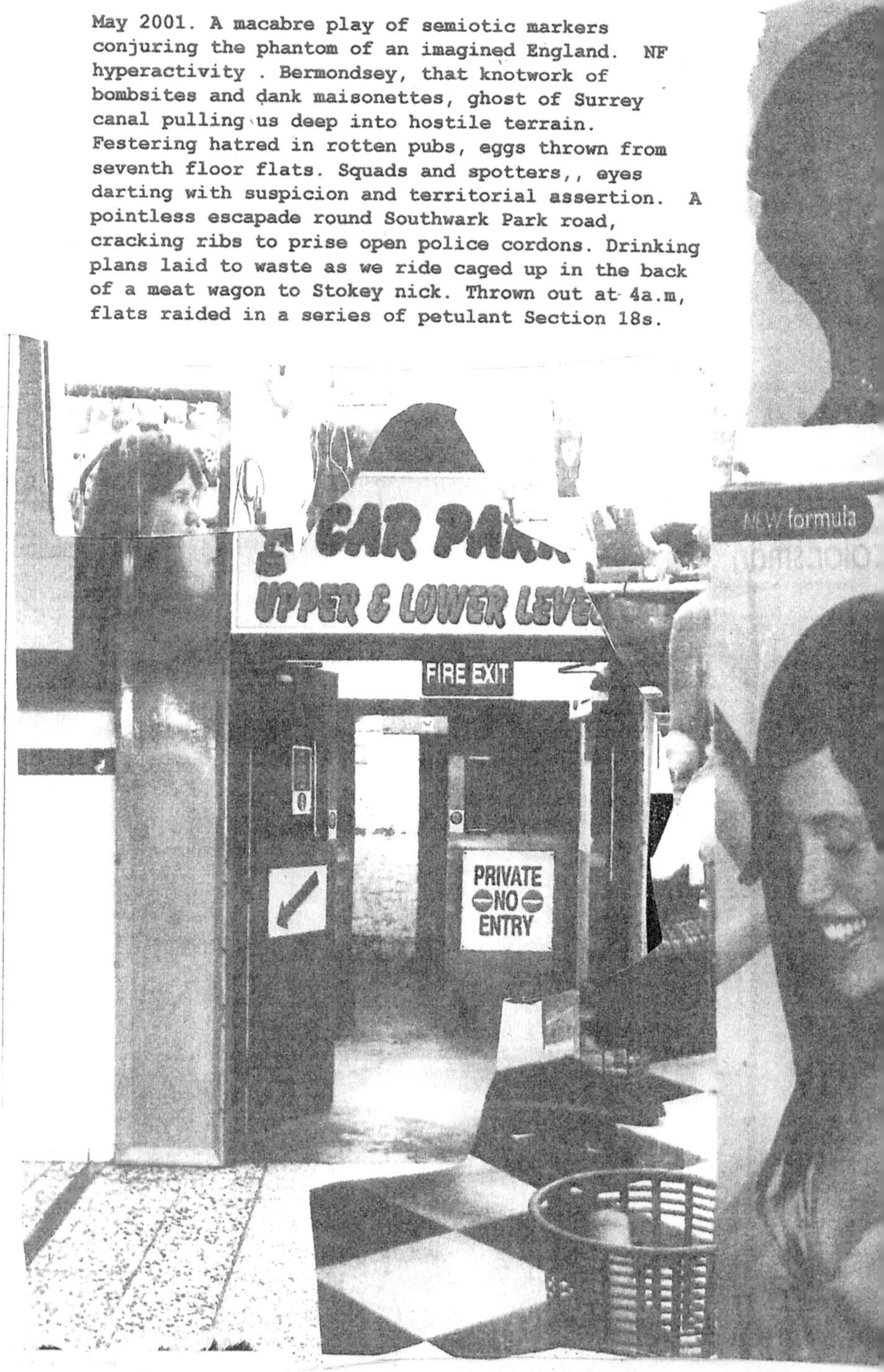
CAR PARK
UPPER & LOWER LEVE
FIRE EXIT
PRIVATE
NO
ENTRY
NEW formula

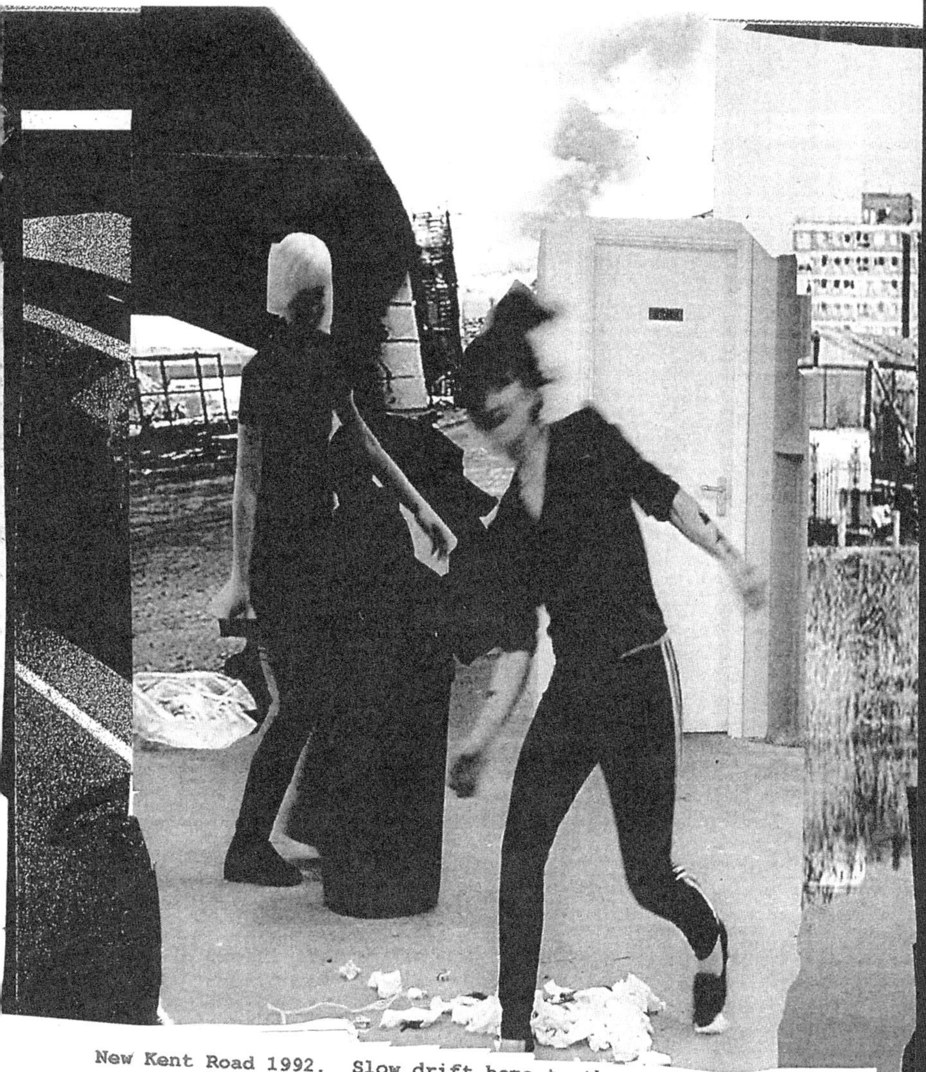

New Kent Road 1992. Slow drift home to the Stockwell Road squat. Killing time before the pub opens. Stifling subways, the yellow glow of decaying strip lights. Alexander Fleming House , domesticated and rebranded. Yearn for its former brutality, to be able to fix it in a Balfron, Tricorn triumverate. The Elephant and Castle Pub. ROOMS AVAILABLE UPSTAIRS, haunted by the demolished Odeon, wrecked in one weekend in 1988, two days before it was to be listed.

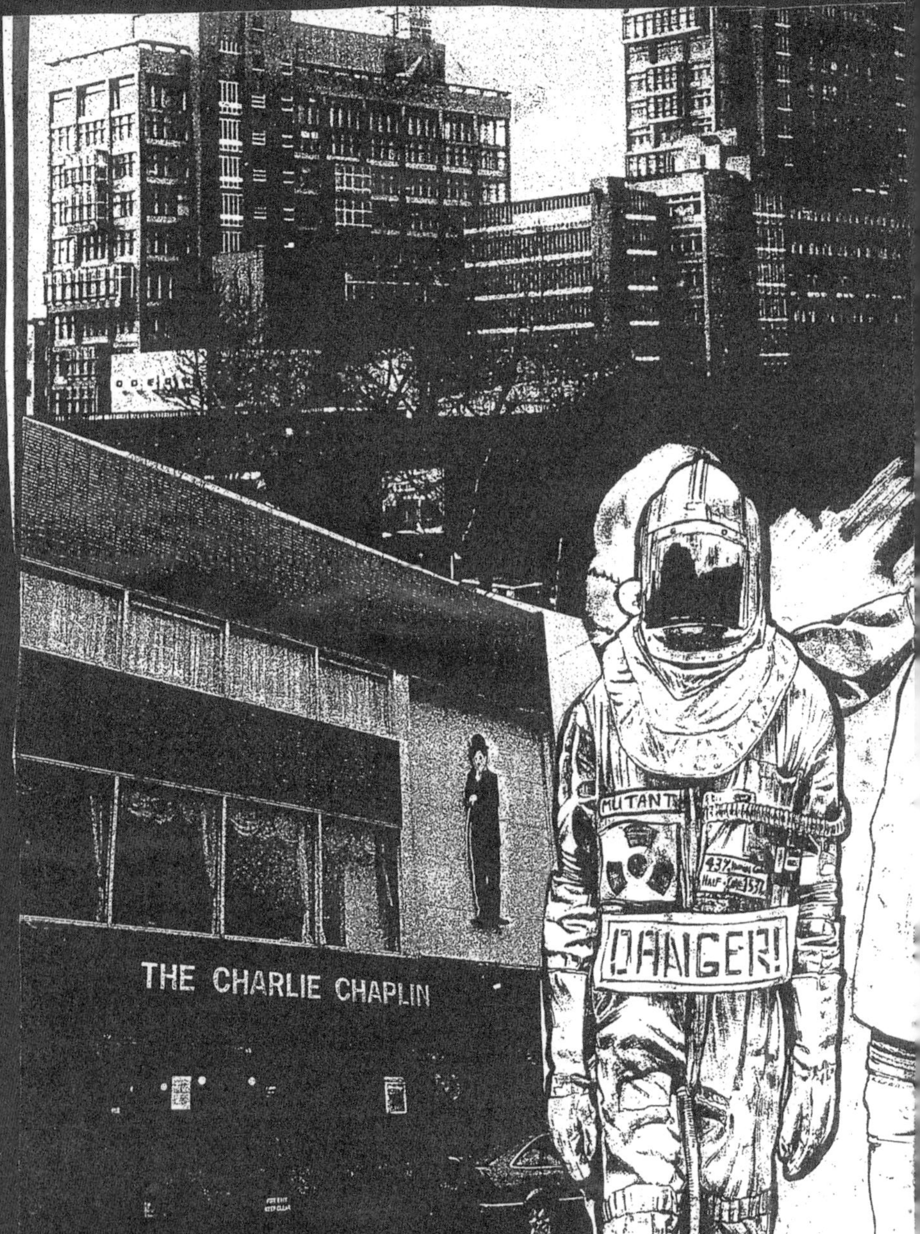
THE CHARLIE CHAPLIN
MUTANT
DANGER!

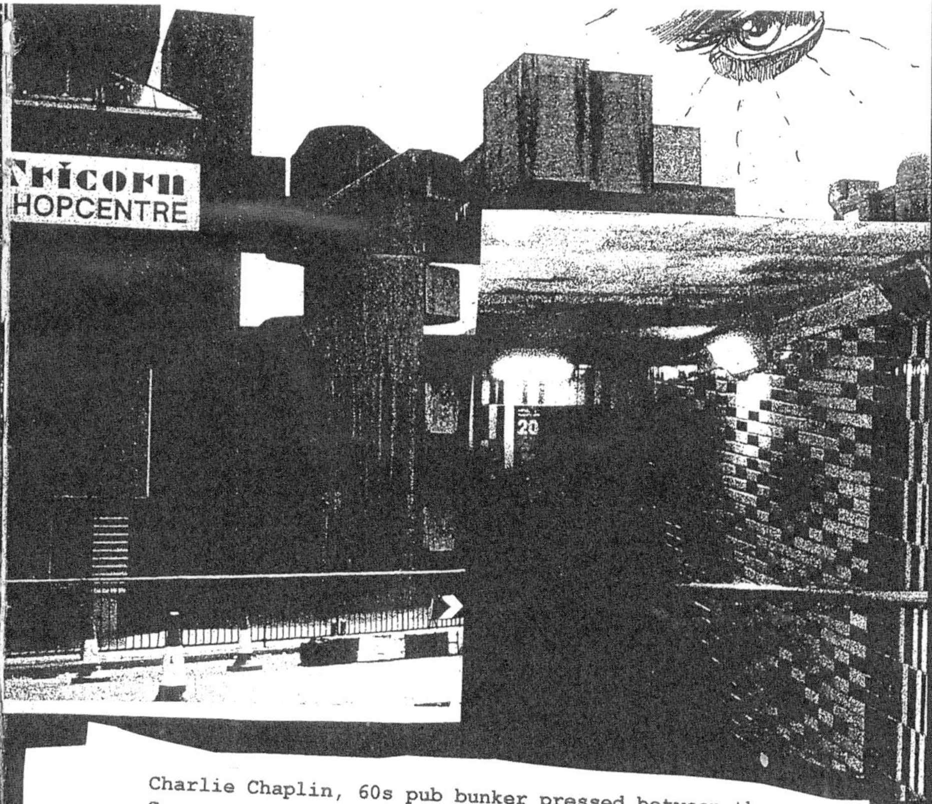

Tricorn
HOPCENTRE
20

Charlie Chaplin, 60s pub bunker pressed between the Coronet and the shopping centre. Lurid pink like worming medicine. /

Nobody, Gaslamp, Killer D-Styles
Junglist mayhem. Kicking up at Ministry, AWOL , Randall, double impact mixing. //
Semiotic reconfigurations and the shifting topographies of Lovecraft.

The ghost of Rodney Gordon's design for the centre, submitted in 1959 , imagined a Kasbah interior with pinnacle tower block , concrete domes and spirals. The plans for this brutalist extravaganza, akin to his other hallowed idyll the Tricorn centre were cast aside in favour of the inferior Willets group design.

Outside there's all these lost ravers, staggering through the dusk since Shoom! Glo sticks, white gloves luminous garb. Jacobs optical stairway-- spatial disorientation.

We stagger into the magenta haze of the
tavern. Lozenges of yellow light dart across black
walls. Silver ribbons sparkle over a gum blistered
stage. A red haired boy, malfunctioning marionette,
does a broken dance in a clown wig and lycra shorts.
Kinetic clack clack /
              disembodied _ vocoder words hover.
         70s furnishings mould around , red dreylon,
peeling flock…
      benylin, Fosters., tramadol/

a slow drift to the fire exit leads not to the lost
alleyways and tenements of a pre blitz Newington but
on to the decaying fabric of a 60s precinct,
jewelled mosaics now coated in a film of black
grease.

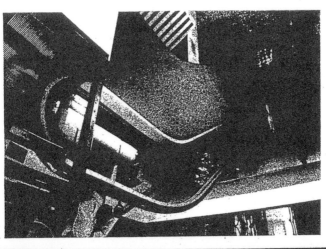

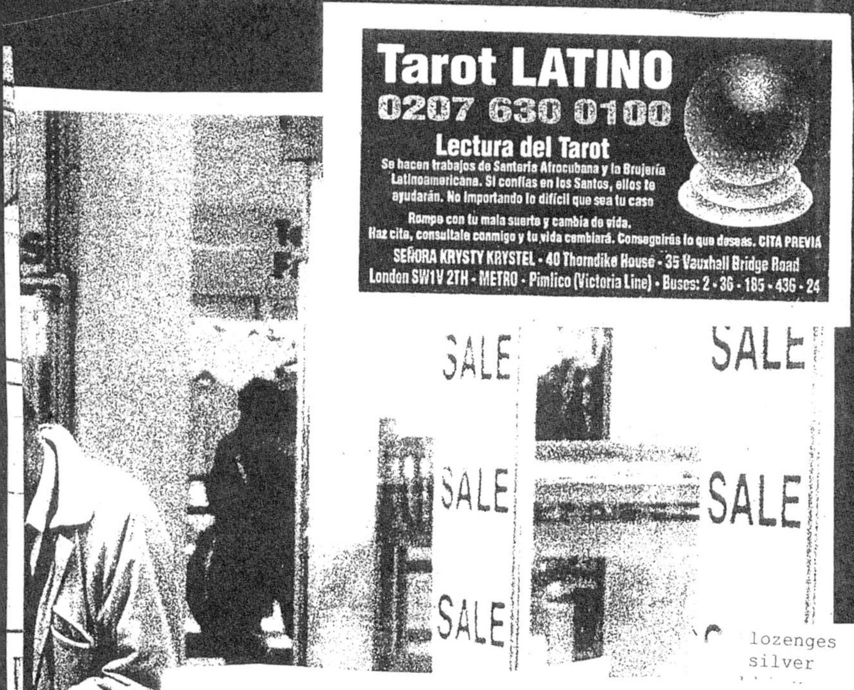
Tarot LATINO
0207 630 0100
Lectura del Tarot
Se hacen trabajos de Santería Afrocubana y la Brujería Latinoamericana. Si confías en los Santos, ellos te ayudarán. No importando lo difícil que sea tu caso
Rompe con tu mala suerte y cambia de vida.
Haz cita, consultale conmigo y tu vida cambiará. Conseguirás lo que deseas. CITA PREVIA
SEÑORA KRYSTY KRYSTEL - 40 Thorndike House - 35 Vauxhall Bridge Road
London SW1V 2TH - METRO - Pimlico (Victoria Line) - Buses: 2 - 36 - 185 - 436 - 24
SALE
SALE
SALE
SALE
SALE

lozenges
silver

The hidden eyes of this panoptican monad scan the arcades, despotic managers and private armies run the arcades that replace city squares.
The state deterritorializes.

This is 2013, a bindweed dilerium, Japanese knotweed and Russian vine, convolvulus creeping over walls. The glittering scheme of the PFI consortium lies in ruins,; Foster and Partners, Tibblads, TM2, Gehl Architects and Space Syntax; mystical names from another era.

Of the two skyscrapers destined to flank the new plaza only one stands, the Hamzah and Yeang bioclimatic tower. It is sitexed up on the main concourse and in the abandoned reception area there is no concierge.
Starlings line the security fences .
Graffitied eyes spray painted on curving glass walls herald a violent return.

This skyscraper was supposed to be a 'tripartite living solution' implementing vertical zoning in an unwitting parody of a Ballardian High Rise. Ideas of drawing street life up vertically to the 'spectacular sky gardens' have collapsed as the botanical outcrops are choked with ragwort and ivy strangles the ventilation shafts.

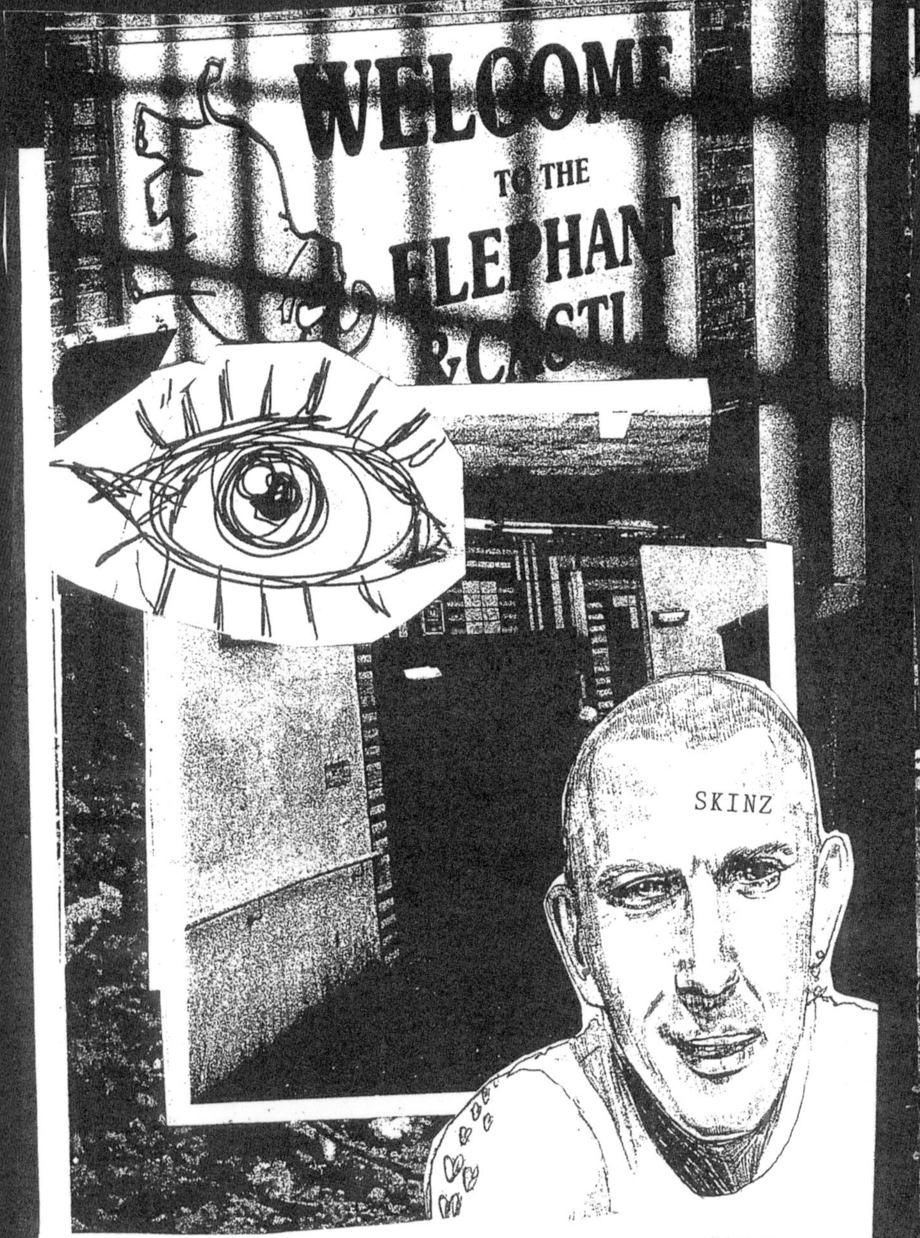
WELCOME
TO THE
SKINZ

The investors backed out long ago after an intensification of terrorist activity in the run up to the 2012 Olympics. The rich don't want to live in zone 1 now, instead they demand exurbia, gated citadels, avenues of guarded comfort.

And so the abandoned scheme, the phantom city.
Relics of the 60s remain as I pick my way over the
rubble of a traffic intersection and excavated
subways. A JCB stands motionless above the maw of
the labyrinth, fragments of yellow tiles glisten in
the dirt.

I step tentatively across wire and pink dust
glancing across at the shopping centre relic, its
foundations visible through the shell of the upper
floors. The escalators are still grinding in empty
deliverance.

And next to it the beginnings of a new retail city
with its glazed canopy. Wiring and circuitry hang
exposed , so too the service tunnels, pipes and
conduits.

Excavations and a burst main, the Neckinger rises
again.

The Faraday metal box has survived, a cage where no
electrical signals can be received. Luminous runes
and glyphs have appeared on its studded surface. .
Cryptic notation. Space to channel, for other
selves to come. Faraday, a Sandemanian, saw nature
interconnected in a single entity, electricity and
magnetism interlinked.

The new Heygate boulevard is desolate but still
holds the traces of the old estate beyond the glass
fronted Foster embarrassments. I try desperately to
find the locus of the estate, the sunken garden in
Deacon way. The gleaming edifices of the new plaza
are smashed now, buildings turned inside out, a dark
and frenzied carnival has spun through these malls.
The desolation of the sunken garden sends me reeling
into reverse.

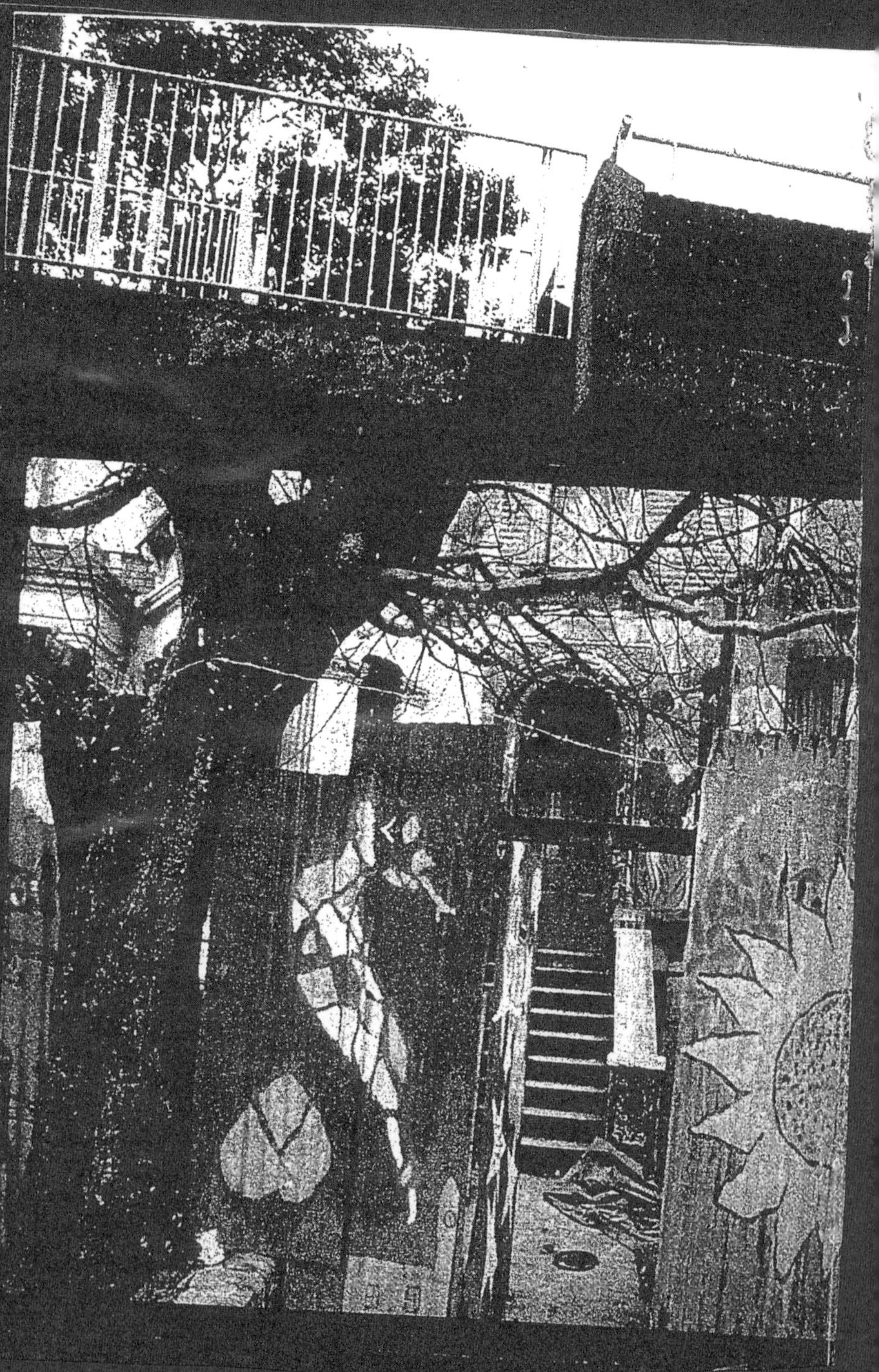

enclosing a sunken garden. Another chalked eye
appears amidst neoclassical figures and fading
roses. I drift through intimate walkways , crossing
Heygate street on a concrete footbridge,
particles of dust float in the warm golden air.
The Archduke Charles stands derelict on the corner.
Encrypted palimpsests, peeling layers of text creep
over boarded windows.
1992, last throes of convoy culture. A balmy
Summer night. Beneath an elderflower canopy, the
beer garden is suffused with indigo light and a
heady confection of woodsmoke and weed. Punks in
studded leather sprawl on discarded furniture.
Radical Dance Faction, Back to the Planet, Gene
October, Chelsea,, zealous ranting from a wrecked
saloon bar.

I'm wearing a yellow dress as I conjure a 60s
phantom. Neon hearts spring ceaselessly from
reinforced concrete slabs as we fall into the back
of a van for a joyride escape North of the River.
Bridges warp and barriers fragment in the rush. 777
flashes up, spasming and dissolving, muscles taut
and skin bruising fast in the heat. The sky glows
red, sweet embers signalling the next episode.

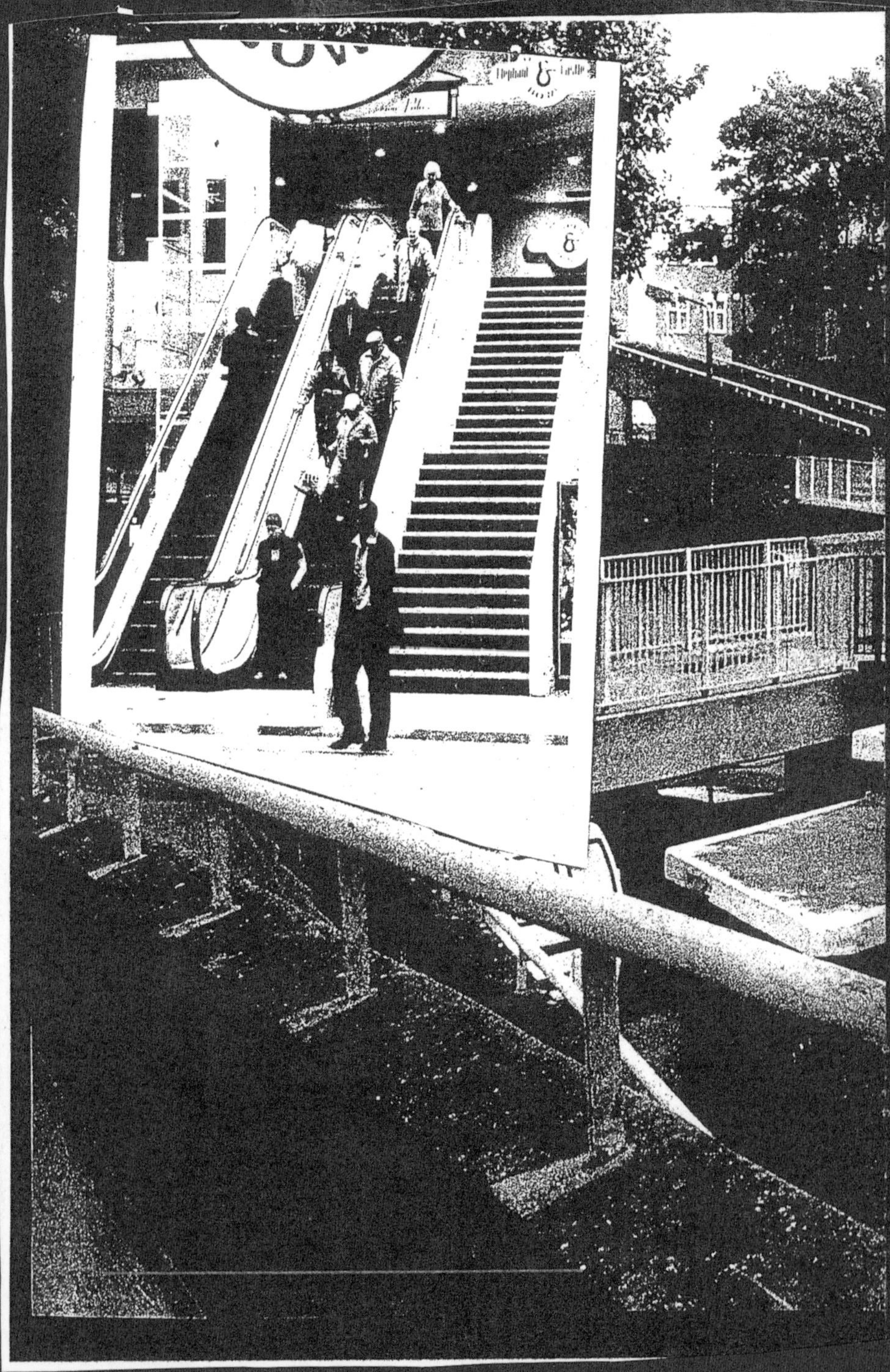

A truncated walkway, a perilous drop onto a bombsite of red campion and dog daisies. Red starts line the telephone wires. I walk through the sickly sweet smell of the doughnut factory to a rooftop enclosure of barbed wire and black doors. The words FEAR==POWER are scratched above ghoulish representations of Bush and Blair.
Up concrete steps, through stacks of plastic chairs, the door is pushed to reveal codes in flux, a world hidden from the uninitiated. A seventh day Adventist church is concealed within a janitorial supplies building. Immersed in systems, invisible most of the time, the veneer is momentarily torn affording a glimpse into those other worlds we walk through. Unseen forces, the National Grid, ethereal mazes of mobile phone signals. Cherubim and Seraphim, English Martyrs RC club, ambiguous orientation.

Fluorescent bibs, bones and burgers. East Street Market, chicken shacks and empty oil drums. The council try to shut it down, running horror stories in the South London press. Planners want to factor in 'colour' in a new 'character market' where Londoners can be paraded for the amusement of home counties and City types.

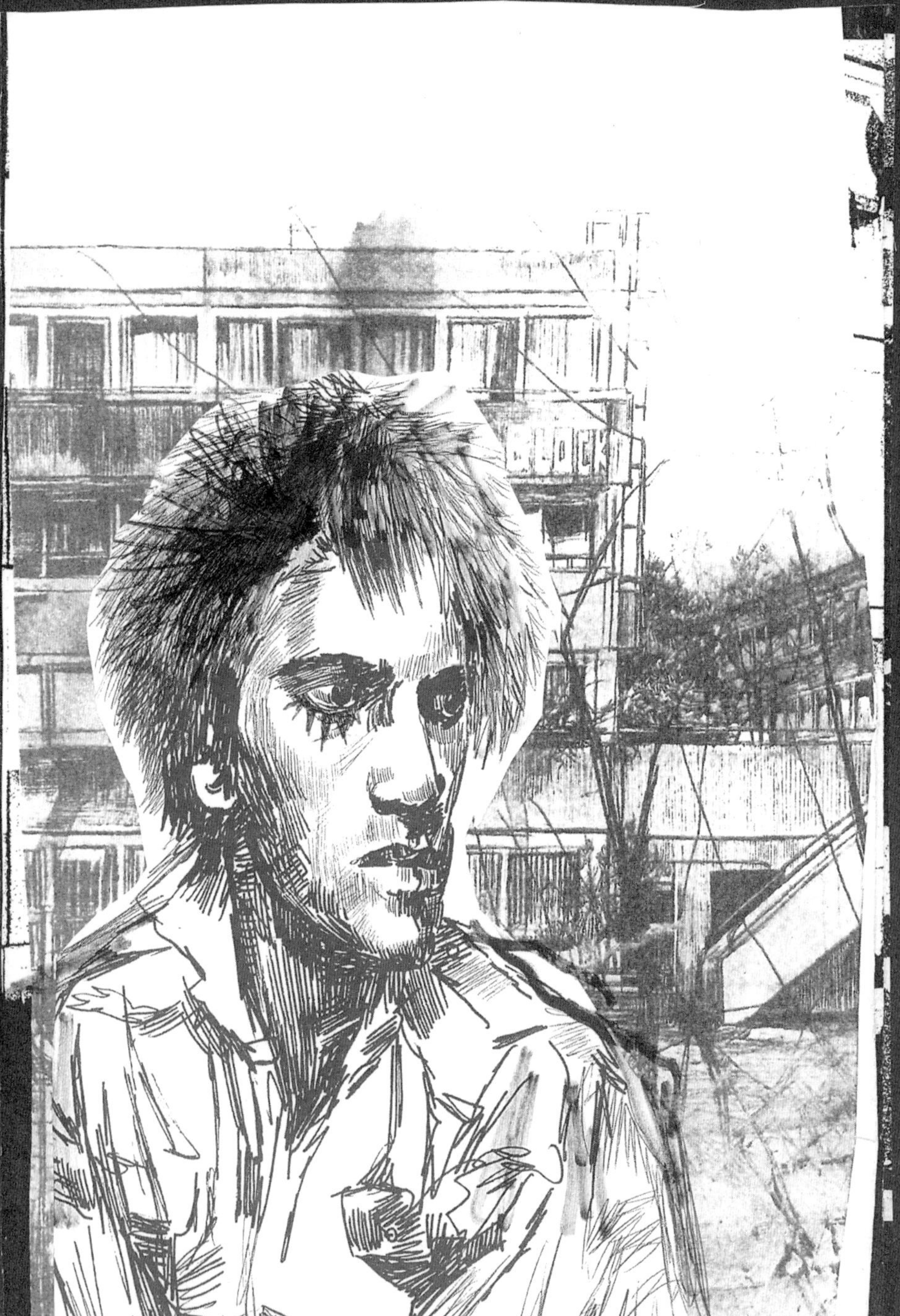

The Aylesbury estate. Redevelopment plans were thwarted after a no vote in 2001. The Heygate are denied a direct ballot.

Taplow , my old block. Rows of George crosses blocking smeared windows. Old Testament names, Ezekiel , Ephraim graffed in the lifts. There were yellow signs outside the block when I came in at 6 in the morning after an ugly night on ketamine in a New Cross squat. Police tape spanned the stairwells, the lifts were out of order and the Old Bill were on the landing.

Door to door.

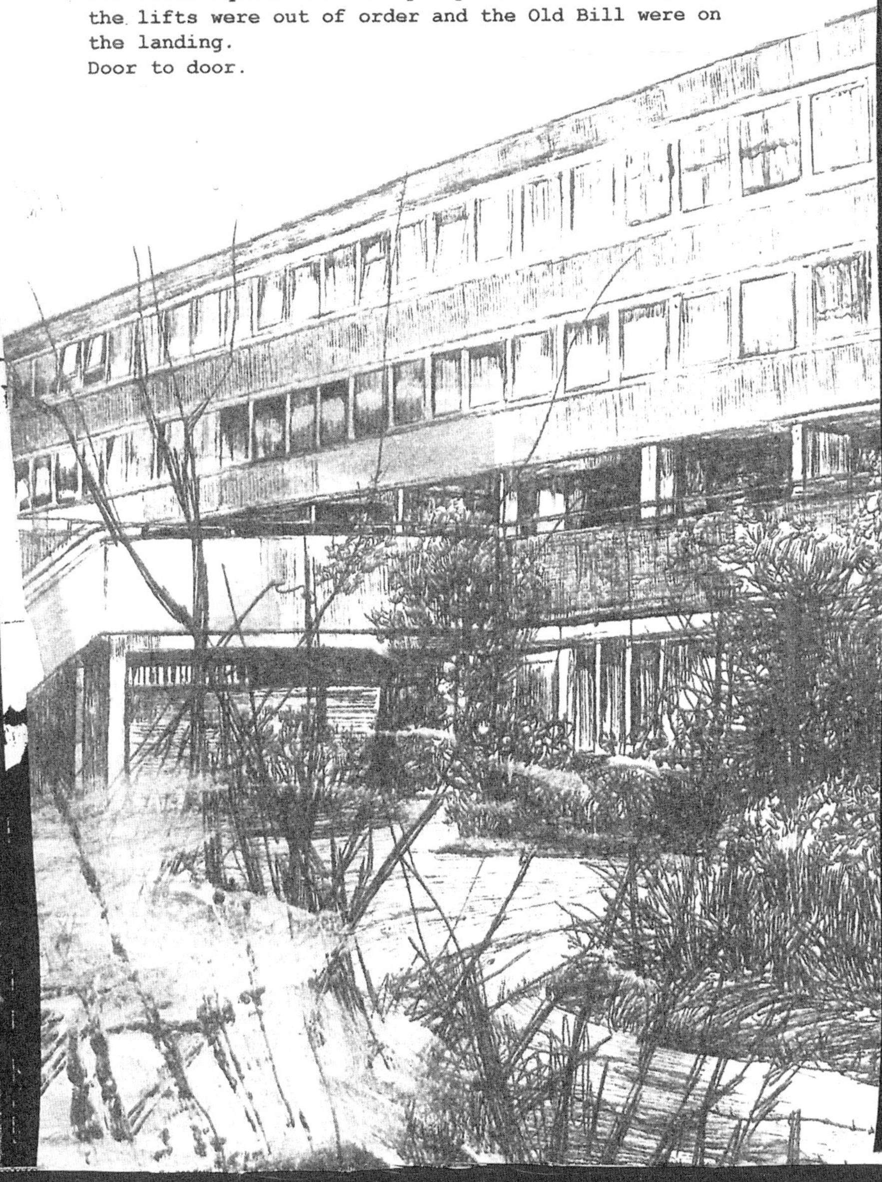

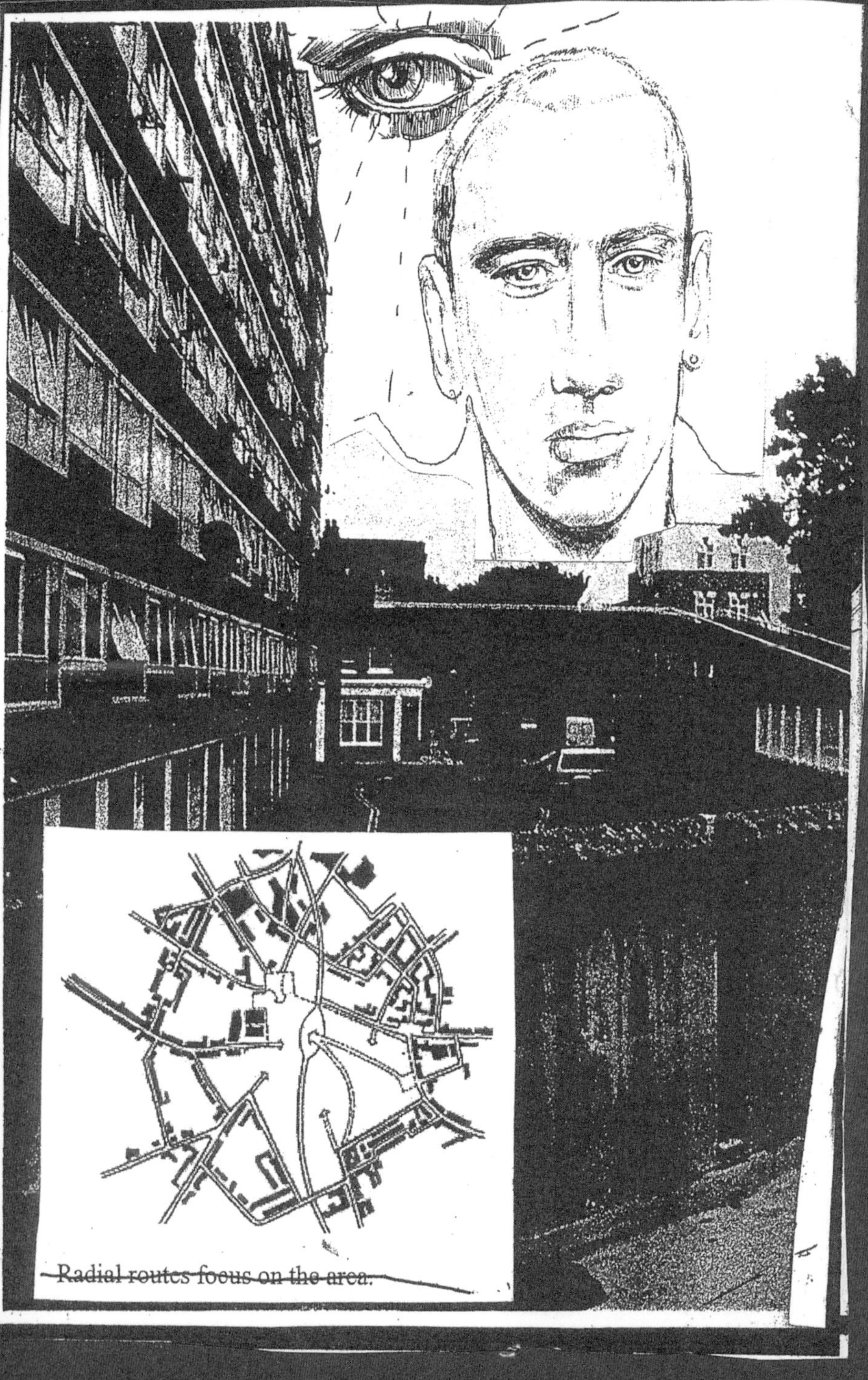
Radial routes focus on the area.

Wendover, mirror image Corbusian slab. Someone I
know burns out their flat in a bid to be rehoused.
Spiral tribe on the roof of that 12 storey block
setting off red military flares. The Irish
contingent from the squatted North Peckham estate
making Super 8 films, smashing sitex panels with
sledge hammers. Military detritus, smoking lift
shafts , windows daubed with black commands,
THATCHER,GIVE BACK THE NORTH! SMASH H BLOCK!
UP THE RA!

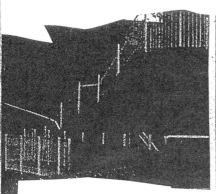
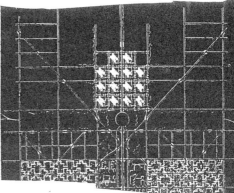

Armed response unit come crashing up stairwells, the
cast is hauled off on firearms charges.

Under the concrete stilts of the block there's a
charred patch of wasteground. The squatters are back
from the convoy, ambulances and horseboxes line the
perimeter of the estate. This hybrid style is just
starting to happen, it is 1985. The gig is an ALF
benefit, Flux of Pink Indians have transmuted ino
Hotilaccio after being called on to play Tube
disasters too many times. The lightning bolt symbol
replicates across shadowy courtyards.

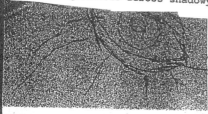

LE CORBUSIER'S DESIGN FOR THE FUTURE

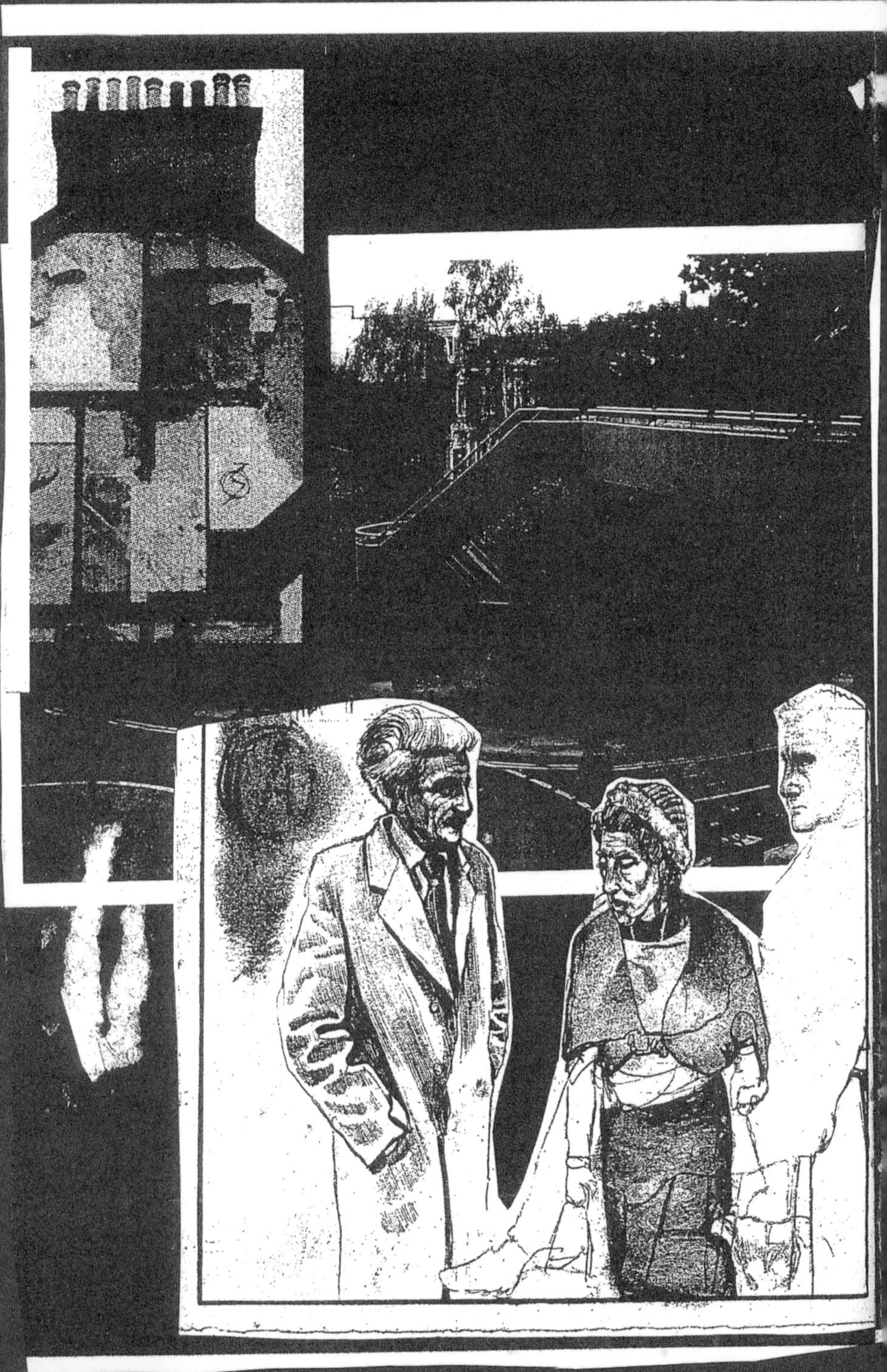

That nexus of dissolution. My loss. Of self.
Absenting myself from the life I had ended up with.
Burgess park, empty landscape of 70s slum clearances
.

Sitting on a crumbling wall scarred yellow with
lichen, contemplating my escape to the bawdy
drinking dens of Deptford and Peckham. The path of
the ghost canal, desire lines slipping under foot,
I remember that year, do you?
 The Montague Arms, dashing brains out of pumpkin
lanterns. Trashed in Nunhead cemetery, little piles
of sacrificial bones. Bun House, Drovers, October
nights hazy with bonfires. The squat on Stuart Road,
drawing red lines on the map connecting all our
hidden bolt holes. His kisses were fierce. I
remember arms and legs scratched and tangled from
briars in the graveyard. The first bite of winter
black.

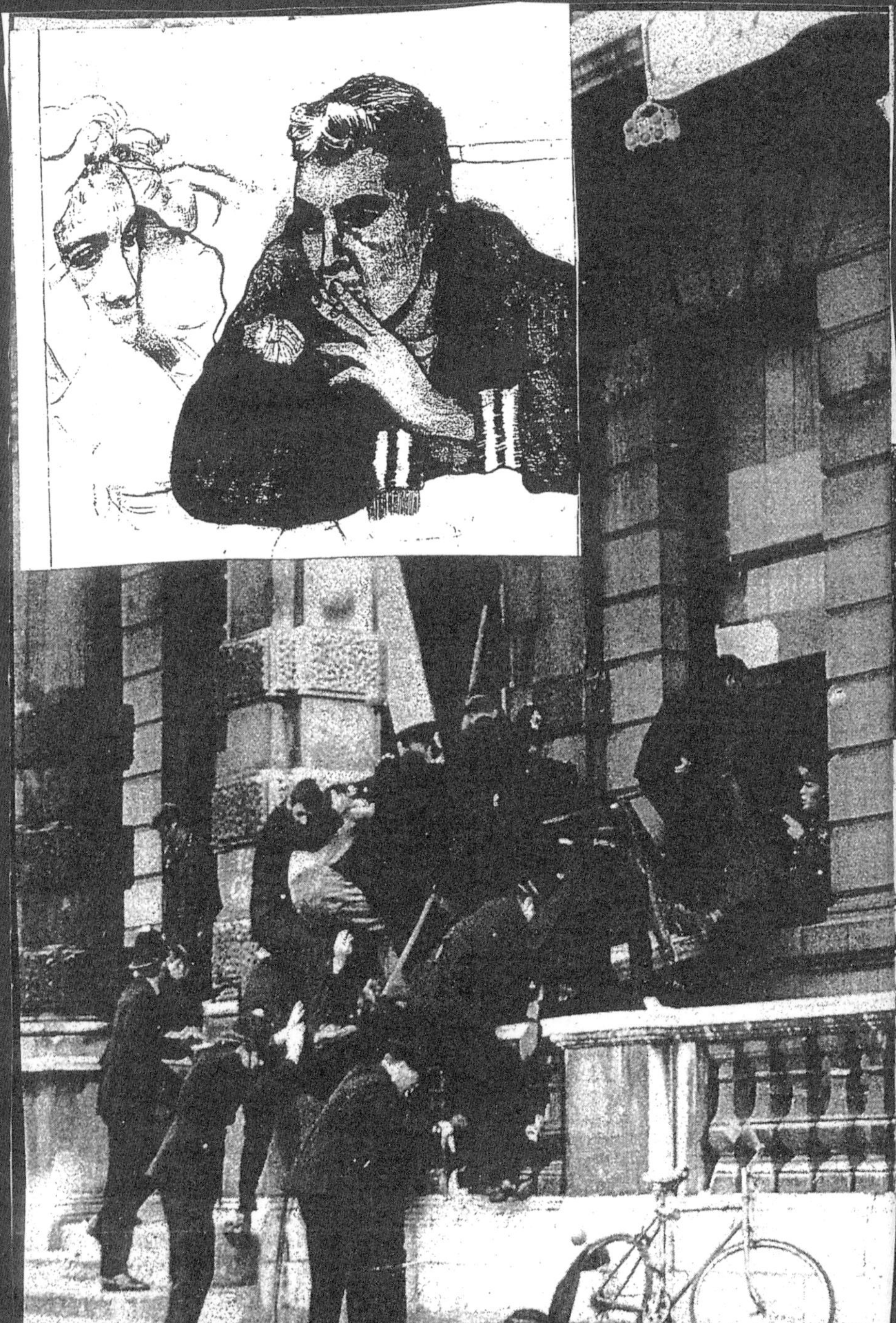

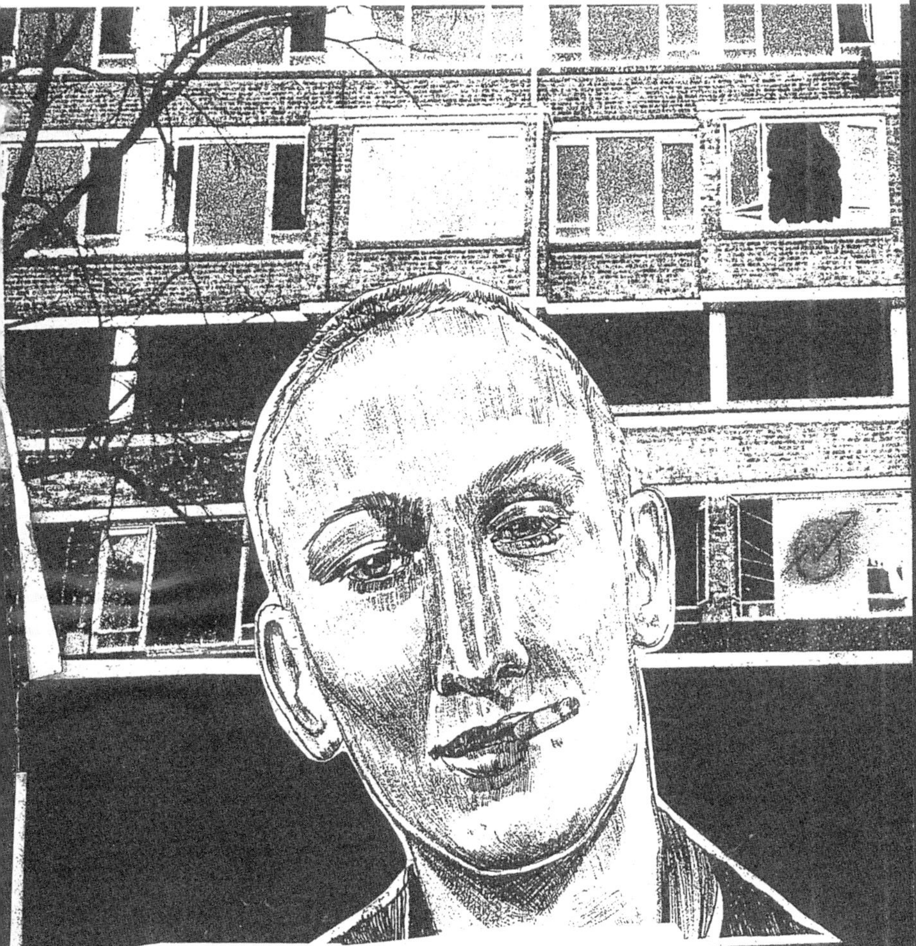

1984, Class War benefit. Squatted fire station, Old Kent Road. Surly faced Anarchos roaming mahogany corridors , bands on the Crass label , white noise and short circuits.

Ghosts of places we imagine, pushed into myth and drunken brags. Always yearning for the time that just eluded us.

Thomas a Becket, public house, site of telescoping misery. Public hangings , , relics of ripper murders, men brain damaged in the boxing ring. Always at the crossroads so their spirits couldn't find the way back.

A brawl spills out. Millwall F Troop tearing up the Old Kent road. Heads smashed into Black Mariahs, iron bars brandished and bollards coated with carmine pigment.

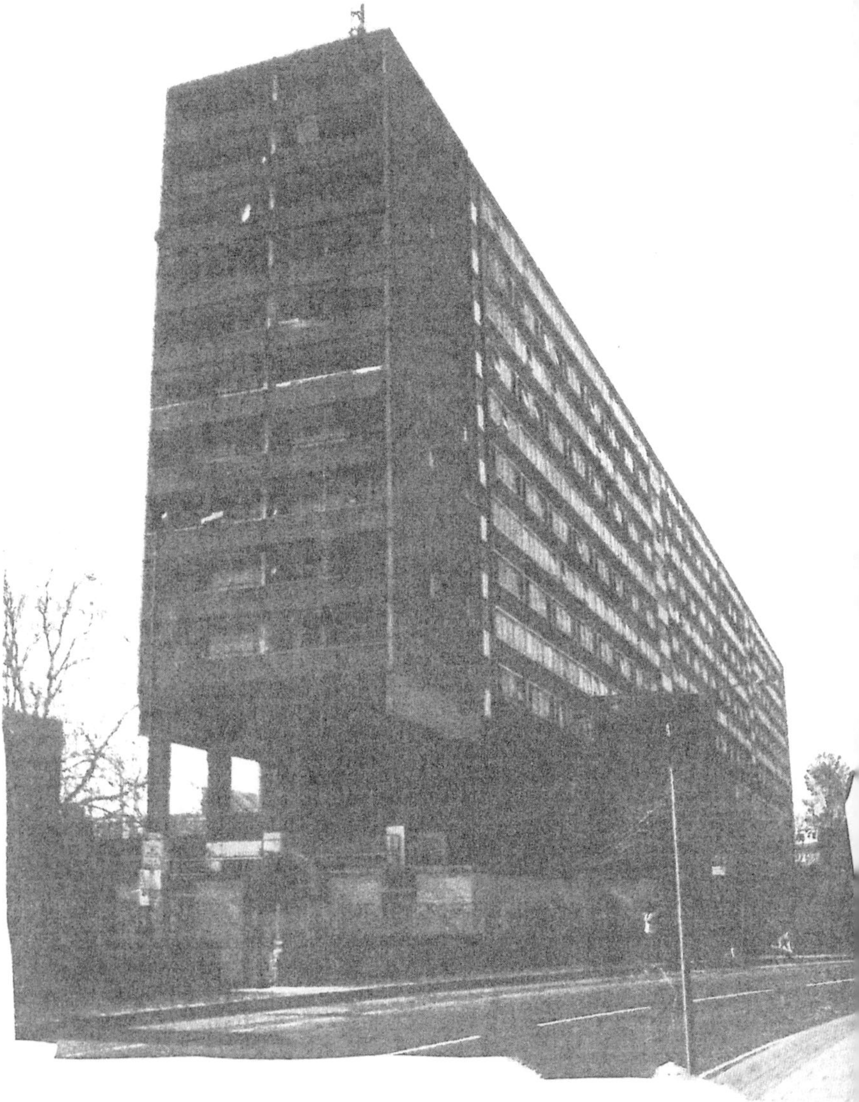

A tainted landscape. The deserted lake on Burgess park , heart pounding and the taste of blood strong in my mouth.
My fate,
never to be content with the present,
to walk perpetually through that elegant wilderness.

Shuttled back along the Old Kent Road it becomes a
tree lined boulevard. The Heygate has gone. I am
immersed in a holographic world, in a zone that is
now 'South Central',' Mid Town', West End and City.
'Radial routes focus on the area', the Elephant is
the missing link. 'Young professionals' sit outside
gently conversing in sympathetic tones. The
translucent edifices of Starbucks and Costa become
shimmering promenades.
The people in this hushed space feel a sense of
entitlement. Their groomed heads and high end
attire create a sinister harmony, immaculately and
perfectly attuned to the order and sanitation of
this 'new quarter'. I am escorted invisibly from
the central plaza, past the Eco tower in full bloom
and the happy couples drinking champagne in the sky
gardens.

1973, 1974, 1981, 1990, 2013.
Always a return. A Mirror touch. A different way
out.

w.l become the focus to a
RGE TO DESTROY

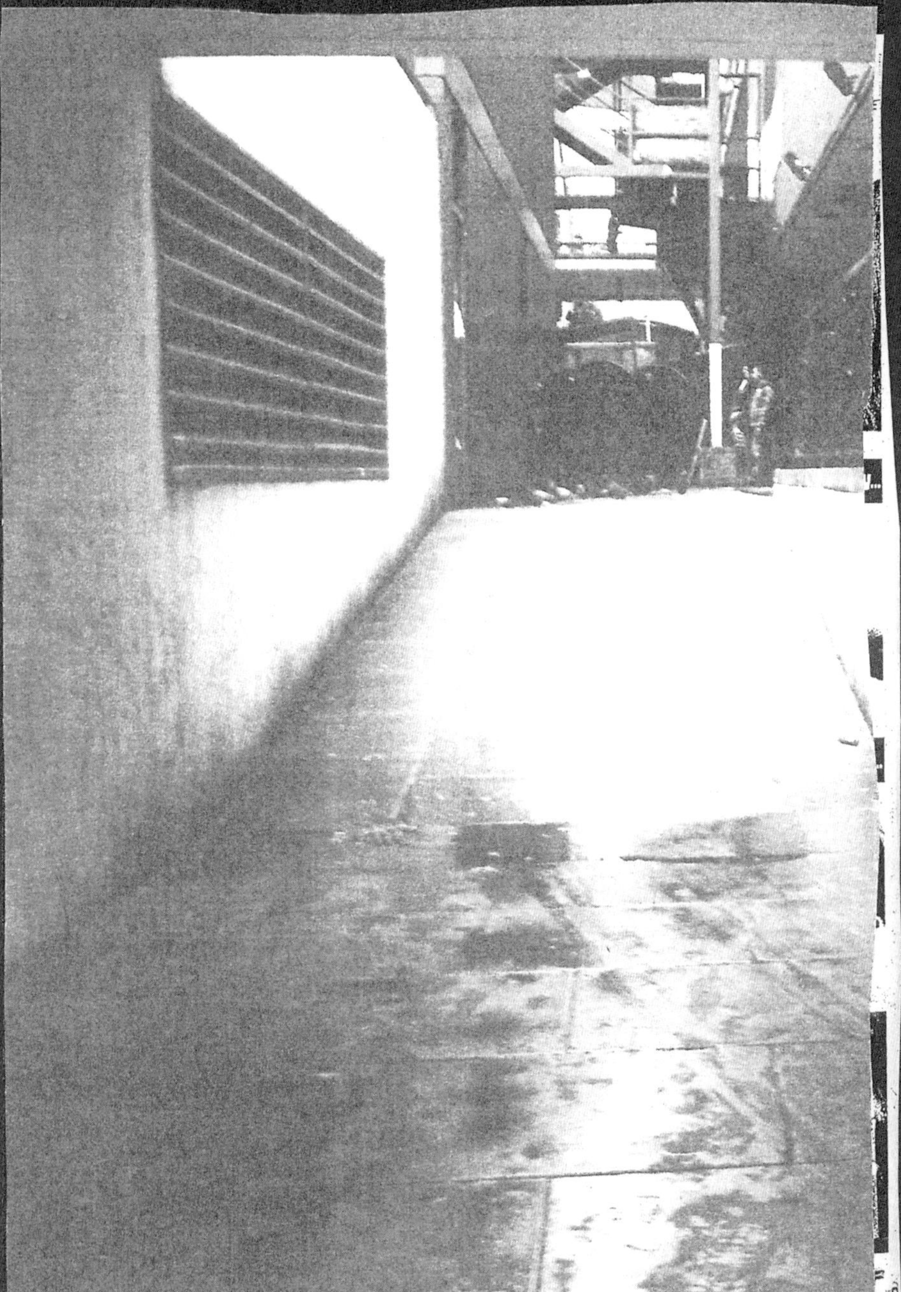

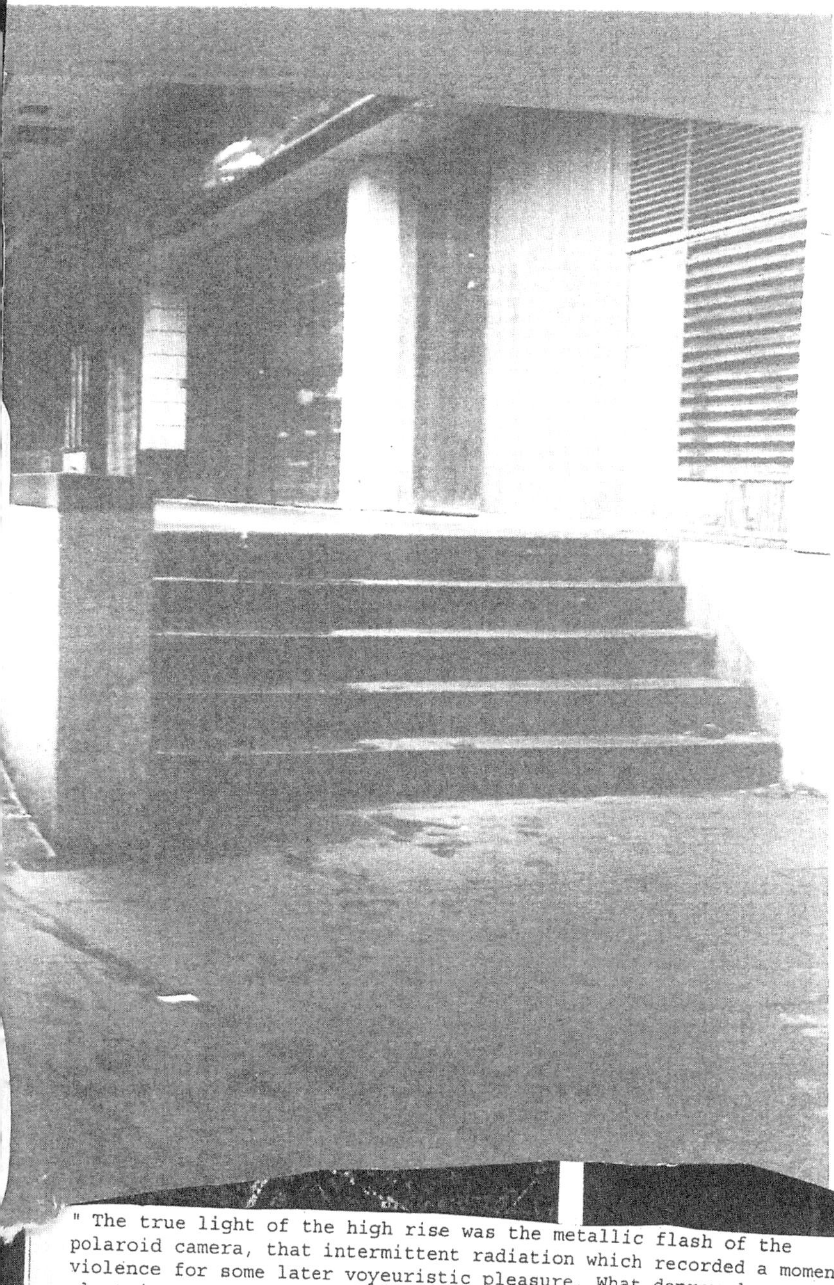

" The true light of the high rise was the metallic flash of the polaroid camera, that intermittent radiation which recorded a moment of violence for some later voyeuristic pleasure. What depraved scenes of electric fauna would spring to life from the garbage strewn carpets and corridors in response to this new source of light? The floors were littered with blackened negative strips, flakes falling from this internal sun". J.G. Ballard. Highrise.

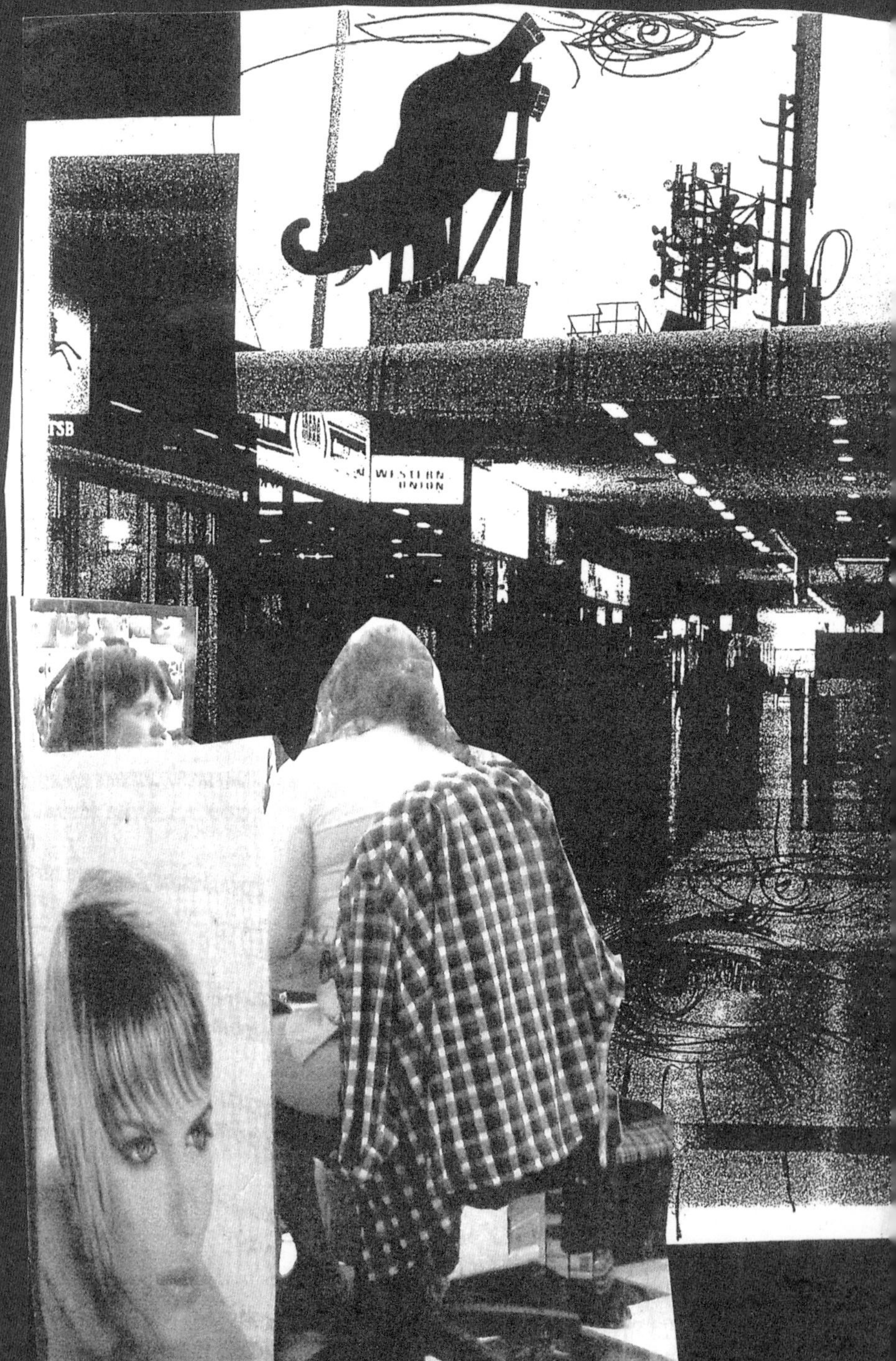

TSB
WESTERN
UNION

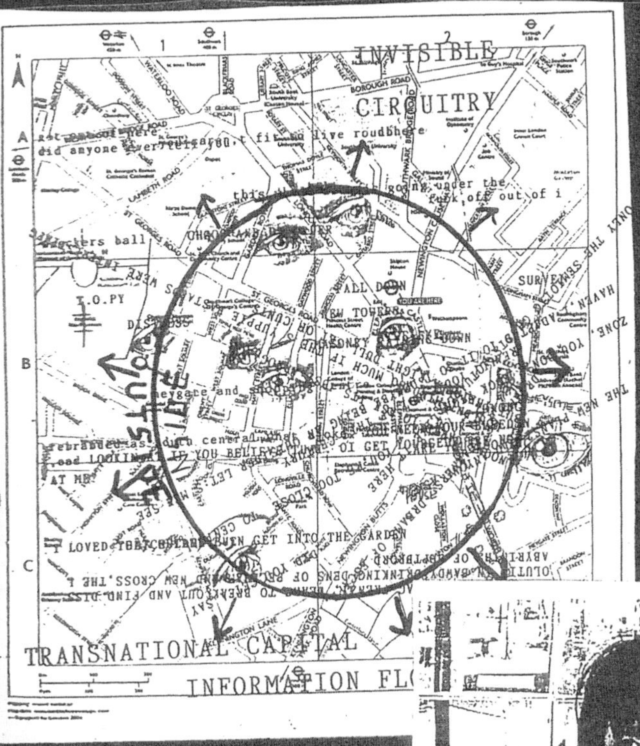
INVISIBLE
CIRCUITRY
TRANSNATIONAL CAPITAL
INFORMATION FLO

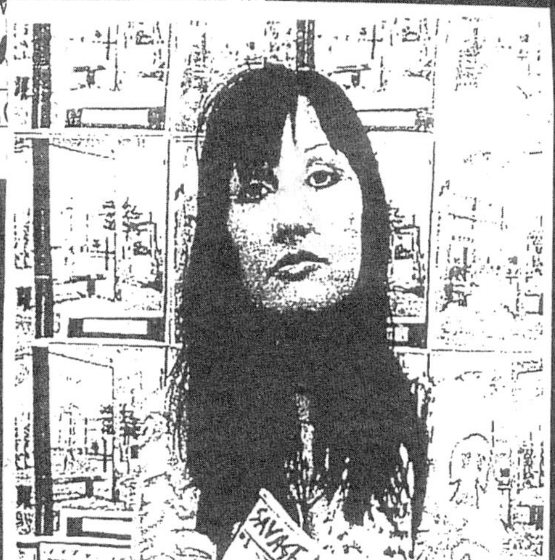
SAVAGE MESSIAH

contact and info

savagemessiah@hotmail.co.uk

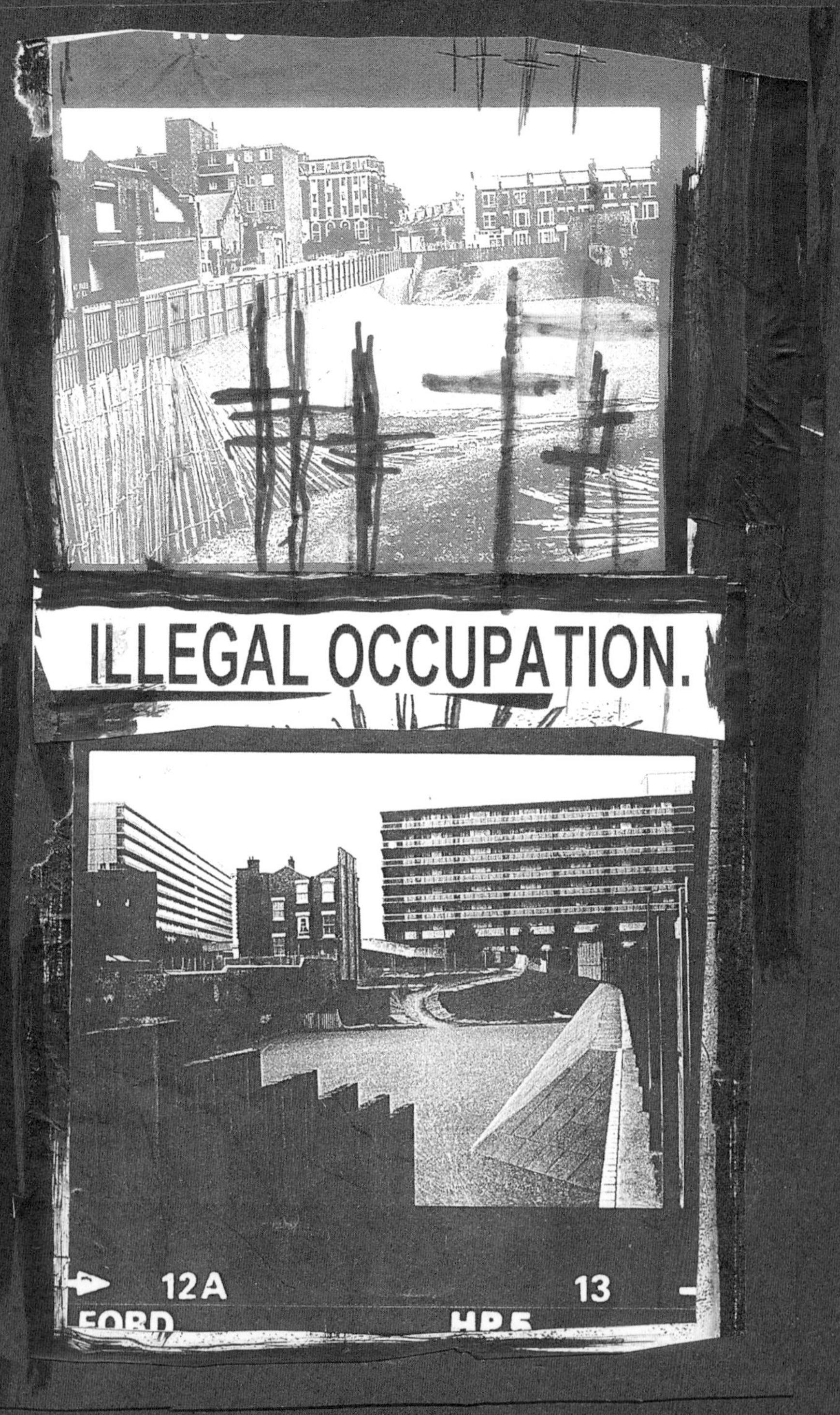
ILLEGAL OCCUPATION.
12A
13
FORD
HP5

#3 DECEMBER 2005

£1.50

"MARYLEBONE FLYOVER, HARROW ROAD, TRELLICK TOWER, POST HUMAN SENTRIES, STEPTOE + SON WESTWAY RIOTS, ST. MARYS OPIUM DRIFTS----;

SAVAGE MESSIAH

♡ ♡ ♡ ♡ LAURA OLDFIELD FORD ♡ ♡ ♡ ♡

A PERAMBULATION THROUGH THE SHADOWSCAPES...

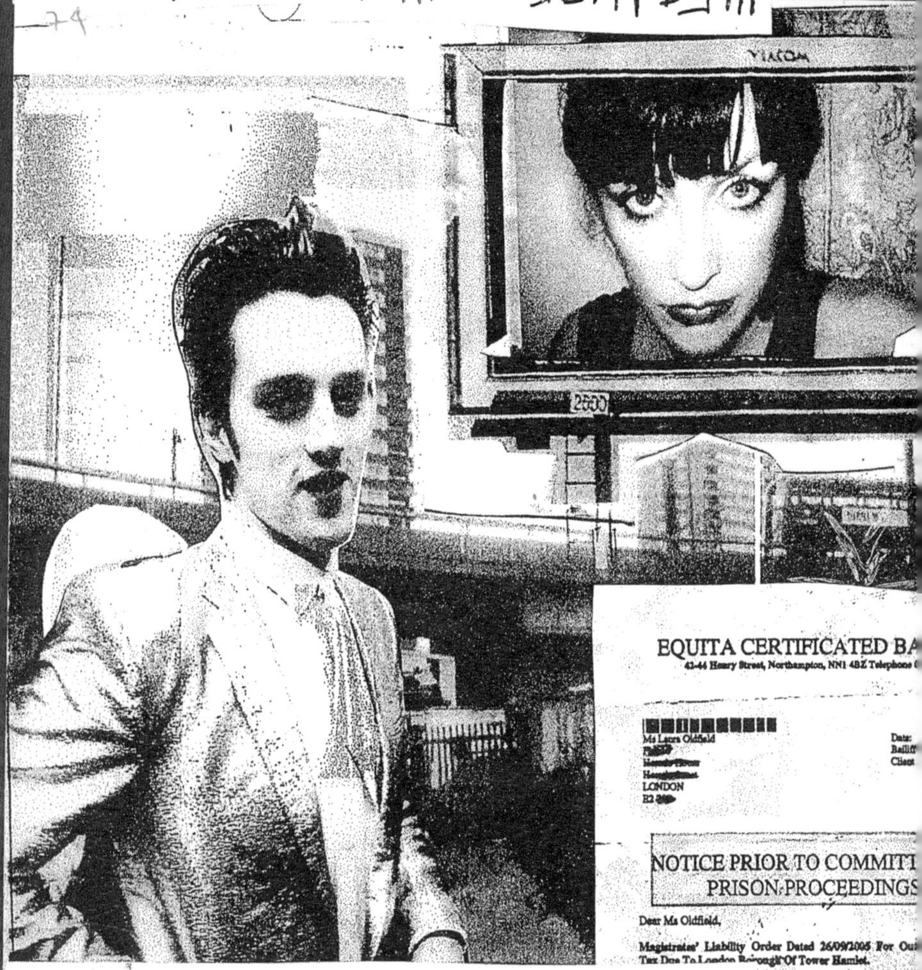
VIACOM
2500
EQUITA CERTIFICATED BA
42-44 Henry Street, Northampton, NN1 4BZ Telephone 0
[redacted]
Ms Laura Oldfield
[redacted]
LONDON
E2 [redacted]
Date:
Bailiff
Client
NOTICE PRIOR TO COMMITT
PRISON PROCEEDINGS
Dear Ms Oldfield,
Magistrates' Liability Order Dated 26/09/2005 For Ou
Tax Due To London Borough Of Tower Hamlet

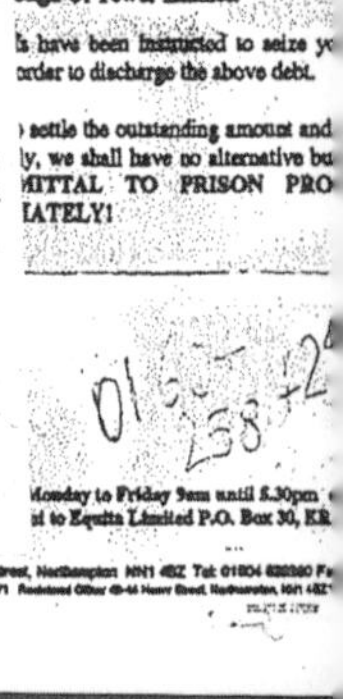
s have been instructed to seize y
order to discharge the above debt.
settle the outstanding amount and
y, we shall have no alternative bu
MITTAL TO PRISON PRO
IATELY!
Monday to Friday 9am until 5.30pm
d to Equita Limited P.O. Box 30, KE

" An invisible occupant seems always to have left before the visitor arrived, and though he may be followed he will never be found. The visitor soon comes to the end of this offputting, objectless labyrinth when he realises, in a flash of lucidity, that he is remembering what has been happening : it was he, erratic and disorientated, who has left each room in the very moment he himself had come in."

Josep Quetglas 'Fear of Glass'.

Issue 3.

WESTWAY

Sunday 9.15 . West London. Top deck drifting to escape bailiffs
and the residual traces of a slow come down. It's a
crystalline winter morning and the rooftops shimmer in pink
light. The Edgware Road becomes a glittering citadel, brutalist
blocks and North American high rise hotels erupt in clusters
around the Marylebone flyover.
And laid out beneath them , rupturing the veneer, are the
tawdry shop fronts, ubiquitous buddleia and the homeless with
their marker pen pleas.

Off the bus at Church Street to my maze of secret hideouts.

Paddington Green nick. No photos here, a whirring of
surveillance cameras as I look up and scan the blank façade.
State of exception. This is where they hold the terror suspects
. The architecture of an ugly premonition.

Metropolitan café, seeking warmth in a steamy cave of shouts
and furtive glances. It's that cusp zone between Halloween and
Christmas. Tinsel waits in boxes at the back ready to be woven
around diamond mirrors.
Formica tables, plastic irises, the smell of bacon and bubble,
liver and onions. I rub a hole in the condensation to watch a
demolition site guarded by the plywood simulacrums of a
Georgian street.

9.45. Traverse the precarious point where Marylebone road becomes the Westway. Slope down a subway of violet tessellations, little tiles glowing like amethysts beneath a film of grime.

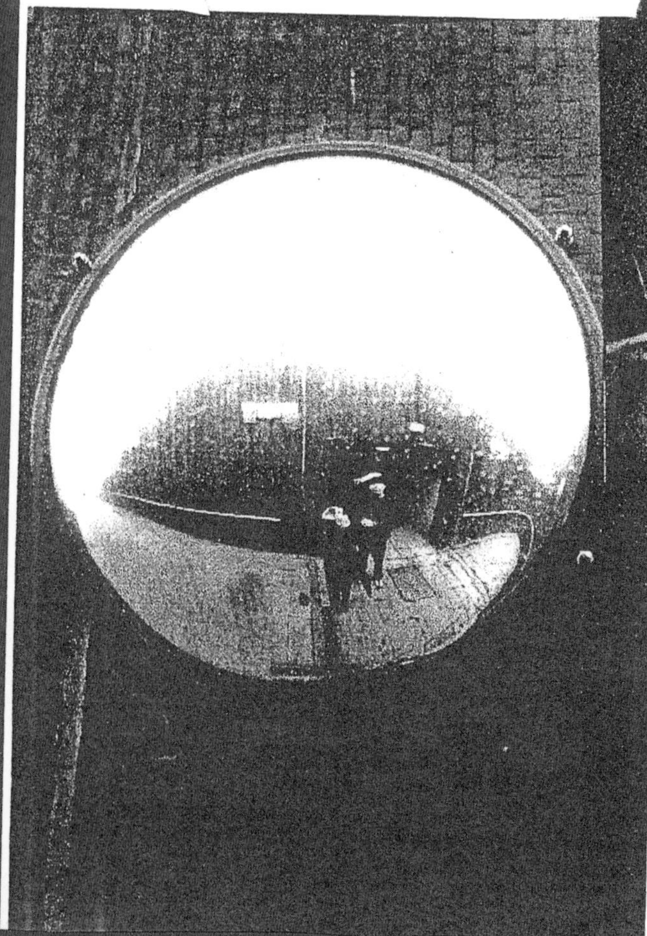

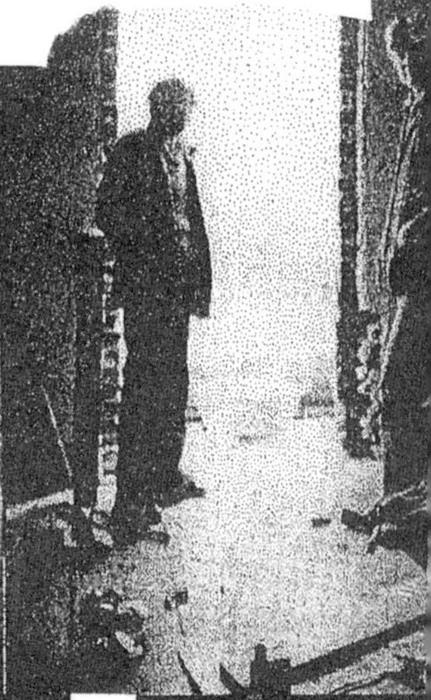

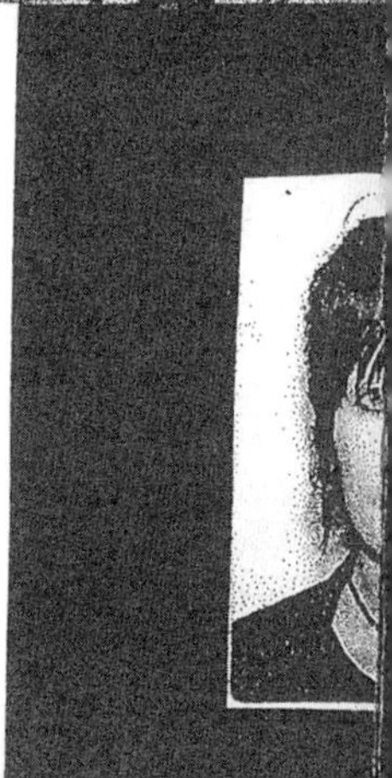

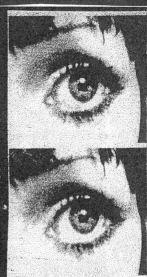

A sign points to North Westminster Community school. Faces distort in a convex mirror. The site is trapped between Hermitage street and the Westway awaiting demolition. Massive steel girders, reinforced concrete and scaffolding cages , the shadows of Piranesi's Carceri.

Emerging on the narrow stretch where the Harrow Road and A4 intersect we are tugged into the fake Manhattan sheen of Paddington Basin. It feels abandoned, a showpiece of a future that never happened. As we cross a tangle of millennial footbridges we are monitored by security guards in luminous vests.

1983 Einsturzende Neubaten.
Centro Iberico , Spanarchist squatted school on Harrow Road.
Mob, Poison Girls, Conflict.
Throbbing Gristle, 1979.

A barge is moored in the shadow of a 70s office block. Black felt is draped across mossy windows and spindles of red geraniums trail from earthenware pots. I remember that sparkling April in Hackney when the scent of hawthorn blossom was heavy on the towpath. A crew of punks called to us, trying to get us drunk. It was the day of a benefit gig at the Arsenal tavern, there was a feverish charge oscillating in the run up to Mayday. Everyone was still up on the euphoria from J18 believing we could have it all again.

Crossing the canal we come to the construction of the new bridge. I've seen this from the other side , from behind the station where it swoops up like a stunt riders ramp. Saw it when I roamed through the maze of St.Mary's hospital floating on benylin through the fraying service tunnels and kebab shop round the station.

I got invited up for a cup of tea in one of those Tecton flats on the Harrow road, one of the old men from the day centre I work in. I took him up Kilburn High road shopping and watered the fuscias on his balcony. We talked about the Blitz and hospitals mostly. He used to be a scientist and wrote shopping lists on brown envelopes dated and filed in a stack of biscuit tins.

I miss him.

I miss them all.

Peer through the hoardings, territories of commerce and control.

Breakages and levels, ladders and lamps; dank chambers stretching out, geometric disorientation, convex mirrors filtered light .

The towpath curves and we get our first sighting of the Westway
as it rises in sublime brutality. They started the clearance in
1964, hundreds of houses demolished, streets left stranded and
bereft in the noise and confusion. In 1966 Paddington and
North Kensington became a gigantic building site.
Pile driving. Demolition.
Unearthly horrifying noise
  like a subterranean attack.

This went on for four years until the road was opened in 1970
by Heseltine , parliamentary secretary of the Transport
Ministry. Arriving the wrong way up one of the slip roads,
protestors on Walmer Road and Pamber Street evaded a police
road block and advanced down the motorway causing total
disruption.
    HESELTINE YOU RICH TORY SCUMBAG WE'LL GET YOU!
  The ministerial cavalcade was pushed back along the length of
the twin dual carriageway where it stopped opposite a row of
three storey houses on Acklam road.
GET US OUT OF THIS HELL ! REHOUSE US NOW!

Elevated on concrete stilts the Westway sweeps over the canal
edging towards the old Paddington maintenance depot. Looking
something like an art deco cruiseliner it was nicknamed the
Battleship. The depot sits wedged between the three levels of
the Westway.

  This sombre place is haunted by the sounds of lost acid house
parties and the distant reverberations of 1986. Test
Department . 303. 808. Traces of industrial noise.
  The roundhouse was easy to get into, and the depot itself,
disused for years is lit up with tags and dubs.

You can hear these deserted places, feel the tendrils creeping
across the abandoned caverns, the derelict bunkers and broken
terraces. Mid summer, blistering heat under the concrete,
Armagideon Time(s), a hidden garden, to be found ,and lost
again.

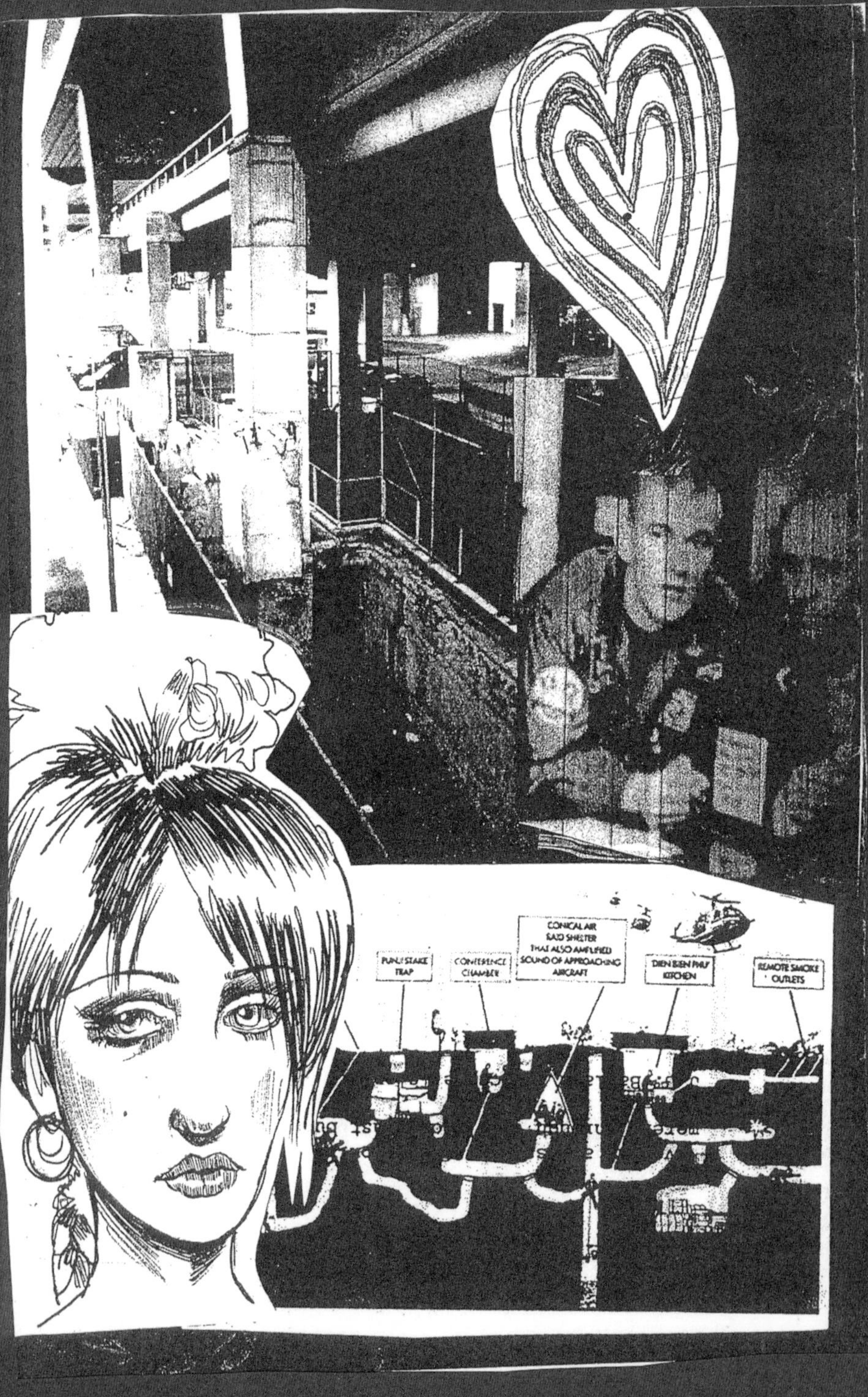
PUNJI STAKE TRAP
CONFERENCE CHAMBER
CONICAL AIR RAID SHELTER THAT ALSO AMPLIFIED SOUND OF APPROACHING AIRCRAFT
DIEN BIEN PHU KITCHEN
REMOTE SMOKE OUTLETS

The Family Home, a catacomb of concrete chambers. The sky, livid
pink and turquoise striations,
  the bleeps and electronic distortions of a kinetic
soundsystem.

1984 mutoid waste company happening, Steptoe and Son meets
Mad Max, military hardware scavenged in East Berlin strewn
across factory yards.
  Tower block silhouettes, light almost green now. Tab wearing
off , stepping anxiously through the ruins,
  the occult worlds beneath the Westway.
Splintered images of that lost trogladite flash up. Envelope
modulation, imperceptible frequencies. Pink and black paint
spanned the walls in checkerboard formations. He was immersed
in those underground chambers, a feral guardian of the last
relics of acid culture. Five years since the last party but he
held his plot, scavenging for food like a Ballardian crash
victim.

Terra Incognita, this world is hidden from view, dank corridors
defying panoptican mapping .The A-Z shows the Westway slicing
through the Paddington rooftops but not the shadowscapes
beneath. I watch the glowing particles of my desire float and
explode across the city. In that underpass, a ghostly
portakabin, names etched with fervour and destruction.
The fabric of the city is erotically charged, a multitude of
red dot locations on the map. The tissue between desiring and
acting disintegrates. Schizoid antics, a matrix of
possibilities, those dangerous moments when promise is pushed
forward and all the little fragments of desire scuttle across
the face.

Paddington Central, a slick rebranding. The crumbling
infrastructure forms a texture of resistance to this North
American banalization.
Voices reverberate softly, an undercurrent gently pulsating.
Slope down to Royal Oak, black cabs hurtling up and down
service roads. The hinterland of the goods yards.
  Concrete embankments , caravans and frying onions. Abandoned
security shacks and empty plastic chairs.

Climbing back to the canal we stop to smoke a cigarette . I can
hear men shouting from somewhere in the brutalist curve of
Warwick Crescent .

Westbourne Green.
Beneath the concrete stanchions there are derelict basketball
courts with empty benches, a black wall with pink hearts,
skulls and horns. I sit still and decipher codes. I write my
own, a chalked eye on the powdery floor.

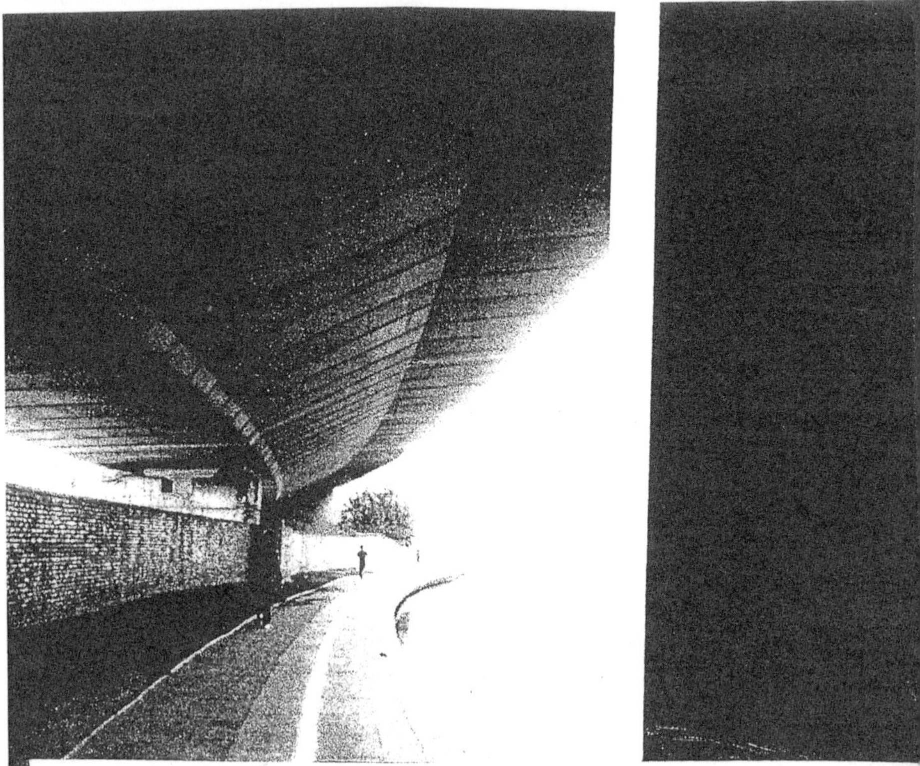

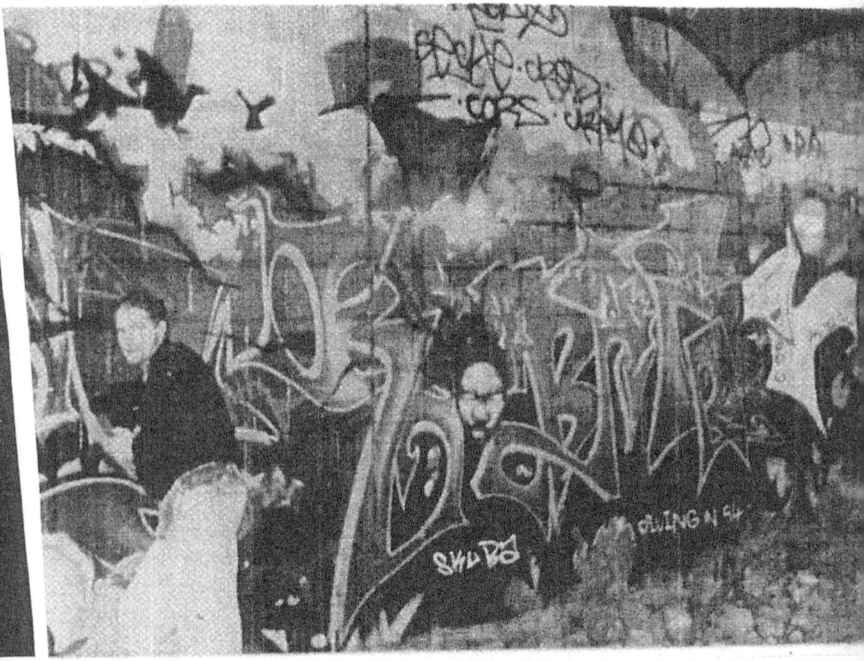

Pass the Warwick estate, peer up at the 18th floor of Wilmcote House where Mick Jones lived with his Nan. The Westway tilts as it skims the Grand Union. I drift slowly in its shadows, the towpath is broad here, elegant graffiti slinks across a high brick wall.

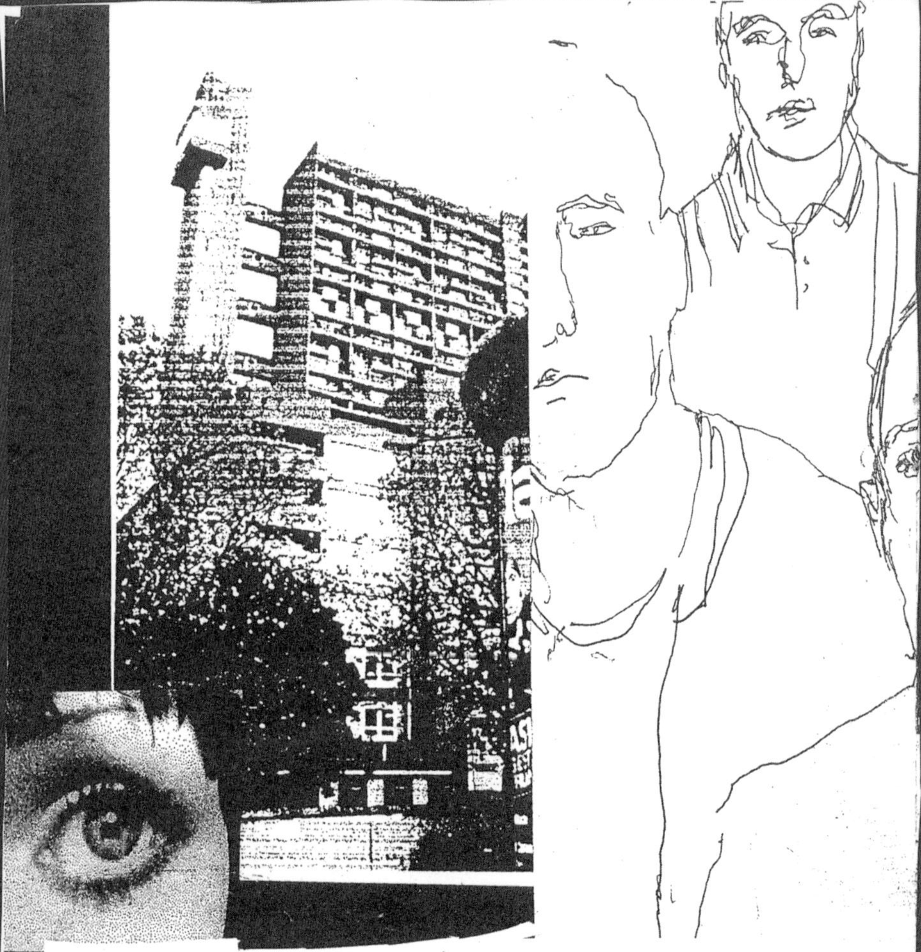

Trellick Tower, Goldfinger's brutal masterpiece. Echoes of its prototype Balfron Tower by the Blackwall Approach hover over the estate map.
Remember Sean's gaff on the 24th floor? The stained glass foyer and us standing about smoking on precarious walkways. Sean's flat was at the top, I would stand on his balcony looking out over Wormwood Scrubs, staring at the prison while him and his mates got stoned watching Countryfile. They weren't what I'd hoped for. My swooning imaginings had populated the corridors with Paul Simonon look-alikes, post skin/suedehead hooligans, not this motley crew of long hairs in Soundgarden T shirts .

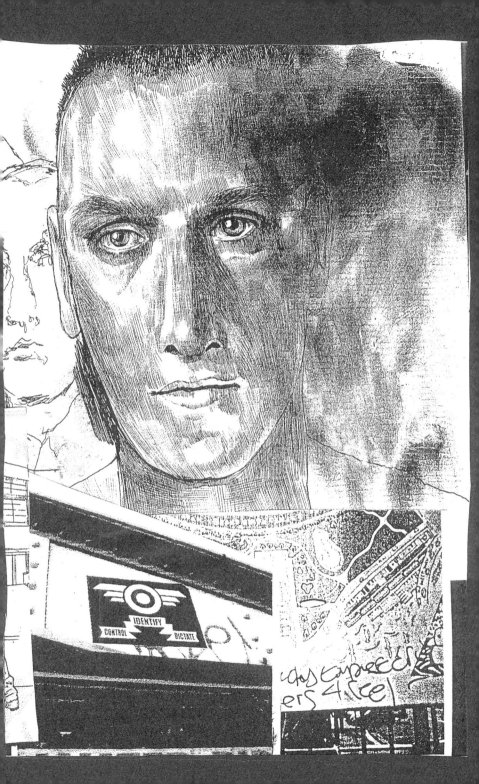

IDENTIFY

CONTROL   DICTATE

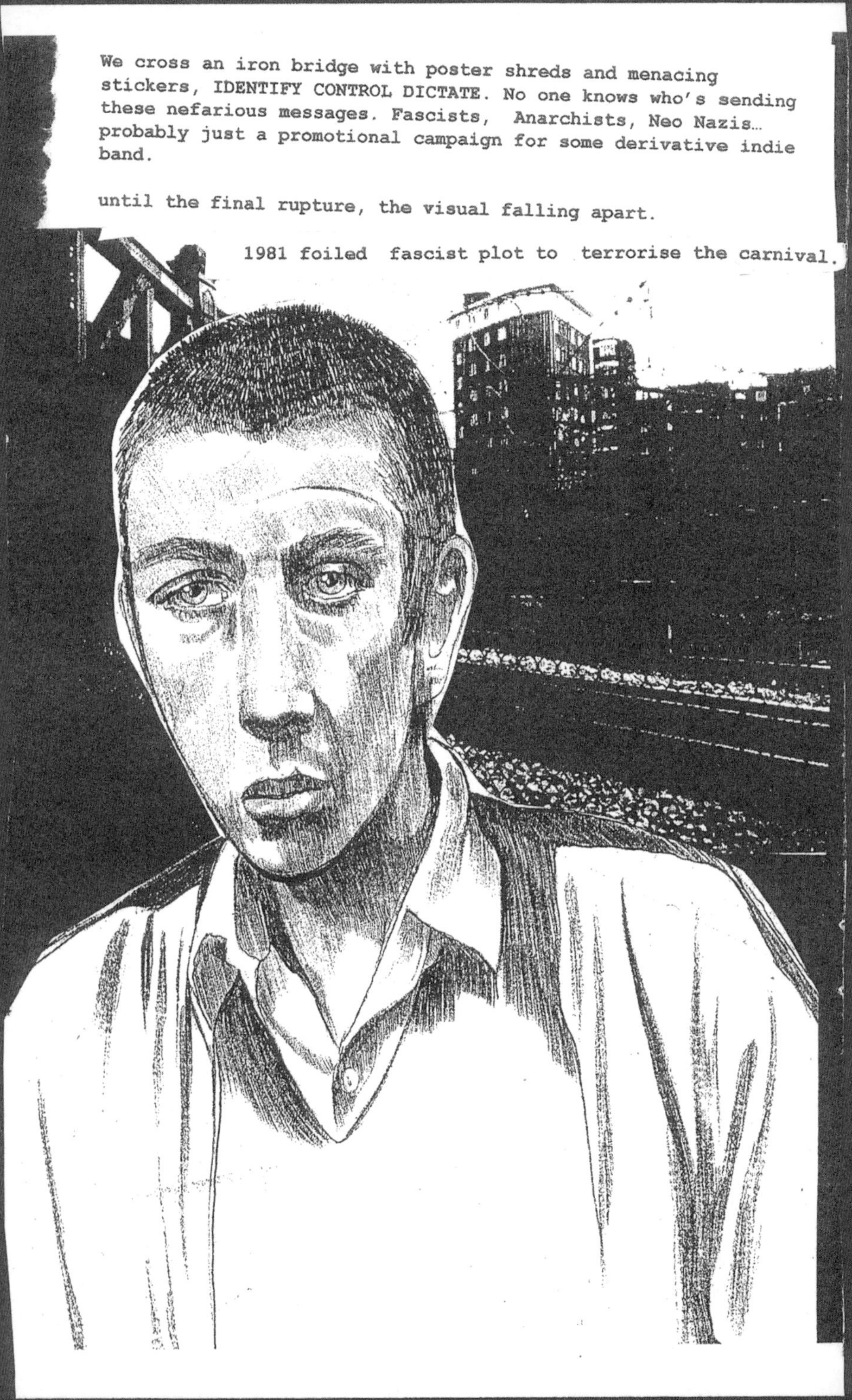
We cross an iron bridge with poster shreds and menacing stickers, IDENTIFY CONTROL DICTATE. No one knows who's sending these nefarious messages. Fascists, Anarchists, Neo Nazis… probably just a promotional campaign for some derivative indie band.
until the final rupture, the visual falling apart.
1981 foiled fascist plot to terrorise the carnival.

We step across Golborne road , stopping for strong coffee and pastries at one of the Portugese cafes. We sit outside in pale lemon rays letting conversations and cigarette smoke drift around us . Sharp turn down Wornington road, the sky is a shrill blue , dusty diamonds shimmer underfoot.

The Westway again. This liminal territory, cast in a negative light in the 70s was recuperated by MTV and boring media types in the 90s. The Westway became the backdrop for Gorillaz imbecility, bland drum & bass record sleeves and photo shoots in corporate skate parks .

Cool Britannia. Old joke.

'Space' becomes the over arching commodity. Notting Hill. New Age cranks peddling expensive junk. Homeopathy and boutiques, angel cards and crystal healing.

The Subteranian, the old Acklam hall, site of shootings, riots and skinheads meting out violence.

. A tumble down concrete steps, ,a beautifully choreographed brawl at a malevolent intersection. Red Skins versus NF skins in a flash up riot.

My new dress is covered in blood.

I'd only been seeing him for a week or two. They knocked me on the floor and set about him. Swarms of teddy boys, skinny drainpipe legs and snide comments thrown sideways from mean little mouths. Said we don't want to see that coon round here again. I remember the dress, dusky rose lace , diamante buttons on the bodice. I got up and I shouted back, pulling them off him, getting knocked to the ground again with a slap to the side of the head. One of them punched me in the stomach and I fell on all fours retching. And the cardigan, pink mohair, real soft, all ruined with the blood.

Fun to be alive.

2001, eight old bill injured in a riot and two shot outside the club .

Photos of the Clash, romanticised and tinted in that little yellow room.

Rebranded with a 2 o clock curfew, 'Neighbourhood'.

Under the Westway and over a footbridge we cross the Hammersmith and City line. The metal railings are graffiti lit by an agitator, manic laughter ricochets around abandoned corridors. Threats of violence, The Shining and getting your head smashed into a fresco.

REJECT FALSE ICONS

CONTROL
DICTATE
CONTROL
DICTATE
CONTROL
DICTATE

REJECT FALSE ICONS

1982. ZigZag squat. Xmas all dayer with Crass, Conflict,
Dirt, Flux of Pink Indians and Poison Girls. Soon it would all
shift east to Wapping and the Central line. Steve Ignorant as
charismatic leader, Stratford Mercenaries and Schwarzeneggar,
pushing closer to the slow dissolve of the forest. Something
had germinated in that moment when the world was darkening with
Reagan and Thatcher. Militancy mutated through the convoy
scene. Spiral Tribe, Mutoids, D.i.Y soundsystem. Paths could
be traced here. A fractured lineage, contestation of space.
Castlemorton, CJB, RTS, J18.

Ladbroke Grove. Market stalls, heaps of dusty bric a brac,
strings of lights glowing pink and yellow. A scratched mirror
in a corner, rows of battered shoes, postcards sent in 1973.
Warming hands on a polystyrene cup I drift through the sweet
smell of candied pecans, rare groove and techno . I sift
through racks of clothes scrambling lost times , prom dresses,
wide flares, leather jackets with long collars. I find a pair
of stilettos, sharp red with black heels. They carry the aura
of future seduction.

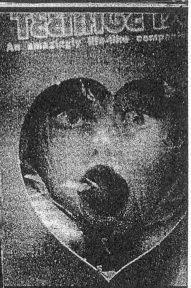

An American life-like compan...

THE WORKING CLASS BUILT THESE HOUSES,

ONLY THEY RE MADE OMELESS

IT 1E... W

ASS   PENIS EN

ZIG ZAG CLU
12 NOON.

I AM
SQUAT
ING HERE
'COS' IVE
NO WHERE
ELSE

5.30
6.00   AMEBIX
6.30   NULL AND VOID
7.00   Soldiers of fortune
7.30   THE MOB → POLEMIC
6.00   POISON GIRLS
8.30   CONFLICT
9.00   FLUX & PINK INDIANS
9.30   CRASS
10.00 DIRT

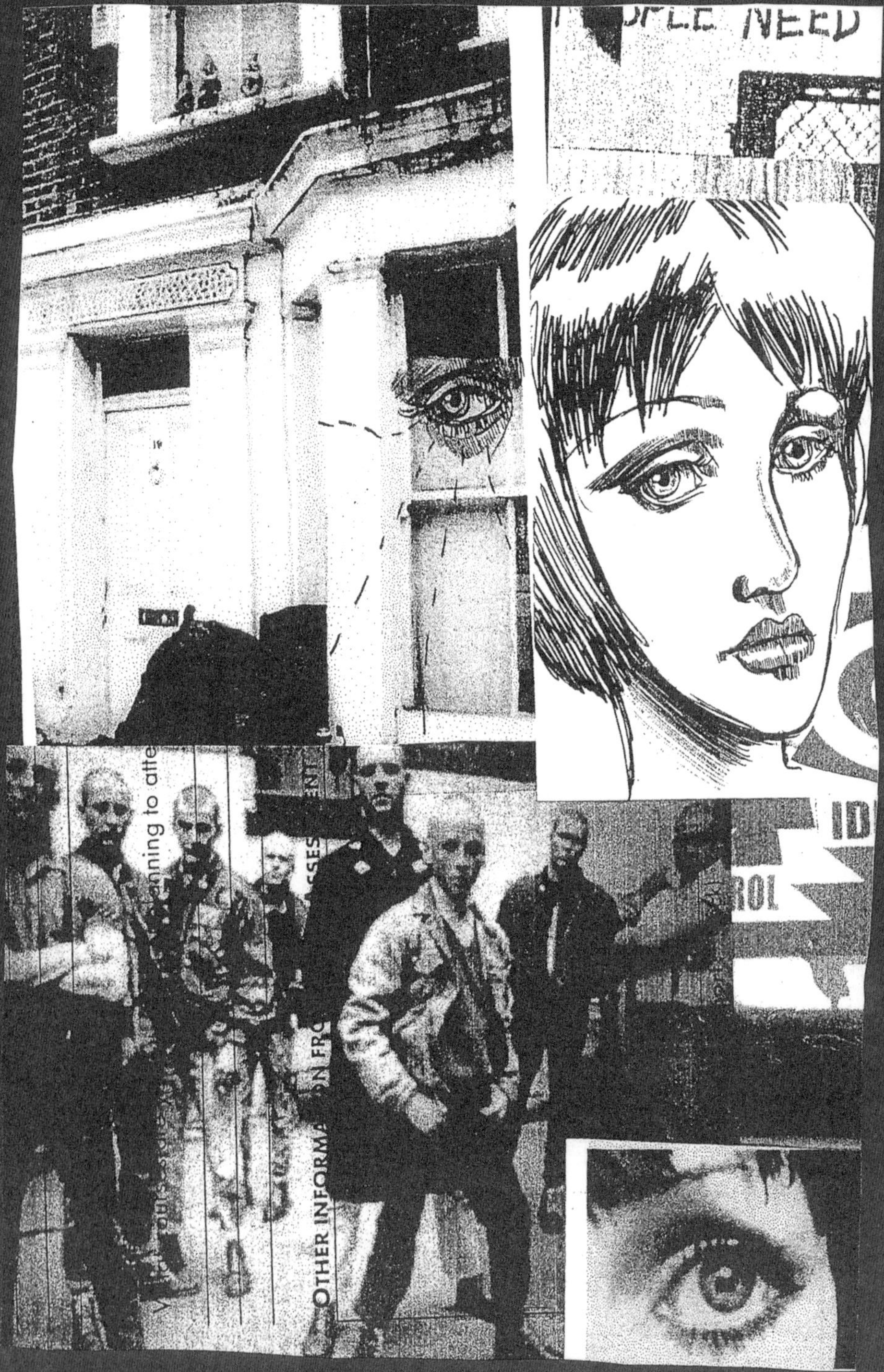

PLE NEED
nning to atte
OTHER INFORMA
ROL

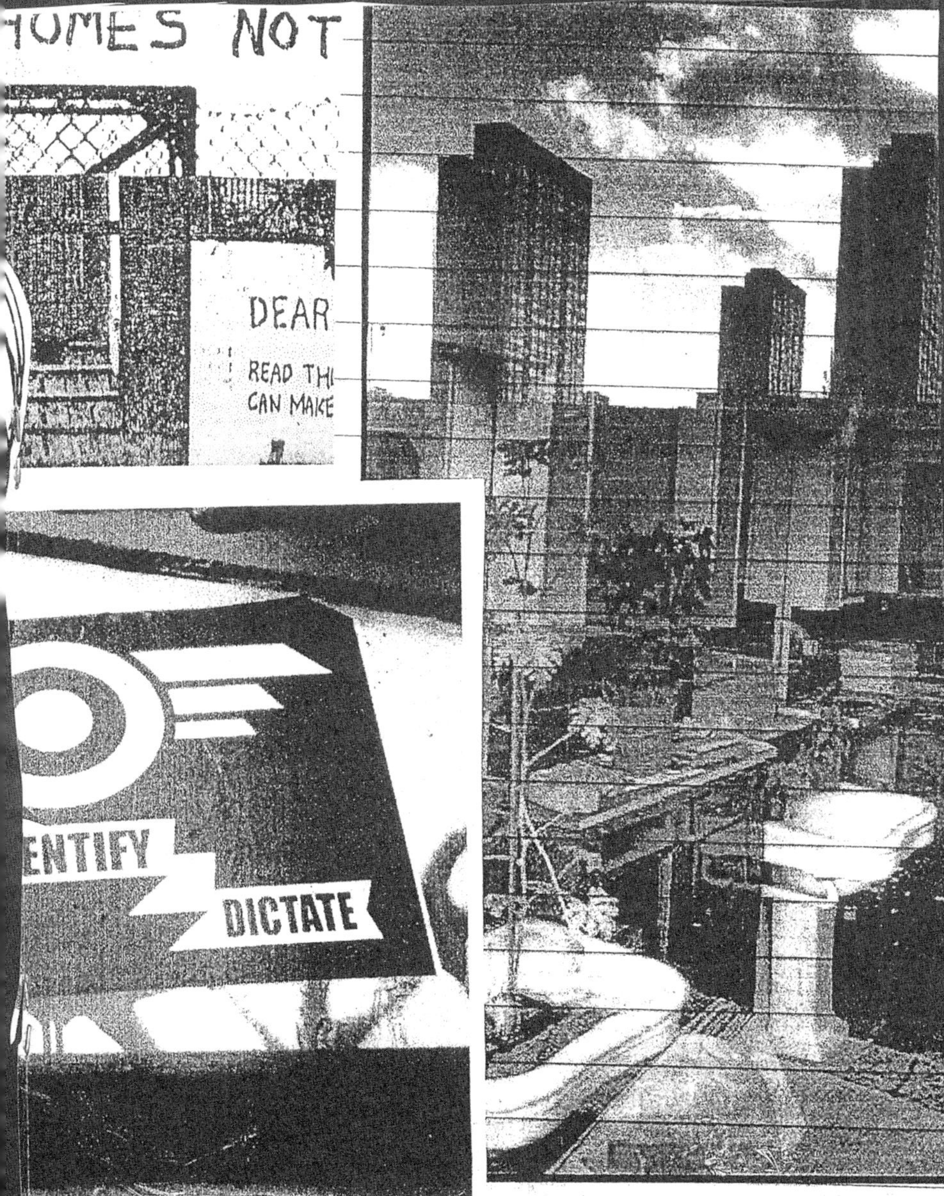
HOMES NOT
DEAR
READ TH
CAN MAKE
ENTIFY
DICTATE

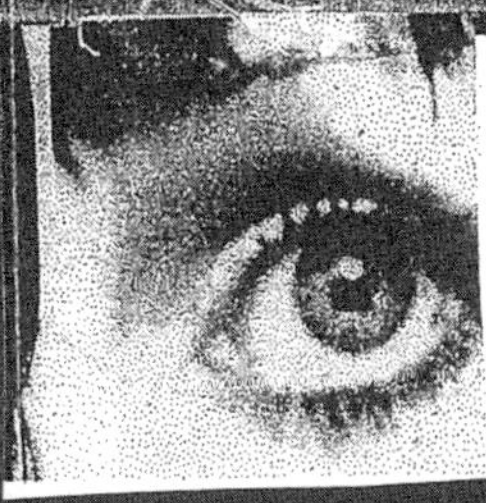

"…the people who make pallets
to carry away the burned body of yesterday
have left chalk marks on the walls
and we follow in their steps along the length of iron
bridges."

Chris Marker

Beyond the breakers yard the Westway is stretched like an animal skin. Orange walls, black glyphs, the haunted etchings of a disturbed prankster. Codes scramble and unscramble through territorial assertions. My biro digs deep in this shifting terrain.

Find a pub lodged under the Westway, hear the rhythmic thud of the traffic above. Fairylights twinkle in a whisky glass. I sense a momentary glimmer of belonging.

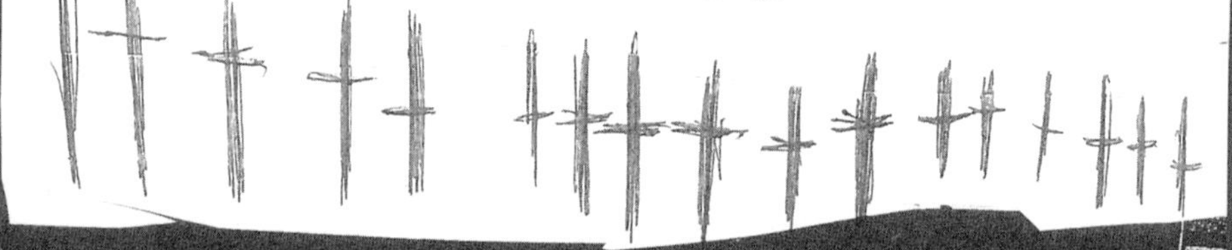

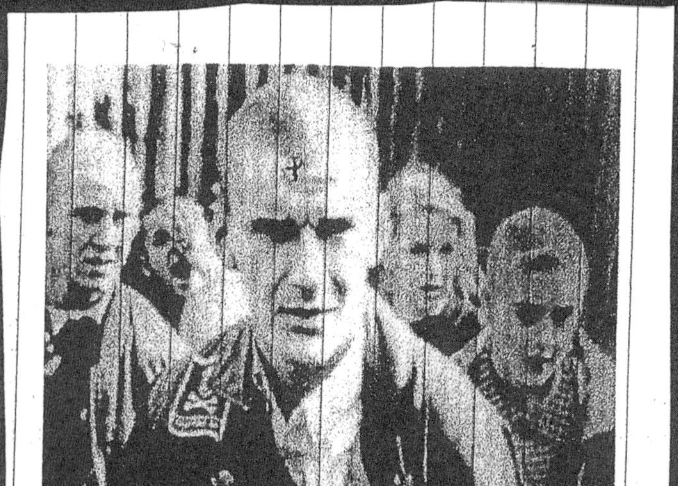

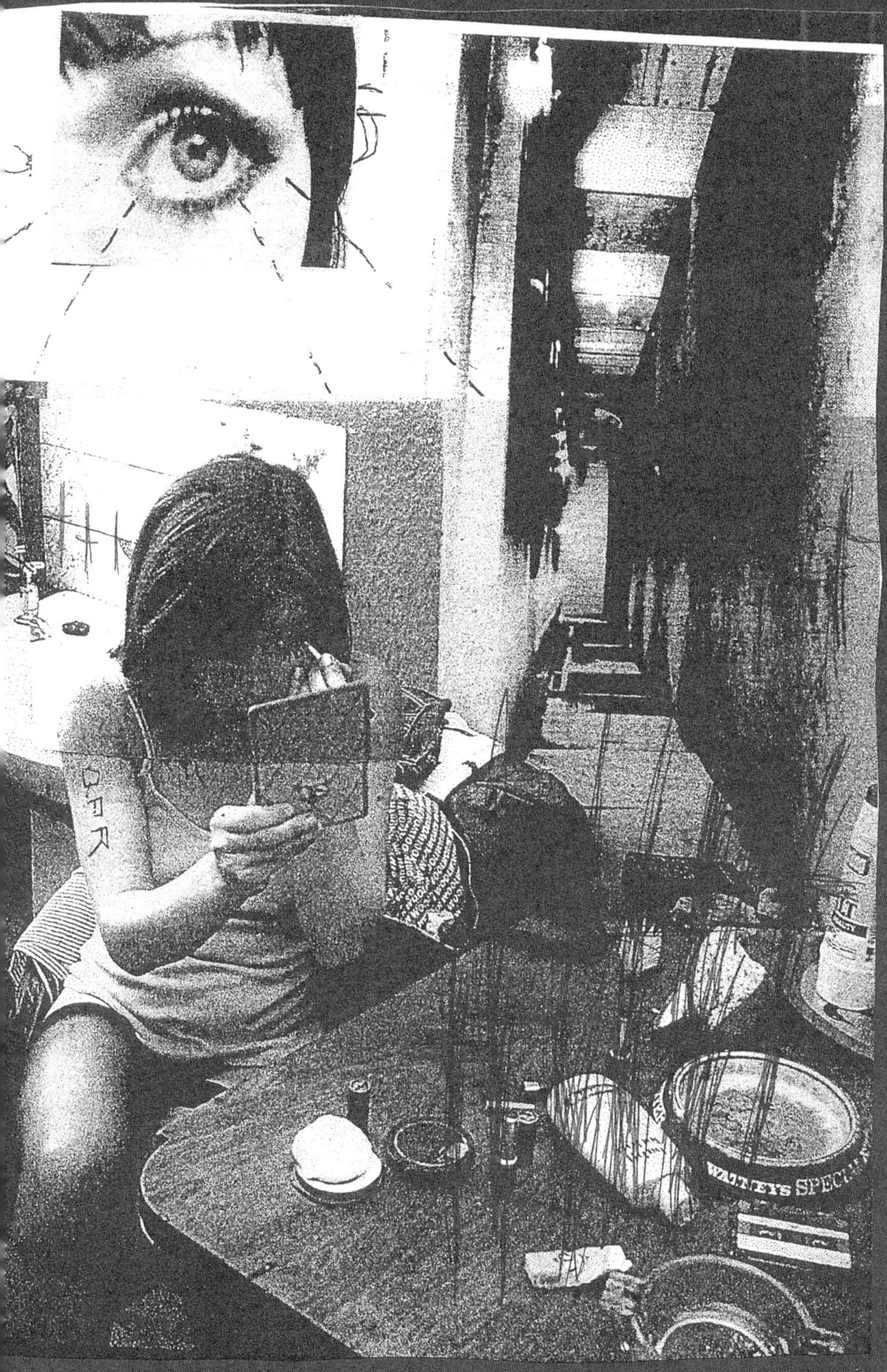
WATNEYS

1976, Michael X has just been executed in Trinidad and Darcus Howe presides over a militant Carnival committee. The police presence is overbearing, tempers fray and the area goes up in an echo of the situation in Jamaica .
Coke cans, traffic cones and bricks are thrown. The Old Bill charge at the rioters with milk crates, dustbin lids and wire fencing. Violence cascades in sporadic flashes under the Westway.

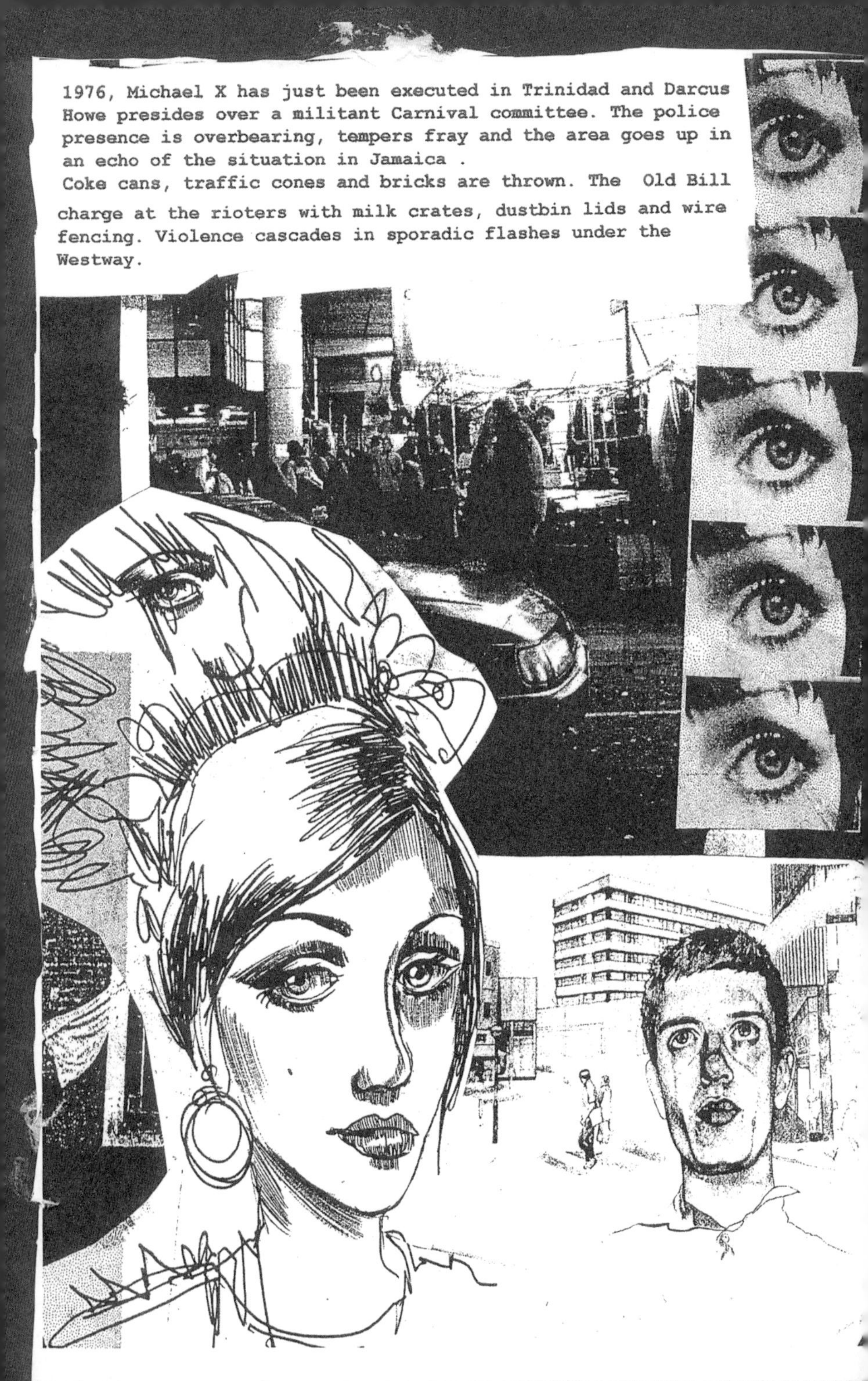

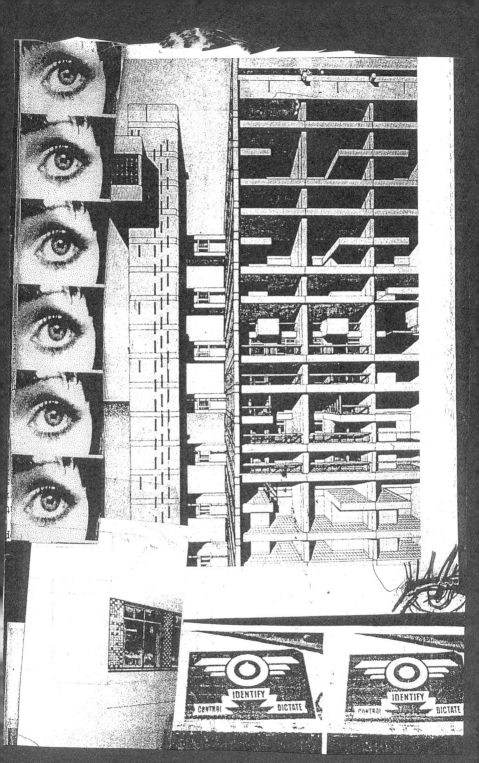

IDENTIFY

CONTROL DICTATE

IDENTIFY

CONTROL DICTATE

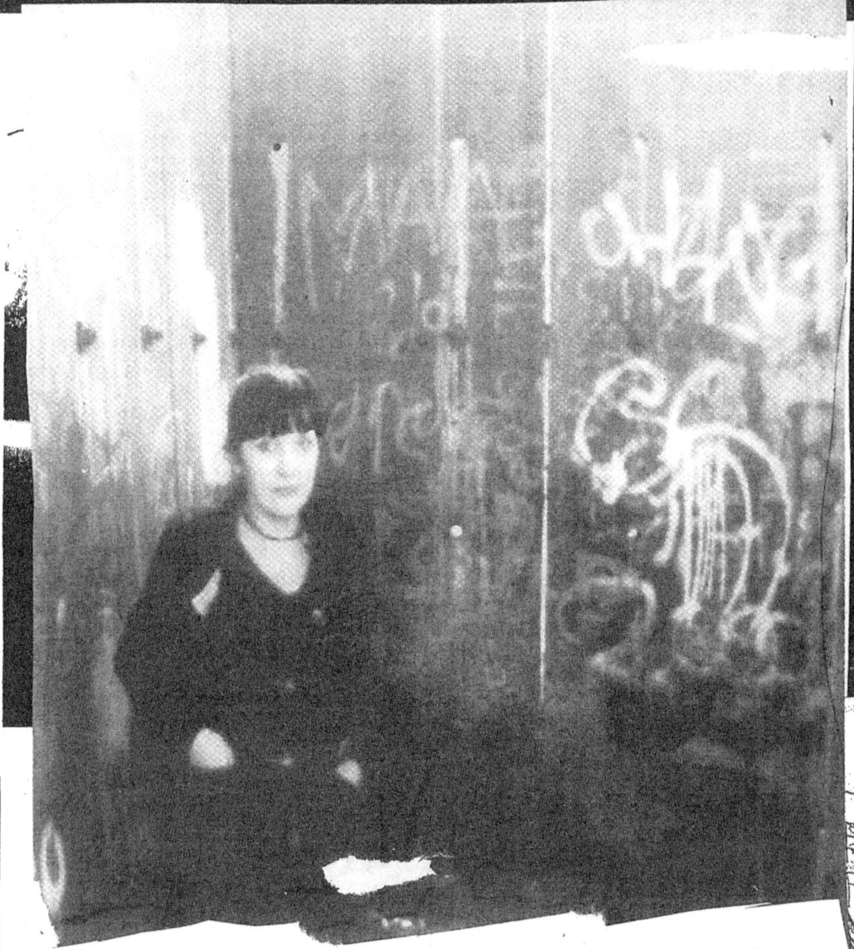

An apocalyptic rhetoric reverberates under the flyover. It emerges in the 70s as stencil graffiti and an all out assault on the 'straight world'. The English section of the Situationists and subsequent King Mob obsess over 'deviants, psychotics and the mentally collapsed'. As active nihilists they carve out the aesthetic of insurrection .

A pyramid evil eye stares out through an ivy canopy as I veer west under concrete columns. My fingers trace the surfaces,, old Situationist stencil graffiti, "SAME THING DAY AFTER DAY…. ."

Hippy free shop on Acklam road is trashed.

A truncated terrace gapes obscenely 20 feet from the motorway. Peeling paintwork and shreds of fabric flutter in sash windows, shadowy figures move within.
Encounter the day glo panels of a derelict working men's club. Once it served pints to locals in scant compensation for the demolition of their houses, now the garish bunker stands abandoned ,illuminated inside by filtered orange street glow and empty aerosol cans.

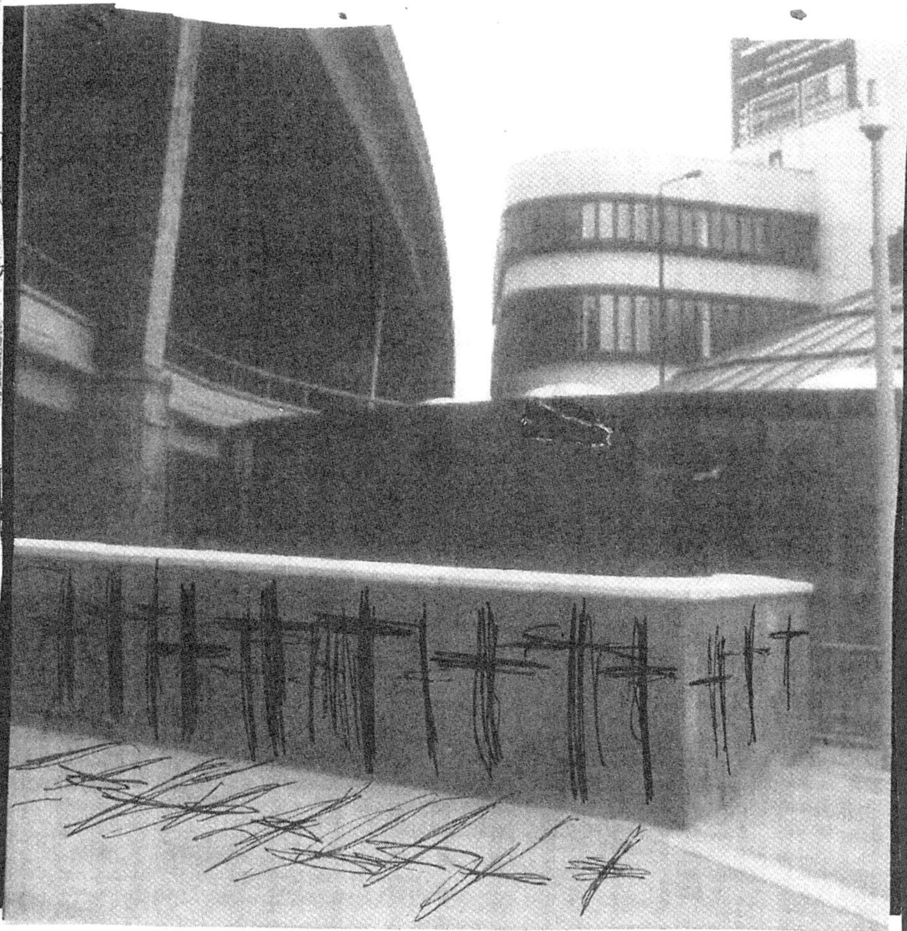

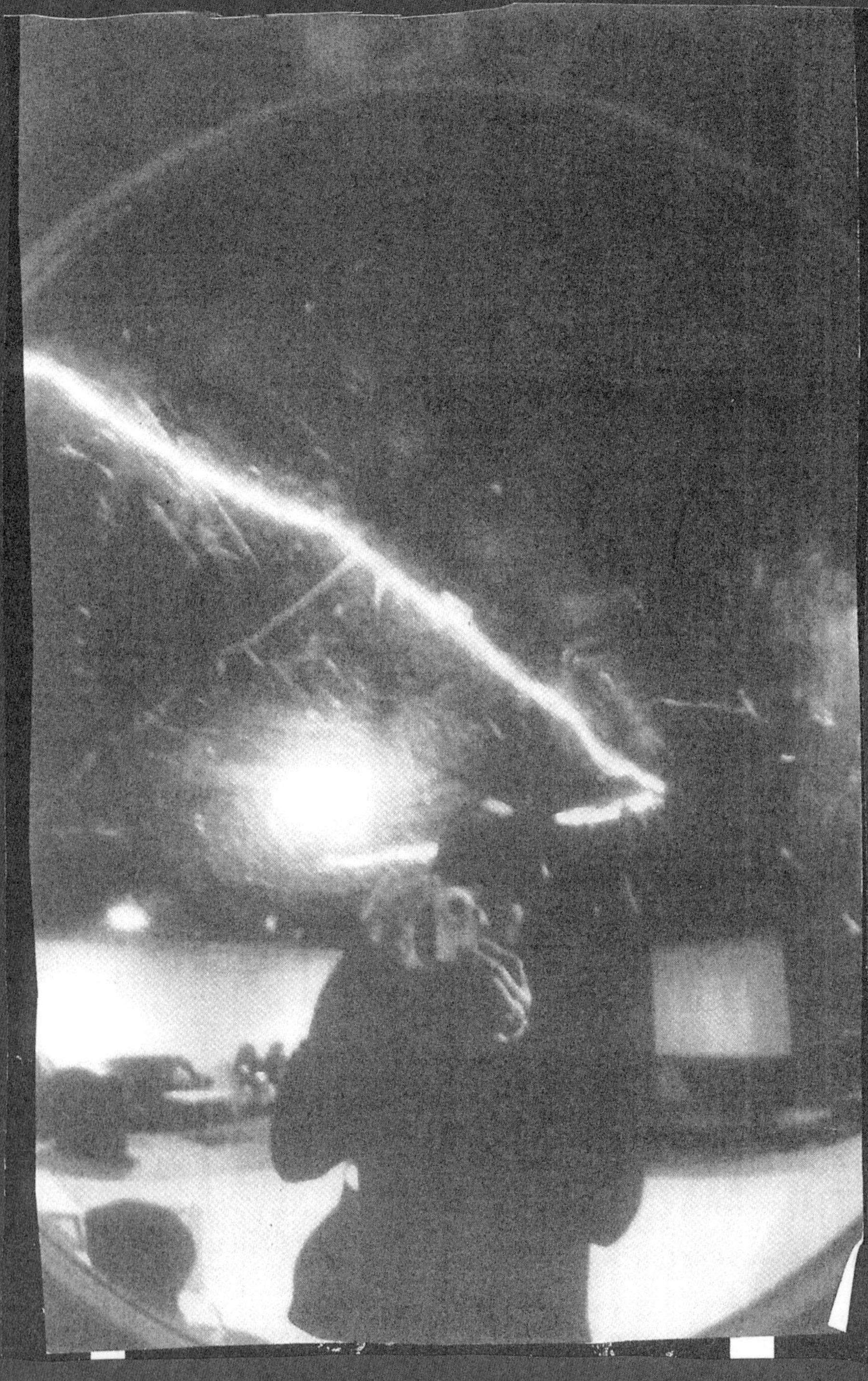

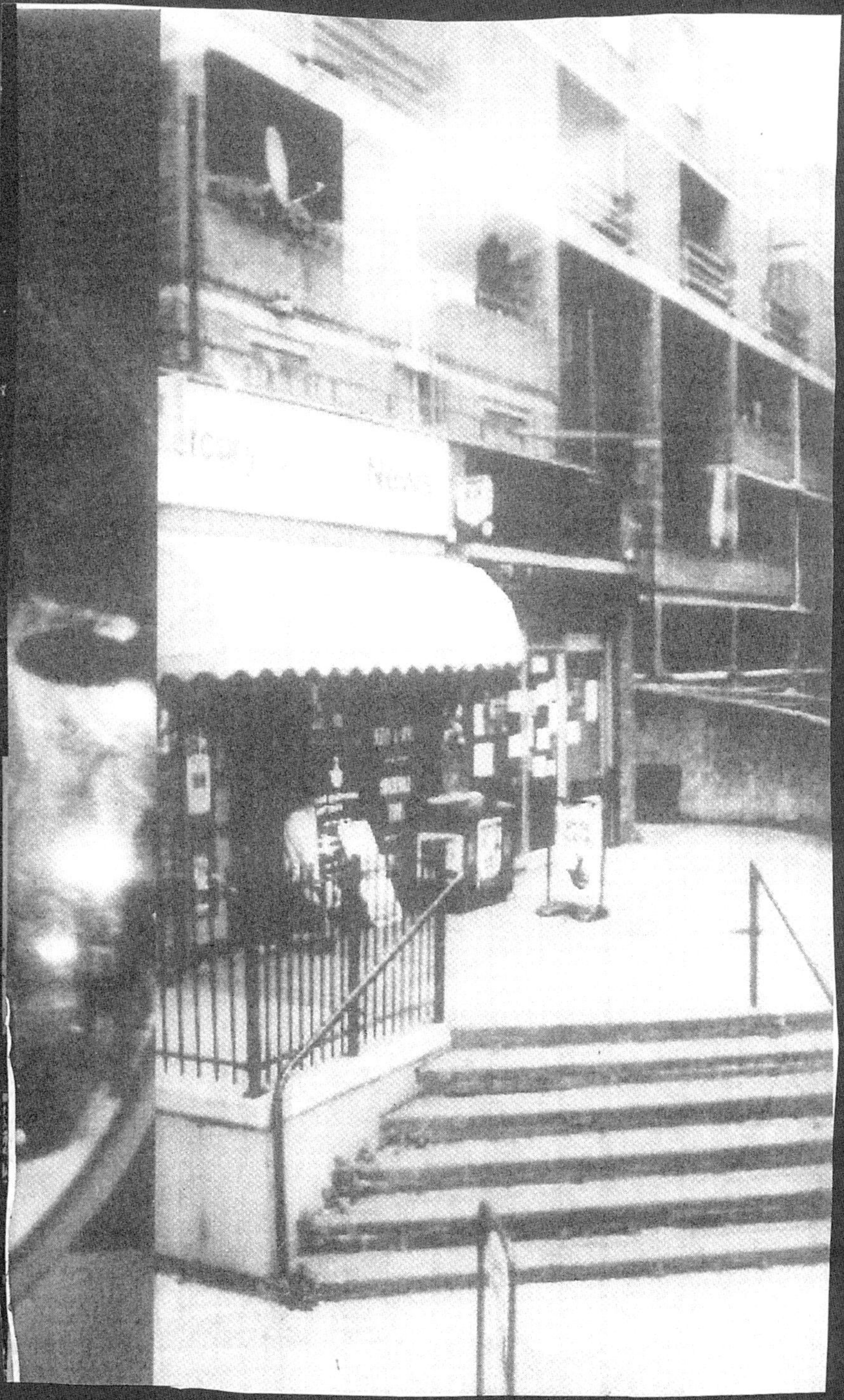

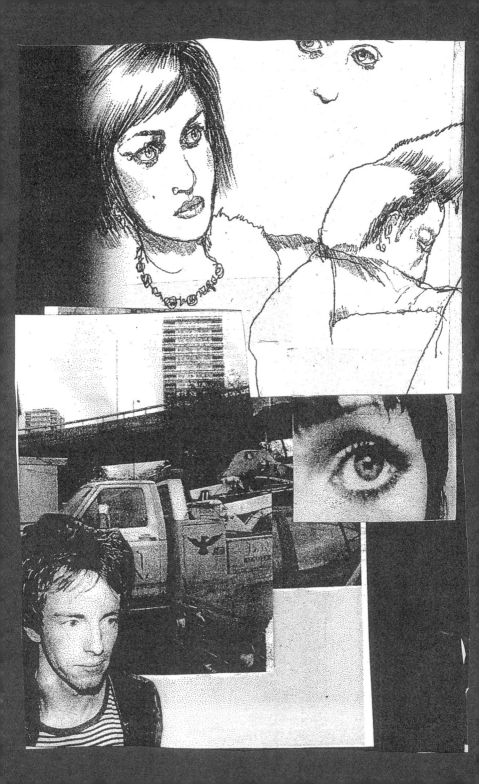

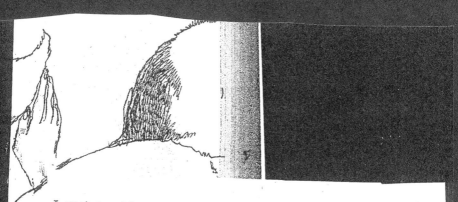

I meet an old tramp . He tells me his woman has gone and offers
me the wine she has left behind. His eyes stray in zigzags as
he clutches my cold hands.

Sweep towards White City, site of the Franco British Exhibition
and 1908 Olympics. There were palaces and halls on stilts and
stations opened amid fanfare and ceremony. The complex was used
to make aeroplanes and parachutes in the war and eventually
laid to waste. Dreams of 2013, overgrown velodromes and
derelict stadiums shimmer in this dirty construction site. The
past holds tight the kernels of repetition and destruction.
The White City was disused for years, part of it became a dog
track, the rest was left as a vessel of the imagination. In
1984 the last greyhound race was run and it was demolished. And
now dust clouds are kicked up again as the site is turned into
a 1.2 million square foot shopping city. Look here for the
future of the Lea Valley.

Shattering drops, senseless truncations. Stables Yard, ponies
trotting in concentric circles beneath the motorway. Latimer
road. Bisected by the Westway it lost its identity. A slow
abandonment, fortress pubs, dilapidated windows, ornaments
you get in amusement arcades . North Pole road, a peeling
corner of North Kensington. Holed up in a brown café circa 1986
, blue cigarette smoke and the mawkish strains of Radio 2.
Eggs, toast and coffee, he wants to treat me to a proper
breakfast. We watch ladies getting their hair done over the
road.

Kensal Rise. Wood Lane, wasteground of pockmarked billboards.
Climb concrete steps to the railway line and marshy tracks of
Wormwood Scrubs. I get a call from Hackney Class War . They
want me to make them an effigy of Thatcher for their bonfire on
London Fields. Over the Mitre bridge, we're drifting through
the Willesden hinterlands, skirting round the cemetery past the
rows of industrial dry cleaners.

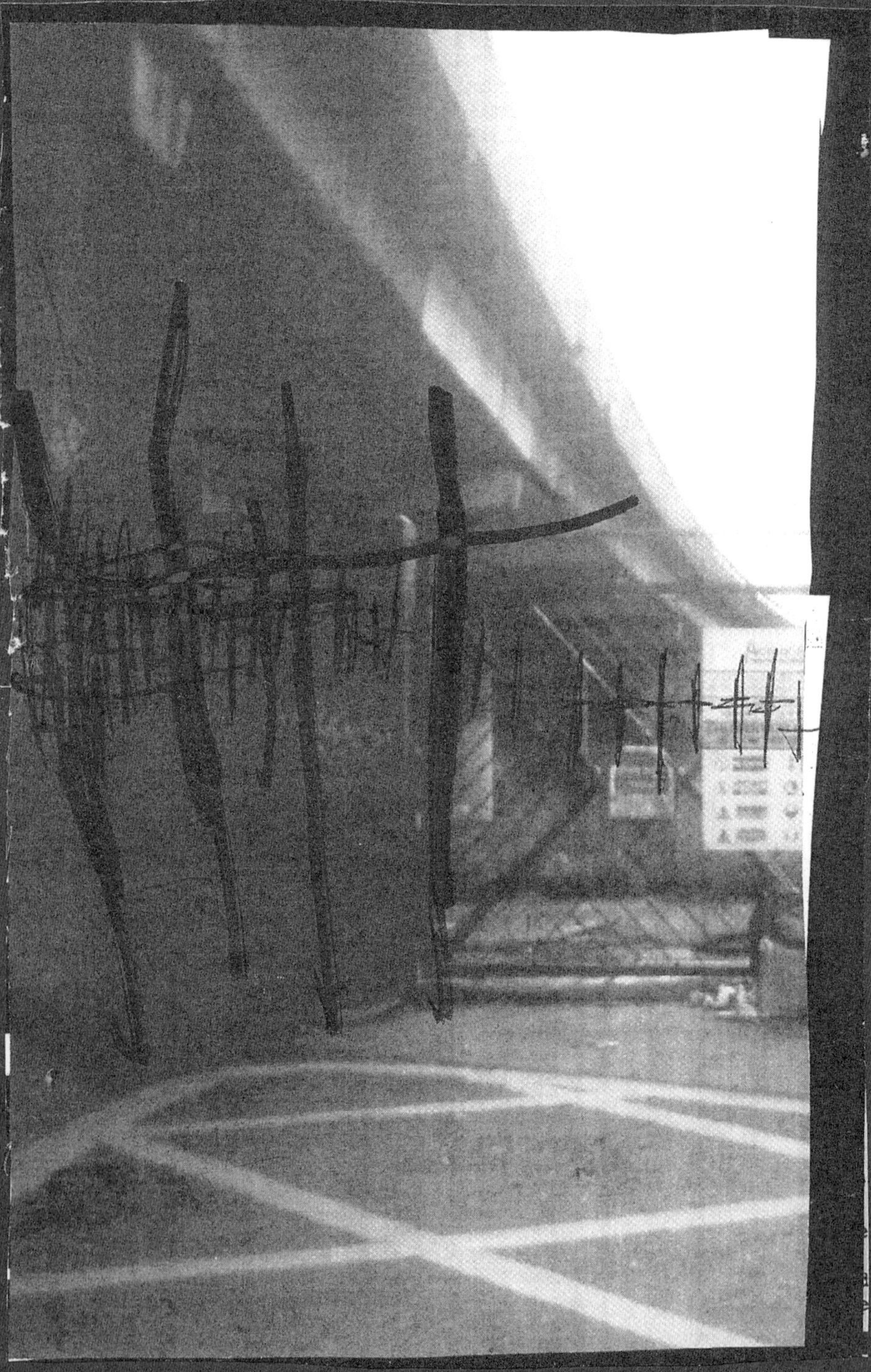

Back to the Westway along Mitre way, to the breakers yard where my friend lives in a caravan with three Rotweillers and a prized crate of punk sevens. He's a roving itinerant, doesn't want to be shut away, likes it here with the door open on a scrapyard vista. We drink sweet tea and smoke as we wait for my phone to charge up. Men huddle around braziers, dark stink of smoke, sweat and paraffin. A dinted portakabin houses a pirate radio station, nocturnal Grime scene . Dj Fang, UK Funky, Lost Souls, MC Gambit. A tantalising link with Grenfell tower, pink lights glowing in balcony windows. 106.9, Laylow FM.

The gypsies live in static caravans under one of the feeder roads. Their homes are adorned with displays of silk flowers and pale figurines. Small allotments of broken bikes mark the edge of their territory.

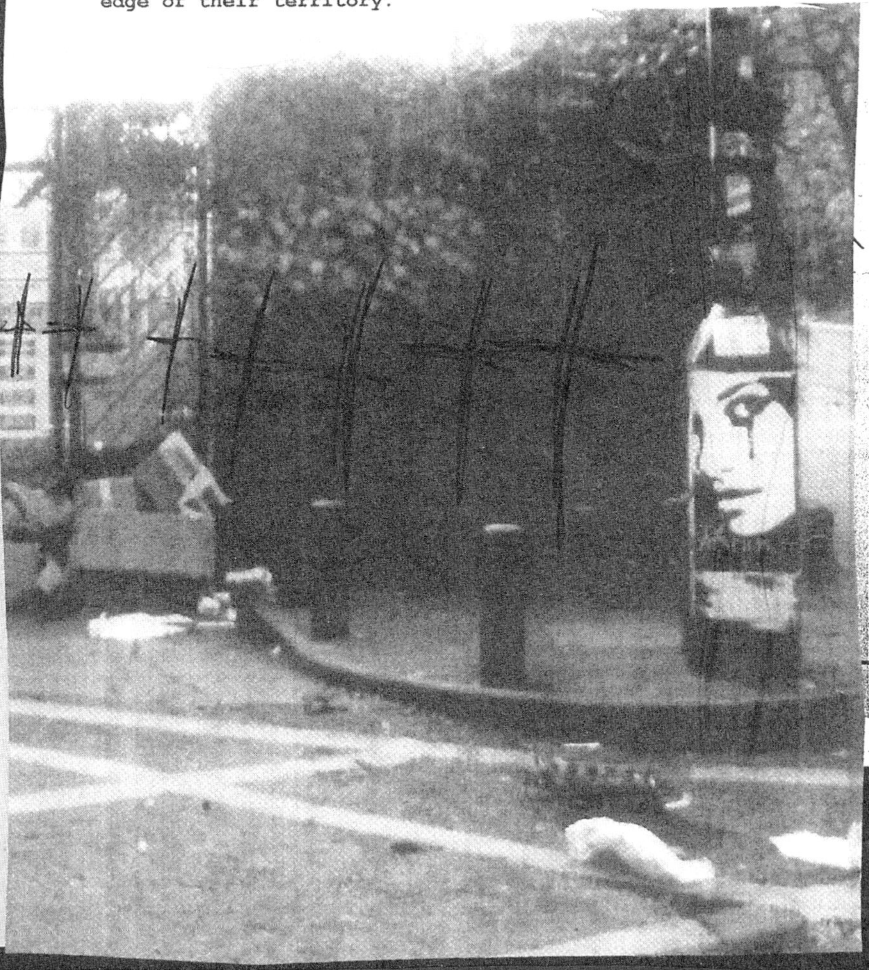

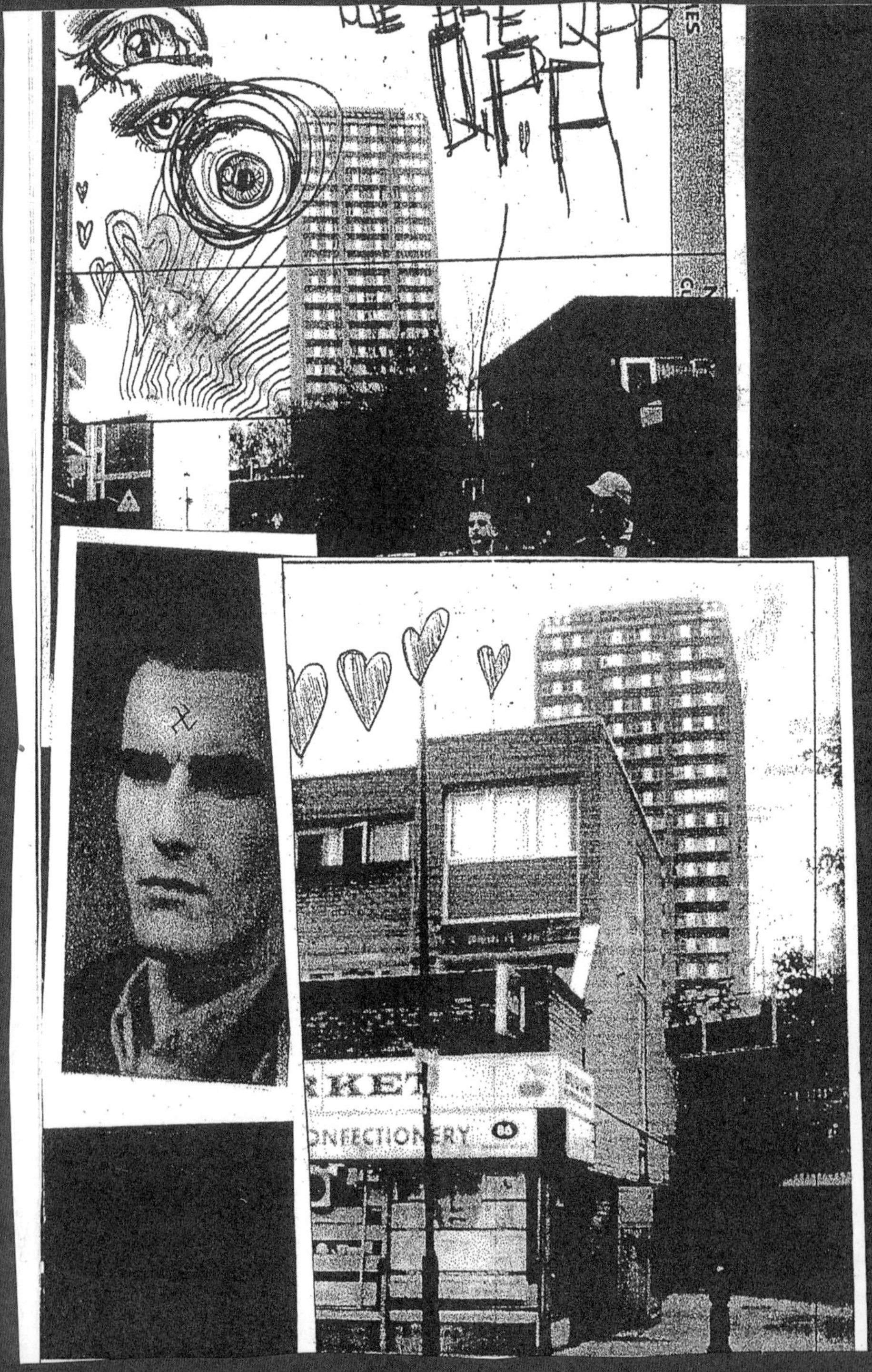
RKET
ONFECTIONERY

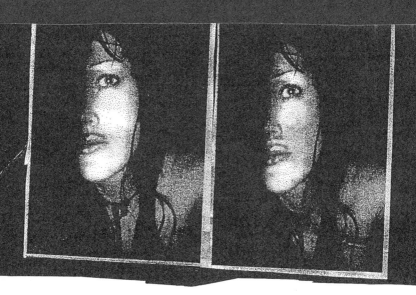

Cross to the estate on Silchester road. WE ARE Q.P.R
ricocheting round the maisonettes.. 1995, a suffocating July
night in the eye of a heatwave, , wasted in Camden at a
Selecter gig. I can't remember how it happened but suddenly I'm
backseat joyriding with a crew of skins into an unfamiliar
zone. He lives ten floors up in that block with the meccano
parapet and there's frantic kissing in a coffin sized lift,
livid weals and fracture lines emerging on his skin. The next
morning a van turns up in the street below to take him to some
site on the Isle of Sheppey. He says he's not going to bother
going to work so we stay in bed.
I notice him properly.
Big Polynesian, black eyes, soft Kiwi accent.
He wants my number but I don't really fancy him.
Jason.
 He puts a tape on, Welsh Oi from 1981, Infa Riot and Blitz.
The room's a mess, Clockwork Orange poster hanging where the
damp has pushed it off the wall. We go to the pub, a paranoid
perambulation in the shadow of the Westway to the Warwick on
Portobello. There's the rest of his crew there talking
politics, sordid diatribes about immigration. Panicked by a
drunken mistake I pretend to go to the Ladies and run out the
back.
He follows me but I'm already away, tearing through Powis
square out of reach and out of zone. This decaying fabric, this
unknowable terrain has become my biography, the euphoria then
the anguish, layers of memories colliding, splintering and
reconfiguring. Years later I wondered if our paths would ever
cross as I glanced at those blocks from the Hammersmith and
City line.
I think I know, then I'm back to the start again.

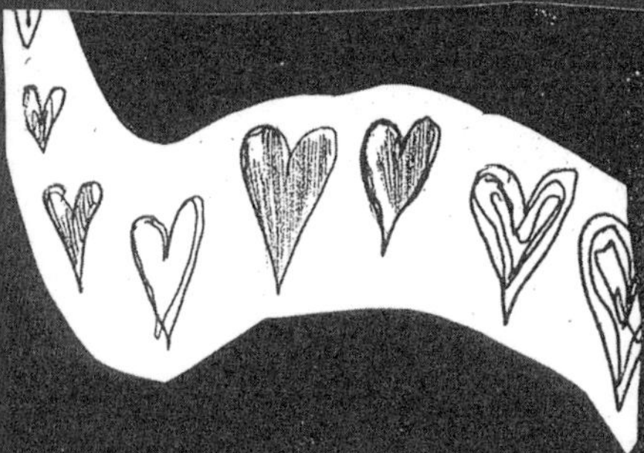

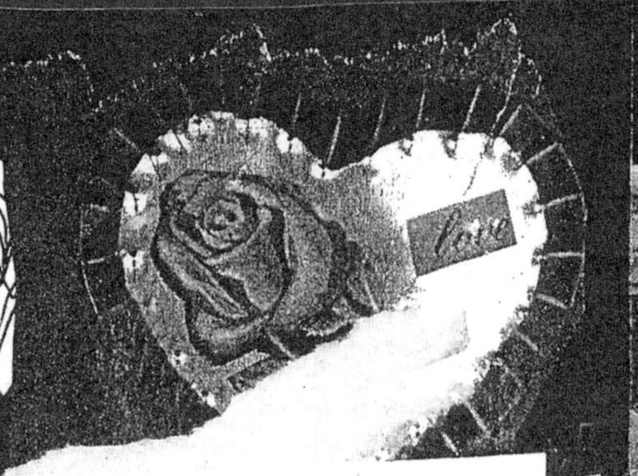
love

This bleak street was the People's Republic of Frestonia. 1981. Combat Rock, Frestonia People's Hall Sessions, the Apocalypse hotel. Some of the Frestonians were rehoused under the councils hard to let scheme in the neighbouring towers. You can sense the aerial surveillance.

Freston road, 70s squatted street. The pub on the corner, Bramley Arms, was once populated by dolelites, punks and hangovers from the hippy era. Looks so innocuous now, tamed by a 90s gastro aesthetic, wooden benches and coffee table drum and bass..

Yards cluttered with DDR hardware and the reconfigurations of Russian fighter aircraft emerged seamlessly as outcrops in this lost industrial landscape.

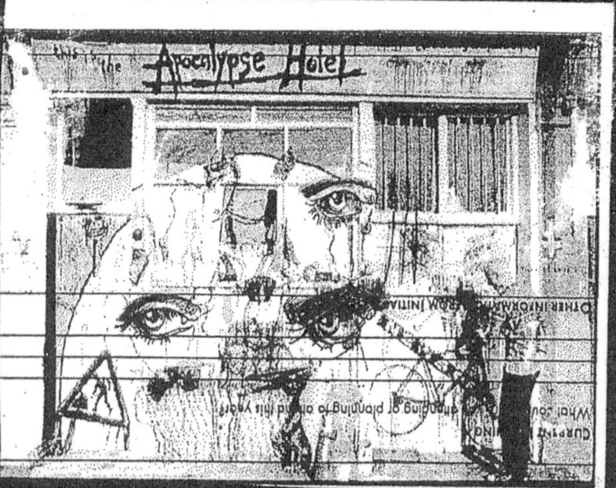
Apocalypse Hotel

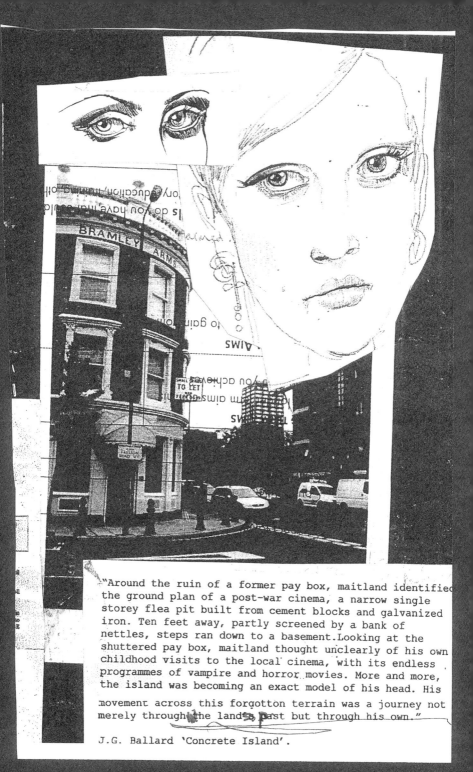

"Around the ruin of a former pay box, maitland identified
the ground plan of a post-war cinema, a narrow single
storey flea pit built from cement blocks and galvanized
iron. Ten feet away, partly screened by a bank of
nettles, steps ran down to a basement.Looking at the
shuttered pay box, maitland thought unclearly of his own
childhood visits to the local cinema, with its endless
programmes of vampire and horror movies. More and more,
the island was becoming an exact model of his head. His

movement across this forgotton terrain was a journey not
merely through the lands past but through his own."

J.G. Ballard 'Concrete Island'.

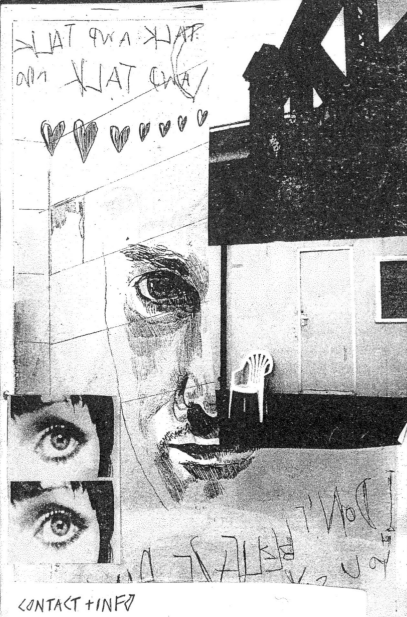

CONTACT +INFO
SAVAGEMESSIAH@HOTMAIL.CO.UK

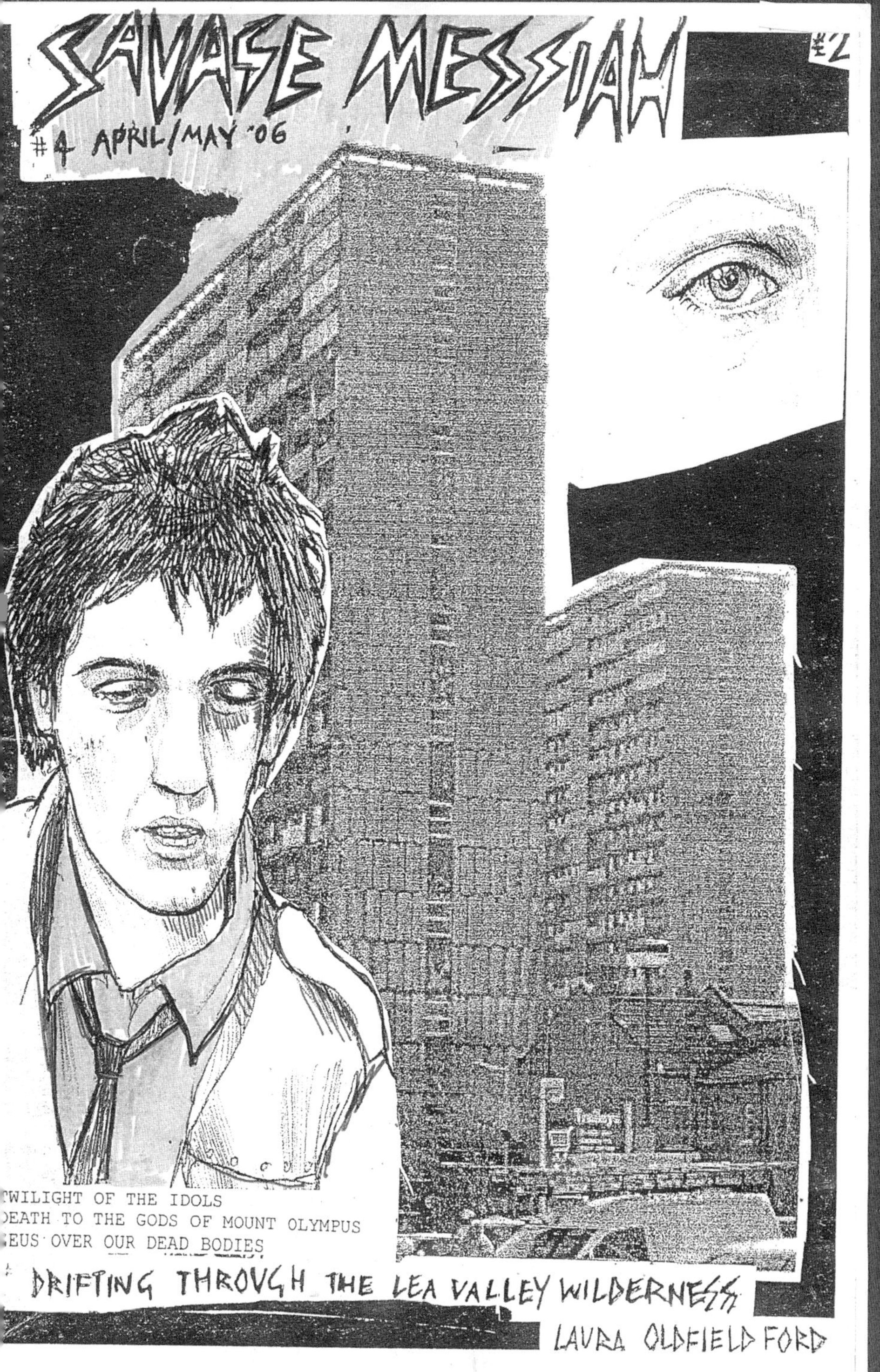
SAVAGE MESSIAH
£2
#4 APRIL/MAY '06
TWILIGHT OF THE IDOLS
DEATH TO THE GODS OF MOUNT OLYMPUS
EUS OVER OUR DEAD BODIES
DRIFTING THROUGH THE LEA VALLEY WILDERNESS
LAURA OLDFIELD FORD

A DÉRIVE FROM LEA BRIDGE ROUNDABOUT TO GREEN MAN INTERCHANGE......

"A lightning-flash...then night!- O fleeting beauty
whose glance all of a sudden gave me new birth,
shall I see you again only in eternity?

Far, far from here! Too late! Or maybe, never?
For I know what where you flee, you know not where I go,
O you I would have loved (o you who knew it too!)
Charles Baudelaire

" You advance for hours and it is not clear to you
whether you are already in the city's midst or still
outside it. Like a lake with low shores lost in the
swamps , so Penthesilea spreads for miles around, a soupy
city diluted in the plain; pale buildings back to back in
mangy fields, among plank fences and corrugated iron
sheds. Every now and then at the edges of the street a
cluster of constructions with hollow facades, very tall
or very low, like a snaggle tooth comb, seem to indicate
that from there the city's texture will thicken. But you
continue and you find instead other vague spaces, then a
rusty suburb of workshops and warehouses, a cemetery, a
carnival with ferris wheel, a shambles; you start down a
street of scrawny shops which fades amid patches of
leprous countryside."
Italo Calvino Invisible Cities.

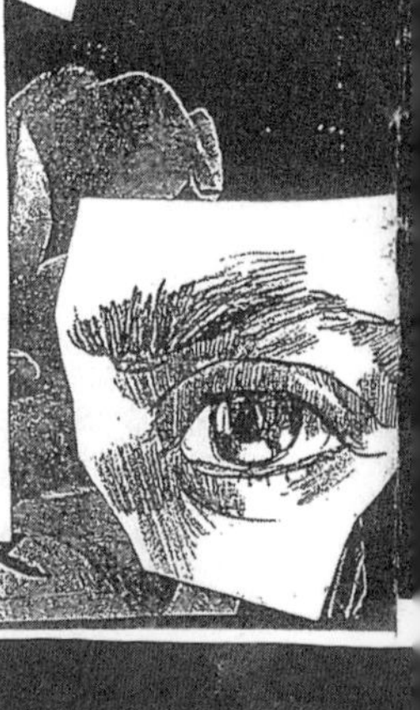

Lea Bridge Roundabout, a relic,
remnants of a modernist dream.
The roundabout is the last sentry before London gives up.

Humid evening in the heart of a heatwave. July 1995/ July 2003/ July 1981. Subways sealed with reinforced concrete. Buzzing and crackling. The Supergrid. Pylons towering over graffiti lit walls.

Clapton Park estate.

London succumbs to the marshes.

A diagonal path pulls me to that other realm. The canal. Bottle green, it shifts beneath a film of grisly flotsam , bulbous bags and rotting polystyrene.
Conjoined.

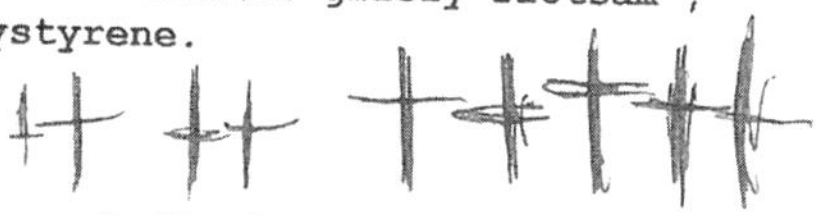

Edge along the tow path, approach the Lea Bridge Road. Trees disintegrate in cerulean light.

Barbed wire. DANGER OF DEATH BY FALLING.
A subliminal fear of falling off the scale, not registering anymore, a zone of displacement beyond the grasp of a signal.

Stepping through a bleached rose garden, petals become scorched tissue in the surreal glare. A tremulous pause, one eye looking back, a configuration in a lilac thicket. He reaches out from 1982, boots and braces, hands held out to the remote stretches of the Lea valley wilderness. We walk beneath the elderflower canopies of the towpath.
A desultory step down from that linear conduit , to the Lea Bridge Road.
Little tracks under briars weave and spiral into the nexus of a lost London.
We follow ancient paths and hidden footbridges.
They are here,
abandoned by the city,
cast into a liminal realm, parched and desolate.
Toxicity oozes from the architectural frames of mutant hogweed, recently appeared and crashing through barbed wire embankments.
We walk through fridge mountains and abandoned factories, boots swinging between lamp posts, threats spelled out in blocks of white paint.

Tyres smoulder beneath a motorway flyover. Stranded shopping trolleys. Circles of black ash.
Psychick TV and the number 23 etched into the concrete in 1985. Spectral traces,, embedded in the dirt.

Leyton. The locus of it lies in pieces.

Terrain vague.
The damp mists of the marshes.
To reassemble it would be black magic, a sleight of hand. It
lurks in the distance, holding something back. There in the
torn and tattered veneers, the peeling hoardings and crumbling
stucco I sense an elegiac emblem, a marker. I am pulled into a
channel I cannot fathom.

Almshouses, regimented and forlorn.
Bakers Arms, frosted glass in a skip outside.

Lea Bridge. The name conjures repressed desires, the
abandonment of reason on the marshes. A violent exchange, face
ground in the dirt on a muddy football pitch.
   Confusion and scarring,
 dreams of another epoch.
 The heady scent of hawthorn blossom beneath the pylons, a
squalid blue carrier bag with cans of casuality strength lager.
Under the shadow of the power station, a biting scratching
encounter , tearing into the scorched ground by the breakers
yard.

 Trapped in the present I conjure these scenes.
   Shimmering tableaux of brutality,
 curious, senseless topographies.
Along the railway sidings on Lammas Road.

 Acid house year zero, the Darkside . Black E zone. Internal
organs melting in paranoia. Factories empty from the recession.
 Intercity firm, " congratulations you have just met the ICF".
Warehouse party nihilism, protection rackets and thugs with
machetes.
 Corruption and organised violence, a matrix of horror zones.
Unit 13 , next to that grisly meat packing factory.
Synthetic Circus party,
A woman lies haemorrhaging under an awning of drilling gabbar.
 Shivering in the yard, the K hole, the Darkness.

Within a year a gruesome repeat. He watched her frothing at the
mouth, eyes rolling into her head with sound systems too scared
to stop.

Lammas, the old pagan festival of Lugnasadh , funeral feast of
the God of light, a time of sacrifice, judgement and reckoning.
Mousetraps carried to spring pickpockets, wraps of Ajax to
poison thieves. It had all gone wrong.
I saw the men hanging around the toilets. In those landings
where there were no lights. Little flies buzzing around fetid
pools of water. Waiting for you, trashed and stumbling, hands
reaching from the blackness.

Security firms standing by watching. Decaying vegetables, the
sharp stink of weed.

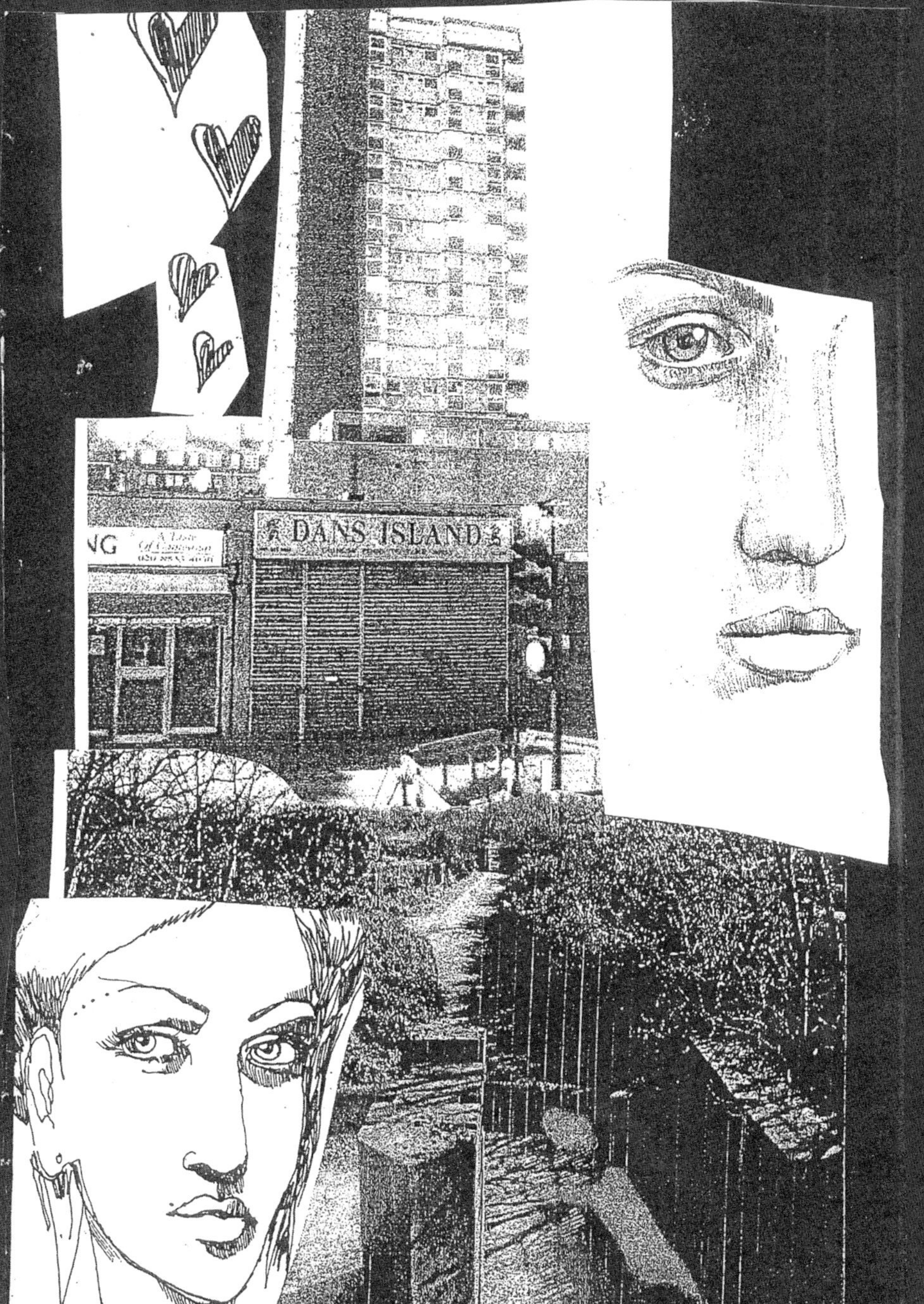
DANS ISLAND
NG

In the halcyon days of the late 80s it seemed possible that these desolate stretches would rise again, the phoenix of East London rising from the ashes.

But something started to claw it back, a malevolent twitching beneath the flyovers and electricity cables, a brooding cruelty.

Cross quarter fire festival, bonfires to power to the waning sun.

Staffa Road. Industrial estate becomes inferno as BritArt burns, tokens of Cool Britannia and New Labour arrogance razed to the ground in 600 degree flashover.

The accursed share, Olympic site as sacrificial zone.

The Dungeons. Dank.
Claustrophobic vaults beneath the Greyhound, reaching under the Lea Bridge Road. A shadow world sealed, gruesome chambers harbouring fear and shame.

Drug money suddenly leaching into the marshes. All these firms, criminal gangs, Hells Angels closing in for a cut. The Greyhound was a front, a sham pub. The Dungeons was where it really happened. Some Merlin automoton serving Red Stripe, moving slowly , and those other bastards trying to put the fear in with tales of torture, electrocuted genitalia.
A screaming, paranoid darkness.
Headfuck and Uglyfunk. Five rooms. Five soundsystmes.
Crossbones, Sick n Twisted Vs Pitchless, Darkside, The Lurker.
 The iconography of horror, 80s slasher movies resurrected.
Rave Enforcer, Necro, Face Hoover.
   Lurching zombified through the wastelands.

 R and B crews move in from Chimes. There are shootings outside and in its final incarnation the Dungeons becomes the last outpost of Murder Mile.

He had blue eyes, intensity crackling in the stifling dark.
A deft exit, down the stairs past the railway sidings and the post industrial glitz hulk of Mondital. Round the back , the buzzing of the electricity generator/
 through a wire fence , a hallucinatory arcadia. Purple shadows, a thicket of lilac, under the pylon.
Biting, frenziedly marking.
. I'm coming down off that pill, zigzag lines, then all these steps, complex shifting topographies, tube lines on stilts lurching through the bogs, the cloying theatricality of Piranesi.. He gives me more, pills, drink, everything, we get a minicab back to some flat in Stamford Hill. Not his, just a place he's borrowed while he's down for the week. Pink walls, black satin on the windows.
His accent is Leeds. His skin pale, flawless under grimy sheets.

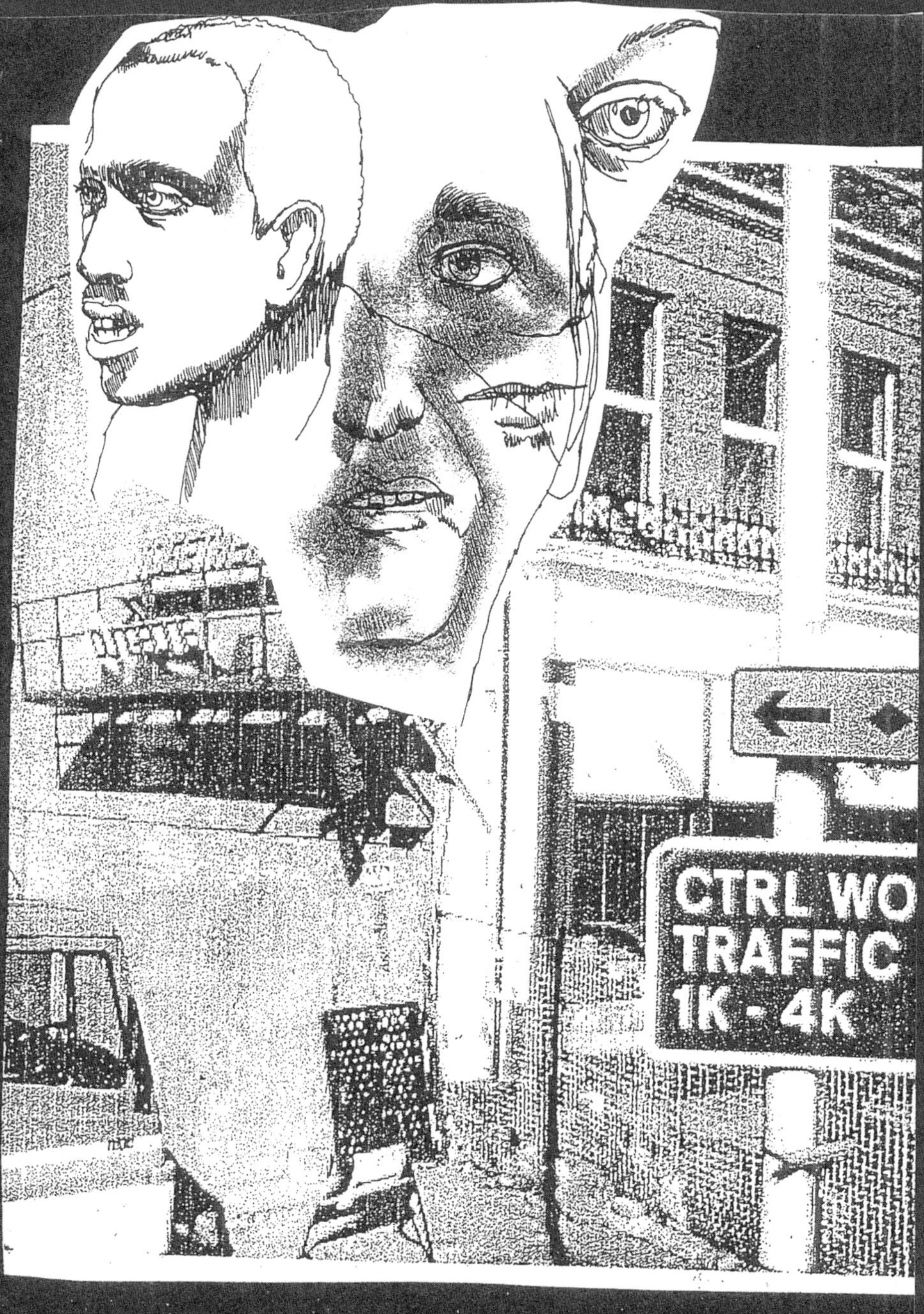
CTRL WO
TRAFFIC
1K - 4K

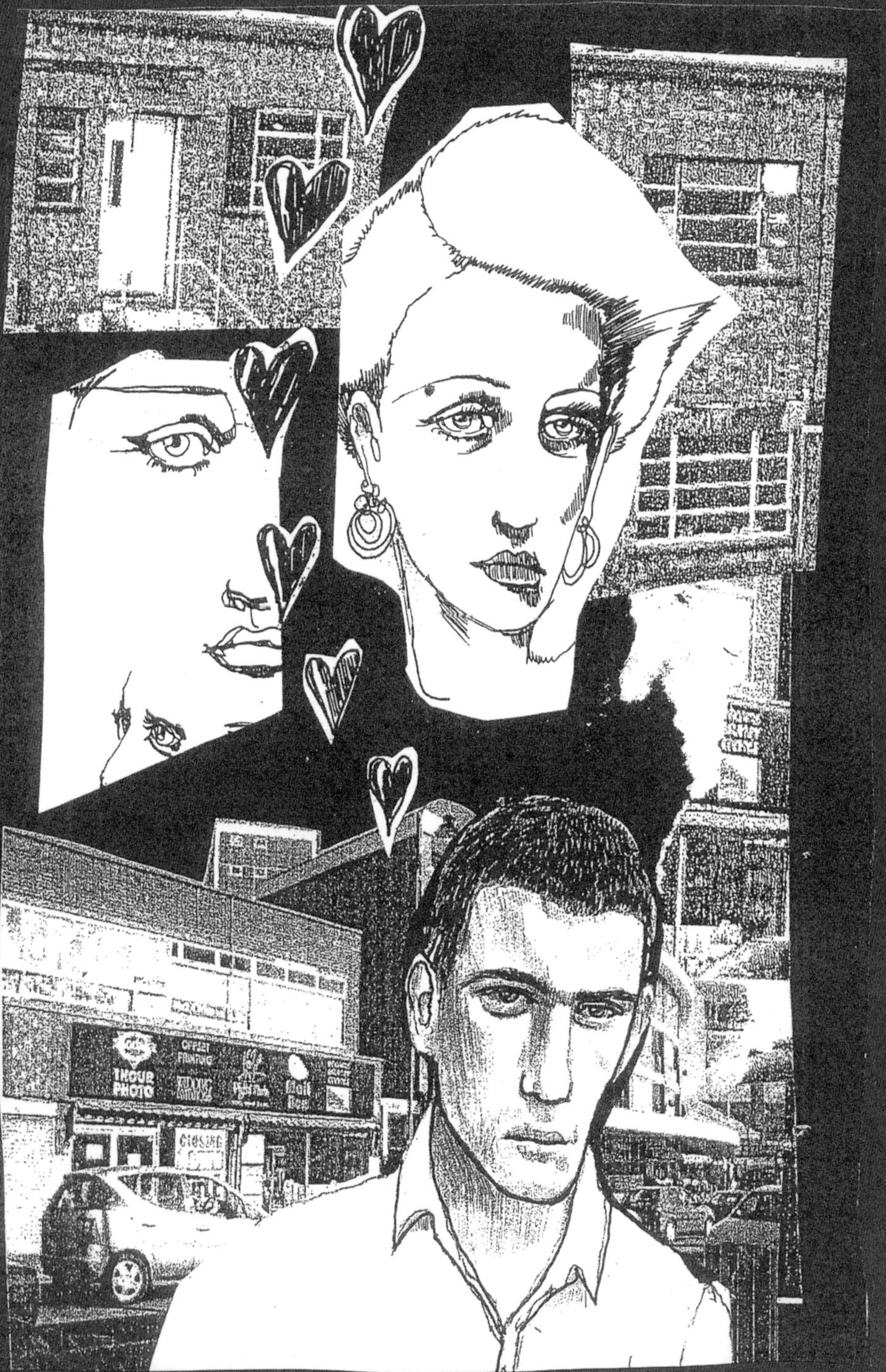
1HOUR PHOTO

I pass by the industrial estates, the Furniture world on Orient
way and fall into some Wetherspoons called the Drum. I'm over
the other side now, a different zone echoing provincial English
towns in the early 90s. Acid hangovers float around, garish
graffiti drug references in luminous yellow and day glo
tangerine. We feel the place drift around us. BAD E in
spraypaint over a bookmakers door, girls trapped in a post
goth/pre rave sartorial dilemma. This isn't London and yet it
couldn't be anywhere else. As I'm smoking my second cigarette
it strikes me that I could hide out here in this place of
forgetting. It would let me lie embedded within it.

The Creator

   Abandoned dreams reside here, unharnessed and unchannelled.
Step over them in carefully avoided cracks in the pavement,
feel them pulsating in the unsmiling eyes of the black cat.

Chain pubs make clumsy stabs at authenticity
Pictures on the wall of Alfred Hitchcock
 A MASTER OF SUSPENSE….
No familiar chains, no sanitised high street,
   little two storey houses next to crumbling tower blocks,
clusters of pawnbrokers next to adhoc churches.
 Aggro boozers, dark caves, flashing screens. A lone woman
hunched over a copy of the Daily Star. Sound of jukebox carries
out into the street.
'*I believe in Angels*' -
' *take the future even if you fall*'

 The Beaumont estate under threat of demolition.

TWILIGHT OF THE IDOLS
DEATH TO THE GODS OF MOUNT OLYMPUS
ZEUS OVER OUR DEAD BODIES

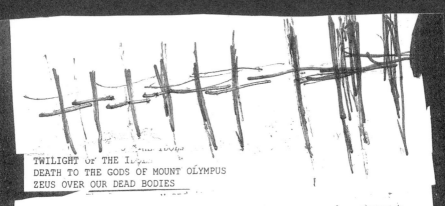

TWILIGHT OF THE IDOLS
DEATH TO THE GODS OF MOUNT OLYMPUS
ZEUS OVER OUR DEAD BODIES

The Lea valley and its peripheral enclaves are an embarrassment
to the moguls and ministers of Whitehall. Leyton is the stuff of
Foster and partners worst nightmares, they look and fail to see
themselves reflected back, their architectural sovereignty
eroded in the entropy and murk of the marshlands. If it seemed
increasingly possible that middle class fools with no
imagination could make a sanitised sweep across the whole city
one must look to Leyton for a last shred of hope. Leyton defies
it, even if the Beaumont Estate and its three majestic towers
lie in dusty heaps Leyton will never become the gleaming vision
of their plans. Look at Temple Mills, millennial mediocrity,
weak parodying of the International style; corrugated curves,
post modern hangars, yellow brickwork and Burger king with
spongy playground all drawn irresistibly back to the dirt, back
to the sucking bogs and greedy marshes. The landscaping has
become a tangle of coke cans and crisp packets, the walls
striated with the black silt of exhaust fumes. Saplings are
snapped in acts of vicious boredom and the shrubs and weeds are
coated in a film of ash. The flimsiness of these buildings,
these sheds, are thinly disguised, a furtive glance into the
loading bay exposes the hastily thrown together service tunnels,
rigged meshes of breezeblocks and plywood. The vistas of pylons
and motorway flyovers cannot be eradicated here as they were on
the planners board.
London 2012, who wants it except middle England pricks in their
executive homes, WPCs with names like Sally and Gaynor and a
raft of deluded idiots who don't realise local opportunities
means shit jobs in the service industry. The Golden Arches loom
large over this grotesque scheme, another gateway, another
fucking Gulag.
Leyton will resist because there is an undercurrent of psychick
viciousness. From Hitchcock to the colonial savagery of the
regulars of Zulu's bar , the violence is always simmering under
the surface. The rage and the manic kick offs, the punch ups to
disrupt the boredom will be channelled into class hate.

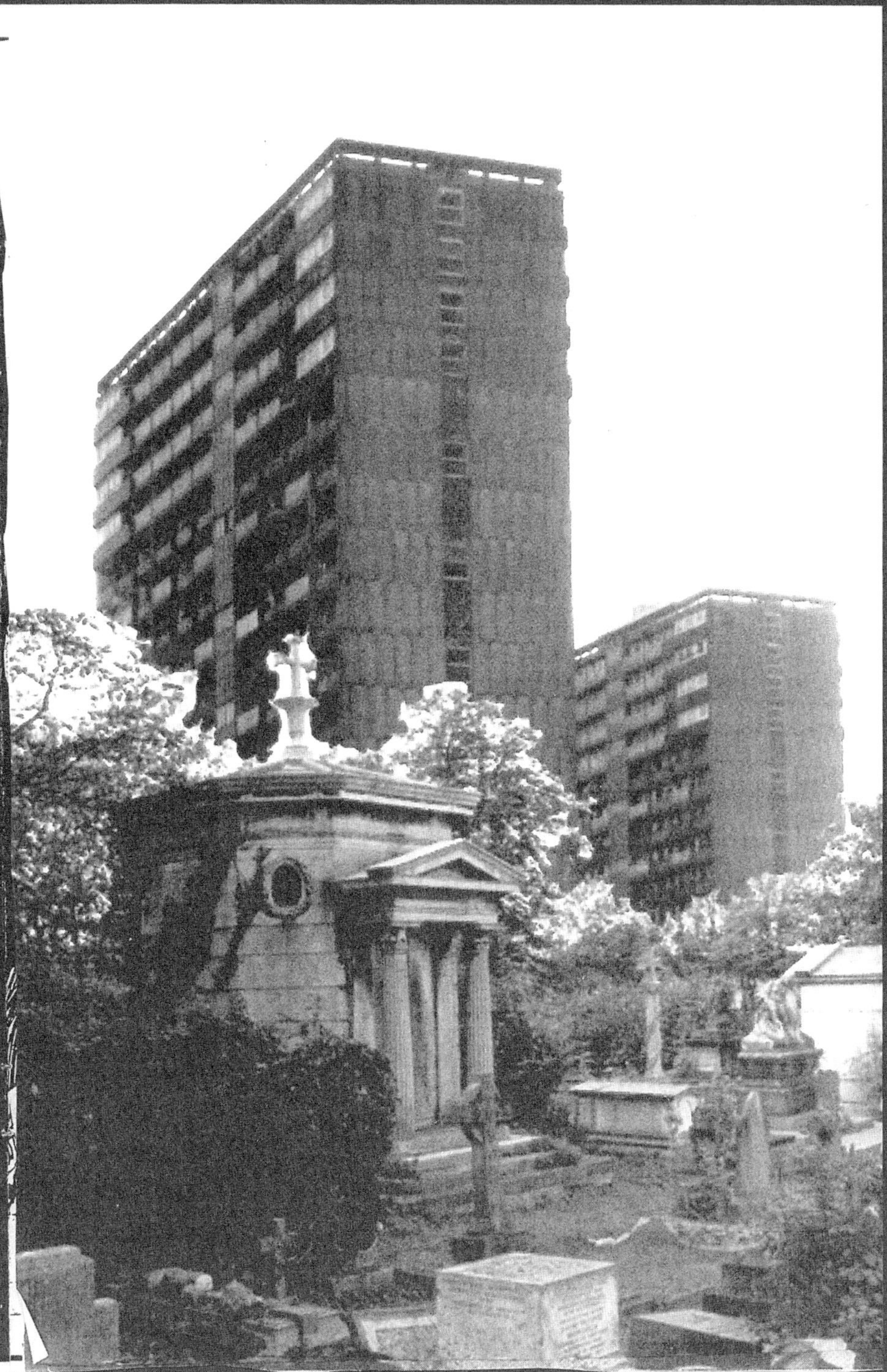

Same genes same daft grimaces. Crumbling faced moron..,
pushes me up slam into a flashing fruit machine. Tilts and I
go chin first into three laughing sevens. Dank smell of stale
booze and grime , polystyrene ceiling tiles, floor festooned
with betting slips. Pushing hard, a miserable cascade to the
face down .
 I'm locked under the fat grinder,
 blubber printing me into the stinking carpet.
Rock rock rock. Meander through the sordid banter of two stoned
simpletons. SAS survival, serial killers , alien abductions.
 Waiting. Listening.
To the fantasies of the brain dead.

Leyton High road .I'm taking some phone snaps of a CCTV camera
. Old Bill constant fucking hassle, don't like it now the
camera is flashed back at them. Hauled in for enforced DNA
swabs..
 Smooth faced home counties dimwits. Grinding. Morons.

 First tender imaginings of Spring,
sweet fragrance after the rain. Cherry blossom and hawthorn,
breaths of warm, perfumed air.

 Keep moving towards Epping Forest. A skinhead leaps from a
peeling door , agitated, face contorted in a West Ham
grimace. *Inside Out /*
Mental Breakdown/ Acid Tracks
Luminous panels, lime arrows in a black tracksuit top. Our
steps are punctuated by a round of staccato expletives, FUCK<
CUNT<FUCK<FUCK. warehouse party reverberating
bass synthesiser,
303 -phuture, accelerating.

On through the seething vortex of the Bakers Arms, Tesco
pedestrian bottle neck, pavement up again , rings of orange
plastic slipping into tarmac pits.
Congratulations you have just met the ICF.

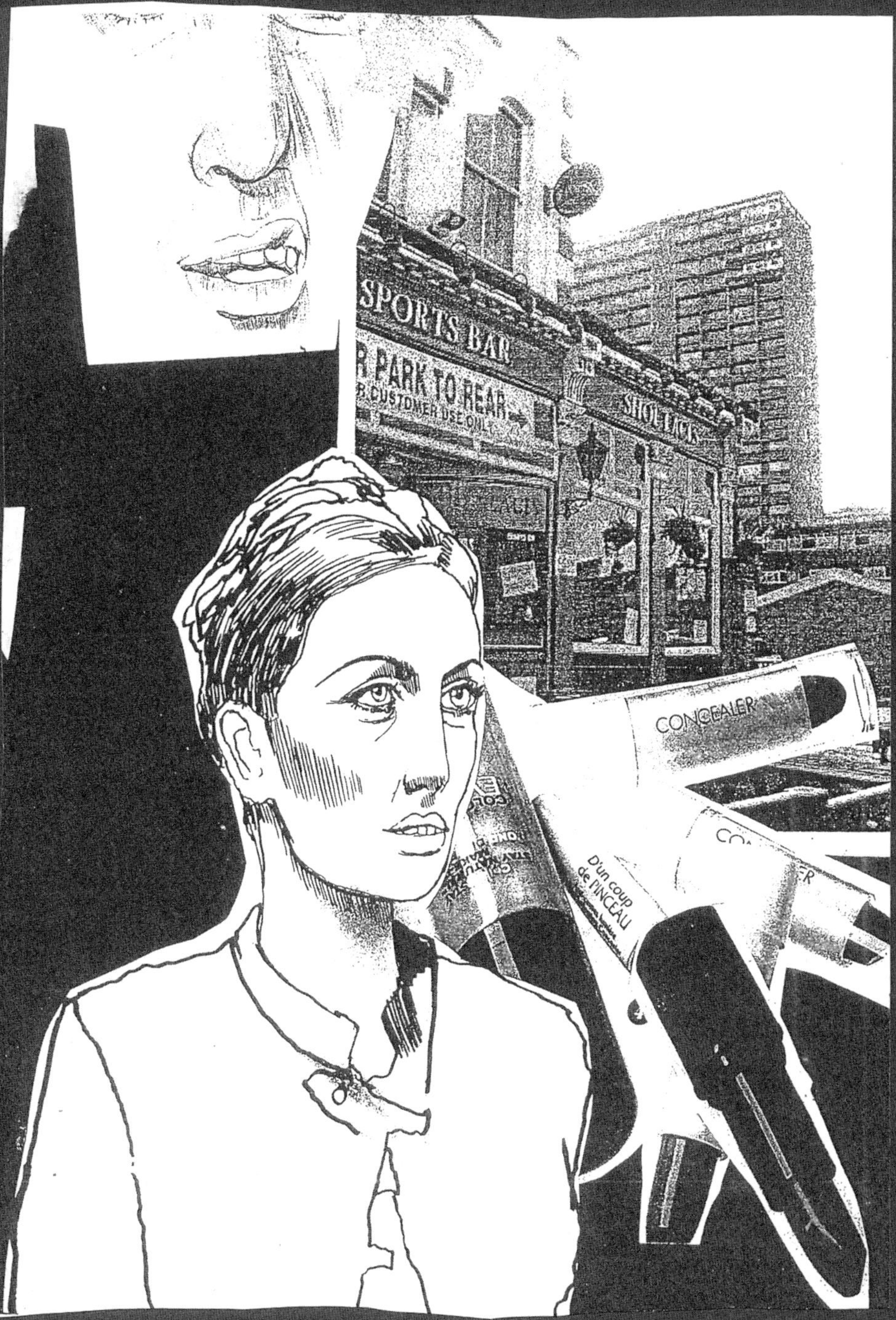
SPORTS BAR
PARK TO REAR
CUSTOMER USE ONLY
CONCEALER
D'un coup
de PINCEAU

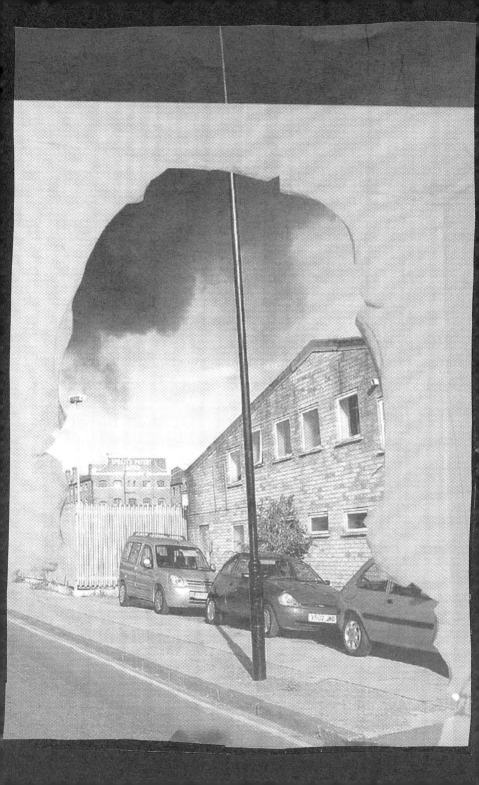

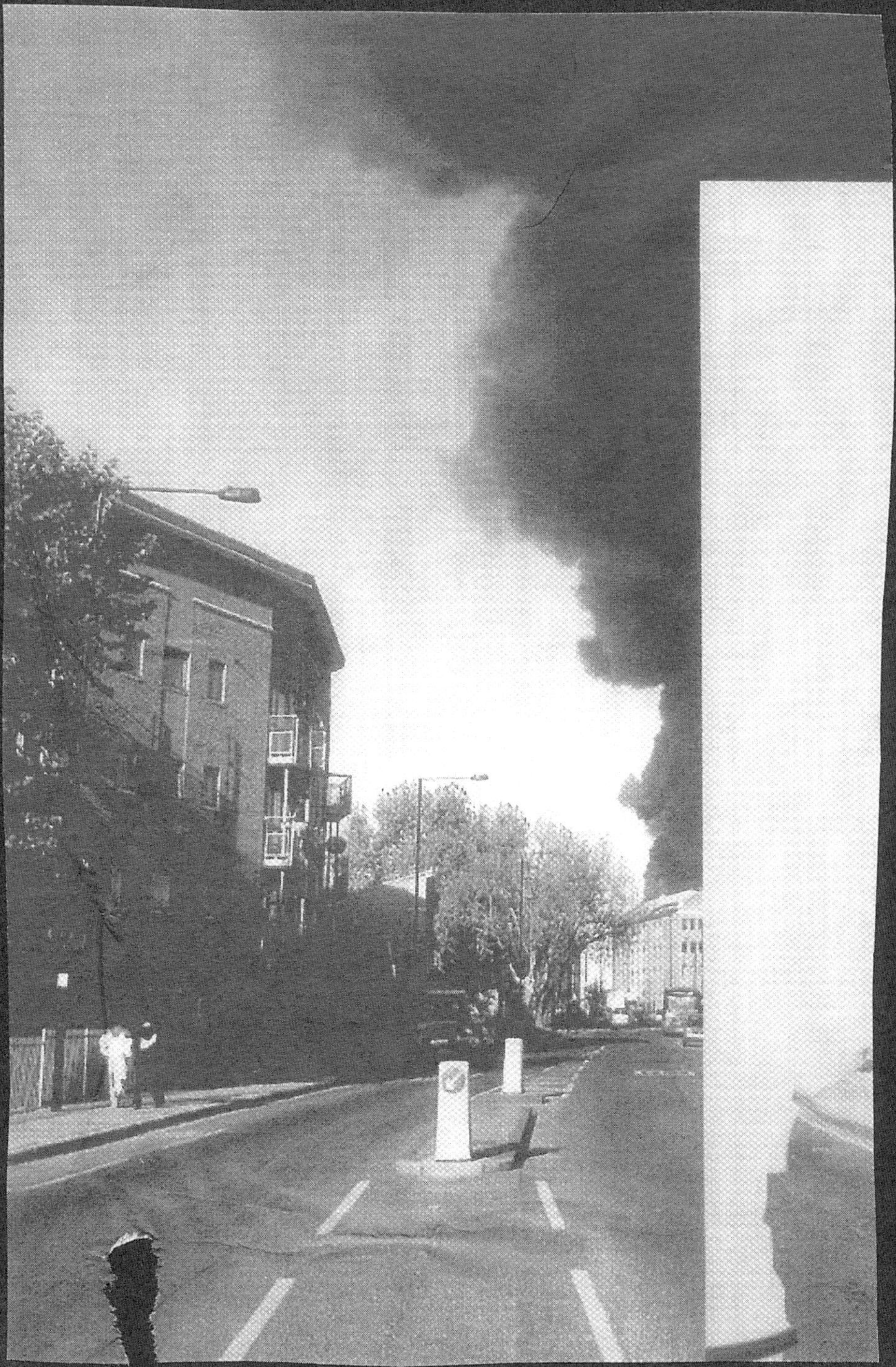

Deke watched,
 behind mirror shades.
 The kind with a greasy oil slick film , murky colours swirling
across where the eyes should be.

Mann's on the High Road.
 Orange rope lights and all them luminous stars in the window.
 Shaved head,, stubby green mohican dreading up at the back,,
smudgy dark sores where he slipped up with the clippers. Could
never handle being a lone drinker., knows he's being mugged off
paying for all the booze but he'd rather sit with a boring
bastard like Troy than be wasted on his own.
Makes Troy stand outside with the dog. Can I have a rollie
while I'm waitin.
 He's asking in that stupid whiny voice . Deke hates that
voice,, despises Troy and all he represents. He smashed the
idiots head into the wall once because he couldn't stand his
fucking whining.
Eight cans of Brew. Deke hands a soft tenner over the counter,
bolts out the shop and up the high road with Troy stumbling and
staggering behind.
Sharp right turn through the Beaumont estate to the Church Road
squat, always walking fast like there's someone after him. It's
made him skinny, all the amphetamines, walking up and down Lea
Bridge Road, wears layers of army surplus to bulk himself up.
Back at the gaff there's Chris and his girlfriend sitting on
the steps listening to Neurosis loud. Deke pushes past them and
puts Richard and Judy on with the sound down, likes the
weirdness of them mouthing mutely to the raucous strains of a
hardcore punk band.

The front room holds the pungent smell of cat piss and mould. A massive poster depicting Ronald McDonald as the Grim Reaper is half coming off the wall leaving a white rectangle in the yellow murk. Beneath that, pinned to the wall, there's an article from the Waltham Forest Guardian about some kid who reckons he's been abducted by aliens 13 times on the marshes. Deke tosses old copies of Class war and the Mirror onto the floor and collapses feet up on the settee.

Troy lurches in red faced and Deke makes him sit on the floor with the dog and some books on military hardware.

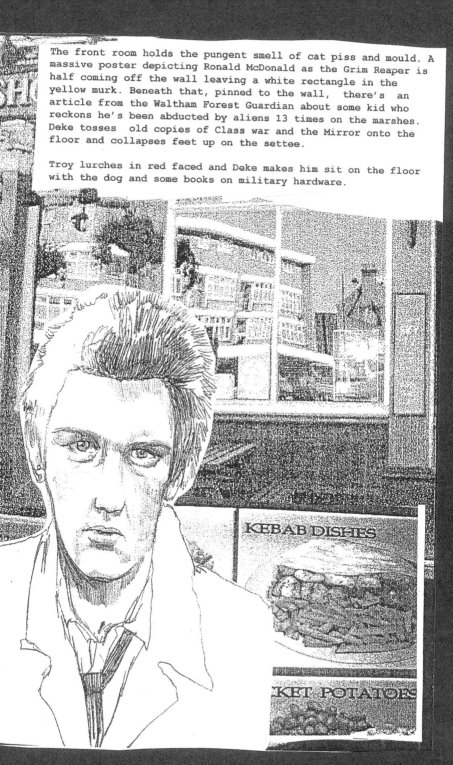

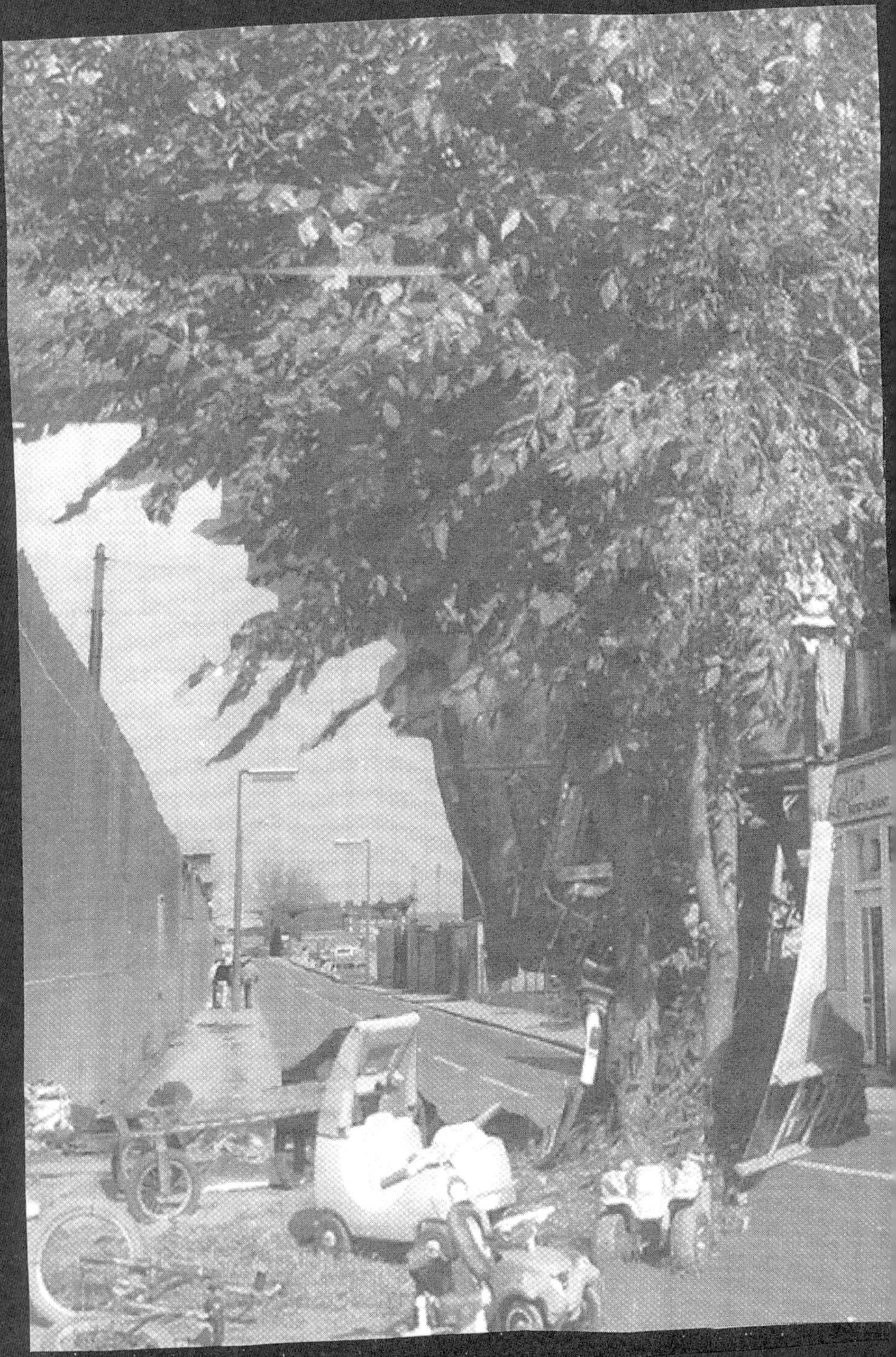

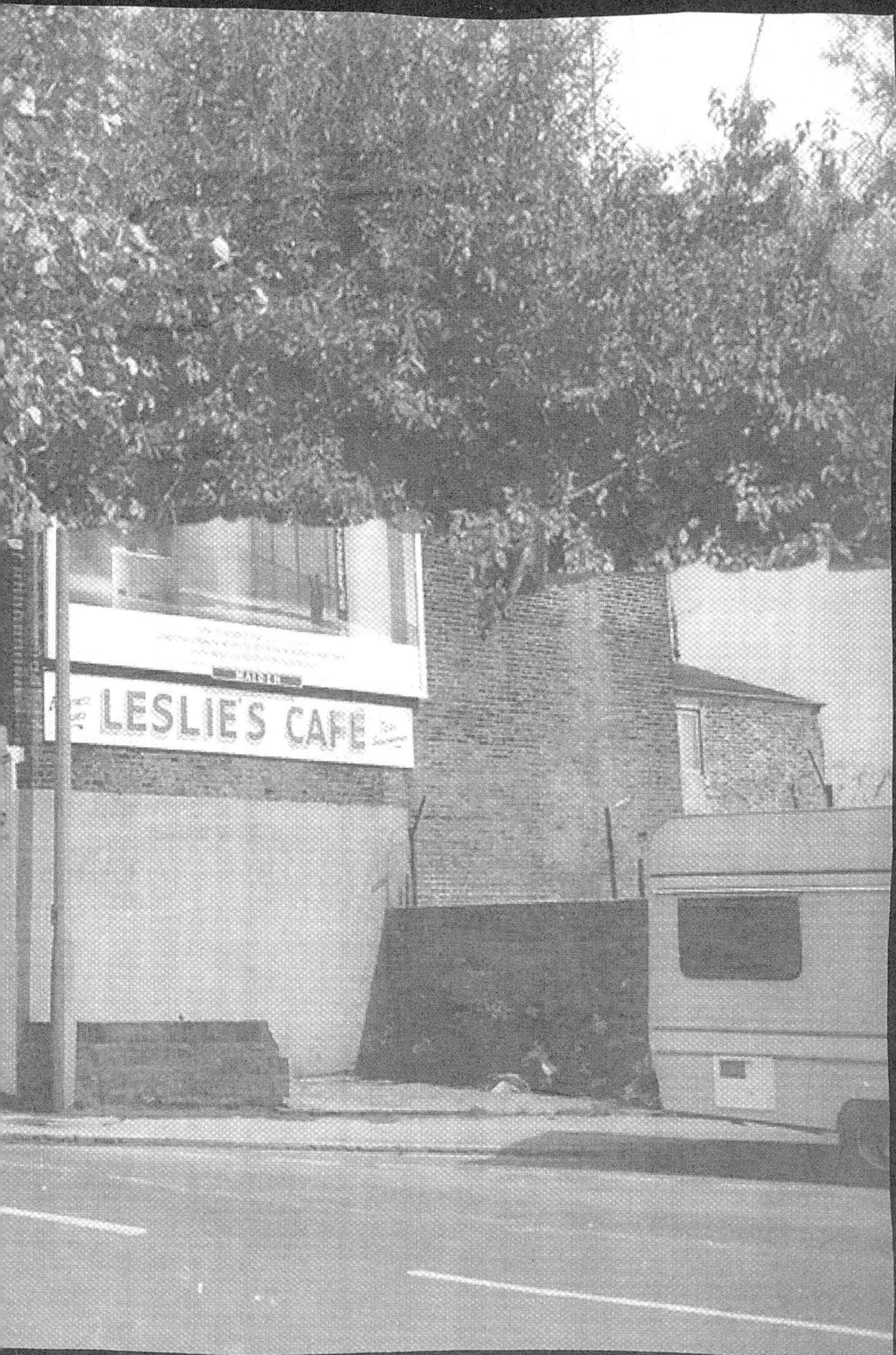
LESLIE'S CAFE

A van pulls up, more crew , mates from Leeds tonight at the Dungeons. A load of them moved down from Leeds together, about ten years ago, all in bands thinking maybe there's more going on down here. Funny how they all ended like this, clinging to the fraying edges of the valley just like it was in Leeds 6 except this feels so much more remote than it ever did there. They were in Hackney first, then Dalston then Stoke Newington.

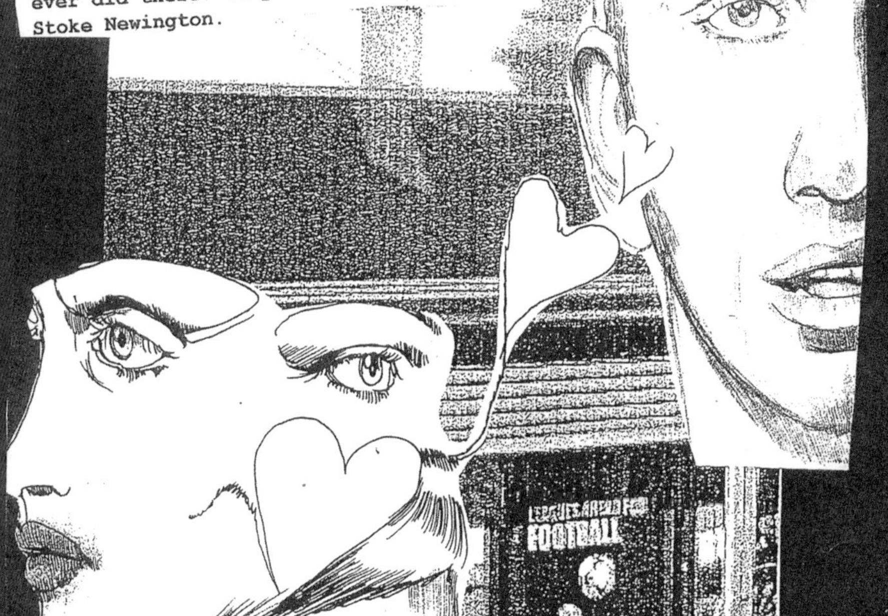
FOOTBALL

It wasn't long before the punks, Northerners and Buckfast swilling scots were pushed out by the three wheeler buggy brigade. Church Street was the first bit to fall, Anarchist drinking dens, radical bookshops and Totem records were replaced by Fresh and Wild and a glut of twee boutiques selling designer baby clothes. The whole of N16 became a property investment for 90s music industry and media types.

Deke watches the mob stagger out of the van into the yard. Nice day, play darts, have some jellies.

He's looking for Marion, green and black dreads and always that overwhelming patchouli stink. She owes him a wrap of whizz, and sometimes when she's in a good mood she gets drunk and stays the night.

He watches the tattoos scuttle across her shoulder blades. Baroque whorls and curlicues twisting and writhing. Mesmerised, he doesn't notice at first as his Nemesis is conjured up in the street.

Craig.

.McDermott.

A monochrome apparition. An ugly fucking doilem.

Cold silence.   All on mute.
Deke bristles. .

Tensed and ready to kick off, adrenaline surging beneath his chest, he stands blocking the door. He'd forgotten that lurching sensation, the last desperate attempt to come up on a drug when deep down you knew there was nothing left to face but the come down.
Marion and him, no chance now with that fucker hangin about.
Why do women go for types like THAT? Fuckin greasers, brylcreem black hair, drainpipe jeans and white slip on shoes, what a retarded look he thinks, what a pretentious fake bastard with that horrific ace of spades tattooed on his hand like he's some fucking hard man.
Marion runs through the yard laughing, grabbing Deke in the doorway. She looks fit in that red dress but somehow her sexiness is tainted by the association with McDermott. He can't fucking stand the thought of her with him, that slimy little bastard. He obviously hadn't taught him enough of a lesson, should have gone in harder, should've ruined his pretty boy face permanently.
She gives him a kiss and grabs his beer off him.
You never said he was comin down Deke says to her with a cold eye cast over the yard.
She looks a bit anxious under the bouncy over confidence, the menace in his eyes has stopped her manic chat. Deke had a serious reputation for violence, he'd spent time in Armley and that was one of the reasons he'd left Leeds, to try and leave old animosities and grievances behind. But for her it was all just rumours, she'd never actually seen that side to him. Until that glimpse. Just now.

The rage was surging up in him. He knew Shelly would still be
around if it wasn't for that bastard with his bad wraps of K.
McDermott was an evil cunt and he should have stayed in Leeds
where people would have properly dealt with him. But no one
round here saw it that way and that's what seared through him .
The injustice. It propelled him towards the raging,
unstoppable violence he knew he was capable of.

 The tension holds fast in the dusty yard. McDermott is pulled
out of sight. Deke silently cracks open another tin , anger
forming in sharp spasms under his chest.
 The shifting of gear and embarrassed chatter goes on around
them until Craig is back in the van. Finally after surveying
the street for a good twenty minutes he allows Marion to steer
him through the tandoori miasmas of Leyton Grange towards the
High road. He knows there is no scope, no vistas open if he
lets himself unravel for the sake of McDermott. Just the sweat
stench and darkness of Pentonville.
Let's go for a pint, she said. The King Harold?
The place holds an air of desolation. There's a darts
tournament being blasted from a phosphorescent tv that looks
like its about to blow up. They;re the only ones in the fucking
place. Settled in with pints of Stella ,Marion passes him some
green eggs under the table. Temazepam. She probably thinks
it'll calm him down. It'll take more than a few fucking jellies
he thinks but he has ·them anyway, help take the jitters away
from the speed comedown.
Anyway Craig was never going to stop at your gaff, she says
later, when they get round to discussing things in a boozy
haze. He met someone last time.
Deke scans her face for traces of jealousy, doesn't see any and
pulls her close. You look fuckin great by the way.

We pass rows of shops, things more subdued now, the kebab
shacks and cash converters have given way to more bourgeois
concerns like motor insurance and Italian furniture. Eyes watch
over us behind greying nets, through gardens hidden beneath
rampant nettles. This is a place to move swiftly through, to
pause is to never leave.
Belmont Place, Knott's Green a thin veneer of respectability
torn away and left fluttering like polythene in derelict
windows. Fragments of council estates, big post war semis
conjure up images of a lost Northern childhood. Whipps Cross
roundabout, the beginning of Epping Forest; it is ensnared,
encircled by white vans, Londons bucolic dream trapped by the
commercial matrix of Essex. The forest has resisted attempts
to push it back , thickets of birch and hazel erupt in suburban
gardens.

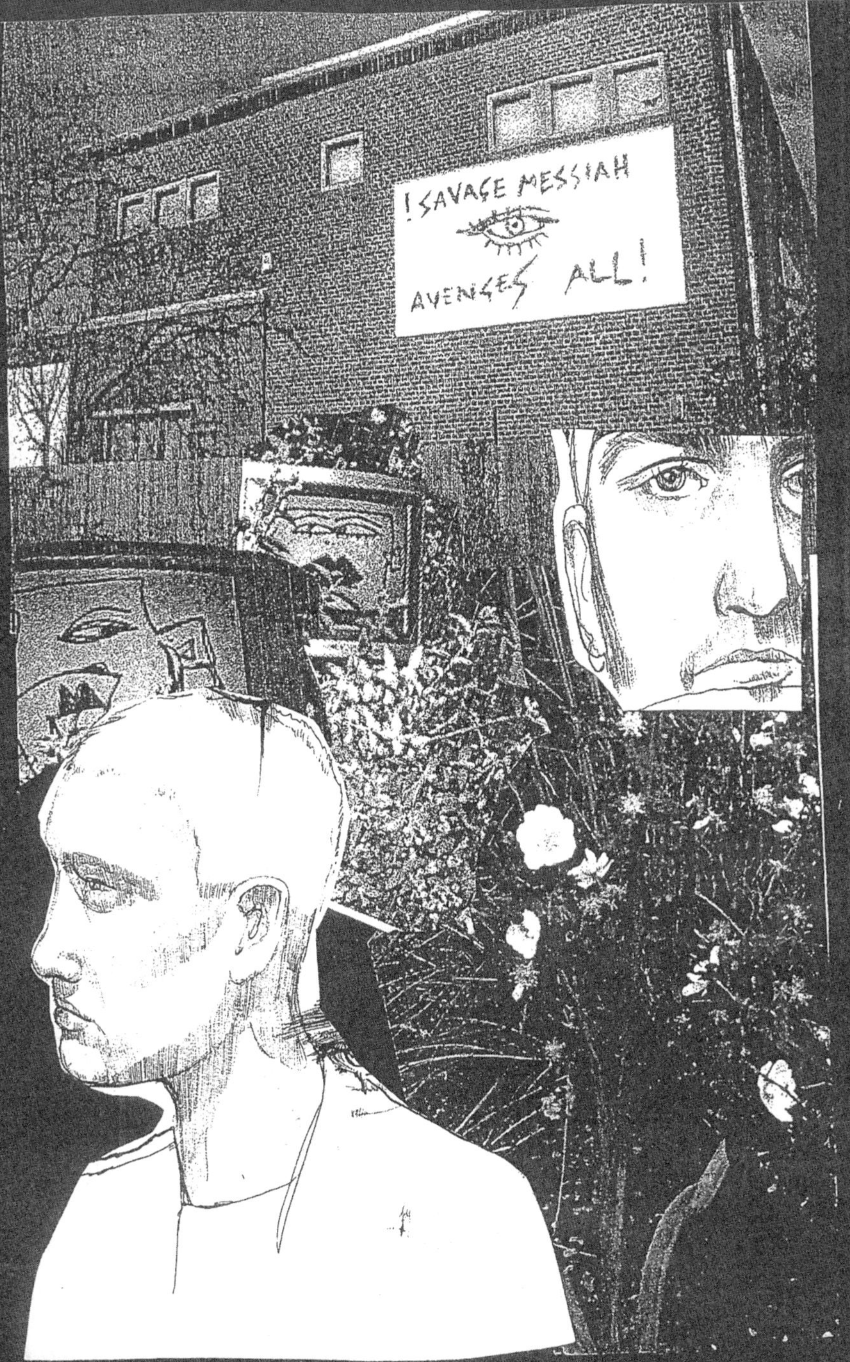
! SAVAGE MESSIAH
AVENGES ALL!

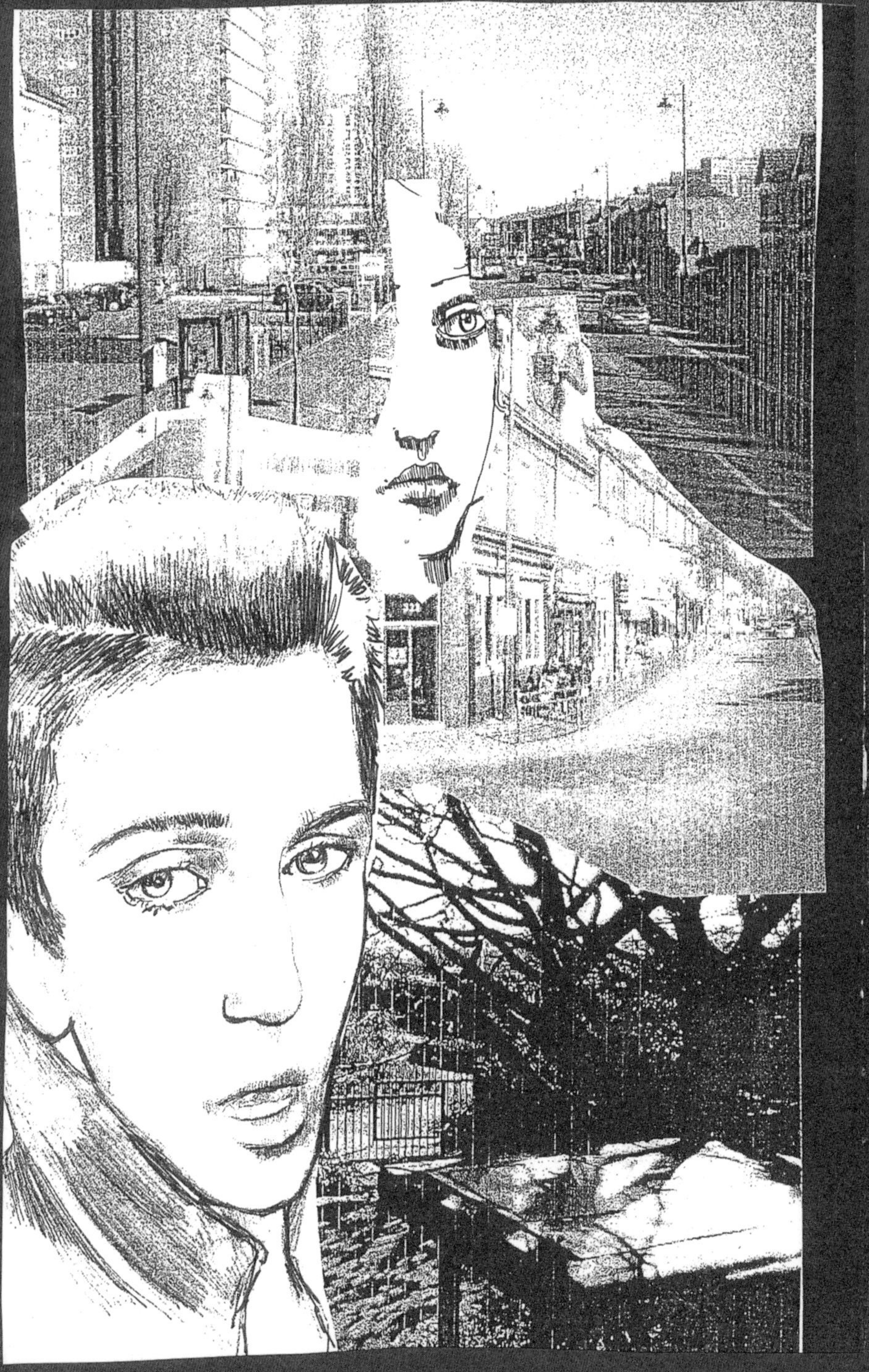

We walk through Whipps cross hospital. I am mesmerised by sprawling Victorian courtyards, arches, the total autonomy of it. We pass through warm canteen smells and the sharp detergent pangs of the laundry. Fractures and fissures appear in the walls, ragwort and campion edge through cracks coated in a soft white powder.

Post war annexes become the nostalgic wanderings of a war veteran. We enter a maze of dark green paint, blistering and peeling.. The topography of melancholia, bullet holes in portakabins, khaki swing doors and mossy corrugated iron roofs.

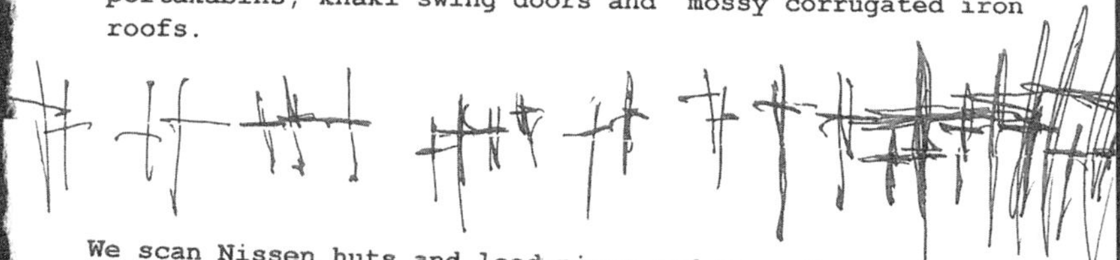

We scan Nissen huts and lead pipes and peer through a padlocked door into a 1940s cell. A woman shakes distraught on stone steps.

The hospital complex is breaking down, the structures that bind it are turning to dust.

McGee was yellow as he watched himself die. Plastic ferns and dusty African Violets, a tungsten corridor of powder and disinfectant. Chair parked facing the Sun Court; salmon pink and curdled yellow. Crazy paving. Nettles marking the fracture lines.

Do I know you love?

Glowing billboards loom beyond the perimeter fence.

All coming down, save for the Clocktower, element of authenticity to maintain a sense of 'place'.

A BRAND NEW HOSPITAL BY 2008, they want to drag it into the 21st century, PFI and organ scandals. Gleaming corruption snakes round, entombing the living, mocking the dead.

Find a way out,
'Through a memorial garden,
a wilderness of roses.

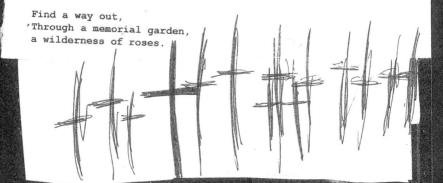

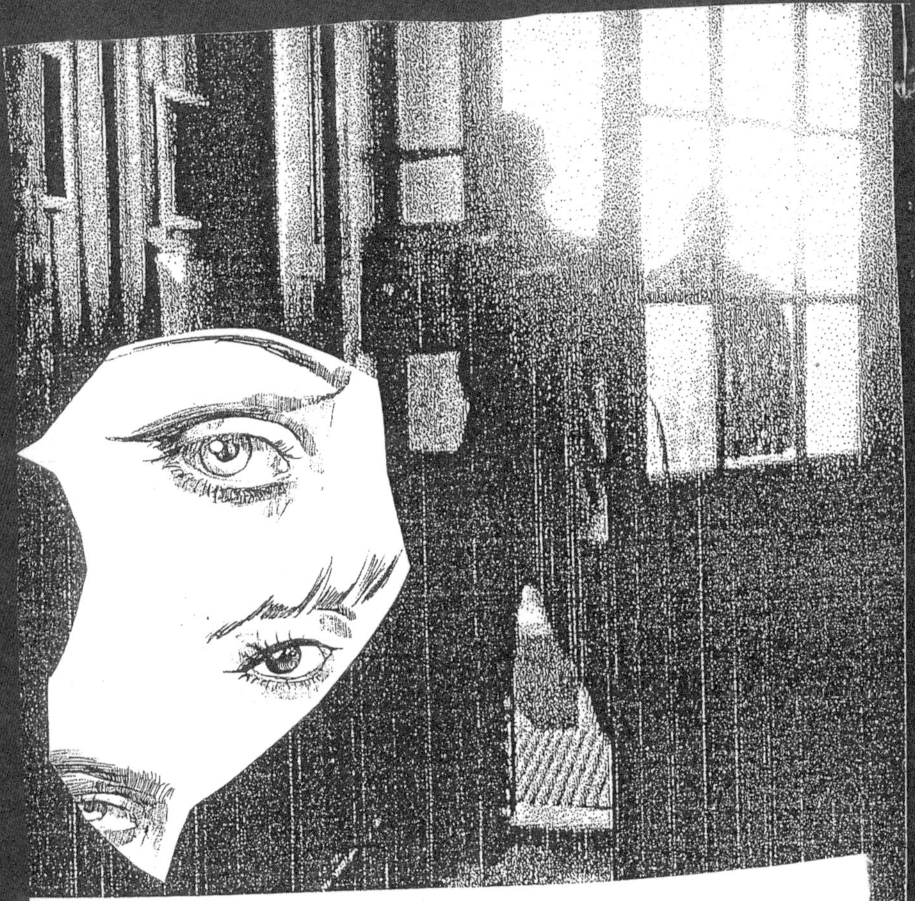

The lake on the other side of Whipps Cross road shimmers pink in the evening light. Flag irises, red dust and mutating islands dissolving in the heat. We edge along its quiet shores, staring across the lake to the turrets and spires of Snaresbrook Crown court.

The forest creeps in, beckoning to us.

Hitchcock Hotel.

Seedy bar, shafts of light slicing the dust. A 90s dislocated world hanging in the reek of chronic depression.

Nicotine walls, blokes sitting on their own at tables strewn with packets of Lambert and Butler and The Sun.

South Africa Times scattered in the lobby, road signs and global clutter. Hitchcock Lager on tap, Sunday carvery in the Spellbound restaurant.

A place for passing.

Step back onto the relentless white van shuttle of Whipps cross road and weave through the gorse and broom of Leyton flats to the Green Man roundabout. The wild terrain and networks of scrubland paths became the last outpost of the road protests. Greenmania, the last effort to undermine t plan. An intensification of Tory road building led to compulsorily purchase orders, destruction of houses and th ousting of entire communities. In response to this theft of territory streets were squatted and veterans of Twyford Dow came to lend a militant brand of Direct Action to the campaig A proliferation of spectaculars emanated from this protest site, Claremont Road as radicalising moment.

I smell the hawthorn, am dizzied by its potency, the rituals the green wood, shimmering red dot locations in this trapped corner of Leyton Flats.

I am hurtling into a flashpoint of dissolution, 5 a.m, delirious in the morning dew. I am enchanted by violet blue eyes, the ace of spades on a pale hand, desire illuminating hi face in the first pink shreds of light.

And on the edge of this mutating scrubland, what is left to guard the forest splinter? The crossroads is undifferentiated, pleromatic.

The stone heap marks the limits of consciousness. Beyond it lies the unknown, the lost zones. Hermes, liminal God, inhabiting the interstices. Aphroditic stealth, sly and amoral, a love gained by theft.

This was always a place of passing, a burial ground for gypsies, suicides, witches, outlaws. Spells and rituals, stocks and gallows repelled those who tried to stay.

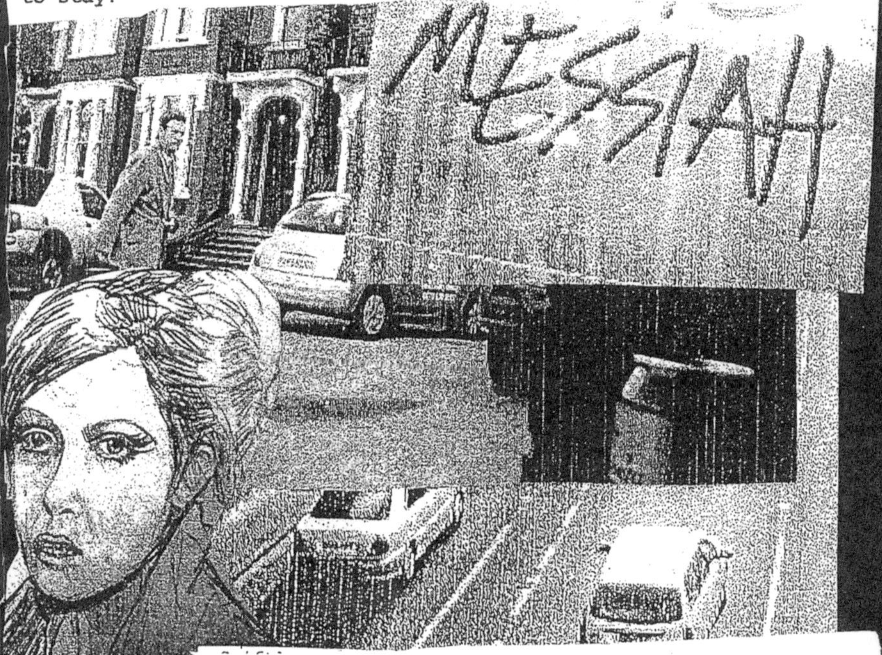
MESSIAH

The Green Man pub, the old coaching inn where Turpin resided, reduced to rubble and replaced by a mobile phone shop called Numast. Now there's an O Neills pub, driven to from all the disparate outposts of the forest terrain for motorway joyrides, layby pharmecuticals and illicit sex in the dark groves of Epping Forest.

A slow sliding back to the dust.

Epping Forest. Site of London's repressed desires.
Gangland killings . Rushed couplings. Pine strewn carpets a
contorted branches .
The Green Man.

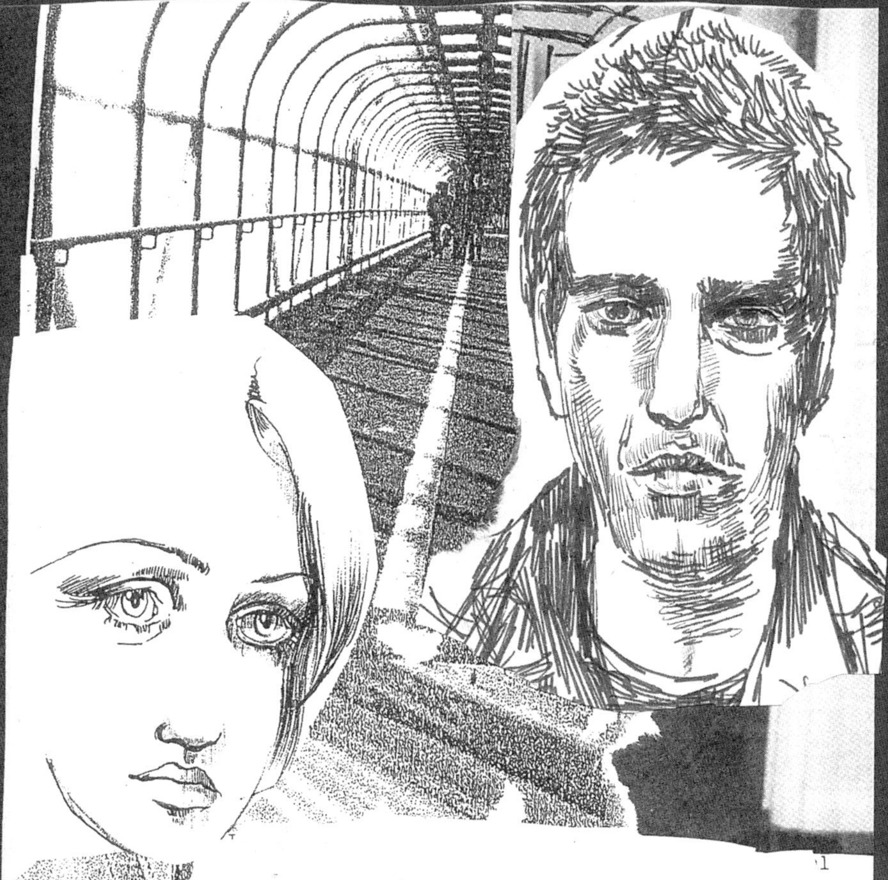

Livid eyes scan the marshes. Dalo says, you been working this shift too long. Radioactive buns in Percy Ingles, luminous pink and the slime of sugary skin. That dumb green uniform, makes you look like a right fucking clown, nearly got sacked for refusing to wear the hat. Two years been here and they're still paying kids wages, £4.80 an hour, fuck that, you gotta take it back where you can. Europop ringtones, Saturday night escapades tumbling through the back, ../ *Times Fade* Phuture- The Next Generation -why wait til 6 o clock? Boyracing on the North Circular ,service station arcade games, banging techno and McDonalds drive thrus. That O' Neills cattle market, anyone can pull in there. They've necked theirs already, he splits his sides when she orders an iced fancy. Spotty and well off it. Fuckin hate this job.

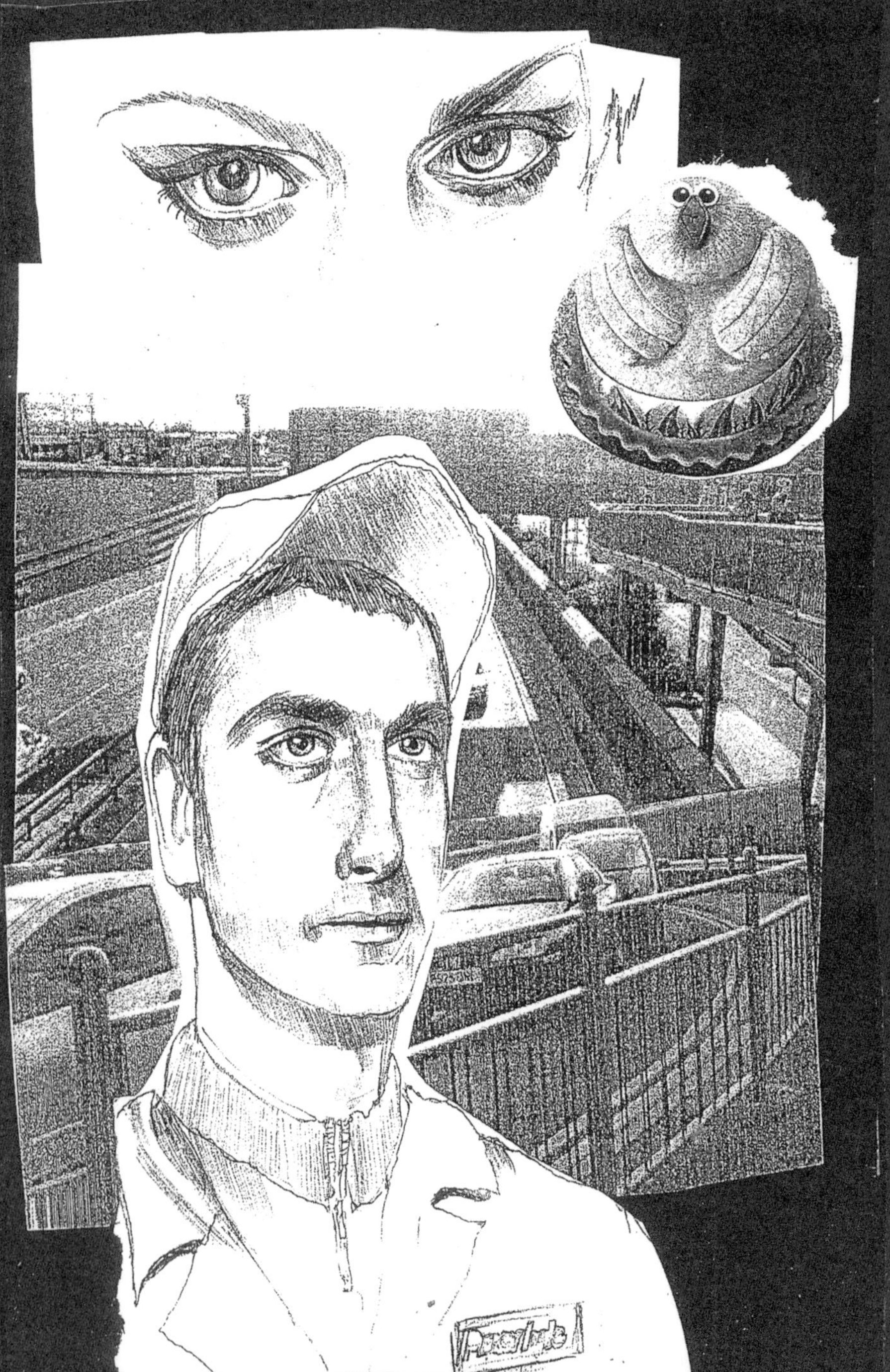

Licentiousness and debauchery, sex as visceral thrill,
atavistic ritual. Saturday night. Bacchinelean revels,
unruliness and binge drinking, ancient rites detested by the
state.   ASBOs and dispersal zones. Know your limits. Safety
first.

But the paths are well worn, the impulse etched deep. These
New Labour gestures are flimsy, superficial, they slide off the
register like the jokes you get in Christmas crackers, read out
once to the grim bemusement of guests then cast out when the
meal is over.

Psychick conveyances, channels ricocheting round the
underpasses of the Green Man interchange. Transitional zone. It
resonates here in this vortex ,, eddies and flows that stop you
settling. The carve up, the M11, Thatcher's contempt for
London. Leyton and Leytonstone divided, a huge gulley gouged
deep in the landscape, a wound always smarting.

Clambering through smeared Perspex the terraces feel
peripheral, fearful of falling into the Eastway gorge. UEL
students, drunk South Africans, refugees with Lidl's bags, a
transient population calculating their escape.

Extractor fan burger stink, signifier of decay.
Mc Donalds hangar, reflective windows guarding a perpetual
present. Immured in a shuttered zone of sensory filtering, the
outside world is blank.
Behind Ronald's Gacey grin sneering marines patrol US gulags.
The gating and enclosure of our land, the robbing of our public
space., they've got away with it for too long.
In the scrambling of codes and the devilment of sabotage, the
euphoria of riots and the thrill of wildcat strikes we hit back
at this magic lantern show of grotesqueries.

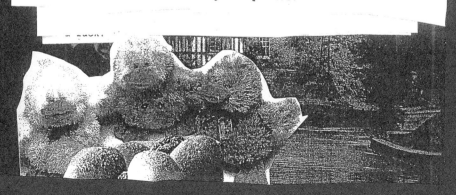

Claremont, the last road standing, a multitude of spanners
thrown in the works . Scene of chaos, resistance and magic. The
491, Grove Green road. Walking there from the stifling room in
Colenso road, diagonal drift across the canal, the lilac
tangles of the marshes, through Temple Mills to Grove Green
road. The mounting excitement, twisting to check make up in
bent wing mirrors, crimson lipstick smeared across face, eyes
flashing with the thrill of an encounter.
A walk half way, meeting the crew, the Northcote, a boozer
beckoning from the outer reaches of 1979.
Wood veneer tv with Jim Davidson and Only fools and Horses
reruns. The pub is brown, except for the day glo explosions of
the fruit machine. I go to the Ladies and am reeling at the
sight of pink and black paint work and a row of round mirrors.
I lean against the cubicle wall.
This becomes 1981.
It could be no other time.
All I yearn for thrives in that place.

We sit outside on plastic chairs. Ancient heathland flora juts
out from splits in the tarmac. The ghost of an abandoned beer
garden ; a skein of ivy, cow parsley and nettles engulfing
wooden benches.

491, last vestige of Claremont road . We approach the squat
from Grove Green road, the shimmering street is suffused with
the scent of honeysuckle and jasmine. Catch my reflection in
the Costcutter window..hair in a bun, lips slicked, Yves Saint
Laurent Red Temptation bought for a fiver from a bloke in the
Rising Sun.

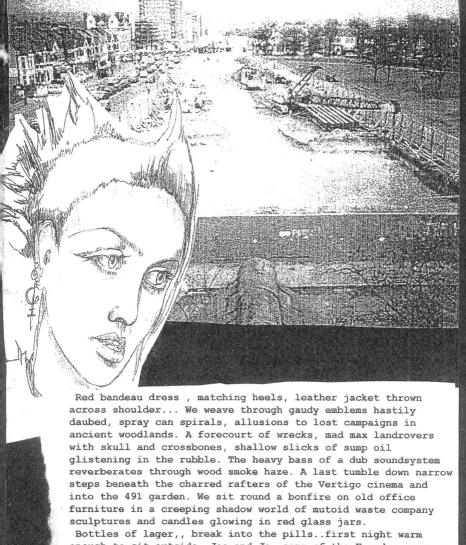

Red bandeau dress , matching heels, leather jacket thrown
across shoulder... We weave through gaudy emblems hastily
daubed, spray can spirals, allusions to lost campaigns in
ancient woodlands. A forecourt of wrecks, mad max landrovers
with skull and crossbones, shallow slicks of sump oil
glistening in the rubble. The heavy bass of a dub soundsystem
reverberates through wood smoke haze. A last tumble down narrow
steps beneath the charred rafters of the Vertigo cinema and
into the 491 garden. We sit round a bonfire on old office
furniture in a creeping shadow world of mutoid waste company
sculptures and candles glowing in red glass jars.

Bottles of lager,, break into the pills..first night warm
enough to sit outside. Joe and Jo, some of the Foundry crew, a
load of people I know from LARC. Hemmed in by the link road
gulley, the 491 perches precariously on the edge. Asim arrives
with the crew in a transit van, Bomb London graffed on dinted
side. Ali, Hasnan, Alex, Atif bundle out the back.   There's a
load of us here, it's proliferating. Ayesha and Iona and some
others from Colenso Road, some of the old faces from the Samuel
Pepys. Nitin builds pyramids with redundant computer
terminals. John Wild roves the terrain with a megaphone. It
becomes 1993, Freak Quency soundsystem, tripping hard and
dancing through strobe lights. Off our heads we renegotiate the
maze of M11 footbridges, the red tubes of Perspex, you can
stand and drink and feel the hypnotic shifting beneath.

The memory traces of a spectral face flit softly back and forth across the motorway bridge/ Someone I met in the early Spring at a punk gig at the Lord Cecil. A monochrome apparition Black hair and royal blue eyes, violet flaring supernaturally from the pupils/

. He was from Leeds, in this band that were like Gang of Four fused with Voivod. You should have seen him, so immaculate, so controlled. He held me in a spellbinding gaze and wrote my number on the back of his hand, the ink creeping over a blazing black ace.

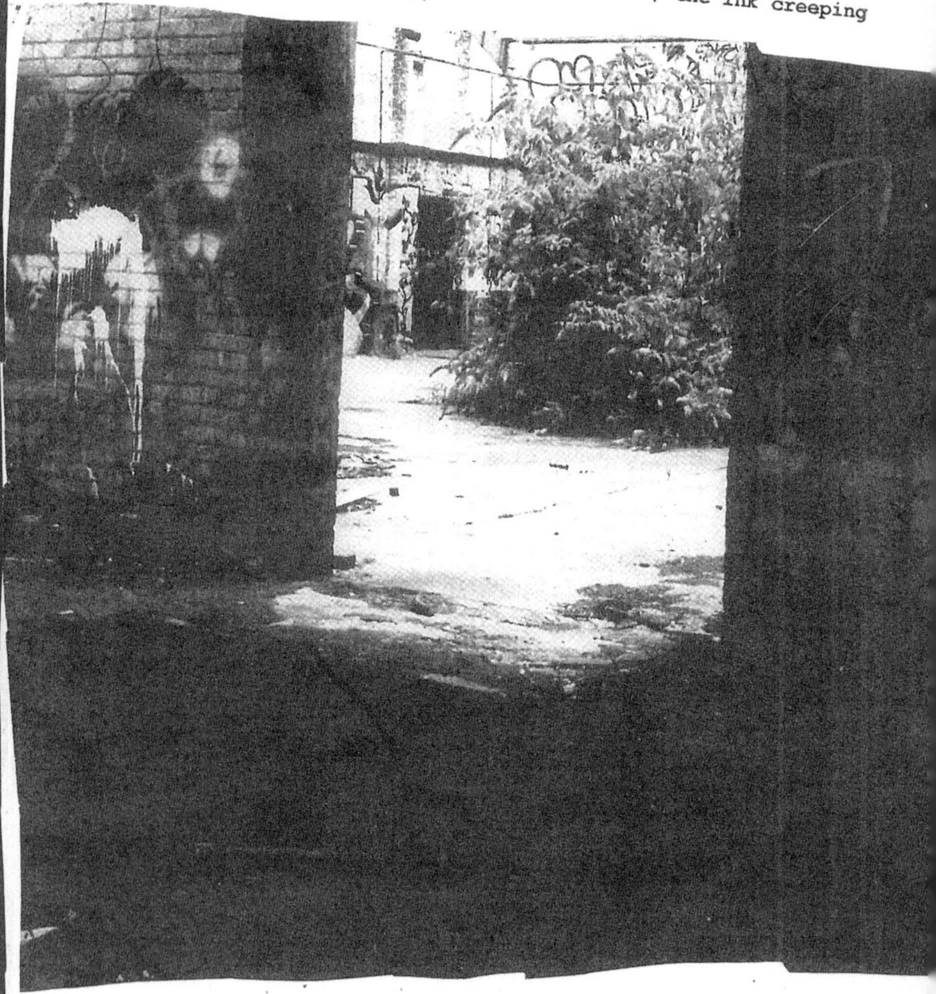

Tonight, the 30th of April, the eve of May Day, the edges of the city generate a constellation of epiphanies

PLEASE BE AWARE THA
CCTV is in operation
Anti social behaviour will not be tolerated
Offender
from Zu
MESSIAH
5/3/06
CONTACT : SAVAGEMESSIAH@HOTMAIL.CO.UK

!SAVAGE
MESSIAH
AVENGES
ALL
(M11)
Wanstead
A12 (East)
I'M SORRY BUT THERE'S
SOMETHING WRONG WITH YOU
IT AIN'T NORMAL...
ODAY'S GATED COMMUNITIES
OMORROW'S GULAGS!

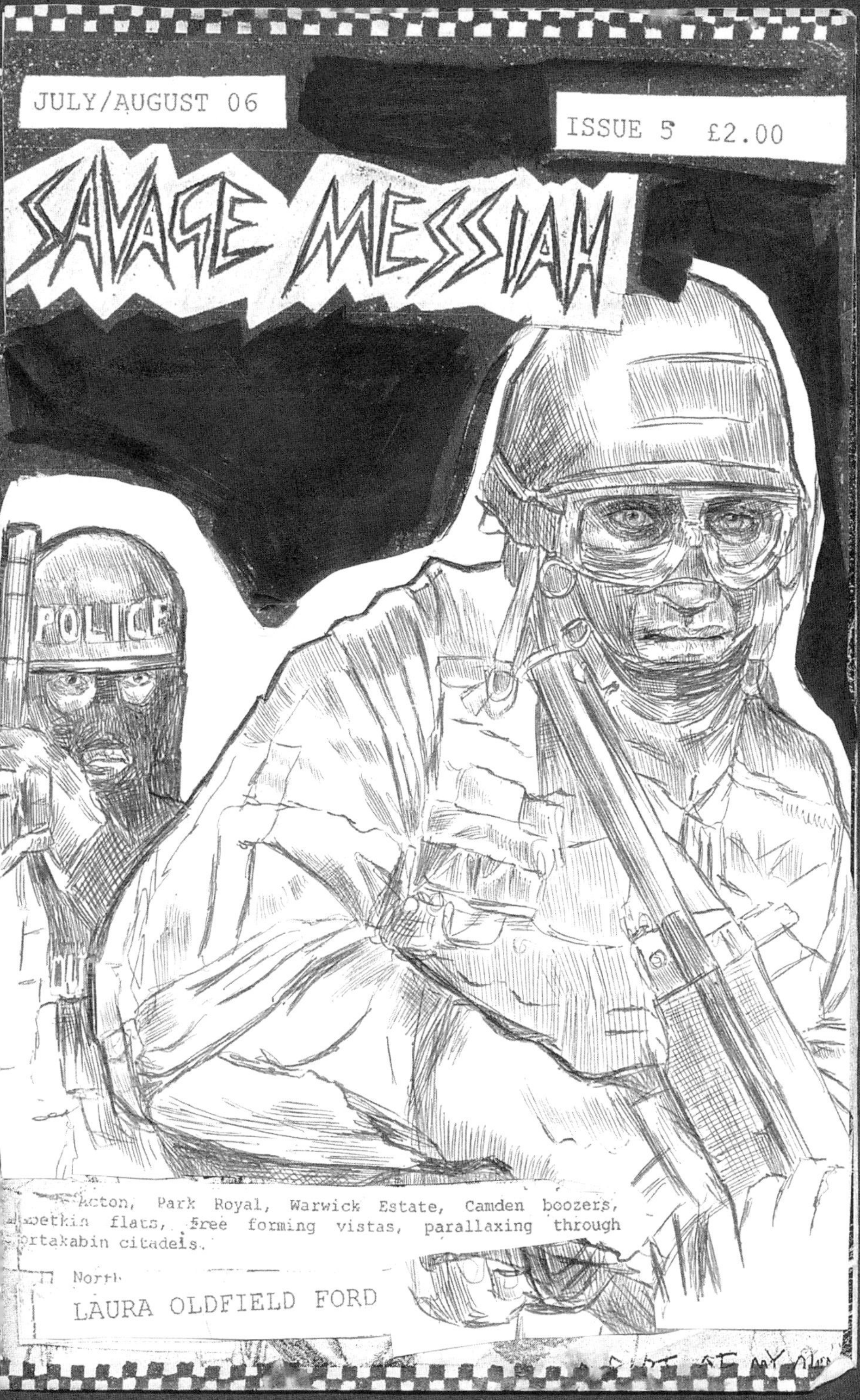
JULY/AUGUST 06
ISSUE 5 £2.00
SAVAGE MESSIAH
POLICE
Acton, Park Royal, Warwick Estate, Camden boozers,
etkin flats, free forming vistas, parallaxing through
rtakabin citadels.
North
LAURA OLDFIELD FORD

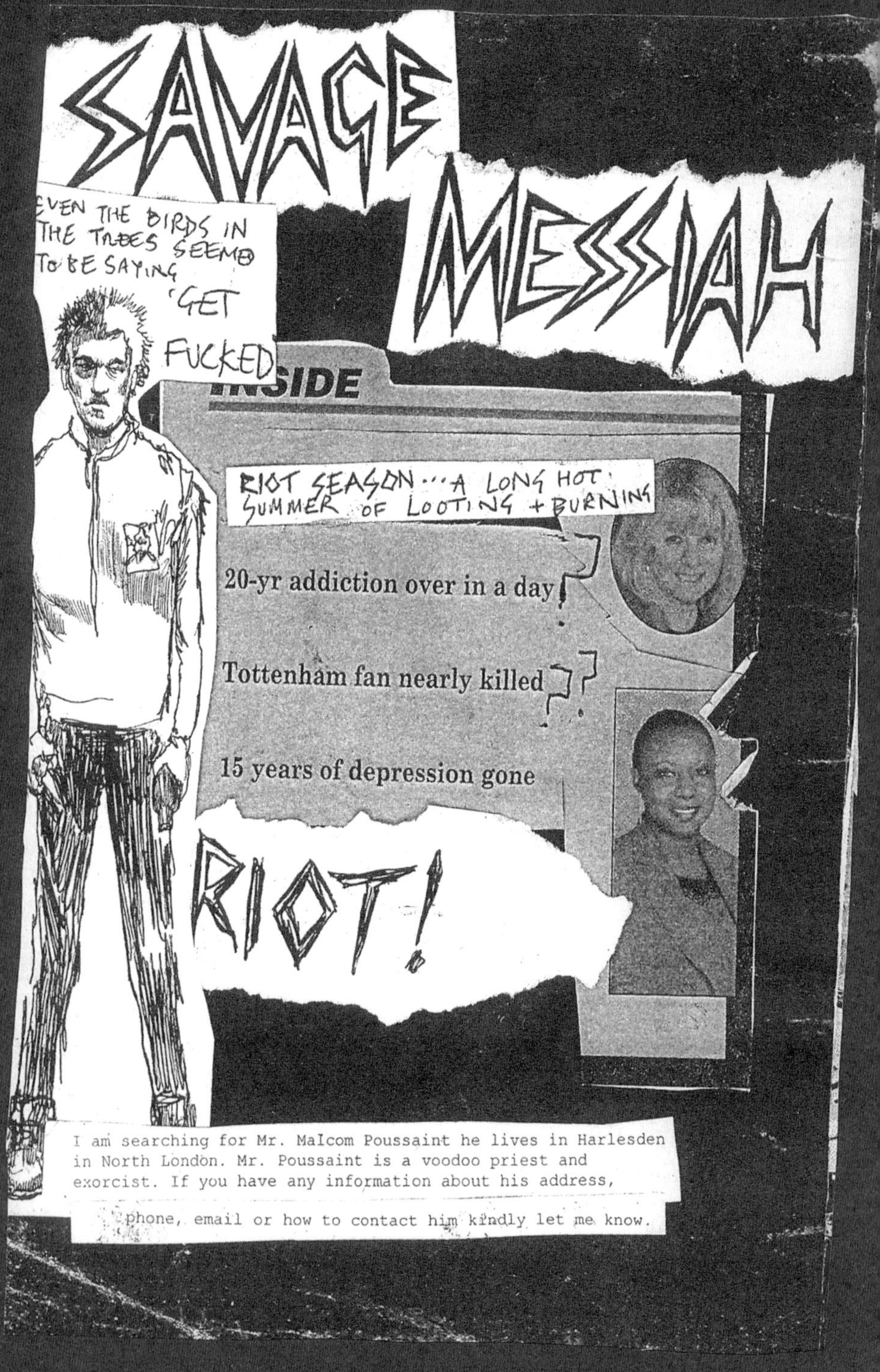

SAVAGE MESSIAH
EVEN THE BIRDS IN THE TREES SEEM TO BE SAYING 'GET FUCKED
INSIDE
RIOT SEASON ... A LONG HOT SUMMER OF LOOTING + BURNING
20-yr addiction over in a day
Tottenham fan nearly killed
15 years of depression gone
RIOT!
I am searching for Mr. Malcom Poussaint he lives in Harlesden in North London. Mr. Poussaint is a voodoo priest and exorcist. If you have any information about his address, phone, email or how to contact him kindly let me know.

Predatory war machines accelerating through the jungle - uprooting arboreal sedimentation - mongrelising 'authenticity'. Feral improvisation displaces arboreal code with a revolutionary - almost cataclysmic - velocity. Speed kills! - the war machine invents absolute speed (Deleuze and Guattari: 386).Mille Plateau.

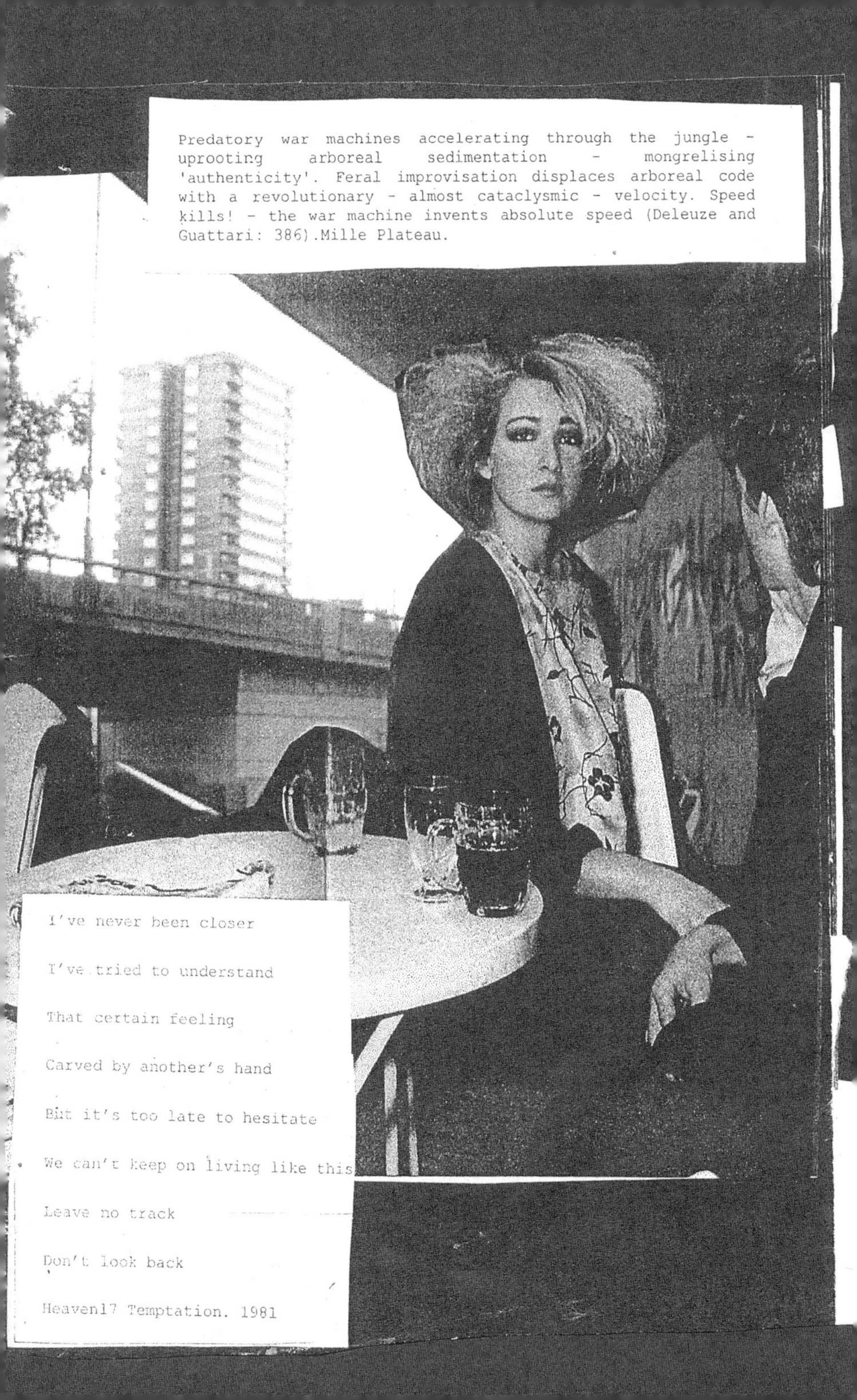

I've never been closer

I've tried to understand

That certain feeling

Carved by another's hand

But it's too late to hesitate

We can't keep on living like this

Leave no track

Don't look back

Heaven17 Temptation. 1981

"The sectors of a city are, at a certain level, readable.
But the meaning they have for us personally is
incommunicable, like the clandestinity of private life,
of which we possess only a few pitiful documents"
Guy Debord critique de la separation screenplay in Guy
Debord oeuvres cinematographiques

September 2003

You remember that afternoon in the Foundry, September, warm
rain, schizoid weather, everyone locked in for the afternoon.
And we were in that corner, faces magenta in the neon.
Saturday, no one caring about anything but getting wrecked,
threshold between thinking and acting dissolved in the mayhem.
On the pints, looking hectically better with each one,
some kid playing Cabaret Voltaire records, scratchy and
distorted, boot sale treasure, voices resurrected from an attic
burial. Rain eases off, soft vapour rises from the streets. A
battered transit, 2000 DS graffitied on the side, skids off Old
Street roundabout and onto the pavement in front of the pub. A
crew of anarcho savages bundle out the back. Straight over the
decks, post punk kid thrown back into the crowd as they
commandeer with a clash of Flux of Pink Indians and demonic
clown step. Our neon corner is colonised by the crew who have
the military fatigues and shaven heads of Spiral Tribe.

Where you lot from?
North Acton.

I look blank, I don't know it. Never been there, can't get it
to register. To me there's a network of squats north of the
river stretching through Tottenham, Hackney and Whitechapel and
a parallel world south of the river in Peckham, New Cross and
Brixton. They look alike with their chicken shacks, punk gigs
and raves in ruined buildings but the two never seem to
collide.

But North Acton, West London generally, I can't picture it, to
me it doesn't exist.
Apparently they've got big squatted factories down there, loads
of sites on breakers yards, industrial estates and cheap
moorings. I'm thinking how come I don't know about this? This
other world is happening, the way they've described it, it
sounds like Hackney wick, and I've never even heard it
mentioned.

Some of the streets down there right, they aint even on the
map, they aint even got names.

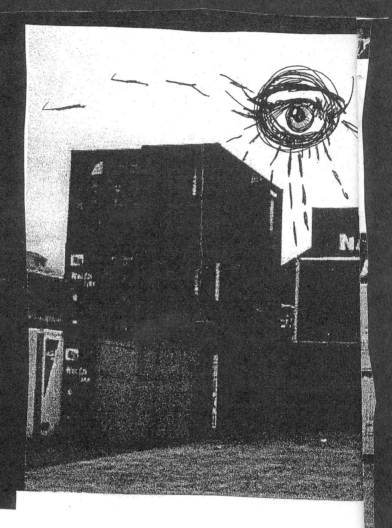

Deptford 1992 Rudimentary Peni. The Venue, New Cross.
Dark and messy, doing the stall, band not looking quite right
in football shirts and tracksuits. Blincoe's disturbed tonal
range is dragged into the common world.
 The vinyl caught his disembodied ghoulishness,
 then you could believe that he didn't exist.
Spiral tribe party going off somewhere in West London, a convoy
outside ready to go, we follow on in a converted ambulance.
God knows where we're going, Peckham, Camberwell, over Vauxhall
bridge, Park lane, Marble Arch, Edgware road and onto the
Westway, past the Scrubs and off at Western Avenue.
North Acton.

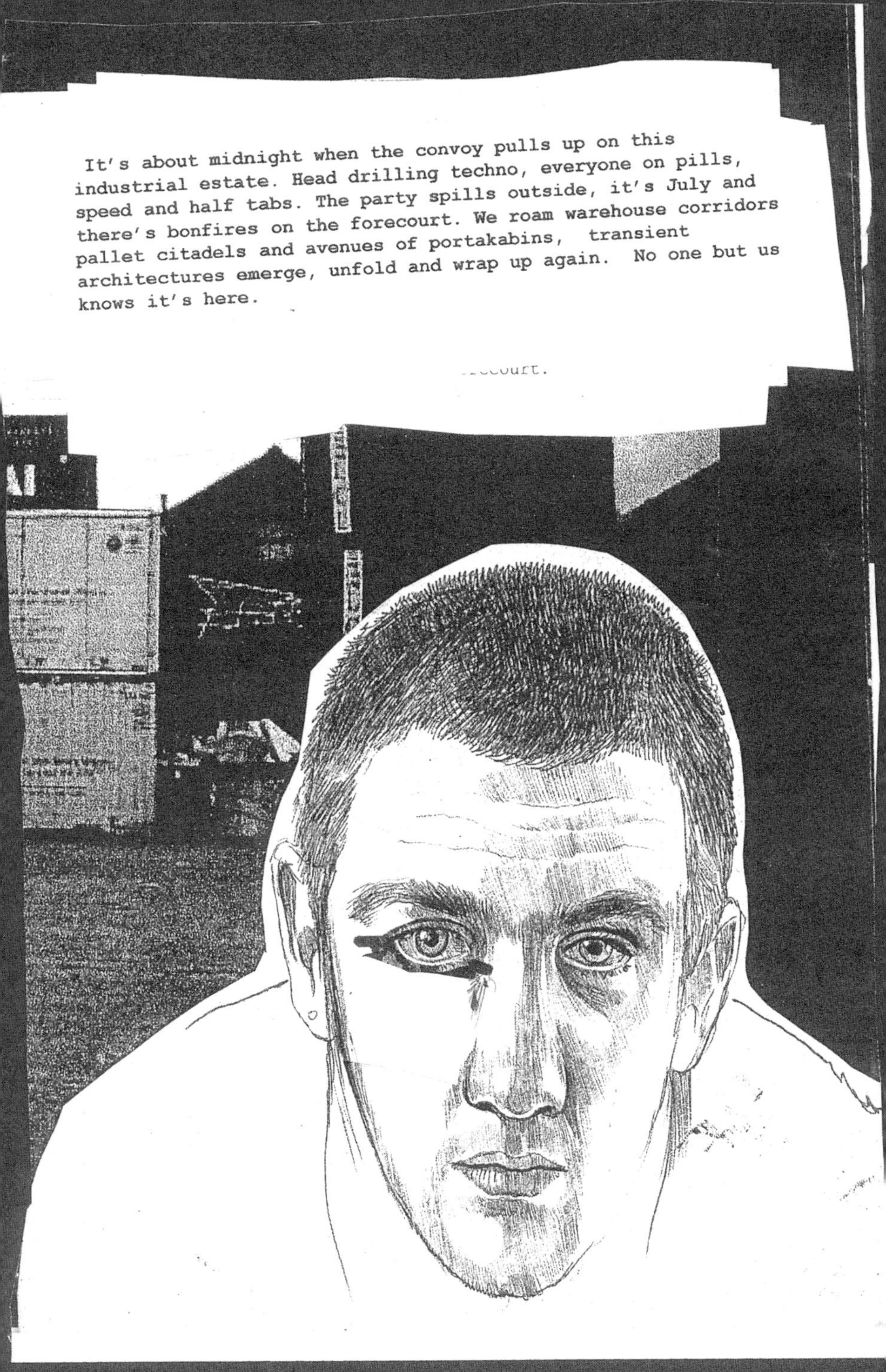
It's about midnight when the convoy pulls up on this industrial estate. Head drilling techno, everyone on pills, speed and half tabs. The party spills outside, it's July and there's bonfires on the forecourt. We roam warehouse corridors pallet citadels and avenues of portakabins, transient architectures emerge, unfold and wrap up again. No one but us knows it's here.

August 1996 Harlseden

"They didn't give another second's thought…They were pouncing
onto the equipment…Pulling apart, breaking everything up…Both
on the same wavelength…smashing every single hook up to
pieces…busting away with hammers…and screwdrivers!...they were
popping pins…going full blast…ripping fragile
membranes!...raging, rummaging it's horrendous…like they're in
the grip of a fever…but booming with laughter, and happy…as
though the gadgetry had gone right to their heads! If I open
my mouth they'll gang up on me…a frenzy of destruction! They
don't give me another thought…they've got a vendetta against
their junk…they lunge on top of it..Savages"
Celine London Bridge

McVitie & Price in 1902 built a biscuit making factory in
Waxlow Road, Harlesden, which employed 1,150 in 1919. By the
Second World War 2,000 workers made 300 varieties of biscuit.
In 1948 the company joined McFarlane Lang to become United
Biscuits. A packing hall and warehouse were built between 1967
and 1969. In 1978 the factory, the largest biscuit factory in
the western world, employed 1,600, with another 1000 in the
offices

So I'm stuck doing the variety boxes in Bindler 5 where your
line managers are these miserable bastards that don't give a
fuck about turning the belt up top whack just to piss you off.
They're sitting next to you one minute packing, the next thing
they're up there at the end of the line, power mad, thinkin
they're a cut above and my God do they put you through it. I'm
stuffed up the nose with that sweet biscuit stink and Terry
bastard Wogan in my ears and I'm getting it all wrong ,hands
all spastic,and there's fucking biscuits all over the floor and
I'm panicking and leaning right into the woman next to me
trying to get them all slotted in and it's chaos. That was when
we were getting them rushed out for Christmas, I hated it, so
when one of the other line managers from upstairs come down to
take people to work on this new line I was glad when I went.
So there we were, eight of us upstairs in this massive
windowless hangar with this one line at the edge of it. I knew
some of the others a bit, a couple of quite lively young ones
and a couple of the older lads from the pub up for a bit of
daft banter. So we were on this line with all these clueless
science geeks fussing round the enrobing machine impatient to
start this new sweet. And then it started to come through the
machine and they'd all be huddled round inspecting some fucking
mess like it was so important, just looked like any other dirty
Penguin bar to me but apparently this one was dark chocolate
with mint fondant inside. They got it going and it was our job
to keep the bars aligned as they went through, slotting them
onto these metal trays. So yeah that was going alright, piece
of piss job, much slower than the lines downstairs cos they
kept having to monitor it.

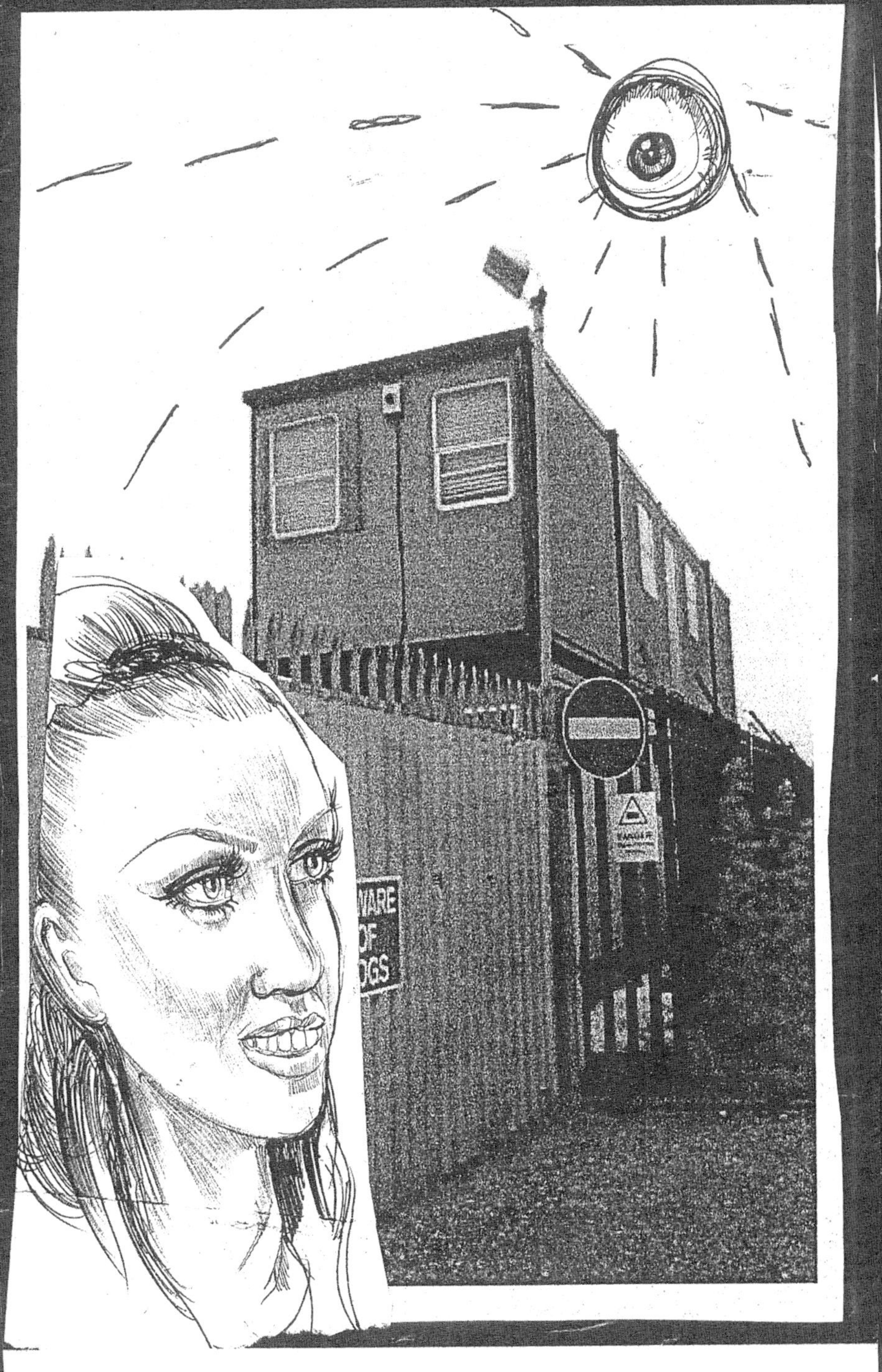

So it ended up we were having quite a laugh really. The Sikh
ladies were right down the end packing, the line managers were
at the other end mixing up this fondant shit and we were in the
middle taking the piss out of each other, making up names for
people in the factory, talking all kinds of shit. One bloke
Daz, I liked him, he was funny, I'd always see him down the
boozer flashing the money about, he had loads of other stuff
going on the side, and he was alright, big QPR fan, didn't mind
the odd bit of brawling so I thought yeah he's ok. And he was
nice to talk to really, he'd say stuff like, if I was getting
grief off some bloke he'd send the boys round to sort it and
once he brought in some really nice watches and said he'd kept
back this nice gold one so I could have first refusal on it, so
 you know I thought, yeah he's a really decent bloke.
But then one morning the line manager comes heavy breathing
round the belt and says he needs Darren down the end with him
to mix this mint slop and man the machine, and so off Darren
goes without looking back, there he is on the controls, at the
helm, and we don't hear much from him til the belt suddenly
starts zooming through at top speed and we all howl in protest.
There's penguin bars scattered all over and we've all missed
them all despite thinking we'd perfected the putting down eight

mint

at once technique. So Red faced Pervert comes storming round
with Darren by his side and he's balling us out and Darren
joins in, shouting directly at Marvin who's a bit fat and not
that bright so I suppose the ideal target for weight throwing
on the factory floor.
So then they fuck off back and Marvins looking at me like he's
about to blub. Don't worry I say leaning over and pressing his
hand, they've just declared war and we can have some fun. Poor
Marvin, he looked up to Darren cos he was one of the blokes who
stuck up for him, then he's gone over the other side, for what?
He's still on the same shit wages as us. It's that little
intoxicating taste of power, straight to his head the dickhead.
So then we're thinking right you bastards and I'm saying to the
others, right all you have to do is nudge the belt a bit, a
couple of millimetres push, it's that fucking simple. We try
it out and it's a marvellous success , biscuit bases no longer
aligned with fondant, enrober squirting chocolate all over the
belt, result a right fucking mess of chocolate snail trails and
viscous heaps of mint sludge. It's hurting to hold the mirth
in, up sweep explosions, eyes red with the crying . Somethings
gone wrong we holler. Red face comes running round, oh for
fucks sake, what the fucks happened here, he's calling us thick
cunts saying why didn't you tell me sooner and runs off all
manic round the back. The machine stops while they try and sort
it out. A lot of fucking about later Darren comes back round
with this stern face and says we're starting up again, we have
to get ready. OK, so we let it run ok for five minutes then I
give them the wink and oh dear the belts sliding off course
again, chocolate slop skidding all over the place..

So they're running round again, completely agitated,
shrieking, hollering, calling us morons and cunts and saying
we're all gonna get fired. We need to make a new batch Red Face
is yelling at Darren, the consistency's all wrong. The machine
stops, a phone call's made, one of the office geeks comes
running down to help them mix this perfumed slime. They've got
a laminated formula book and all these massive vats of stuff.
Mint essence is poured in from a giant oil drum. Darren is
shown how to mix this stuff, power trip tainted somewhat since
it's him under suspicion for it all going wrong. Funny how that
puffed up bit of power vanishes so quickly, it's that kind of
mad uncontrollable laughing you get off mushroom tea and we're
nearly killing ourselves holding it in.

August 1999

  Straight away Arran became my companion in drifts. We would
wake and set out on long walks through the industrial estates
of Park Royal and Acton. Our days together were always
cinematic, they always felt really symbolic, as if everything
was bending towards us showing us signs. Ring tones, stray
cats, china dolls in bedroom windows, it all felt charged with
dreams and chance. Arran would stay with me for a couple of
days, we'd get drunk, go to bed then he'd disappear back east,
round Hackney or the Isle of Dogs or somewhere.
He liked the north west hinterlands I showed him, he said they
were the lost zones, easy to hide out in. He had a real
obsession with terra incognita, unknown places that defied the
map. Our adventures were always spellbinding, always the vistas

of the city enticing us, arcade game violence ricocheting round
the dereliction.

When I asked him to take me round Millwall and Cubitt town he
said he would but we never did.

Mark was bored, OUT OF HIS MIND. Anna was out in the garden
with the baby. He couldn't handle it. He never wanted all this
really, and now he felt guilty for allowing it to happen. I
mean it was all his responsibility . He didn't hate Anna, he
wanted the best for her and the kids but he was letting them
down and they both knew it. He just didn't feel right being a
parent, it didn't fit with the image he had of himself, down
the pub with his mates or on the terraces, always available
women around and money for nice clothes. Kids didn't ever
really figure in his scheme. He considered that it was probably
something to do with his Dad dying that had started this
inexorable slide into family life. Something murky about
identity, keeping the line going .
Anna was the sort of girl he knew his Mum and Dad wanted him to
marry, easy enough on the eye but in a kind of mousy, domestic
way. I mean she was smart enough but her intelligence was neat
and compartmentalised like the house, everything in its place
and no space for deviation. He watched her now in the garden,
white dress and hair smooth and shiny. Why did he have such an
overwhelming urge to mess it up, to tear it out. He thought
when the baby came some feelings for her might come from it but
it just made it worse, the whole pregnancy sickened him. He
hated hospitals, the visceral ordeal of the birth, the ugly
sliminess of it all. He didn't want to be in this scene, he
couldn't bear to be near her, physically, after that.
And the house, that's all she thought about, buying furniture,
decorating rooms. She polished surfaces and ironed clothes all
day, acting like he was an impostor when he came in at night.
He wished she'd go back to work, he always thought being at
home was for dolelites and invalids.
Anna was working in an estate agents when he first met her in
the Lion in Crouch end. He was out drinking with some of his
old mates , she was there having an after work drink that was
turning into a session. She was one of those 90s Britpop girls
with trainers and short hair, not really his type but there
was something about the way he could have a laugh with her,
like she was on his side. God knows it'd been a long time since
he'd felt comfort or security, what with all the class A's and
all the shit that had been going on, him and Andrea splitting
up after months of domestic chaos and the old man dying the
year before. He would have taken up with anyone offering a bit
of solace.
They went out for meals and to the cinema, it wasn't the kind
of thing he was used to. He was more into women who liked
getting trashed, more nihilistic types who he could share his
destructive tendencies with. This was all new to him, walks
round Primrose Hill, Sunday lunches with a civilised couple of
Hoegaardens instead of the usual 8 pints of Stella. But maybe
he needed it, comfort, a calmer life. He felt himself getting a
semblance of order back, his flat looked brighter, things were
even going better at work. He started to feel like he could

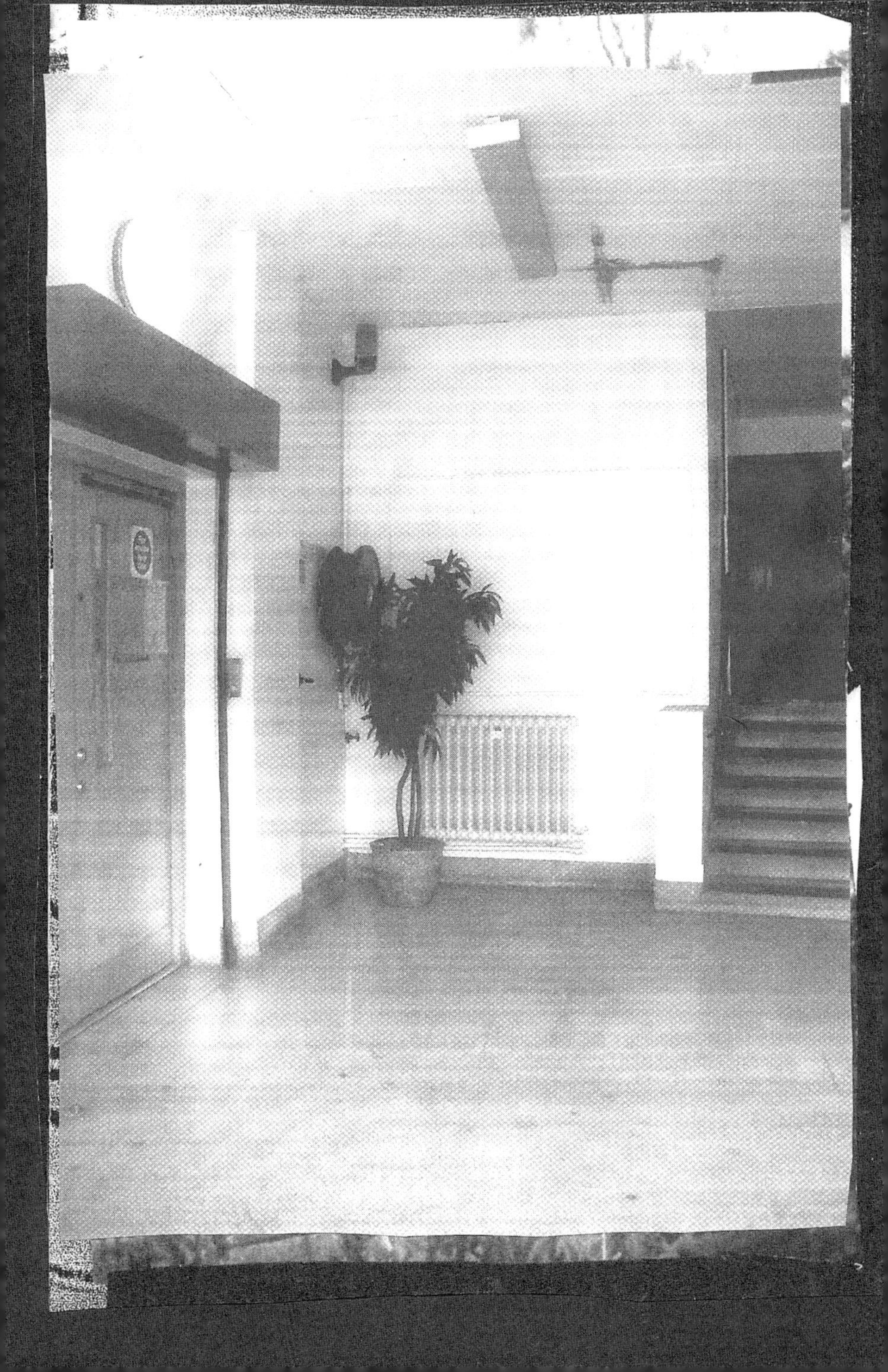

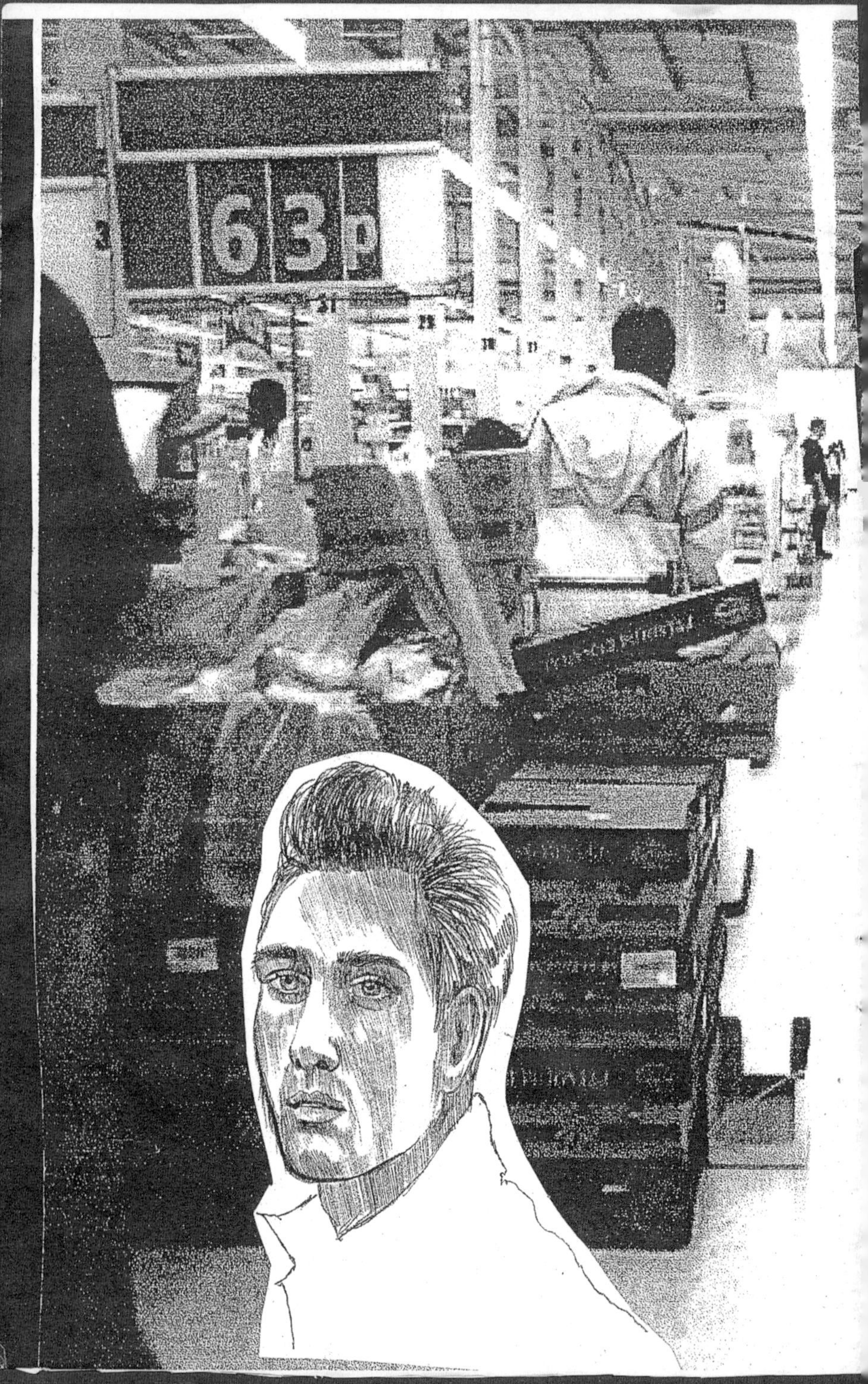
63p

chase promotion and get round the top brass, they'd always gone
on about his potential, got what it takes to rise to the top,
CID all of that,, well he knew that, I mean he'd never have
joined to wallow at plod level.

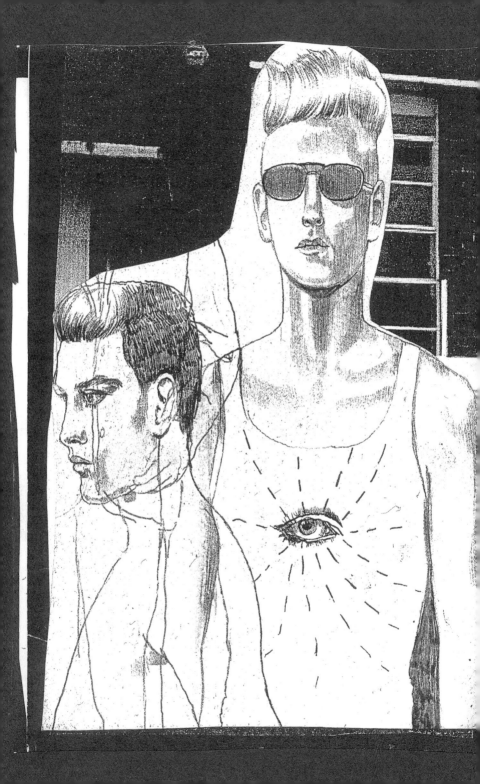

The sex was easy, uncomplicated. She was accommodating, but only because he knew not to overstep the line, he couldn't sully her NEATNESS, her DECENCY with his sadistic cravings. She didn't turn him on in that way anyway, he could kind of project onto her but she wasn't his type. He preferred his women a bit trashy . It didn't take long before they started to talk about getting married, they were as good as living together and it seemed the logical next step. He accepted it as a matter of course, that's what you did, it was expected, you did better at work if you were seen as a family man, normal, reliable, you couldn't go round saying what you really wanted, what you really desired out of life. And he had to admit that, since he'd met Anna and curbed the boozing and the charlie and all that stuff he felt hell of a lot better, he wasn't waking up in the night with the horrors anymore , so that was something, you couldn't discount that.

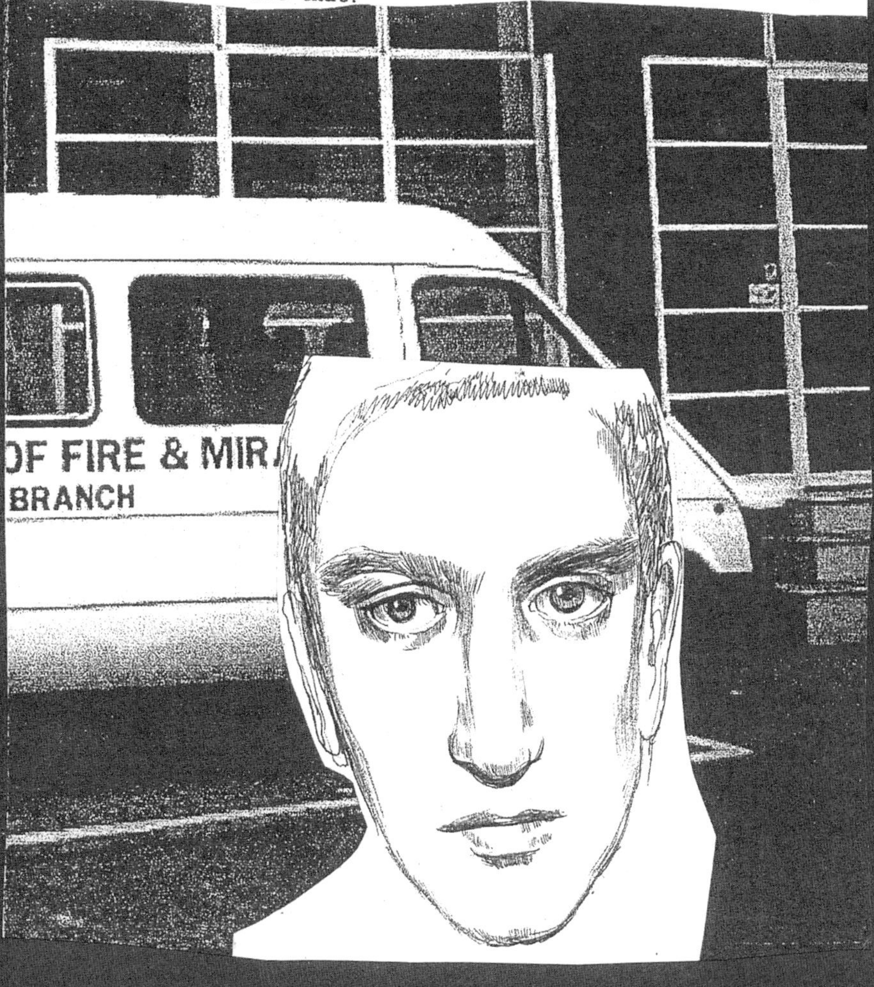
OF FIRE & MIRA
BRANCH

It didn't take long for the first baby to arrive, the second
not long after. The house in Potters Bar was what she wanted,
nice garden, everything knocked through, light and spacious. He
thought of the Acton squat, what Anna would think if she saw
it, the horror. He thought of the black crosses on the walls,
the stack of speaker cabs and the scratch pit tattoo parlour in
the lounge. He allowed himself to scan slowly over the nights
he'd spent there, immersed in an unexpected rush of desire. He
wanted to go back, pacing, frustrated, knowing he was
powerless. There were rumours he was going to be taken off that
job, too much chatter, risk of him getting too cosy and going
native. It was Gannon, he didn't trust him. He thought of her
out there walking, worrying about where he might be, it shocked
him how much he missed her.

*I am searching for Mr. Malcom Poussaint he lives in Harlesden
in North London. Mr. Poussaint is a voodoo priest and exorcist.
If you have any information about his address, phone, email or
how to contact him kindly let me know.*

I haven't heard from him for over a week, it's completely
weird, I'm thinking something's happened. I knew there'd been
some kicking off on the Island, flats getting busted left,
right and centre, something going down on the Samuda estate. I
knew Arran had to be involved, but what the fuck, he could've
just called. I'm skint, it's two days til I get my giro and
there's fuck all going on, everyone listless and moody prowling
round the gaff, and I think fuck this, I got to take flight.
Sometimes I just get overwhelmed by this powerful desire to
take off, on my own, walking. I have to do it by myself, no
transport, completely independent. Got to be fit, getting in
training for the big one, you know when the whole lot goes up
and there's police cordons and its shoot to kill and you got to

get out of London fast. So that's it I just set off along the
canal, his face is looming everywhere, the bloke in the caff,
him on the forklift truck in the pallet yard, there walking
towards me, passing, then ebbing away, a thousand
configurations of his beautiful face rupturing in the humidity.
I'm kicking up dust on the towpath, past the Acton power
station, sickly biscuit stink drifting over from McVities, a
passing cyclist, head shaved; Arran.. The likeness shatters
and scuttles across his face.

Pushing through the pneumatic clattering of the car breaking
plant, the searing heat, glad to see the skull and crossbones
of Mick's barge. He's just woken up when I get there , been
sleeping off a massive bender , snapped into the daylight by
manic barking of three rotweillers. He lets me in, glad to see
me. The crew have been over East London doing some party in a
warehouse near Old Street. I should have been with them.
He's fighting off the horrors, glad of the company. We smoke
and drink black tea looking out onto the canal and industrial
estate beyond. There's a low roar of traffic overhead on Scrubs
lane but it's strangely peaceful down here .We're both lost and
glad to be clinging to someone. We walk to a caf on North Pole
road. He wants to treat me to a proper breakfast, eggs ,toast
and coffee. The world seems easier now.

Swift diversion through the hospital and onto the perfect
savagery of Trellick, reconnect with the Grand Union at
Meanwhile gardens (job creation scheme and riot dissipating

Arran loved the visceral thrill of a riot, the demonic lunacy
of full scale brawl . Where the fuck was he? I'm imagining the
island in flames, it all going up with a load of old bill at
one side and Arran and all his crew chucking bottles and going
beserk on the other.
Encounter my old mate Sara by the abandoned basketball courts
of the Warwick estate. She takes me up 18 floors of Wilmcote
house and we have coffee and smoke B & H on the balcony.
Another hiding place. Soft pink bed and rosé wine. She hasn't
seen Arran, and anyway she doesn't trust him, too good looking.
Daytime TV blaring from the flat next door, smug bilge about
cosmetic surgery. Smell of chocolate and cinnamon, cigarette
smoke and parma violets. A rapturous burst from the 14th floor.
Denise Williams Let's hear it for the boy.

From here the city vistas unfurl in a shimmering eastward
sweep, the Barbican, Canary Wharf glittering in a polluted
shroud, I search for the plumes of black smoke, the helicopters
overhead...
...roam through the labyrinths of St.Mary's hospital, floating on
benylin through the fraying service tunnels and kebab shops
round Paddington. You never know do you? Think about that night
when I first met Arran, one of the drinking dens of Portobello
road. It wasn't full of yuppies then, more itinerants, déclassé
deviants on smack, a lot of failed musicians. We were holed up
in some boozer, probably the Star, yeah must've been cos it
felt so small, so claustrophobic that night, I remember my eyes

smarting with the smoke and thinking that all my mascara was
going to be messed up. There was an impromptu Class War meeting
going on, loads of fuelled up anarchos excited by the success
of J18, still intoxicated by the sight of flames leaping over
the ransacked city. I'd made a little side street diversion to
be there through the rows of pastel houses and now I was among
them, the jail birds in crombies, anarcho skinheads with a
taste for violence. Arran was hanging about at the back, a blue
eyed, brutal looking skinhead . Anyone unaccustomed to the
nuances of deviant subculture might have mistaken him for a
Nazi.

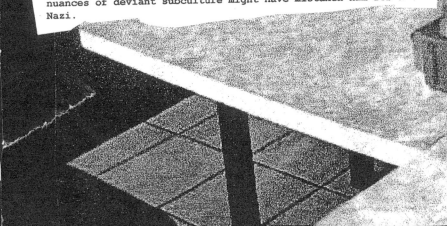

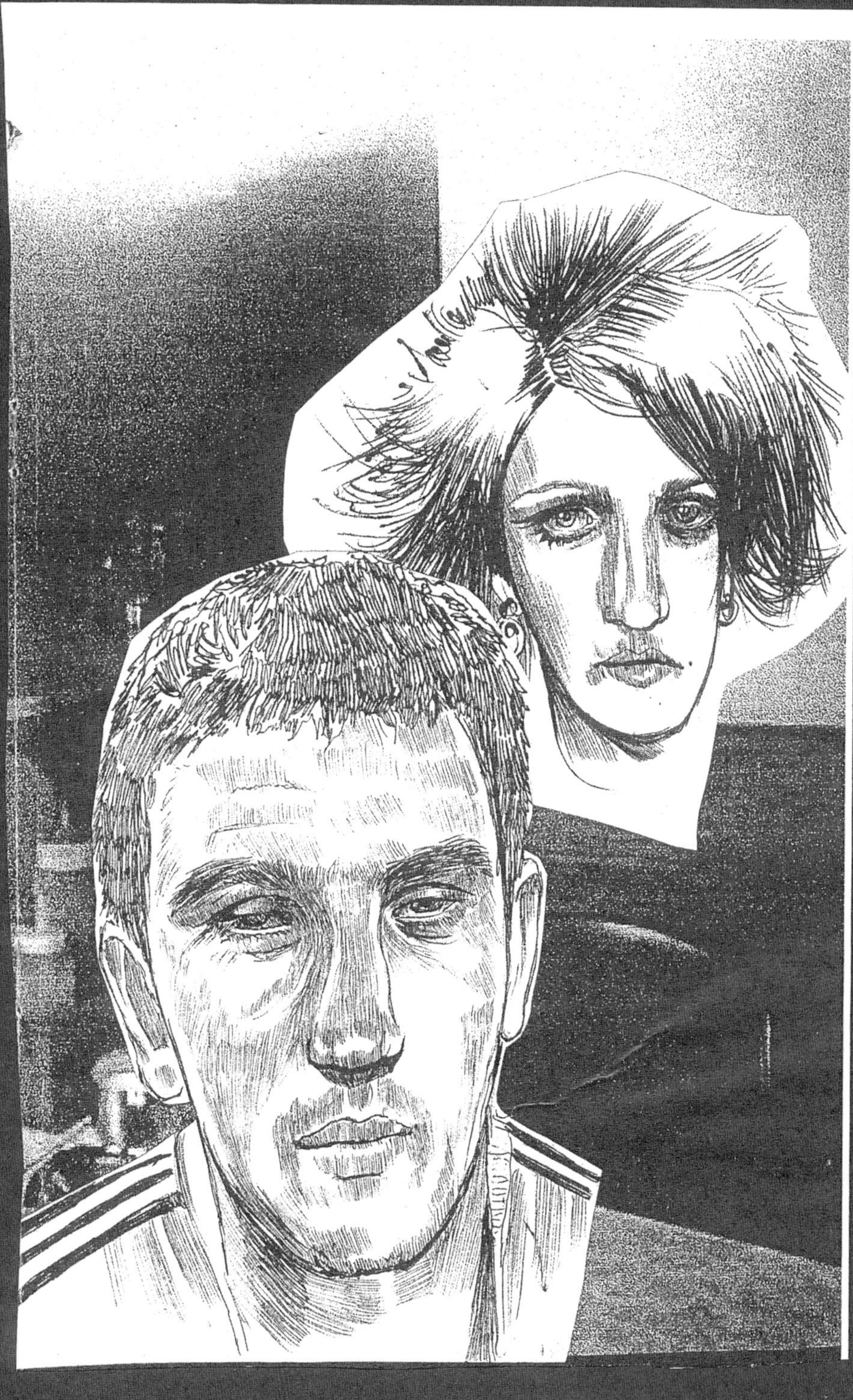

... tracing hidden paths through Little Venice, scarlet geraniums
trailing over cracked earthernware pots, skimming under the
Westway, Edgware road, Regents Park.

Emerge in the brash din of Camden Lock and steal into the
Dublin Castle for a quiet drink. Stale booze reek and dark
alcoves, gold flock wallpaper glimmering under red lights .
Lonely men, eyes glancing up on the off chance, watch as I
stand at the bar.

 Do any of you lot want dvds? Got fucking loads of good stuff,
proper an' all not like that ropey shit the chinks are
flogging, good deal an' all, some geezer down Park Royal, all
straight out the back ,none of yer backrow camcorder shite.
Alright darlin, you look nice.

I feel all the possibilities radiating out, he's in reach now.
We used to get drunk in the factory yard with the sound system
blasting out Clash. I loved the way he looked at me when we
danced, flashing desire, the elderflower and yellow roses, the
depots behind kings cross.
York Way, havoc erupting with Scots and Geordies after a booze
up on the train ride down. Caledonian Road, the Hemingford,
Limerick people.
   No time. Could get stuck into a session but need to keep
moving, over ground, to The Angel.

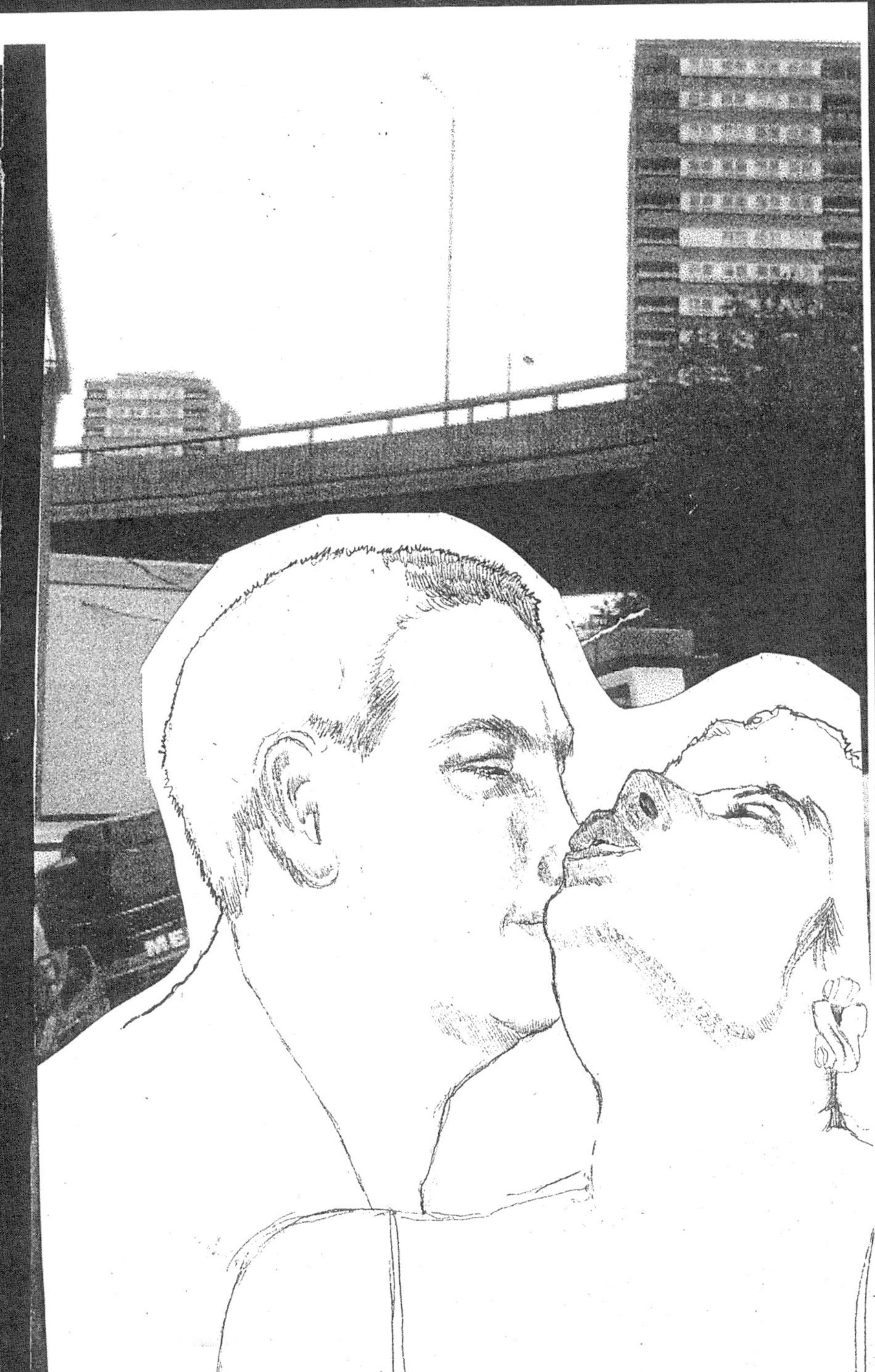

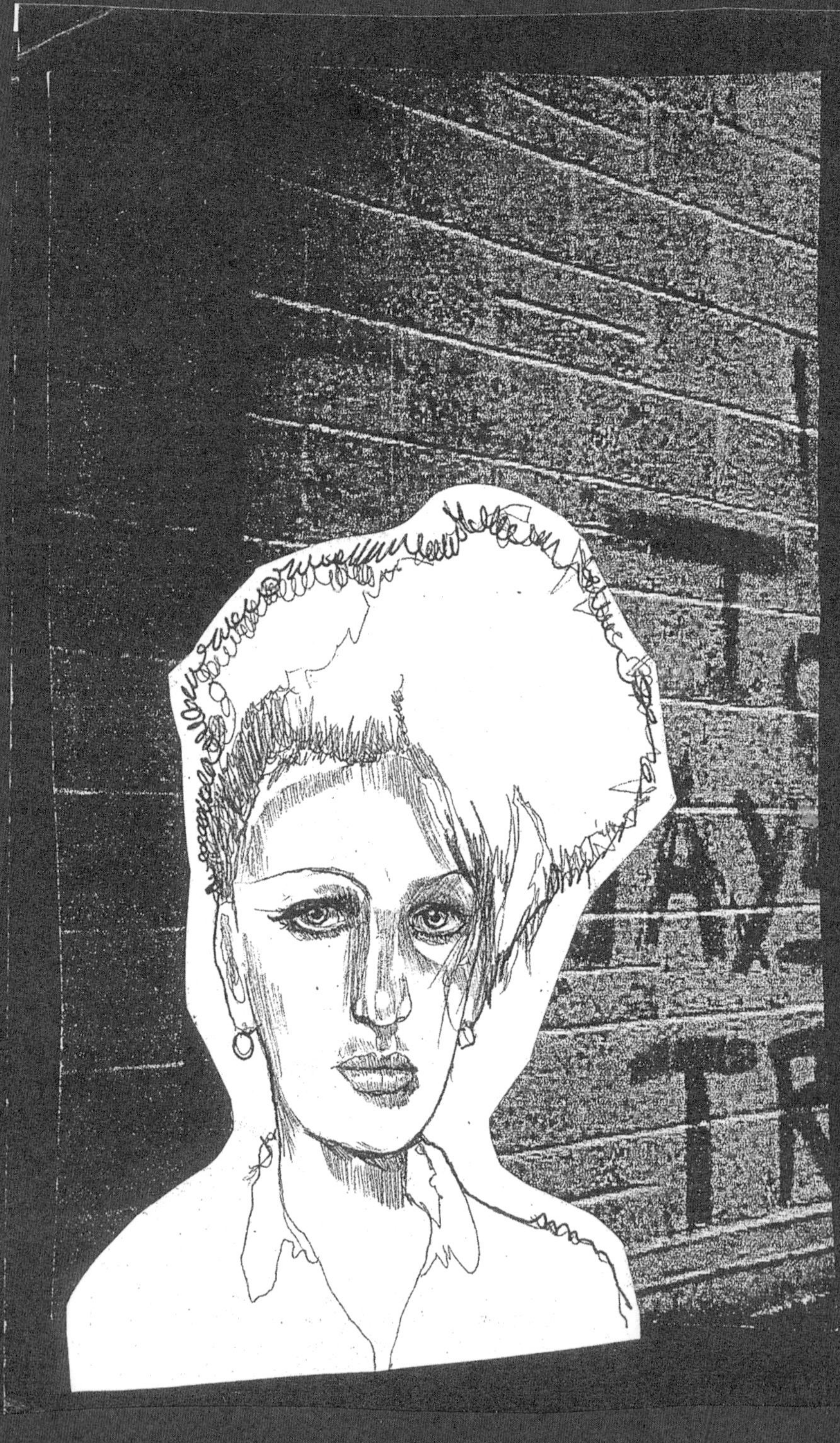

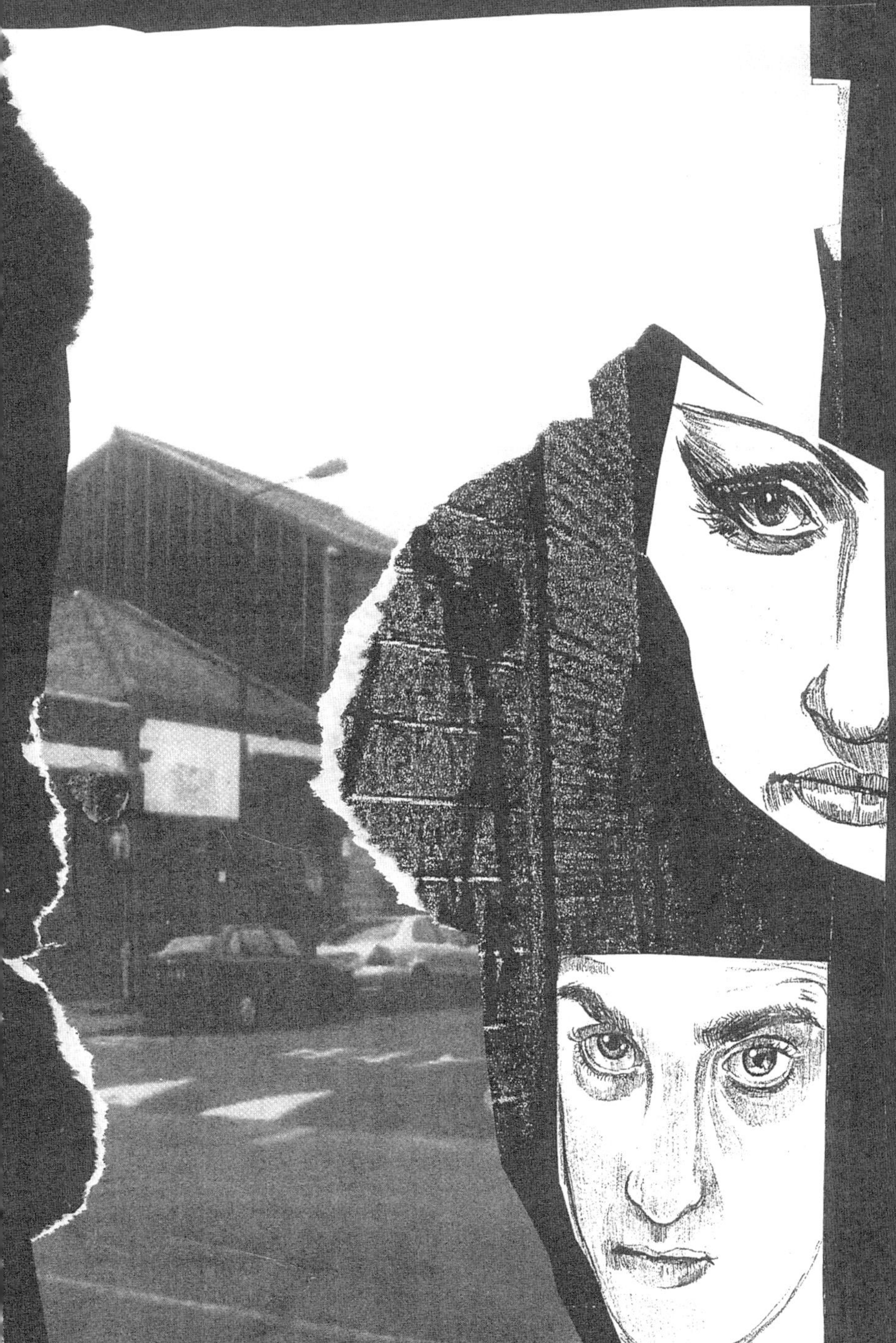

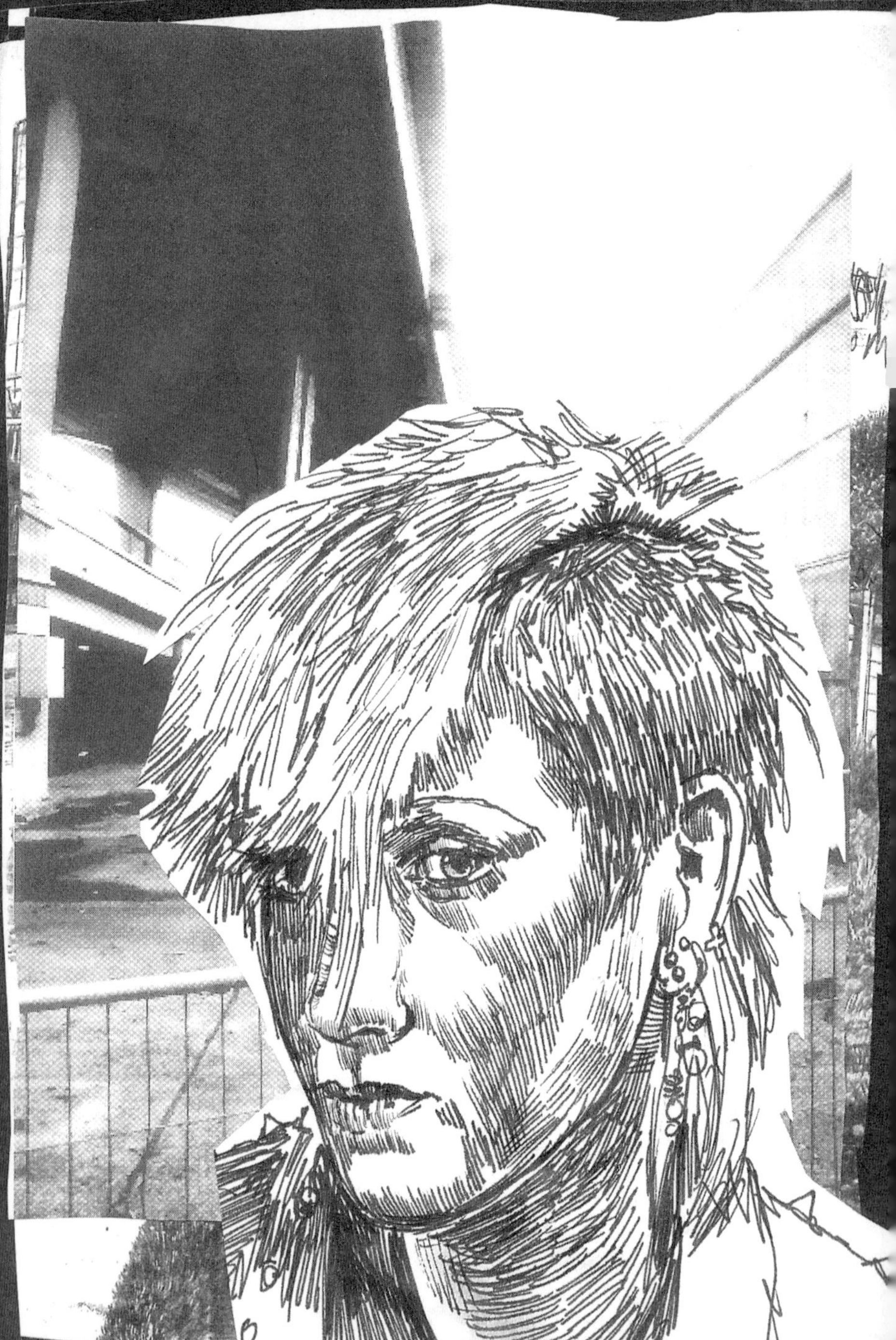

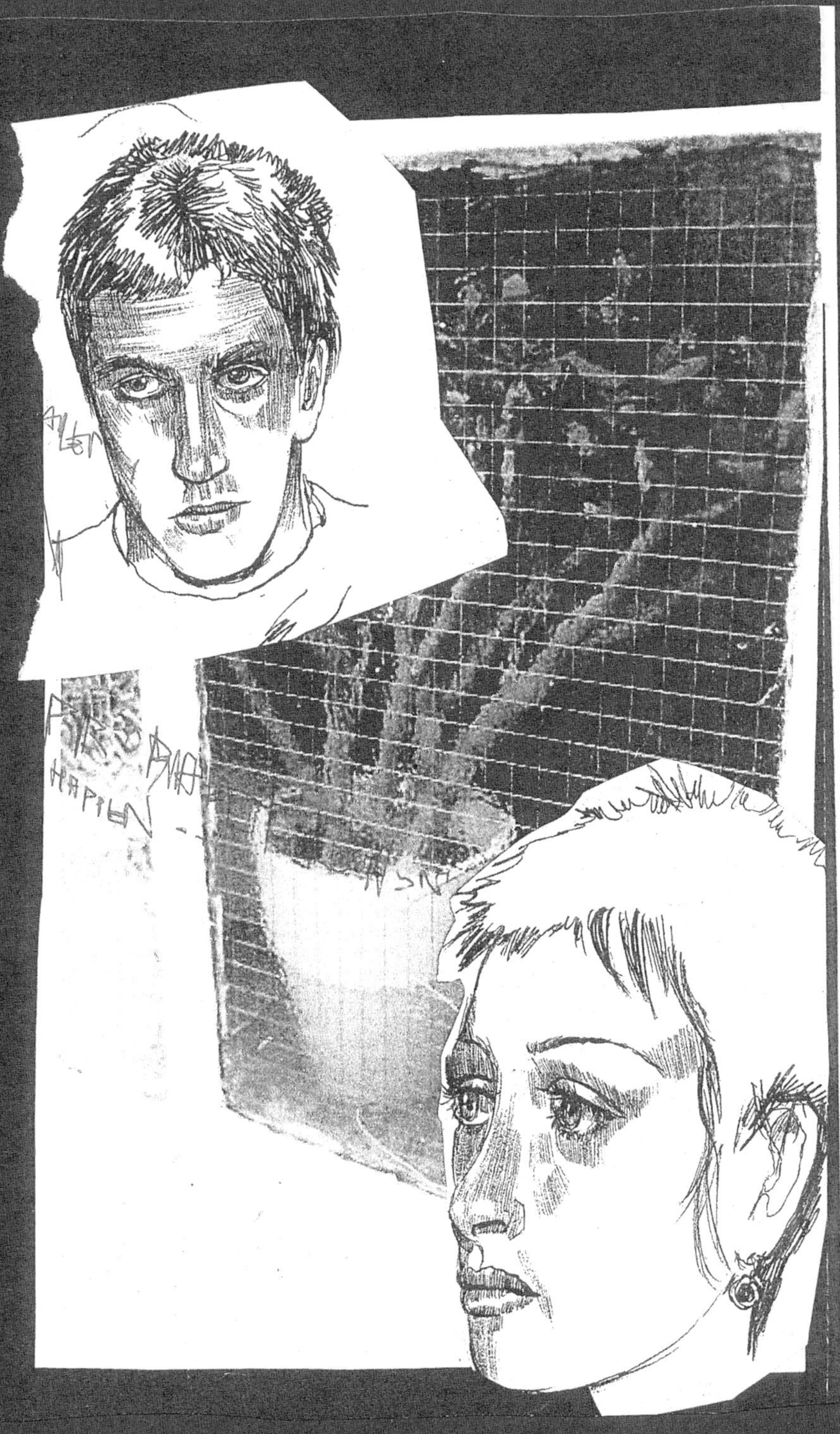

Priory Green estate, Lubetkin showpiece and modernist arcadia. Shortcut through Exmouth market to a brutalist pleasure garden. Barbican towers and Spa Green Estate, parallaxing through concrete shells. Cherry blossom and fragrant lawns, vistas free forming. Golden Lane, hazily European in the Spring sunshine.

Backstreet boozers. Bottle green tiles. I've been here before.

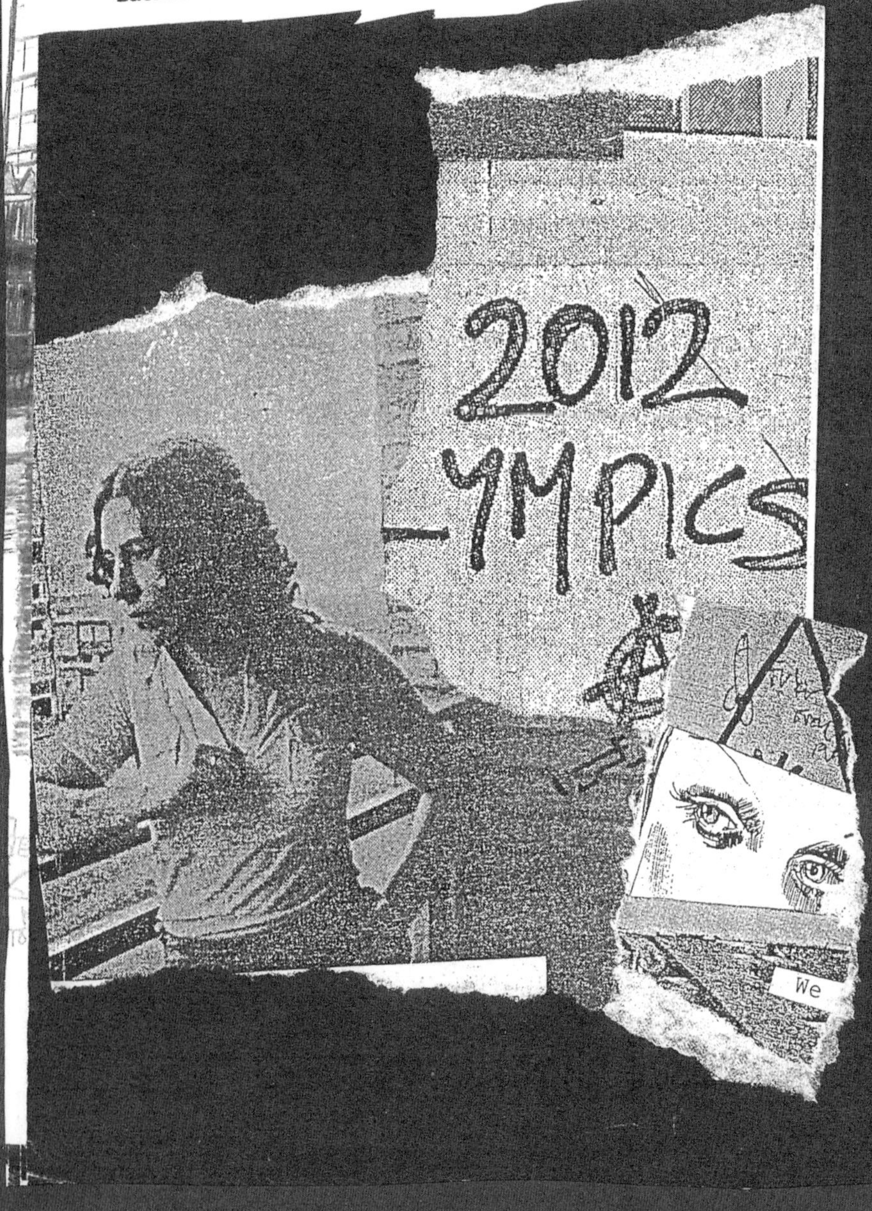
2012
YMPICS
We

And then it really starts to rain, torrential, and there's
people running in the boozer soaked to the fucking skin, and
we're all pretty off it now, and one of these lads has just
passed round a bottle of mushroom tea so you know you can
imagine, we're totally wrecked, laughing at fuck all. Someone
kisses me, beat up skinhead, face a lattice work of scars, nice
one, no one cares. And we're all in the back of that bashed up
van heading over East London, a joyous bundling rush as we take

off on the Westway, peering over the whizzing parapets at the
lost streets beneath.

I find a gap in the railings and drop down onto the towpath,
spectral memories radiate in the hawthorn scent. City Road
basin, Shepherdess Walk, Ox eye daisy and red campion.
De Beauvoir. SMASH H BLOCK . Free Birmingham Six. Through the
backs of Haggerston, under Kingsland road, cutting across
Queensbridge.
Fires in barrels on the industial estate, plastic chairs in
circles. I know some of this crew. A chance to stop and
consider. Tonight I'll sleep in the squat on St Marks Rise.
Orange fences, crew from the old days. Jean and Alessio, Martin
and some of the Whitechapel lot. Barbequed lamb and Lidls
lager. ESTATE AGENTS UP AGAINST THE SOUTH FACING WALL.

Broadway Market and Globe town, the troubled edges of Victoria
park. Scented rose garden , I lost myself there. With him. That
night, I could see from the look in his eyes. His feelings for
me had intensified.

Mile End park, The Palm tree. Outside in violet shadows, his
hand, a black tattoo. Red wine. Mirages on the canal. Drifting
into sleep, dreams opalescent, erotically charged.
 This is the last stretch, futuristic citadel of the Wharf
glittering on the skyline. Limehouse basin. Nerves fraying.
And the heat, the scorching heat.

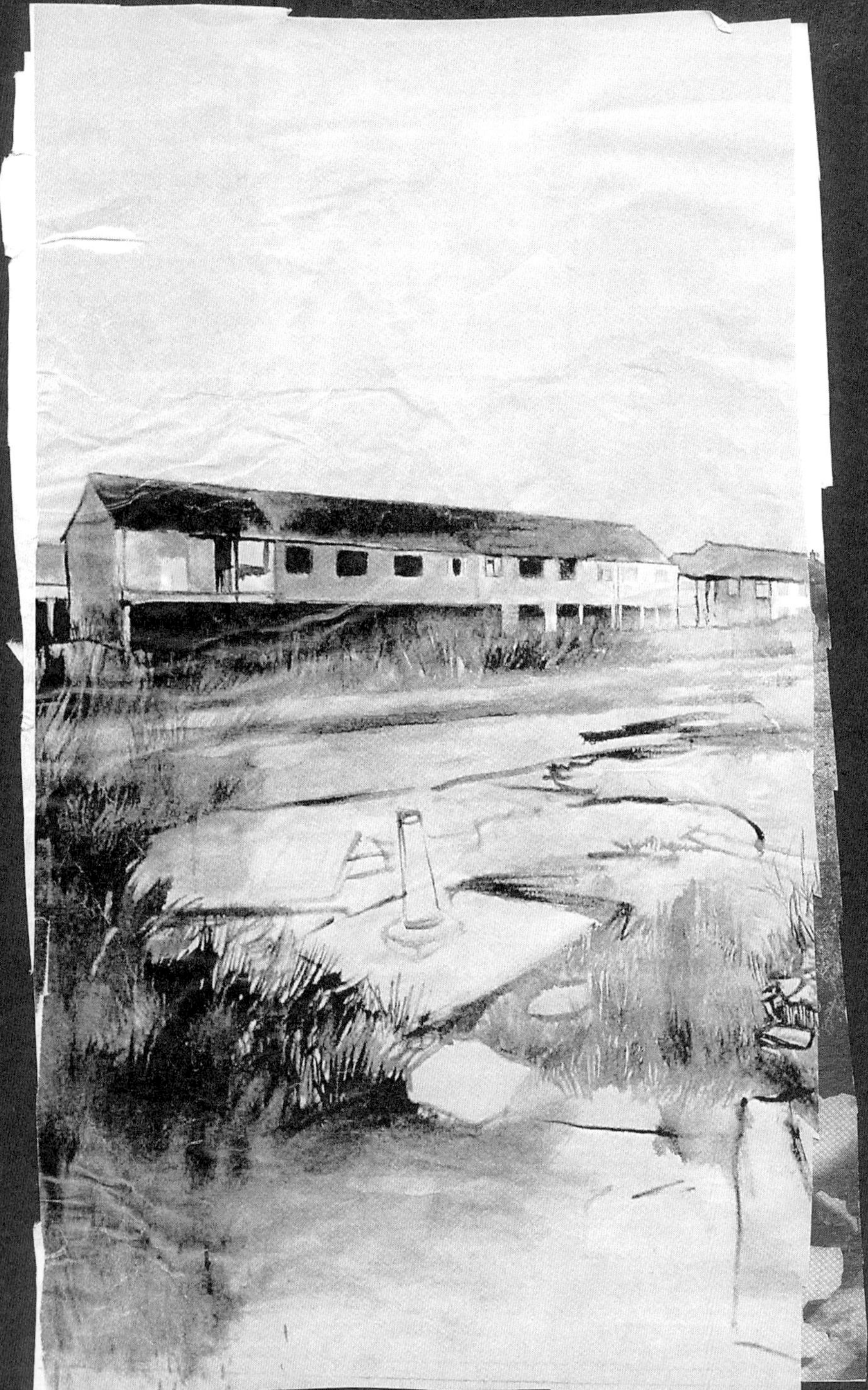

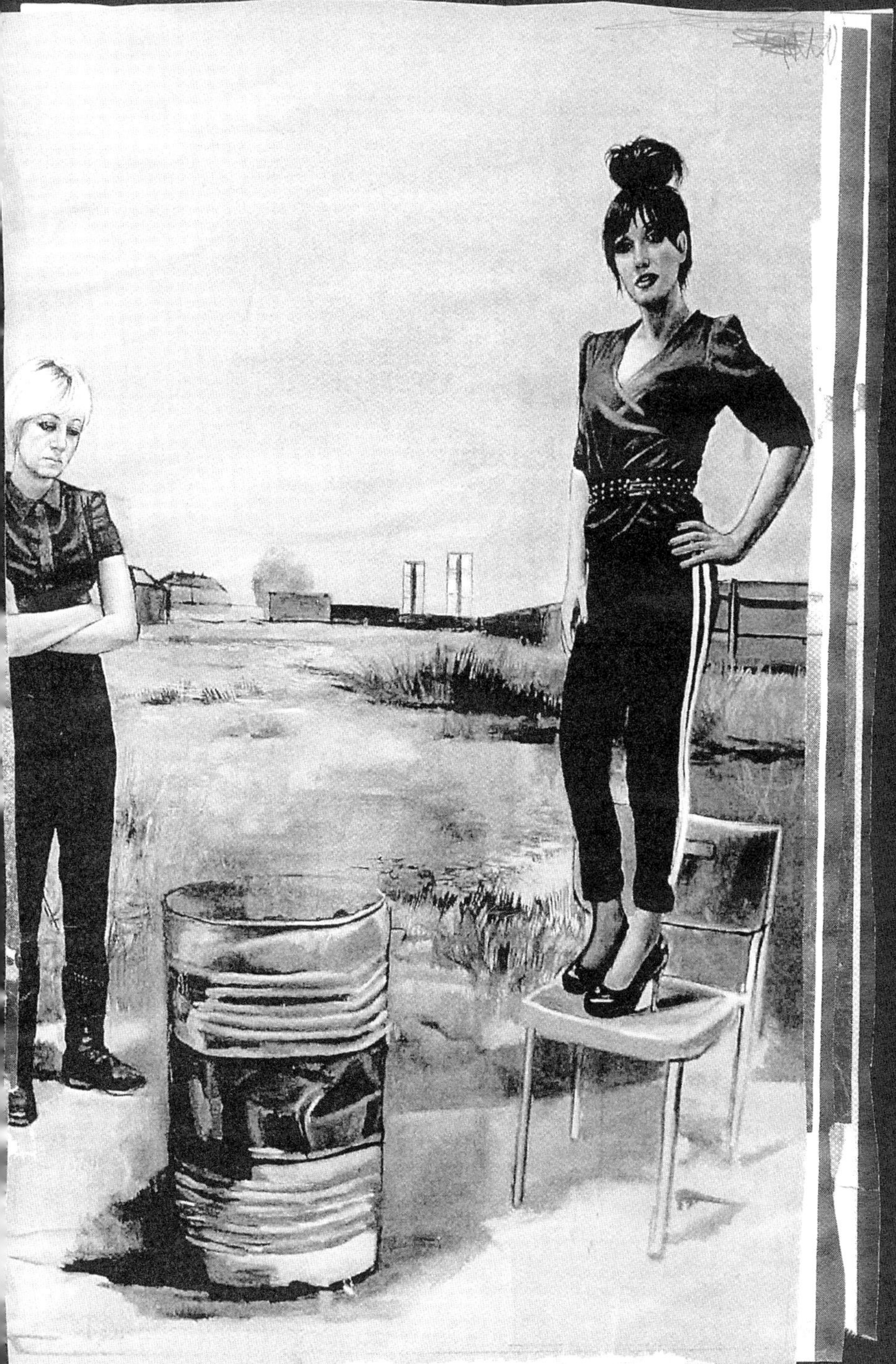

Visiting someone on a knackered Peabody estate in the shadow of the Mint. 8th floor dossing. Bottles of beer in the fridge, another little bolt hole. I have a bath, backcomb my hair while he watches the racing.

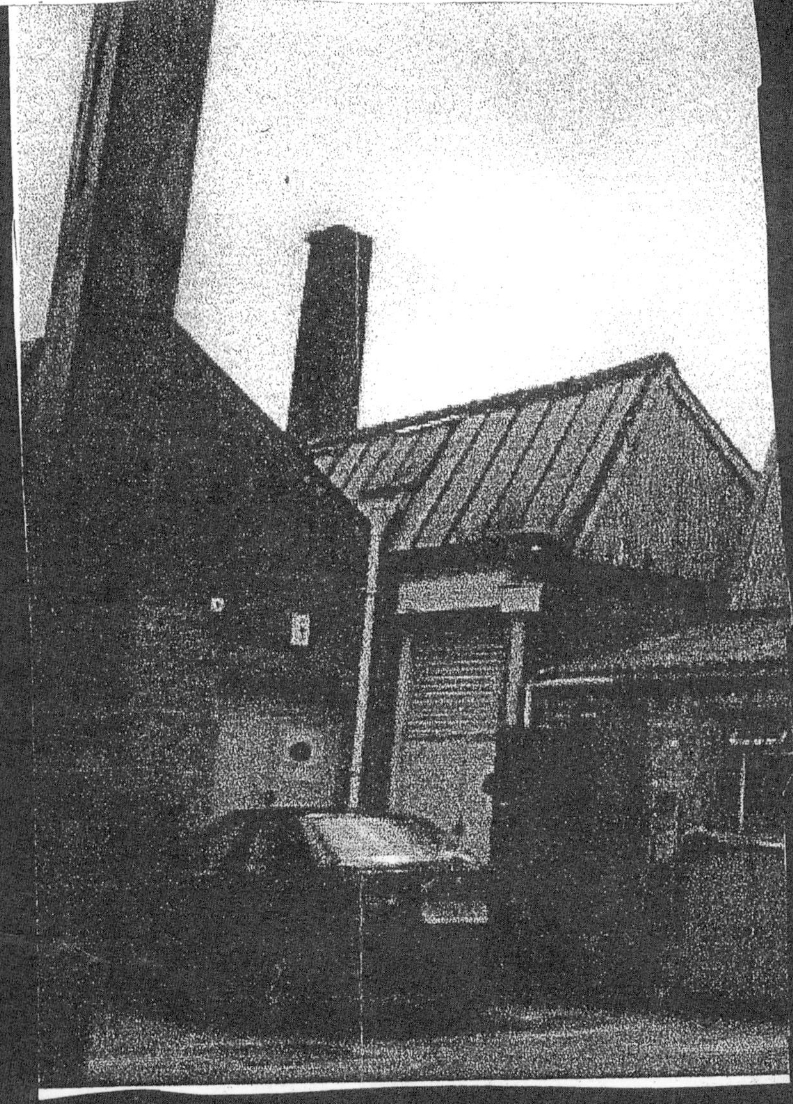

He knows all the Class War crew, knows Arran by sight but hasn't seen him round here. I'm asking him about the Island, the situation since J18. Old Bill been raiding flats, section 18s. Getting people on really heavy charges, violent disorder and stuff.

The network of squats from here to Poplar are pulsing with tense jubilance. There are still people partying down here since J18 but you have to be careful because you never know who's watching. Beer dissipates the anxiety. One more glug of codeine linctus and the maze of streets round Aldgate shimmers in the palm of my hand, Thames becoming crystalline life line.

777 Commercial road.
We emerge from the flats and walk down Cable Street,
 ...swift diversion through the churchyard of St Anne's. Place my palm flat on the pyramid, tilts everything towards me, chalk dust on my fingertips. Dome laid to waste beneath a convolvulus matrix. To the Thames, push through empty yuppie blocks and the Samuda estate. A labyrinthine weave through elevated walkways and I find his empty room, curtains drawn, rest of the lads playing Cockney Rejects, drinking cans of stella. Arran, Mark, an old passport in a dusty wallet.

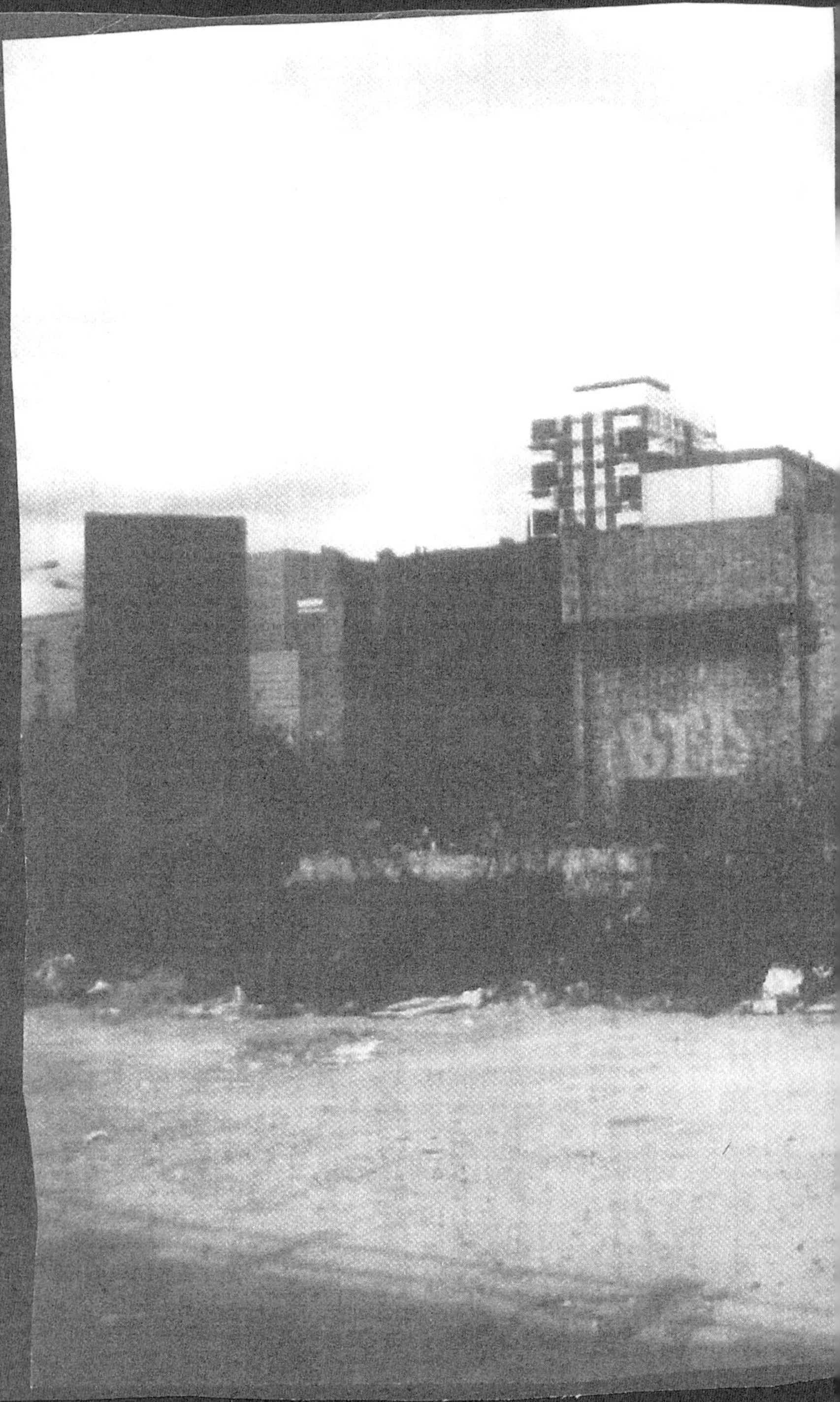

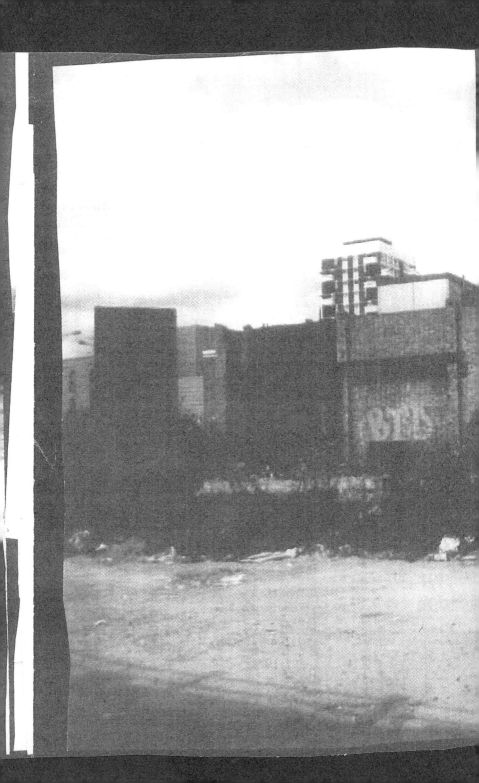

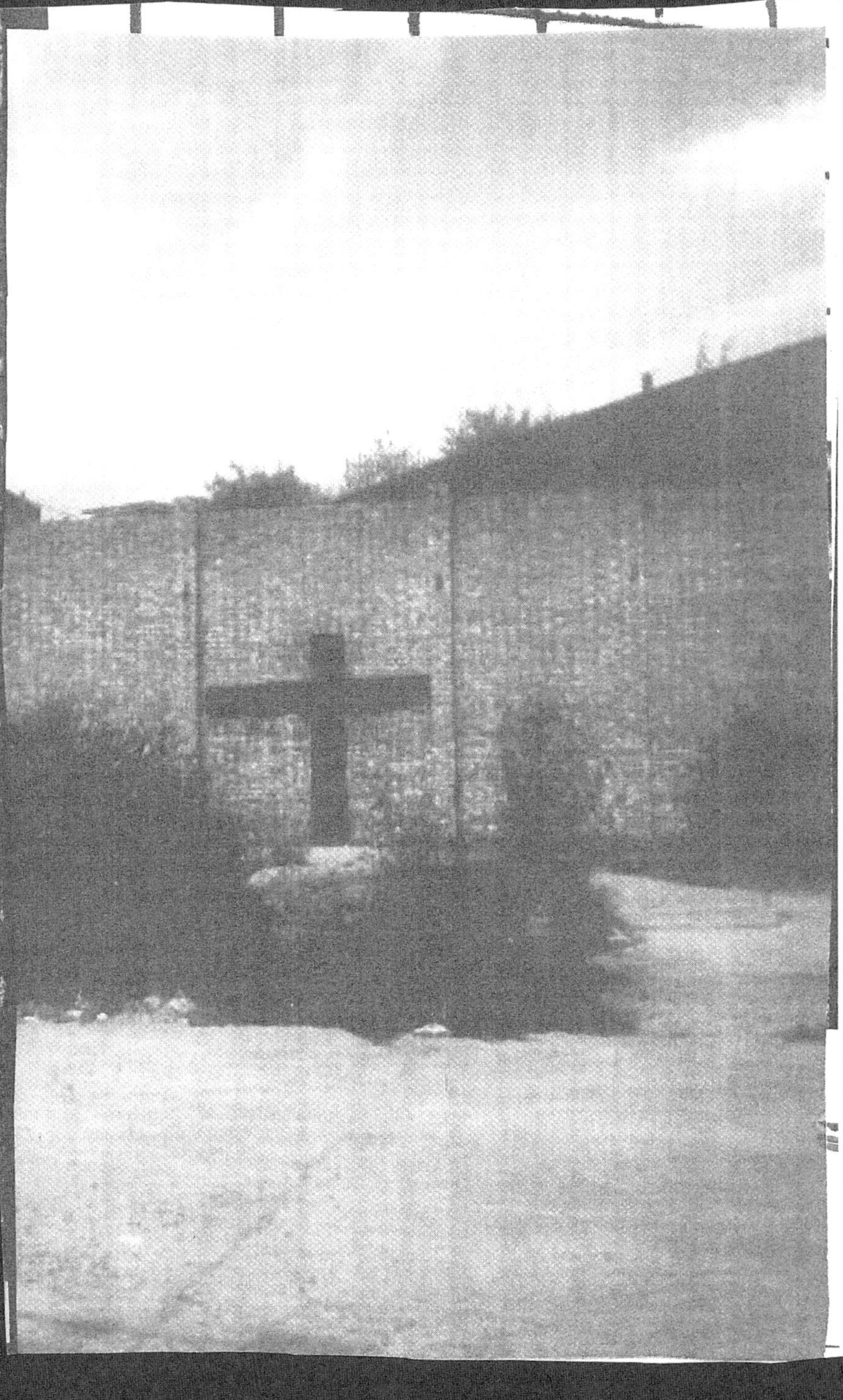

"Such harmony only he can relish whose long experience and detailed knowledge of the niches are such as to permit a perfect mental image of the entire system. But it is doubtful that such a one exists."
-Samuel Beckett *The Lost Ones*

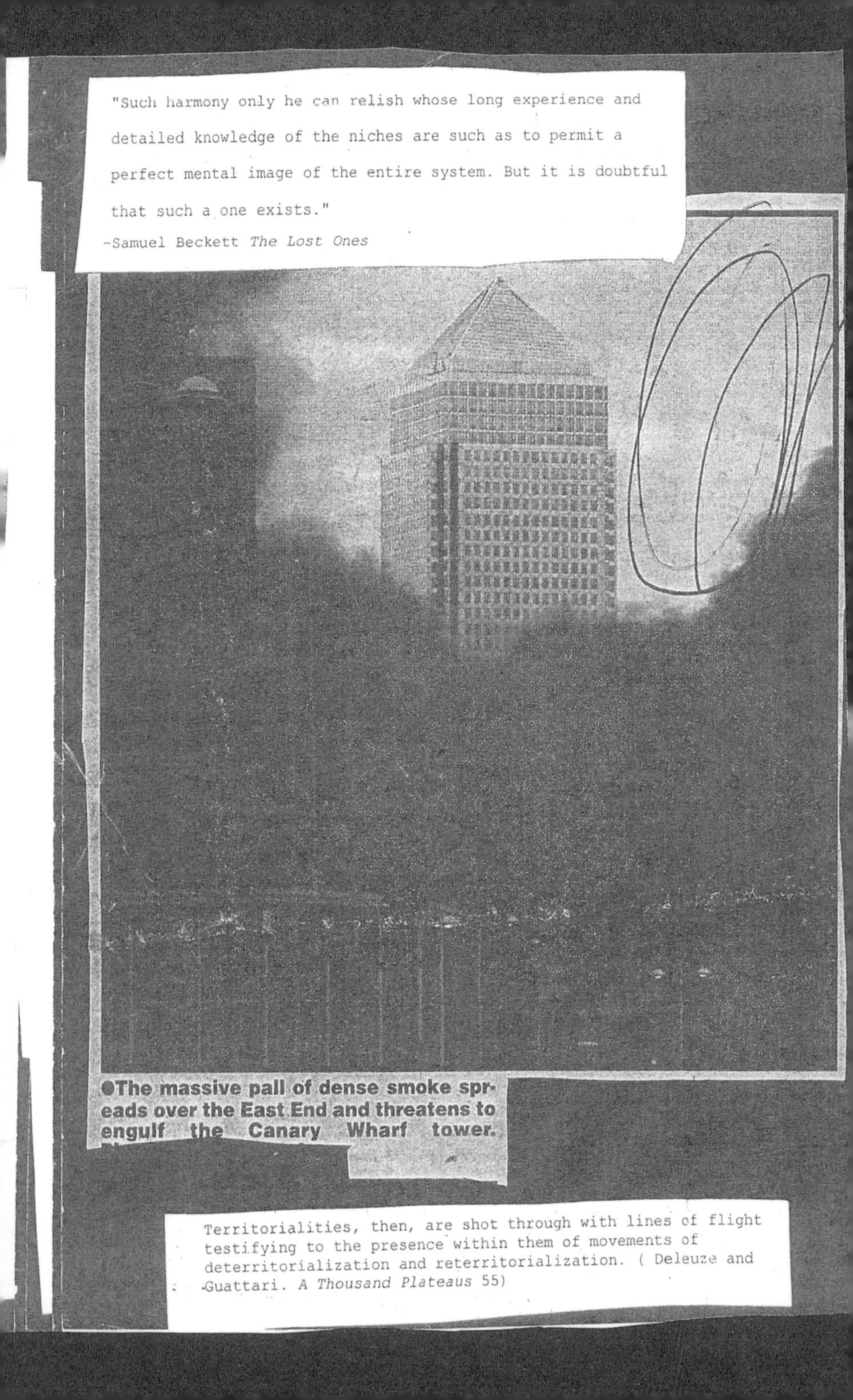

●The massive pall of dense smoke spreads over the East End and threatens to engulf the Canary Wharf tower.

Territorialities, then, are shot through with lines of flight testifying to the presence within them of movements of deterritorialization and reterritorialization. (Deleuze and Guattari. *A Thousand Plateaus* 55)

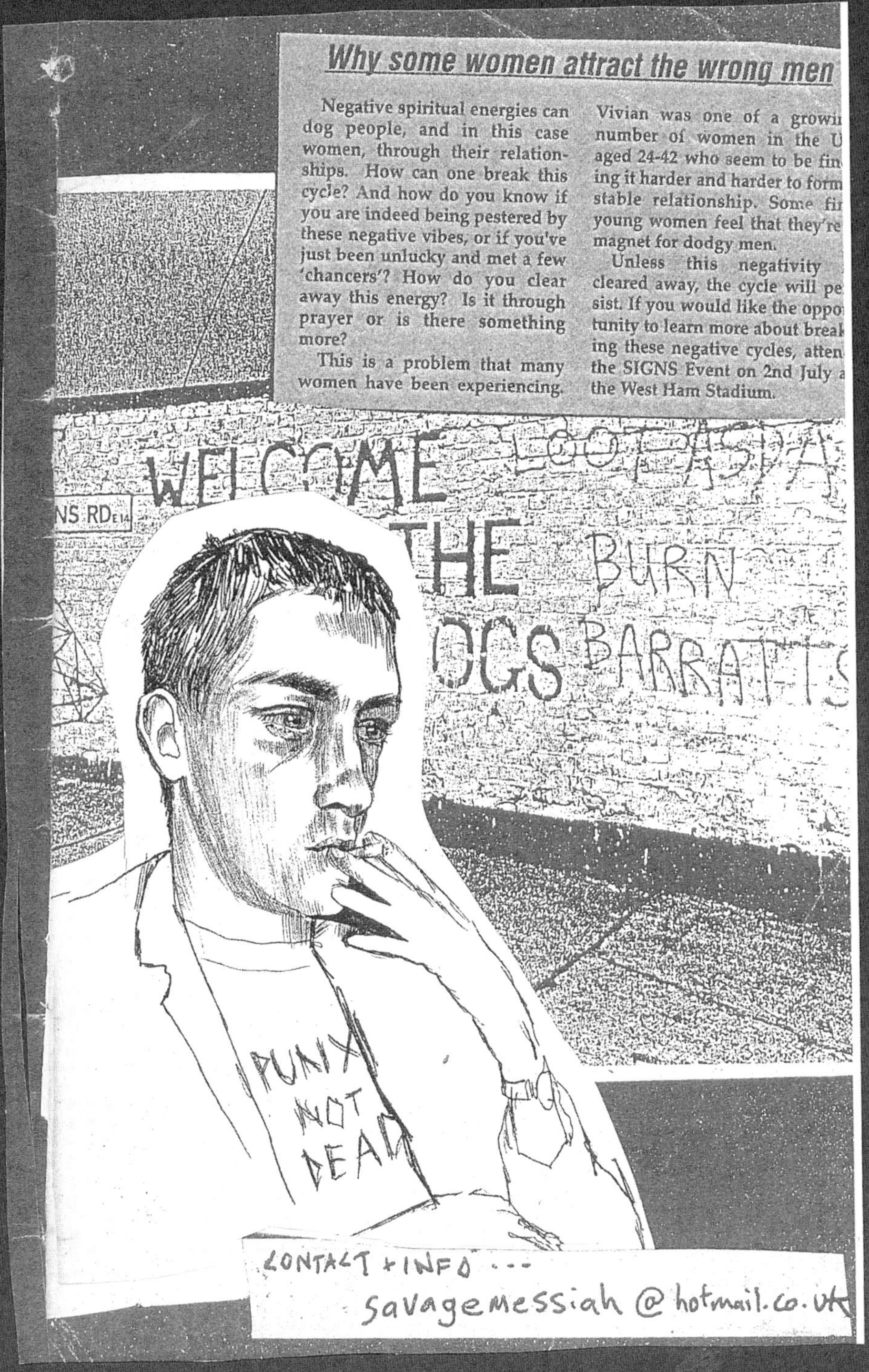

Why some women attract the wrong men

Negative spiritual energies can dog people, and in this case women, through their relationships. How can one break this cycle? And how do you know if you are indeed being pestered by these negative vibes, or if you've just been unlucky and met a few 'chancers'? How do you clear away this energy? Is it through prayer or is there something more?

This is a problem that many women have been experiencing. Vivian was one of a growi number of women in the U aged 24-42 who seem to be fin ing it harder and harder to form stable relationship. Some fir young women feel that they're magnet for dodgy men.

Unless this negativity cleared away, the cycle will pe sist. If you would like the oppo tunity to learn more about break ing these negative cycles, atten the SIGNS Event on 2nd July a the West Ham Stadium.

WELCOME THE OGS
BURN BARRATTS
NS RD E14
PUNX NOT DEAD
CONTACT + INFO ...
savagemessiah@hotmail.co.uk

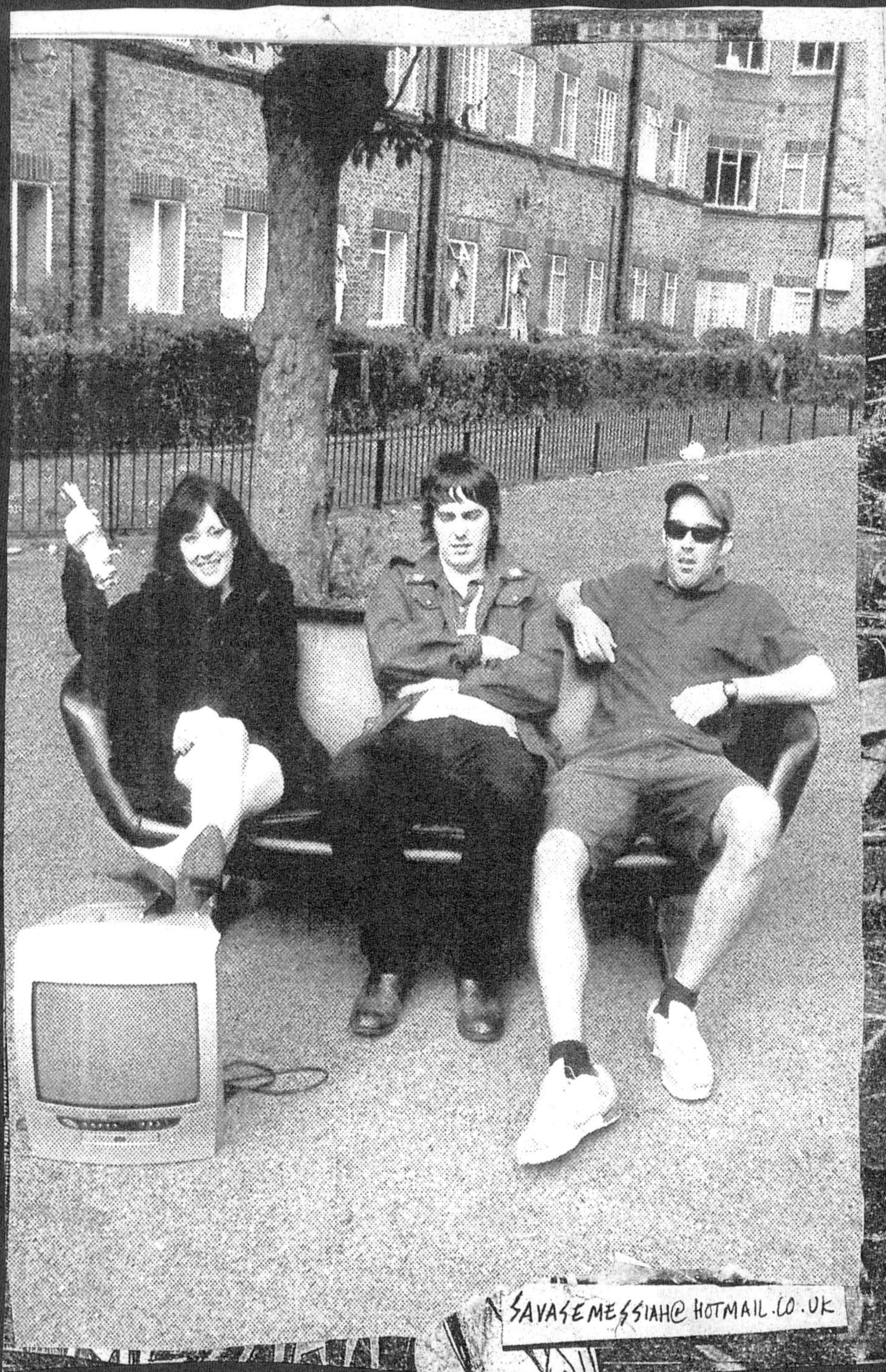
SAVAGEMESSIAH@HOTMAIL.CO.UK

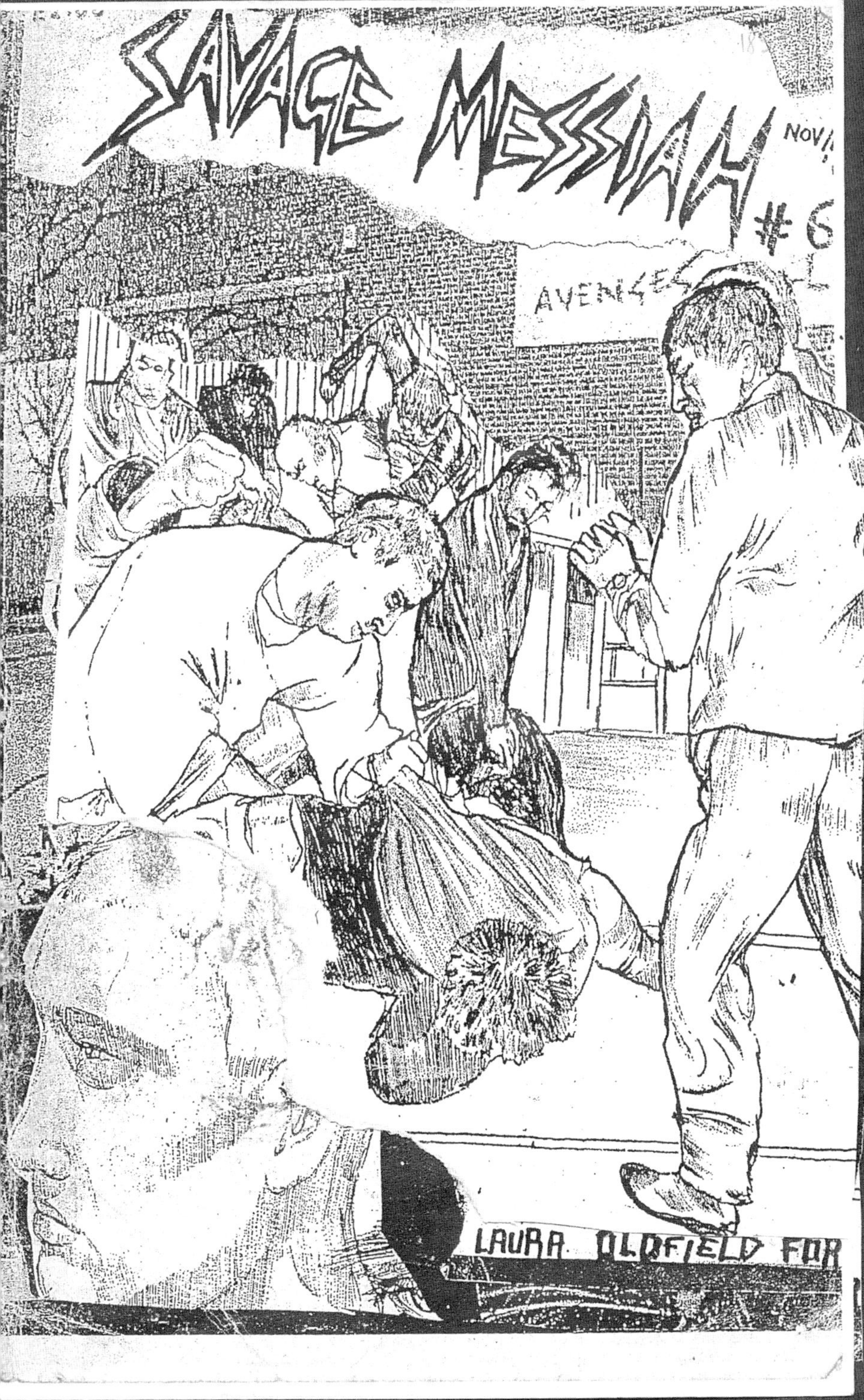
SAVAGE MESSIAH
NOV/
#6
AVENGE
LAURA OLDFIELD FOR

WALKING THE PATH OF THE RIVER FLEET: A JOURNEY THROUGH LONDON'S REPRESSED DESIRES ----

Walking the path of the river Fleet: a journey through London's repressed desires.

"As for flirtation, it gives to Benjamin's moment of hesitation a bipedal dynamic. It is an endless closing and opening or oscillation between two positions: flirtation is 'the act of taking hold of something only in order to let it go again, of letting it fall only to take hold of it again, in what could be called the tentative turning something on which the shadow of it's own denial already falls.' George Simmel: On Women, Sexuality, and Love.

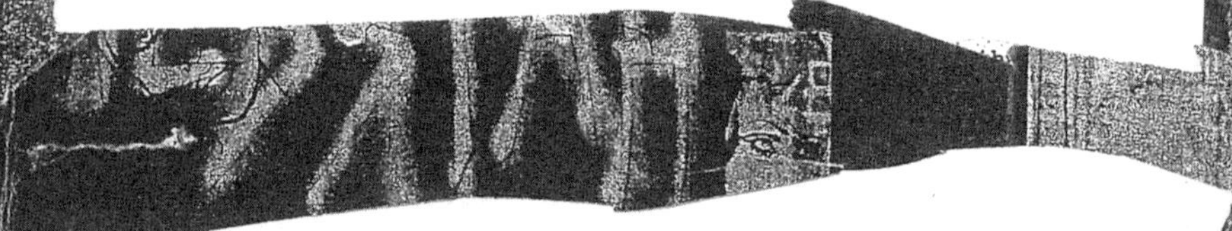

"Love affairs And endless strategies.
I don't believe in a word they said.
City limits . No more information.
Go follow navigation in your head."
Japan . Suburban Berlin.

I walk the path of the Fleet as it runs through the city as a buried current. The repressed desires of the city flow through hidden pipes and conduits and become counter narratives, a described jouissance in a euphoric engagement with the city.
A balmy July evening ,standing outside the Coach and Horses in Clerkenwell.
Laughter and shrieks ricochet around the Fleet valley.
I hear the sound of rushing water in a grate under my feet. The river perpetually threatens to break out of its confines in a volatile, intoxicated state.

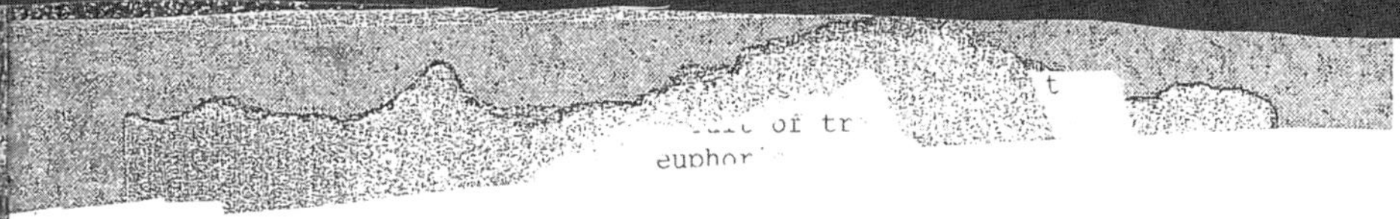

HAMPSTEAD.
We drift in circles around each other. Threads untangle in the memory flashes of an uncanny landscape.

One night in a pub on Rosslyn Hill I witness three skirmishes, three explosive grasps at violence. We end up in a cab to Camden, shifting over the path of the Fleet, and I feel London cascading, cinematic and charged. Inverness street, carnivalesque loopiness .It's a feverish Summer night and there are hordes of screechers and brawlers, a real demented din. We weave through a maelstrom of dodgy loiterers and onion fryers , delighting in the thrill and degeneracy of the fairground.

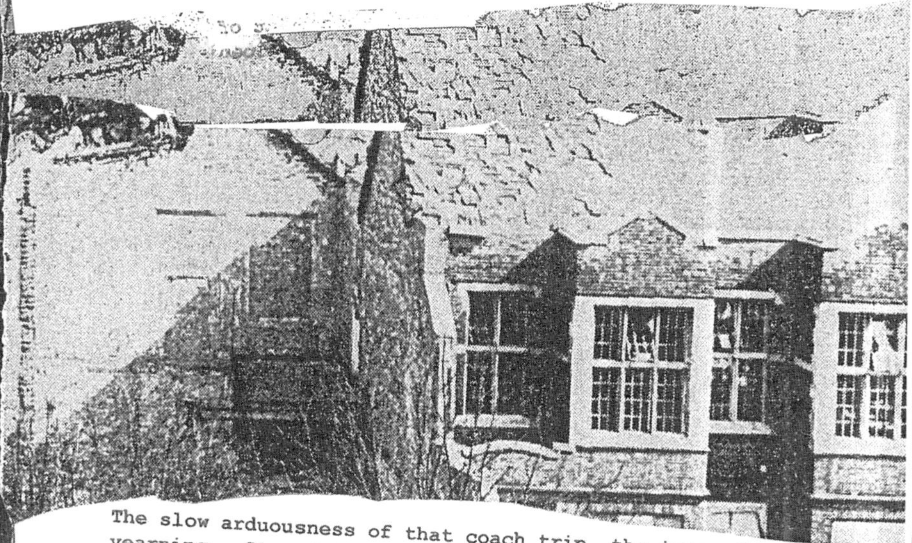

The slow arduousness of that coach trip ,the impossible yearning. Stranded up North, I saw our first encounter played out in such vivid clarity, the frantic kisses, it was the most alive sequence, I just watched it unfold, didn't even have to focus or try, all that plotting and dreaming, eyes pressed to the window to see the first ragged boundaries of Edgware. Drill holes in rock, ravines gouged out in the cliff face, envelopes of blocks opening one on top of another.
In Wooley Edge services I yearned for the whorls and spirals of the labyrinth, smearing red lipstick in the fluorescent glare of the mirror.

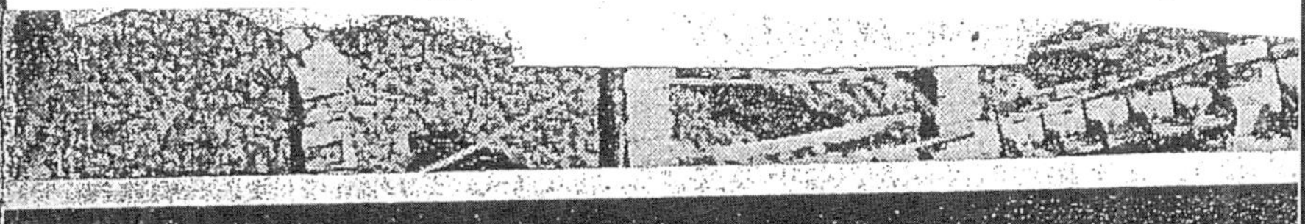

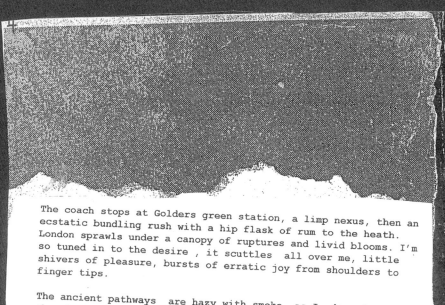

The coach stops at Golders green station, a limp nexus, then an ecstatic bundling rush with a hip flask of rum to the heath. London sprawls under a canopy of ruptures and livid blooms. I'm so tuned in to the desire , it scuttles all over me, little shivers of pleasure, bursts of erratic joy from shoulders to finger tips.

The ancient pathways are hazy with smoke as I drop down to the glowing windows of the Vale of Health. I search in the November dark for the traveller site behind corrugated iron, briars and hawthorn. A big crew of skinheads smash up cars, defying the dead time of the Barrat estate. Caravans and trailers are reconfigured as mobile architecture. .
        To desire placelessness is to defy authority.

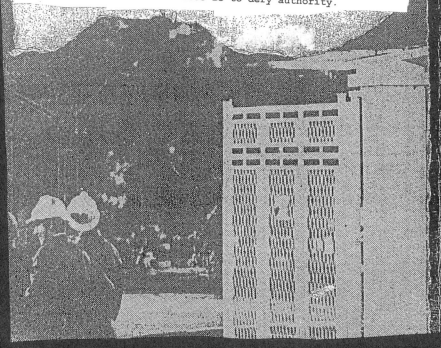

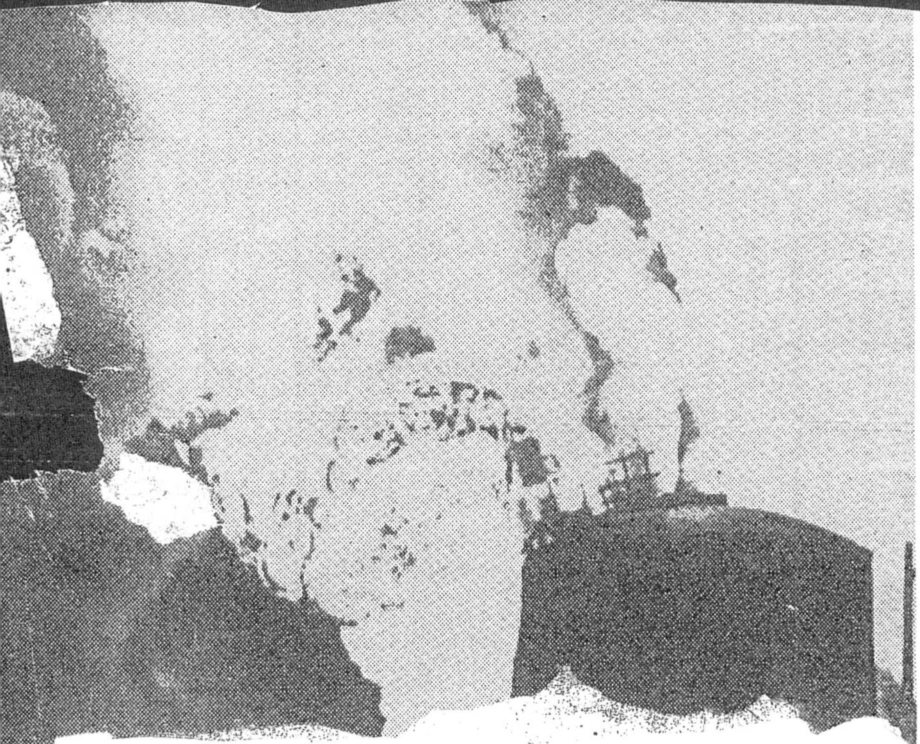

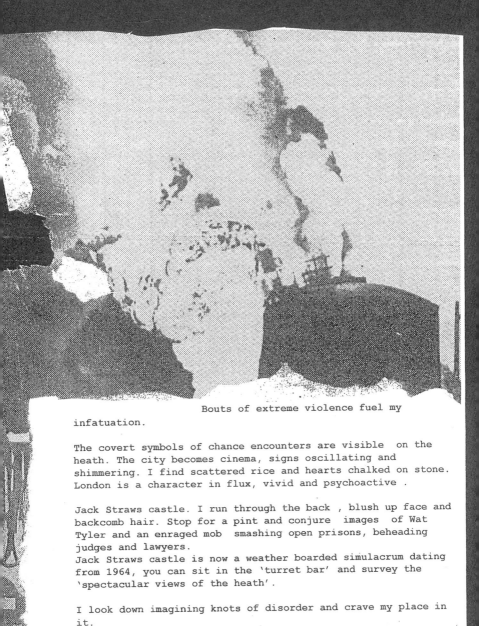

Bouts of extreme violence fuel my infatuation.

The covert symbols of chance encounters are visible on the heath. The city becomes cinema, signs oscillating and shimmering. I find scattered rice and hearts chalked on stone. London is a character in flux, vivid and psychoactive .

Jack Straws castle. I run through the back , blush up face and backcomb hair. Stop for a pint and conjure images of Wat Tyler and an enraged mob smashing open prisons, beheading judges and lawyers.
Jack Straws castle is now a weather boarded simulacrum dating from 1964, you can sit in the 'turret bar' and survey the 'spectacular views of the heath'.

I look down imagining knots of disorder and crave my place in it.

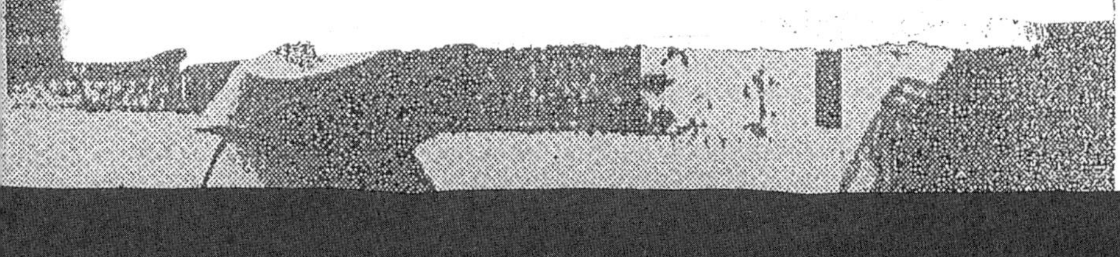

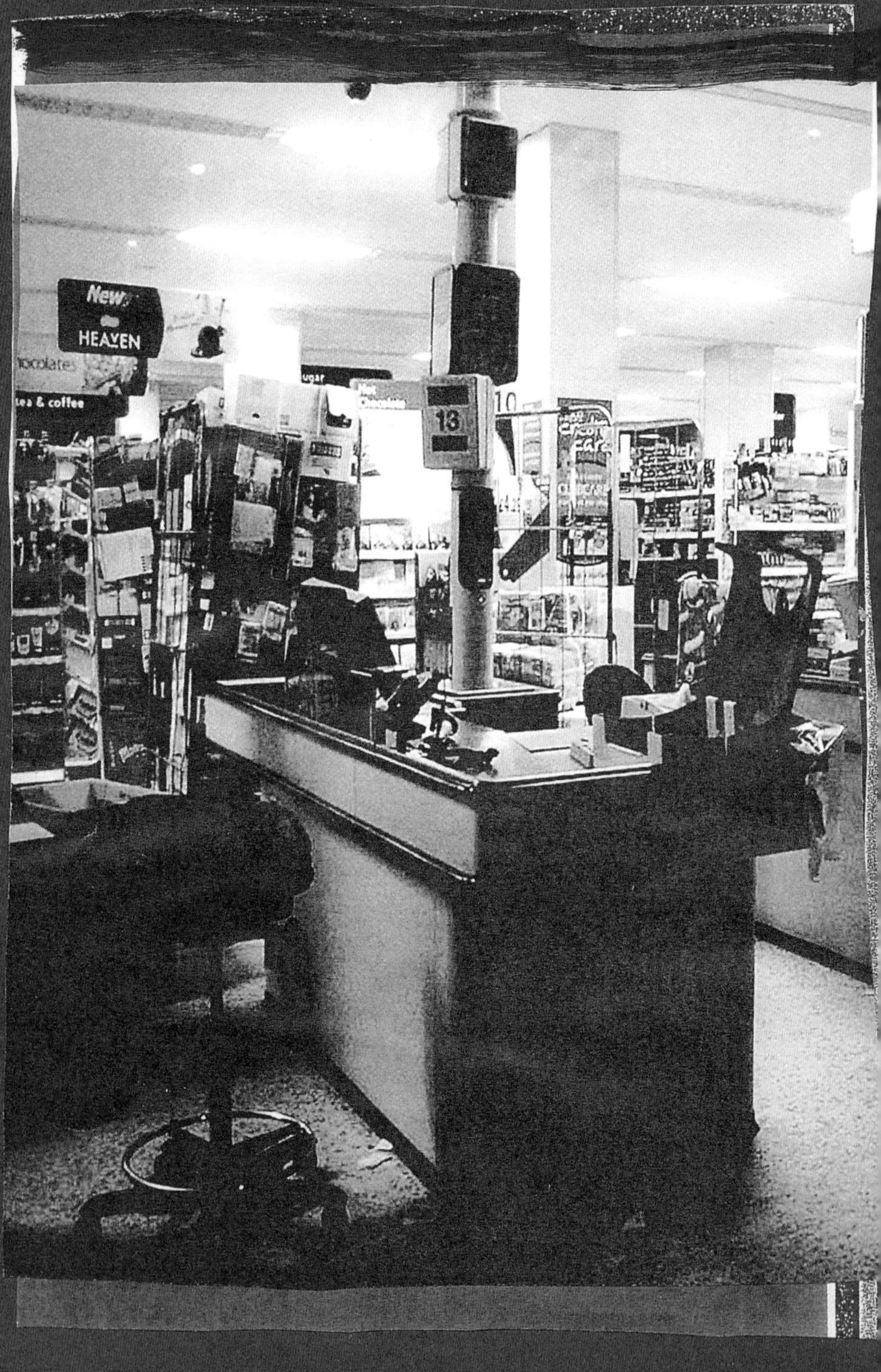
New
HEAVEN
tea & coffee
13

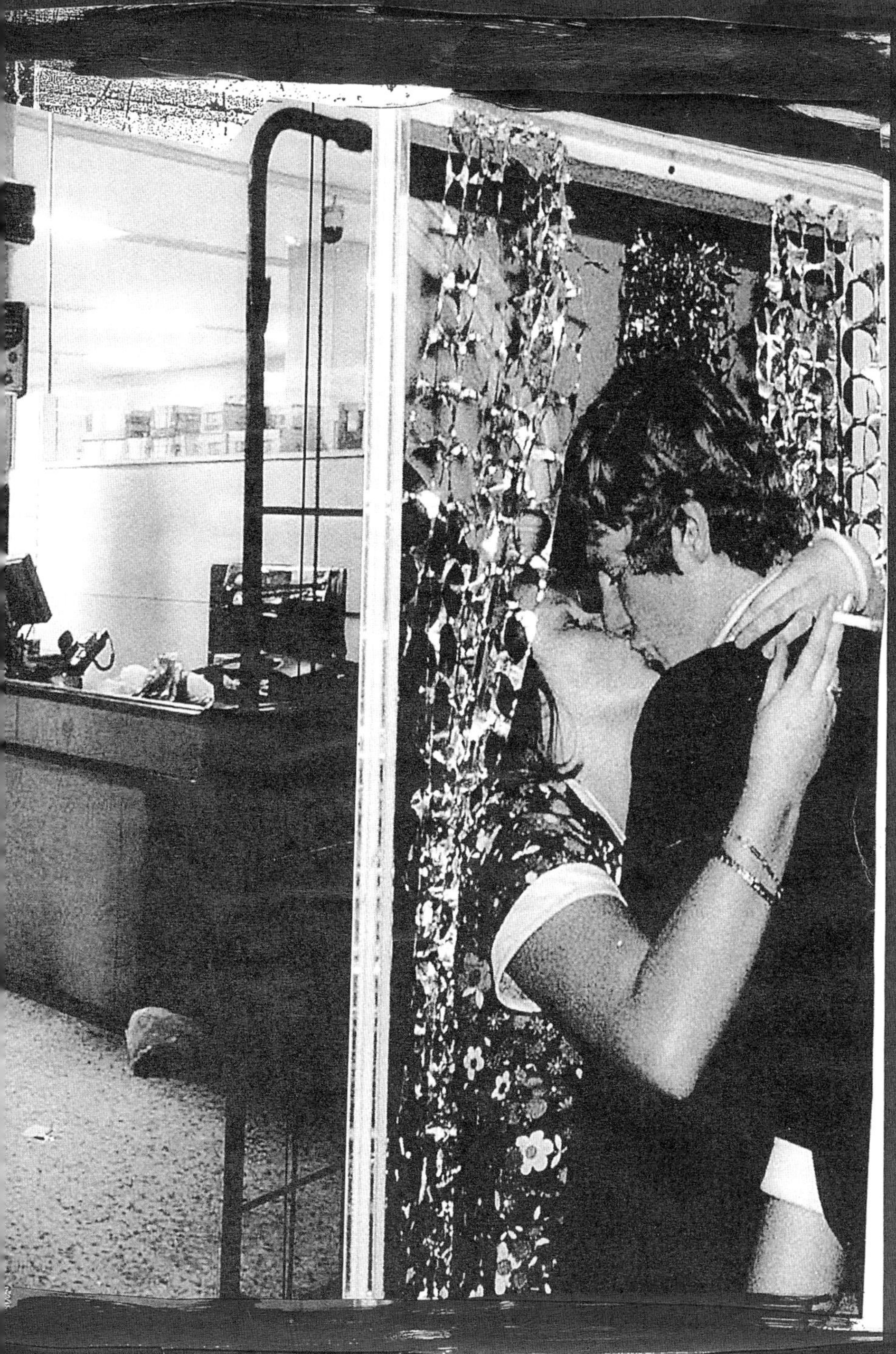

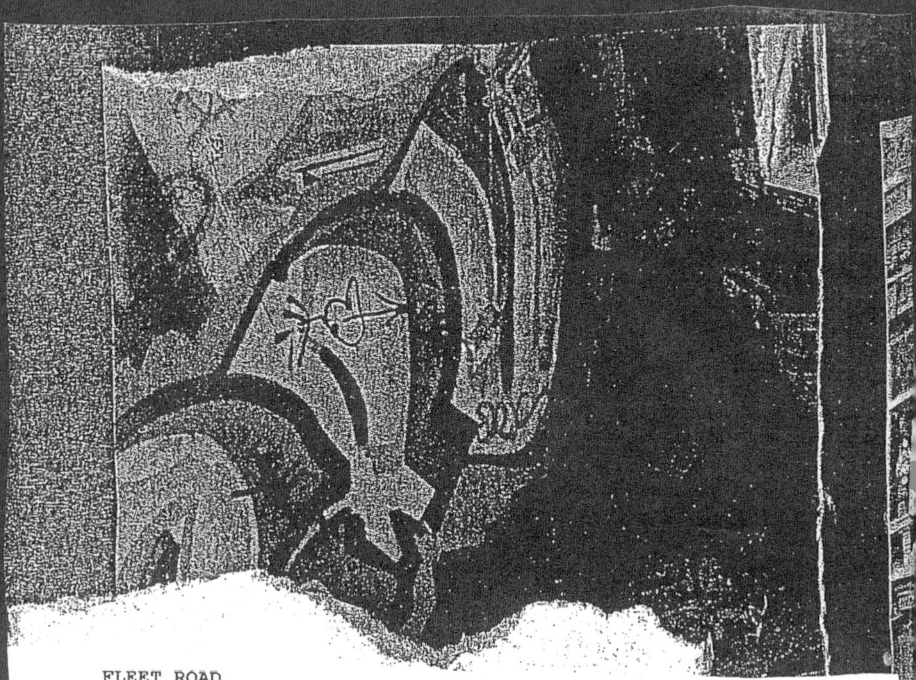

FLEET ROAD.

The Stag on the corner of Fleet road, a marker, the crossing of an imperceptible boundary that takes me beyond the grasp of affluent Hampstead into the realm of chaos and spontaneity.
Pass the council yard on Cressy road, sweepers memorizing contours of the Fleet valley. The hidden river asserts itself in street signs, shops and cab firms.

the city

I pause to call on a lost acquaintance in Polgrave house and push through amusement arcade kitsch, tainted nets and falling dreylon. There's a cat in the communal launderette dozing between geraniums pots.

This place is a nest of junkies, the dank pain of boredom spans the threshold.
I haven't been here for 9 years but everything's the same, even the scorched teaspoon on the gas fire is still there.

I drift out of those flats with the dislocated feeling you get when you emerge from a matinee, those film noir treble bills at the Everyman.

1960 , Peeping Tom, Michael Powell,
voyeurism,the ubiquitous eye and covert surveillance. The main character was a TV studio serial killer who prowled around Hampstead secretly filming people.

Hysterical darkness, Party party, a day glo explosion of glitter balls, balloons and Killer Clowns from outer space.

Alright darlin, you look nice!

The Gospel Oak estate is a beacon of modernist architecture. There's a warped Cartesian logic at work ,an attempt to eradicate the erratic flare ups of the street. Got to keep moving to escape the striations of control.

Chtcheglov said of Le Corbusier, "His cretinizing influence is immense. A Le Corbusier model is the only image that arouses in me the idea of immediate suicide. He is destroying the last remnants of joy. And of love, passion, freedom"

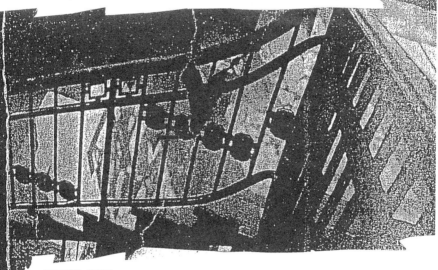

MALDEN ROAD.
I nip into The Westport for a glass of Murphys. I know the place from way back. Mayo people. This is the corner where all the fellas will be conjured up at 6 in the morning looking for a start, then all the vans will come and they'll just vanish as though they'd never been there.

When apples still grow in November/ When blossoms still bloom from each tree/ When leaves are still green in December, It's then that our land will be free./I wander her hills and valleys,/ And still through my sorrow i see./ A land that has never known freedom/ And only her rivers run free.

I sit at the bar absorbing the maudlin sentimentality that will precipitate bouts of violence.

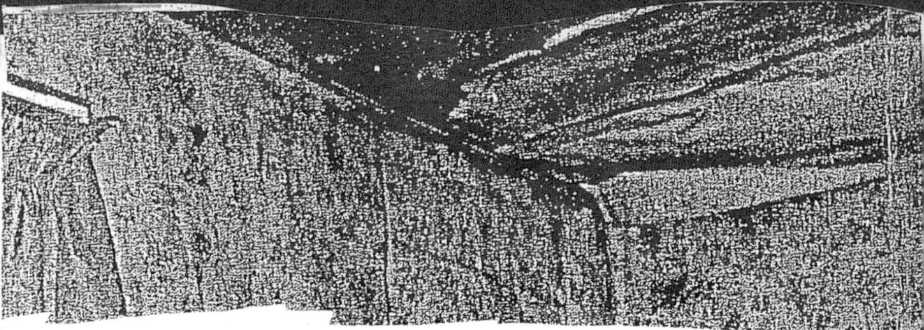

Grafton terrace, Marx's house, a dilapidated unmarked villa.

"The reform of consciousness consists entirely in making the world aware of its consciousness, in arousing it from it's

rienced as

dream itself, in explaining its own actions to it."Karl marx in a letter to Arnold Ruge ,1943

On the corner of Herbert street I find unintelligible glyphs on peeling stucco, a tally of condemned men. This is the yearning f the mythical homeland, the invisible cord.

of

QUEENS CRESCENT

"A landscape haunts, intense as opium." Mallarmé .

Queens crescent is the nexus of knife crime, a flashing matrix of Sheffield steel. There's a scene outside William Hill, a tableau of imminence. In the searing July heat men hang around. The homeless blokes sit in a cluster on the opposite wall , waiting . Something might happen. The dispossessed know plenty about the drift through the city. Benjamin called the streets, the 'dwelling place of the collective'

Queens Crescent is suspended somewhere between 1968 and 1981, and I sense my darling there, on the corner of Baset st and Allcroft road. I'm searching the brickwork with dusty fingertips for the first Sex Pistols graffiti of 1976. He was here then, and possibly now, we drift in circles around each other.

Japaneses animation, white explosions of gunfire, 80s synthesiser soundtracks.

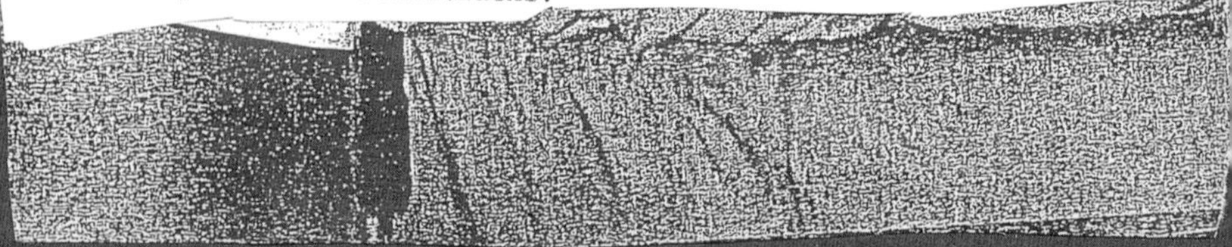

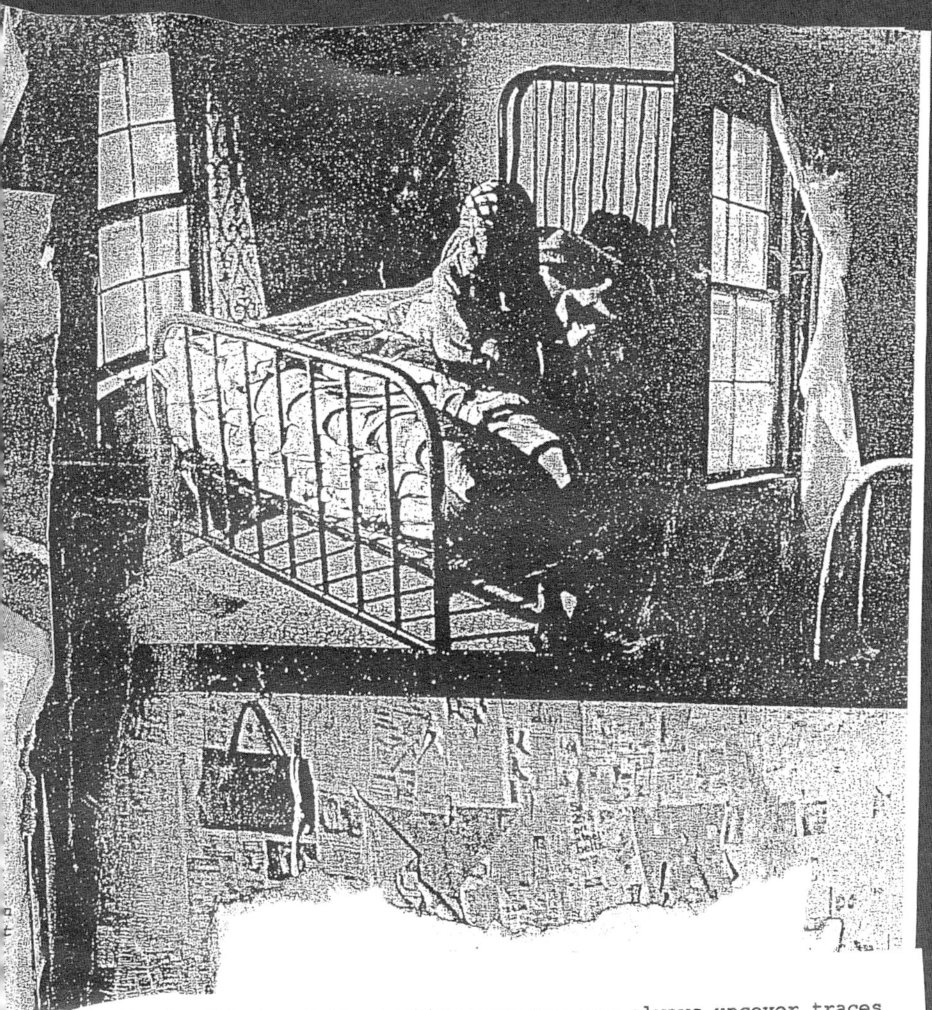

In the fabric of the architecture you can always uncover traces and palimpsests, the poly-temporality of the city. As I lay my palm flat against the wall I grasp past texts never fully erasing the traces of earlier inscriptions. The polychromatic riot of London's histories travel in shimmering, tangled lines.

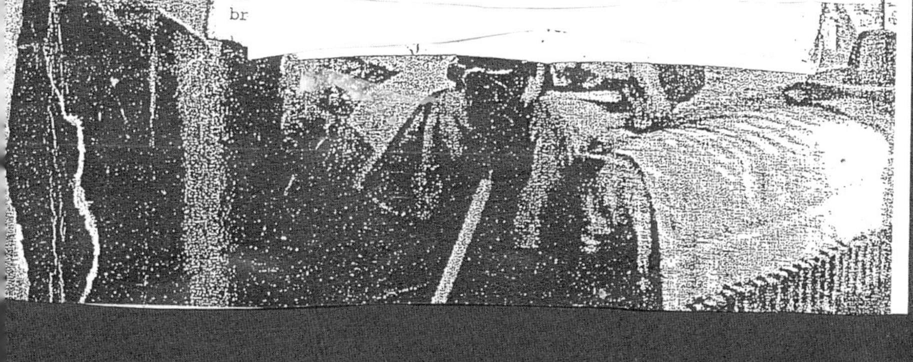

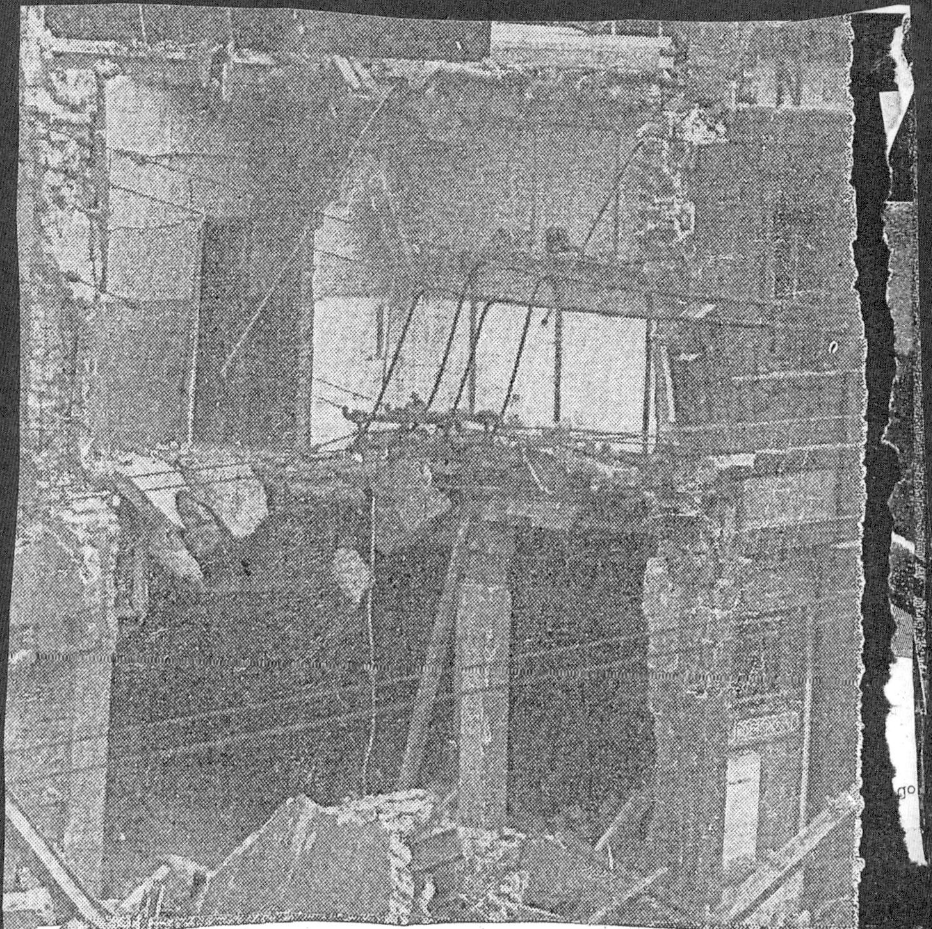

I gravitate as always to the late night linctus apothecaries. Can't get a grip on this thing, keeps turning up, impossible to walk in a straight line. I'm floating through the vistas, De Quincey scag meanderings, dizziness, inner ear malfunction, swaying like I'm out at sea.

A glance across at Bulls pizza and bagels takes me to 1982. The diamond patterns in bleached pastel colours leave me choked with sadness. I feel sick. Drawn in, chamber after chamber, worlds unfolding like a computer game. Someone shouts wotcha! And I don't think I've ever heard that outside the cinema.

serious assault 18th August. 2 males involved in stabbing incident. We are appealing for witnesses,can you help us?

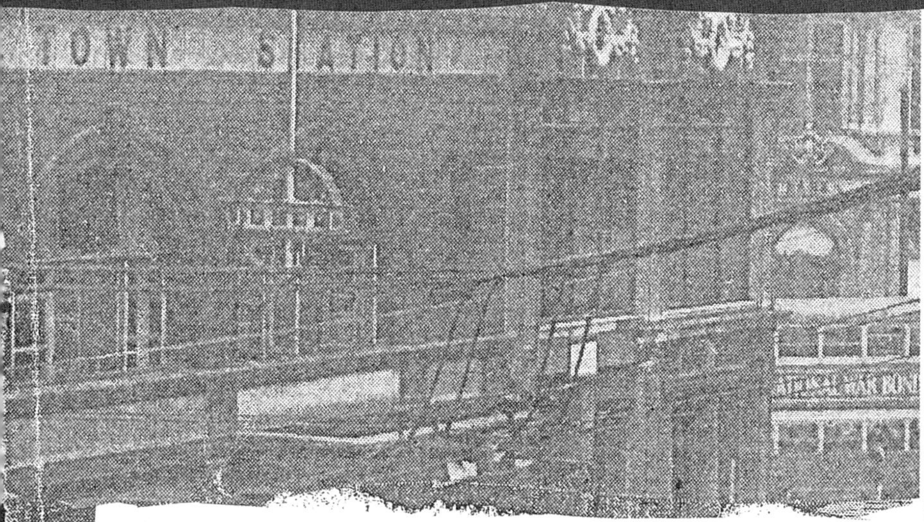
TOWN

Arcade game violence seeping through the cracks, threshold disintegrating.

The Man of Aran pub. I feel alright in here with the flashing fruities, slashed up leather and red pillars. It carries an air of seedy abandonment, no one cares that I'm too wasted to speak on shoddy scag derivatives. John Legend on the jukey,

We're just ordinary people,
We don't know which way to go

cold scuttling sensation of cathexis, Proustian flashbacks, something about walking around Highbury Barn at 4 in the morning , a drowning guilt,

the loss of someone I loved.

This enclave is steeped in nostalgia for the Crimean war, Inkerman, Alma, even this pub, the idiocy of the officer class .

Sex crime 1984.

Weight lifting, video shacks with Jackie Chan fixations.

And all the guilt I harboured, all the shame, the walk around Highbury with so much hanging in the balance, the tyranny of choice and the crashing cruelty of desire, it was all locked into that one anodyne song.

Song ends, bag open, rummage ,find money, on again.

Beyond the pub lie corridors of industrial ruins. Crumbling pathways open up between 50s factories. Dislocated bontempi rhythms come cascading through an abandoned coffee grinding factory.

Jesus loves me! He will stay, Close beside me all the way; He's prepared a home for me, And one day His face I'll see.

Crawl beneath cables and graffiti lit walls. There's a massive squat party in one of the industrial units with all these speaker cabs stacked up in pyramids. Townships of portakabins span the railway arches like a Gustave Doré etching. I drop through a trapdoor and descend into an appropriation of Imperialist fanfare, Throbbing Gristle broadcast loud.

My skinhead companion looks like a New English Library classic. Bootboys. Skinhead Returns. Lured by curiosity and desire, I play the game for the sake of playing, endless inescapable configurations, Homo Ludens with a diseased mind. I take him under a bridge in Arctic street, pushes me hard against a wall emblazoned with THE JAM and FLUX OF PINK INDIANS.

CAMDEN TOWN.

Under the cobbles, Sid Rawles.
Squatter king, maverick anti property tycoon and tabloid folk devil. He cracked hundreds of houses round here.

Weave through the ramshackle alleyways and takeaway miasmas of Camden dodging packs of drugged up kids. Canal Collective Squat is now derelict but still quietly breathing under heaps of detritus and giant hogweed . There were always punks necking cider outside the front, a little nexus of mayhem, doors leading to unknown pleasures and symbols painted on broken windows.

Camden is that cess pit playground you are permitted to degenerate in. With its filth and grime, the fabric of it is unmistakably London but the people possess a provincial air. It's something about the haircuts, the Brit pop and Goth thing never going out of fashion, a ghoulish parade of recuperated rebellion.

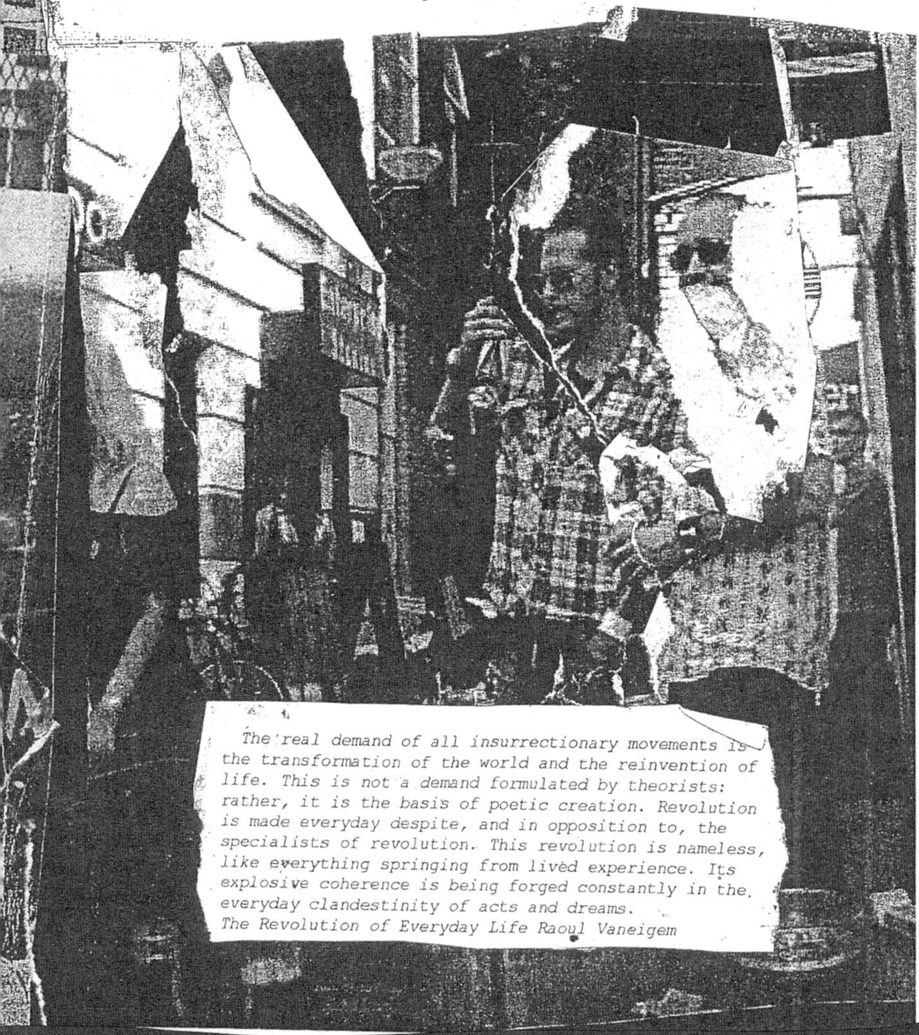

The real demand of all insurrectionary movements is the transformation of the world and the reinvention of life. This is not a demand formulated by theorists: rather, it is the basis of poetic creation. Revolution is made everyday despite, and in opposition to, the specialists of revolution. This revolution is nameless, like everything springing from lived experience. Its explosive coherence is being forged constantly in the everyday clandestinity of acts and dreams.
The Revolution of Everyday Life Raoul Vaneigem

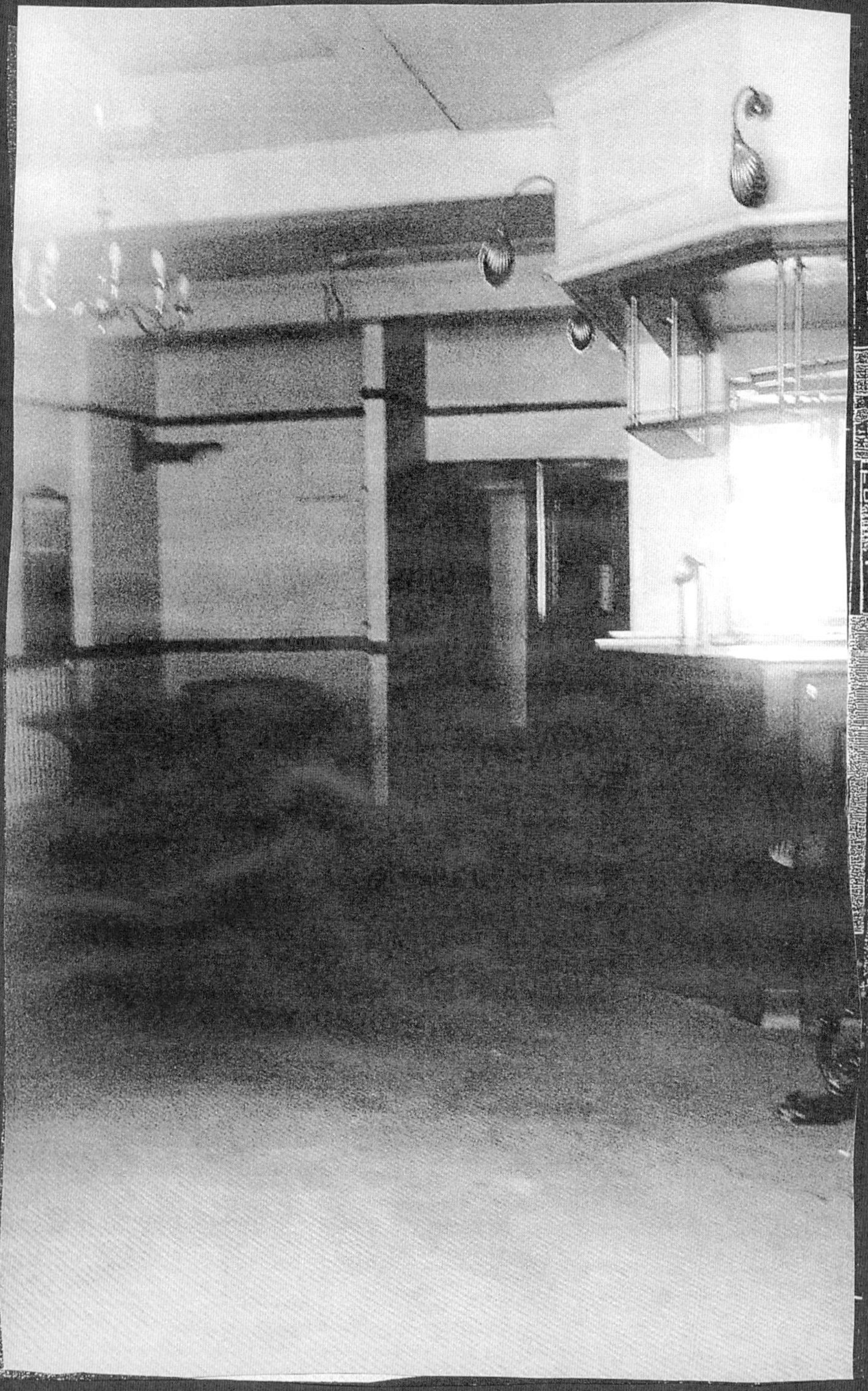

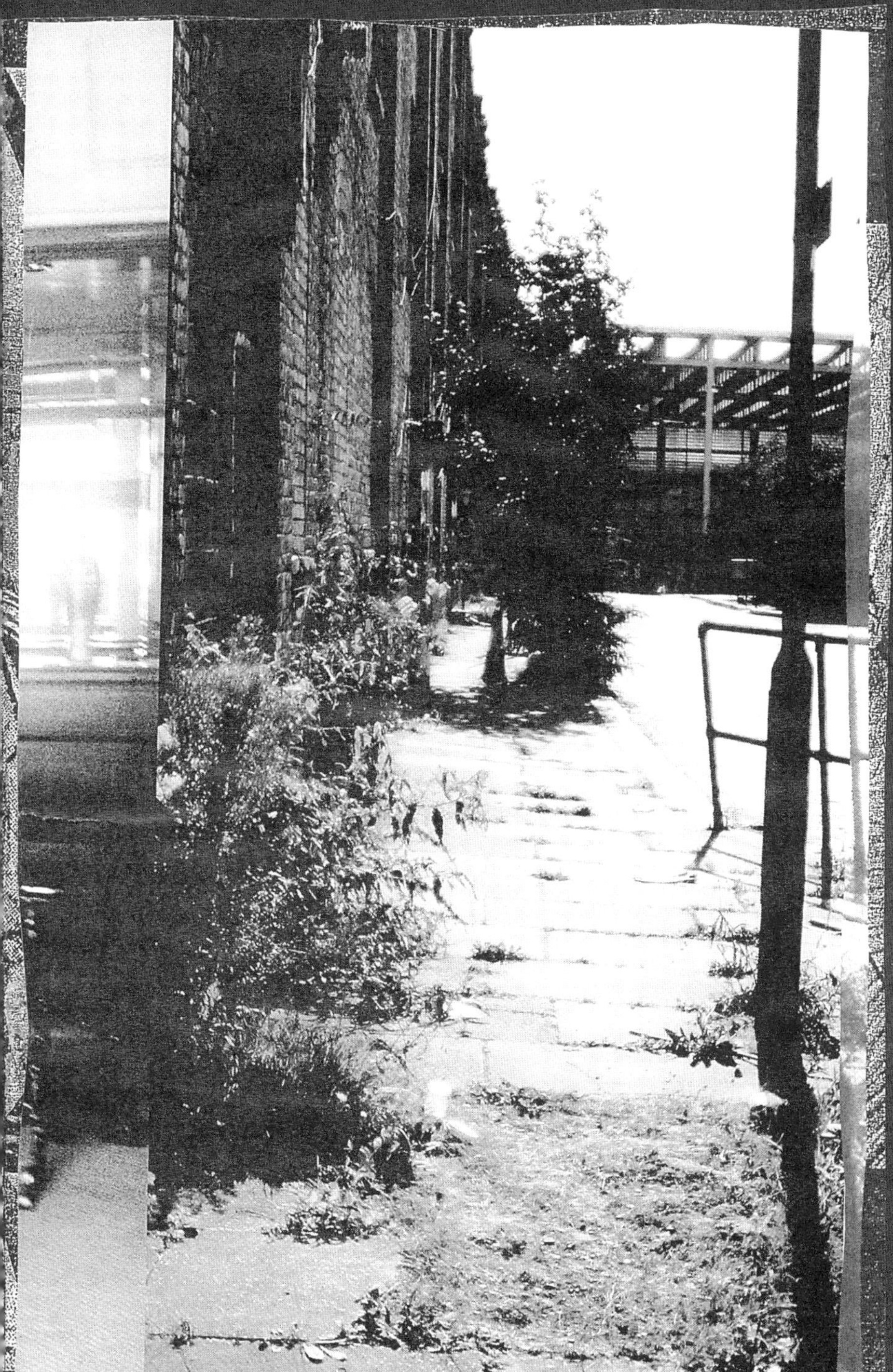

As we enter the maze of market stalls I think about Aragon and the inhabitants of the Opera quarter at the time of Haussmann. Developers were accused of corruption and robbery and groups of people were led by exasperation to dream about the return of rifles and barricades.

Camden new journal, 31st August 2006.
"£12 m Stables plan is 'the end as we know it'. …Fears the proposals will turn the market into another Bluewater shopping mall with Starbucks cafes and Top shop have terrified traders. They say they are frightened to be named in case the market's owners thrown them out- their contracts require only a week's notice for them to be evicted. One woman, whose shop will be forced to move by the scheme said: "this is going to be the end of Camden as we know it. The arches, one of the most integral parts of the buildings will be revamped. All the traders will have to leave. The Victorian horse hospital, the catacombs and the arches are all in for a facelift,..Glass frontages will be built in front of the arches."

Is it possible to hope resistance is brewing?

Camden Lock, the glasshouse 1984, there was a gig down here, Crass and Flux of pink Indians. In an attempt to destabilize their position as a formulaic sub genre of entertainment they unleashed a futurist nihilistic noise under a canopy of glitter balls and balloons.

join with the friends of kebba 'dobo' jobe who was killed last saturday - 15 may 2004 - while being arrested by police.

friends and relatives of kebba jobe and the local community are incensed both by his death when he was attacked by a plain-clothes police anti-drugs squad, and the lack of action taken by the police to find the truth about what actually happened.

"Without traffic, cities could come to life. Gigantic roundabouts in city centres could become public forums once more, planted with trees and gurgling with fountains. The br highways that slice our cities into fragments would become genuine thoroughfares, linking communities rather than dispersing them." -flyer for first Reclaim The Streets (RTS party, Camden 1995.

KENTISH TOWN

I went down there with all my crew from the squat in Dalston Lane, French punks with scowling faces and black tattoos. I remember all the skirmishes breaking loose, us taking half tabs and dabs of whizz and dancing on the asphalt. I just remember looking and thinking, I've never been here before, because the street had been utterly transformed . And I thought then about splintering and subverting , escaping constraints to disrupt the flow.

OFF LICENCE
OPEN
TILL LATE

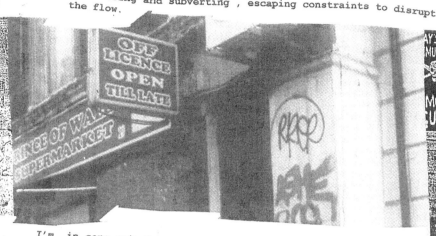

I'm in some grim R and B basement dive with mirrored ceilings and toxic looking drinks, doing some proper dirty grinding to some tune, maybe Kelis, when I turn round and it's this bloke I met last night in some dive in Hackney and he's looking sexy as I remember him and we just start kissing and its frenetic and wild and I know we've got an audience so that just makes it better. We make slip through the giddy viciousness of Camden, weaving through potholes, road works, pavement excavations and drunken hordes. I lead him to Rimbaud and Verlaine's house.

TODAY'S GATED COMMUNITIES, TOMORROW'S GULAGS.
I'm having a swift one in The Constitution casting an eye over the newly rebranded 'Star Wharf'. Laid out beneath me are the old Camden squatlands of Georgiana street, Ossleton road and Torriano Avenue.
I pause over the shocking montage of Carol street, a brutal dichotomy. Skrewdriver and Scritti Polliti.

The greasy rebranding is in its final stages, 'Star wharf',,
faux heritage, something left over for the sake of
authenticity. I suppose this is the cosmetic veneer that is
meant to distinguish it from the tabula rasa brutality of
modernist architecture or the high octane demolition tendencies
of Haussmann .

Royal college street . The Falcon . Soft musings of .
melancholy.
An empty shell waiting to be filled with vacuous 'executives.'

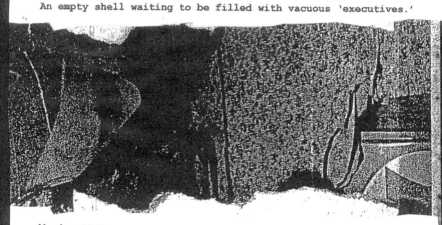

Mayday 2000 , mid bender, there was a punk gig in here and I'd
been on it three days. Suspended in delirium,, sleep
deprivation.
We'd walked from Blackstock Road after an all dayer in the
Arsenal tavern.

Tons of old bill with telephoto lenses.
. Back room
benefit gigs, meetings, conspiratorial chatter///
black walls,, red flock peeling beneath luminous posters,
Class War banners draped above bar.
Saturday afternoon,
   warm alcove of euphoria, pints of lager and whisky chasers,,
bomber jackets, hooded tops, eyes darting as old animosities
sparked amidst collisions of emerging desires.
         number

Walking,, fierce on psychoactives, mild April. Perfumed
streets,,,past the tower blocks on Tollington road,, through
the dilapidated villas of Holloway and Camden. Bold in a crew
of five,, hair erupting, flamingo pink,, bleached white, eyes
flashing
   black kohl,,
silver leather, knocking back supermarket vodka.

Seeking more episodes, more encounters before the crash.

And now it's a sanitised sweep and the Falcon's next in line to
be turned into flats, destroyed,
   all our North London boozers, The Pembury, The Samuel
Pepys, the Albion in Stoke Newington... gone.
   The screws are turned with noise complaints and licensing
problems. Everything anarchic, everything slipping off the map
has to be forced back in.

The battle is on to get us all living in some Thames gateway
dead zone, but, you know there are still a few of us left
holding out.

I squeeze through broken hardboard and break in round the
back. There's a pretty intact boozer in here and I sit on a
mildewed banquette smoking a cigarette thinking about having
this place as my own yard. I imagine it packed out with
juvenile delinquents in crombies, you can't beat that look,
Borstal dots and cherry reds. I brush masonry dust off the juke
box and let the ghostly strains of Cockney Rejects ricochet
around.

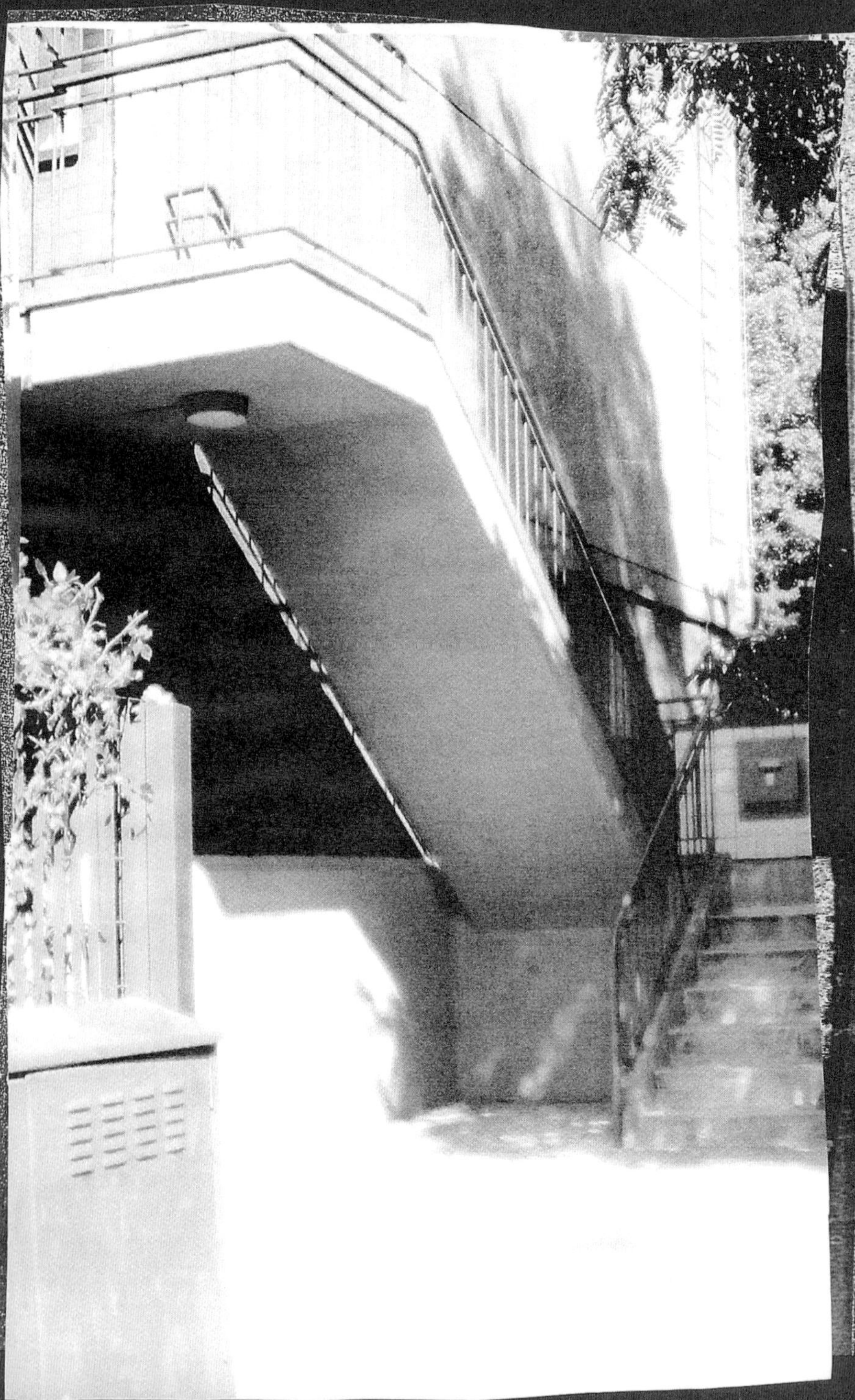

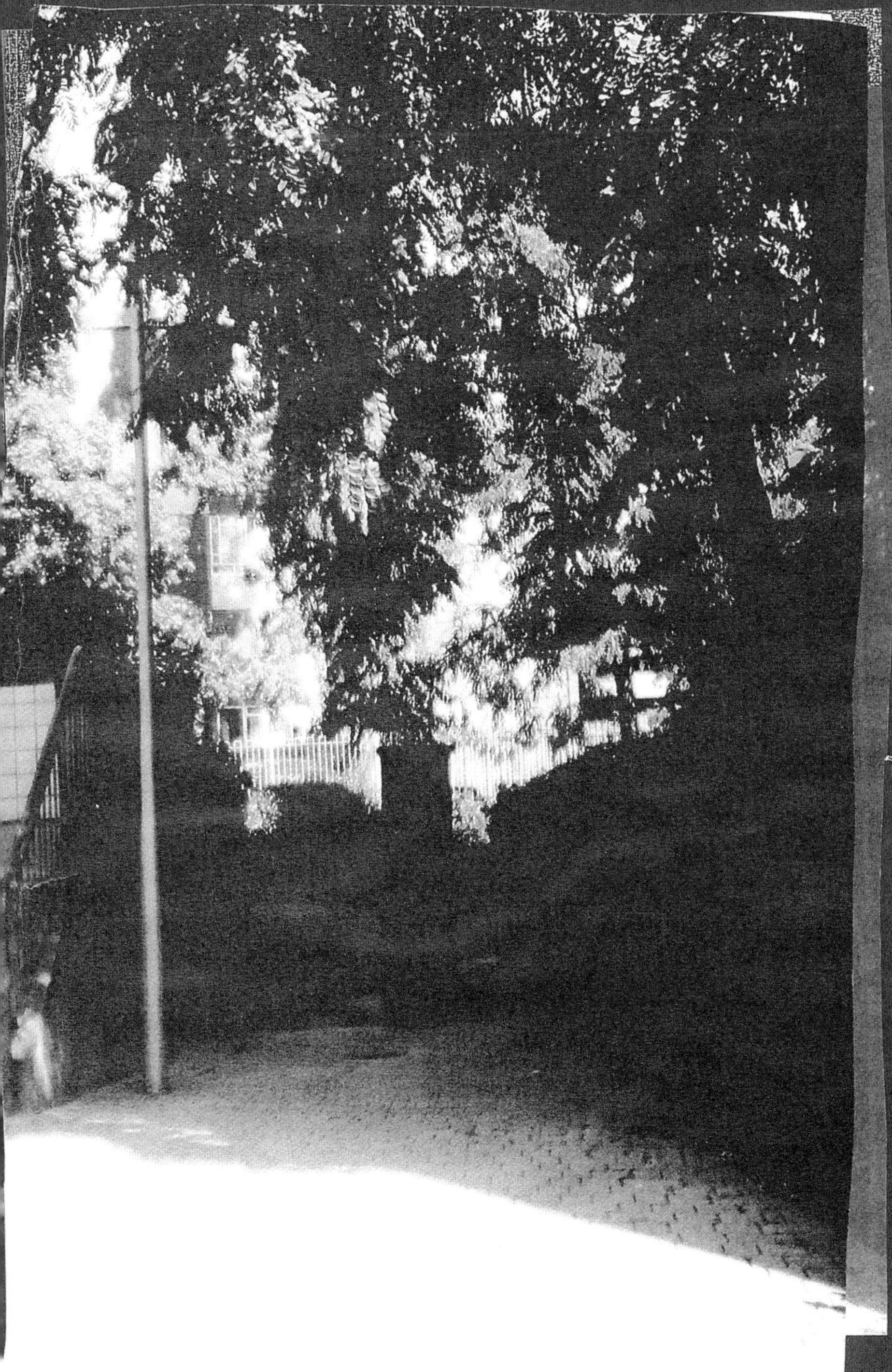

If u
Waht
2
kill me
I still
Love
u.

We trace names carved in soft red brick.

Royal college street is quiet and strangely depopulated .

THE FRENCH POETS PAUL VERLAINE AND ARTHUR RIMBAUD LIVED HERE
MAY-JULY 1873
Their rooms lurk behind a façade of peeling stucco and violent
eruptions of budleia . I discover some graffiti in the sodium
glow of the adjoining alleyway ,
W MSI. Vote Italian social movement. MSI , a fascist group
associated with the Bologna bombings of 1981 and the P2 Masonic
lodge .There's some link with the Ferndale hotel, and Roberto
Calvi, the feverish tracings of conspiracy theorists draw lines
from here to Blackfriars.

Rimbaud and Verlaine were proto flaneurs. They walked through
the shifting perspectives of the Dockyards, intoxicated by
glyphs and a heady confection of gunpowder, tobacco and rotting
wood.

We kiss on the steps, he wants me to go back to his, I want to
break in here. In the alleyway, oh dear another undoing
encounter, climb the fence.   You sure? Yeah. The greying
nets, a slight flutter, the grime and mess, a room with falling
wallpaper, faded roses, mildew and moss, he cuts his arm
getting through the window. I don't even know him, but that's
how it works, then there's a pause, but I've never known a full
stop. In my life. there's always an adjunct, a sequel, a little
bit more.

KENTISH TOWN.

'poets find the refuse of society on their street and derive
their heroic subject from this very refuse. This means that a
common type is, as it
were, superimposed upon their illustrious type. ... Ragpicker
or poet -- the refuse concerns both.'
Walter Benjamin.

Thrust out of the mossy corridors and into the turmoil of
Kentish town high street someone reaches out and beckons me
into O Reilleys bar.

 all changed now , it's not the place it was. If you stay for
long enough you can lose yourself. I lose myself in the cells
of the honeycomb ceiling. Do you love me? What you ask that
for? Idiot. No fool. Thought it was me you cried for/ only cry
for meself now, but not this time..over that , old episode,
hark back/ No more, an old episode.
And for what/

 I got new pies,
all bubblin.
 it's catching, I'm running, somebody shut her up, shut up,
mouth runs off, think idiot , don't you have enough to regret?
No nothing. Eyes to the side, oh dear, another undoing
encounter there's no point shedding tears.

Ah there's the young ones just starting out not knowing any
different, but you know the young people are stopping at home
now, it's a different place altogether,oh it's a young people's
town now.

And then he smashed the truncheon, smash like that, right into
me, right here, and then he said to me, and this is honest to
God, no word of a lie, he said this is so you can't produce no
more filthy fenian bastards. And that went on then for three
days, three whole days, two of them kicking me up and down,
using me like a football.

There's a tramp in the middle of the road with bags of junk, shouting and stopping the traffic. And an old lady mournfully talking to a dead husband with all the soil of neglect daubed across her bundled frame

The pound shop at Halloween is a garish display of luminous plastic and theatrical horror, a demented clash of plastic pumpkins, bleeding axes and glow in the dark eyeballs. *You wanna loot that? You fucking wanna loot that?*
I remember one year, probably '89, going up there and seeing market stalls full of pumpkins. You got 20p there? Or a roll up? 20p for the Captain? .
I got caught up in an encounter with a chancer in a hat. He had that New York punk look, black hair and block print Black Flag tattoos on his arm. We saw each other once on the tube and glanced at each other all the way to Highgate, he wouldn't let me go without my phone number.

Best café. I came in here once and cried. I couldn't bear music then, I couldn't bear be stirred up. And some song came on that opened it all up, all the stuff I'd been hiding, the sobbing, sleepless nights, the futility in waking. But now, with desire proliferating it's impossible to remember how that really felt.

I rub a hole in the steamed up window to scan the cylindrical tower above the Assembly rooms. They got some pretty lurid graff up there, territorial warnings to those piling down from Tufnell park, Anarchy and Kentish town! Petty tyrannies, vendettas spiralling, bastardised honour. This was once the domain of the Camden Tongs, they got the name off Hammer films about Chinese gangs, the Terror of the tongs! And the Torriano mob, fracture lines and territories, contours carved up in mass bundles.

Conflict were doing an all day gig at the Forum and we were doing a Class War stall there. It was boring so we smashed up the table and burnt all the pamphlets. The Forum used to be a Cinema it was always packed out, Bonnie and Clyde, Dirty dozen, the Mercenaries.

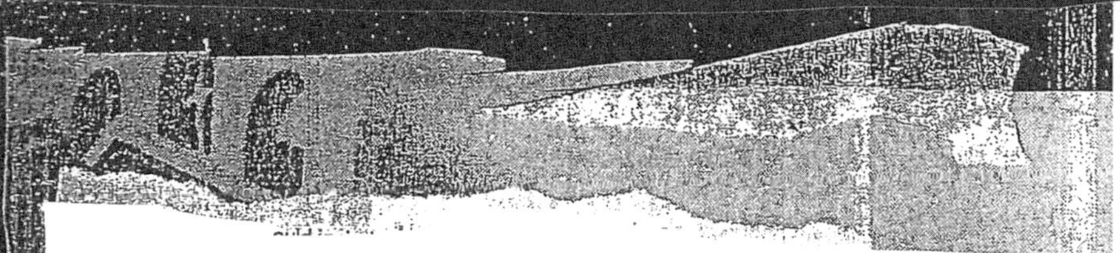

Coin laundry. Bull and gate

It unnerves me to chance upon the ghostly carapace of the Tally Ho. We used to go there at the end of 80s before gigs at the Town and Country. Now it's derelict with dead ivy and scorched hanging baskets.

Smashed windows. Velvet curtains sun bleached and faded, the uncanny announcement *Foster and kronenburg £2 a pint* in that swirly writing that's supposed to look like chalk.

Let's go for a walk then,
cajoling, persuading,
violet eyes flashing with intent.

We pass an abandoned fire tower and veer off down a cobbled alley way into a millennial cul de sac. It's like a miniatur Poundbury , model for the Thames gateway, a bland congestion

of architectural imbecility. Bellina Mews. *You know all you want to do is wreck it, graff it, fuck it over.* They're all crushed in there oblivious.
It used to be a squatted factory before the shove up to Gr banks.

There was a party above the Co-op, 2004,a load of punks from Bologna had abseiled down to get in. The place was a filthy cavern , I just remember a lot of slack jawed lolling and erratic clatters of activity when some crew rolled up with a knackered soundsystem and wraps of k.

A swift side step into Fortess grove leads to little pastel streets heavy with the scent of pink roses, campanula and yellow snap dragons.

On a Sunday night they have the music. Leighton road, you know that boozer, they have the dancing in there. The landlord is fucked, no lads, I've fuckin told you, face bloated, red eyes googling round the side of his head. Then his son comes and kisses me and we all pile in.
Tiocfaidh ár lá
Come on then! The repeats the repeats, still it all comes back, all the tumbling and cascading in one long sweep, seen it before, dragged there, squeezed there, taken the rap and beat up proper.

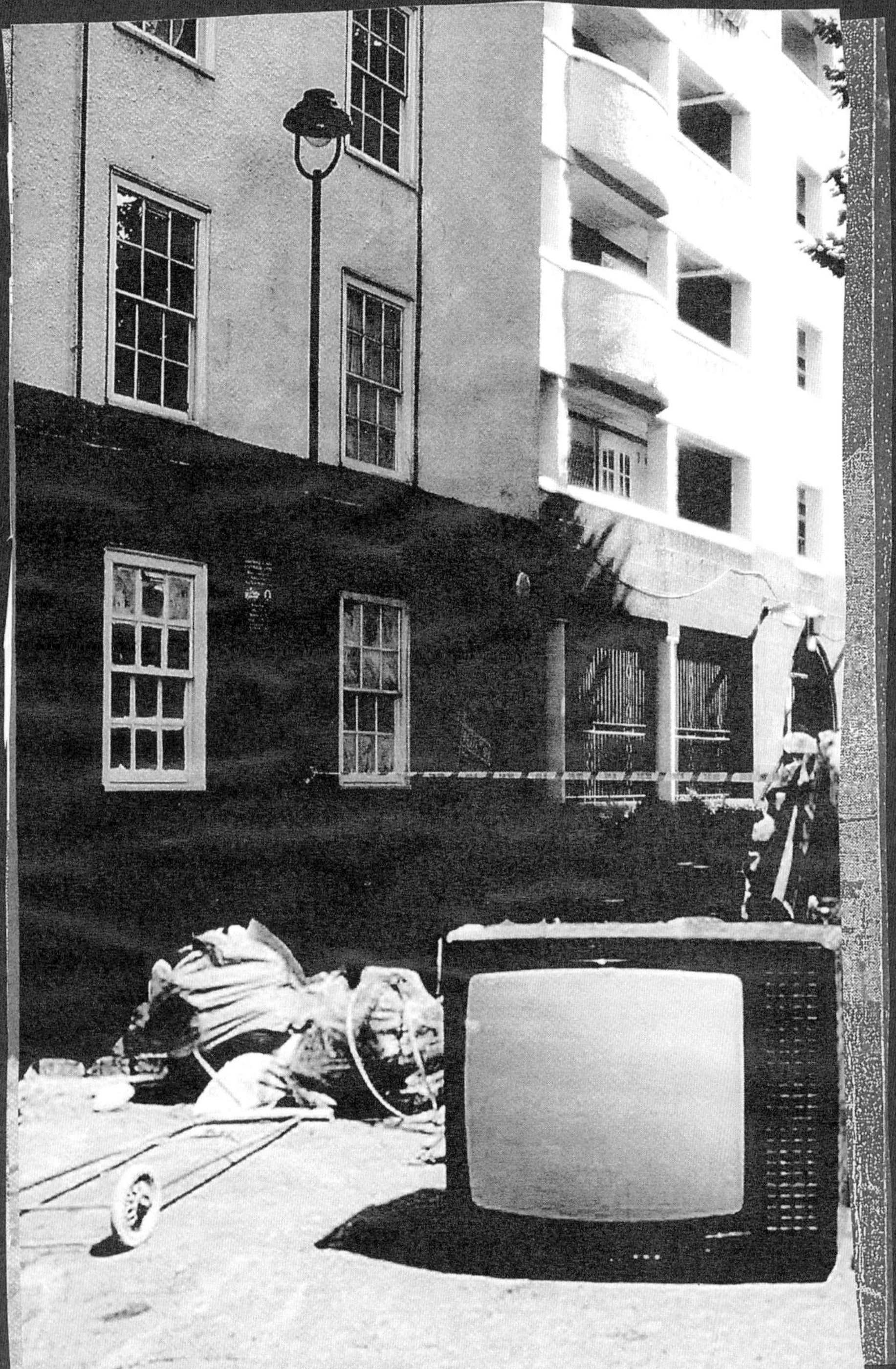

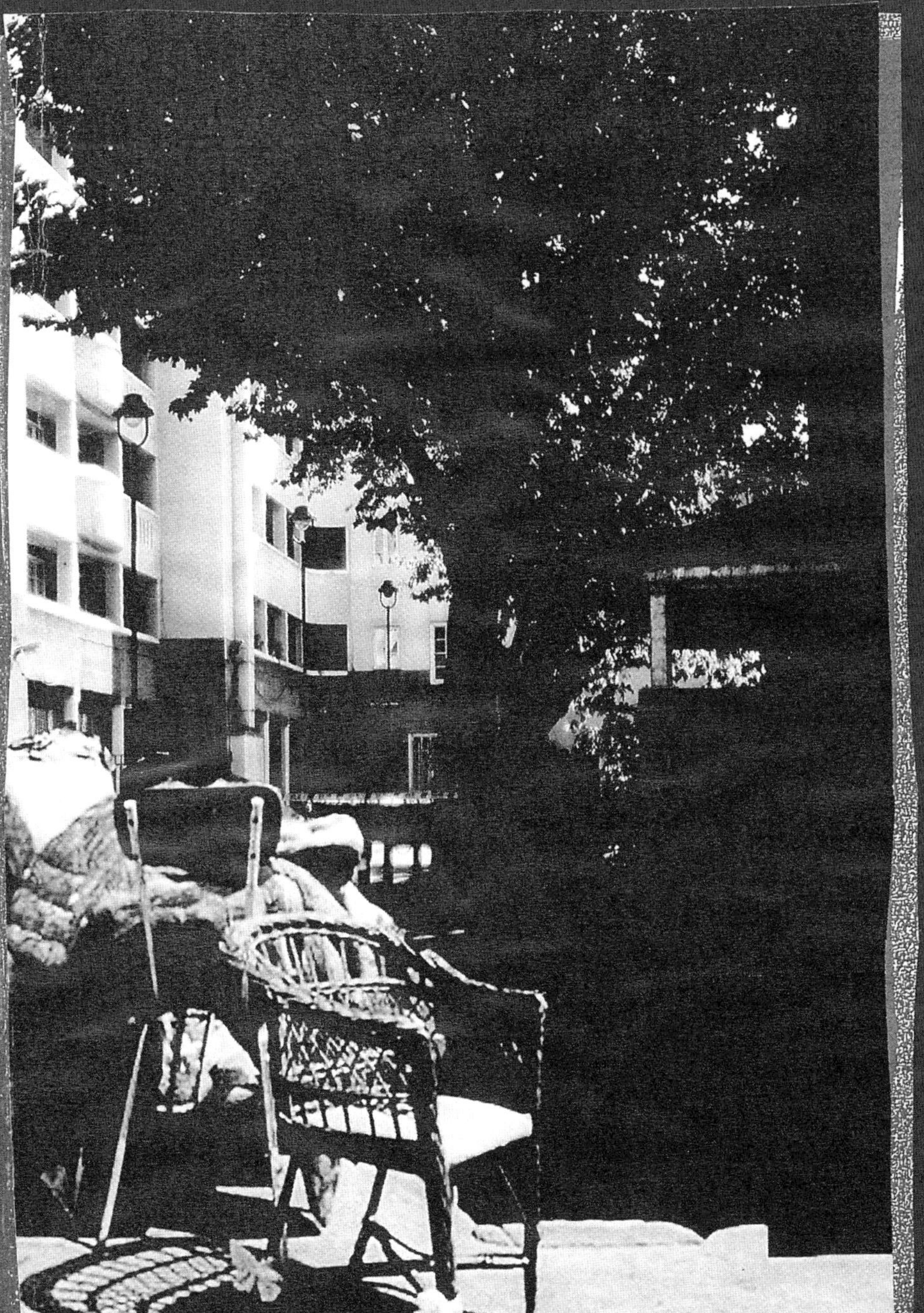

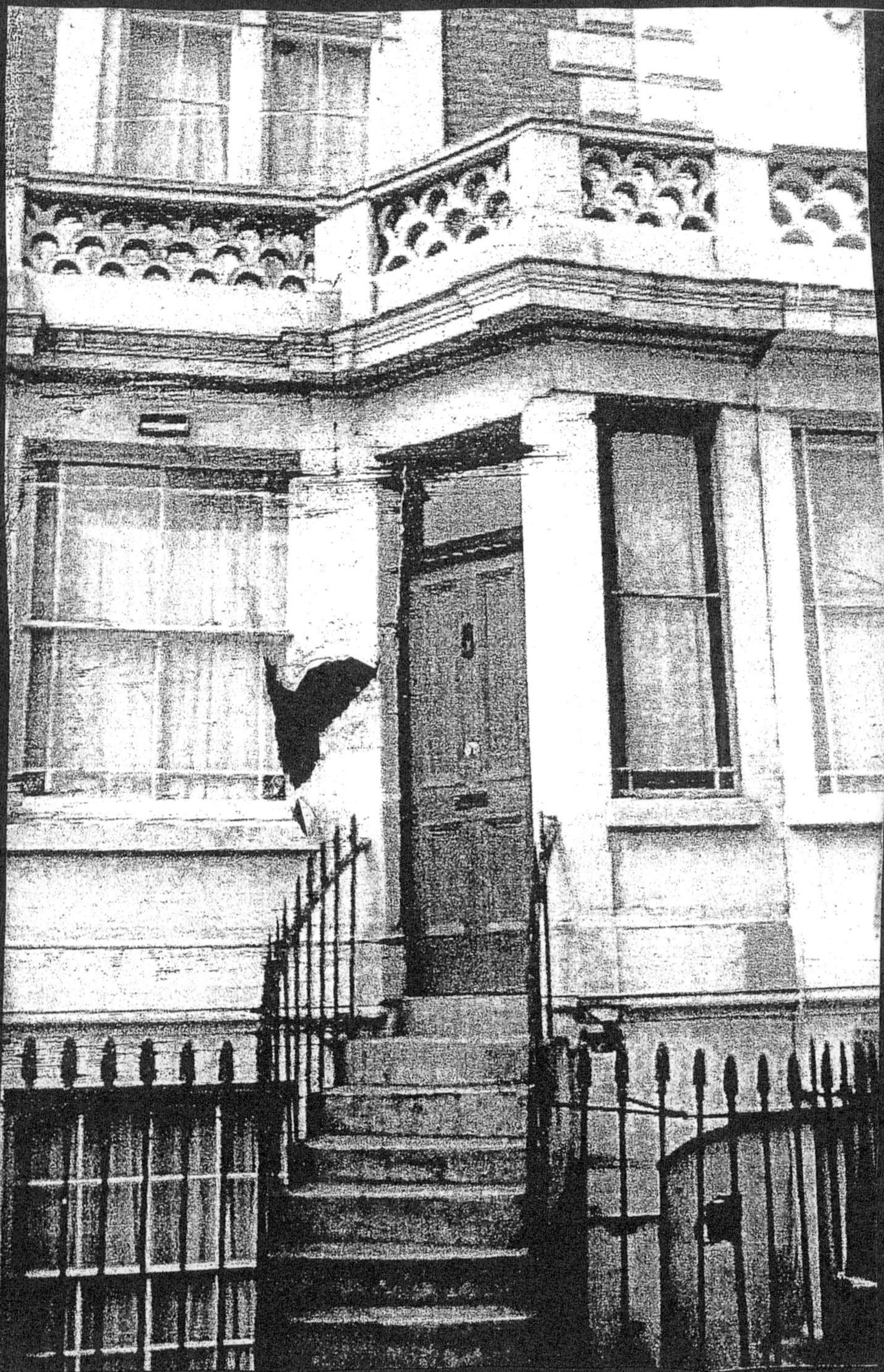

The touching and flirtation on Farringdon road, cascading images, erotically charged;
an abundance of heightened moments, ruptures in normality. Old bill, fucking move it.
Turkish caf, armful of eye amulets. Swerve out the back. NF pickets , mass evictions, old bill in riot gear , brawls erupting and cascading onto the street….

The paths of The Fleet converge under Quinns. We stop for a Jamesons, a welcome withdrawal from the street to the dislocated realms of afternoon boozing and Setanta sports. I descend into the underground maze of distorted mirrors, a 60s dream of a Ladies, you do your hair and see an infinite parade of reflections.

A woman in a black headscarf sits on a step near the Oxfam and shouts.

St. Pancras and Somers Town.
We slip through the churchyard railings and lie in the shadow of the Soane tomb. The imaginary vistas of Piranesi's carceri stretch as far as Lincolns Inn and the bank of England .I dream of mob violence at the Bank, the exhilarating rush to the eye of the riot.

That's how you want it?
Is it? Is it?
Really is that how you want it?
Tell me now before I can't stop myself.

A cluster of headstones radiate form the buckled trunk of a sturdy ash. This is the shadow side, the coroners court, the morgue. Reeling through the Tropical hospital and the tenement arches, there's a pin eyed scramble to get to those windows where plastic sheets slap and clatter . We push through walls scale chimney stacks and tear through the roof to an abandoned attic room.

A frenzied encounter of bruising and blinding.

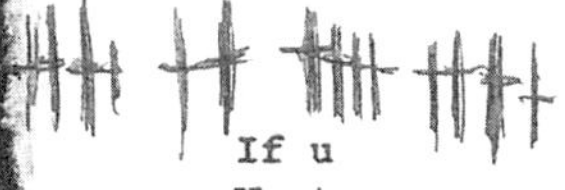

If u
Want
2
kill me
I still
Love
u.

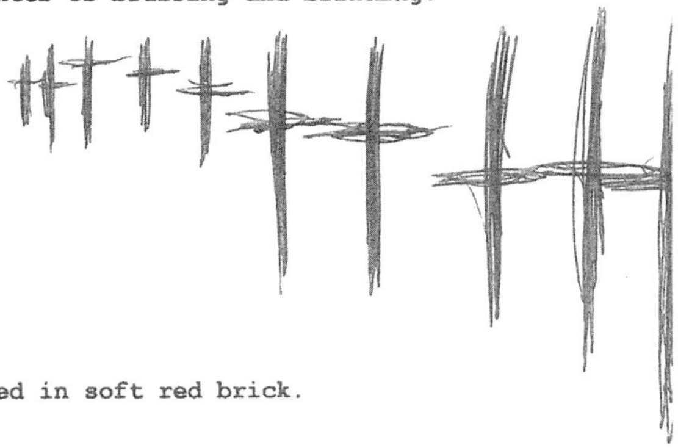

Trace names carved in soft red brick.

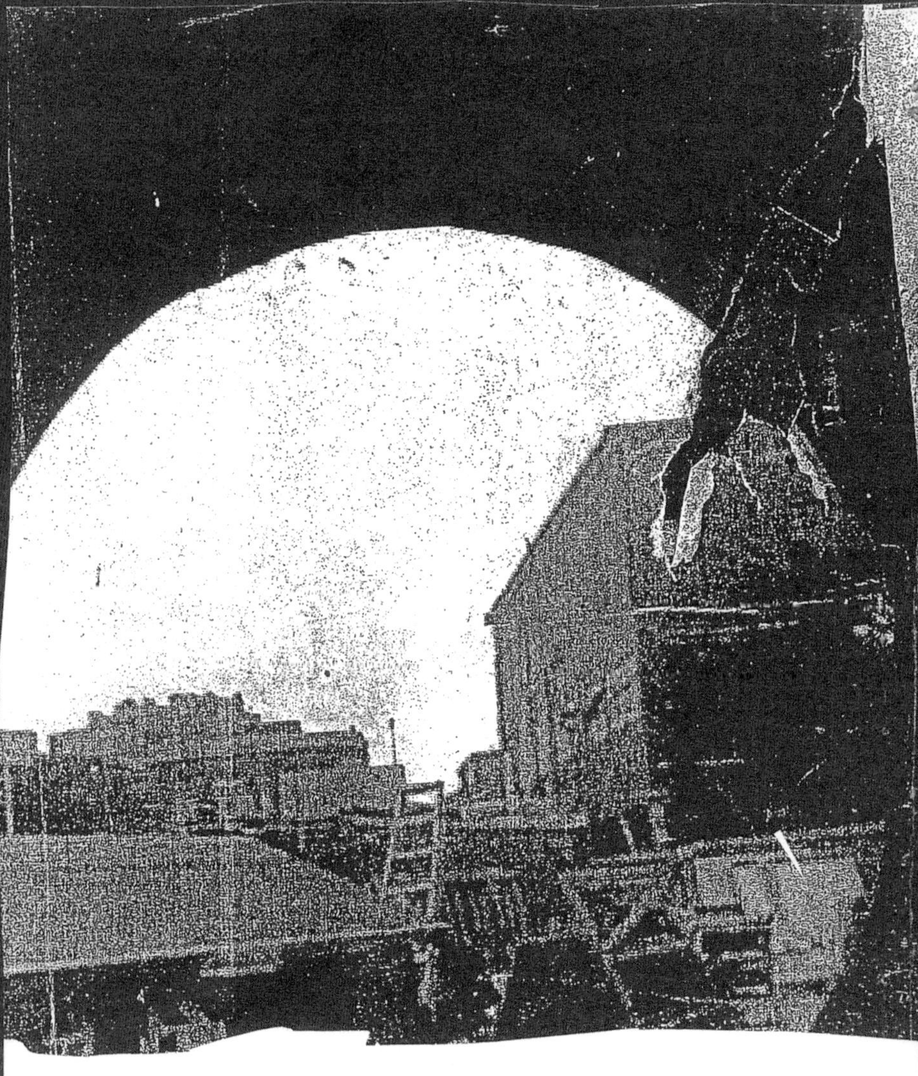

I'm picking through the relics of an abandoned London conjuring up The Polygon and the Brill.
These dusty shadowscapes are the product of bomb damage and slum clearances.
I drift through three towerblocks.

The Cock tavern.

HANDS interlocking on top of head and turn around!! is there anything in this room we should know about?IS THERE ANYTHING THIS ROOM WE SHOULD KNOW ABOUT? .

The Cock tavern is an Irish boozer. They used to have RTS
meetings there.
  In the back room..Meetings sprawled for miles in search of
consensus… 90s squat rave aesthetic, dreadlocks, day glo
spirals and tele tubby clothes .
  Then the flash up memory of 9/11. This was where we headed
after the Arms Fair in Docklands to watch events unfold on a
big screen TV.

If our future has been stolen now is the time to look back with
vengeful intent.

I'm living in a squat in Grays inn road, my room's a mess,
  orange and brown and cream,
  70s wallpaper, torn turqoise curtains , red lampshade. Stale
smoke, dust. I'm getting done up for a night in Merlins Cave.

  Marker pen graffiti, UK subs and Sham 69, a view of tenements
out the back. It is 1980, one face staring at Europe , the
other to America. I yearn for the abandoned dockyards.

1797 . St Pancras Church and Battle Bridge flooded by River
Fleet. 1818 it happened again, shocking resurgance. That which
"ought to have remained secret and hidden but has come to
light" (Freud 1955: 225).

"Sacrificial slaughter: head thrown back, mouth twisted
with pain/joissance at the body's pinnacle." Hollier

Uncanny rupturing.

St Pancras hotel, survived the sweep of the 60s, now it will
stand as a glowing example of Victorian gothic architecture to
add heritage to the Eurostar terminal development.

KINGS CROSS. Once the area was known *as* Battle bridge. .
Boudicea fighting the Romans, London burns.

*"The labyrinth is basically the space where oppositions
disintegrate and grow complicated, where diacritical couples
are unbalanced and perverted etc., where the system upon which
linguistic function is based disintergrates, but somehow
disintegrates by itself, having jammed it's own works.The
labyrinth we discuss cannot be described. Mapping is out of the
question."* Against Architecture The writings of Georges
Bataille, Denis Hollier.

The masterplan should include:
> Proposals for the retained heritage buildings and fabric,
showing
how their restoration, adaptation, and reuse protects, and
where
appropriate, enhances them and their setting, and preserves or
enhances the character or appearance of the conservation areas,

Kings Cross is in a state of confusion, it is in gripped in the foolish tyranny of the masterplan. The telescopic gasholders of Agar Town have been realigned. One has been allowed to stand as a token of heritage while the others have been dismantled and left lying in Hemel Hempstead.

Old bill come over, what do these cunts want?

The Culross buildings were built for railway workers. It became an autonomous zone, a self contained area, no one mixed outside block, all piled down the same boozer. Surrounded by heavy industry and transport infrastructure it became an island community, intimidating to the outsider.

There's some red stencil graffiti on the pock marked wall, *the song is over but the melody lingers on..*

Clarence passage is a strange juxtaposition of old tenements with the gleaming new architecture of an international airport.

All places become surfaces that can accept the neo liberal stamp.
Representations of places are decontextualized. These are placeless places. Little alleyways boarded up, windows opening on tenement ravines.
Costain portakabin slabs,
    damp construction,
        Stalinist penitentiaries

Security guards sit watching. Bored. No longer able to see.

4 am. Construction workers loom like day glo apparitions. Portakabins emerge as illuminated citadels. A maze of Perspex and plywood tunnels afford glimpses of skips, cones, barriers and the ad hoc, rambling constructions of Lebbeus Woods. Yard after yard of detritus, sentry boxes lit up with strings of lights.
A circus world of flux and transition.
Impermanence.
Warrens hastily rigged.

I remember that night in the Great Northern hotel, prowling the corridors like the kid in The Shining, me and some New York punk opening up doors. We used to chase around London wrecking and burning, smashing stuff up.

These are the enchanted places that slip out of sight, re emerge and reconfigure somewhere else. There are numerous portals, fluctuating and reversible like a Baroque ceiling, lenses opening onto other realms. These settlements and reconfigurations of forms become nomadic subjectivities, taking off on lines of flight, denying classification and fixity.

And then it starts, just slowly, little tentative suggestion at first. I can't help stealing little glances over, I catch him looking back with a smile on his face. I yearn for the abandoned shopping complex, Owen luder, the Tricorn centre, glorious, resplendent in it's dereliction. The labyrinthine corridors, the lost chambers, the walkways and roundels. A place to hide, to seek out exchanges.

An observation tower looms over the rush hour havoc, The Kings Cross lighthouse, the old bill use it for covert ops. Billion dollar brain. Harry Palmer. The stuffed Bentham in the case at UCL. York Way where some semblance of sleaze still clings to the fraying edges.
The Scala, we used to go there in the late 80s for Schwarzeneggar treble bills. Blade Runner. Post apocalyptic nightmares accelerating the come down. Kings Cross is symbolic, it was the archway that I stole through to get to the promised land only to be hurled into a maelstrom of chicken bones and congealed blood.

We take a swift turn into Birkenhead street,a decrepit string of DSS hostels and halfway houses. The Violet hotel, number 55, and the flats on the corner where binliner curtains slap and rattle.
I want a jar in McGlynns, that hidden Irish boozer on corner. You can trawl the hostile ravine of the Euston road, but to find the gems you have to deviate from the path. There's a roaring crew of miscreants sitting outside.

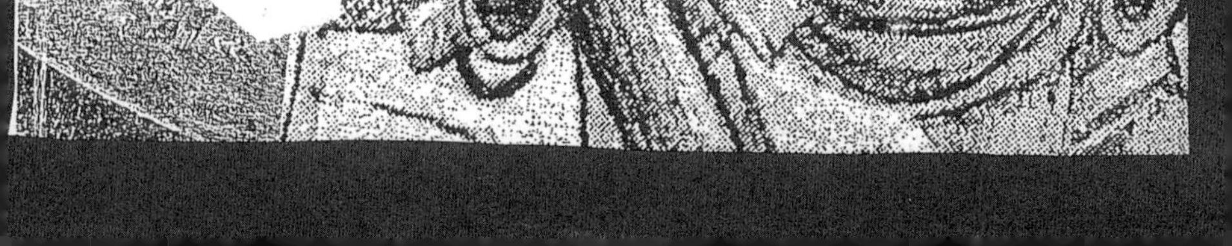

You meet me in that Italian caff on Pentonville rd, massive
rubber plants, a psychotropic nightmare. The assembling of the
crew, funny as fuck, deviants of all stripes. October, sharp
air, copper blue skies. Get some breakfast down in preparation
for the session. Follow the path of the fleet, Brittania road.

21-22 Argyle square . 1981. The Ferndale Hotel was run by the
NF, Bologna bombing suspects were harboured there, links to P2
and Gladio. Ian Stuart lived there permanently from 1981..
Strength through oi!
A desolate Union Jack hangs in an upstairs window.

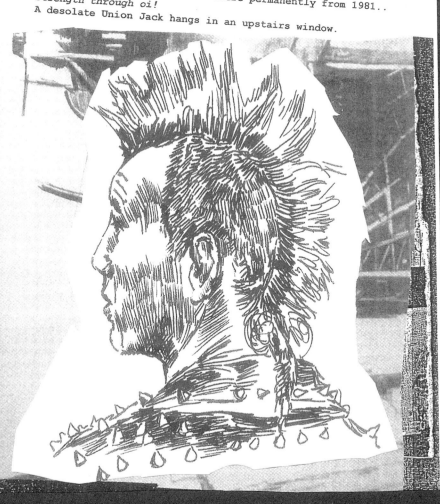

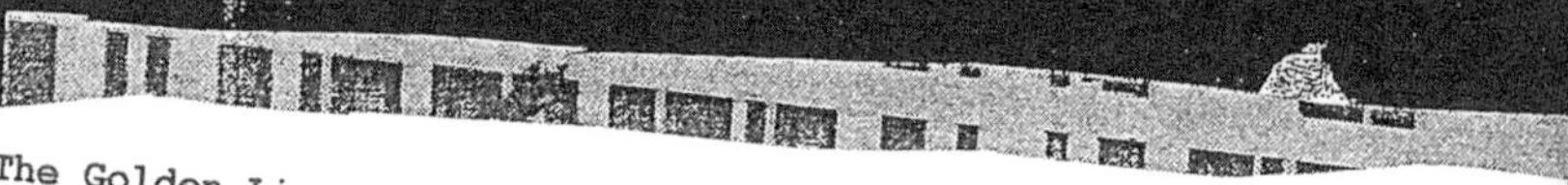

The Golden Lion on Brittania st, 90s pub done up, horrible,
fuck this. We're done up for a bit of the old ultra, a Bakunist
wrecking spree on every gastro pub travesty we can get our
hands on. Flick knife activates at sight of swaggering prick
whose class background assures him of lording it status,
dirty jeans and scruffy t shirt only serve to reinforce it.
Laminated flooring, best brawled over Ikea settees .
All I want to see right, is the Clinique counter at Selfridges
smashed up with Paul McCarthy abjection, Robert Gober
mannequins trashed in a Ballardian make up counter frenzy.
Sean, have it, have it go on.
Don't know what he's doing, head splitting with the hysterical
banalities of Saturday night tv.

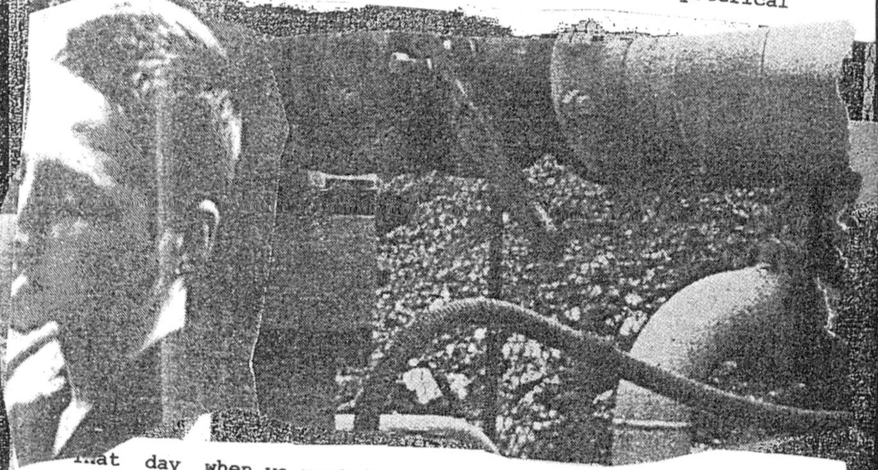

That day when we went in search of the Groaner, we had to
scour The Boot. We scanned the orange paintwork, bottle green
tiles and Guiness trinkets. It was a Saturday afternoon booze
up, brawls erupting, hilarity and shouting, but the Groaner
wasn't there.

Dickens, Barnaby Rudge, rioters' headquarters is The Boot,
also HQ of local mob in Gordon Riots.
I saw a Scottish girl outside who I hadn't seen for five years,
she said her Aunty had just been murdered on Clapham Common.
You wouldn't see it on the news she said, she was a working
girl , no one cared.

In the 1960s London regularly exploded in vortices of mass
brawls, eruptions of elegant Clockwork Orange choreography. The
Cromer street mob could muster 100 to a 150 for a big ruck,
spilling on the streets with bike chains and razors.

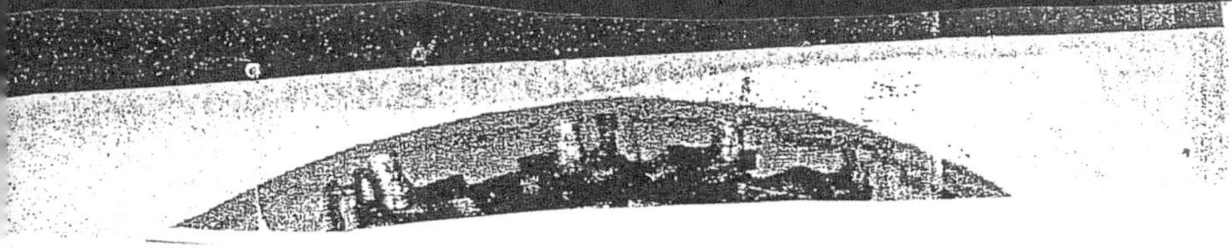

There's a Euro feel down here, could be the coffee smell and continental looking blocks over the road, looks like Berlin,

Kreuzberg maybe. Used to be a white area, a few Maltese and Italians, most of the pimps were Maltese.

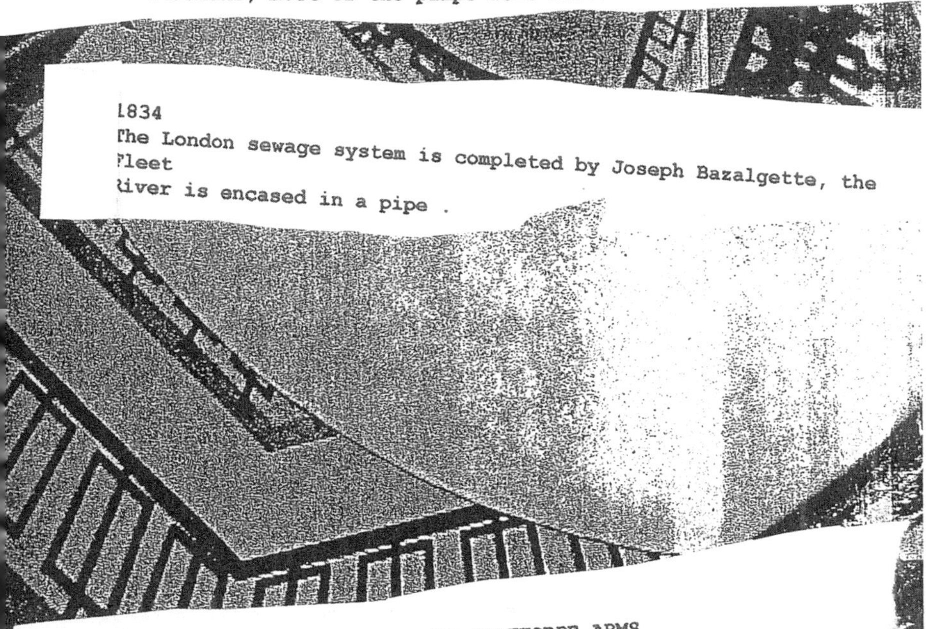

1834
The London sewage system is completed by Joseph Bazalgette, the Fleet
River is encased in a pipe .

COLDBATH, MOUNT PLEASANT AND THE CALTHORPE ARMS

The Calthorpe Arms. The afternoon drinkers are all men, I recognize one of them from the Justice for Harry Stanley campaign. In 1833 there was a riot outside here, The National Union of the Working Classes rally was attacked by the New Police. There was a massive battle between the 'Blue lobsters' and the 'London Mob' and one old bill was killed. There's a plaque on the wall commemorating the jurors who let the rioters off.

LUNCHTIME drinkers at a backstreet pub in North London were suprised to find themselves being photographed at the weekend by police using telephoto lenses.
An upstairs room at the Calthorpe Arms in King's Cross had supposedly been booked by ringleaders of a May Day protest to finalise arrangements for paralysing the capital. TUESDAY APRIL 17 2001 the Times.

As we prowl under the viaducts and bridges, in and out of secret boozers, the Fleet asserts itself. The Acton studios squat, HARMONY QUALITY SAUNA and Travelodge slide softly into the valley.

Farringdon road. Amwell st. Percy Circus,

Lenin 1870-1924
Founder of USSR stayed in 1905 at Percy circus which stood on this site.

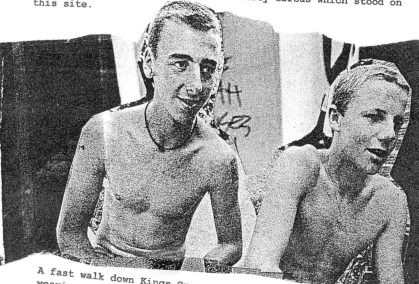

A fast walk down Kings Cross road, freedom of the streets, weaving through commuters, get to the station at exactly five past 6. S is there waiting for me at platform 2 smoking a cigarette. It's a really warm evening, wild and bold. We want a drink. There's madness going off in the Courtyard, Christine and her friend on the steps, some of the K'd up lads out as well and some black geezer I'd never before asking for cigarettes. Fuckin tons of old bill, don't know what's happening but they're jumpy as fuck and start pullin people in. I'm out of there quick when the sirens start going and all these orange lights start flashing over the barriers.

In Great Percy street there are melting steps and cars smashed up in the middle of the road, the aftermath of a Bakunist wrecking spree. We scale the tilting perspectives of the staircase in Lubetkin's BEVIN COURT where a memorial statue to Lenin once stood. It was repeatedly smashed by fascist gangs exploding the myth of blitz,, the idea that everyone pulled together against a common enemy.

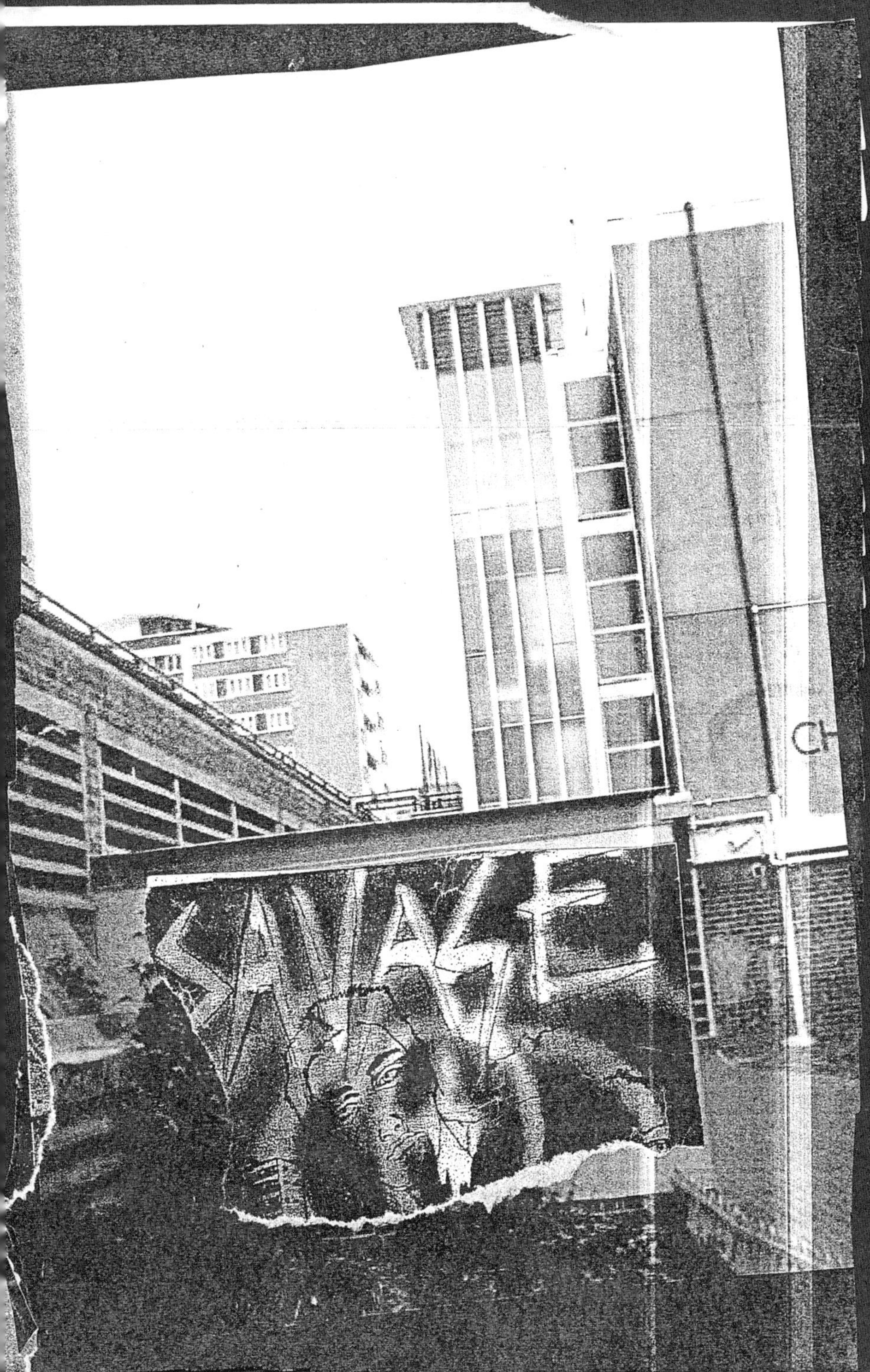

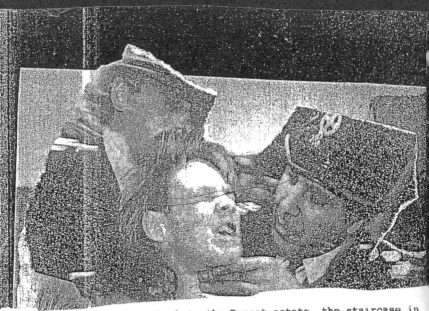

I get another flashback to the Dorset estate, the staircase in George Loveless house is the same. The BNP have meetings in the pub above the library

S disappears behind a Greek Orthodox church plastered with 70s graffiti, CYPS OUT! and the BM hot cross bun. She has been drawing on the wall, looks like little marker pen droogs engaged in some kind of production line scene, I write SAVAGE MESSIAH over the top.
We carve a path through walkways, hidden staircases and tower block landings.

I know the potency of desire, the cataclysmic power, how everything can come hurtling off it's axis, everything risked to satisfy the craving. Desire like that is always seething under the surface threatening to take over.
 He leans over me.
Say now if you want this to stop,
 you've got more to lose than me.

It's been one of those seamless days , episodic, epic almost, hundreds of adventures, a massive cast, no surprise in turning a corner and facing another lost acquaintance. It was almost as if the city broke free of its alienation, we all knew each other.

I'm assailed by the raucous strains of punk rock as I'm shoved into the seedy red glow of the Merlins cave. It's a tableaux of mirrored alcoves, tiled walls, distorted acoustics and Goths on cheap speed. I'm sent reeling onto the dancefloor by a load of crew off the estate .Drinking fizzy piss, dancing on little diamonds of broken glass, I get pulled back to the velvet banquettes by some Scottish psychopath who promises that if I come home with him I'll get a proper beating, " I can see you're the kind of girl who would really like that, I wouldnae mark you up mind."

I'm fractured with anxiety as I drift down Amwell street. I'm wondering whether to stop for a swift one in Filithy Mc nastys when I see my mate Tony outside. We were both wasted the night before in the Victory demanding that they turn the jukebox up full blast so we could dance to Chaka Kahn.

Fleet Prison 13th June 1381
Burned by peasants and London rebels.

Clerkenwell

 Green eyeshadow , red lipstick , enveloped in the hi nrg exaltations of Bronski Beat, I'm in a good mood, wanting the mayhem, willing it to happen. Strutting down Clerkenwell in emerald stilettos, desire swarming right on the surface, it's giving me a rush just being on the street.

We're massing outside the Three kings and it's getting a bit tense. I feel weird on arrival but after a couple of jars I'm ok. Then I'm glancing around haphazardly and he's there. Shock jolts of electricity surge through me.
We're observing the gangs of Kurdish communists and SWP hacks. I'm dreaming of the teeming multitudes, the black flags and the proper kicking up, hordes of brutal skinheads booting fuck out of banks and rich bastards. I go to the garage for cigarettes and get followed by two old bill.

Then it's cinematic as we drift from one enchanted interior to another through a labyrinth of narrow streets and sloping valleys. We wander through the shifting topographies of Lovecraft and Escher , the old rookeries of Saffron hill.

SMITHFIELD

Trace names carved in soft red brick.
The city harbours repressed desires and fears.

Smithfield, site of animal slaughter and religious killings,
has always been known for its rowdiness and rioting. Bataille
talks about an economy not of conservation but of waste and
expenditure.
These are the counter narratives of the city, the Rabelaisian
splurging, drug taking, blowing all your wages in one night.

Smithfield was a site created specifically for the ritual of
sacrifice. When Smithfield is sanitised the destruction happens
everywhere, all the time, a boundless, limitless wrecking
spree. The sacrificial site was intended to contain it, losing
a part to keep the whole.

Smithfield .6 a.m, The first shimmering moments of a July day;

post clubbing delirium , The Hope, Cowcross street.
Licensing laws are turned on their head. Pub opens 5.30 a.m.
There's a scramble for more drugs as pint pots smash and high
voltage shrieks ring out across the meat market.

Bloodstains leach into concrete slopes.
A concealed staircase leads to the subterranean Cock

The Old Market,   had two pur
dusty assemblage with eruptions of tenacious ferns. Crumblin
red brick turrets,,, Gaffer tape Anarchy signs still visible i
the upper portholes. He kisses me with unusual tenderness,,
black hair, royal blue eyes, violence never far from the
surface.

need for

The city
The Fleet river used to run red from here, a pestilential
stream, the canal and Holborn viaduct were built to sanitise
it. You could call this a form of denial, the blood and filth
hidden beneath the surface, the poor dispersed and hidden from
view.

and fears.

blow

Blood flows everywhere, riots erupt everywhere,
the endless performance of a ritual without consciousness.
Alright darlin, sexy, you comin for a drink with me?

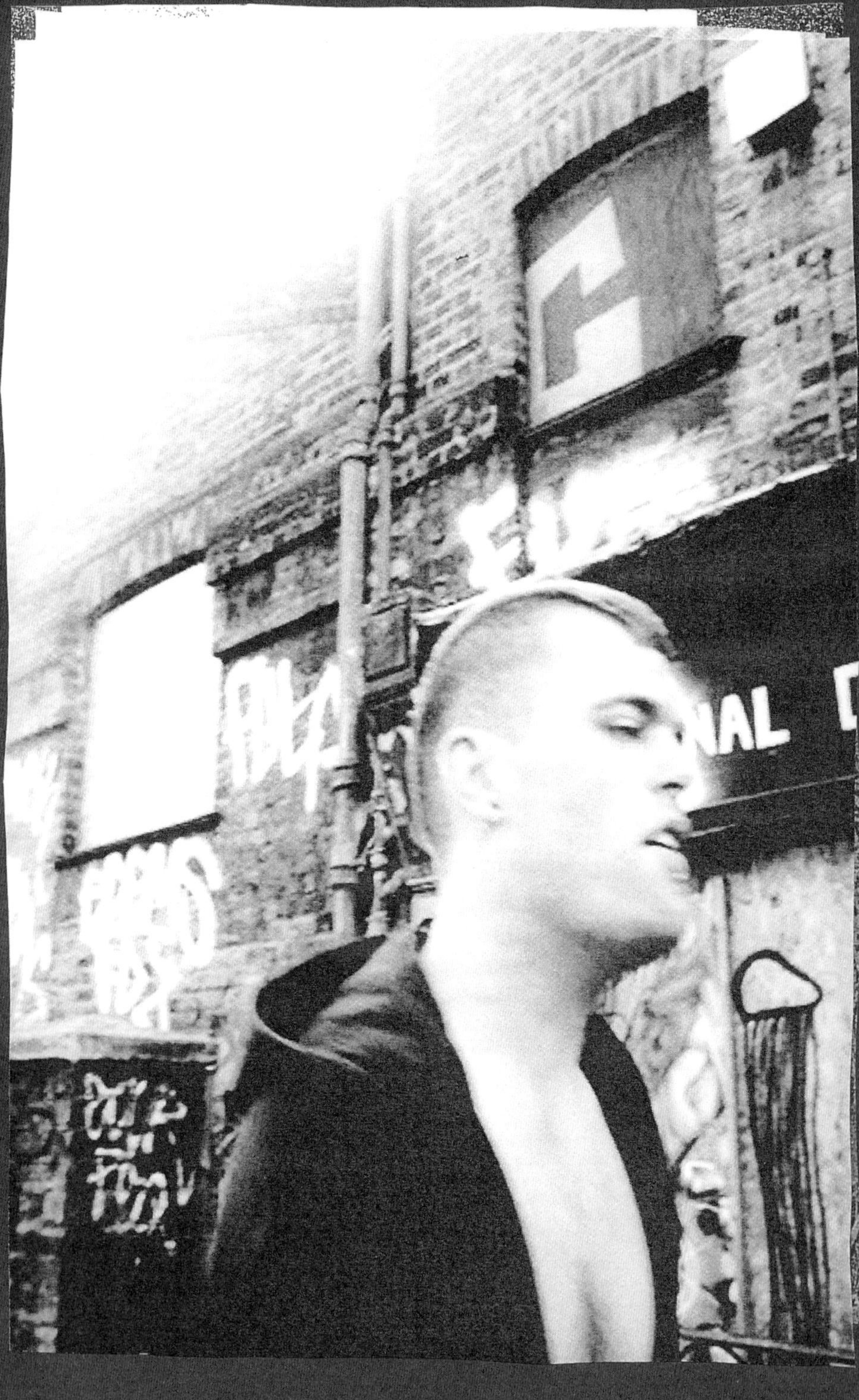

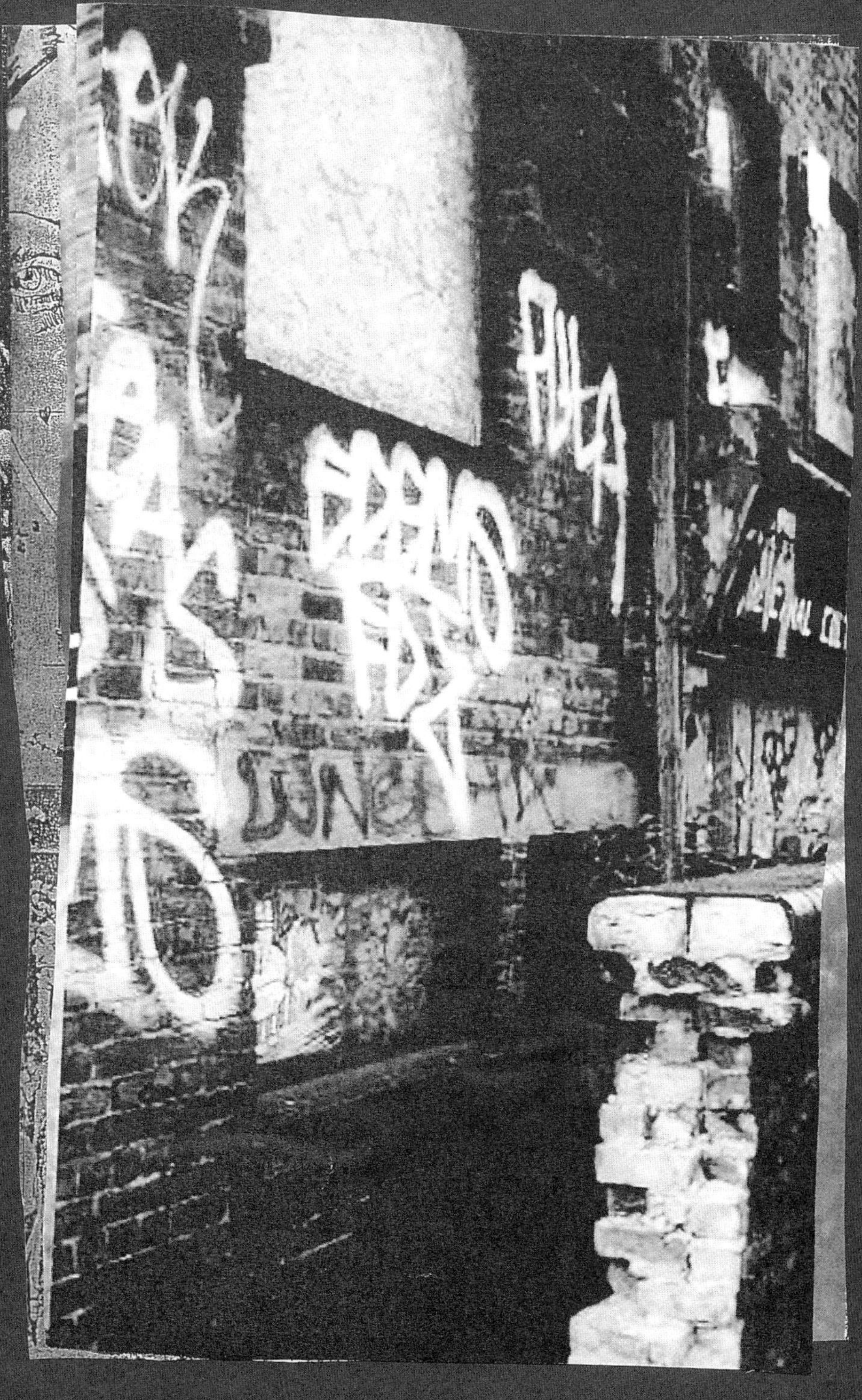

HOLBORN BLACKFR

OKFRIAF

A slow shifting down the sloping banks of the Fleet , a deviation through the staircases of Holborn viaduct. I'm struggling with the weight of the codeine, it would be alright if I could just lie down. Each touch feels like thousand particles of pleasure skimming across my skin. He tries to pull me to my feet but I just slump back, so happy, no strength to stand, falling into him, a smile I can't help smeared across my face. People work so hard, striving in the pursuit of happiness, what's the fucking point.

The viaduct was built in the 1860s, the rookery was destroyed and thousands evicted. Slums were considered a threat, dangerous hives of insurrectionary impulse . The destruction of the rookeries did not erase the poor but dispersed them. Thousands of little rookeries cropped up all over in unexpected places. The attempt to eradicate leads to an uncanny rupturing. The accursed share, nothing divided neatly but always a remainder, something that can't be erased. Once you lose the sacrificial altar the whole world becomes an altar...

Rivulets of burning gin.
1780 Langdales gin distillery burnt out.
Rivers of raw gin flowed, hordes wriggled face down to suck it up. Drunkenness, debauchery and death throes. Sly diversions

on the stairwell. Can you keep a secret?
I saw his tactics, they were good, but transparent . Sometimes its best to let things flow, chance meetings, small coincidences all adding up to a cinematic unfolding.

I guide us through narrow gaps in walls .We smash through masonry, Gordon Matta Clarke becomes Israeli Defence Force.

The Blackfriars pub is a maze of alcoves, a haven for crazed conspiracy theorists. The murder of Roberto Calvi (Gods banker) was a case of real state conspiracy shifting into imagined conspiracies. The hanging of Calvi under the bridge was linked to P2, Gladio and the MSI. He leans back off the bar stool and grabs my waist, digging his thumbs hard into my pelvis, I kiss him on the cheek and he tilts his head back for proper kiss.

The hushed chatter reverberates along the valley of the fleet. We find them huddled in a snug with a pack of tarot cards 'The hanged Man. Ideally, he is a willing sacrifice, though life sometimes demands sacrifices of the unwilling. The Hanged Man is the initiate into mysteries. He understands the truth because he sees it from a different angle. The most common interpretation of the card is of an outcast of society that appears to be a fool but is actually in complete alignment.
The Hanged Man's association with the Empress can be ennobling or pathological. If the Empress is the object of desire, the Hanged Man is the one who desires. That desire can be destructively consuming or defining. If the Hanged Man appears with the Empress, it can signal consuming longing.'

He follows me through different houses, hallways and parlours.
We climb the fire escape and break into an unoccupied riverside
apartment .
Four in the morning,I'm awake listening to a strange soundtrack
that pulls me in and out of other realms . He sleeps in my
arms, defences temporarily dissipated. I dream but don't stray
far, can't bear the separation of sleep.

Then all hell breaks loose in the courtyard, gated communities
explode, people just wander in and out of each other's gaffs,
he goes away and I end up in a heated sexual entanglement with
a long forgotten ex. Everything is boundless, structureless and
chaotic.
.
A *door opens onto a glowing cavern of 60s kitsch.* Orange
plastic, perspex lampshades in concentric circles and all these
trinkets on every ledge and surface. It opens up in strange
ways, like my flat with another half, the mirror image
included. There's an old lady at a formica table playing
patience. I used to be her pride and joy, now she doesn't know
me.
 I stand above the past and survey the constellations of
light, the feint glows then the dark blankets thrown far and
wide, the interminable stretches of darkness.

I climb under the bridge where the Fleet disgorges into Thames.
Spaces, voices and ideas dissolve into an oceanic realm. This
is the dissolution of everything into everything else, the
channeling into the collective unconscious. This is the
unraveling of the two month bender, everything dissolving into
an undifferentiated mess. I stand and look out across the
Thames. Water is the universal solvent, everything dissolves.
A perpetual shifting, tides go back and forth. I consider the
frail promise of the Thames barrier, a spring tide and a
strong easterly that the barrier can't hold. Storm drains back
up, sewage systems collapse, the Fleet bursts its banks and
London becomes New Orleans.

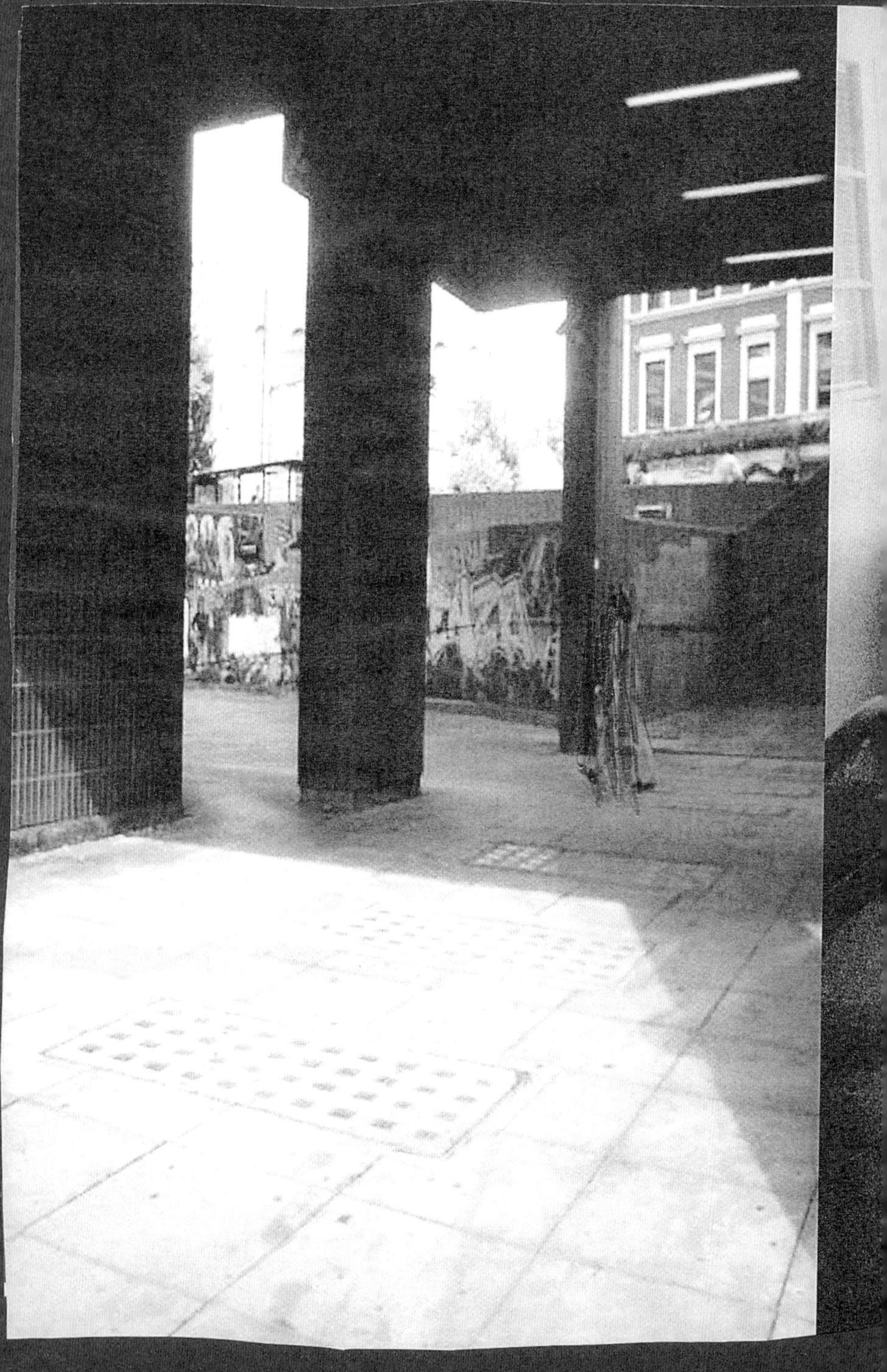

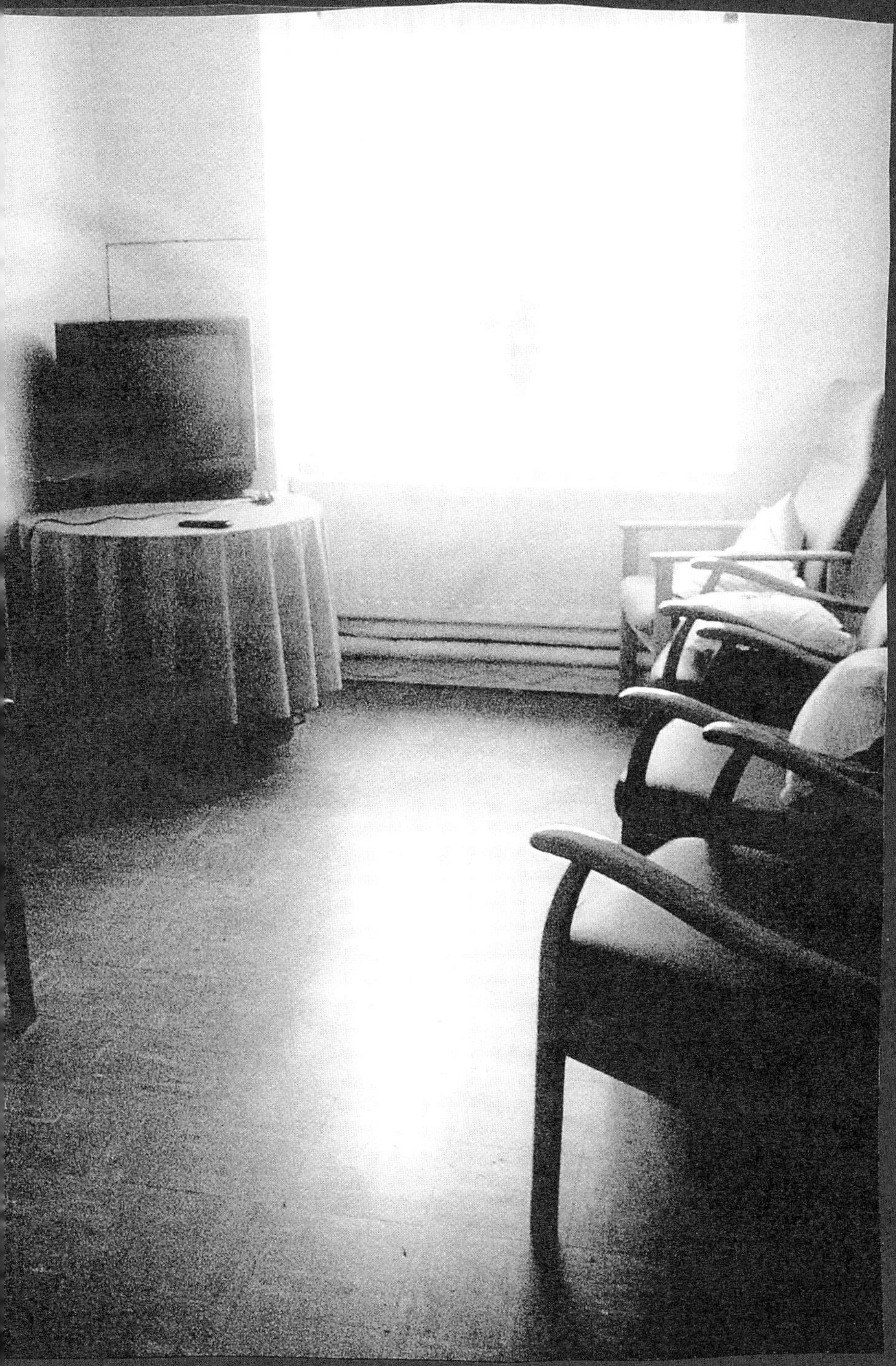

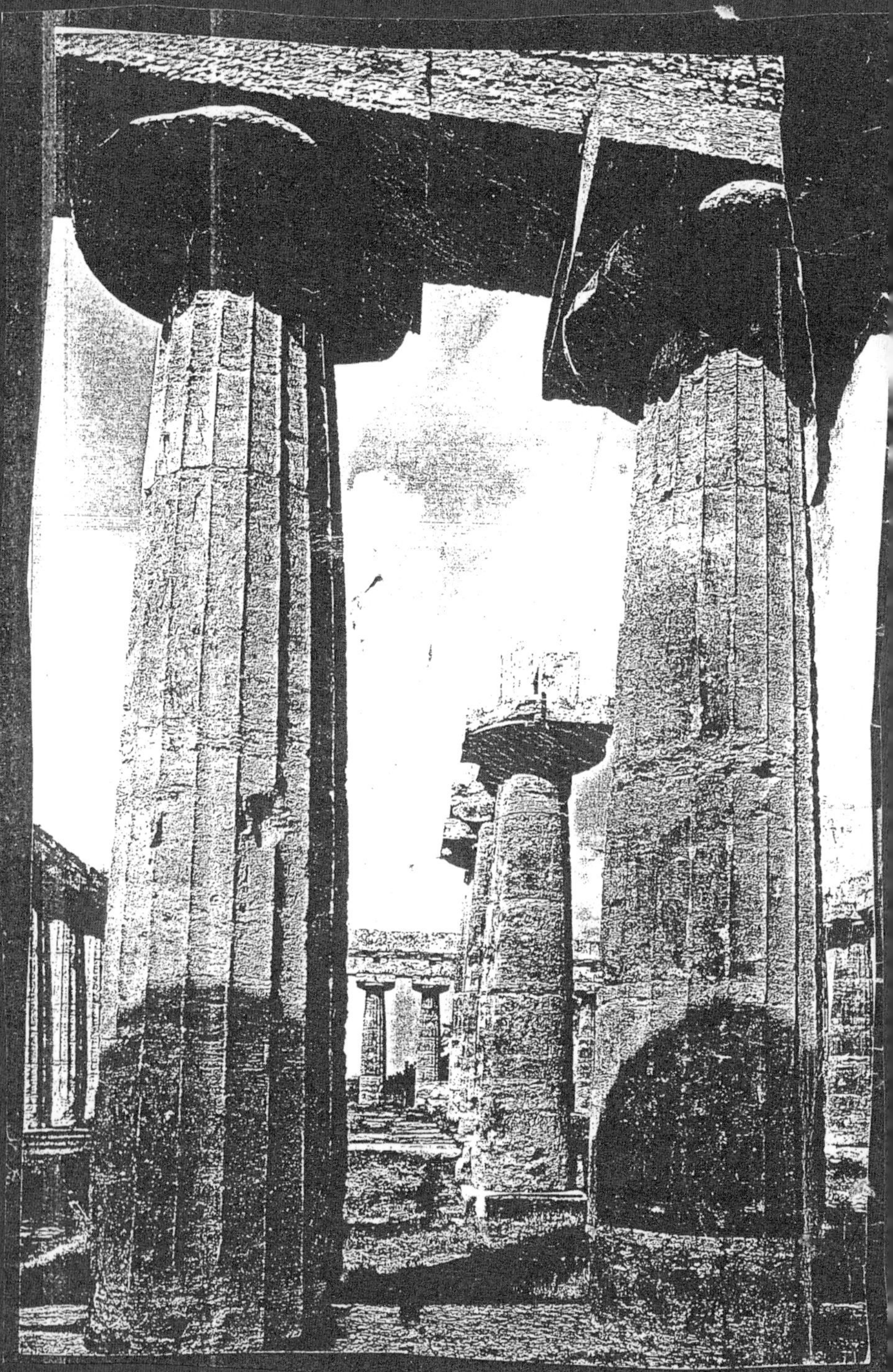

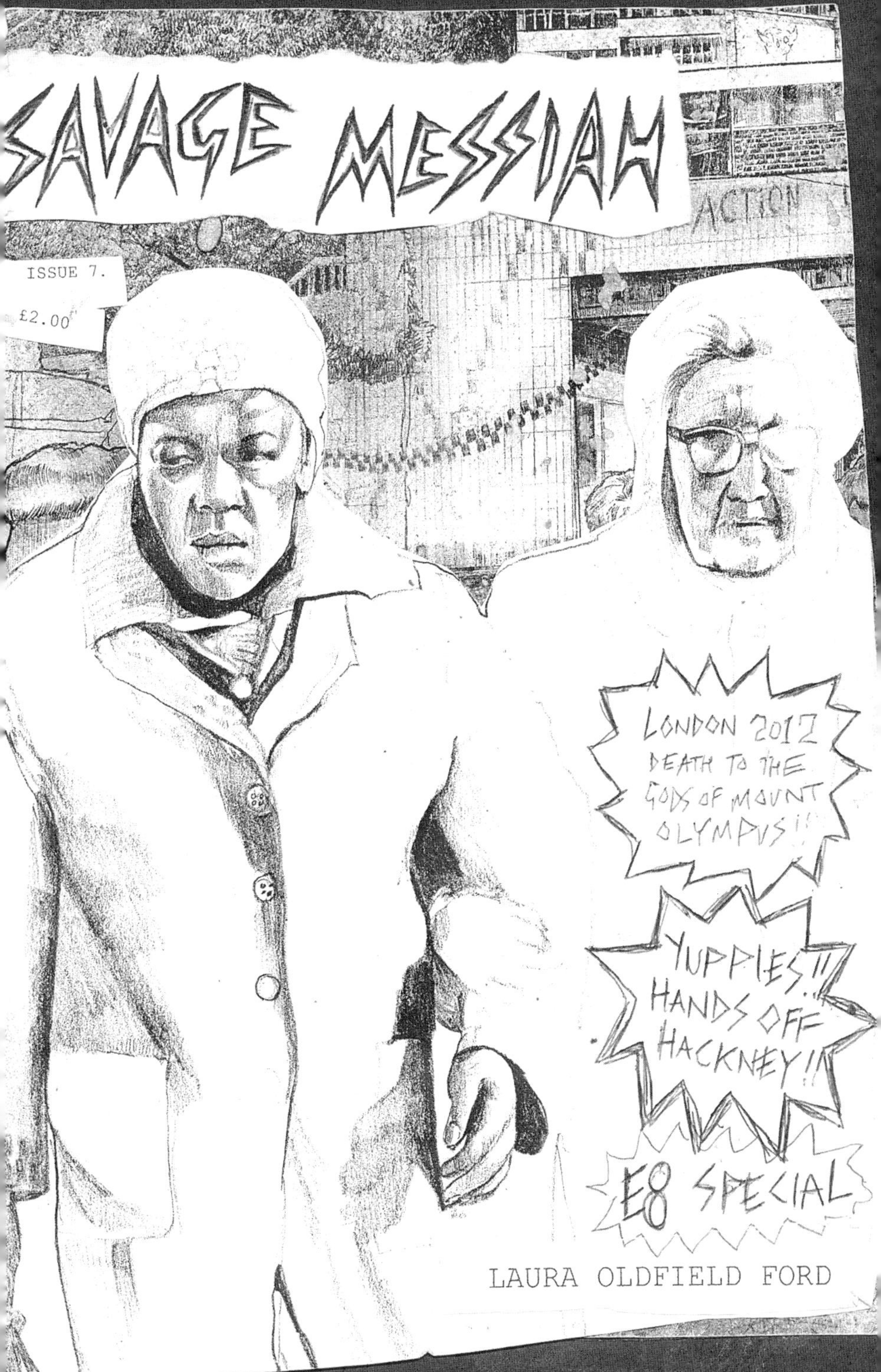
SAVAGE MESSIAH
ISSUE 7.
£2.00
ACTION
LONDON 2012 DEATH TO THE GODS OF MOUNT OLYMPUS!!
YUPPIES!! HANDS OFF HACKNEY!!
E8 SPECIAL
LAURA OLDFIELD FORD

! WARNING ! YOU ARE NOW ENTERING SAVAGE MESSIAH ZONE!!

BANK HOLIDAY CHEAP THRILLS AND ULTRA VIOLENCE

" The first man who, having enclosed a plot of ground, took upon himself to say 'this is mine', and found people silly enough to believe him, was the real founder of civilisation. How many wars, how many murders, how much misery and horror would have been spared if someone, tearing up the fence and filling in the ditch had cried out to his fellows: 'Give no heed to this impostor; you are lost if you forget that the fruits of the earth belong to all, and the land to no one."
Rousseau 1753

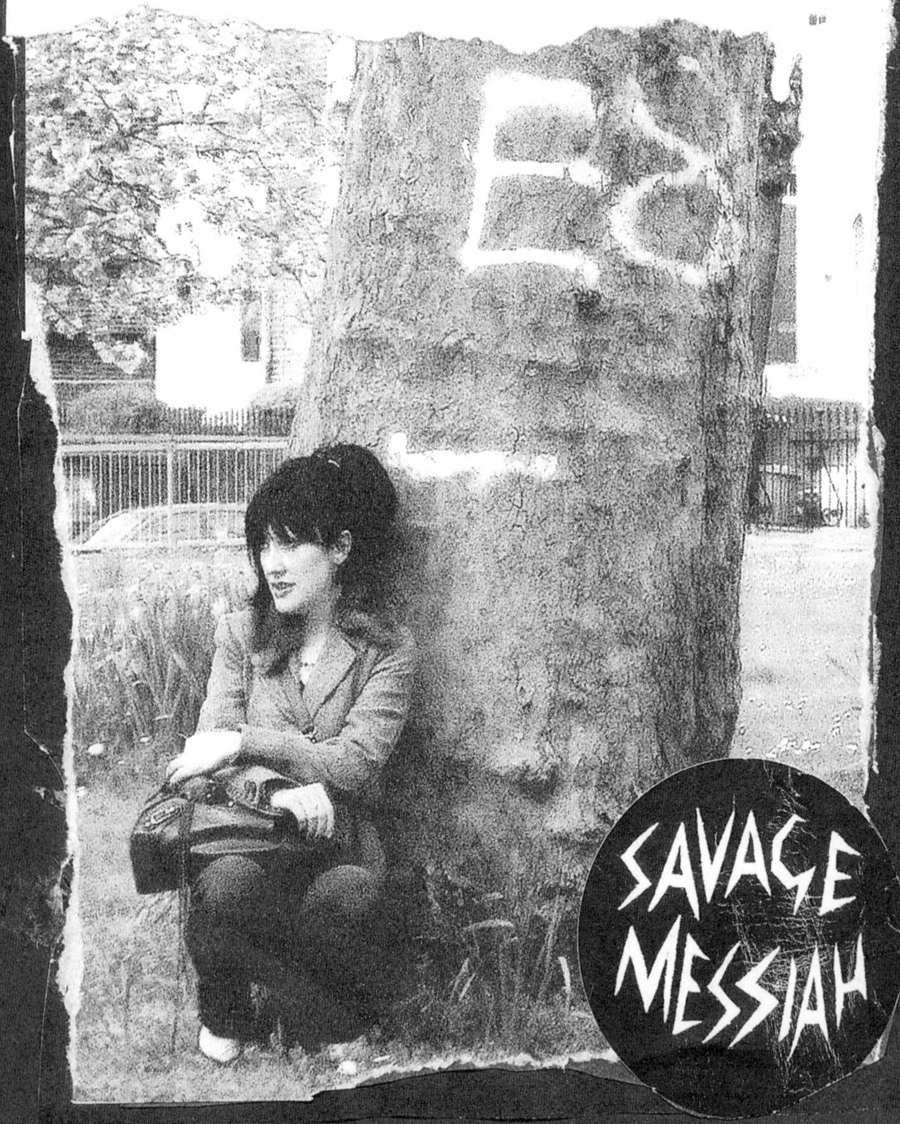
SAVAGE
MESSIAH

7. DALSTON E8
! WARNING ! YOU ARE NOW ENTERING SAVAGE MESSIAH ZONE!!

BANK HOLIDAY CHEAP THRILLS AND ULTRA VIOLENCE

" The first man who, having enclosed a plot of ground, took
upon himself to say 'this is mine', and found people silly
enough to believe him, was the real founder of civilisation.
How many wars, how many murders, how much misery and horror
would have been spared if someone, tearing up the fence and
filling in the ditch had cried out to his fellows: 'Give no
heed to this impostor; you are lost if you forget that the
fruits of the earth belong to all, and the land to no one."
Rousseau 1753

HACKNEY TOWN HALL, site of sedition.
An intoxicated walk through Hackney. The night is cinematic as
we drift from one enchanted interior to another through a knot
of narrow streets. A balmy July, colours shift, images cascade.
Discontent simmers in the yards.

ESTATE AGENTS UP AGAINST THE SOUTH FACING WALL!!.

 Industrial estate, engines running, air lilac and soft grey.
 The Oval is desolate and abandoned until a clashing encounter
     with an African church.. Place of Victory in a disused
printers. "You have dwelt long enough at this mountain ... see
I have set the land before you; go in and possess the land...."

Deuteronomy 1:6-8.

Running up and down glass stairwells kids carrying babies done
up in Sunday best. Azure and canary yellow, green and gold
proudly wrapped. Bontempi backdrop, swaying, clapping. Fire
and miracles.
Megaphone threats.

A stagger through the detritus of Cambridge heath road,
everything Sunday shut like it was in the 70s when you looked
forward to the antiques road show and boiled eggs and ham for
your tea. Drop another half, *pink uns yeller uns*, quick jar in
Dolphin and a go on the fruity, slammin bar, caning
Marlboroughs. PSYCHO CASH BEAST . Ha ha ha, glittering
heirophant. Bronski beat, ABC, us lot broken dancing.

And so we drift through mossy corridors, roam through lost industrial estates. All that remains of the works,(toys, matches, tanning) are factory shells turned yuppiedromes. Pub on the park. Can't move in here. Another bag of pills on the table. In and out the bogs, inane jabberings, big fake compliments. Crew in fine form, bawling shouting kind of pissed, got the whole boozer, waiting for it to kick off. Started the whispers hours ago, now the events unfold by themselves. The last night of the Pepys before it disappears under a pall of mediocrity. The mood is militant, angry, carnivalesque.

Middle class hippies plead with us not to let violence mar their special night, not to let ugly scenes overshadow their memories of such a great place. These are the 'fluffies' you have to contend with when mass demos shift towards wrecking sprees. These are the types who try to physically restrain you and chant 'no violence' when you're about to smash a window. The crew lunges forwards to the town hall where fury at council greed erupts and human battering rams are used to storm the town hall.

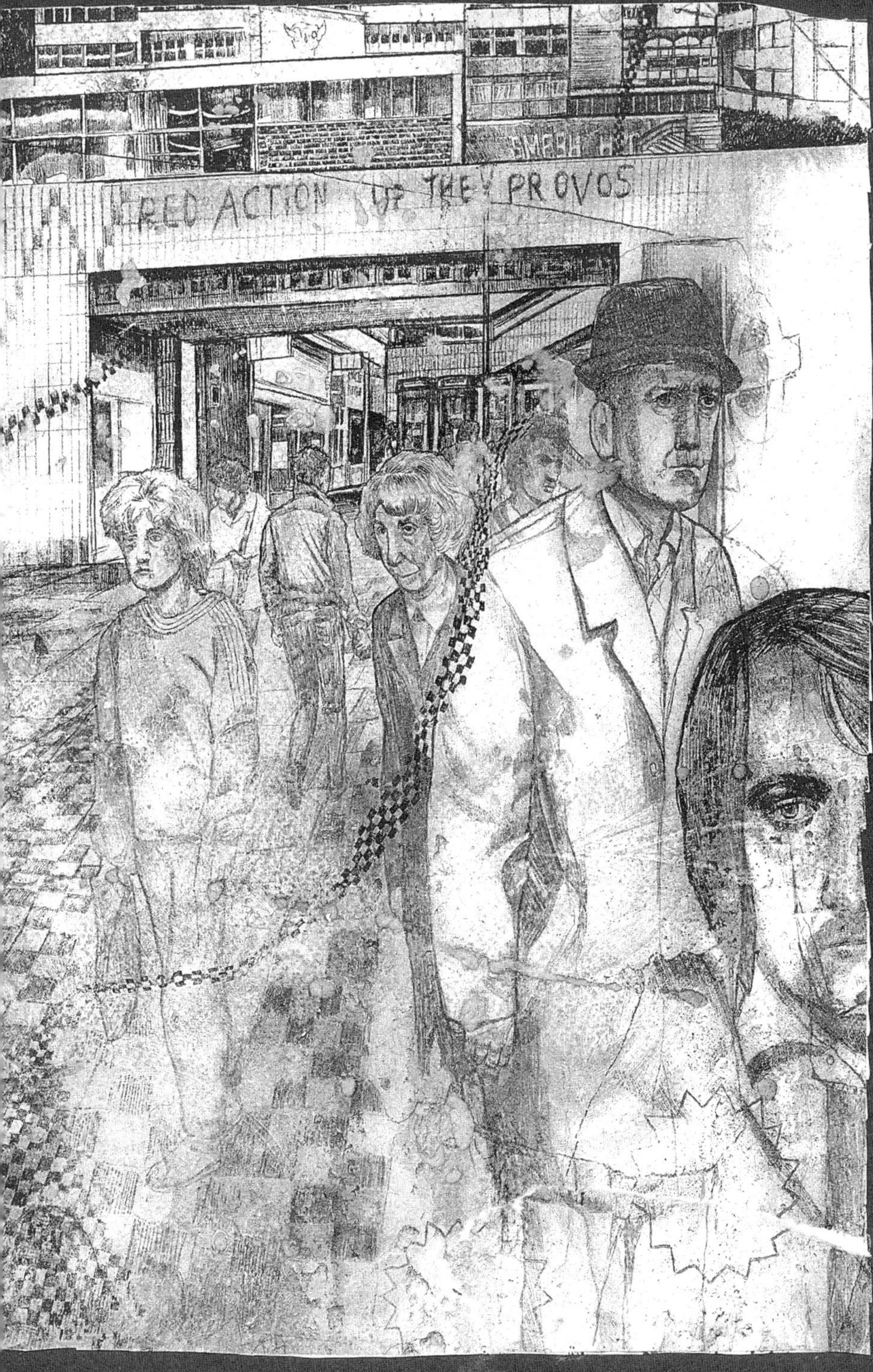
RED ACTION UP THE PROVOS

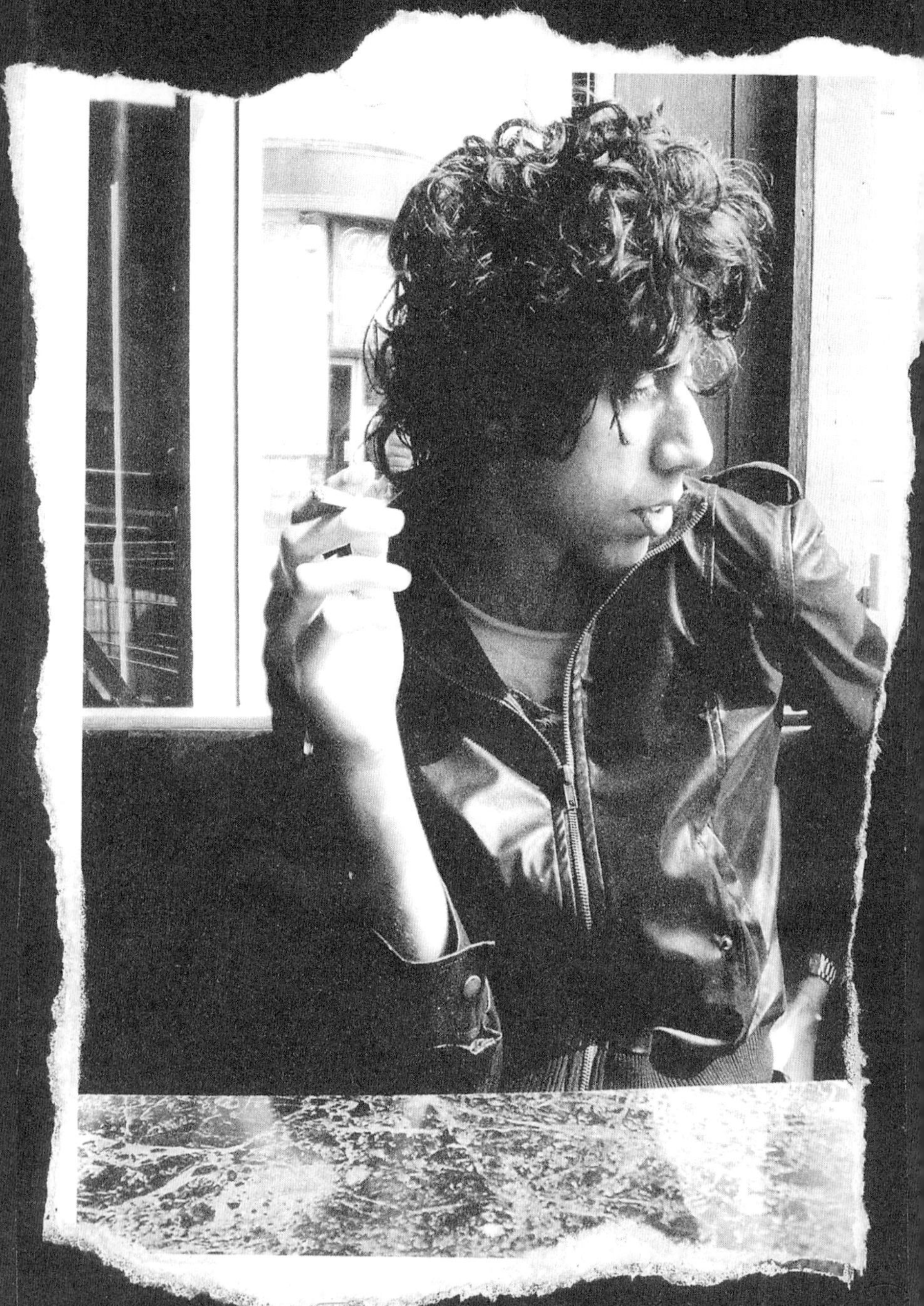

WHERE HAS DALSTON GONE?

Drifting through Dalston is to traverse a network of holding
patterns, a city in stasis. It is a series of film stills,
waiting rooms, a world behind it and another yet to come. We
escape surveillance by slipping in and out of bolt holes,
dilapidated shops and bombsites.
Subverting colonised spaces and master planning strategies we
carve out other realms beneath the eye of the cctv.

Sites left derelict and six major fires suspiciously engulf the
neglected row.
4-14 Dalston lane, 4 aces club, Labyrinth, ten rooms of
luminous glyphs emanating from 1989, disorientation in black

corridors, day glo spirals, fractals pulsating beneath
knackered eyelids.

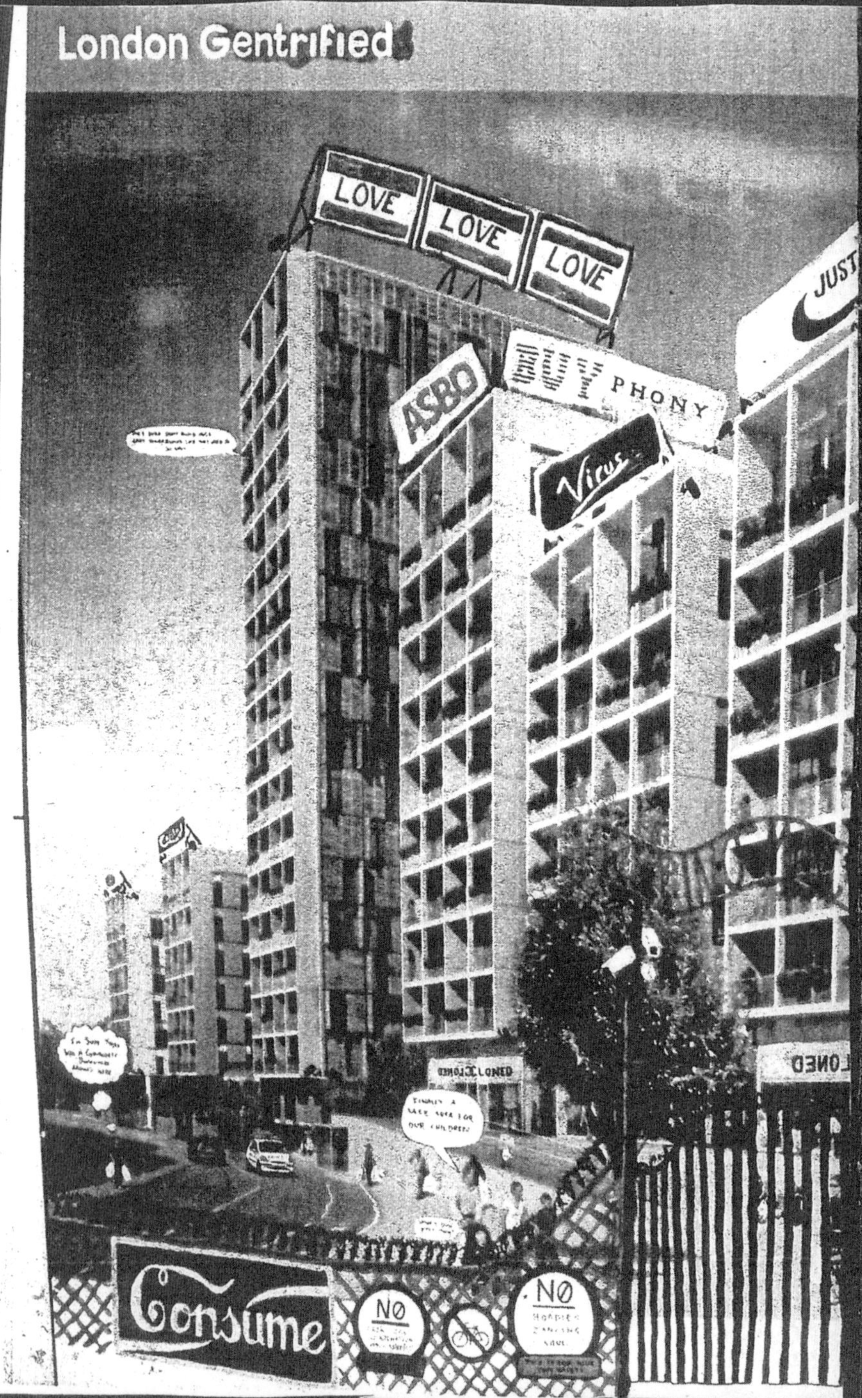
London Gentrified
LOVE
LOVE
LOVE
ASBO
BUY PHONY
Virus
JUST
CLONED
CLONED
Consume
NO
NO

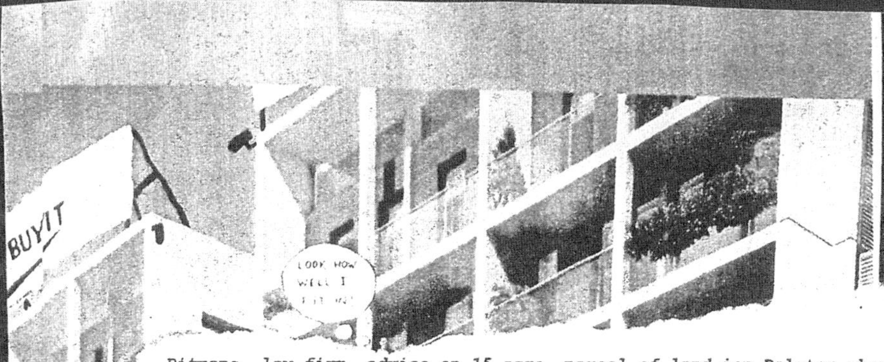
BUYIT
LOOK HOW
WELL I

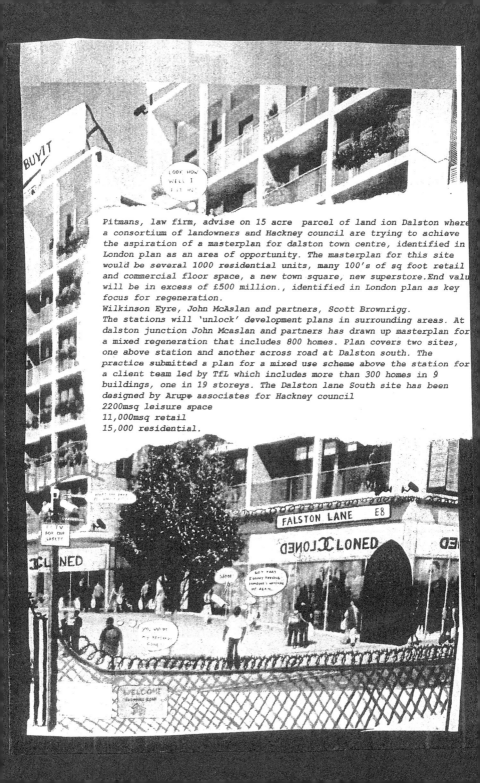

Pitmans, law firm, advise on 15 acre parcel of land ion Dalston where a consortium of landowners and Hackney council are trying to achieve the aspiration of a masterplan for dalston town centre, identified in London plan as an area of opportunity. The masterplan for this site would be several 1000 residential units, many 100's of sq foot retail and commercial floor space, a new town square, new superstore.End valu will be in excess of £500 million., identified in London plan as key focus for regeneration.

Wilkinson Eyre, John McAslan and partners, Scott Brownrigg.

The stations will 'unlock' development plans in surrounding areas. At dalston junction John Mcaslan and partners has drawn up masterplan for a mixed regeneration that includes 800 homes. Plan covers two sites, one above station and another across road at Dalston south. The practice submitted a plan for a mixed use scheme above the station for a client team led by TfL which includes more than 300 homes in 9 buildings, one in 19 storeys. The Dalston lane South site has been designed by Arup associates for Hackney council

2200msq leisure space

11,000msq retail

15,000 residential.

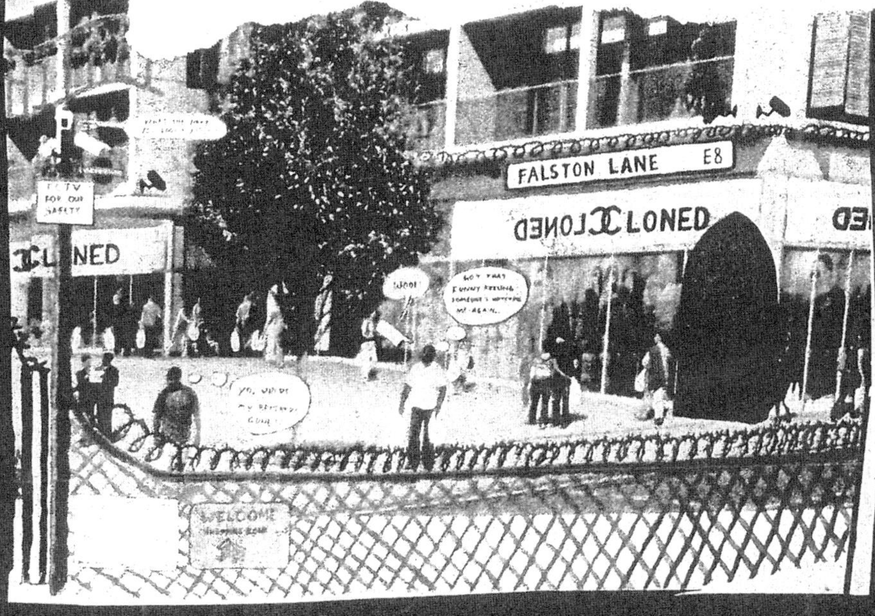
FALSTON LANE E8
CLONED
CLONED
CCTV
FOR OUR
SAFETY
WOO!
WELCOME

The Dalston masterplan. Class cleansing. Aerial surveillance, streets marked.

These megamall structures have eclipsed the postwar precincts and highlighted their obsolescence; the veneer is torn away to expose crude mechanisms.

Perhaps it is here that space can be opened to resist this neo liberal expansion, the endless proliferation of banalities and the homogenising effects of globalisation. Here in the burnt out shopping arcades, the boarded up precincts one might find the truth, new territories might be opened, there might be a rupturing of this collective amnesia.

Four Aces, Labyrinth, the scene went Dark, horror movie samples, queasy sound effects, metallic breakbeats reflecting the collective mental state. Duff pills flying out of Latvia, everyone monged, incapictated in heaps.

London 2012. Darkness. Paranoia. London 2013.

International broadcast and press centre in Hackney and indoor sports arena. Growth areas art and culture industry. Dalston, Nov 2006 High court order banning destruction of Dalston theatre but still the wreckers ball comes. The Dalston theatre is occupied, there's a frenzy to save it, white letters writ large ,barricades, Spanachists breakfasting in café Bliss with baillifs and law firms. Old bill buzzing overhead, monitoring ,filming, iris recognition and tracking technology.

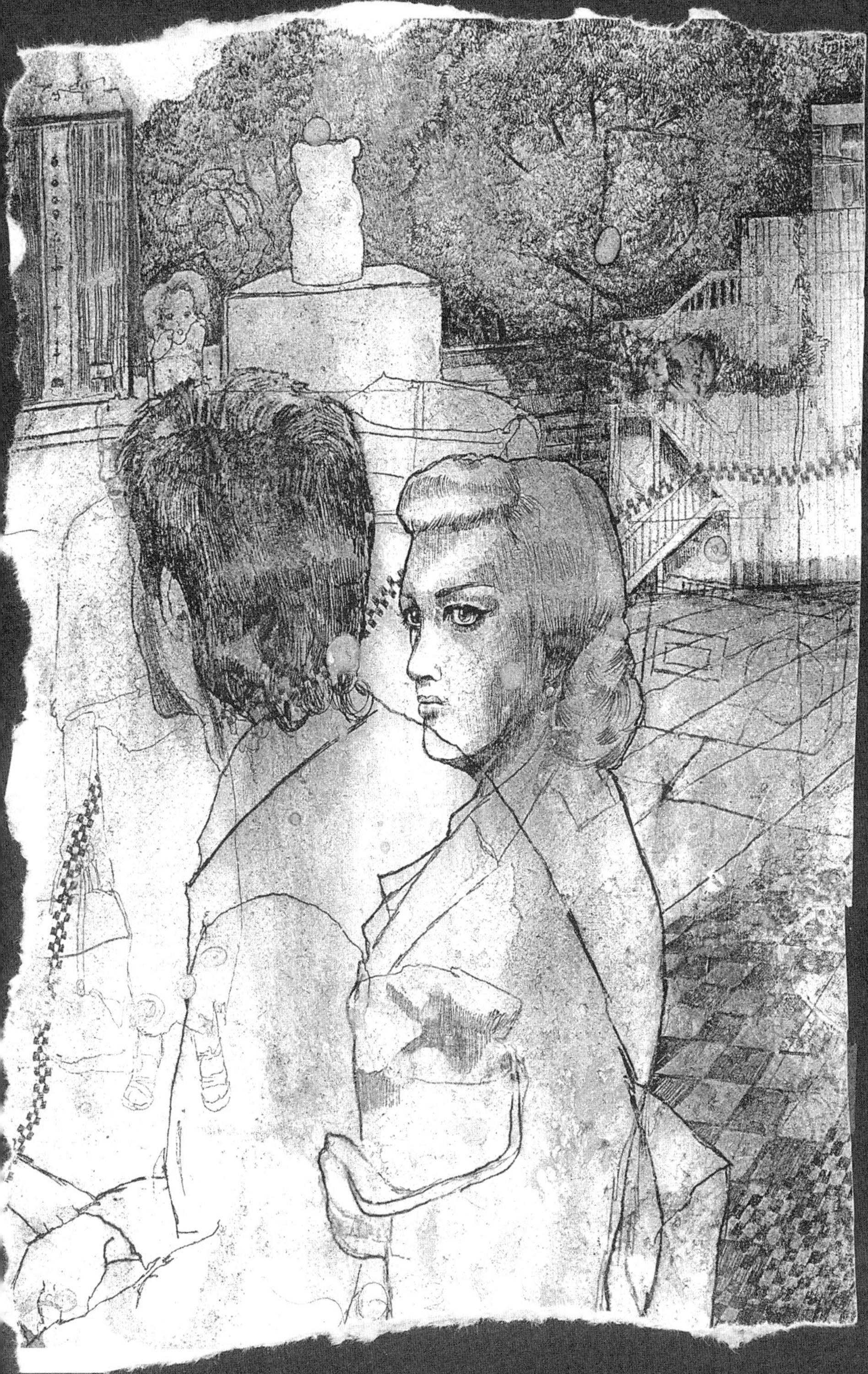

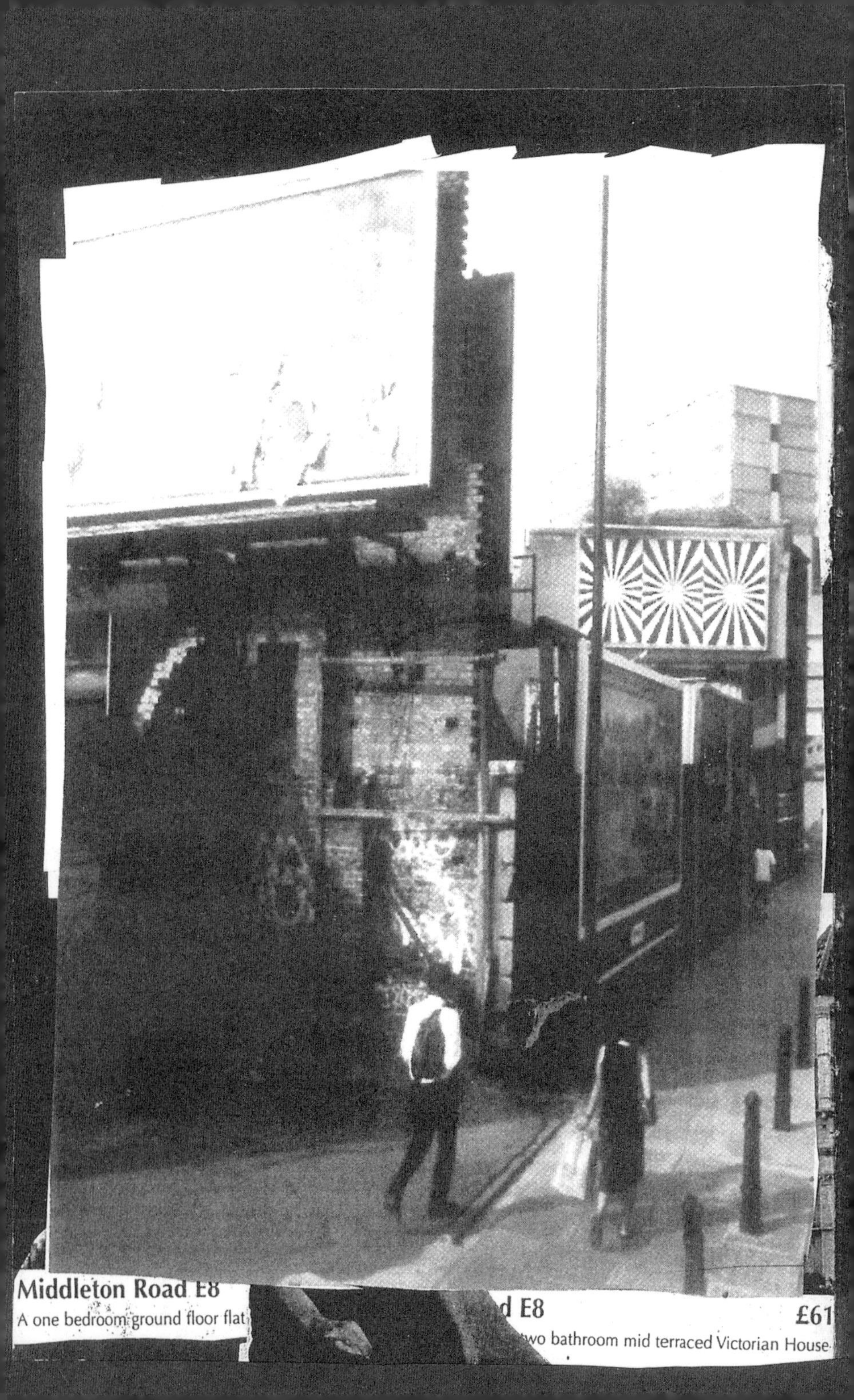
Middleton Road E8
A one bedroom ground floor flat
d E8
£61
two bathroom mid terraced Victorian House

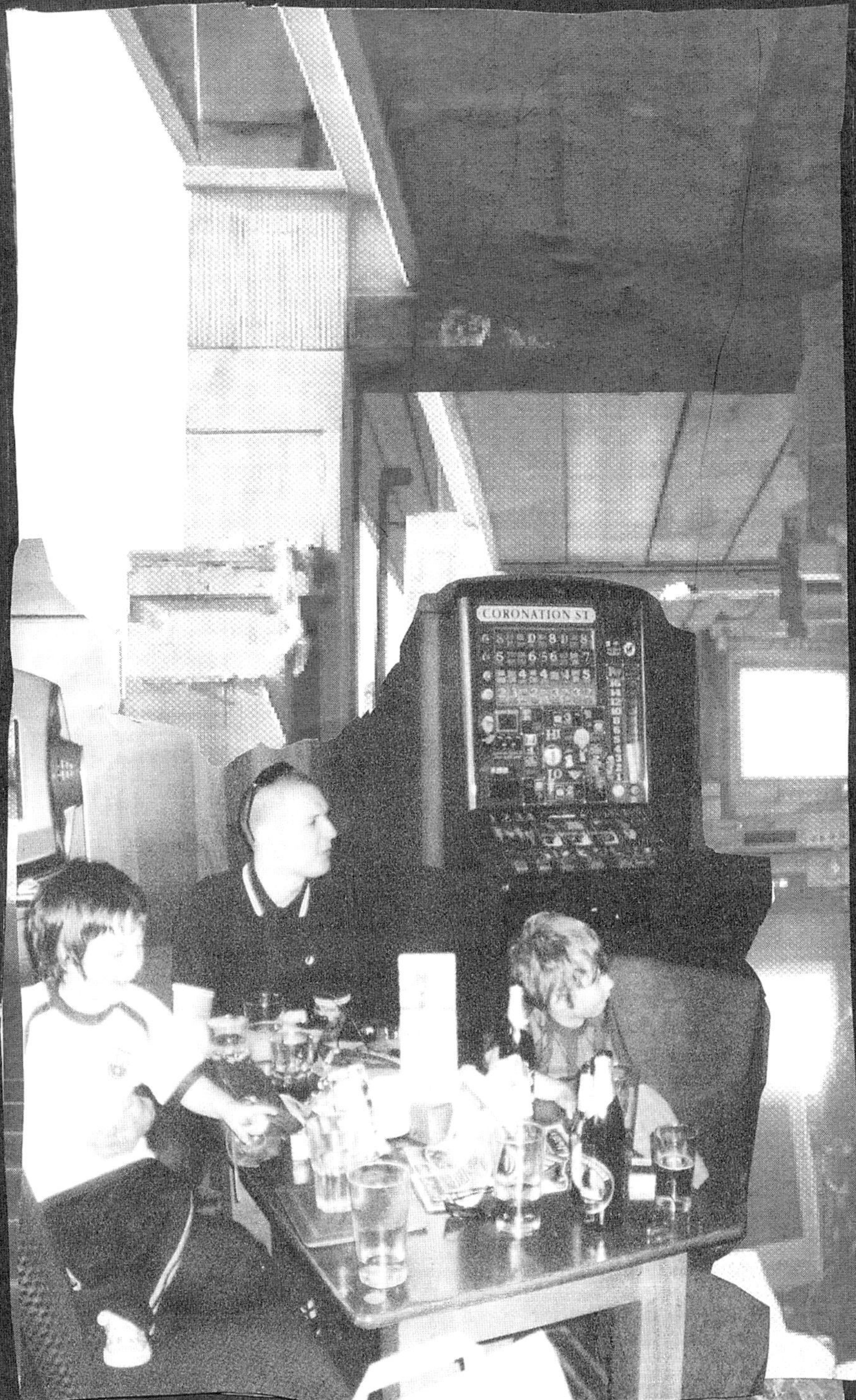
CORONATION ST

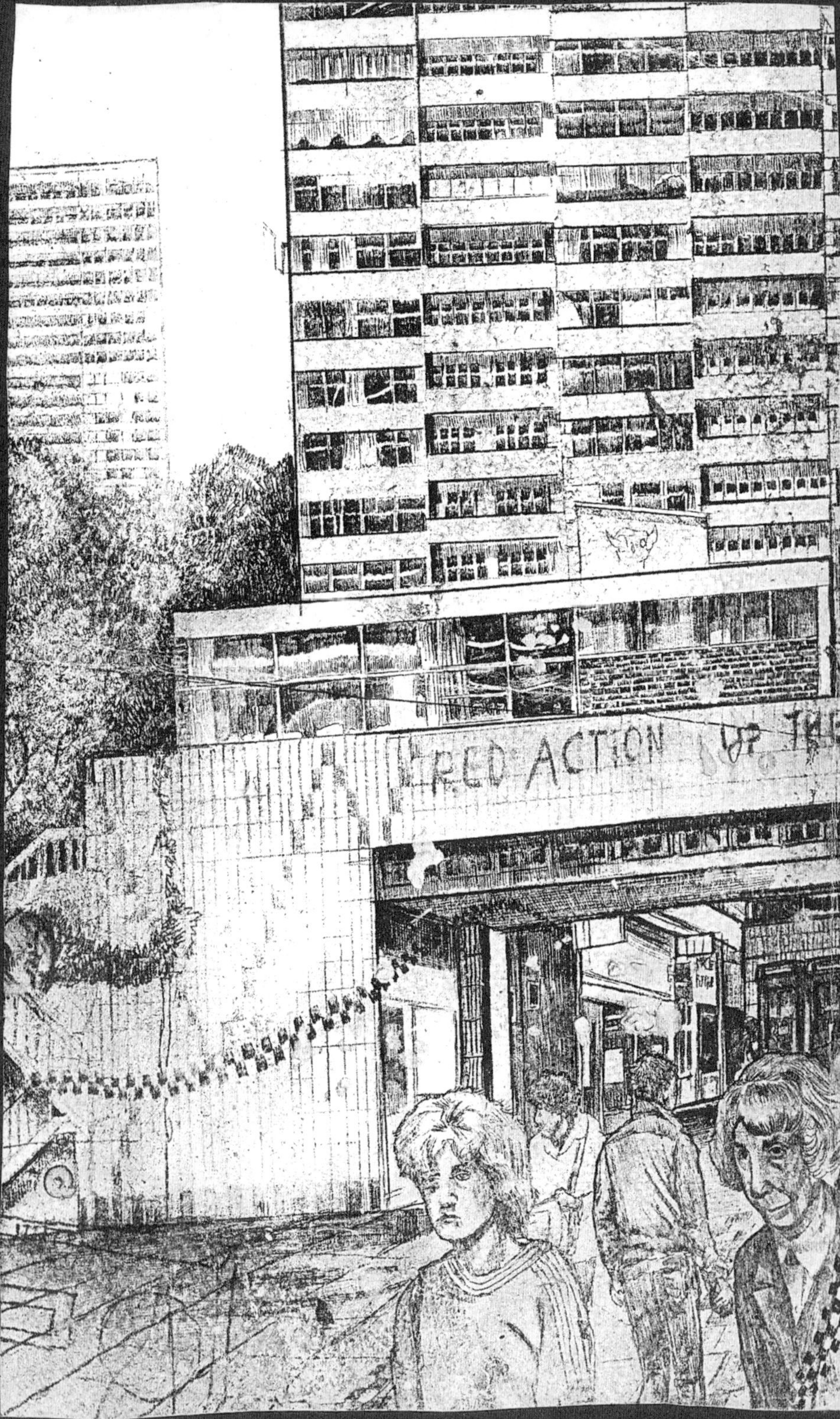
RED ACTION

"The universal and ineluctable consequence of this crusade to secure the city is the destruction of accessible public space. The contemporary opprobrium attached to the term 'street person' is itself a harrowing index of the devaluation of public spaces. To reduce contact with untouchables, urban redevelopment has converted once vital pedestrian streets into traffic sewers and transformed public parks into temporary receptacles for the homeless and wretched. The American city, as many critics have recognised, is being systematically turned inside out- or rather outside in. The valorized spaces of the new megastructures and supermalls are concentrated in the centre, street frontage is denuded, public activity is sorted into strictly functional compartments, and circulation is internalized in corridors under the gaze of private police."

Mike Davis City of Quartz

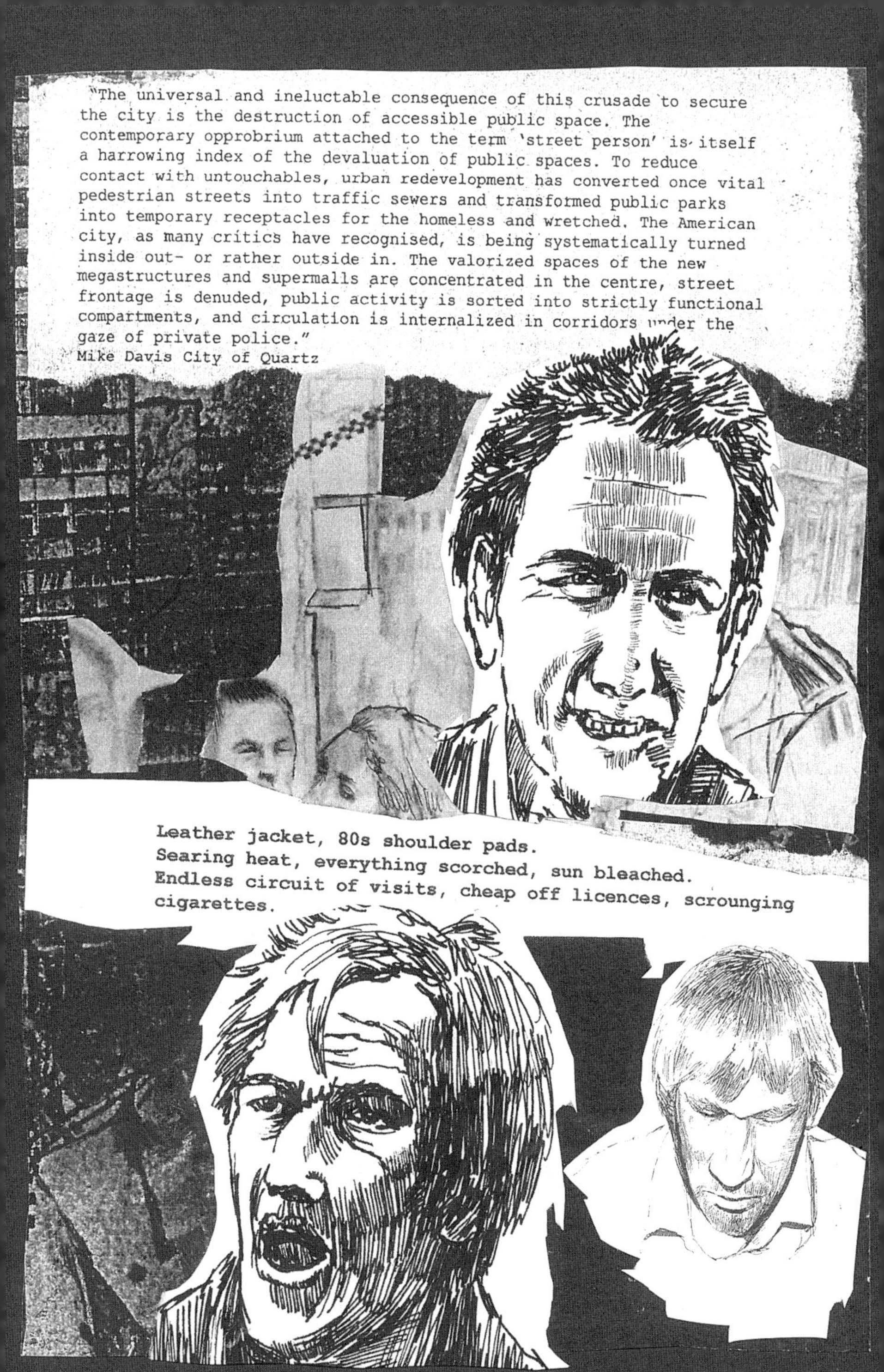
Leather jacket, 80s shoulder pads.
Searing heat, everything scorched, sun bleached.
Endless circuit of visits, cheap off licences, scrounging cigarettes.

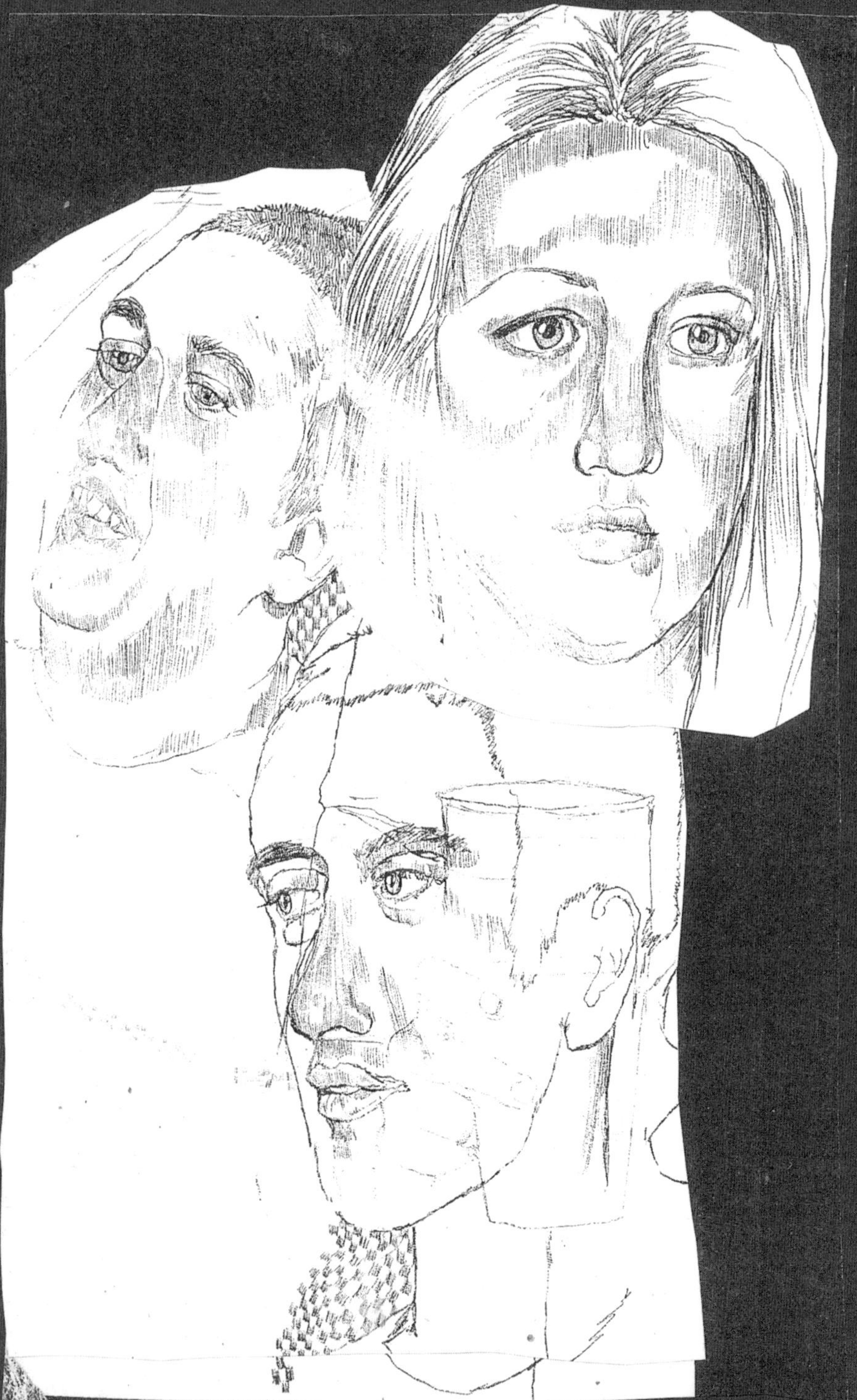

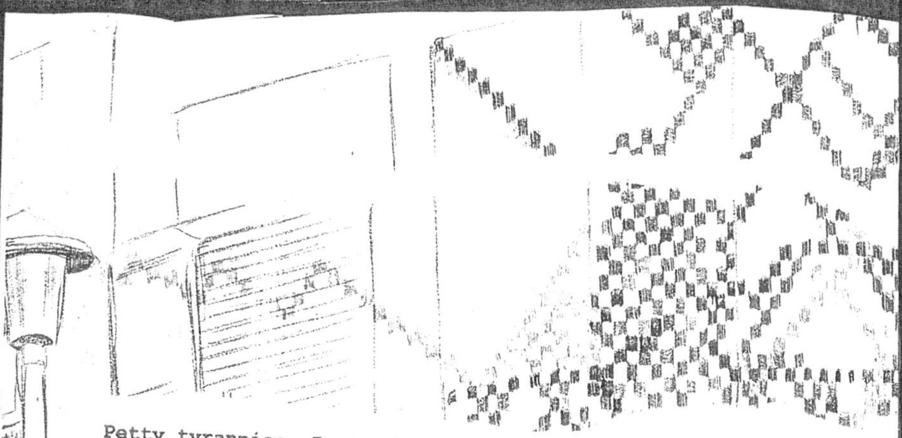

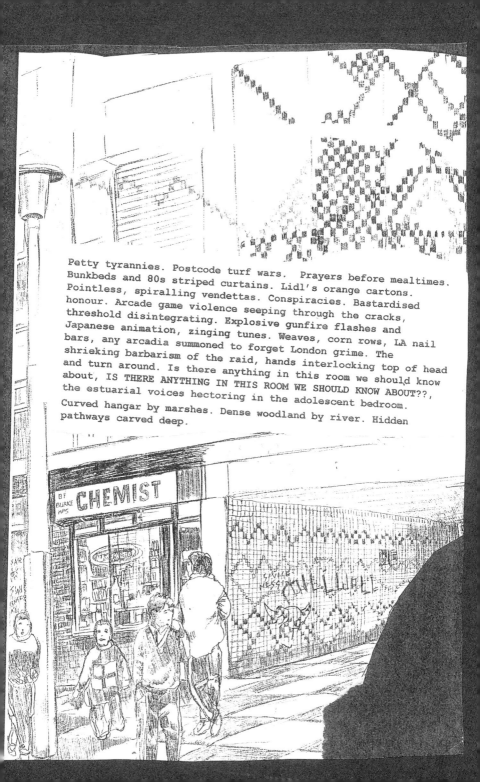

Petty tyrannies. Postcode turf wars. Prayers before mealtimes. Bunkbeds and 80s striped curtains. Lidl's orange cartons. Pointless, spiralling vendettas. Conspiracies. Bastardised honour. Arcade game violence seeping through the cracks, threshold disintegrating. Explosive gunfire flashes and Japanese animation, zinging tunes. Weaves, corn rows, LA nail bars, any arcadia summoned to forget London grime. The shrieking barbarism of the raid, hands interlocking top of head and turn around. Is there anything in this room we should know about, IS THERE ANYTHING IN THIS ROOM WE SHOULD KNOW ABOUT??, the estuarial voices hectoring in the adolescent bedroom. Curved hangar by marshes. Dense woodland by river. Hidden pathways carved deep.

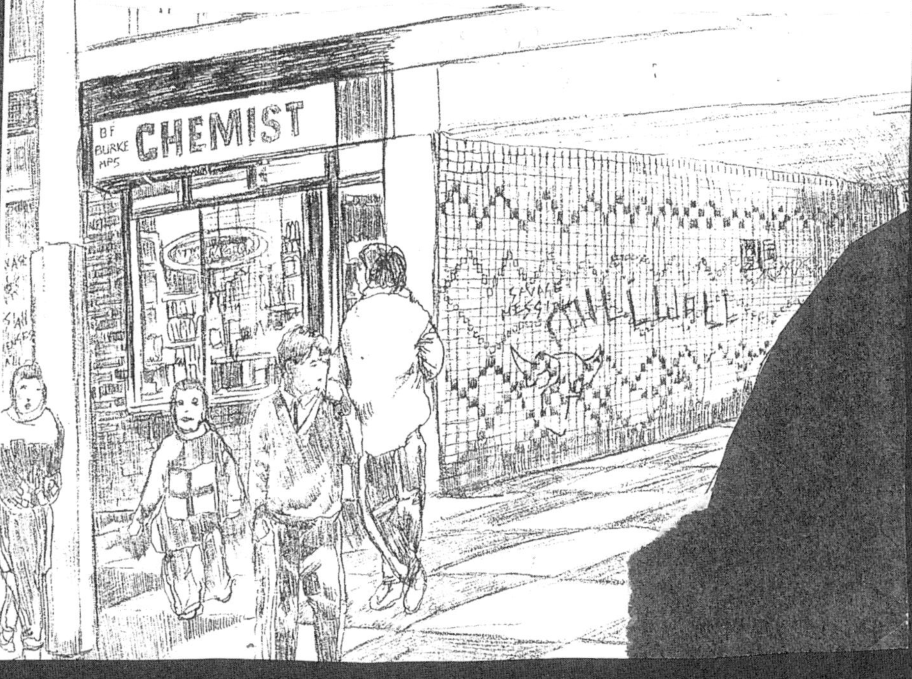
BF
BURKE
MPS
CHEMIST

Cigarette smoke ,coffee and plain chocolate, a continental
smell, a London smell. She remembers, Covent Garden 1981, the
unfamiliar warmth, spring advanced, and that luxurious scent.
Balcony doors open over marshland vistas. S is lying on the
bed. Soon she will make some coffee and they'll get ready to
go out. Candi Staton, Rozalla, Snap! Looks out over sweep of
Olympic regeneration, cranes puncturing the wilderness. She
smokes and watches, the heat intensifying. Going to be a long
hot Summer. Puts make up on at the kitchen table, 18 floors up.
Damask, the heavy scent of elderflower, mutant strains of
hogweed crashing over barbed wire.
 London, she can feel it now, she is on the brink of good
times. She can leave the flat again.

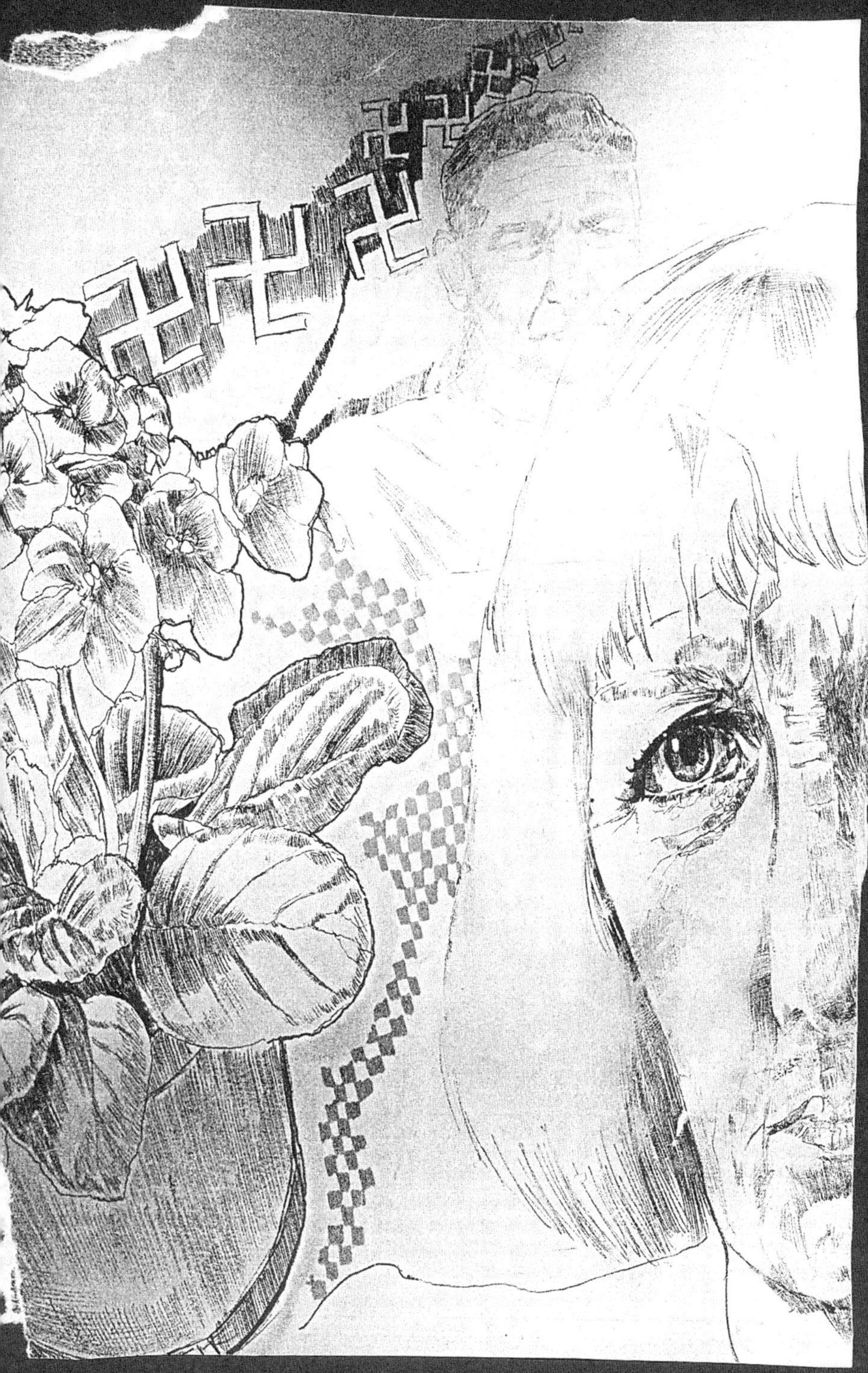

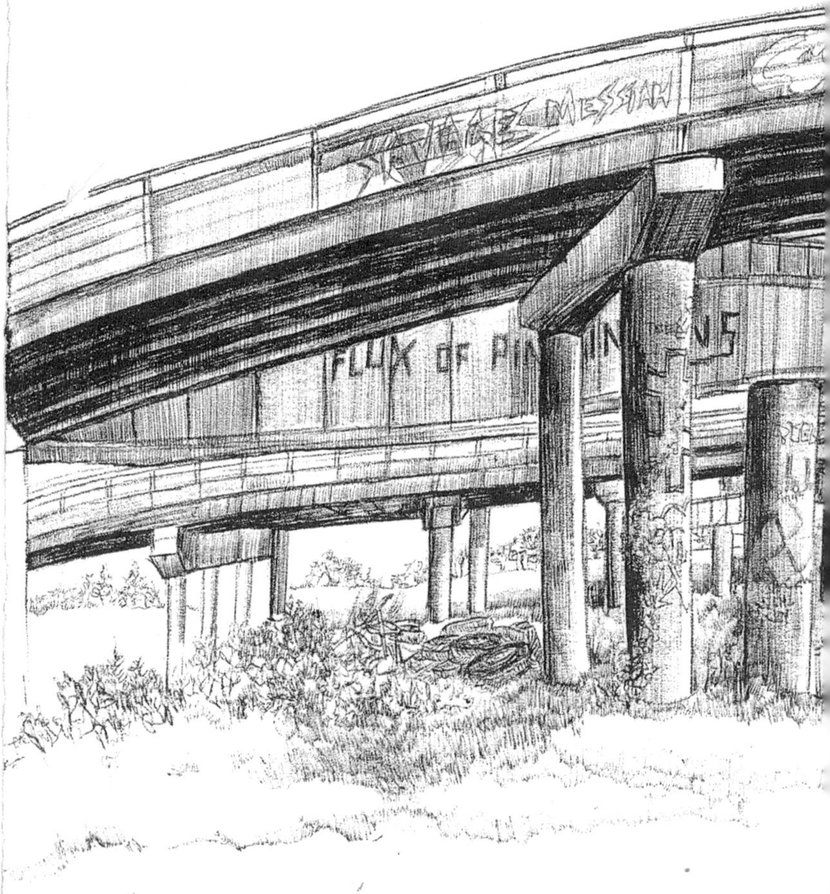
SAVAGE MESSIAH
FLUX OF

There are untold magical places he will show me, collisions of sweet memories and the walking of new ones.

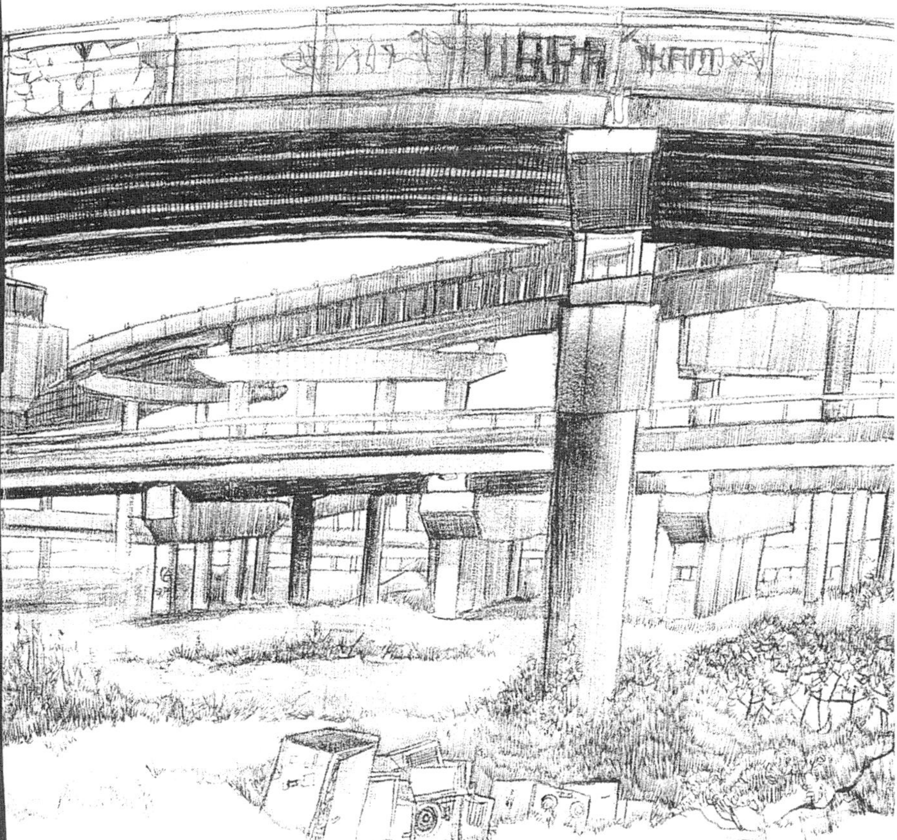

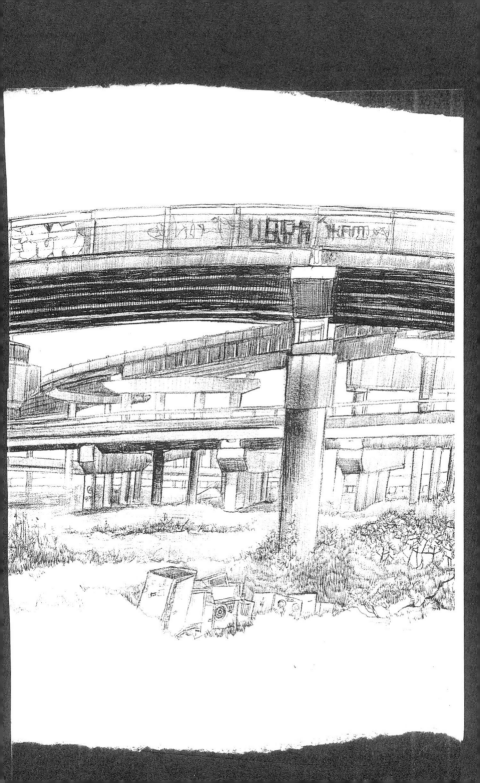

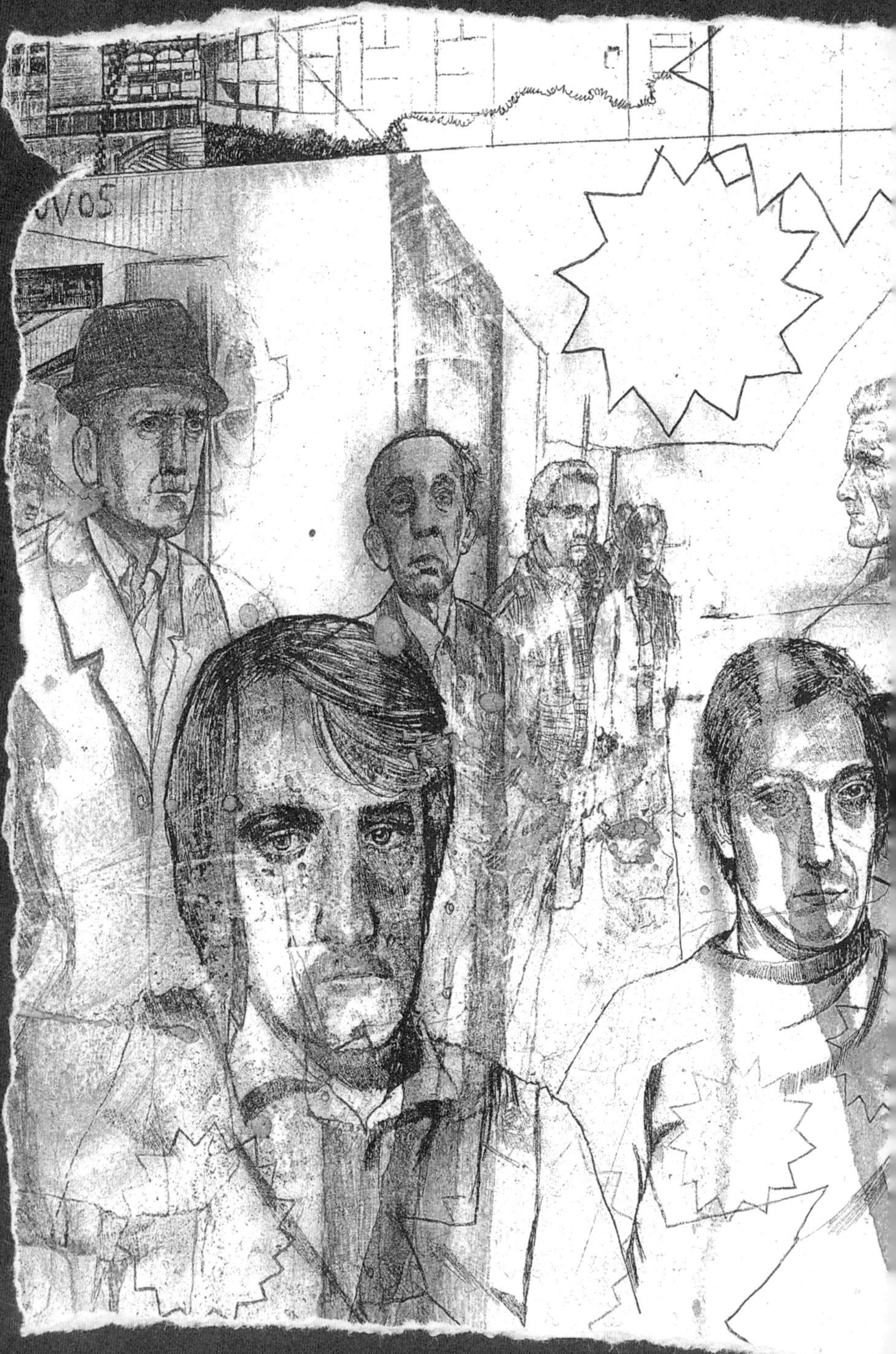

Collide with another crew on Broadway market, frontline of extreme gentrification. Residues of an all dayer outside the Perseverance, Declan stands arms raised bawling about estate agents being cunts and THE LOSS OF HACKNEY. Tony's caf smashed, Spirit fighting eviction, what next for Haggerston? NO T MOBILE sprayed up on the wall, FUCK OFF MIDDLE CLASS WANKERS on another, but you know, doesn't it just add a bit of edgy chic to the area. Wratten and his bunch of henchmen continue to empire build with the assistance of Hackney Council, BOYCOTT LA VIE EN ROSE.

This party, anyone know the address?
 Yeah a site by the gasholders on the canal.
   London becomes wasteland ruptured by erratic flare ups of
euphoria.
Chance encounters,
    drug binges, the softening effect of opiates.
 The squat party on a derelict industrial estate, sky glowing
luminous yellow, pylons and electricity generators, banks of
nettles by the service canal.
Thickets of briars.

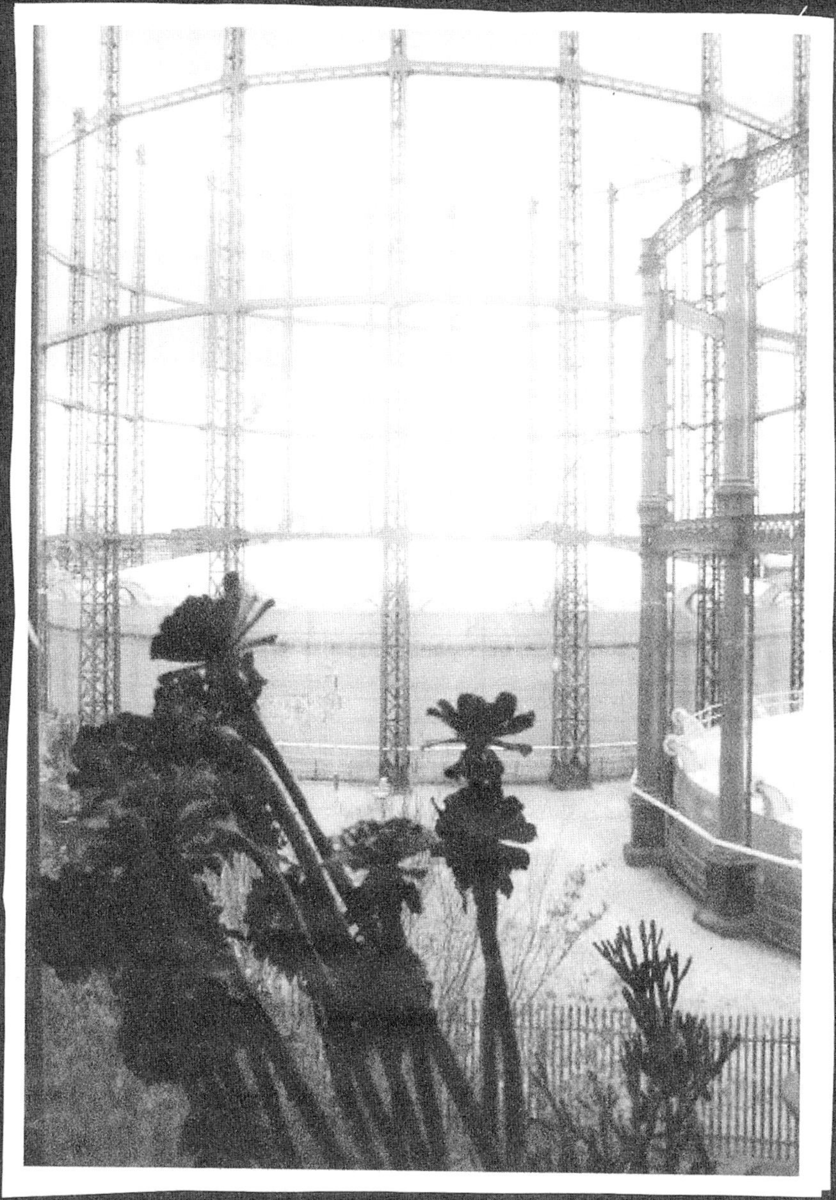

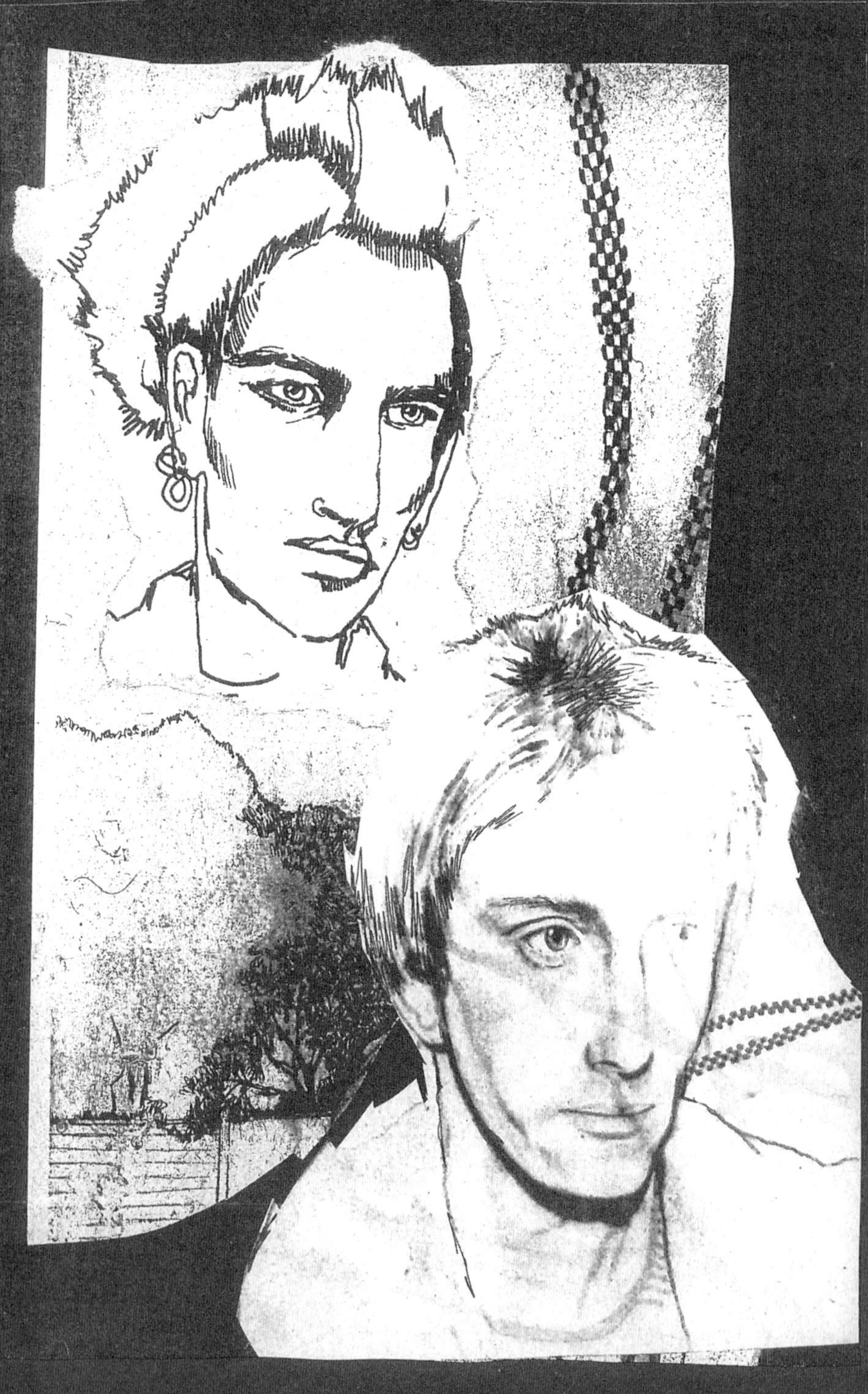

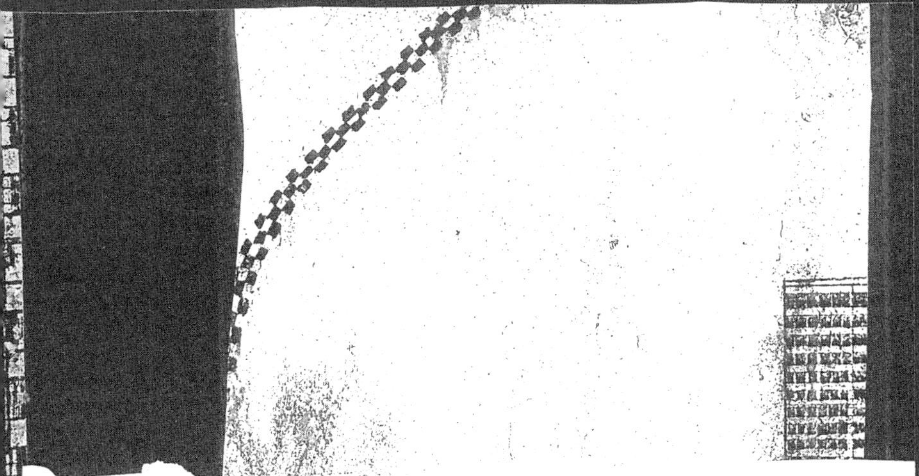

The corrugated iron gate gives way, a dazzling neon interior opens up, fleamarket kitsch, office furniture, dayglo fabric draped from factory ceilings. He follows me through yards, levels, staircases, hallways.

Don't forget me,

let these iridescent moments glitter embalmed in our memory.

We could have lived, loved and desired.

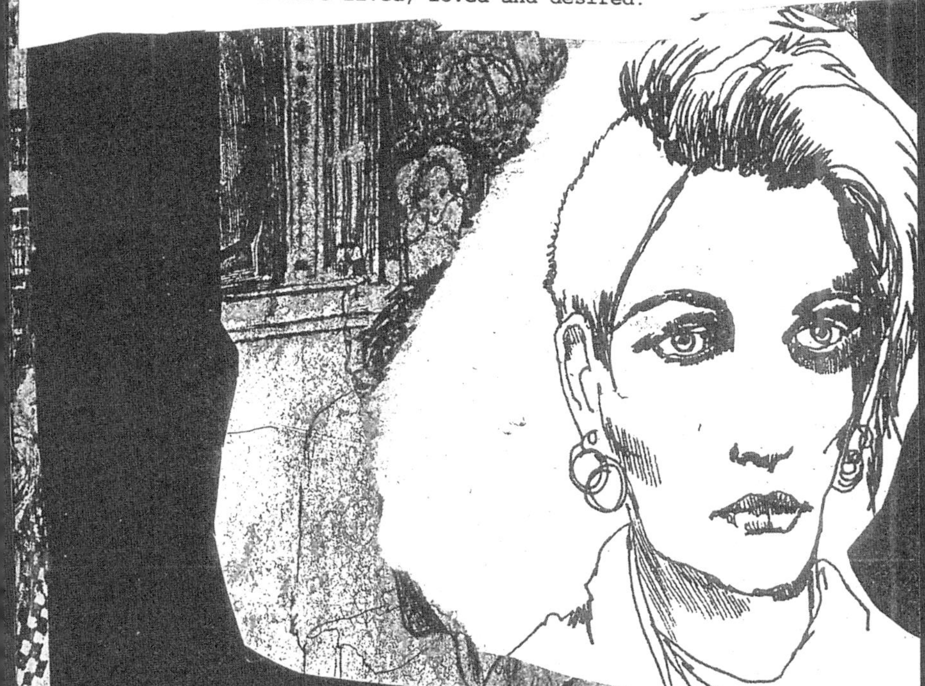

Drawn East, the marshes, footbridge over the Lea.
 Mounting excitement, intoxicating dizzying syntax, endless
architectures.

London is not only the backdrop but the fabric of adventures,
drifts, encounters. Love erupts and emerges as a subversive
force.
Real engagement ruptures and tears at veneer of spectacle and
threatens its stability. The chimera, illusion or manufactured
construction of love and desire is shown up as hollow, wretched
and malign in the moment of encounter with the real,
uncorrupted experience.
 We pick through ruins, an abandoned rose garden, bleached
landscapes; we roam under motorway flyovers, towerblocks
cascading down embankments.

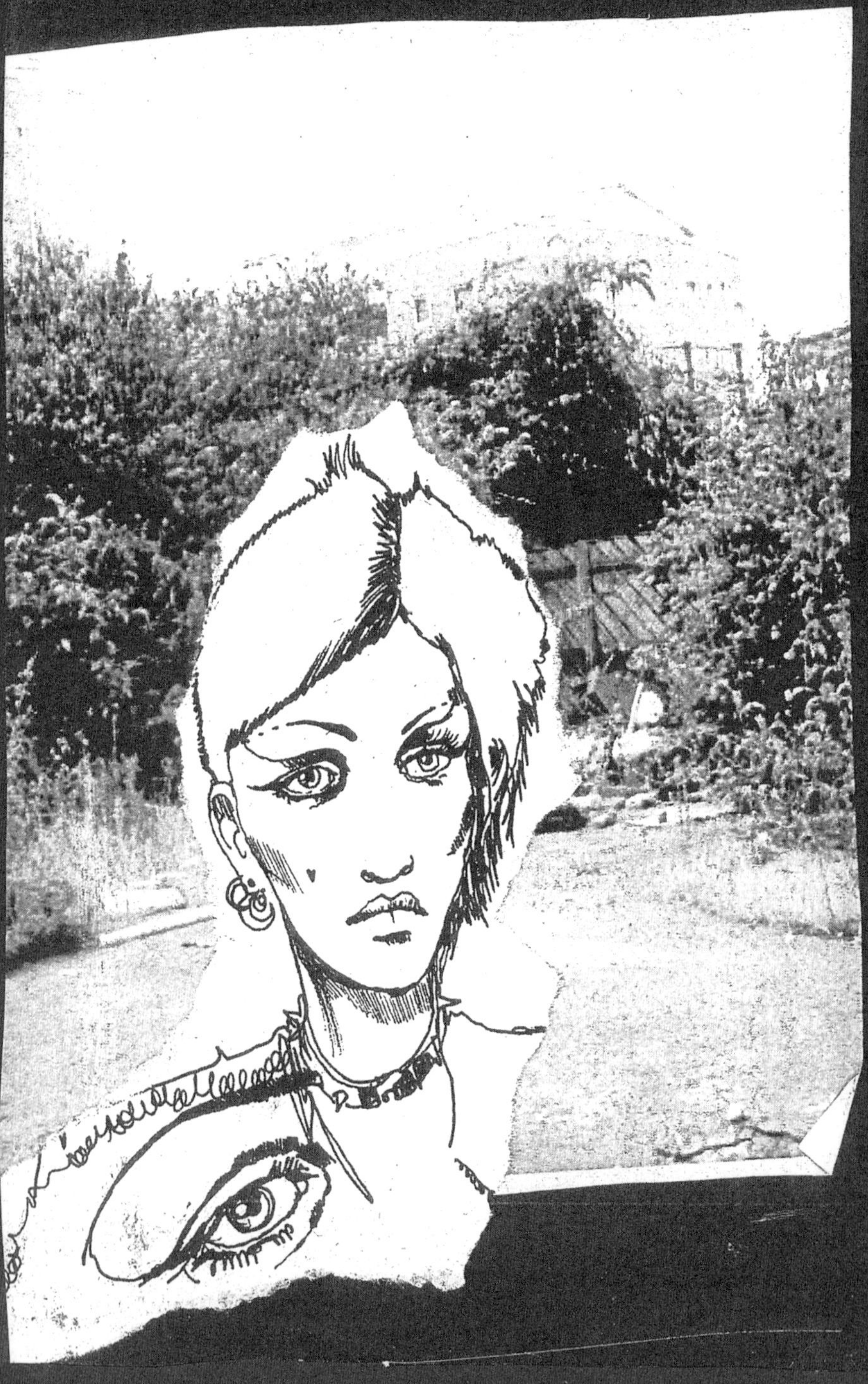

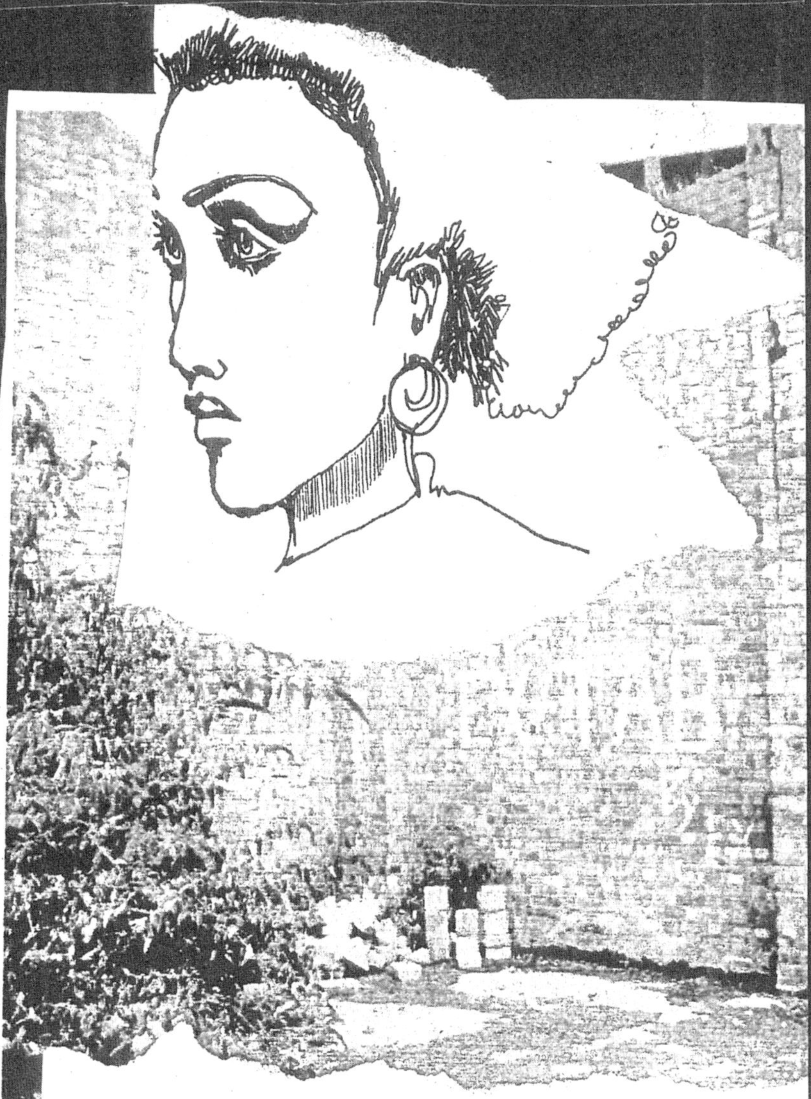

Beyond the heaps of dusty bricks, the crumbling walls a huge steel structure rises ,spanned with ivy and graffiti traces. This is the abandoned Olympic stadium, this is London 2013. A chance encounter, in the midst of a heat wave, London burns. Taking off. Occupation of space in multiple temporal zones. Projections into a dystopian future, harking back to a romanticised past, carving out territory in the present. Time, multi faceted and crystalline. Language shifting. Heaps of tyres smoulder, nuclear bunkers echo beneath soft ground. Sky glowing violet...stranded in the midst of luxuriant foliage.

The air is perfumed , the sky pink. My hair is loose, unkempt, I am in a red dress descending into the chlorine scent of a disused pool.
Riot season begins.

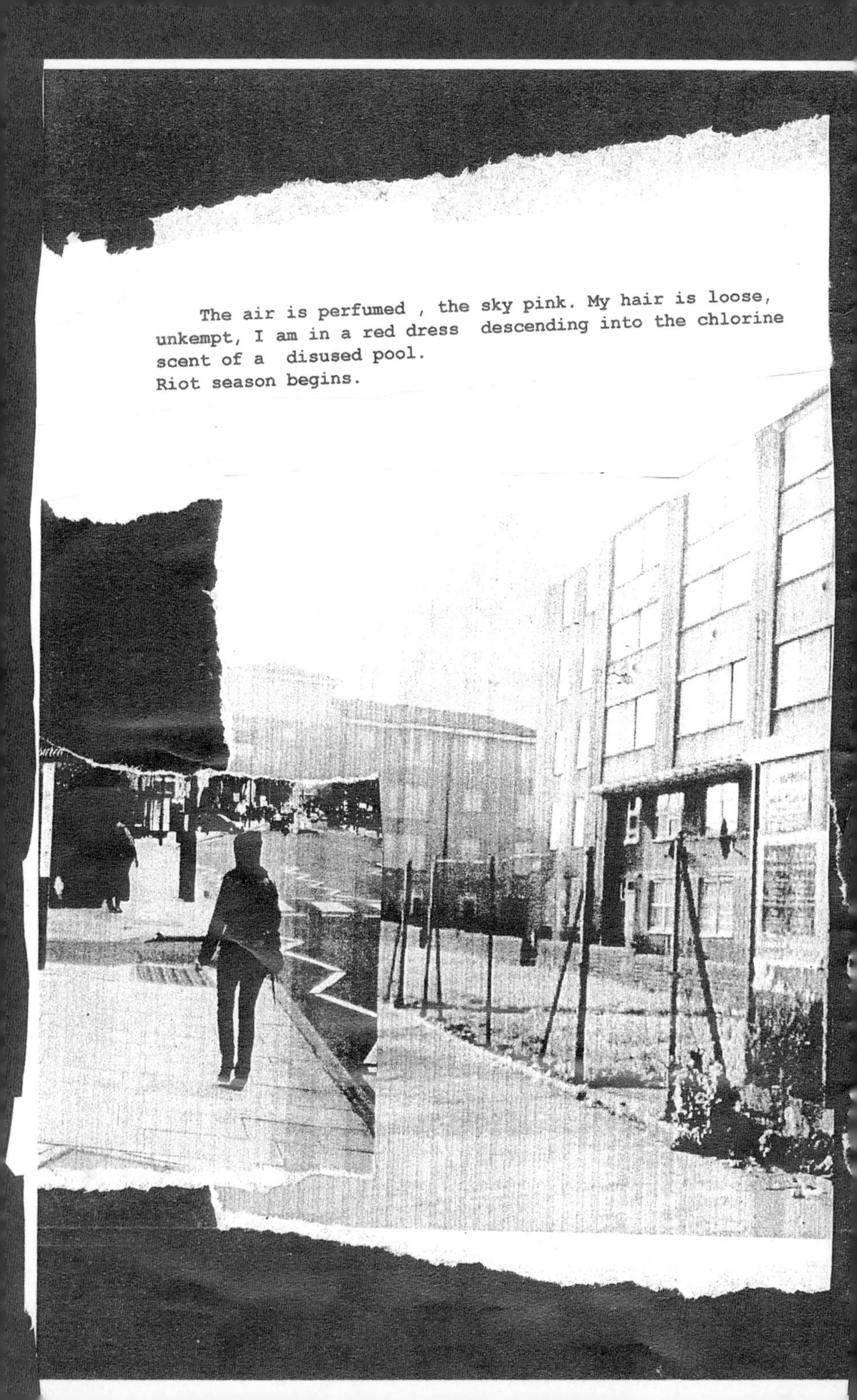

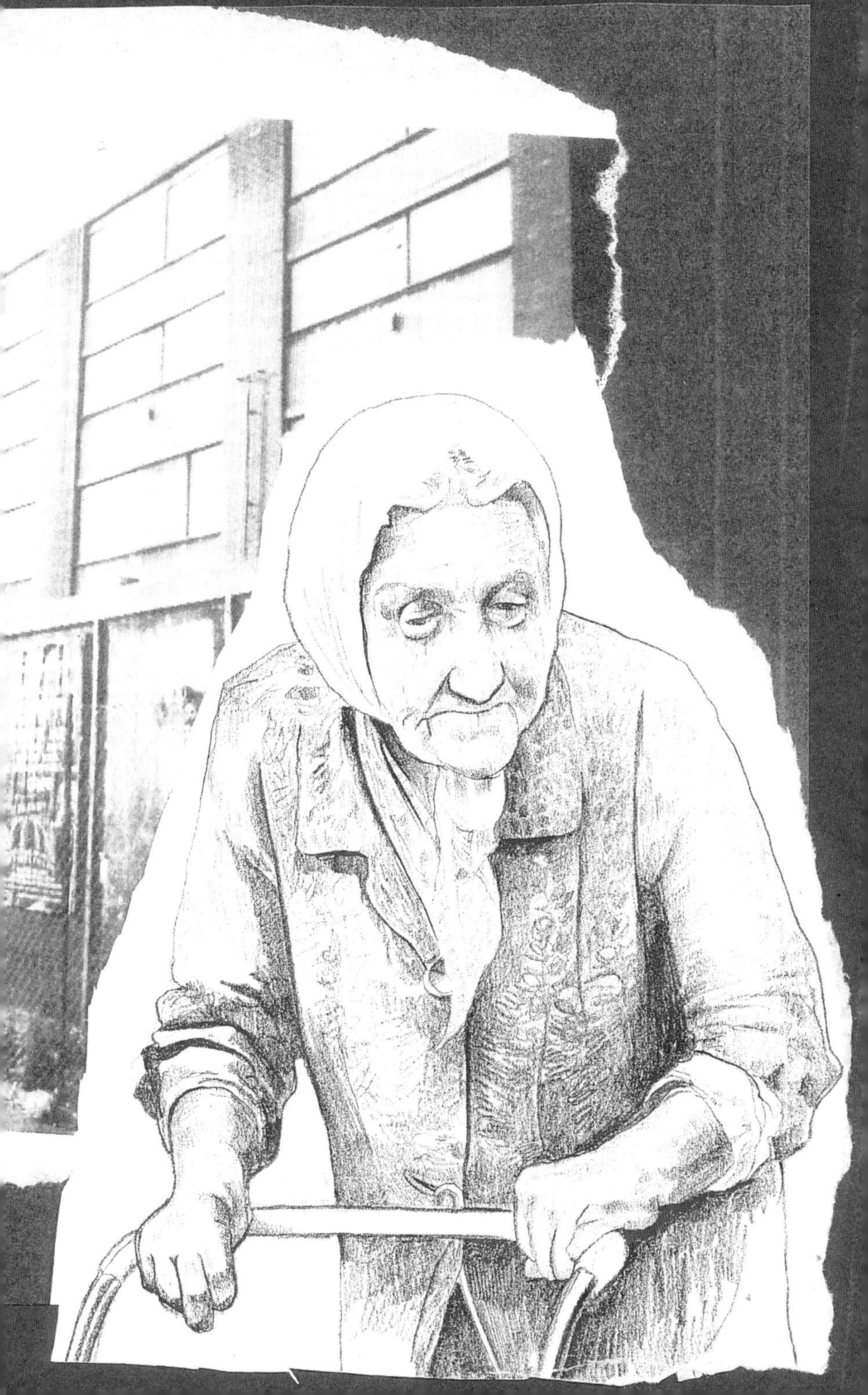

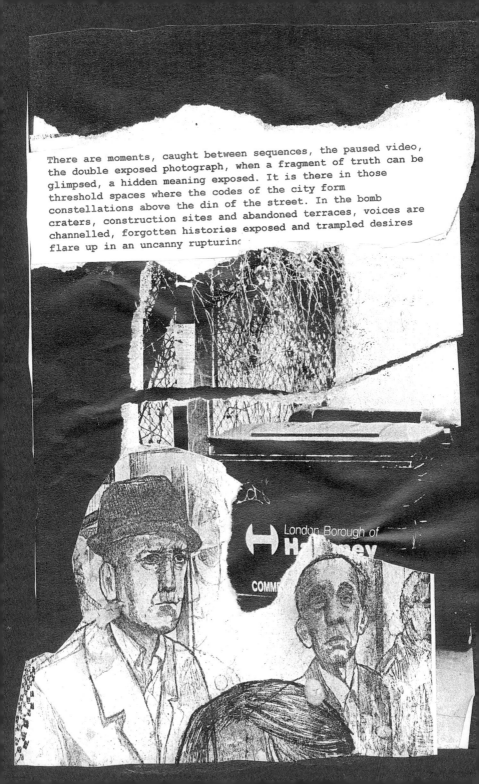

There are moments, caught between sequences, the paused video, the double exposed photograph, when a fragment of truth can be glimpsed, a hidden meaning exposed. It is there in those threshold spaces where the codes of the city form constellations above the din of the street. In the bomb craters, construction sites and abandoned terraces, voices are channelled, forgotten histories exposed and trampled desires flare up in an uncanny rupturing

London Borough of Ha ney

COMM

This is one of the enchanted places that slipped out of sight, only to emerge and reconfigure elsewhere.

1973/1981/1990/1994/1999/2001/2011/2013

DEVELOPERS!!HACKNEYCOUNCIL!!YUPPIES!HANDS OFF OUR ESTATES!!!!
FUCK OFF TO THE THAMES GATEWAY!!!!!!!!!

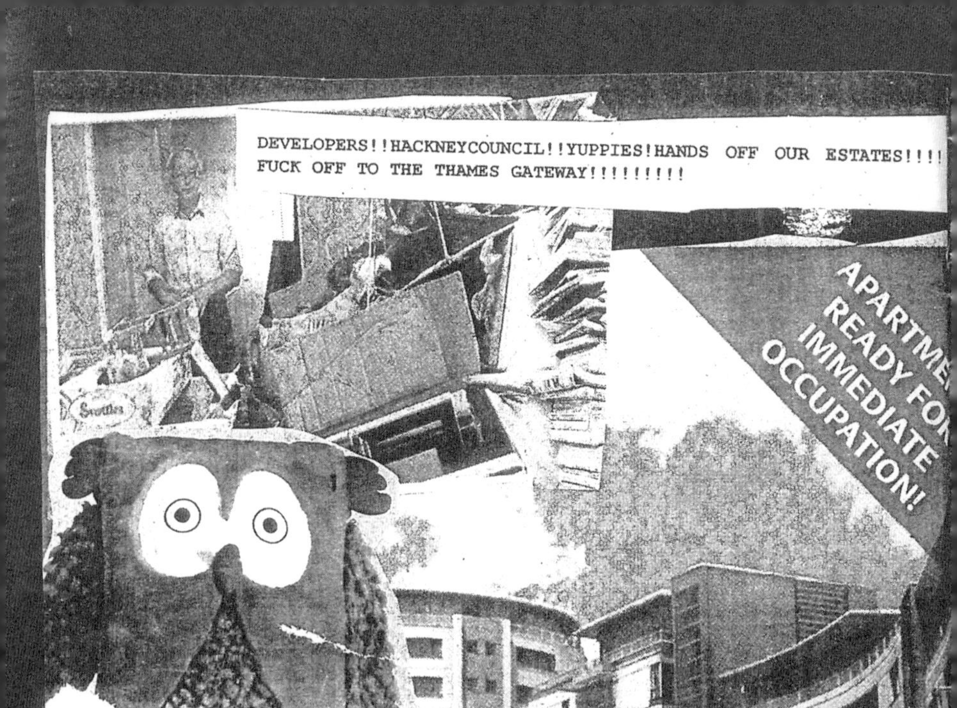
APARTME
READY FO
IMMEDIATE
OCCUPATION!

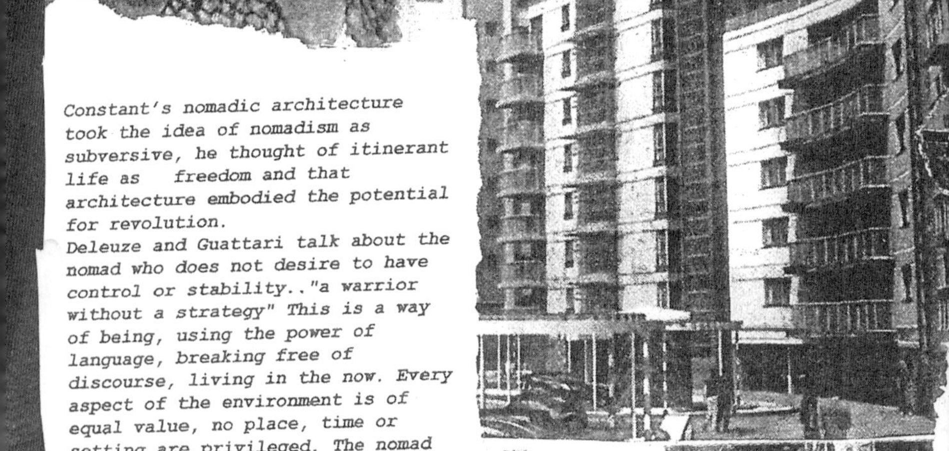

Constant's nomadic architecture took the idea of nomadism as subversive, he thought of itinerant life as freedom and that architecture embodied the potential for revolution.
Deleuze and Guattari talk about the nomad who does not desire to have control or stability.."a warrior without a strategy" This is a way of being, using the power of language, breaking free of discourse, living in the now. Every aspect of the environment is of equal value, no place, time or setting are privileged. The nomad is always becoming, with a line of flight ever open, of "choices and chances, commission and omission, opportunities taken and missed" Fox 1999

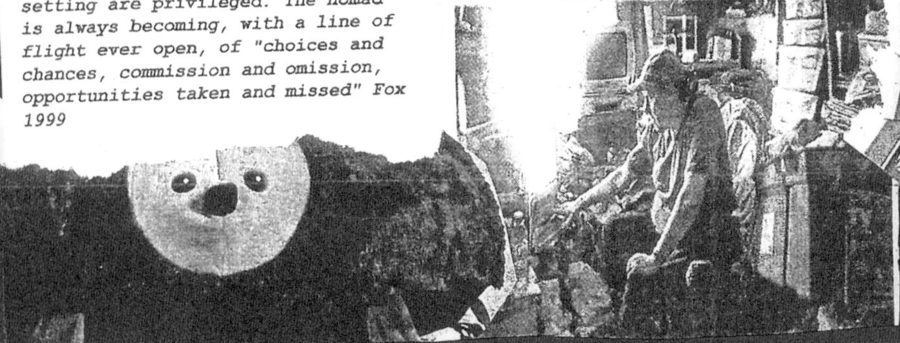

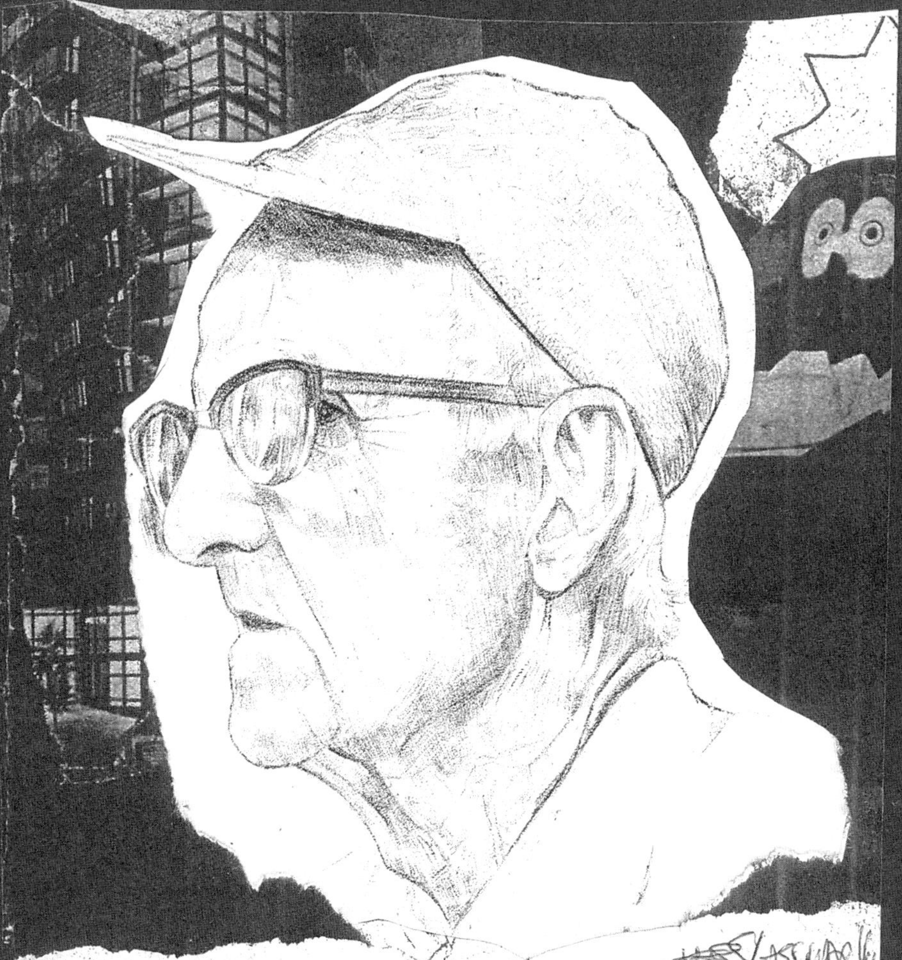

! VIVA SAVAGE MESSIAH !
SAVAGE MESSIAH DEMANDS THE ABOLITION OF ALL ZONES!! [illegible] SAVAGE MESSIAH IS CALLING FOR A MASS [illegible]! SMASH THE VILLE RADIEUSE, RETURN TO THE LABYRINTH!!!

YUPPIES!!! Hands off our houses! There's plenty of space for you in the THAMES GATEWAY! GET OUT OF HACKNEY!!!

Demand an end to boring, mediocre architecture, build your own social housing. DESTROY THE MASTERPLAN!

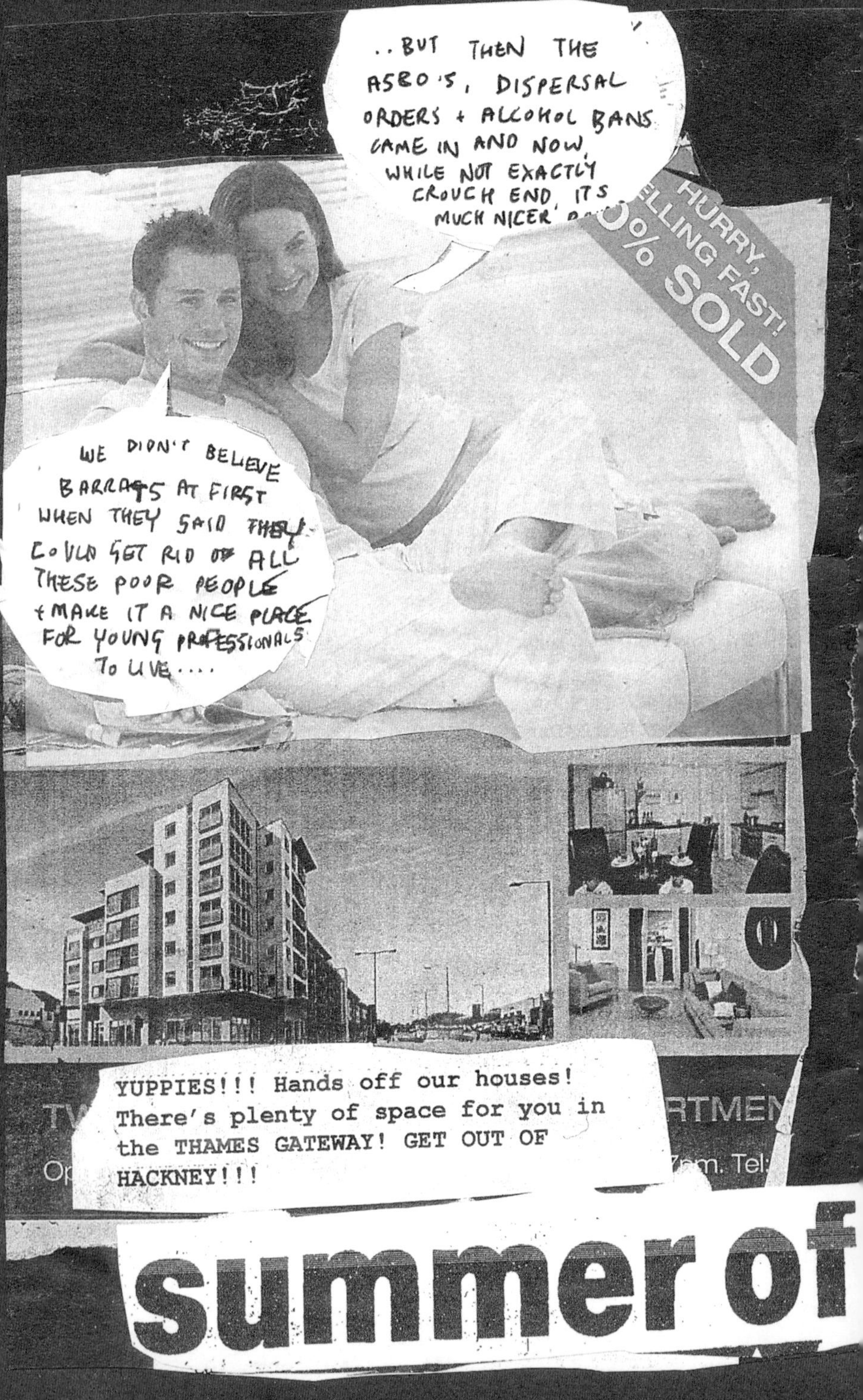
WE DIDN'T BELIEVE BARRATTS AT FIRST WHEN THEY SAID THEY COULD GET RID OF ALL THESE POOR PEOPLE + MAKE IT A NICE PLACE FOR YOUNG PROFESSIONALS TO LIVE....
..BUT THEN THE ASBO'S, DISPERSAL ORDERS + ALCOHOL BANS CAME IN AND NOW, WHILE NOT EXACTLY CROUCH END, ITS MUCH NICER
HURRY, ELLING FAST! % SOLD
YUPPIES!!! Hands off our houses! There's plenty of space for you in the THAMES GATEWAY! GET OUT OF HACKNEY!!!
summer of

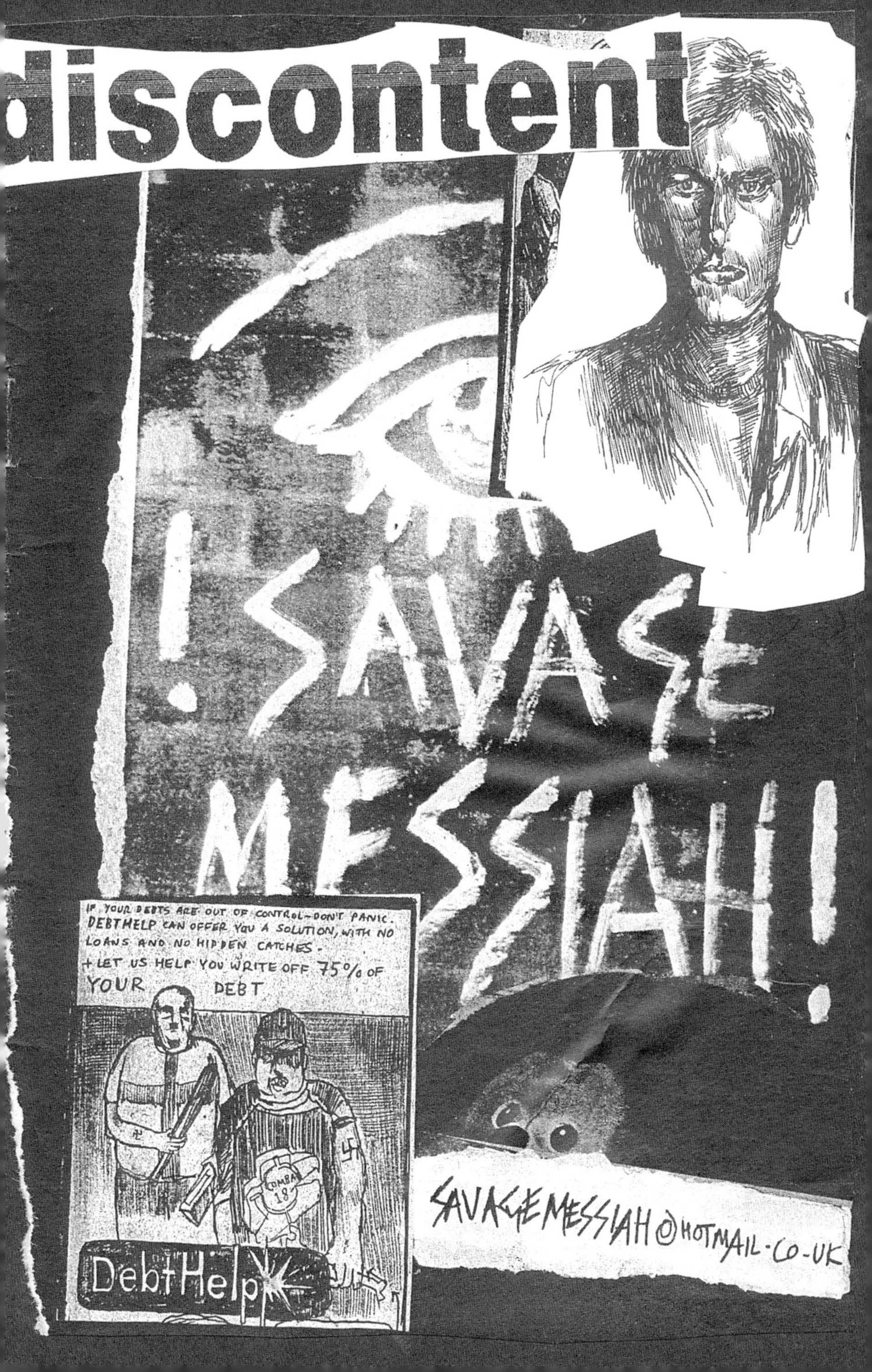

discontent

!SAVAGE MESSIAH!

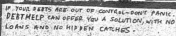

IF YOUR DEBTS ARE OUT OF CONTROL—DON'T PANIC.
DEBTHELP CAN OFFER YOU A SOLUTION, WITH NO
LOANS AND NO HIDDEN CATCHES.
+ LET US HELP YOU WRITE OFF 75% OF
YOUR   DEBT

DebtHelp

SAVAGEMESSIAH@HOTMAIL·CO·UK

MOSS SIDE, MANCHESTER
7-8 July 1981
20 police injured
53 arrests
WOOD GREEN, LONDON
7 July 1981
8 police injured
21 public injured
43 arrests
FINSBURY PARK, LONDON
20 April 1981
60 police injured
32 public injured
91 arrested
LONDON
BRISTOL
ST PAUL'S, BRISTOL
2 April 1980
49 police injured
100 arrested
SOUTHALL, LONDON
3 July 1981
105 police injured
30 public injured
23 arrested
BRIXTON, LONDON
9-13 April 1981
144 police injured
58 public injured
224 arrested
sick of yuppies encroaching on your territory?
are you thinking NOT ANOTHER FUCKING YUPPIE DROME?
THE SOLUTION LIES IN YOUR OWN HANDS!
WRECK IT! LOOT IT! BURN IT!
0870 005 3749

SAVAGE MESSIAH

ISSUE 8 £2.00

LAURA OLDFIELD FORD

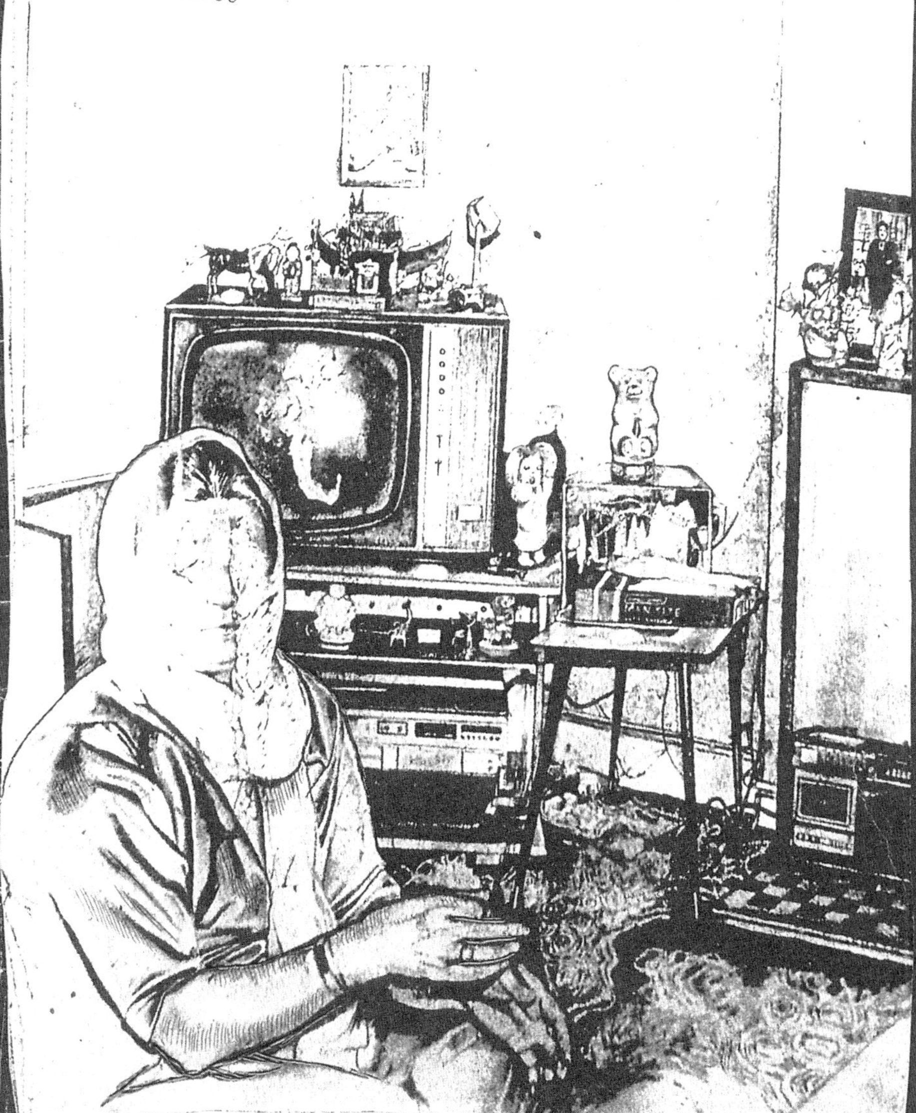

KINGS CROSS TO HACKNEY WICK.

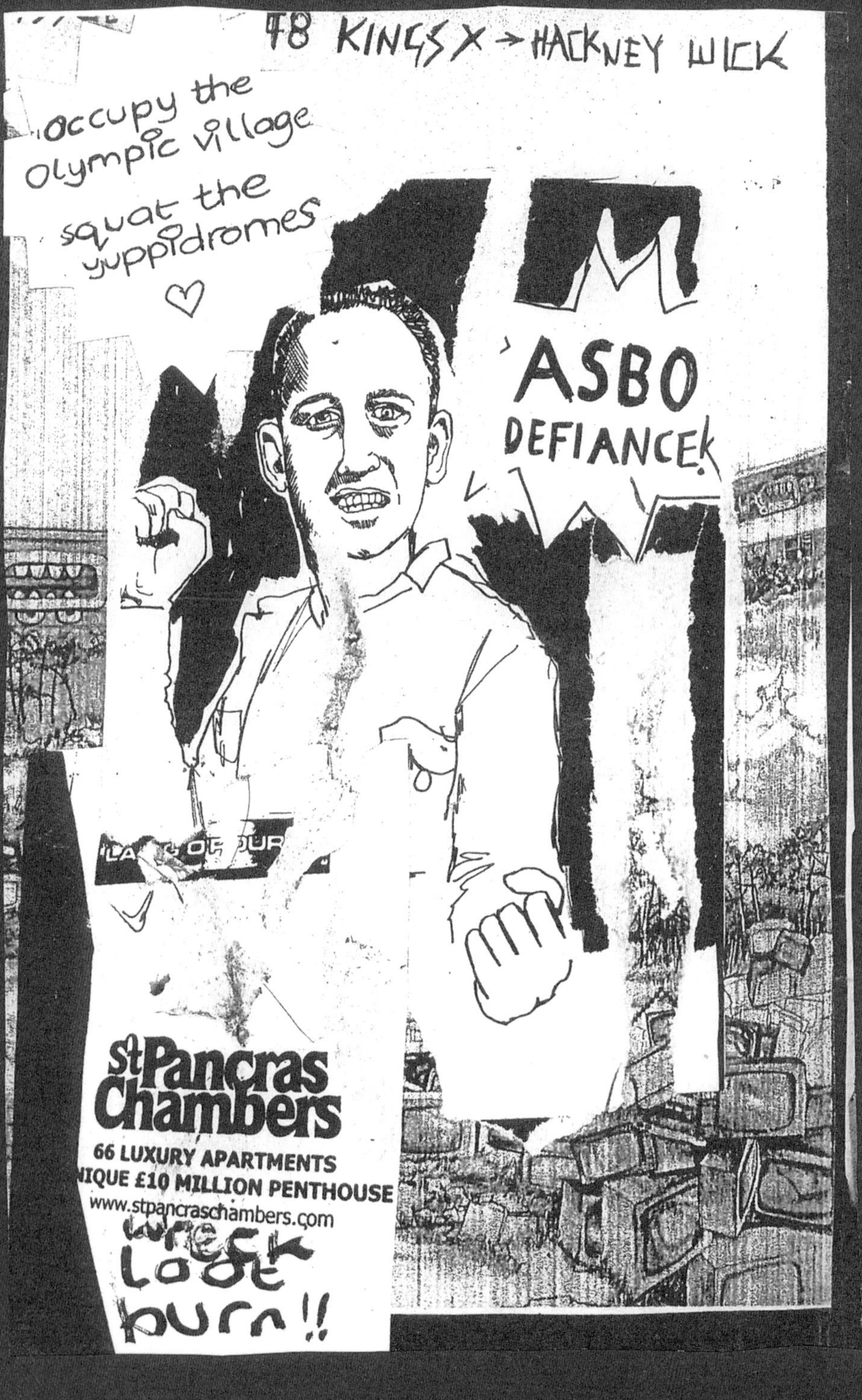

48 KINGS X → HACKNEY WICK
occupy the olympic village
squat the yuppidromes
ASBO DEFIANCE!
St Pancras Chambers
66 LUXURY APARTMENTS
NIQUE £10 MILLION PENTHOUSE
www.stpancraschambers.com
wreck loot burn!!

Louise Road, E15 £352,500 Fhd
Lovely house boasting many fine features
and situated in a quiet residential turning

Trumpington Ro
Charming brick fron
home located in this
and offering spaciou

£289,950 Fhd
boasting no onward
should be viewed
appointment

Geere Road, E15 £310,000 Fhd
three bedroom recently converted Victorian
house that should appeal to a variety of
purchasers. Close to excellent transport links.

Bridge Point Lofts, E7 £299,950 Lhd
Stunning live/work apartment situated on the
fourth floor of this highly desirable modern
development and boasting a huge terrace

I'VE LOOKED INTO THE FUTURE
~~AND I CAN'T FIND MYSELF~~
ANYWHERE.

E11
ed to a
er this
use.

Louise road, E15 £330,000 Fhd

SO HE SAYS TO ME, GET THIS RIGHT,
HE SAYS, 'STOP GOIN ON ABOUT MIDDLE
CLASS WANKERS, YOU KNOW MATE WE'RE
ALL MIDDLE CLASS NOW, ~~WE'VE ALL GOT
HARD NOT GARDENS~~' AND I SAY, YOU
WHAT PAL? YOU THINK I'M GONNA TAKE THIS
SHIT IN MY OWN GAFF? AND HE SAYS, 'YOUR
GAFF?' ALL SNEERING LIKE SO I SAYS
'YEAH MY GAFF, ITS MY FUCKING NAME
ON THE RENT BOOK'. SO HE SAYS 'RENT
BOOK, HOW QUAINT' AND I AINT GOT NO
CHOICE THEN TO SMASH HIS FUCKING
FACE IN, CHEEKY LITTLE CUNT

Road, E15 £350 PW
West Ham Park, this delightful
ree double bedrooms over
rly viewing recommended

Adriatic Apartments, E16 £330 PW
Keatons are delighted to offer this stunning
one double bedroom apartment, boasting
fantastic views over London's Royal Docks

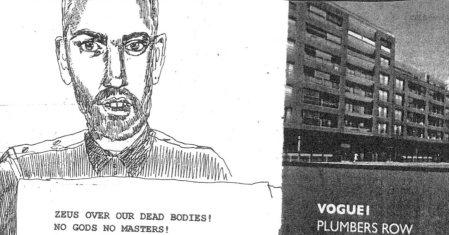

ZEUS OVER OUR DEAD BODIES!
NO GODS NO MASTERS!
DEATH TO THE GODS OF MOUNT OLYMPUS

VOGUE I
PLUMBERS ROW

He was drawing a map for me on a torn up fag packet, it was of
the streets and industrial estates before the mass demolition
had taken place.

LOFT LIVING VICTIMS
OF FUTURE CRIMES!

The preparation for the Olympics involves systematic social cleansing. An attempt to sanitise the market on Bethnal Green Road and Brick Lane has already begun but is proving unsuccessful. There will be a battle for the entire East end.

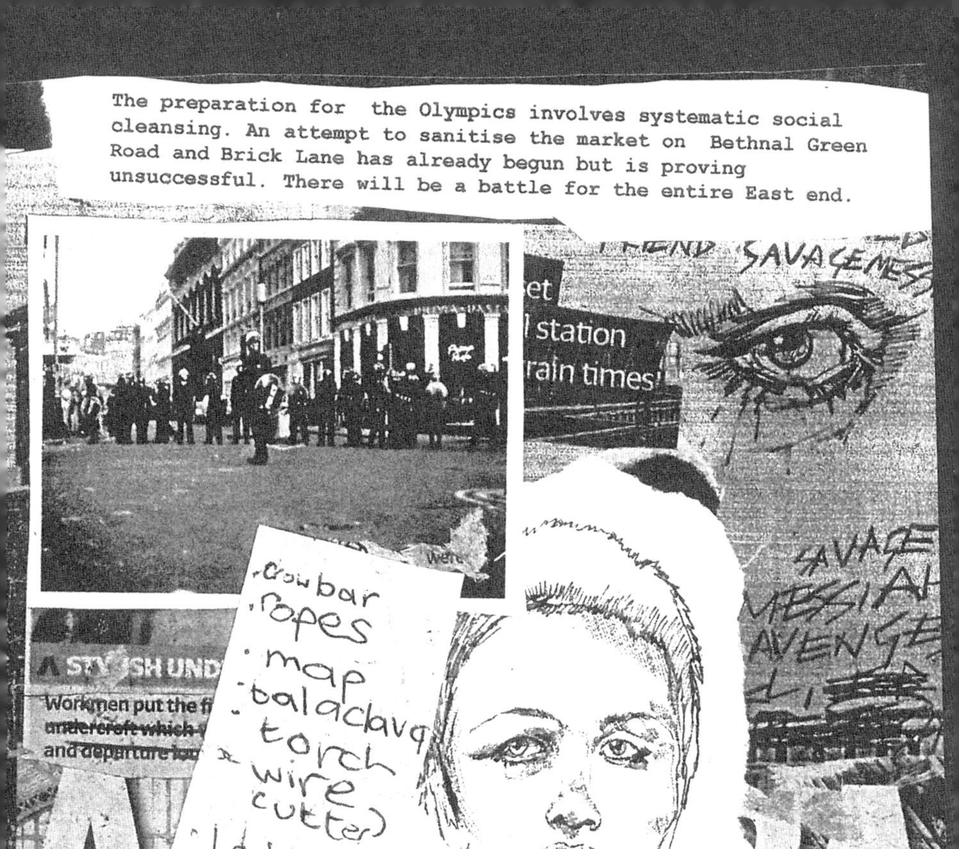
SAVAGE MESS
station
rain times
crowbar
ropes
map
balaclava
torch
wire
cutters
Ladder?
van
Johns
phones
SAVAGE
MESSIAH
AVENGE
Workmen put the fi
Wembley football p

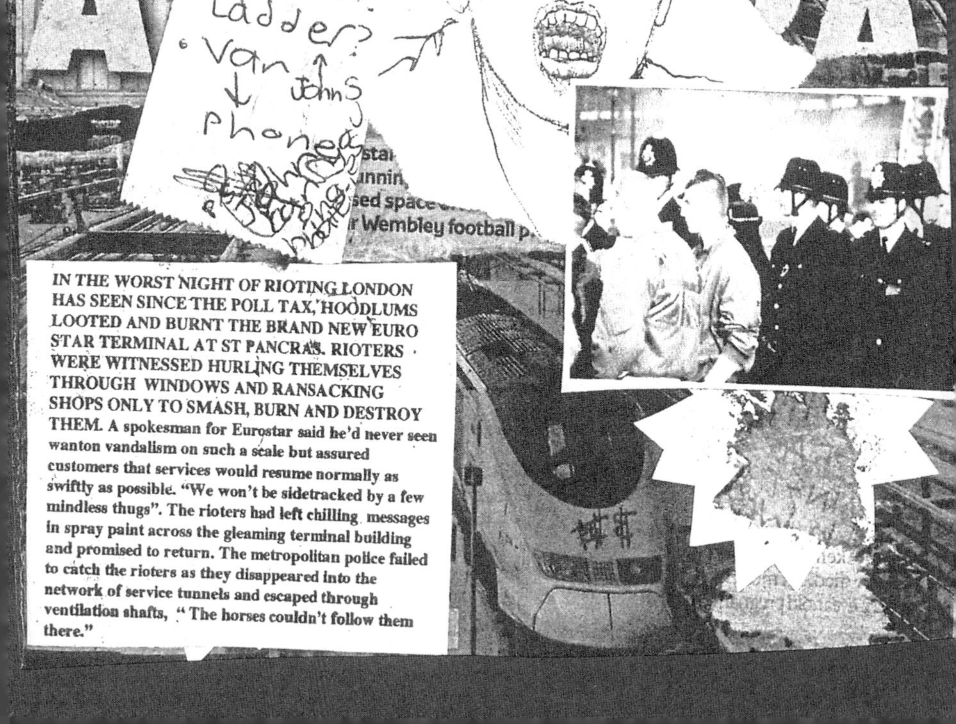

IN THE WORST NIGHT OF RIOTING LONDON HAS SEEN SINCE THE POLL TAX, HOODLUMS LOOTED AND BURNT THE BRAND NEW EURO STAR TERMINAL AT ST PANCRAS. RIOTERS WERE WITNESSED HURLING THEMSELVES THROUGH WINDOWS AND RANSACKING SHOPS ONLY TO SMASH, BURN AND DESTROY THEM. A spokesman for Eurostar said he'd never seen wanton vandalism on such a scale but assured customers that services would resume normally as swiftly as possible. "We won't be sidetracked by a few mindless thugs". The rioters had left chilling messages in spray paint across the gleaming terminal building and promised to return. The metropolitan police failed to catch the rioters as they disappeared into the network of service tunnels and escaped through ventilation shafts, "The horses couldn't follow them there."

So then I had to sign everyday in this open plan office that
looked like a Starbucks with plants and coffee machines and
soft chairs in primary colours. That was the punishment, the
compulsory visit to a building droning with resentment. They'd
tried to erase it when they ripped out the strip lights and
metal grilles, but there it was, dyed in the fabric, the
perpetual low buzz of coercion.
I was pretending to make lists of job vacancies when he invaded
my peripheral vision, this massive bloke in a pin stripe suit
with a weird, probing stare.

It was around the time when the pound shops were just gearing
up for Halloween.
   The windows were full of garish tat, glow in the dark
eyeballs and plastic pumpkins. I escaped for an hour from the
flat pack blandness of Working Links
   to Astro Caf,   Genesis crackling through the kitchen.
Oh think twice,
   it's just another day for you, You and me in paradise ......

Hanging round in cafs was better than going home, even the vile
job centre was better than that at the moment. I hated the
flat, it still held the smells from when Jim had gone beserk
and barricaded the place up. The floor was criss crossed with
smears of blood, whisky bottles smashed in the kitchen. He'd
gone, eventually, but the place was wrecked.
   We were all out in two weeks anyway.
Every morning I got up and walked the streets.

I was stirring the heap of Nescafe into the frothy milk when
the text came. A number I didn't recognise.
Hi it's Paul, the tall skinhead from Working Links, you are
gorgeous, fancy a drink?

        the devious bastard was sitting at his desk spying into my
file. He knew where I lived, full name, date of birth,
everything. I stared at the phone and left it.

I walked back along the canal to the Dorset Estate. The towpath
was glittering from an early frost and I felt invigorated. I
climbed the twisting staircase of Loveless House to see if K
was in. I hadn't seen her since all that shit finally went off
with Jim, not that I really wanted to talk about that. I
wanted to rekindle the old times, the times before I got stuck
in sordid isolation. I missed all that, going down the boozer
half pissed already, maybe the Birdcage, half trashed and
falling, singing old songs.
K looked rough when she answered the door but smiled enough to
make a welcome. She gestured to the bedroom door and pushed me
in the lounge.

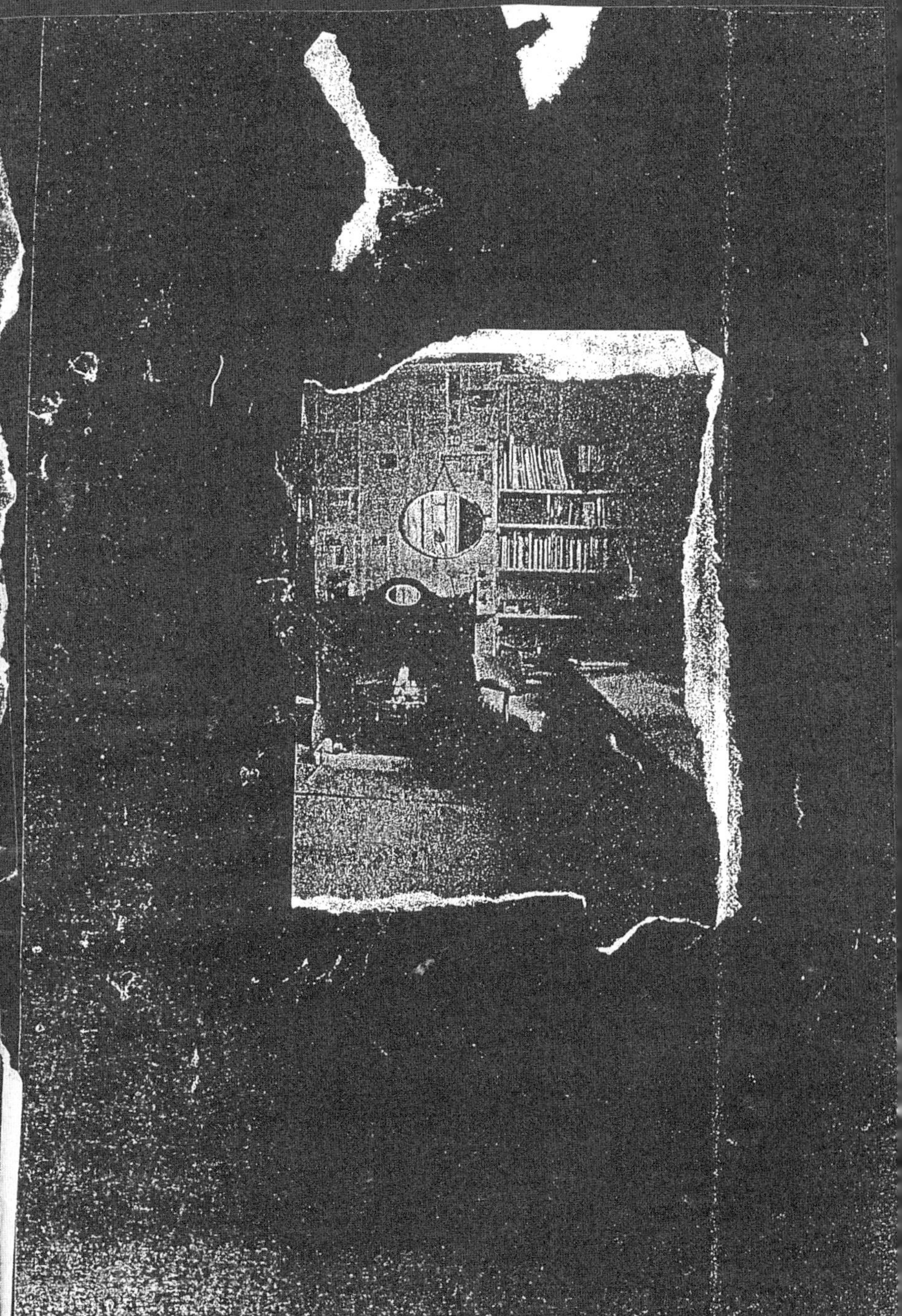

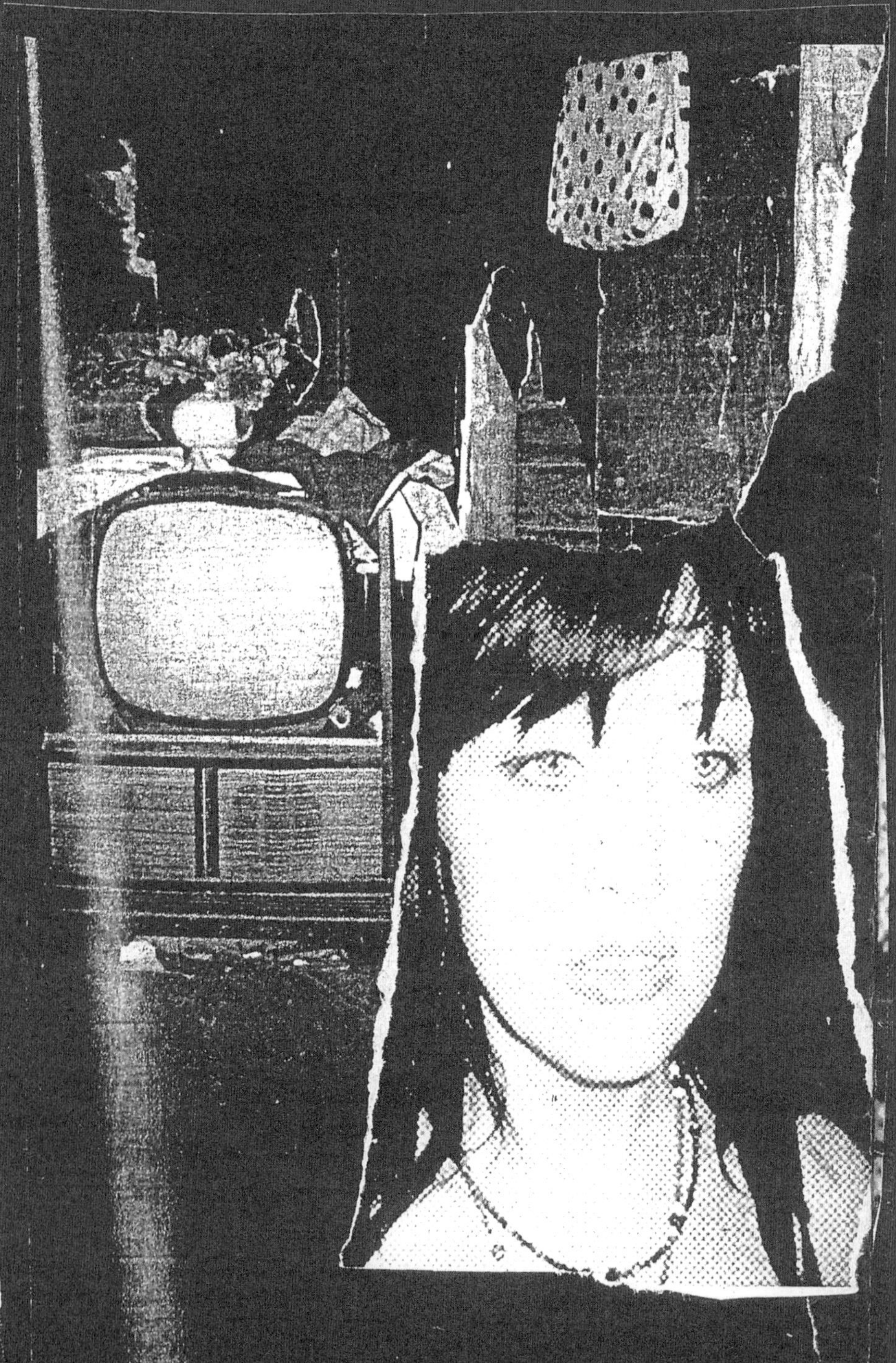

I sat awkwardly while voices dipped and rose next door and
wished I hadn't come. I let myself out onto the balcony and
cast my eyes over the giant building site that London had
become. I could dream then, searching towers and bridges,
arches and narrow lanes, scaffolding spanning the horizon. He
had to be in there somewhere, my true ally, my partner in
crime.

Then the door banged and K was out on the balcony with me
sparking up a Marlboro light laughing her head off in a pink
fluffy dressing gown. Oh my god, thank god you turned up, I
thought he was never gonna go. We went back into the lounge
with all K's trinkets, an ad hoc mixture of charity shop and
Ikea. Let me get some slap on and we'll go and have a drink
yeah, it's been ages.

Things were quiet in the Vic, Tuesday afternoon not much doing,
Kelvin and some of his boys were hanging about in the other bar
watching horse racing on a big screen.

Then the phone bleeped and I got a jolt when I saw it was him
again, the bloke from the dole course.
 Hey gorgeous.
 I was a bit pissed now and grabbed Kay. Look at this, some
perv down the dole office. Wants me to meet him, been sending
me these mental texts.
Kay was quizzing me about him. What's he like, why don't you
meet him, might be a laugh, might be funny, get him down here.
Don't be daft I said I but didn't put it straight from my mind.
 And the pints kept coming and the chasers kept coming.
Countdown was on the big screen and Kelv and the lads kept
coming round putting songs on the jukey trying to get us to
dance.

     Rhythm is a dancer, it's a source companion, people feel it
everywhere

And as K got up to dance the phone beeped again, another
message.
 ,Oh my god, I looked over at Kay holding the phone up but she
was getting squeezed tight and dragged round the room.

Don't be shy gorgeous, we both know you'd love it.
 I felt a shiver of desire scuttle across me and instantly felt
disgusted with myself. Why would I feel excited by some dirty
scumbag lording it round the dole office?

I'm wondering about later. How much I've got left in my purse.
Can't face the flat yet, don't want to be off my head on my
own. But anyway, K and them were there so maybe I couldn't see
the harm, might be a good laugh like she said. We could let
him get the drinks in. And so I sent it, the text telling him
where we were and I just thought fuck it, who cares, I won't be
on my own with him, and the halves kept coming and the breezers
kept coming and the news on the big screen went blurry and
soft.

And then there he was, suddenly taking up the room ... with a
long leather coat over the pin stripe suit. He strolled
straight over, bold as brass.
 He was flashing the wad about the moment he saw us, the
fucking geezer, the big man. K was suddenly sitting up ,
pushing her tits out, putting on a big sexy smile. She's fallen
for it, I thought, straight away, his overbearing mockney
charm. And then he sat down between us and stared at me again,
the eyes boring in, making me feel a bit uncomfortable, despite
the booze, despite the half a pill I'd just necked with the
lager.

On the shots and serious this time, they're doing trebles for
singles tonight on the vodka I said, so he got straight up and
went to the bar turning round to stare back with that leering
grin as he waited.
You gonna fuck him or what? K said as soon as he got up to be
served.
Are you joking K, the geezers from the fucking dole office!
He's a right ugly weirdo!
   She's thinking of blue drinks, an endless parade, lined up at
the bar.
And so the drinks kept coming and I was dancing with some of
Jerome's crew who were all drinking in this side now the
football had finished,
that song 'Breathe', Sean Paul and Blu Cantrell.
And the dirty bastard, Paul, his eyes were boring in, all over
my body, with that malevolent, intense stare saying if I wanted
I could have you.
 And all the while K was laughing.
And you know that I'm going to take you home tonight., he said
as soon as Kay went to fix up her make up in the ladies,
 His hand rested on my thigh and I let it stay there, eyes
unfocused, head fuzzy and multicoloured with the booze.

Walking along the Northern outfall is a melancholy experience.
The phantom of an invented, slickly choreographed future haunts
the landscape. Photoshopped families, the joyful inhabitants of
the new yuppiedromes are not here yet, but their avatars stalk
us.

Amidst the rubble and chaos, Polish construction workers in
luminous garb bundle in and out of vans for papers and fags.
 Oily leatherskins deconstruct the rusting heaps.
        Sometimes there's a group of kids with a nicked
scooter, always the same, taking apart, a destructive urge;
 sections examined and strewn across the Greenway path.
 The area is cut, scrutinized, destroyed, not rebuilt but cast
off as parts hurled across a flat expanse.
                    The sewage pipe is the conduit, it
slices through the wreckage and gives a Gods eye view of the
marshes.

I didn't really see the point, I mean, the struggle, day to
day, to get by, when you know, it seems a bit unnecessary, I
mean work, you know, what's the fucking point?
There were loads of crew shacked up in the Marshgate trading
estate, the vehicles were parked up by the Bow flyover, been
there a while, trucks, vans, ambulances amidst the oil drums
and broken pallets.

Sometimes, when you had a party down there you could end up
with 500 people.

Do we have to watch this?
Oh I love Montel. I love Trisha. I love them all.
Sick of it here.
The caravan is warm. There are red fairy lights and silk roses
from the market. The TV flickers in the corner, colour
saturated, turquoise glow.. Adele watches the disclosure cult,
she has become a part of it.

Go then.

 He liked it round here, they'd been on the site for two
months and the life was pretty good, not too many casualties
and the money was easy enough to find.

Do you want me to bring anything back from the Offy he asked ε
he grabbed his leather jacket. She barely glanced up as she
murmured something about tobacco.

 He felt that strange mix of euphoria and guilt as he jumped
down from the caravan to the dusty tarmac beneath. He was free
again, roving the alleys and yards in search of encounters.
She used to go with him once, walking, drifting, exploring new
zones. Hard to really remember those days now. Back then it was
always her, dressed up, trashy and beautiful, getting people
onto warehouse rooftops with soundsystems and wraps of k. It
pained him to leave her nervously watching TV while everyone
else was hammered in the yard.

He found Jim sitting outside his van, blood glittering in a
smarting head wound. The rest of the crew were hanging around
drinking stella waiting to go to a party somewhere. He felt
reckless as they started the walk east along the Northern
Outfall, overwhelmed by the desire for a catalyst, something
dramatic to shake up his life.

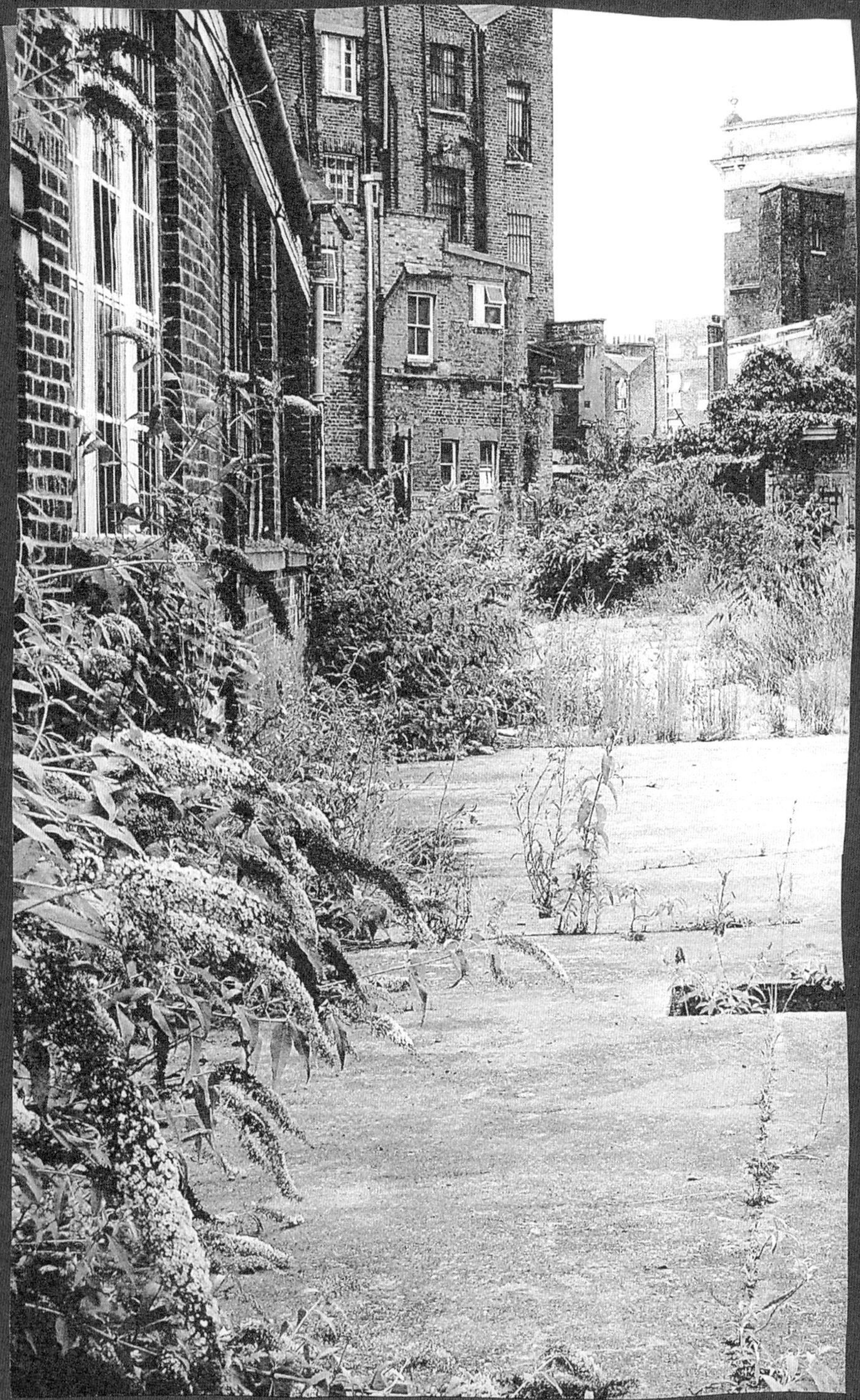

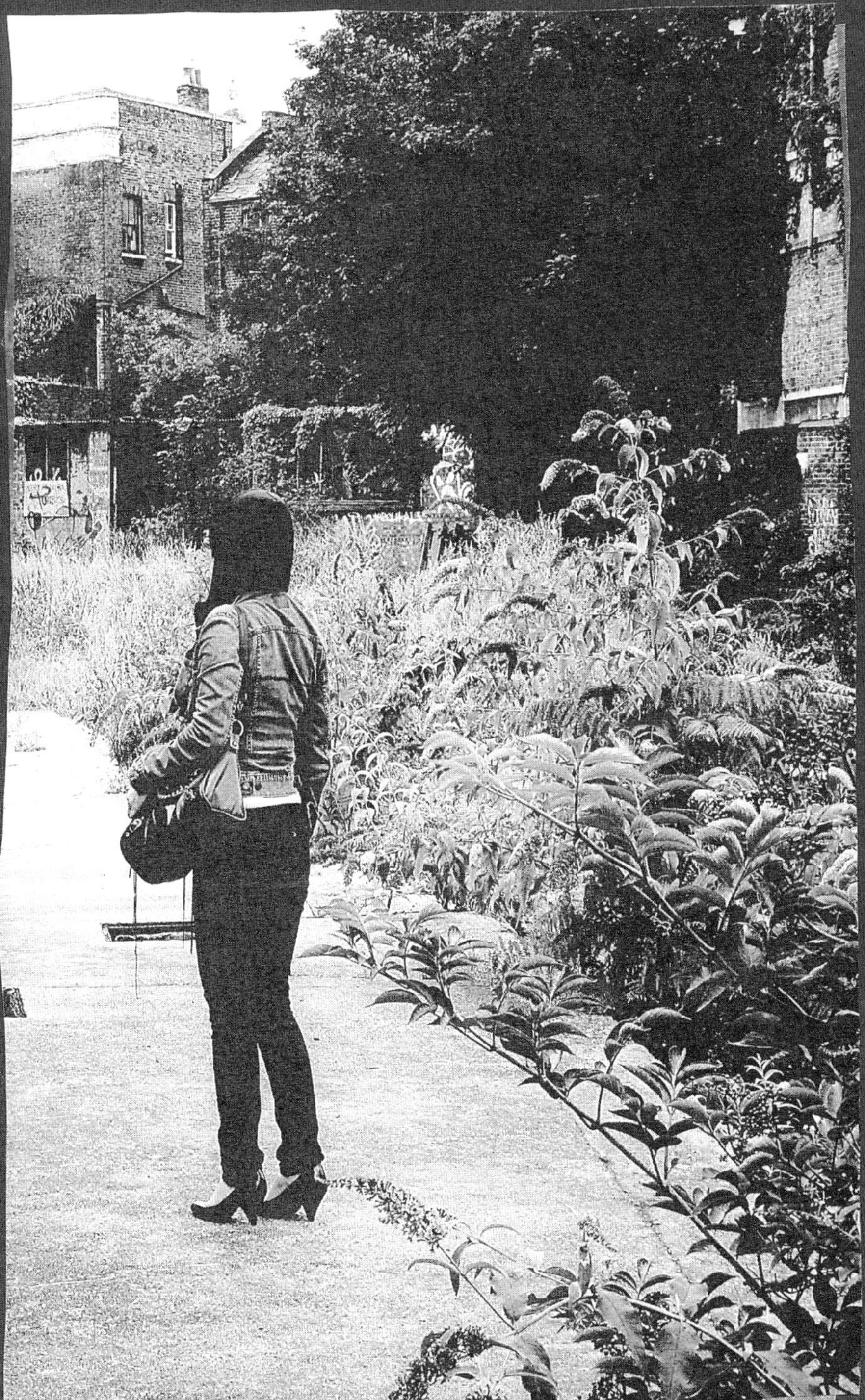

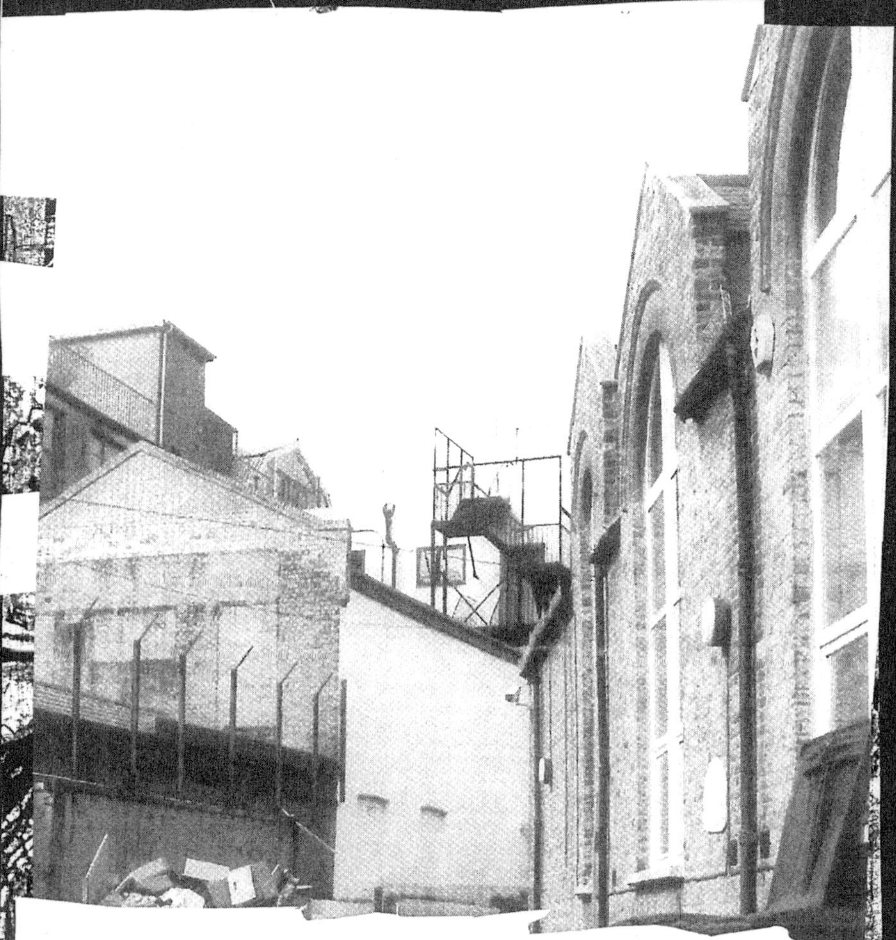

Of course, she knew she'd let him go, not pushed him exactly, just let him drift away gently, without making the effort to pull him back in. There wasn't really an exact point when the malaise had started, when it didn't matter anymore that he saw her without make up, looking dishevelled in the morning, bloated and tired and rough with a hangover. She couldn't even figure out when it was that she'd stopped wanting him to desire her, when did that start, that feeling of just not being bothered anymore.? It had gone on a long time , that feeling of heaviness, the weight under the ribs, of being pushed deep into a bed kept for sleeping now. It all became futile. Waking. Living. There was no rhythm, no thrills to shred the tedium. It was all condensed in a grey dread that made every hour, every day the same. It surrounded her, no past no future, just suspension in the fog.

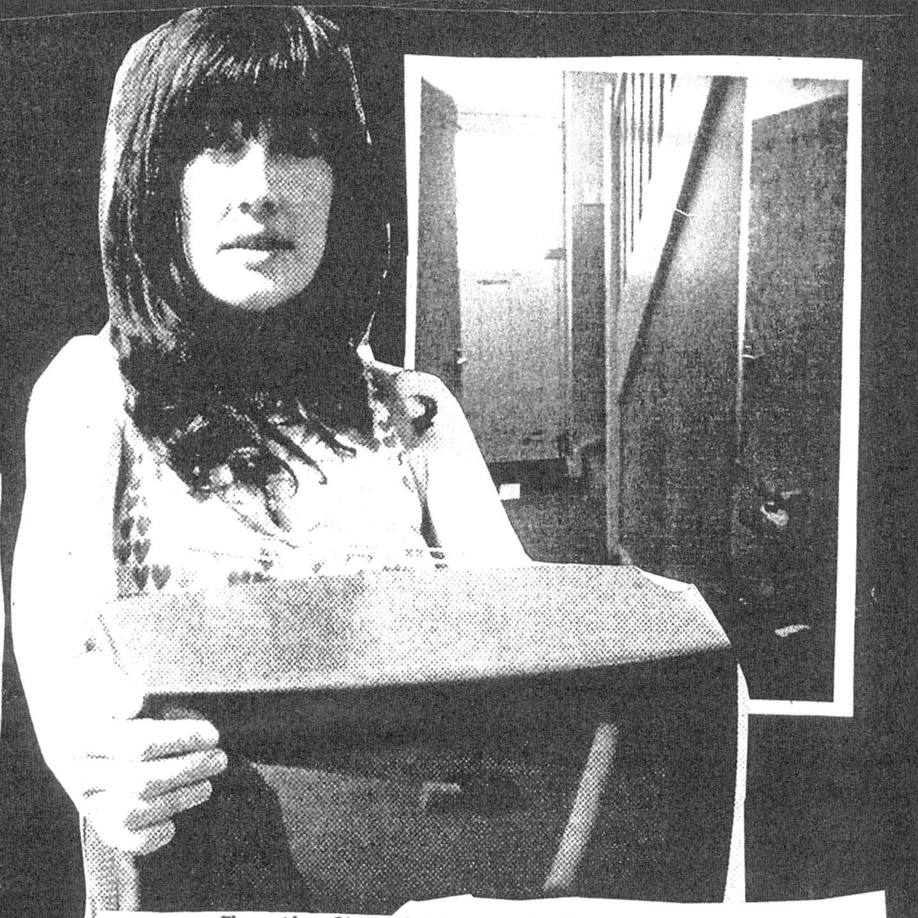

Then the first letter arrived, she could pinpoint that date ,it rose sharply in her mind.
, a brown envelope stamped first Glasgow then Peterlee, PLEASE REDIRECT.

where you been? been missing you, me especially

haven't been the same since you
disappeared, and so I'm wondering where the hell are
I hope you get this

Love always,

There was a photo of him outside by a fire with Scottish hills in the background. She studied his face, unchanged, still the same thick dark hair, pale skin and dark eyes, Scots-Italian. He was still handsome, still had that way of smiling that made you think of kissing him, of hiding away in some cottage for the winter. What would he think of her now. She couldn't bear to see his disappointment, he'd recoil at the sight of her. She nipped her thighs and looked with dismay at the dimpled flesh, and her face, she peered deep into the mirror and

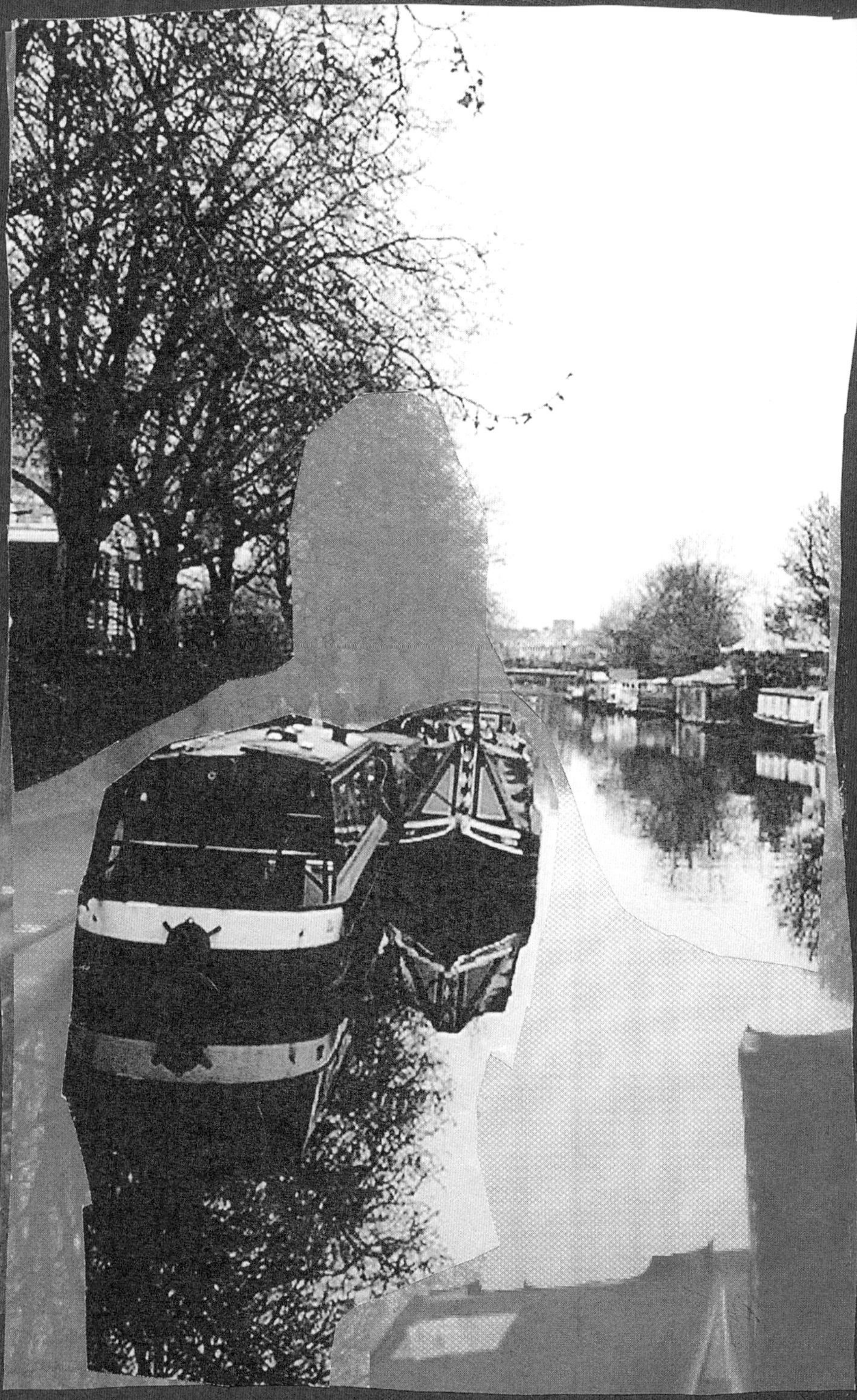

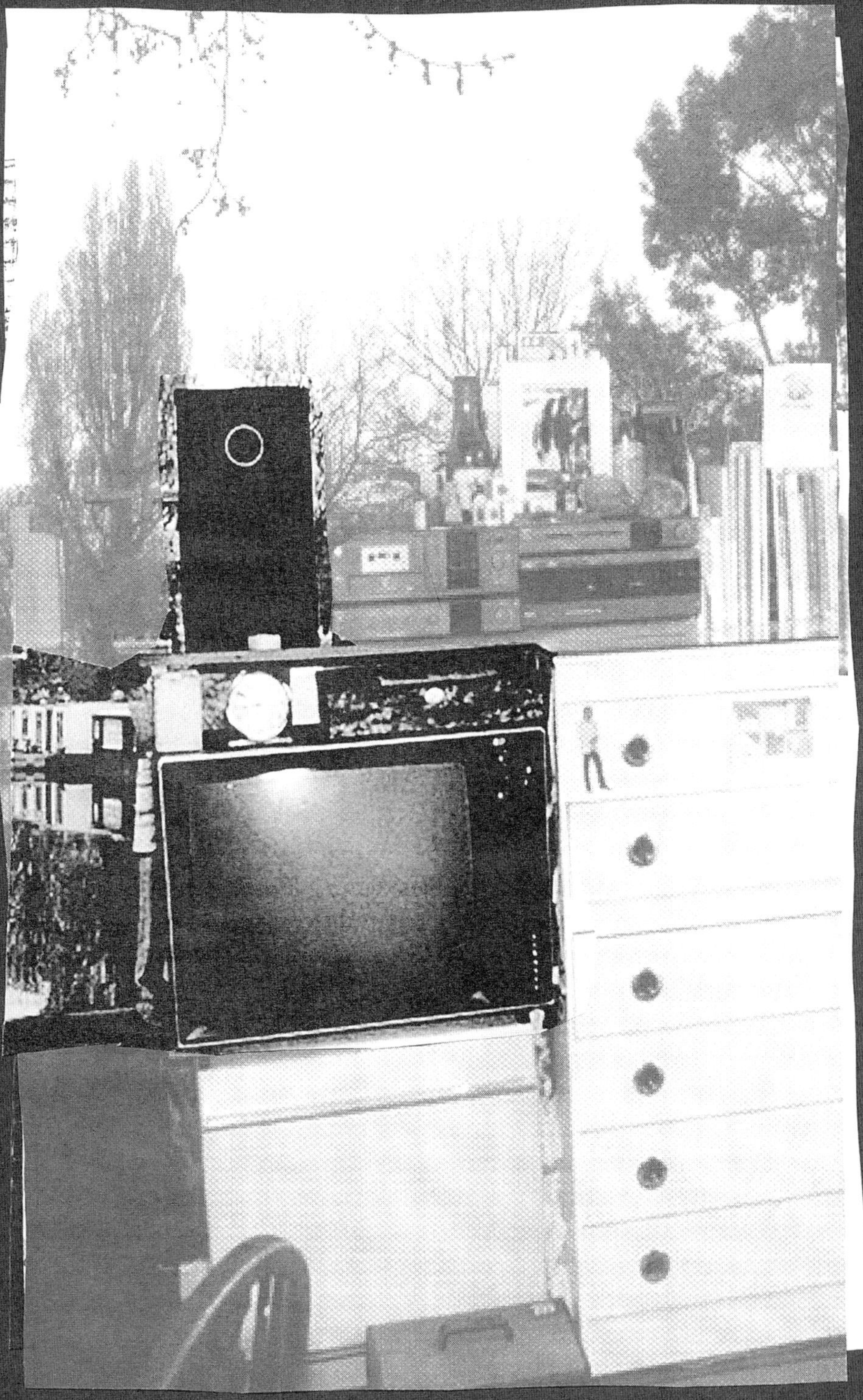

She felt sick, couldn't stand herself. She wasn't the girl that had flirted and messed around with that handsome boy.
He wouldn't feel the same if he saw her now.

But still, that letter had touched her in a way she hadn't felt for so long. It pierced the fog like flashing head lights in a dark lane. She was alive, someone from that other life had addressed her directly. He was reaching out to her.

The air was October sharp, dusk now.

Stratford was seething beneath an orange lamp glow. They took a convoluted route through the shopping centre, through 60s mazes and dark alcoves, corridors of sullen mosaics. It felt like a video game to him as odd shambling figures loomed up suddenly from dim corners. The light was phosphorescent, an arcade of the past trapped in the wrong time.

There was a lively scene when they walked in the Edward VII, a few old punks, some Anarcho types and a few Goths from UEL. He knew he looked good in his leather jacket and black hair quiffed like Cosmo Vinyl.

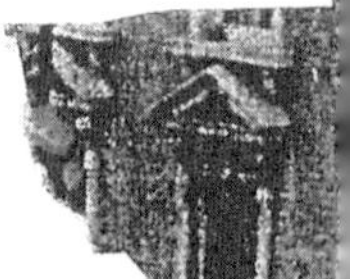

They pushed through the back to a snug corner of yellow light and cigarette smoke. The fruity was blitzing out multicoloured noise.

She was there, suddenly at the bar getting pushed and squeezed, and he felt it again, that jarring *sense that he'd known her before*.

climb the fence. You sure? Yeah. The greying nets, a slight flutter, the grime and mess. A room with falling wallpaper, faded roses, mildew and moss. Cut my arm getting through the window. You sure? A stranger, but that's how it works, always an adjunct, a sequel, a little bit more.

He felt anxious. He was lagging behind her, or somewhere in front. He searched for the time and place but it kept sliding beyond his grasp. His eyes brimmed with her, the peroxide hair, the dark eyes. Drifting through the fridge mountains of the Wick, the landings round Hackney road, in and out of boozers and cafs, alone, always somewhere just ahead, tracing the steps he was about to make.

And she looked directly over at him and smiled.

The memories surged over him, a future summoned or an atavistic impulse. She was here now, flesh and blood, but he was struggling with the images replicating furiously in his head, the corridors opening, the vistas shifting and reconfiguring.

He couldn't think straight anymore.

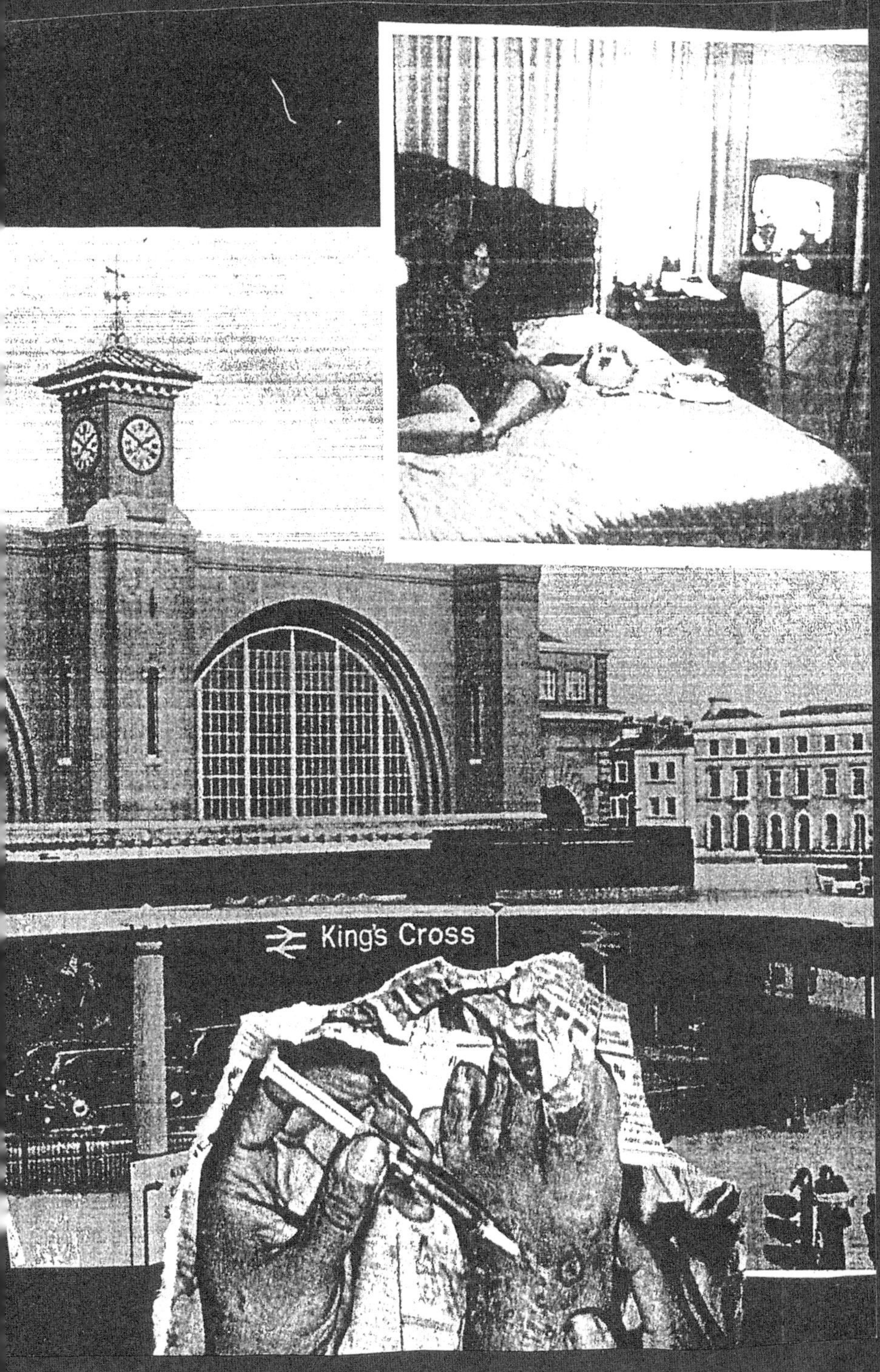
King's Cross

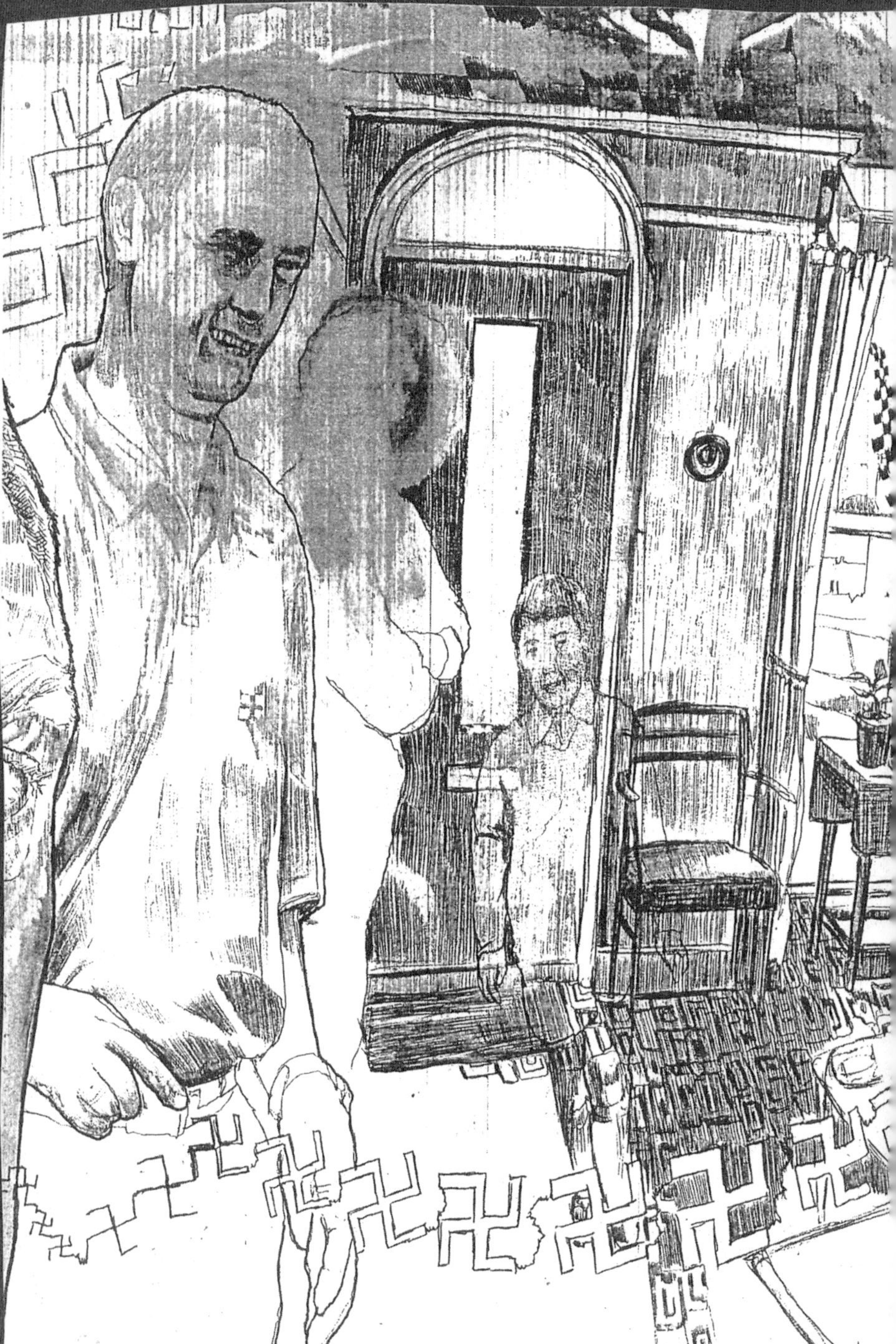

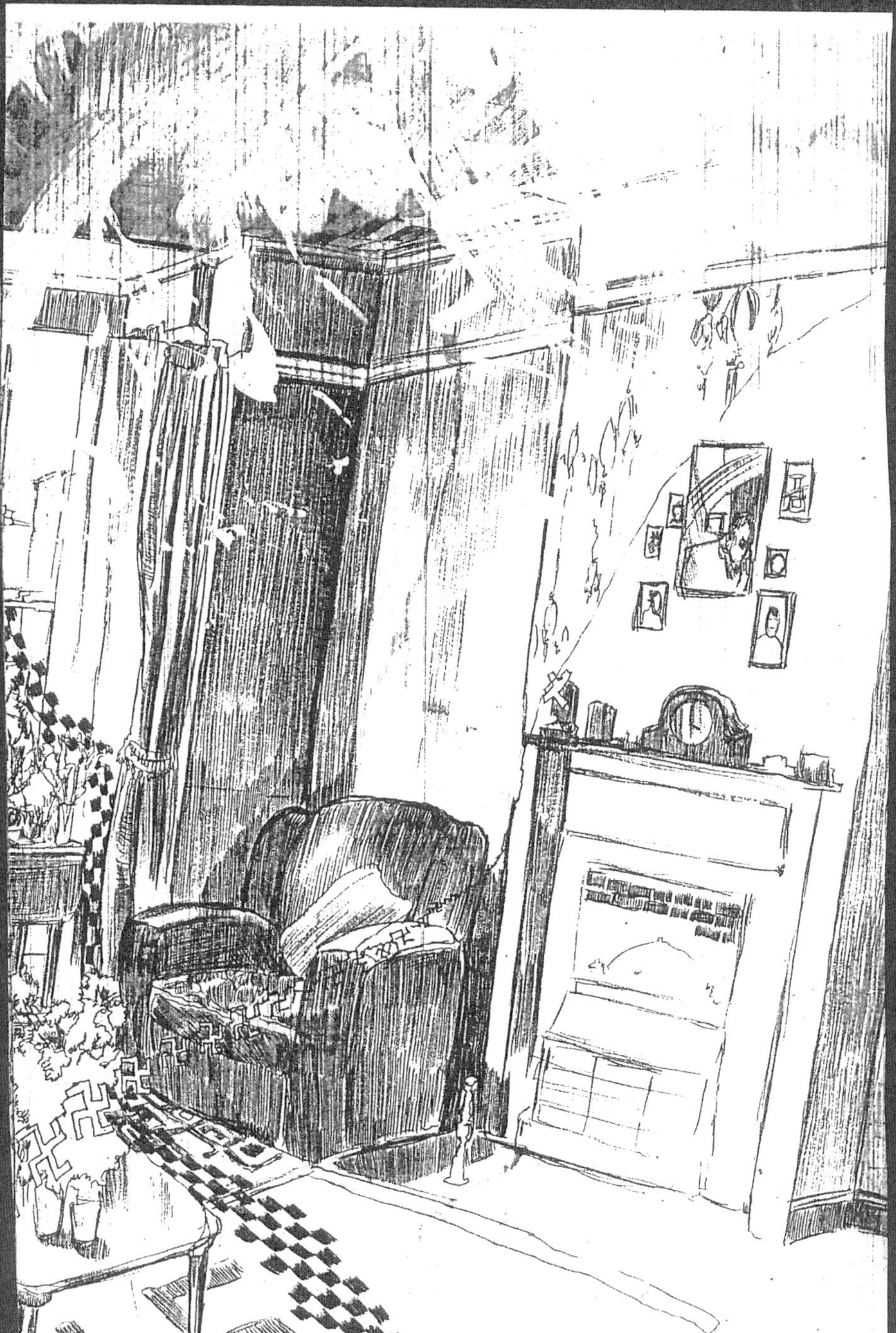

And so I began plotting . It started the moment he slung the leather coat over the pin stripe suit and left the flat in the morning, never smiling unless he'd just rolled off me, hot and grunting. He was the only white bloke in that dole office and he strutted round the place like he owned it, you know, superior. He laughed at the rest of them, their dreams of careers, for him it was just a temporary dip below station, a means to and end because of course it was only a matter of time before a monumental talent like his was discovered.. and someone had to pay for the massive recording studio he'd set up in the front room . He thought he was elevated high above the rest of the herd, his public school education had given him that. Snooping around in the dole office ,,he felt powerful.

I looked out from the 18th floor balcony over Kings Cross, watching the trains edging out through the canals and goodsyards. Kings Cross, mythical London portal. I saw the hordes daily, crushed round the departures boards clambering over each other to get back to Yorkshire or Scotland, and the rest of them sucked in for the first time , jittery with anticipation.
And the minute I started plotting in earnest , I felt better, more real. I'd been a kind of dream of myself, haunting the streets, overlooked and transparent. After all those months avoiding my reflection I'd got myself back.

A walk up to Camden would do it, my hair had woken up really good, a proper bleached mess in the 70s punk mode. I rushed the
  pink lipstick and felt the notes folded in the jeans pocket, yeah, some fun in the market with that bastards money. Sometimes when he came home hammered stinking of cheap perfume and booze, out cold on the settee with half a spliff hanging out the ashtray I'd raid his wallet. The thick bastard never knew, couldn't remember who he'd been flashing his money with the night before. But when he was smashed like that, skin waxy and toxic, I could lift a tenner here and a twenty there and the stinking drunk never mentioned it. I'd started stashing it away,, my little emergency fund.
   I left the tiled mosaics of the foyer with a delicious feeling of excitement, adventures were rising to meet me in the tower blocks of Somers Town.
  I drifted through the rubble of bomb damage and slum clearances. The sky was ultramarine, the gas holders bleached spindles. I headed through the estates on Ossulton Street in search of a drink.

The slob came home from work every night storming into the kitchen lifting pan lids and making demands. Then he'd crash down on the settee and reach for the gold tin with the fractal design and pull out a record to use as a rolling mat. It was the same boring ritual every night, tear up king size rizlas , break cigarettes all over the smoked glass coffee table, turn on TV, get stoned. But I was counting the days now, marking a tally and it was less unbearable.

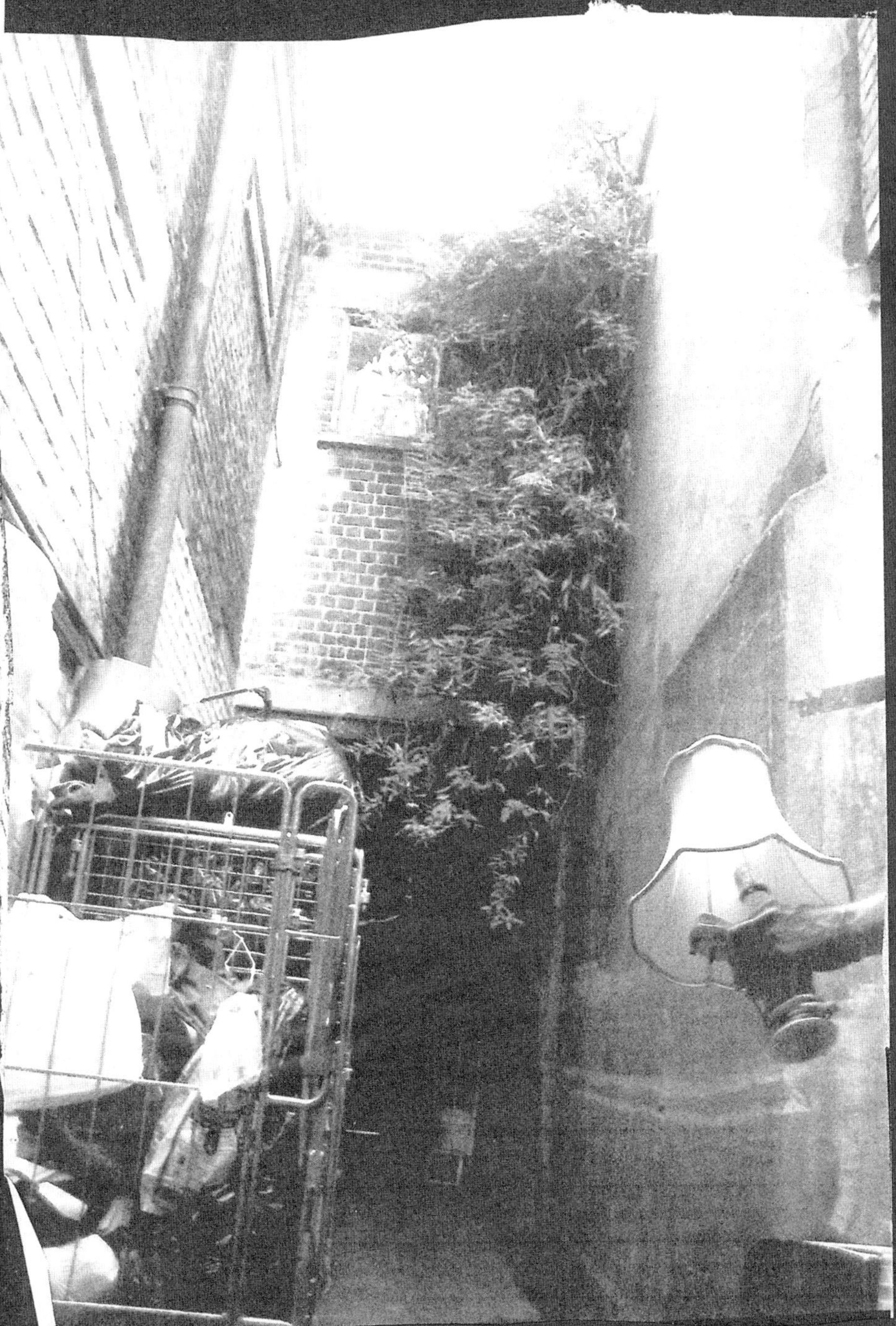

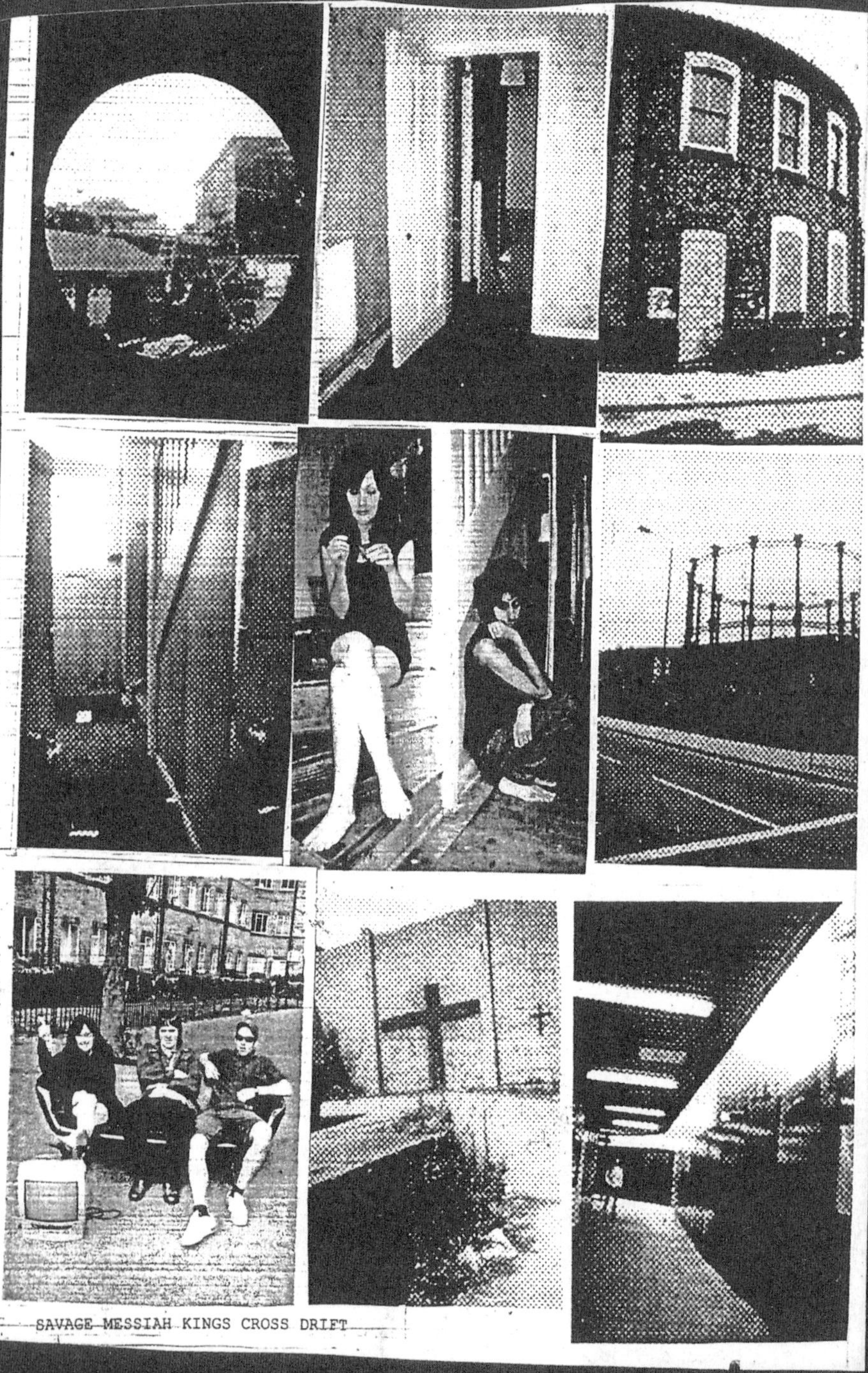

SAVAGE MESSIAH KINGS CROSS DRIFT

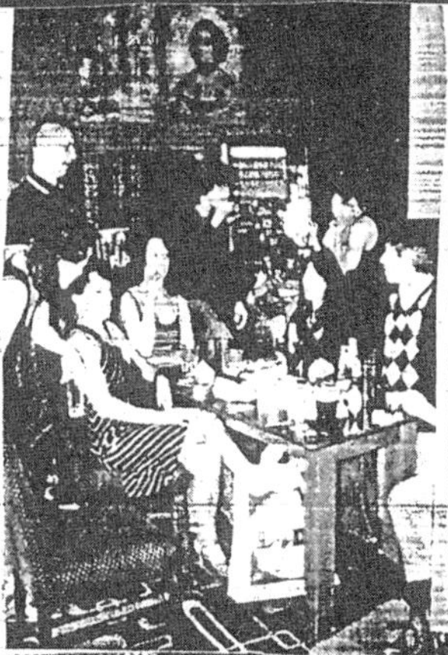
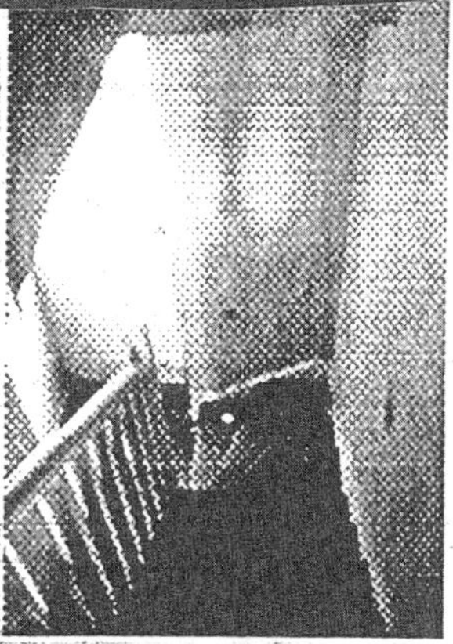
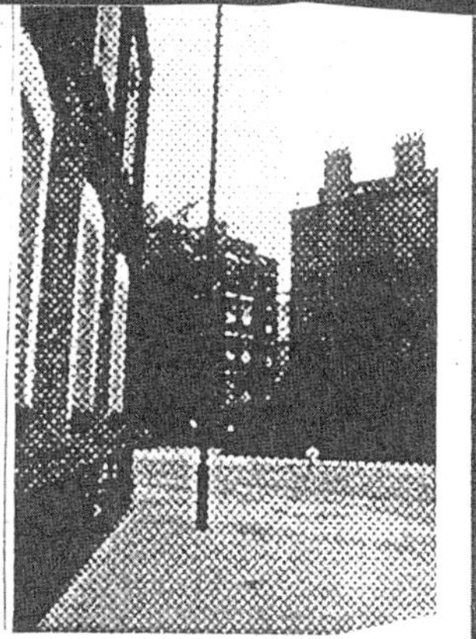
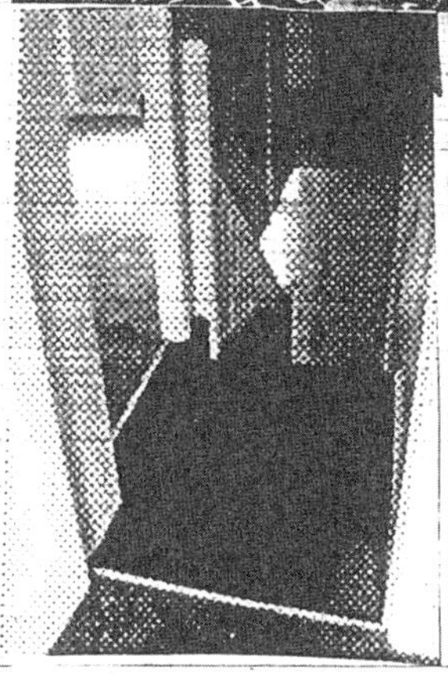
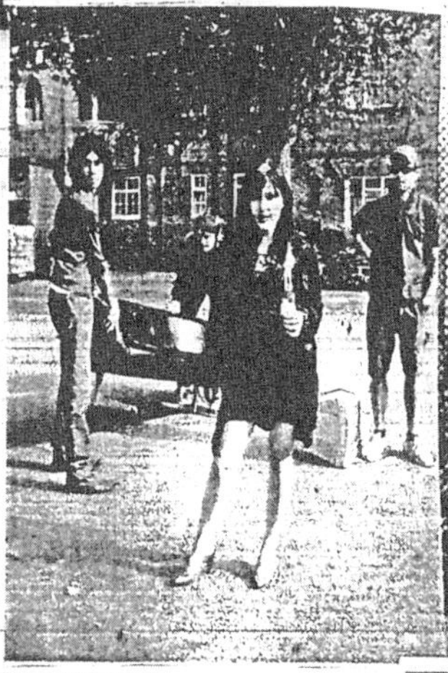
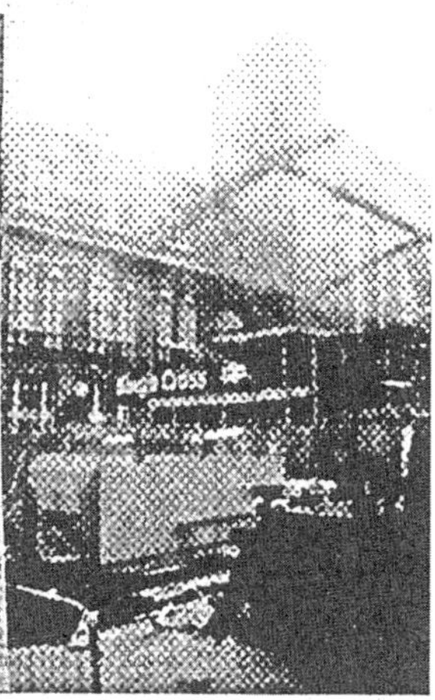
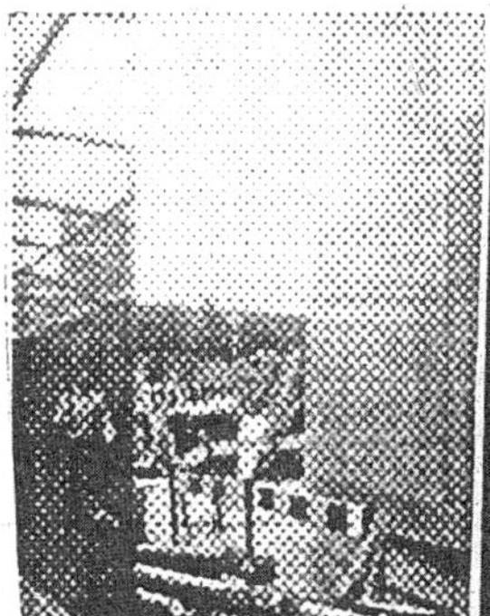
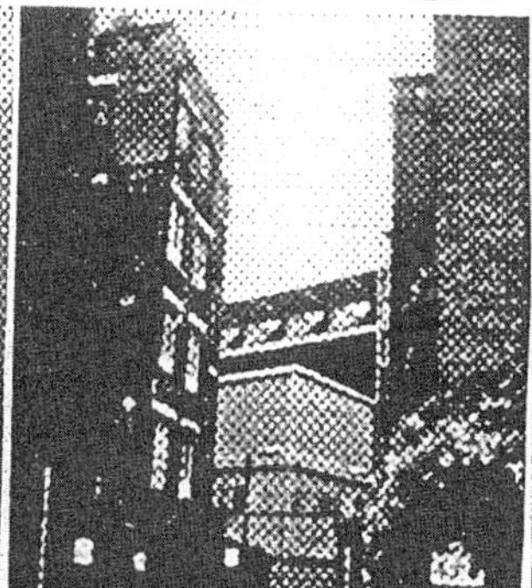
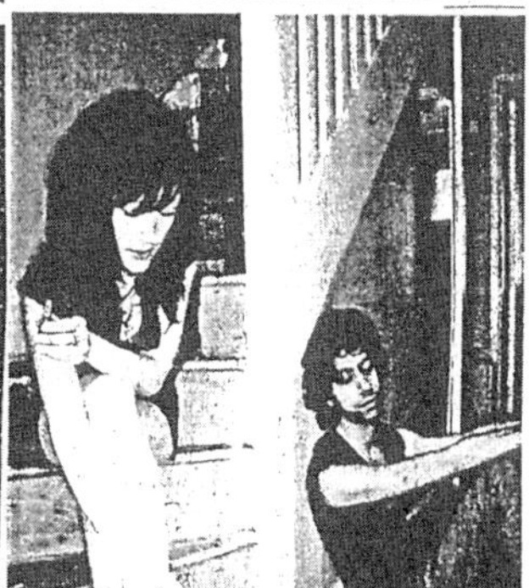

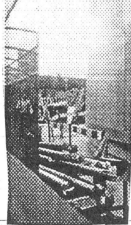

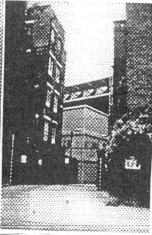

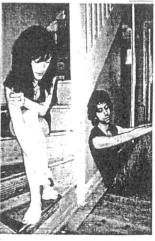

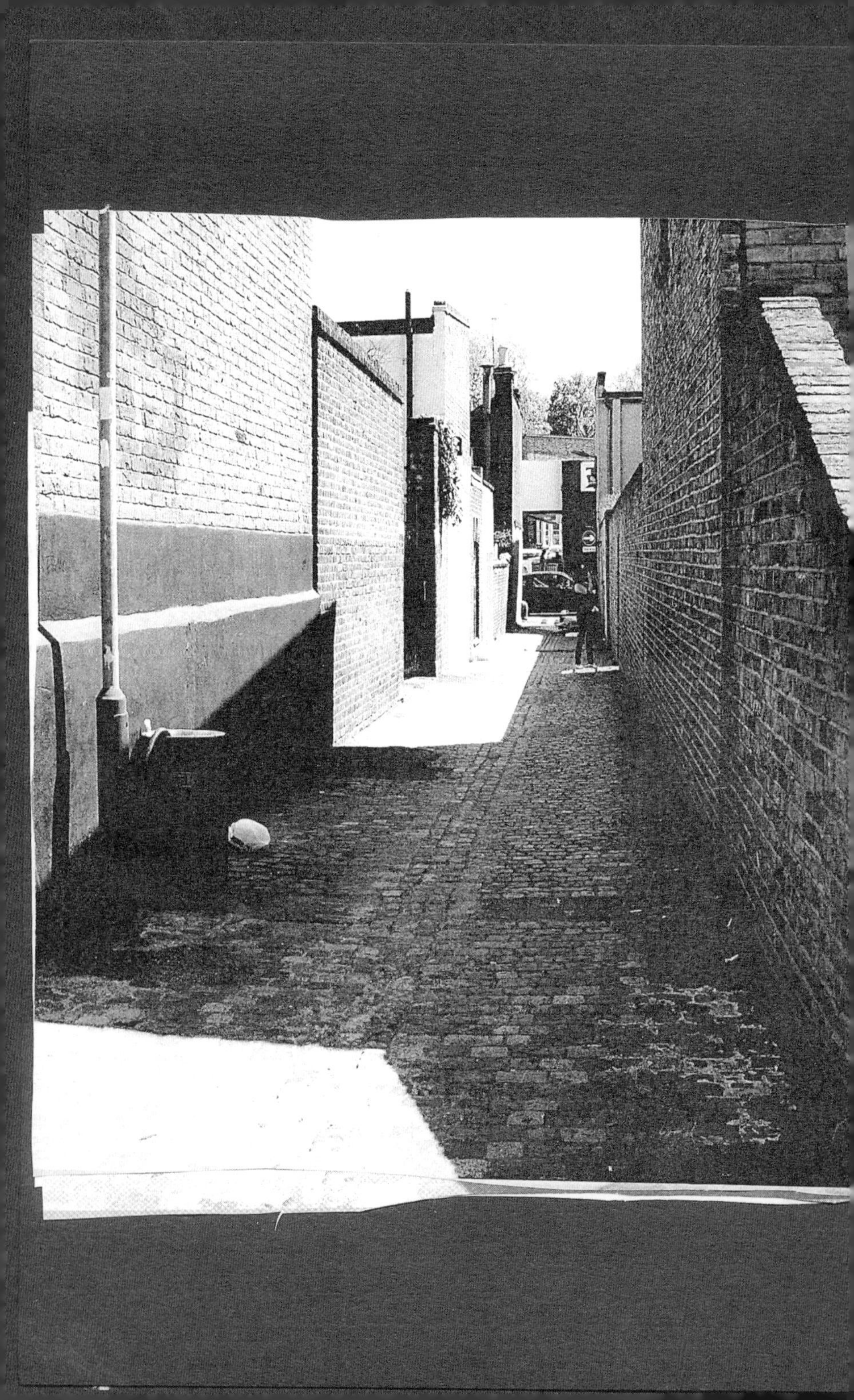

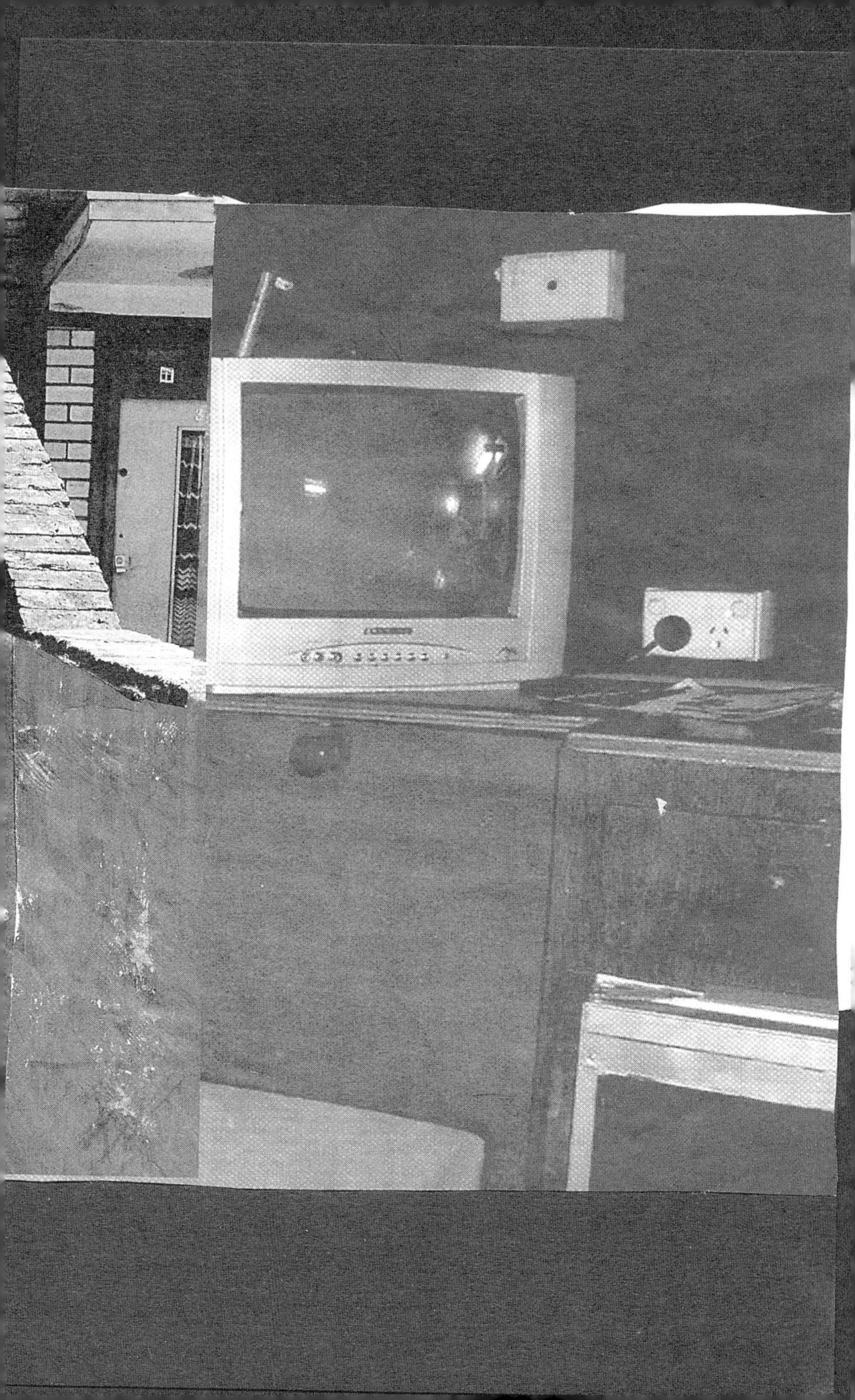

And usually after a couple of beers that was it, the familiar
desire to walk east along the canal overwhelmed me . I loved
that walk ,that conduit shuttling me back to that desolate
landscape. Over the tunnel through Priory Green and the little
alleyways in Half Moon crescent, and on to the Angel, sometimes
stopping for a cup of tea in that caf near Duncan terrace. I
walked it most days, sometimes getting off at Broadway market
and walking round London fields, other times going on to the
Hertford Union and the Lakeview flats. I roamed through old
territories, bumping into people I'd missed, hiding out in
boozers with lost acquaintances.

I passed through the ramshackle alleyways where the North
London line cut across the street, glancing up at the pale
figures in the carriages above. A girl clutching a letter looks
back at me. A last journey from Hackney to Kings cross, a
farewell to the city.

  If u
  Want
  2
  kill me
  I still
  Love
u.

I wandered through the sugary doughnut smell of the market
with its fairy lights and carved pumpkins. Young punks, goths

in black plastic and raver kids in neon yellow were hanging
about outside the Devonshire. That boy with dark hair looking
across at me. I thought maybe i knew him, from somewhere else.
Another time.
He had amazing hair and eyes that seemed to glow violet.

And I felt the particles of pleasure scuttle across my skin. We
found an alcove in the seedy glow of the Red Lion theatre bar.
 There in that snug, in those exquisite moments of plotting and
flirtation ,I felt the desire radiating, I would be hidden,
adrift in terra incognita.

    "Those vows, those perfumes, those infinite kisses,
    will they be reborn, from gulfs beyond soundings,
    as the suns that are young again climb in the sky,
    after they've passed through the deepest of drownings?
    -O vows! O perfumes! O infinite kisses!"
    Baudelaire

I'd been drifitng around Leyton for a while, it was 1999 or
sometime around then. I'd walked from Lea Bridge roundabout to
Chobham road passing Mobeens and Leyton Leisure lagoon and all
these little churches and pawnbrokers set up in people's
houses.
There were loads of little takeaways and kebab shops and all
these bric a brac stalls spilling odd shoes and broken toys
over the pavement. And on the bus shelters and lamp posts I
kept seeing these little flyers stuck up with selotape,.
drawings of fly agarick mushrooms and litt
le doodly spirals advertising an all dayer in a pub in Chobham
road. It was so strange, even then it seemed to emanate from a
lost time.
I walked into the industrial zone between Leyton and Stratford
where it wasn't really anywhere, a liminal zone with gypsy
sites and garages and light industrial units.
I found the pub soon after that. From the outside it looked
ordinary, an estate pub from the late 60s, early 70s, a bunker
with fortress windows at the front, plastic hanging baskets and
St George flags . I could hear the thudding of synthesised bass
drum, 220 bpm and pitch shifted samples. There were skinheads
outside wearing tie dyed t shirts and temple of psychic youth
symbols tattooed on their arms. I couldn't really believe it,
there wer
e massive groups of them staggering about, lighting fires.
 This party was the continuation of a Saturday all nighter at
one of the massive abandoned factories on Carpenters road.
dark and brooding

speed down,
short, staccato- They were all off it, topping up on psilosibin
after a big weekend of acid and flyagaricks.

overdriving   sinusoidal
aggressive sound, amplitude envelope….

I walked into a large room split roughly into two sections by a
bar in the middle. On one side there were families from the
neighbouring estate, babies and kids running in and out the
door. A marching
Industrial hardcore Big screen was showing some football match
but no one seemed to be paying much attention. The blokes were
drinking pints, grabbing the kids now and again, jeering and

 shouting fast hoover-patterns.
 cleaner, detuned supersaw lead,
 obscenities at each other. And on the other side much the same
 pandemonium, ketamine fuelled antics, erratic bursts of
 dancing, people in heaps on the floor. Some bloke was shrieking
 about the second coming , necking some pills , washing them
 down with blue alcopops.
 Fucking hell this was amazing.

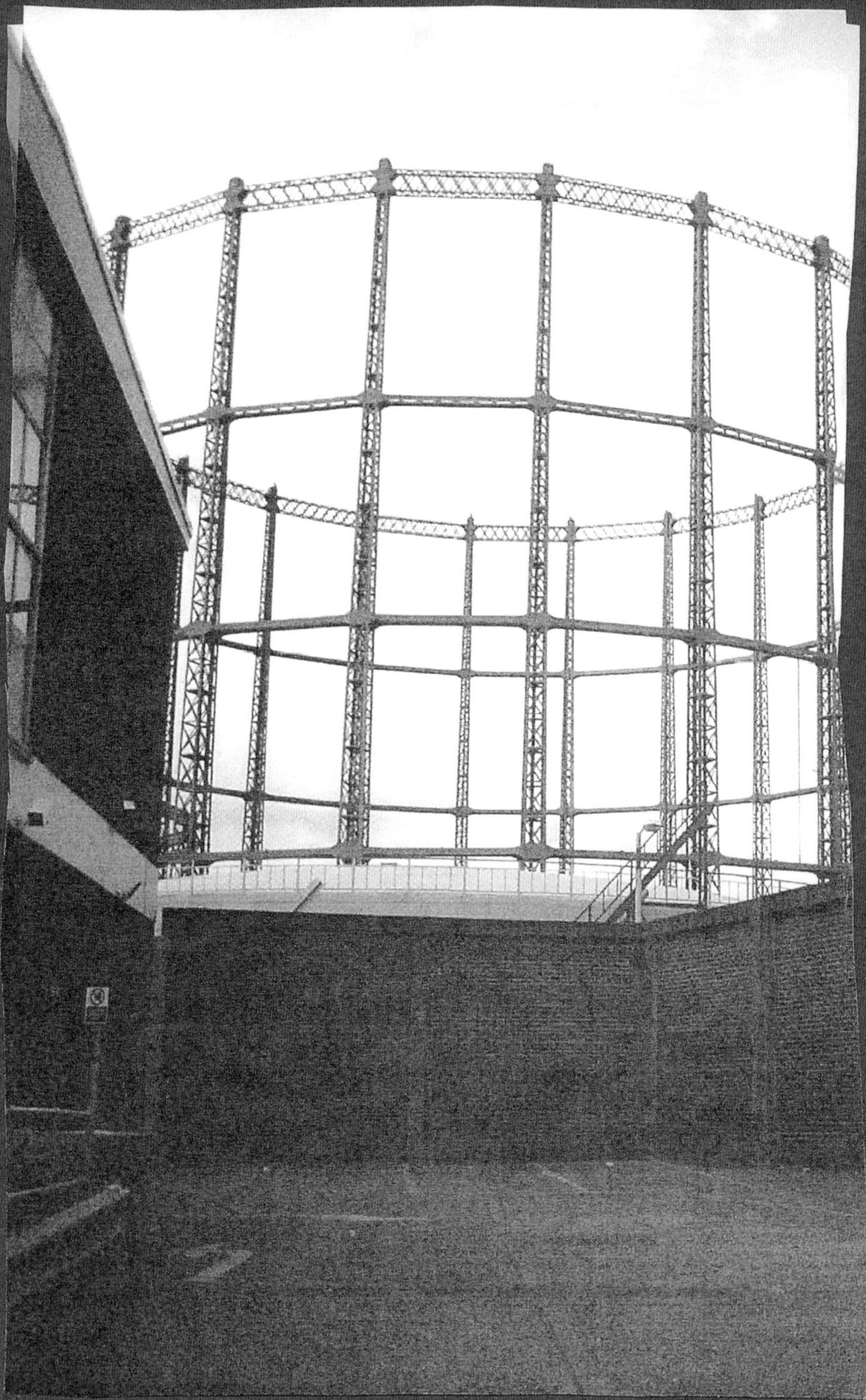

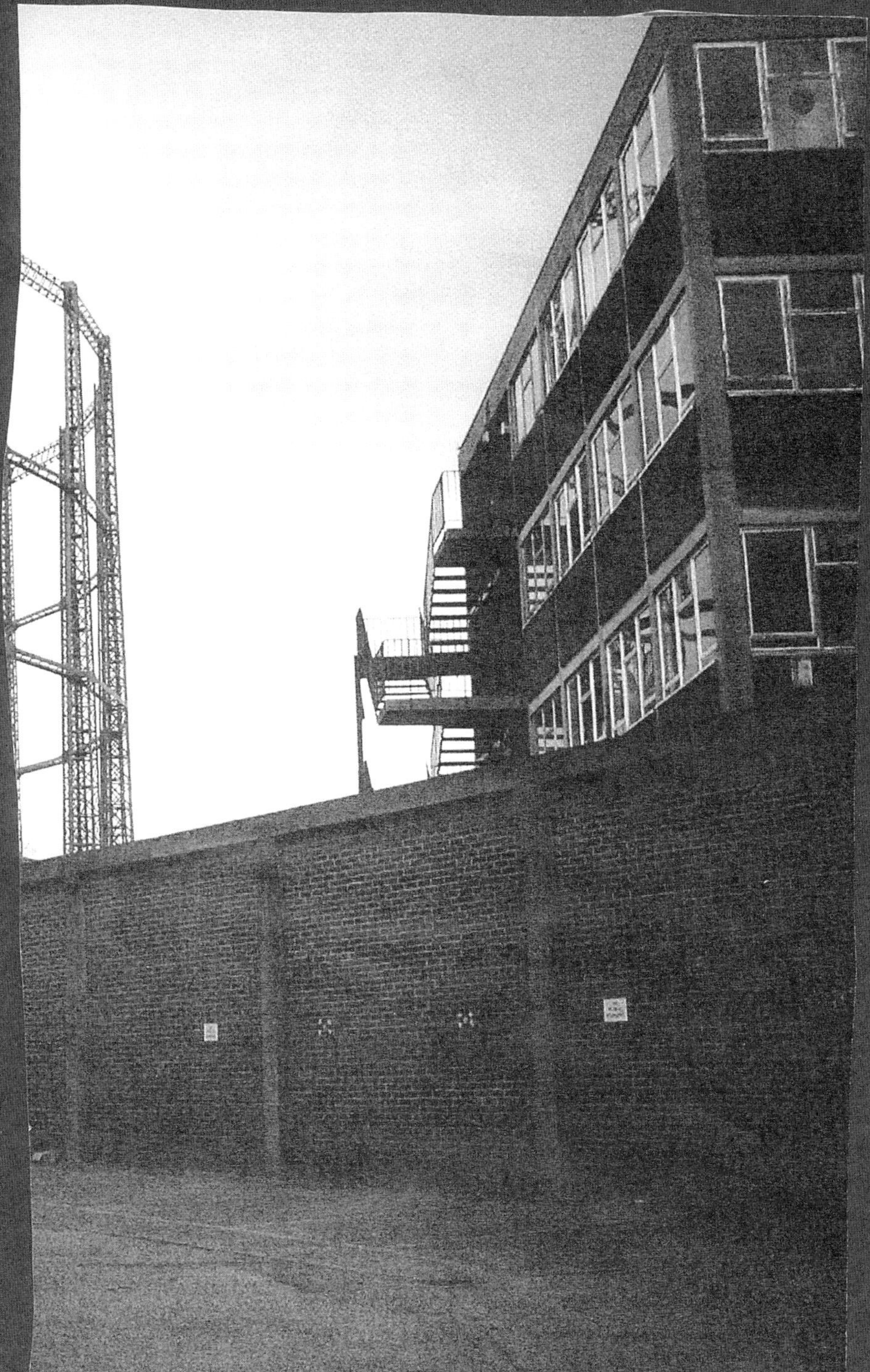

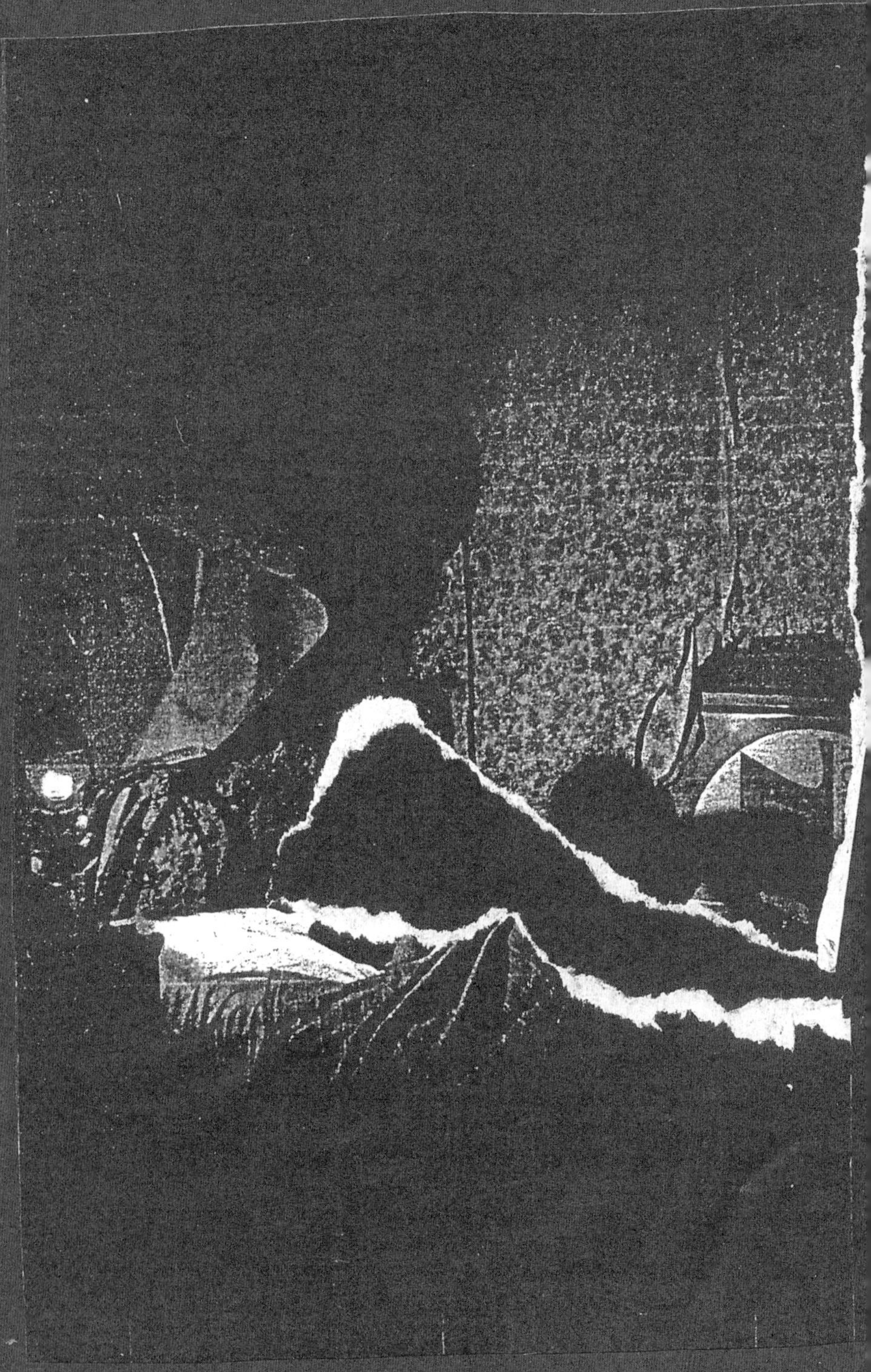

of

I looked for a payphone to get the Hackney crew down here. Someone had said the landlord of the boozer was quite happy fo us to do what we liked, reckoned the old bill never really ventured down this end much. There'd been a wave of vigilante attacks on the site over the past few months, nasty stuff stoked up by the BNP. Old animosities between travelling factions were temporarily suspended and newcomers welcomed.
Screeching sample ,

square wave falling pitch.

A big group of dread locked blokes with orange overalls walked in, I recognised some of them from the old days in South Yorkshire. Drawn into an embrace, recounting the old days of Wath On Dearne, we got the pints lined up on the bar. It was warm outside and groups were sitting out the front with bottles of cider.

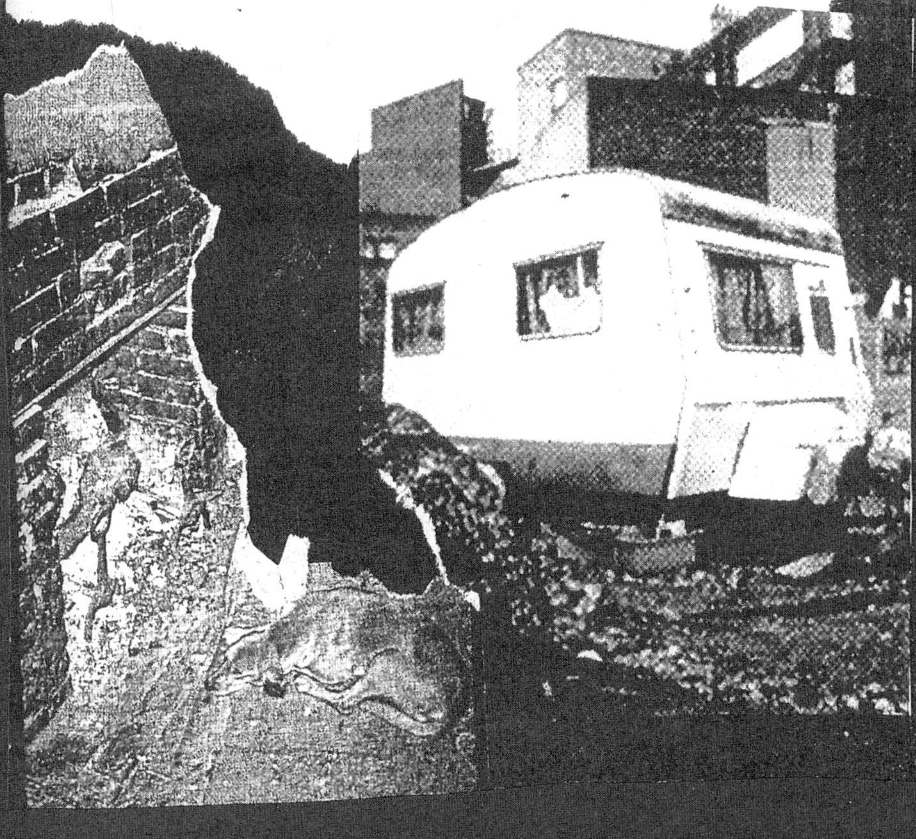

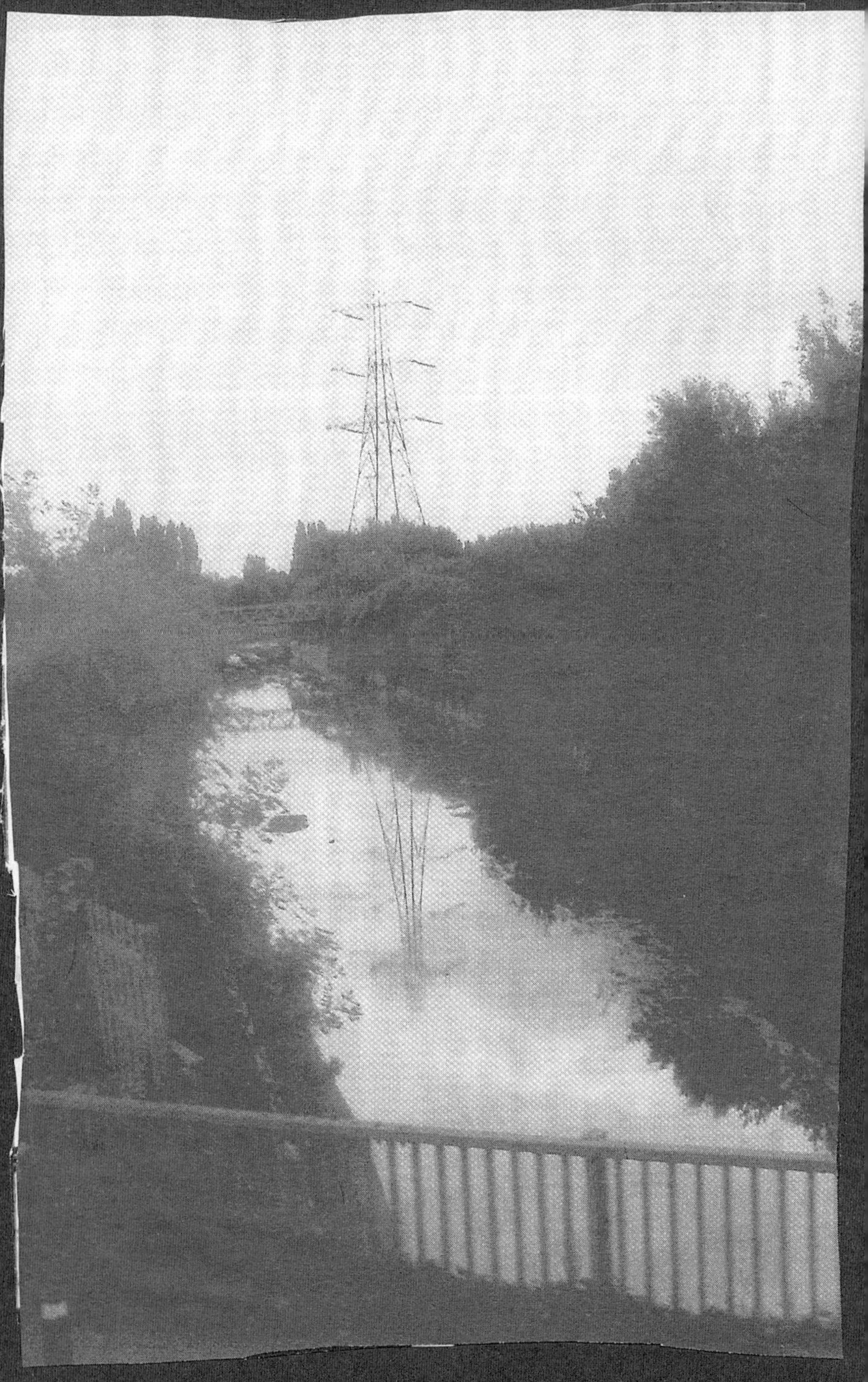

The atmosphere inside was manic, pounding Belgian New Beat,
skinheads forming circles, moving closer to each other then
spreading out in menacing ripples. I hadn't seen anything like
this for at least seven or eight years, not since maybe Spiral
Tribe parties round the Isle Of Dogs.
Frequency spectrum spreads out
I was watching and revelling in it, totally intoxicated. I'd
had a few the night before, nothing on the scale of these lot
but enough to make me start feeling a bit off it straight away.
There were blokes crawling around, hoovering the floor for
dropped pills. I watched them get up and march on the spot,
drilling themselves into the floor. They wore black military
uniforms and all seemed to know each other. I heard some
shouting in French, Dutch and Italian, there were a few from
Dublin as well.
  bass-frequency resonance
          . increasing the sustain
As the evening wore on my mates from Hackney had started to
arrive. There was an amazed look of delight on all their faces
as they realised my frantic urgings to get them across here had
not been exaggerated. The beats had stayed frantic, hoover
becoming an aggressive, shrieking lead. You couldn't really
move to it, not in a sexy way, you just had to jackhammer
yourself into the floor.

It was like going back ten years and intensifying it. Rotterdam
, Berlin, Ruhr Valley.
The families on the other side of the pub didn't really seem to
care. I noticed some of the little kids get up and start
jumping up and down. Some bloke came staggering out of the
mens toilets with an England shirt almost colliding with a
three year old, sorry son he said while some other bloke

smacked straight into him and spilled half a pint on the kids
head.
As the afternoon turned to dusk, the sky became a golden pink
and some of the crew dragged a load of palletes round the side
of the pub and started a bonfire going. Someone else wheeled
some speaker cabs round and the party shifted outside. You
could still hear the thudding bass from inside but out here
they were playing dub, it wasn't as hectic.
Everyone was sitting round on beer crates and tyres. The crew
from south Yorkshire were there and more and more were turning
up from Hackney. Some mushroom tea was being passed around. It
was 1999, the beginning of Summer, and the talk was of the City
of London, of a riot in the heart of it, meeting at Liverpool
street station on June the 18th. I'd heard a lot about this, and
seen the orange stickers everywhere. Someone said that a lot of
these skinheads in the pub had come over from Europe just to be
in London while all this was kicking off. There'd been benefit
gigs and meetings round Hackney, the word was out on this one,
there was a sense it was going to be massive, bigger than the
Poll Tax.

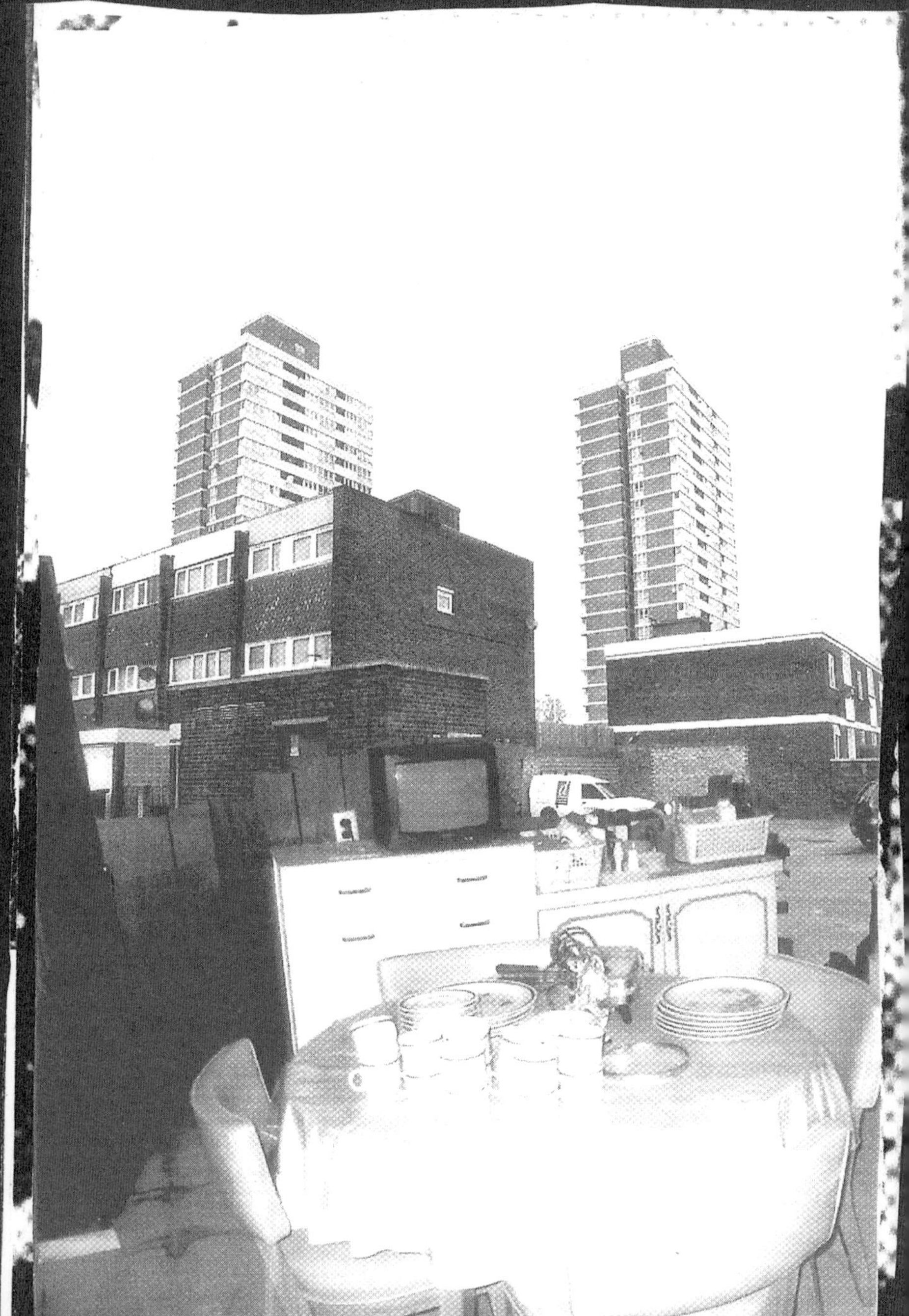

I was confused on the walk up Angel Lane, disorientated, I
recognised fragments, the wall with shards of broken bottles on
top, the tower blocks in Maryland looming across the 60s
maisonettes. But I'd lost my bearings as all the paths by the
railway sidings, all the little side streets had disappeared.
And as we walked up there, watching the construction of the
doomed Westfield shopping city I felt a sense of regret. I
passed the Wheelers pub where the young men form the relocated
Clays lane traveller site gathered in clusters outside. I was
in search of that other pub where piebald horses pawed the
ground at the edge of the car park, that one that had loomed up
so often in my dreams and reveries but still could not be
found. I searched on maps, I scoured aerial photos but it had
gone missing, or it had never existed. I was still amazed by
that day, amazed that we were able to get away it, wondering if
I'd imagined it all. For years I had sought out other
witnesses, wrote about it hoping someone would step forward and
say yes I was there. But they never did, and the crew that were
with me that day had drifted away years before. I wandered
through a yard where car parts lay strewn under the watchful
eye of an Alsation, a last dismal remnant of the lands of the
past.

I walked by the Major road Methodist church, through the flat
green expanse around it and headed towards the Leyton road. I
was sure this is where it had been. The new traveller site had
been constructed recently, it was neatly compartmentalised
behind high sandy walls. You weren't supposed to peer in and
they weren't to venture out. It was a sort of compound.

Distortion,.
1973-1974, 1980-81, 1990, 1994, 1999, 2001, 2008/9/10 2013.
hoover distorted, grainy, sweeping
low key.

I wondered with a jolt if the pub I remembered so vividly in
all those psychoactive colours had been bulldozed to
accommodate the new site. As I wandered around I could hear
the faint reverberations of that soundsystem, I could smell
the woodsmoke from the bonfire outside. I pushed on through the
dusty scrubland at the back of the site and found some old
graffiti, the temple of psychick youth double cross and all
these faded pale yellow 'J18 Carnival against Capitalism'
stickers. I knew that it was still there, spectral and
pulsating, locked into so many perfumes and sounds. And it was
all to come, another epoch, a mass return to the labyrinth.

'poets find the refuse of society on their street and
derive their heroic subject from this very refuse. This
means that a common type is, as it
were, superimposed upon their illustrious type. ...
Ragpicker or poet -- the refuse concerns both.'
Walter Benjamin.

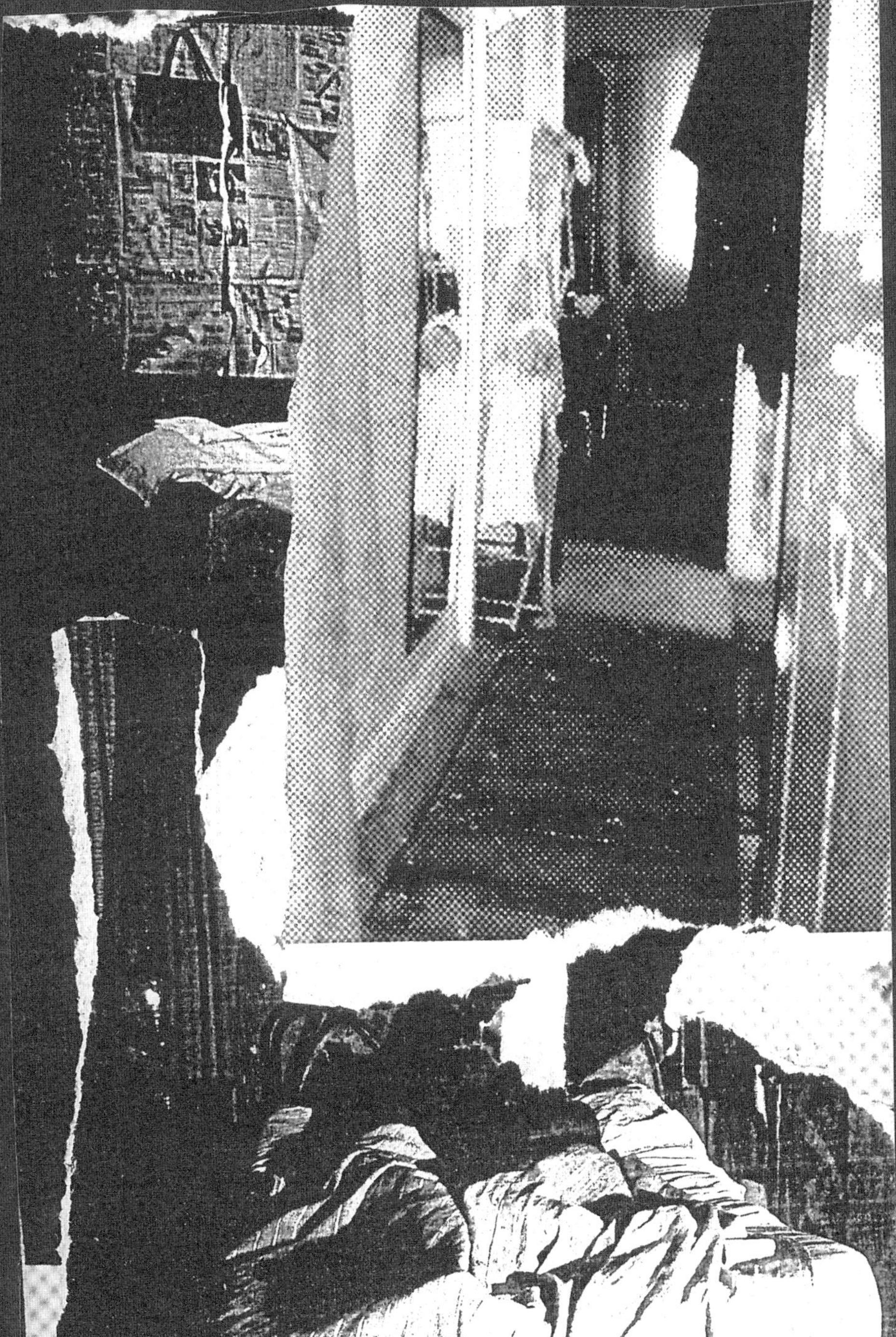

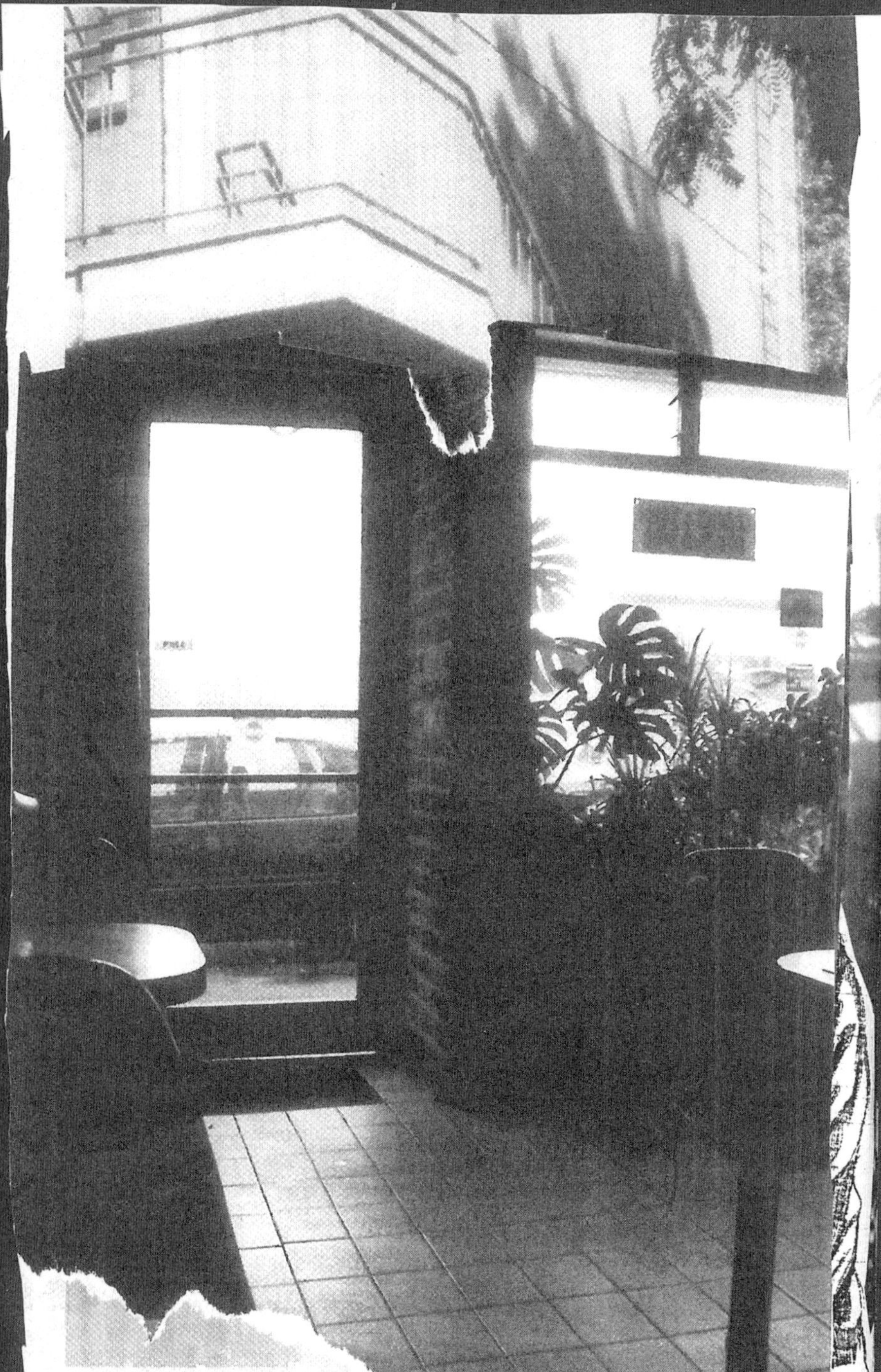

THREE COLTS LANE.

Old Bethnal Green Road,

.

Immersed in the anticipation of a big night out, white spot
lights , smell of shampoo, air heated with tongs and dryers.
Germaine Stewart on Heart FM, Barcadi breezers, fluffy pink
towels, cigarette ash dropping onto heaps of shorn hair. I'm
dreaming of our next meeting, the high speed deranged chat,
afternoon drinking, walks across heaths and marshes. I'm
thinking about his eyes, beautiful burnt umber.

I meet him in The Pride of Spitalfields, the lure of the snug,
the open fire, fairylights twinkling in a glass of Jamesons.
There's Boyzone on the jukey, we're getting pissed, cajoling
one another to misspend the afternoon. City boys strut back to
work, turns into a session.

Silenced in 1985, window panes scorched and etched , a slew of
angry cries. Broadwater farm, empty promises and a leather
settee for 49 pounds.

Bethnal green road.

Back room of Café Alba.
Crystalline December morning.
Usual assortment of moody pensioners, mini cab drivers and
market stall traders. Traces of the Blitz, housing association
tension and every day frustrations loop and barb in the
agitated vowels.

Round the back I clamber through concrete bunkers, steel
cages,to maisonettes upstairs that are always catching fire.
 Cardboard and plywood in the windows, Macdonalds stench rising
    through grilles on the stairwell.

    Cash converters, Money shop. Rise of religious zealotry,
    proliferation of pawnbrokers.
    When you emerge at the tube station it feels hectic and
    erratic, radios blaring ,market stalls and pound shops
    exploding on the streets.

    Capital Radio channels vicious boredom.

Tinsel, fairylights, garish tat.
The smell of pine on Columbia road.
Abandoned pubs

He leads me to a secret room above a pound shop, a grotto,
Matthew Barney deluxe, glitter, baubles, trinkets, golden
sequins, black walls. His room. An afternoon lying in bed
before the next onslaught,
 of boozing antics.
It's blue with frost outside, we go to Rosa's caf and the
Golden heart, the little room at the side. Steal back into our
hideout, my desire for him intensifying with every moment, we
crush each other, the frenzied tearing and scratching. Bedside
table smashed to the floor.

Voss street,a tiny alleyway punctuated with portals,
letterboxes opening on other dimensions, mirror distortions and
House of fun spatial confusion. He kisses me. The way he looks
at me, the way he holds me, I don't think I've ever felt so
cherished.

Ainsley street is flavoured with vanilla. Those tall streets
hold the scent of jasmine and blackbird song and I'm sent
hurtling six months hence.
The courtyard behind is vast, a desolate armchair is stranded
by a tree.
The haze of a balmy summer evening, we hide away with a bottle
of wine, escaping the party to seek out the pleasures of long
grass and the scent of wild roses. The sky is pink, he is
beautiful, tender. Whatever I sought in brutality has been
given to me now.

A chimera, an illusion, a finely woven narrative in the absence
of a reality that doesn't seem to exist.
The Arches café.

  Under the railway arch, formica tables. Fruit machine by
door. Snooker hall at back.
Looking out through 70s rubber plants . Magic Cut barber.
 M.O.T here.
Luminous stars, mince and onion pie, chips and peas £3.20.
Cascading plastic plants. Train rumbling overhead. Shiny brown
chairs.
 His head's done in, but then there was no need for the
Tramadol after all that booze.

We're ready for the next round . Maybe call in at Birdcage on
the way back for a livener.
Colour TV. I'm seeing double. Millwall.
 I'm nostalgic for Northern Saturday afternoons, pea soupers,
football results on TV, fish and chips on the knee.

There's a derelict pub on Headlam street, with grey paint
splinters and orange fabric in the window. I want to go in.
There's got to be someone squatting upstairs. Curiosity lures
me through the broken railings to a brazier in the abandoned
beer garden. A neon Youngs sign lies smashed on the ground . A
young punk draws distorted faces on the wall. I've seen him
before, he plays bass in a band called Wrath of God Syndrome.

It's dark at 4, real bleak Winter dark. The newsagent has
become a glowing cave, coloured bulbs hang around the awning
.There are tunnels opening up under railway bridges, caverns
and alleyways revealing themselves. Pools of oil,the smell of
paraffin,the sound of dripping on glistening cobblestones and
always that heady scent of Nag Champa.

Orange sheets at the window, stencilled sound system graff
outside. Eagle House. Calum striding purposefully across the
courtyard.

Whitechapel high street, the search for the pound shop with the
grotto.
.
We find a demented cacaophany. Pink fairylights, fiber optic
Father Christmases, singing trees. A real bonkers din, black
walls, flashing lights, neon signs, a Jason Rhoades
installation without the staging. He loops an arm around my
waist, steering me through the market hordes.

Bradford circa 1985. We cross the bridge behind Whitechapel
station to the bus depot that looks really northern.
New builds, vernacular travesties.
Voss street, my darling kisses me.

As itinerants we are treated as subversives and criminals in
our pursuit of the drift through the city.
Tourism grows, transit is encouraged within the confines of the
industry. Monitoring, surveillance,ID and iris recognition
technology are piloted at airports.
I get a marker pen and join all his moles together making a map
of my drifts on his skin.

There is a myth that our future has been taken, that no other
future is possible. do you passively accept that?

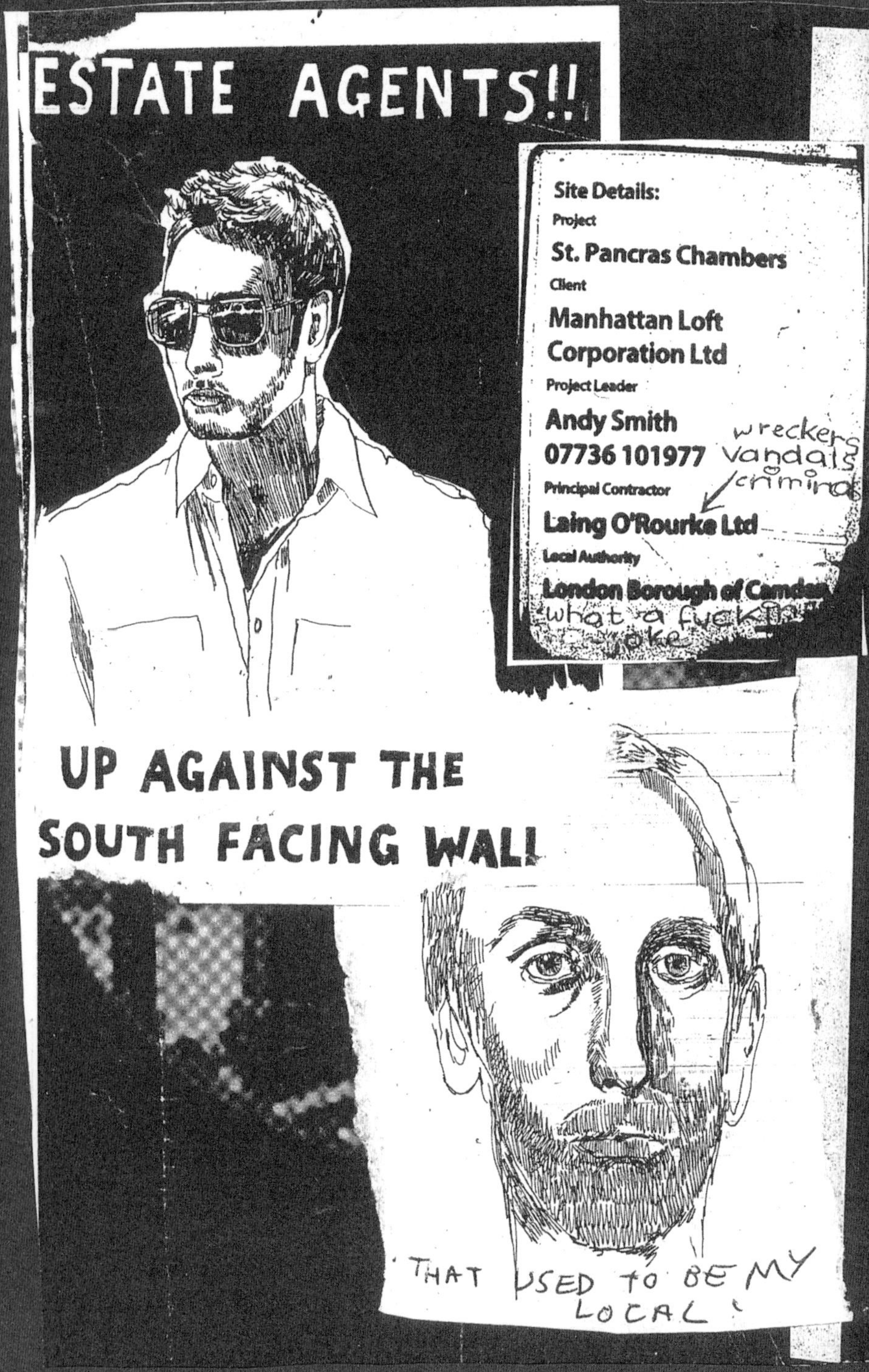
ESTATE AGENTS!!
Site Details:
Project
St. Pancras Chambers
Client
Manhattan Loft
Corporation Ltd
Project Leader
Andy Smith
07736 101977
Principal Contractor
Laing O'Rourke Ltd
Local Authority
London Borough of Camde
wreckers
vandals
crimina
what a fuckin
UP AGAINST THE
SOUTH FACING WALL
THAT USED TO BE MY
LOCAL

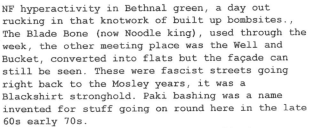

NF hyperactivity in Bethnal green, a day out
rucking in that knotwork of built up bombsites.,
The Blade Bone (now Noodle king), used through the
week, the other meeting place was the Well and
Bucket, converted into flats but the façade can
still be seen. These were fascist streets going
right back to the Mosley years, it was a
Blackshirt stronghold. Paki bashing was a name
invented for stuff going on round here in the late
60s early 70s.
Paper sales, top of the lane ., split into
factions, late 70s ,early 80s , NF, the New NF, NF
constsitutional movemnt,the BM, each had different
corners. They were only booted out after rioting
around Brick Lane when Beakon got elected.,
petrol bombs and police cars torched.

Drill holes in rock, ravines gouged out in the
cliff face. Burrrowing into it, hidden in the
catacombs,the exhaustion, dimly lit streets,
alleyways, silent through the train window. Beck
road, Cambridge Heath, Three Colts lane. Thirties
estates, shadowy, orange street glow, layer after
layer, envelopes of tenement blocks opening one on
top of another.

A row of suburban houses, trapped in an
architectural clash, forests of tower blocks,
knots of maisonettes. Cars parked out front,
padlocked gates. A chalked eye glowers up, Masonic
navigation. Bethnal green overground station,
tangle of circuits, overhead wires, aerial mazes.

You were meant for me.
The song is over but the melody lingers on.

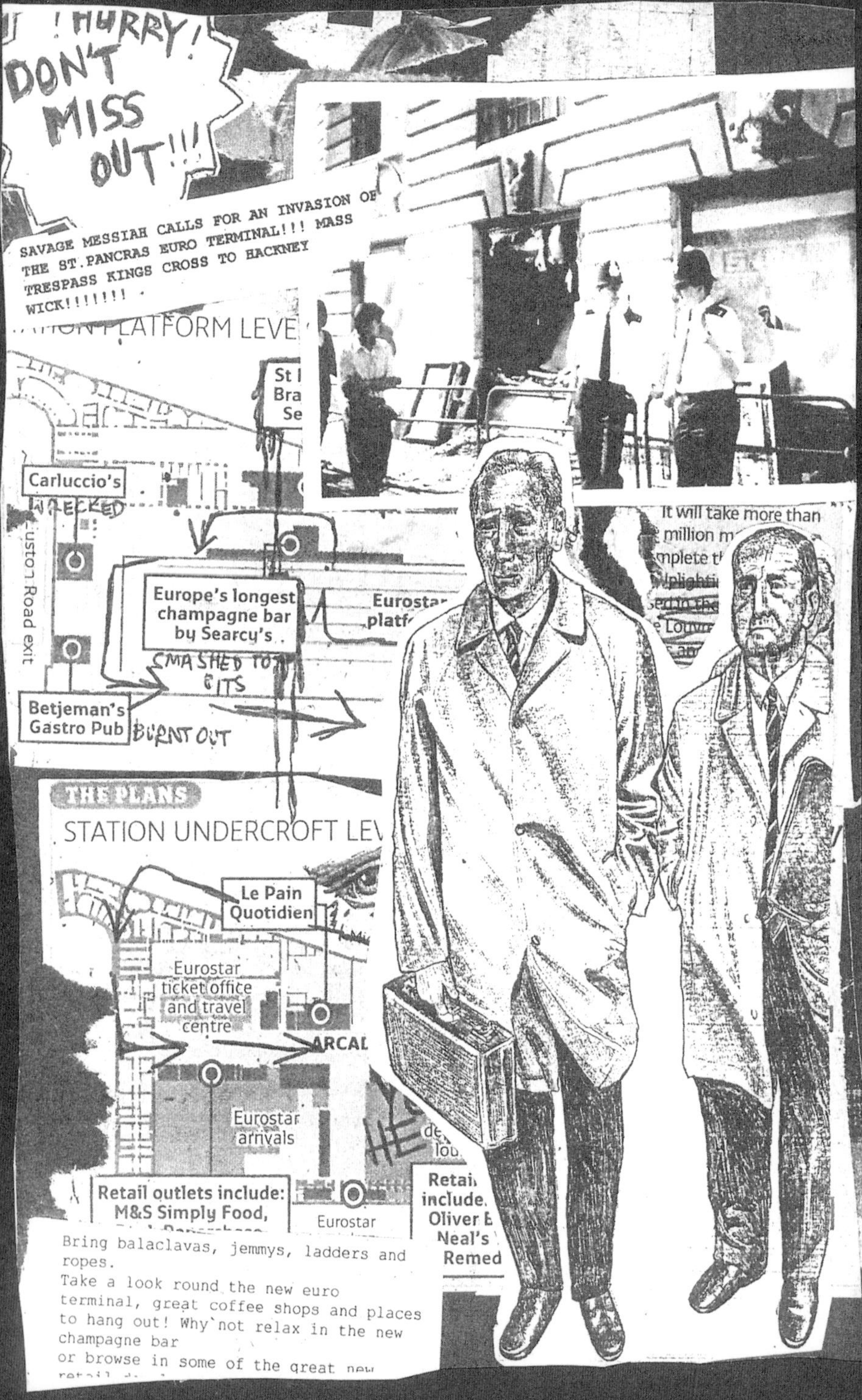
! HURRY! DON'T MISS OUT!!!
SAVAGE MESSIAH CALLS FOR AN INVASION OF THE ST.PANCRAS EURO TERMINAL!!! MASS TRESPASS KINGS CROSS TO HACKNEY WICK!!!!!!! .
PLATFORM LEVE
Carluccio's
WRECKED
Euston Road exit
Europe's longest champagne bar by Searcy's
SMASHED TO BITS
Eurostar
Betjeman's Gastro Pub
BURNT OUT
It will take more than
million
THE PLANS
STATION UNDERCROFT LEV
Le Pain Quotidien
Eurostar ticket office and travel centre
Eurostar arrivals
Retail outlets include: M&S Simply Food,
Eurostar
Bring balaclavas, jemmys, ladders and ropes.
Take a look round the new euro terminal, great coffee shops and places to hang out! Why not relax in the new champagne bar
or browse in some of the great new

SAVAGE MESSIAH

Bow, E3
...bedroom riverside apartment • Heated flooring
...En-suite...

Bow, E3
...Modern 1 bedroom apartment...

CE APARTMENT
WOOLNERS WAY
STEVENAGE

LAUNCHING SOO...

£38 one and two bedroo...
apartments and penthou...
...et within a cosmopolita...
development close to
Stevenage town centre.

ULTRA VIOLENCE

RIOTS!

CAT
cuddle me
& I will
purr

...BO
...FIANC...

...LENCE, MOB VENGEANCE, MOB RULE!

but, if you pull
my tail, I'll hiss

Bow, E3
• Two bedroom maisonette
• Laminate flooring
• GCH
• Walking distance of...

• Laminated flooring
• Open plan living/kitchen
• Security entry phone system
• Walking distance to Mile End park
• Close to Mile End tube

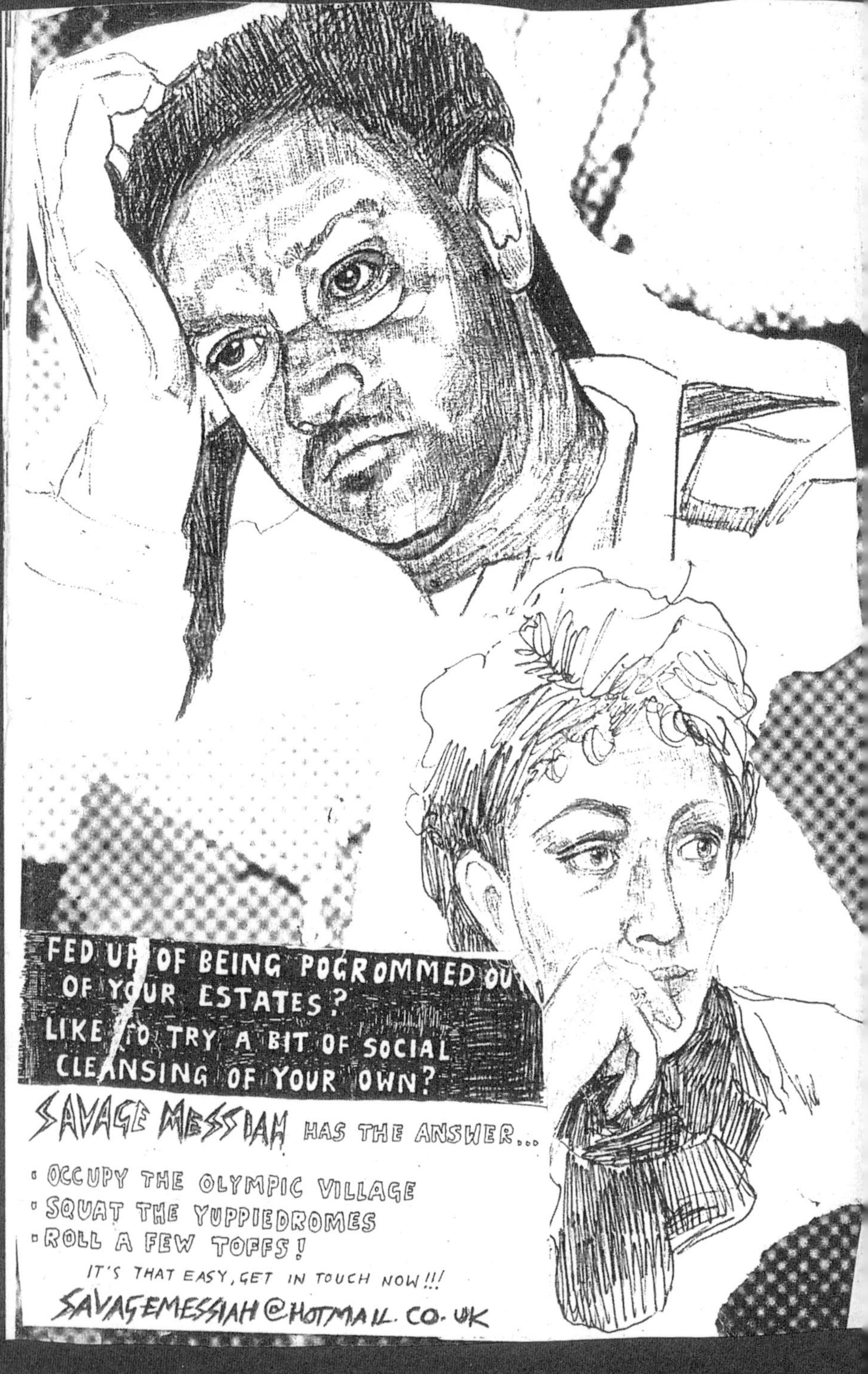
FED UP OF BEING POGROMMED OUT OF YOUR ESTATES?
LIKE TO TRY A BIT OF SOCIAL CLEANSING OF YOUR OWN?
SAVAGE MESSIAH HAS THE ANSWER...
• OCCUPY THE OLYMPIC VILLAGE
• SQUAT THE YUPPIEDROMES
• ROLL A FEW TOFFS!
IT'S THAT EASY, GET IN TOUCH NOW!!!
SAVAGEMESSIAH@HOTMAIL.CO.UK

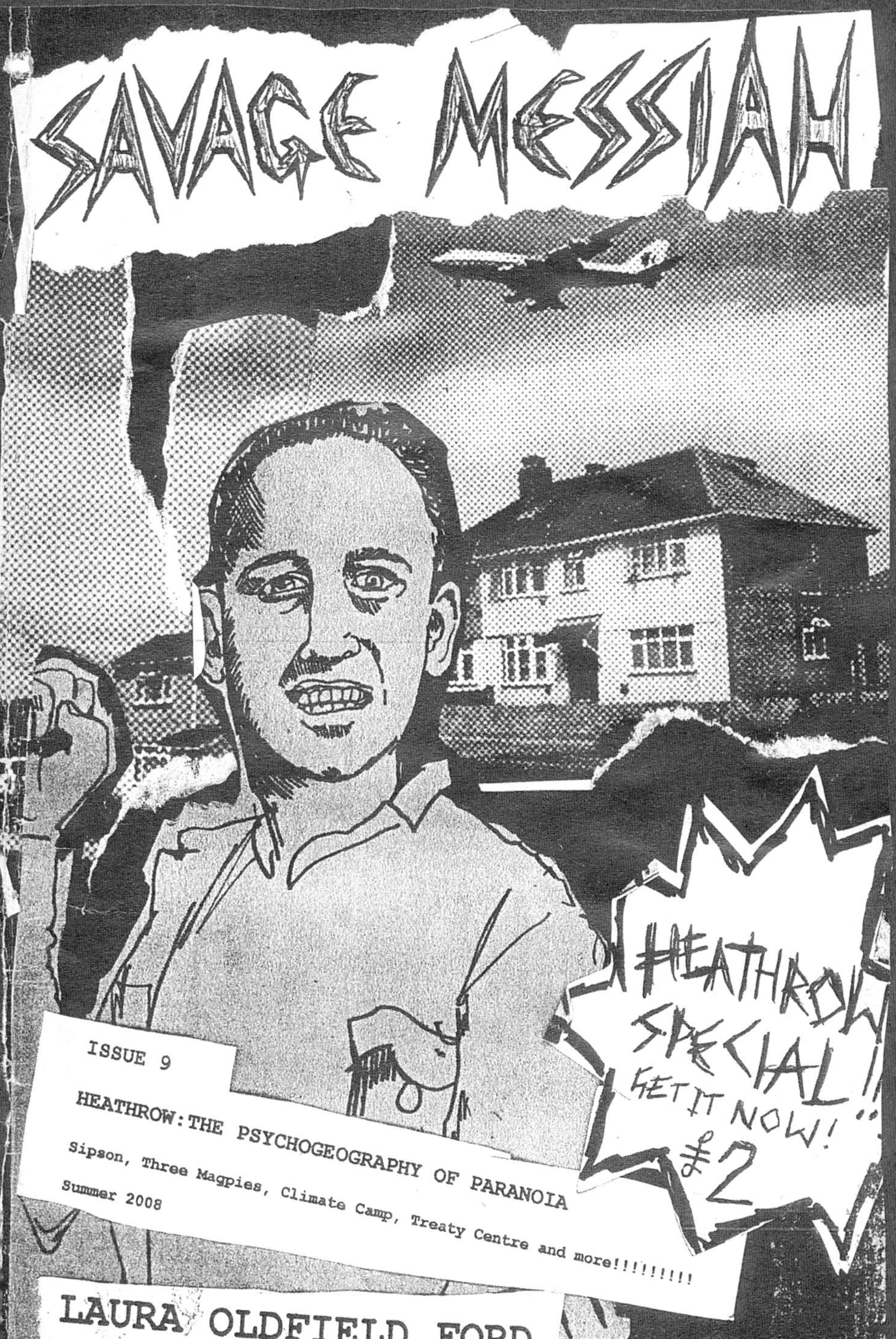
SAVAGE MESSIAH
ISSUE 9
HEATHROW: THE PSYCHOGEOGRAPHY OF PARANOIA
Sipson, Three Magpies, Climate Camp, Treaty Centre and more!!!!!!!!!
Summer 2008
HEATHROW SPECIAL!!
GET IT NOW!
£2
LAURA OLDFIELD FORD

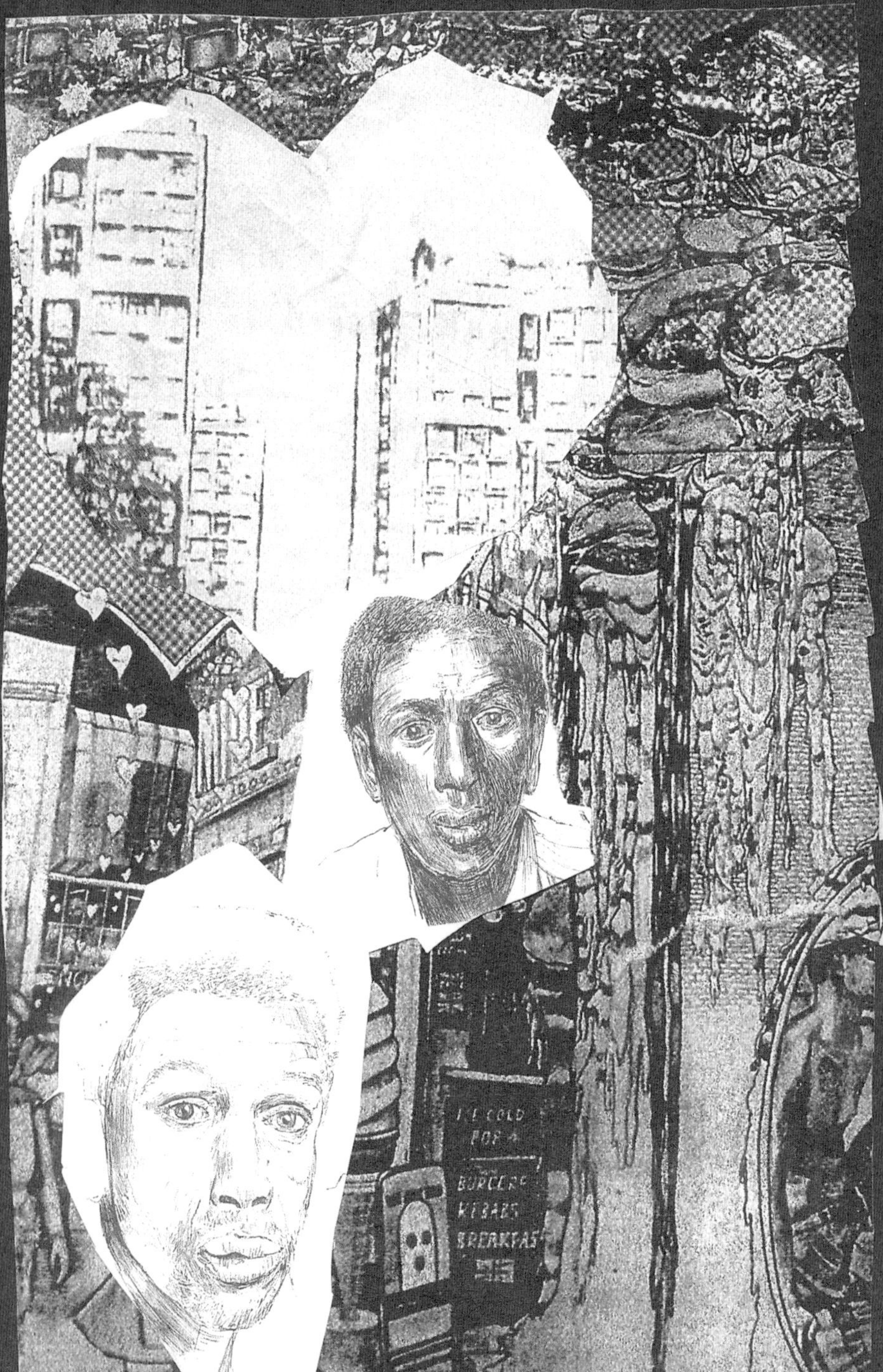
COLD
BREAKFAS

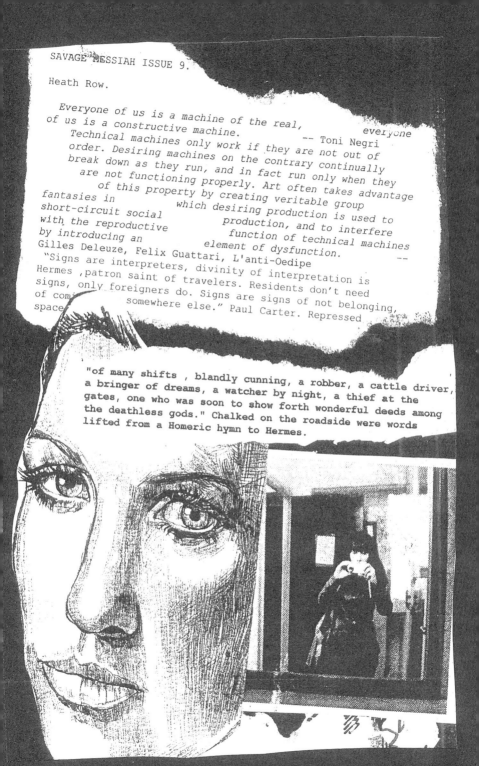

Heath Row.

Everyone of us is a machine of the real, everyone of us is a constructive machine.   -- Toni Negri
Technical machines only work if they are not out of order. Desiring machines on the contrary continually break down as they run, and in fact run only when they are not functioning properly. Art often takes advantage of this property by creating veritable group fantasies in which desiring production is used to short-circuit social production, and to interfere with the reproductive function of technical machines by introducing an element of dysfunction.   --
Gilles Deleuze, Felix Guattari, L'anti-Oedipe
"Signs are interpreters, divinity of interpretation is Hermes ,patron saint of travelers. Residents don't need signs, only foreigners do. Signs are signs of not belonging, of com͏   somewhere else." Paul Carter. Repressed space

"of many shifts , blandly cunning, a robber, a cattle driver, a bringer of dreams, a watcher by night, a thief at the gates, one who was soon to show forth wonderful deeds among the deathless gods." Chalked on the roadside were words lifted from a Homeric hymn to Hermes.

Heath Row.

"of many shifts , blandly cunning, a robber, a cattle driver, a
bringer of dreams, a watcher by night, a thief at the gates,
one who was soon to show forth wonderful deeds among the
deathless gods." Chalked on the roadside were words lifted from
a Homeric hymn to Hermes.

PSYCHOGEOGRAPHY ,LIKE THE CITY, IS MORPHOGENETIC, IT CARRIES
THE SEEDS OF ITS OWN CHANGE WITHIN IT. IT CANNOT BE MAPPED,
THERE IS NO EXTENSIVE SPACE.

 "In every case, the state of exception marks a threshold at
which logic and praxis blur with each other and a pure violence
without logos claims to realize an enunciation without any real
reference" …………"President Bush's decision to refer to himself
constantly as the "Commander in Chief of the Army" after
September 11, 2001, must be considered in the context of this
presidential claim to sovereign powers in emergency situations.
If, as we have seen, the assumption of this title entails a
direct reference to the state of exception, then Bush is
attempting to produce a situation in which the emergency
becomes the rule, and the very distinction between peace and
war (and between foreign and civil war) becomes impossible."
Giorgio Agamben.

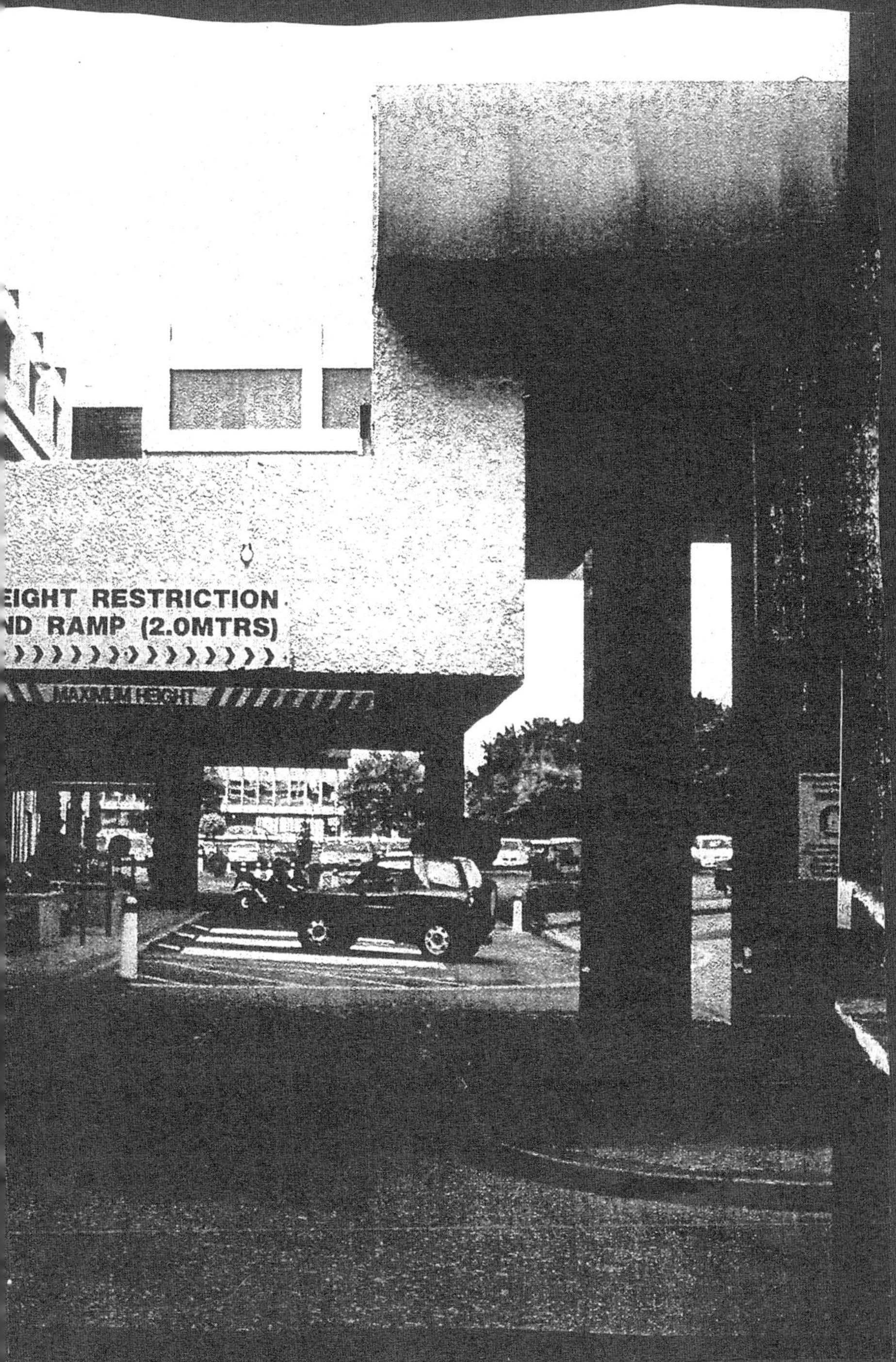
EIGHT RESTRICTION
ND RAMP (2.0MTRS)
MAXIMUM HEIGHT

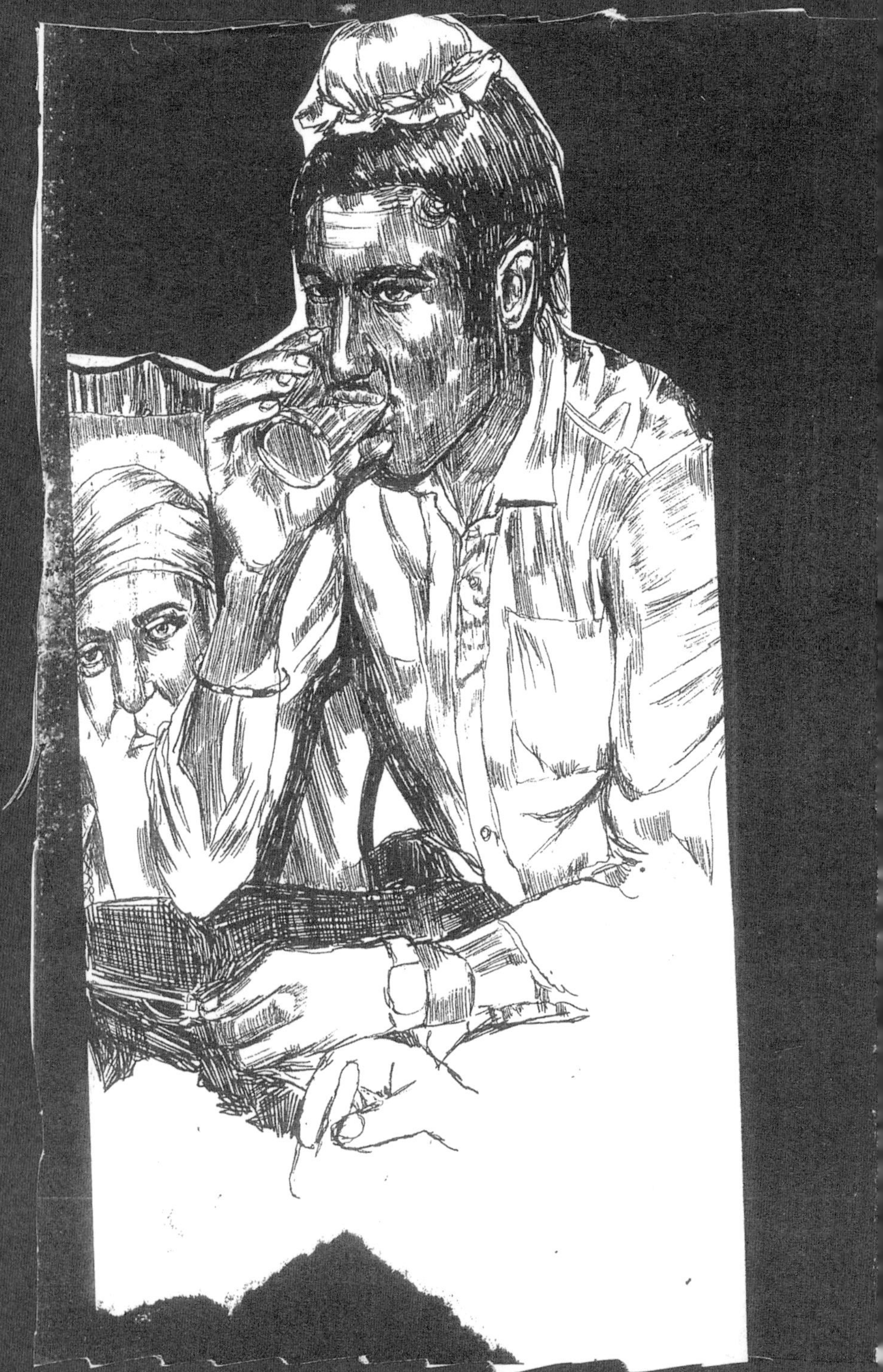

AUGUST 2007.

Heathrow is a mesh of paranoia, clusters of armed police traversing the perimeter.

Edge beneath the razor wire of a forlorn camp , a guarded non space mutating into contemporary locus of struggle. Middle England just this side of the fence, clinging to heritage and hanging baskets, 'No third runway' daubed on George cross banners.

Immigration removal centres, privatised prisons, they're not keen, they don't want them coming in, and they don't like unhealthy proles holidaying in Spain much either.

Terrorism, a word almost drained of its psychotic cravings by the anodyne platitudes mouthed on ABC/

It lurks in the infrastructure. Does anyone really believe in it? Conspiracy theories abound, there's a retreat into the escapism of fantasy lands, the irrational.

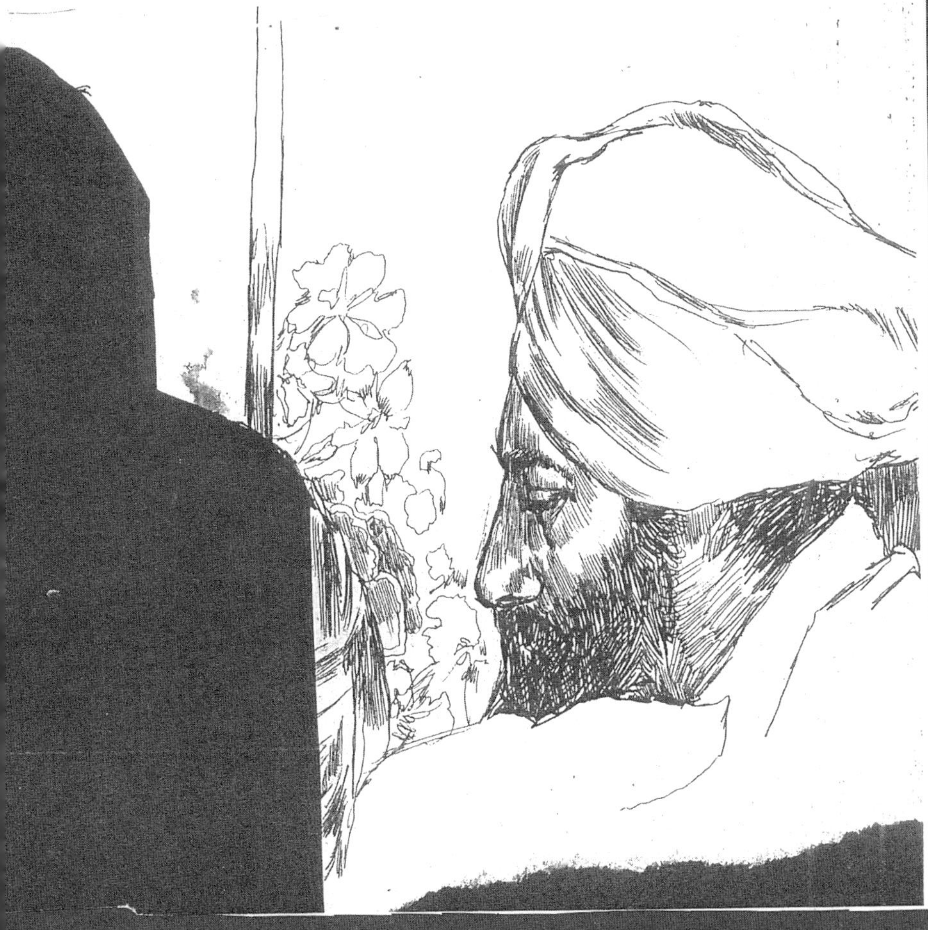

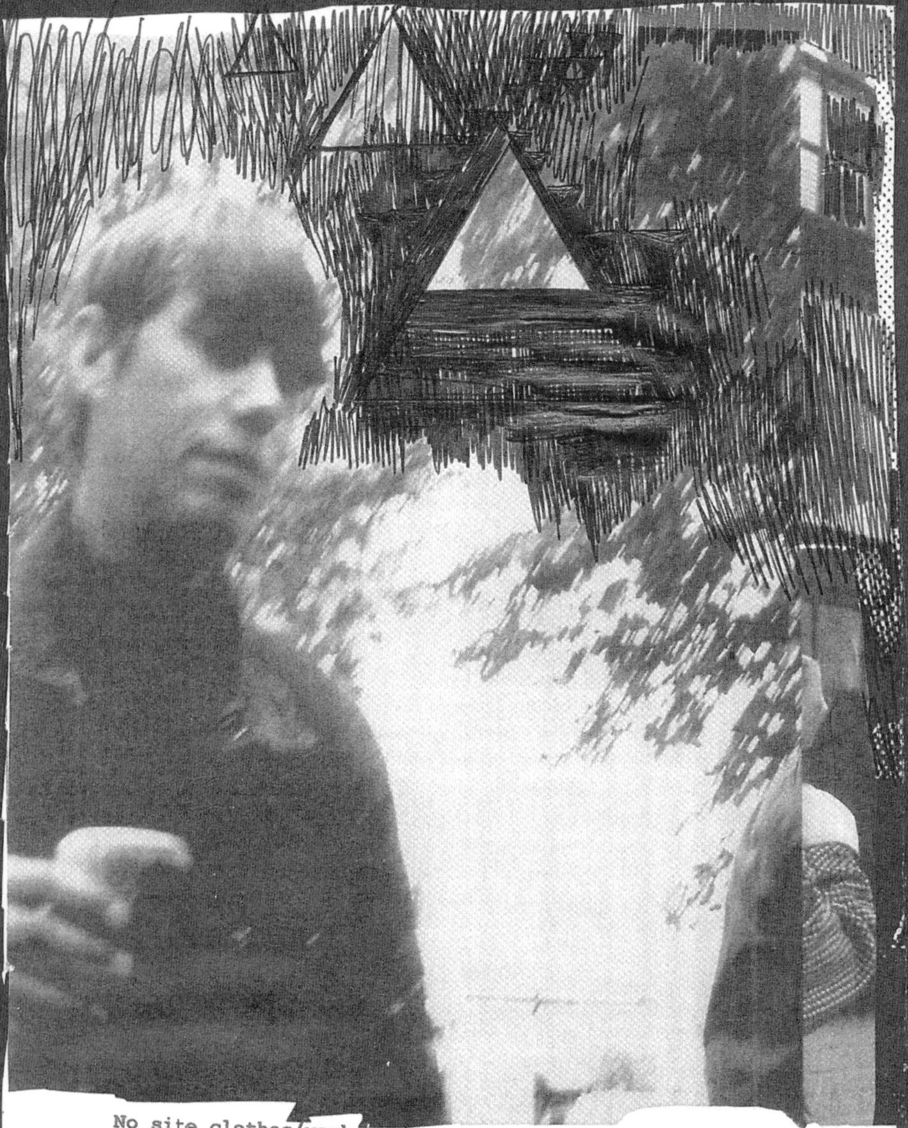

No site clothes/work boots.
The three magpies, relic of its 70 heyday. Nothing really changed. A saccharine rendition of "Silent Night'plays on the juke box.

Monday afternoon . August,2007
just us and a couple of baggage handlers.
We leave the faux heritage of Edwardian Tudor and head for the patio bar,,
some tables beneath a razor wire fence.
Then the airport.

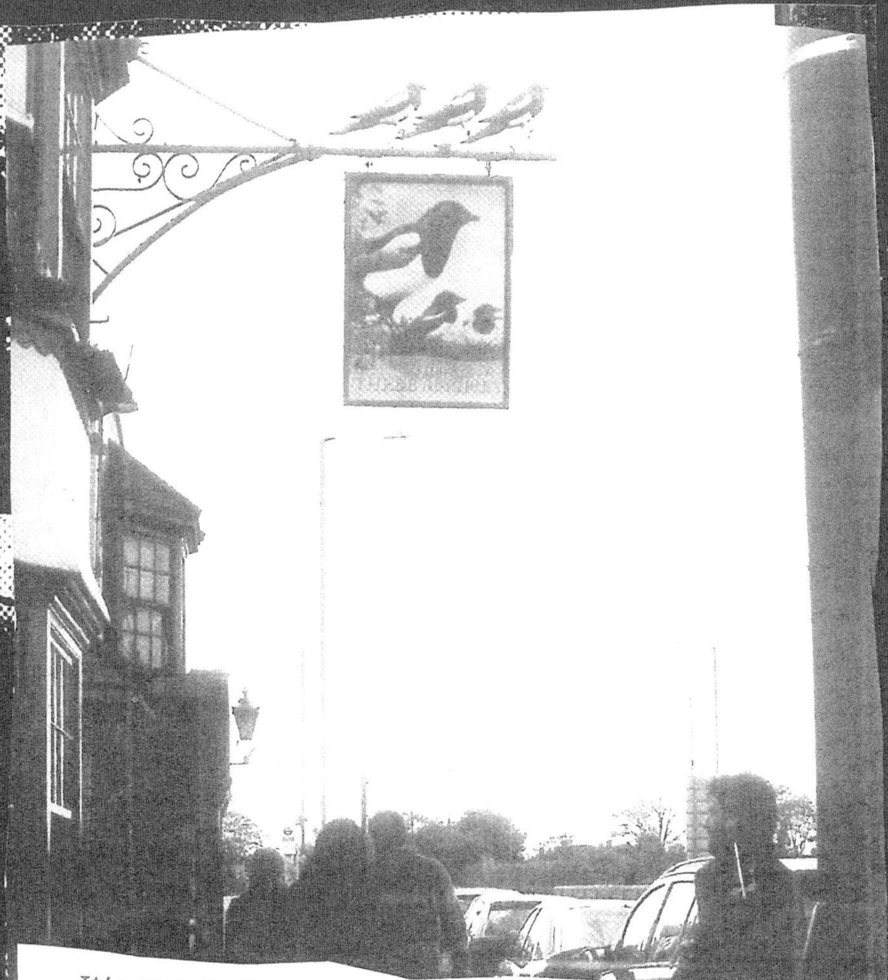

It's an out of time zone, clandestine encounters, a few drinks before a dash to the Renaissance hotel. Its a place of under table powder slipping and hawkers peddling stuff off the luggage truck. You get it now, or it's on its way to the auction house in Tooting.

Had everything in here, mainly perfume and stuff, specially since the ban on hand luggage and liquids, some nice stuff, expensive, all sorts really. Grew up in Leeds, used to be married, swapped council house in Gipton for a flat in Hounslow and just disappeared.

Here in this transit zone everyone was just passing through, it was me and the Somalians and Sikhs and everyone, loads of Polish, Lithuanians everywhere, all the shops, Polski Sklep now. A lot of the pubs closed ,, turned into boring stuff like burglar alarm businesses . Asians didn't really use them so much but now the Poles are bring them back to life. // mobile discos,,

blue drinks,,

Euro mash ups.

The Three Magpies is alright, working there three years. you get your regulars,/

gathering for a while, blokes from the airport. Then there's lads up on a weekend, mainly for the karaoke and late licence, airport means it's easy to get one, funny hours people work and no neighbours to annoy.

Outside this strictly controlled zone we had this little pocket that was almost operating outside the law. We had all sorts going on, a lot of young ones off their heads but the old bill never looking in.

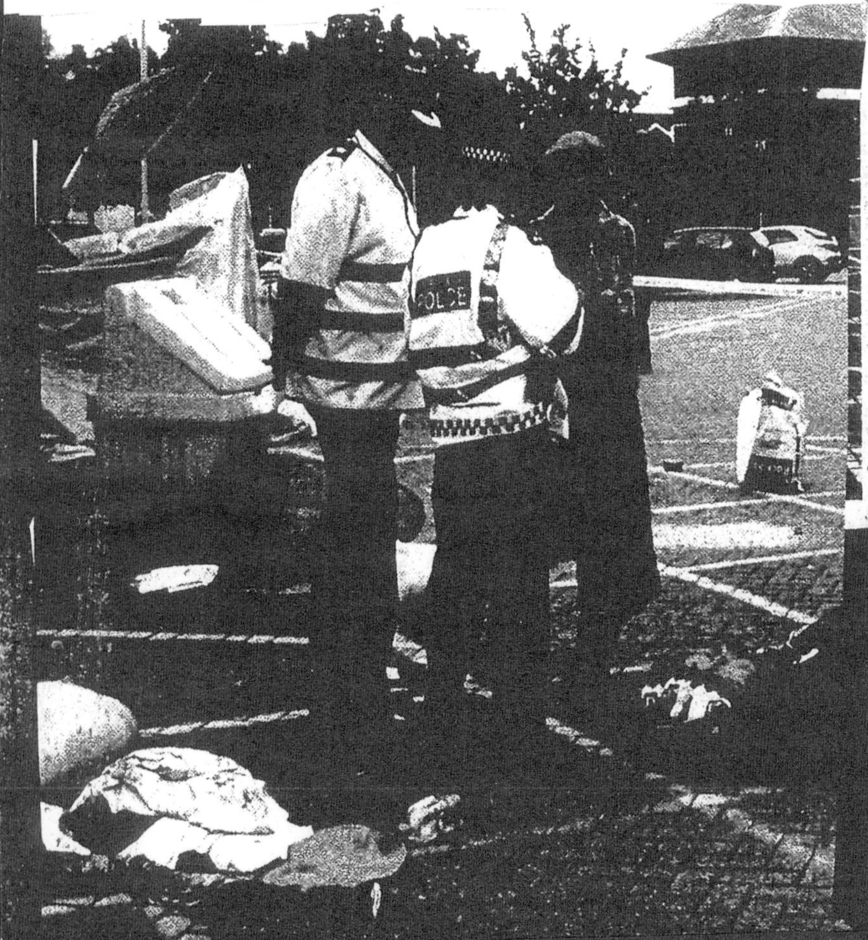
POLICE

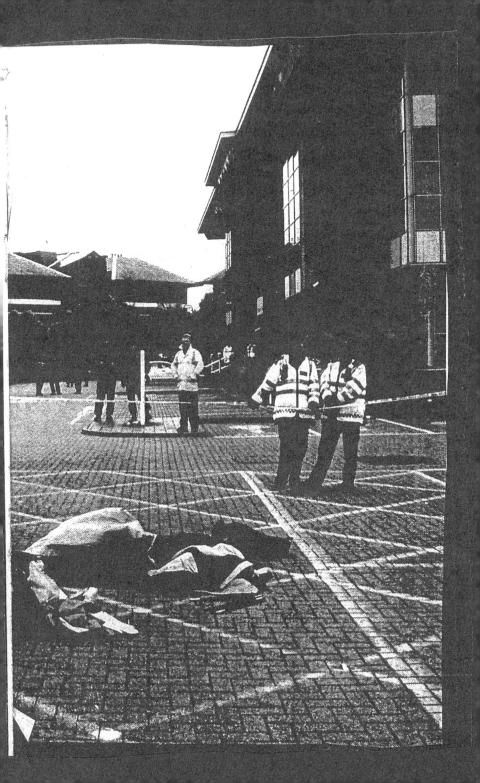

Hounslow, a slump back to lean times when the railway came, a long glance to the Highway men and hostelries of the neglected roads. The Great West Road, The Golden Mile and then, once more, the slow decline.

Treaty Centre, spot of shoplifting, runs into the duke of Cambridge, through tunnels ,back alleys, through corrugated iron gate and into beer garden of pub. Few metallers, old punks hanging about. So much for HBAC, well we wanted their licence so they had to join.

The shopping centre had a Father Christmas in it drinking special brew.

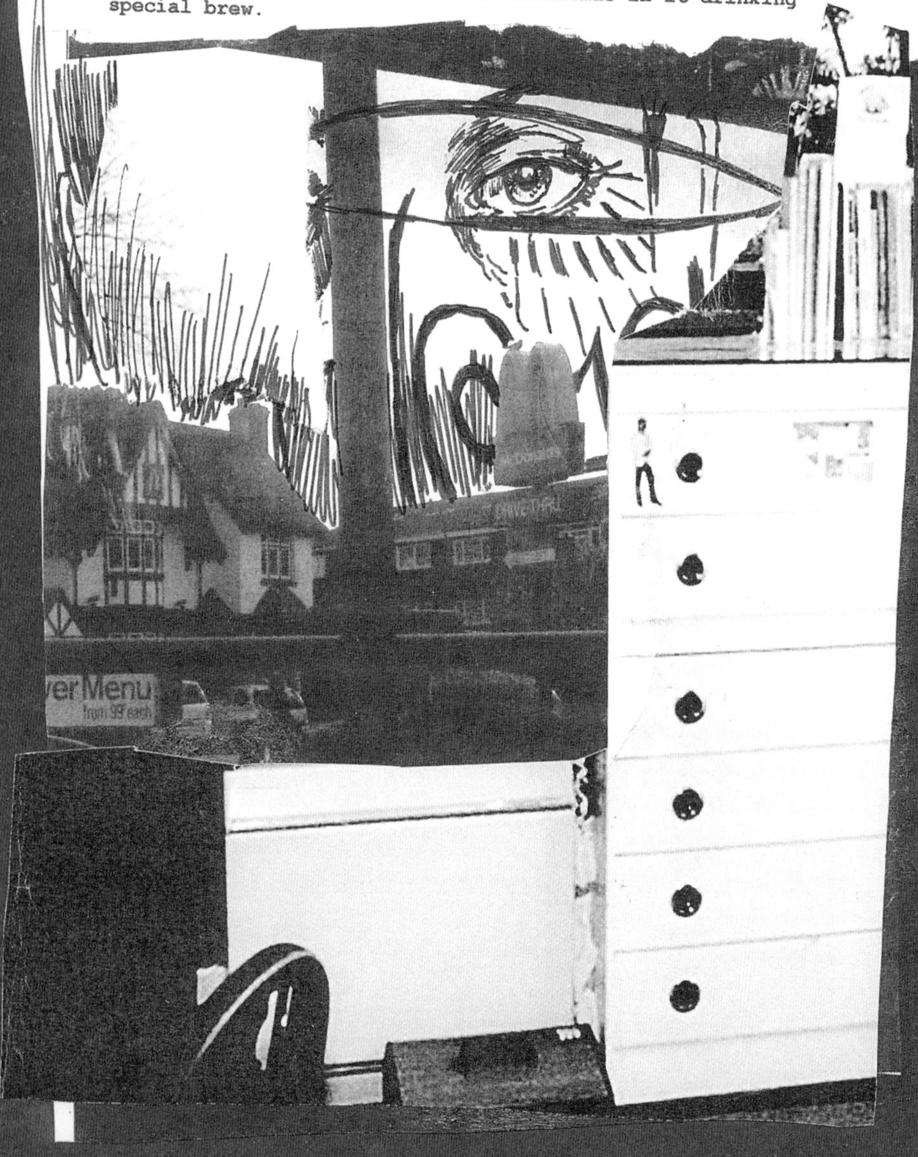
DRIVE THRU
ver Menu

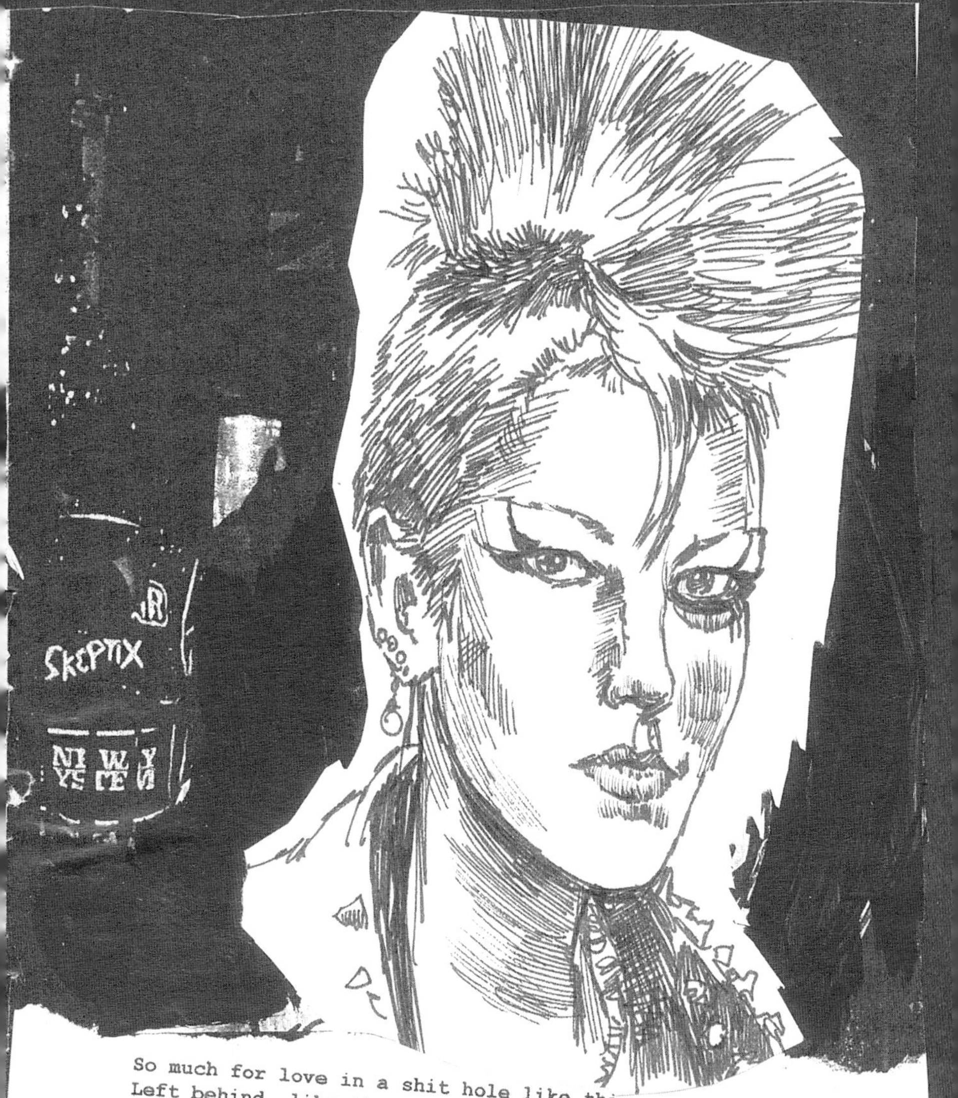
SKEPTIX

So much for love in a shit hole like this.
Left behind, like the summer we never had.
I was so looking forward to it and then the Autumn came in July, a slow Autumn, the longest Autumn. We never had the jubilance, the carnivalesque loopiness. It passed over in a matter of hours.
I did glimpse it, on the way back from Highgate that balmy Sunday, on Shoreditch Park, everyone outside, but there was that creeping melancholia that couldn't be burnt off in the fierce sunshine. I longed for the dissolution, the craziness, but it never came. Instead a catalogue of grimness,.terror alerts, floods and foot and mouth.

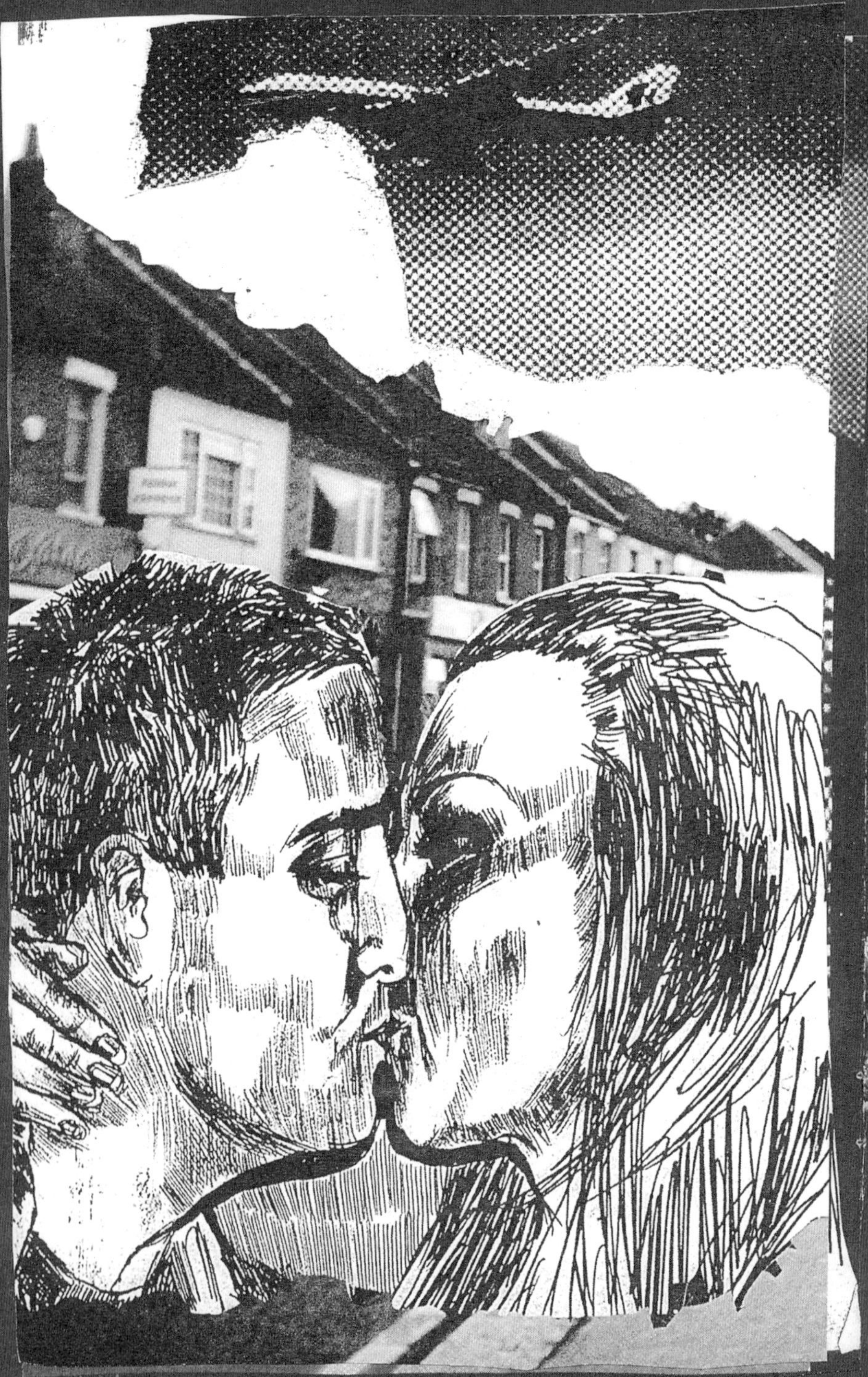

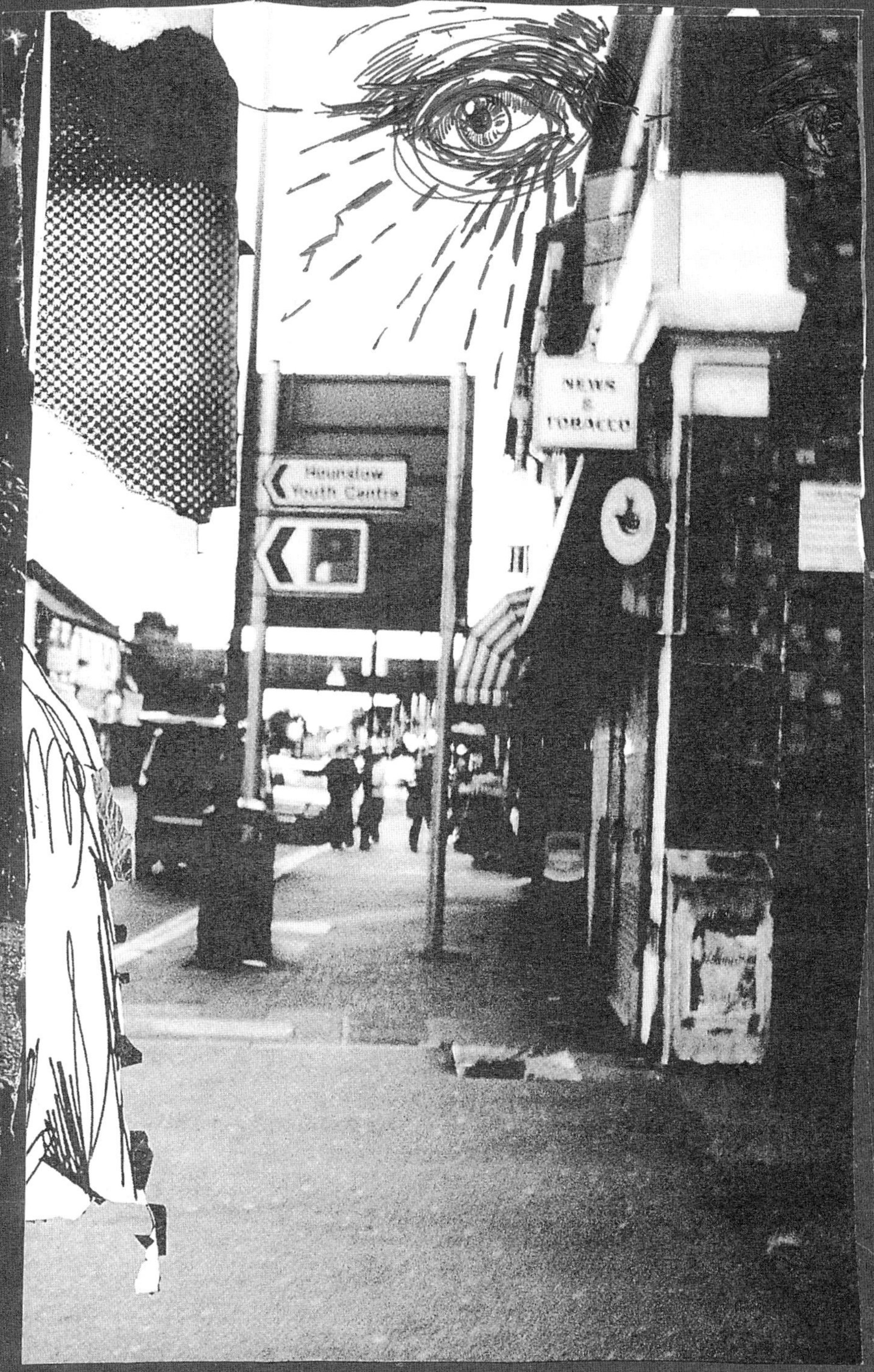
Hounslow
Youth Centre
NEWS
&
TOBACCO

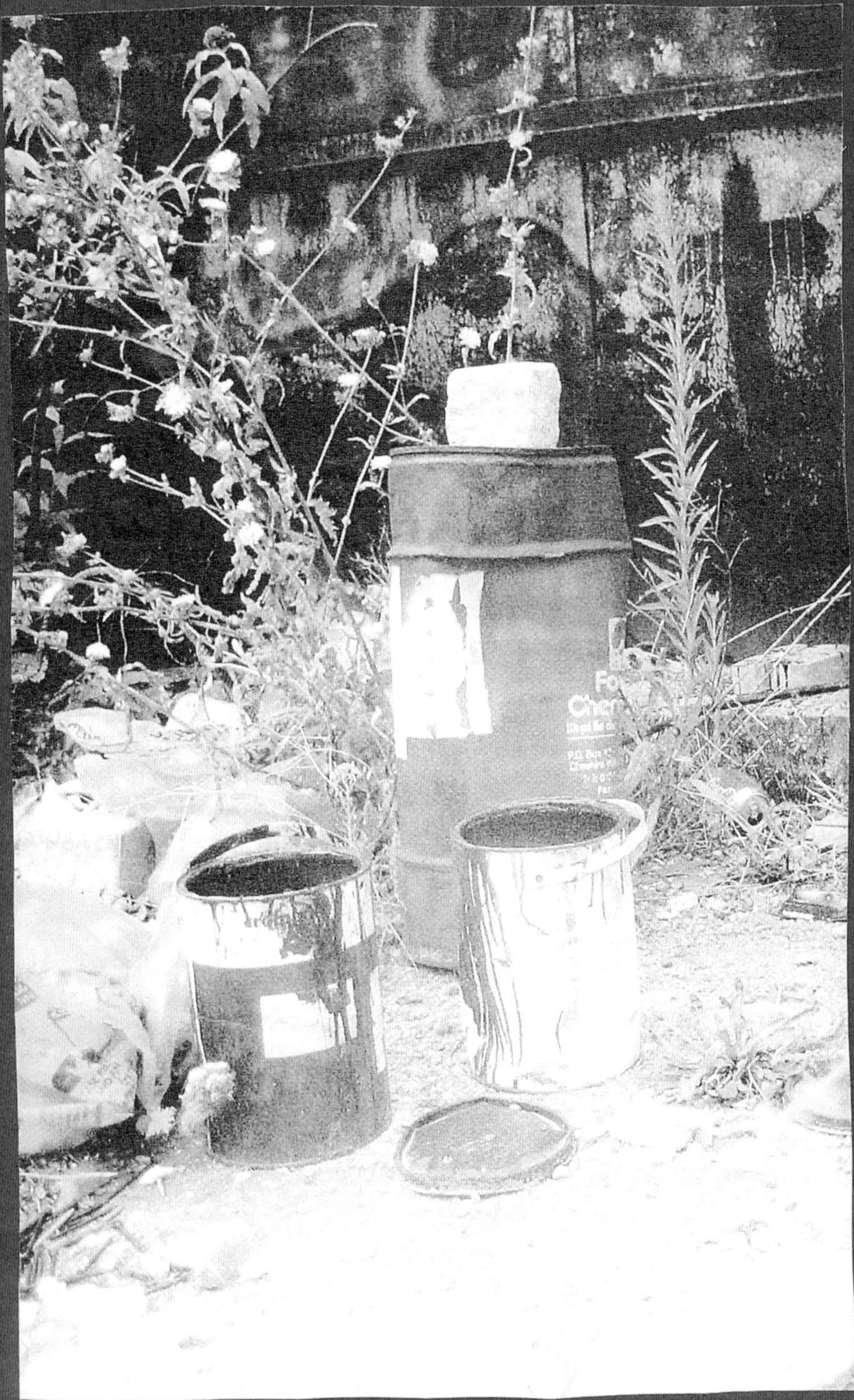

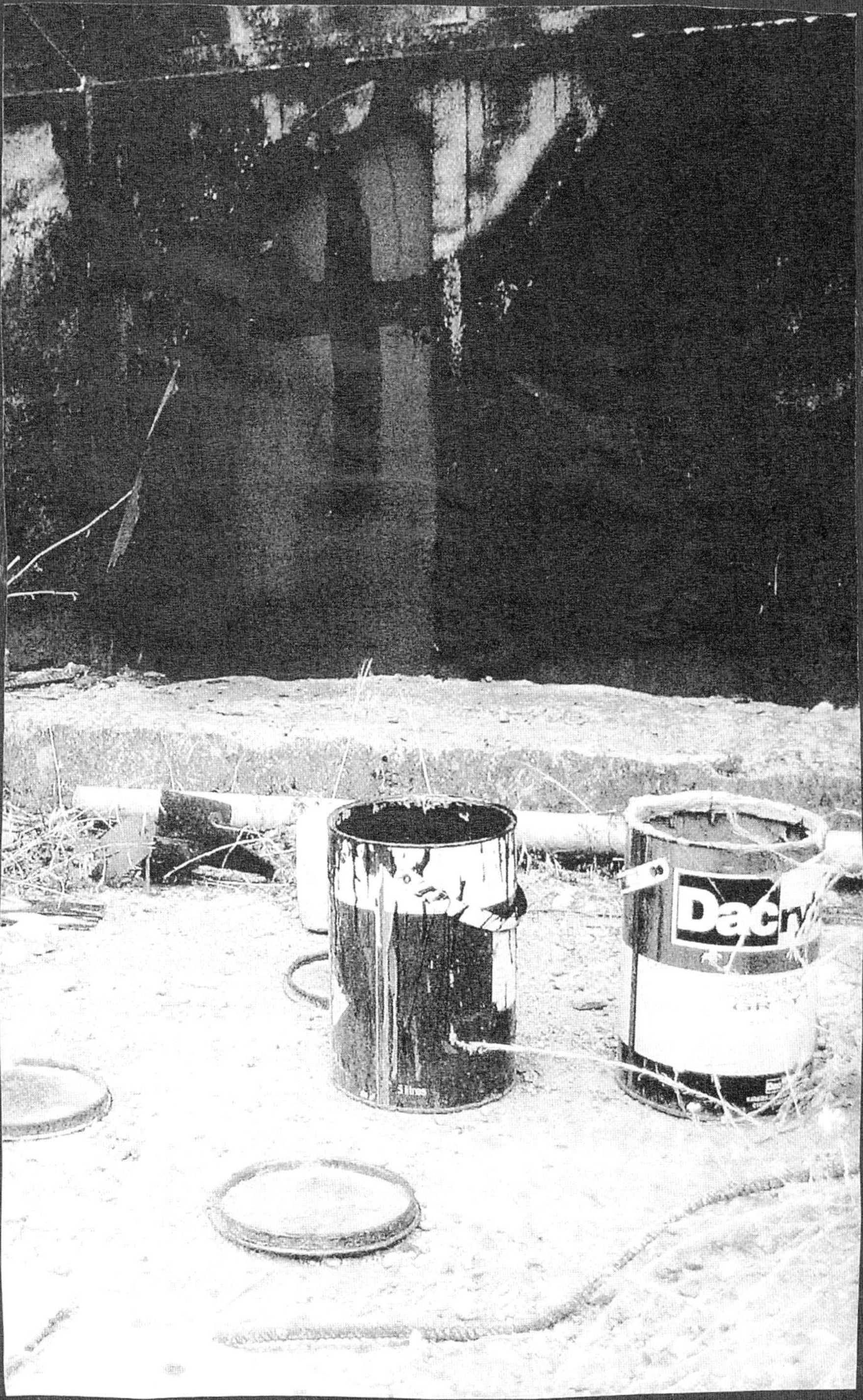
DaCry

The flat was stifling, Mick put the heating on full blast.
Louise made Nescafe for everyone, it was nice to sit round the
gas fire watching tv in the afternoon, it was nearly dark
outside. Sandra was crimping her hair, she'd just dyed it black
and the skin on her neck was dark blue. It was a long ritual,
hair first, dyed,crimped,teased and coaxed in elaborate spikes
and crests, then the make up, panstick white, kohl eyes, a
slash of purple lipstick. And always that patchouli oil stink.
Mick was going to the Offie, it was alright, the one on the
corner, good deals on Stella and that horrible wine Sandra
liked, so he went off with a tenner and came back with two blue
plastic bags. The flat was in a 60s block on the eastern edge
of Hounslow. Mick had let Sandra do what she liked with the
décor, he couldn't be bothered with it. She liked animal print,
red walls, black velvet and weird tapestry stuff from India
with mirrors and stuff. He didn't care, before she moved in it
was a right shit hole, curry cartons and beer cans everywhere.
Then she put lava lamps and red lightbulbs in the hall and
these stupid animals with punk outfits on and trolls from the
pound shop, and he was thinking it's getting a bit much now but
if it kept her happy maybe it would stop her moaning about his
little habits.
Mick was really looking forward to tonight, it was fucking ages
since he'd had a proper massive bender. All the crew was coming
over from Hammersmith and some mates from out in Slough, it was
gonna be a right gathering, a proper fucking weekend. He'd just
got his giro and started a new driving job so he was quids in.
Sandra was up for it, always liked a good booze up, Louise was
staying over, just down from Leeds, yeah things were looking
good.
He cracked open a tin, Weakest Link was on, he kind of liked
that programme cos he liked the darkness of it, you could
really buzz off that studio set when you were coming up on
something, especially with a bit of Scaldic Curse on the
stereo, it was Anne, the way she fixed you, and the leather
trench coat, but fucking hell, he didn't fancy her, no way,
fuck that.

Sandra's going on about who'll be playing in the Duke tonight
. They always rotate the DJ's round in there, some he likes
better than others, he's more into the really dark metal stuff,
Sandra and Louise like it when its more goth and industrial, he
doesn't mind that much but really aint into it when the place
gets clogged up with all these little dickheads in Slipknot t-
shirts. It annoys him when the scene gets full of kids, mind
you Sandra's only twenty, but its not so much of a problem when
it's the birds.

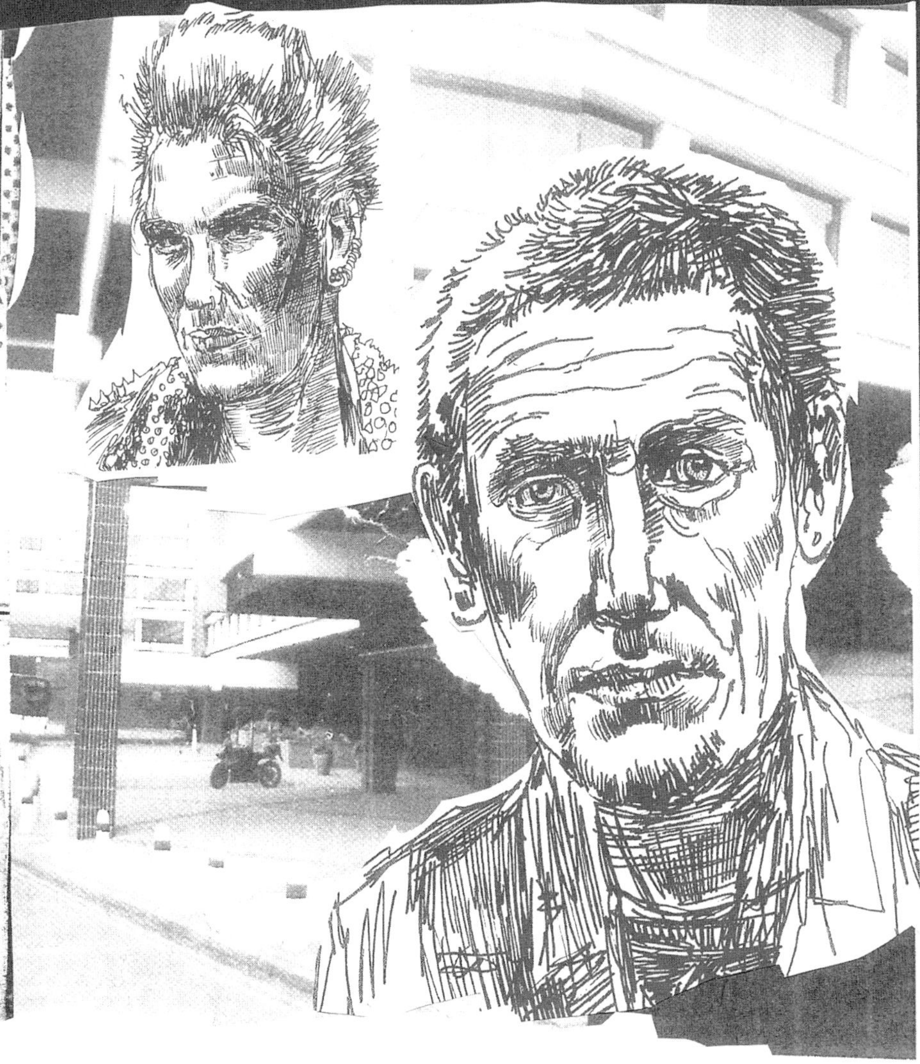

Sandra and Louise are caning a bottle sweet white wine, he don't know how anyone can stomach that shit but still it only cost £2.99 and that'll do em for the next two hours. They start acting daft and pissed up straight away, they're demanding music so he goes up and slaps some Mordred on. Sandra starts shrieking Sisters of Mercy so he puts some on cos he has to admit that the Sisters, in their early phase were good. When it gets to 7 they're all up for it and it's time to go and get the crew together and have a few pre- Duke warm up pints in the fake Irish shit hole round the corner. Mick's well known

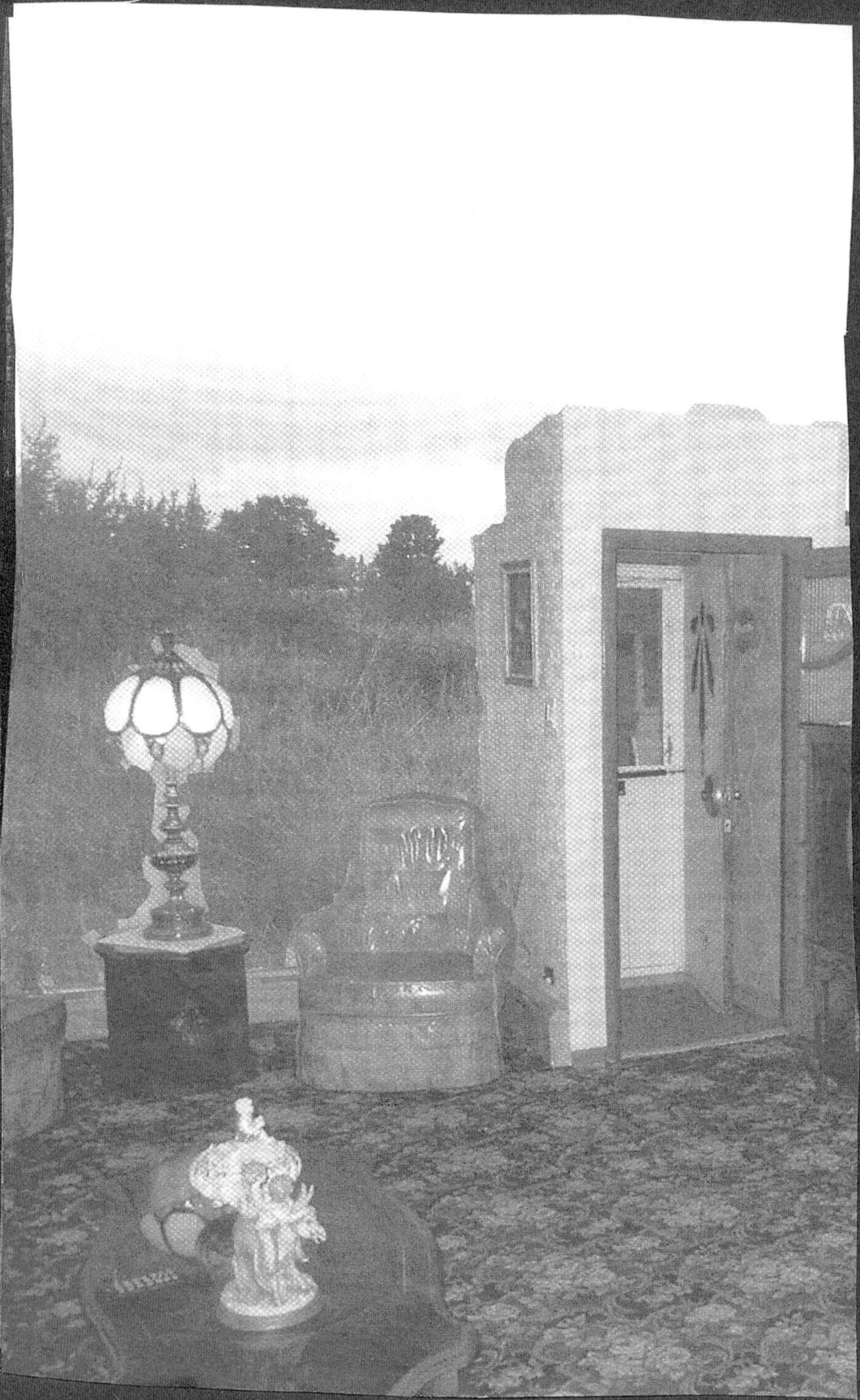

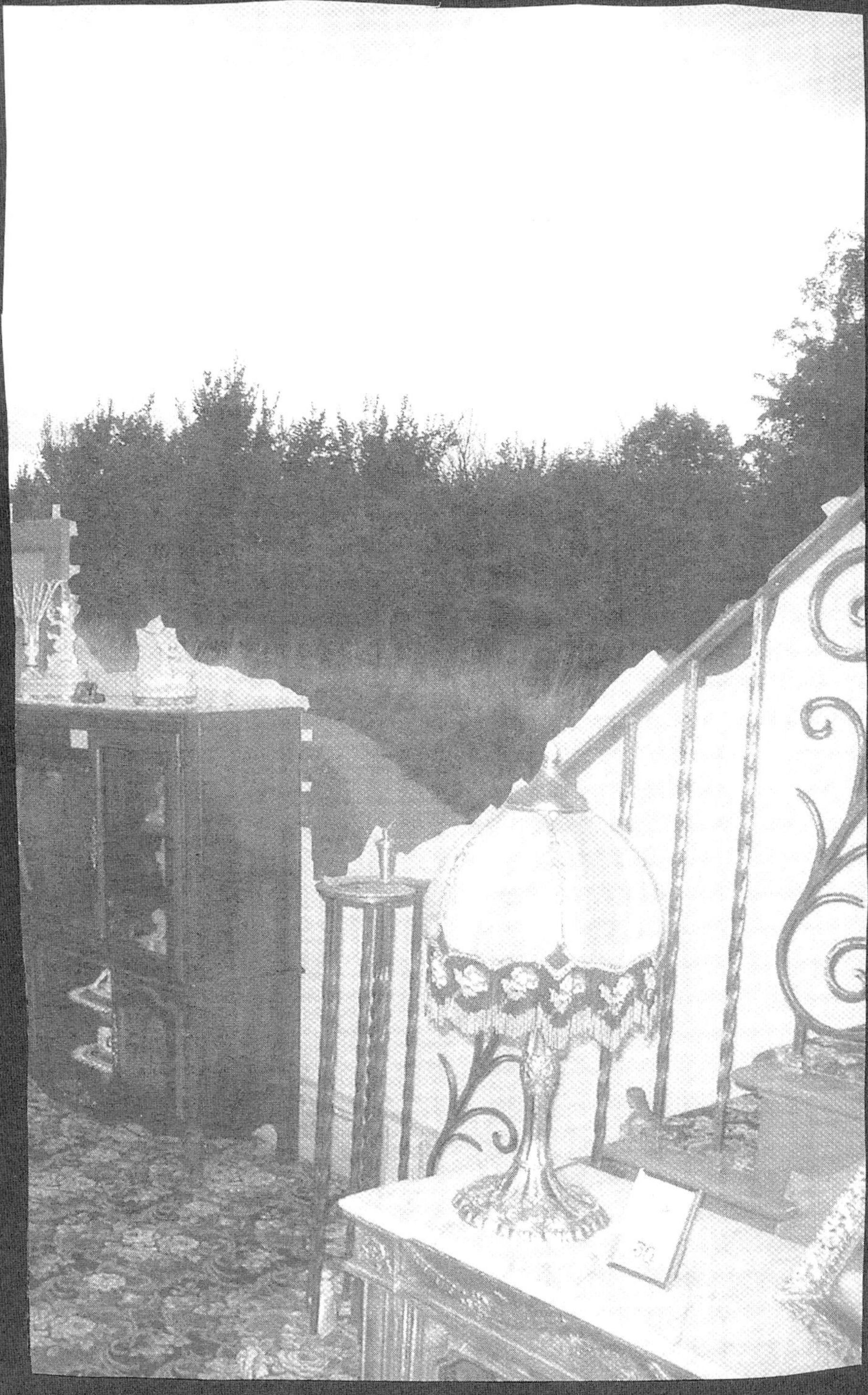

round here and can handle myself with the crew of eastern
European wankers who've installed themselves ~~come~~. He;s
got opinions on that but he aint gonna let it spoil tonight,
infact he has a go on a couple of pints of the Polak lager just
to get into things a bit quicker. There's a big crew assembling
now, a dozen or so of the Slough lot are over and the
Hammersmith boys are on the Picadilly line. Mick likes it in
here, he likes the fruities flashing against the wall, he
likes the bird behind the bar even though she dresses dead
straight she's still fit and he likes the jukebox with the old
metal classics embedded in all the dance shite that the Polaks
like. Yeah its ok, everyone getting off their heads, nicely
uncivilised.

He wonders about Clare, he thinks it might be a bit much if she
shows up tonight, specially after all that stuff that went on
last week. In the mens bogs. Fucking hell he must have been
well gone, thought he'd only had the usual quota, few pints,
dab or two of whizz, but it all went mental, dead hot, all the
lights just going all over, purple and pink glowing all round
his eyes. But he doesn't like all those hippy drugs so it
wasn't that and he didn't feel bad or sick or any of that just
really mental, like invincible, like he could do whatever he
fucking wanted. And he was just coming out of the bog when
Clare was standing there in this plastic skirt and fishnets
with this dirty look on her face, and quick as a flash he was
pushed back and they were all over each other, grabbing and
biting.
 He pushed open the window and climbed out into the yard,
there was a brick wall, razor wire, an orange street light and
a plastic chair. You wannit.,like this//. He hauled her out and
pushed her against the wall, brick dust and blood from a
crushed lip. This scene had been brewing for weeks, him and
her, the glad eye like teenagers over a hot dancefloor, him
thinking he had to bide his time, knowing it was worth waiting
for.
Clare was leaning against the corrugated iron smoking a B and H
.They're gonna notice we've gone Mick said with a sly grin. He
was feeling pleased with himself, Clare was fit, things were
going pretty well, he hadn't embarrassed himself with all the
booze and drugs.
I don't care , do you? she stood there nonchalantly brushing
the brick dust and blood off her jacket. Mick considered it,
well yeah a bit he thought to himself, the invincible feeling
wearing off a bit since he hadn't had a pint for nearly twenty
minutes. A bit worried, he thought, I mean he wouldn't mind
swapping Sandra for Clare, Clare was a laugh and he knew
there'd be plenty of good times, but you know it's never that
fucking simple. He'd ended up letting Sandra shack up with
him, it was one of them daft things, starts off as staying for
the weekend, then a few days, then the weekends blur into one
and she's living there. And that's sort of ok, but now he knows
he can't really get out of it without a whole load crying and
carrying on and he hasn't got the stomach for that. And then
there's AK, who's Clare's fella, and he's a bit of a handy
bastard, been on the circuit for ages, would not take kindly to

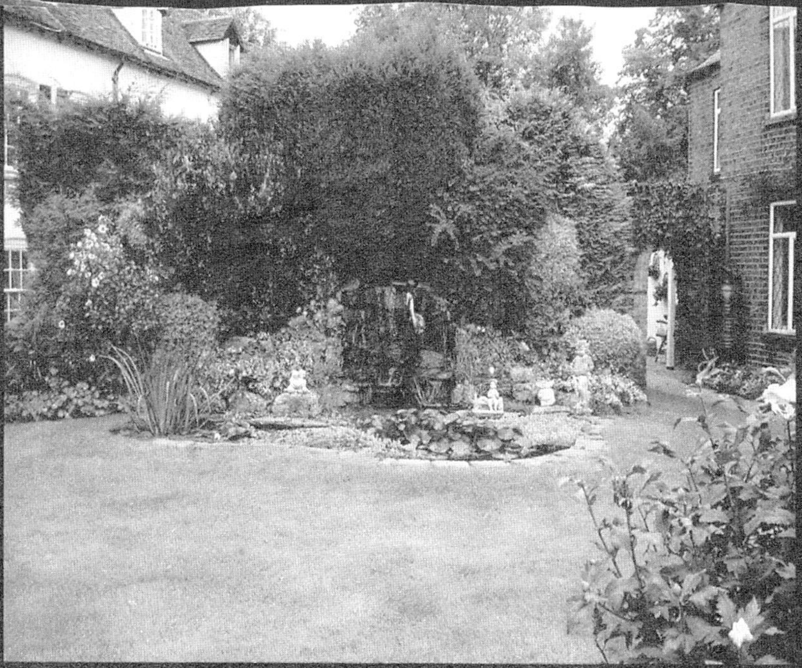

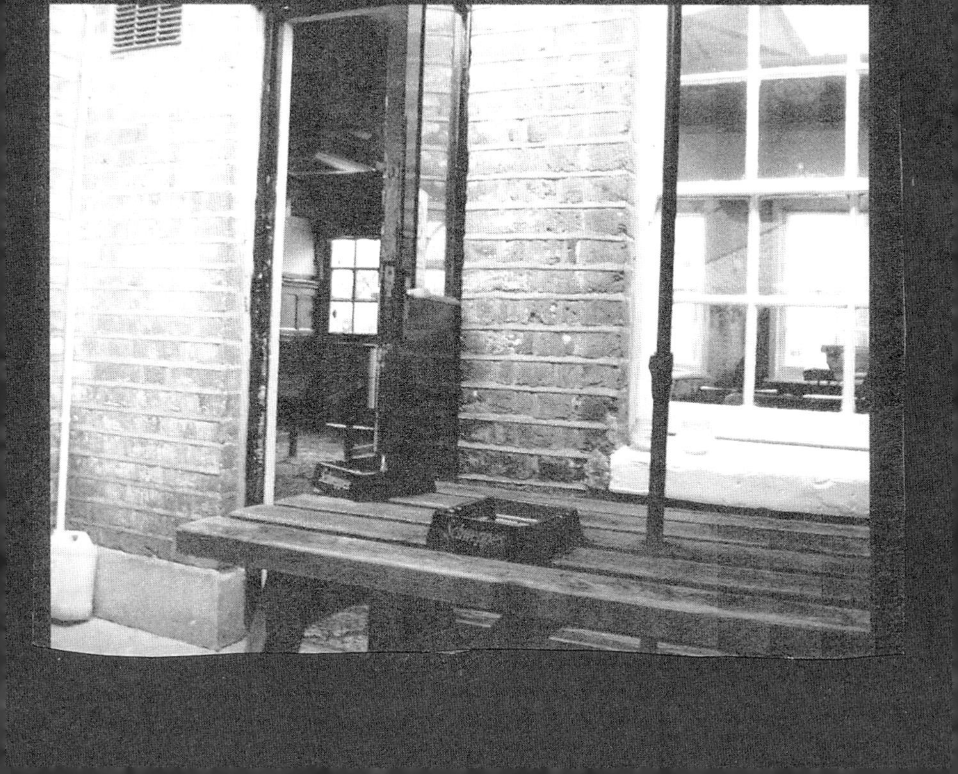

antics of that sort. Could get a bit nasty. He'll leave it he
thinks, they've had some fun, let that be enough.
She leads him down the corrugated iron alley under the orange
lamp glow, checking herself out in a little compact mirror,
putting lipstick on and fucking about. He lights up another
fag. The air is sharp and smells of petrol and a bonfire
somewhere. He shoves a panel of the fence and it gives enough
to let them squeeze through, they clamber through bindweed and
rusting car parts and reach another dilapidated fence backing
onto the Duke beer garden. I'll go back through the men's, you
go through here, I'll see you back inside.

The village, Sipson, sits on the precipice, heading towards the
relic zone beneath the asphalt. There's a couple of activists
lurking. We settle in for a few jars, the high heels and Ikea
bag are already causing consternation.
Blunt faced hacks sit down to give me lectures. Moralising and
hero worshipping this one's trapped in 1994, sometime around
Claremont Road and the first formations of reclaim the Streets.
He can't escape those times, its what defines him, maybe
because, as we see in the photos he pushes in front of us, he
wasn't a largactil tranqued doleite then.

2015.ghosts, revenants, memories haunting the fabric. London
gripped in security cordons. A day out looking at new plans for
projects on a recently evacuated and bombed out suburb.

The staircase. Closed doors, disinfectant on every landing,
fluorescent lights, peeling linoleum, flies round bare
lightbulbs, sometimes a wave of garlic transporting him to the
apartment in Spanish Harlem, sometimes a door ajar, a chink of
red light and the green stink of cannabis. He noticed
everything on those stairs as he climbed them, a slow ascent
into a labyrinth, another chaotic rookery with no exit signs.
He almost turned to leave as he reached number 18. He paused
before knocking.

…,the other night. Well of course. She hadn't forgotten, but he
might have, he was fucked, totally hammered. Let's walk back,
walk back my way. I'll show you a secret roof garden, she said,
we can see down onto airport and watch the planes.. She
clutched a bottle of wine in one hand and linked his arm, he
was pretty trashed but enjoyed the meandering walk through the
hot back streets. London this Summer was like Spain, they
walked through dusty backstreets with heat coming out of the
walls. She knew the alleys, the gaps in fences, the staircases
and industrial estates. She was confident and unafraid as they
drifted through the night. His drunkenness gave way to a more
heightened awareness, she sensed him stop stumbling, he
sharpened up quite suddenly as those last two dabs took effect.
She took him to a factory and pushed a wooden door, he looked
surprised as it yielded to her and they went in. They went up
another dank staircase, suddenly stone cold away from the
stifling heat, they kept climbing, passing doors with
fluorescent lights and the sounds of the radio above the

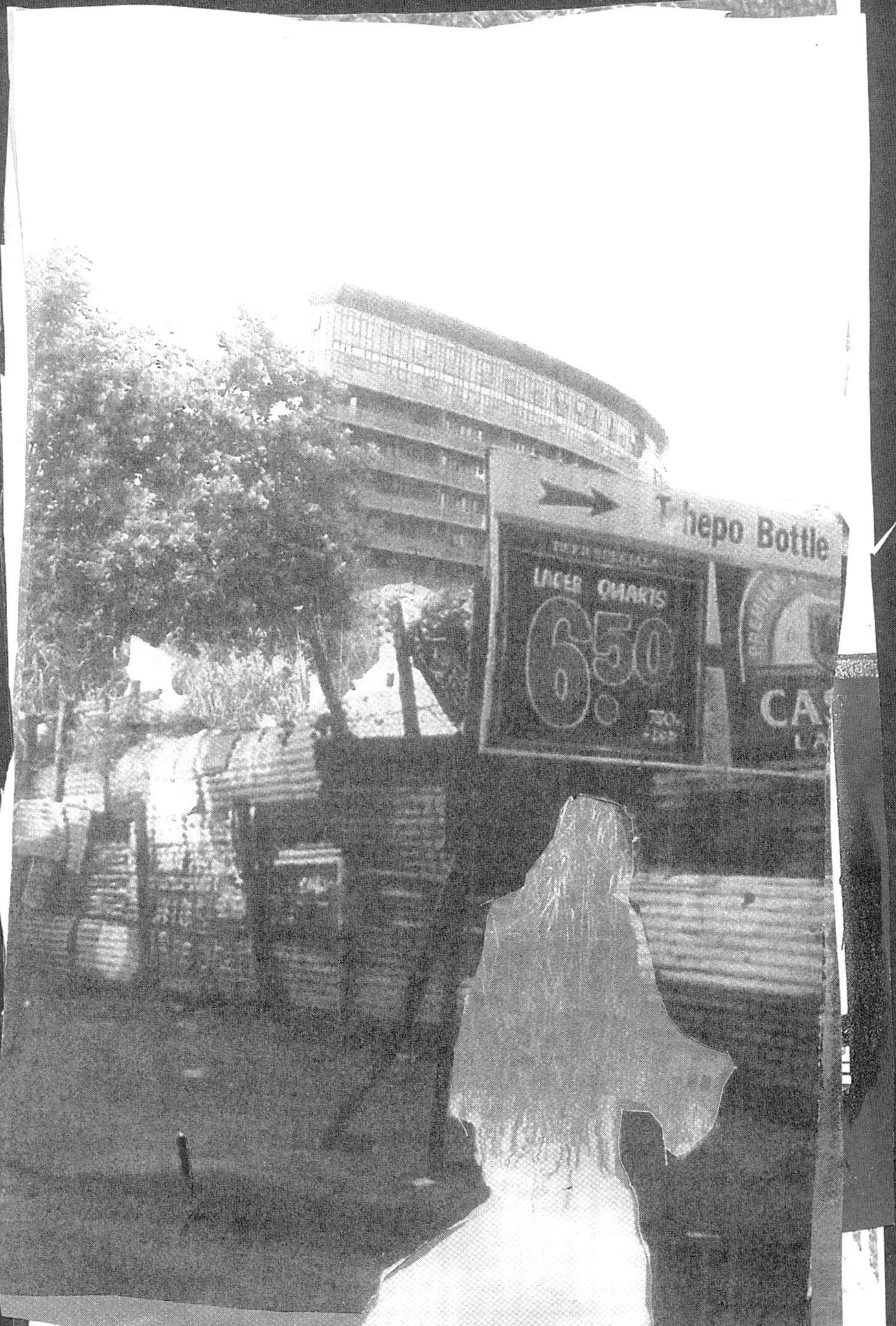
hepo Bottle
LAGER QUARTS

machinery and on every half landing bales of mildewed cloth. Finally they broke out onto the roof, three interlocking rooftops. She sat on the wall and opened the wine. His face seemed to fall apart in that kiss, the red wine, the balmy July heat, the spicy scents of Southall. Once that gate had been opened, once the composure had been breached he dissolved in the moment…,. She wanted this, the moment when the veneer would be split open and his desires would surge to the fore, composure could be thrown to the wall..She wanted the uncensored, uncut version, she wanted to feel what it was to be in him, to be him, to live temporarily behind his eyes.
They'd crossed that line now and she was swimming in all his racing neurons.

They always return, he said eyes scanning the path by the canal, the light was thin yellow now with dusty grains of grey and pink. He watched the monitor as the three figures slipped into a side street. Is it them?
Doubtless.
The security guard nodded and lit another cigarette. The older of the two men tapped a no smoking sign on the hut window.
The cameras had lost the figures, they were momontarily in a liminal zone, a hidden place between the cameras circle of view., them lot pride themselves on knowing where these fucking cameras are.
Tunde stepped outside the hut to smoke leaving Brian to his panoptican and his commentary. Tunde couldn't give a damn about vandals, he agreed with them, why should he care, he wouldn't mind joining in himself.
Brian on the other hand was determined to catch the hooded figures, it was about time head office noticed him, he wanted a promotion to the branch in Surrey, he wasn't comfortable stuck out here in this wilderness, too many Poles and Pakis. Trouble with Tunde, Brian concluded, was he was dim, no fucking spark in him, being stuck with him on a twelve hour shift was purgatory. I'll tell you now Fats I'll get those bastards. They called him Fats on account of him being so straight and skinny. I mean it, they'll get cocky, they always come back.
Tunde thought about the group , he knew nothing of them other than the grainy figures on the screens and the posters with drawings of flats on fire. He liked the idea of making things easy for them, turning a blind eye. Brian though, he took it fucking personal, saw it as a direct insult to him, his patch, they're taking the fucking piss.

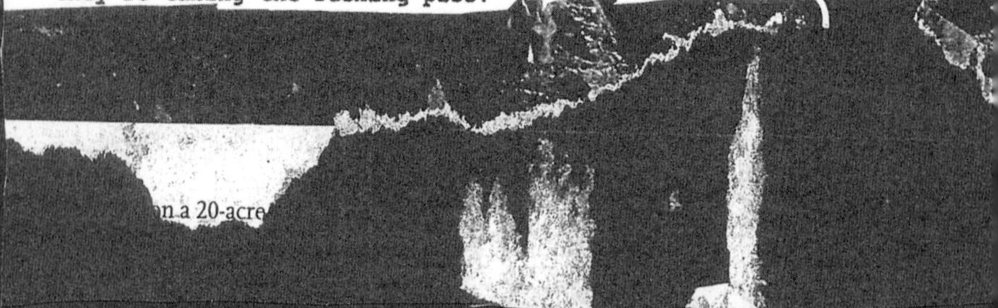
n a 20-acre

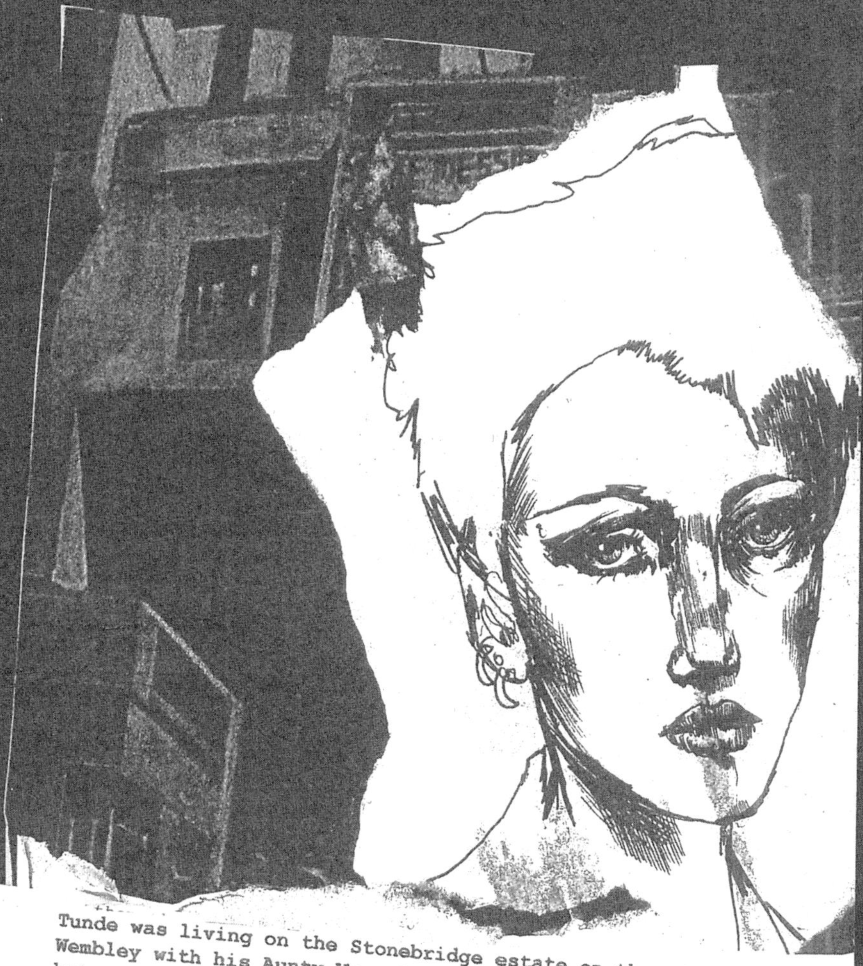

Tunde was living on the Stonebridge estate on the edge of Wembley with his Aunty Veronica and sometimes cousin Anthony but not always . It was better really when it was just him and Veronica, peaceful and easy. Veronica spoilt him, made a fuss, got him all his favourite things from the market. Tunde had an idea Anthony was in prison but Veronica never said. Maybe she discussed it with the priest or somebody ,but never him. Sometimes Anthony stayed away for months and then get a welcome like the prodigal son, other times he'd just fly in for a day here and a day there, but Veronica always kept the room the same, like the teenage boys room Anthony had left eight years

ago, Wu tang posters all over and the iconic Tupac face looking
down over his bed.
The lounge was a small treasure trove, crammed with pictures of
the Holy Mother. The doors were thrown open onto a balcony
packed with flowers and herbs. It was Veronicas pride and joy,
she sat on the little settee with seed catalogues making notes
of all the flowers she wanted to see blooming the following
summer. At night the scent of stocks and honeysuckle would
drift into the flat, in the day the geraniums and cornflowers
blazed red and blue.

Tunde never wanted to do the engineering degree, it was his
fathers idea, back in Nigeria, he was always talking about the
strength of the men in his family, their skill and ingenuity in
engineering. He'd seen his older brothers suffer at the hands
of his father, Kofi the eldest and Adebayo the middle one,
they'd stood up to him a for short time in the teenage years
but his father had been relentless, invincible. You couldn't
fight him, he possessed the brute strength of mind that left
the older boys crushed and humiliated. It was better Tunde
thought, to do what he said, to go England to do the terrible
engineering degree and study in secret for the real passion,
writing.
Tunde hid books beneath the Daily Star when Brian came into the
cabin. Brian favoured the Sun and the Daily Star in the day
shifts, and Razzle at night. He liked to have the radio on,
talk Sport or Five Live. Tunde liked it quiet so he could read.
It wasn't ever quiet at home, the flats on the Stonebridge were
stacked up like little boxes and the doors and windows were all
kept wide open to broadcast as much din as possible. The summer
was the worst, it became a cacophony of R and B, hip hop,
gospel and country and western, added to that the domestic
screech outs, crying babies and the shouts of the young men
congregating on the landings.
He found it hard sometimes to read and took his books to the
library at college.
Today he was reading Borges, he allowed himself to be lulled
into the labyrinths and watching the grainy figures on the
monitor almost felt he could slip in among them.

    Aunty Veronica was dozing on the settee when he arrived home.
    Is everything alright Tunde, did you have a good day today? She
    asked him without opening her eyes. It was fine Tunde said as
    he moved quietly around the kitchen. I'll make you your earl
    grey, Aunty yeah?
    Veronica opened her eyes a little and smiled. You're a very
    good boy Tunde, its what I tell your father every time he call.

    Babatunde
    the father has come back.

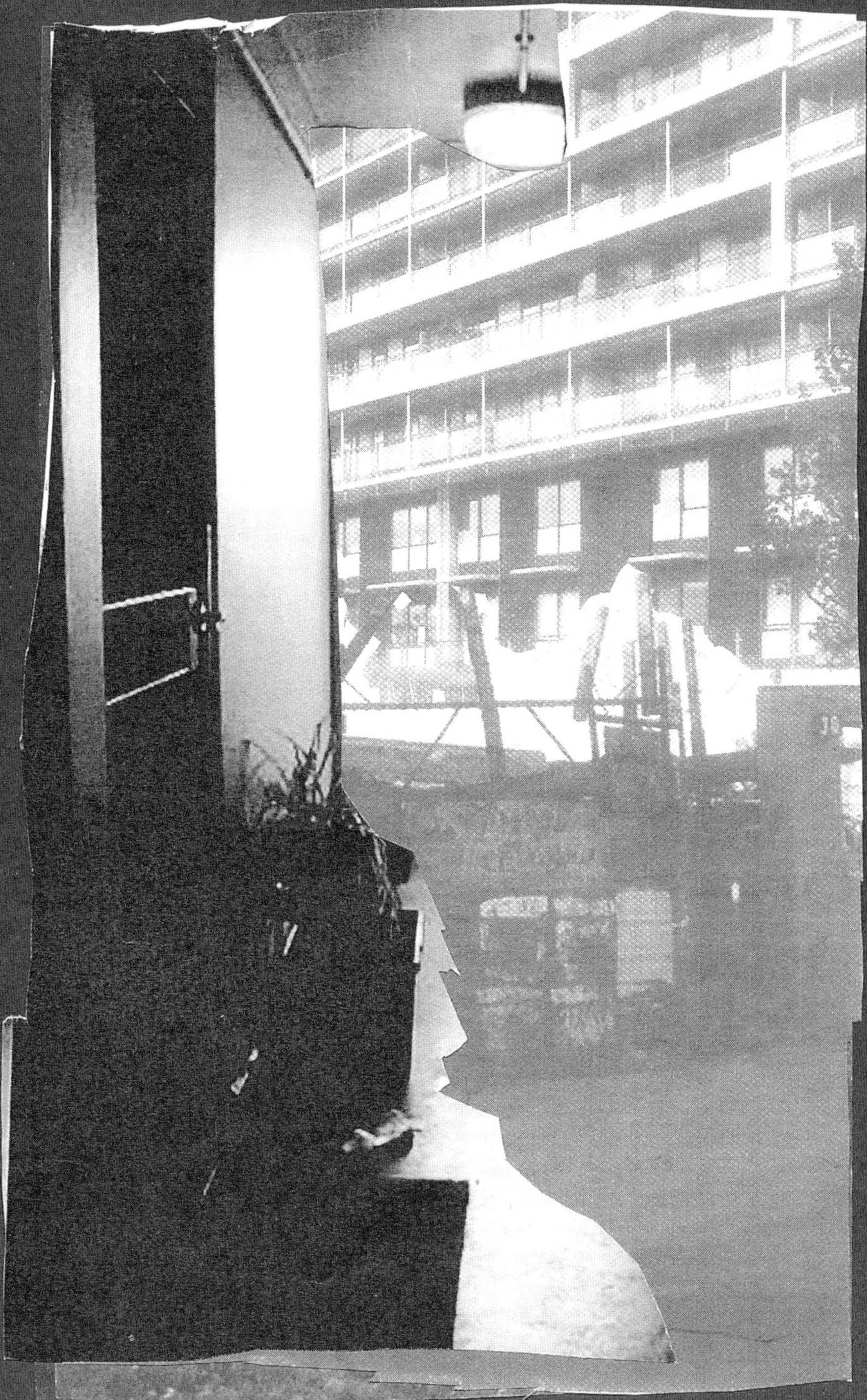

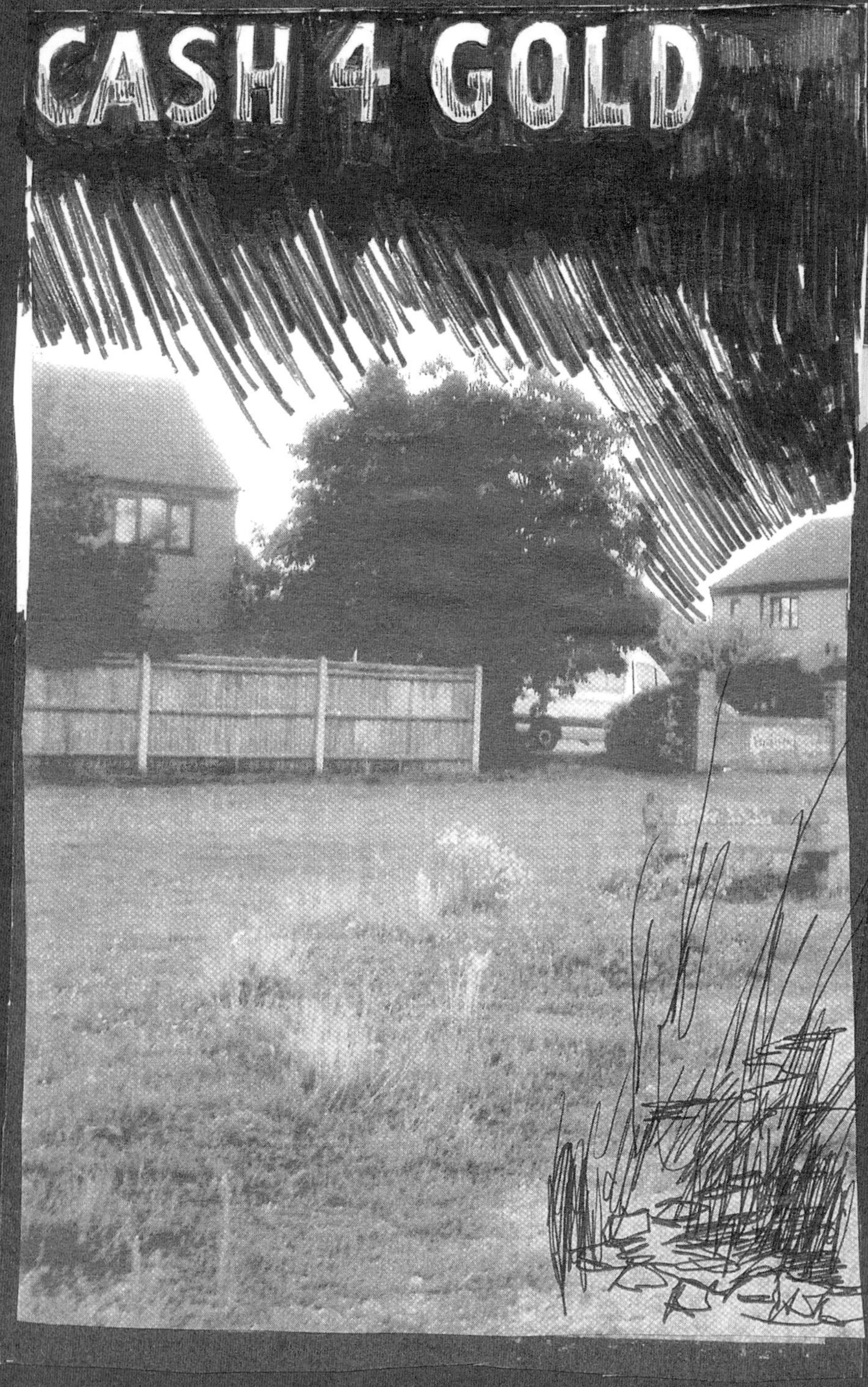
CASH 4 GOLD

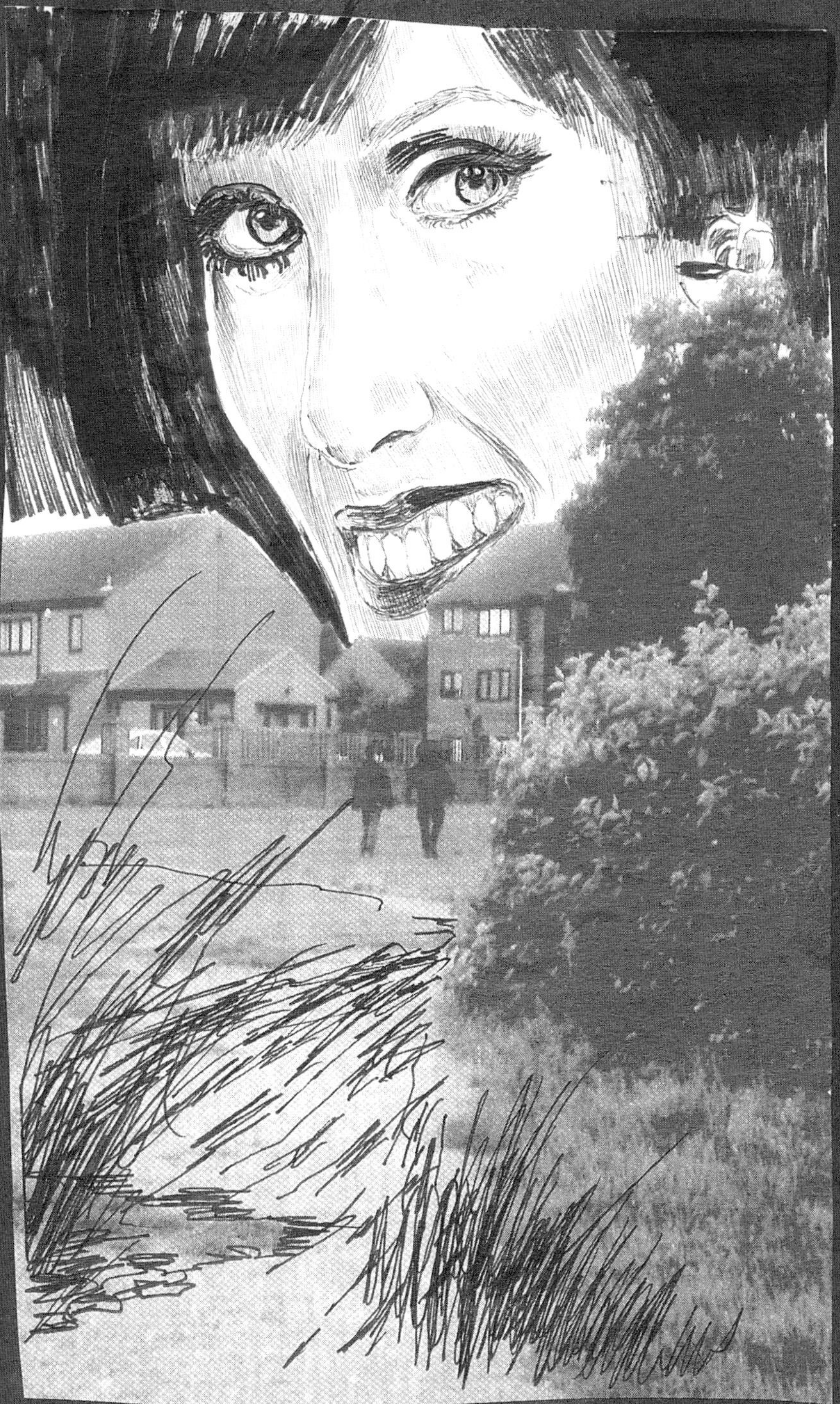

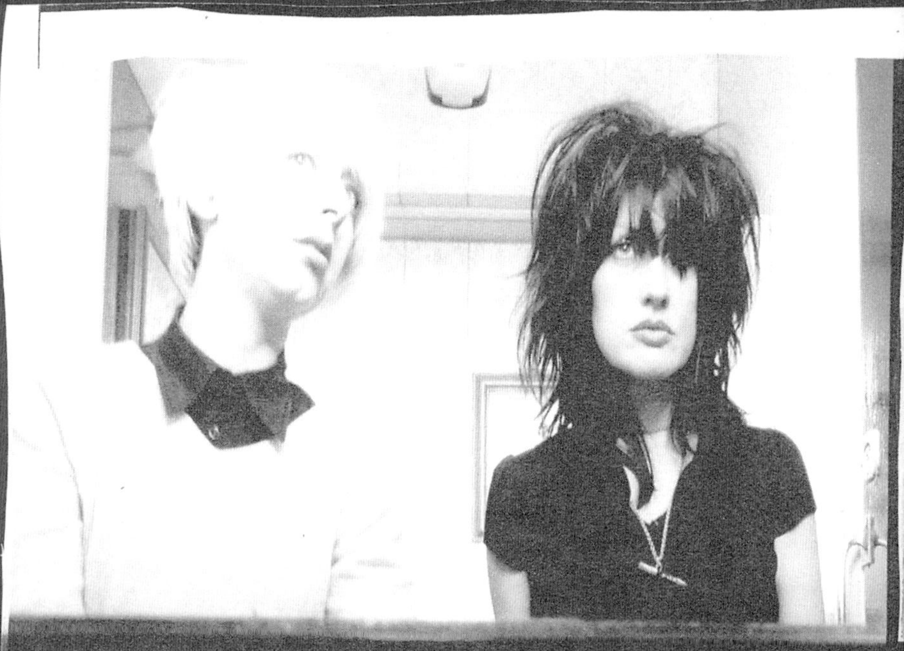

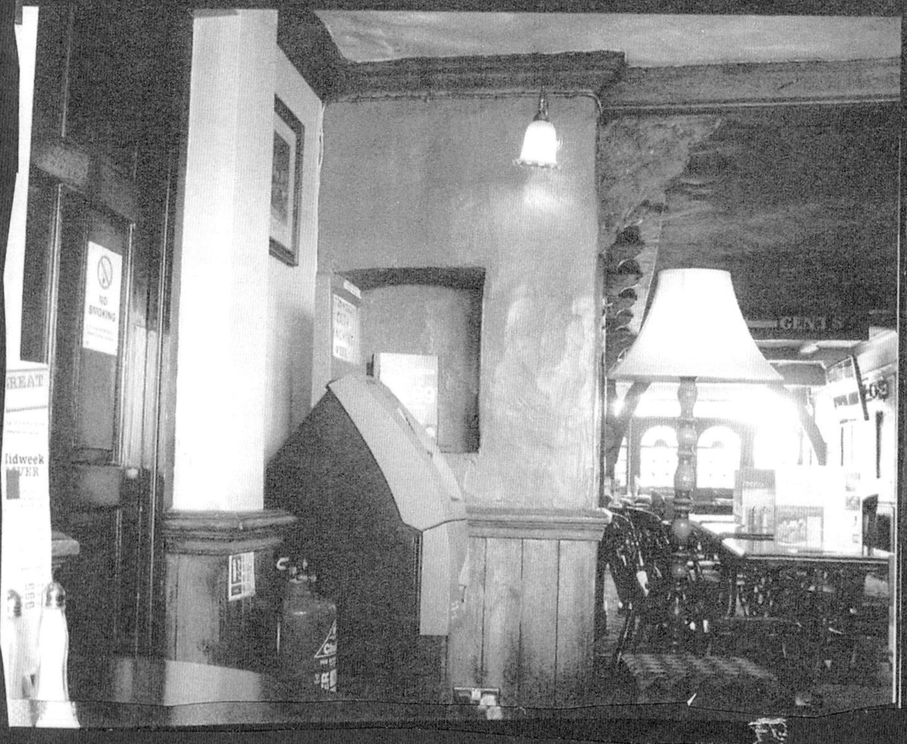
NO SMOKING

"In every case, the state of exception marks a threshold at which logic and praxis blur with each other and a pure violence without logos claims to realize an enunciation without any real reference" .... *"President Bush's decision to refer to himself constantly as the "Commander in Chief of the Army" after September 11, 2001, must be considered in the context of this presidential claim to sovereign powers in emergency situations. If, as we have seen, the assumption of this title entails a direct reference to the state of exception, then Bush is attempting to produce a situation in which the emergency becomes the rule, and the very distinction between peace and war (and between foreign and civil war) becomes impossible."*
Giorgio Agamben.

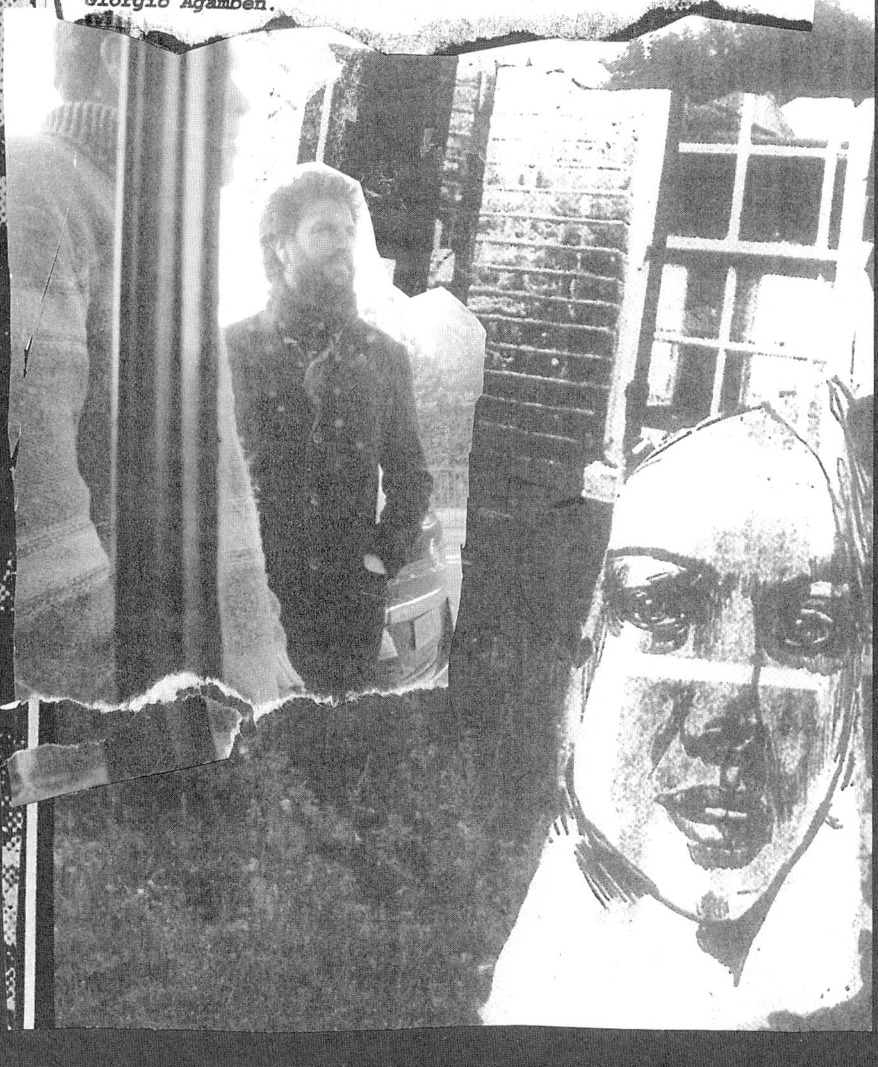

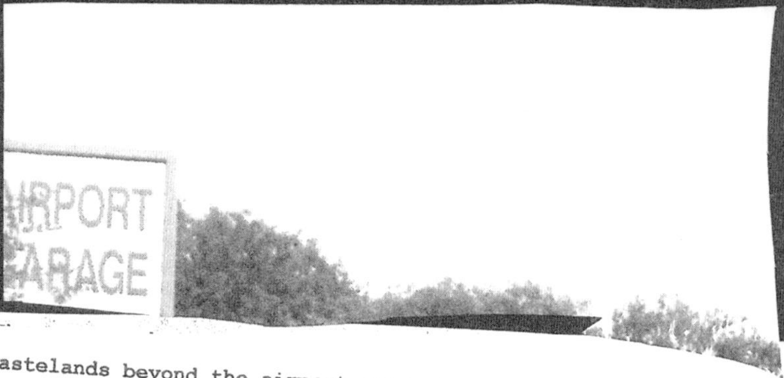
RPORT
ARAGE

The wastelands beyond the airport were stopped by ranks of huge post war factory blocks, mostly in a state of dereliction. In the east End they would have been turned into yuppie flats or studios by now.

They pushed on through the lacerating thickets of brambles and into a mossy yard stacked up with caravans and abandoned vehicles. Once into the building they climbed a large staircase, on every half landing were the strange glyphs and markings of the group.
The floor numbers were marked in heavy black type, they pushed open the swing doors at the twelfth level. A cavern opened up, windows blacked out, walls painted in black emulsion with the erratic writing and the repeated ghoulish head he had come to recognise as their trademarks.

END TIMES FOR THE RICH, the words he had been seeking were there chalked across the ceiling.

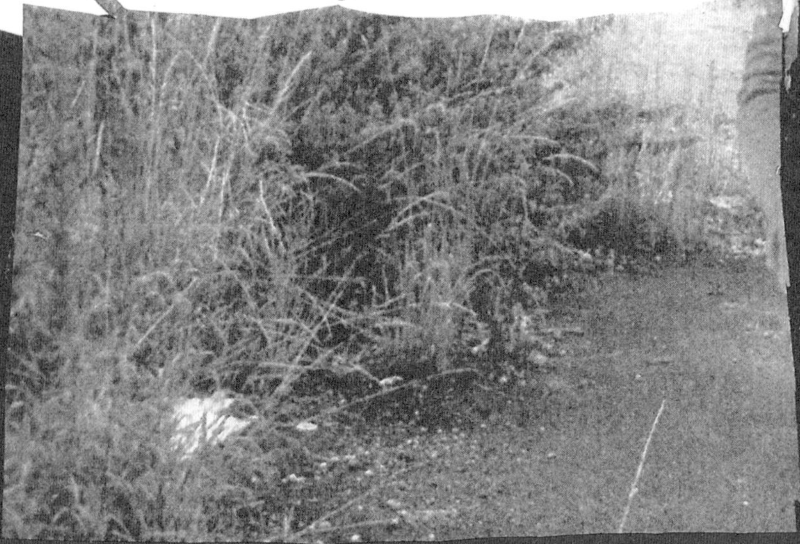

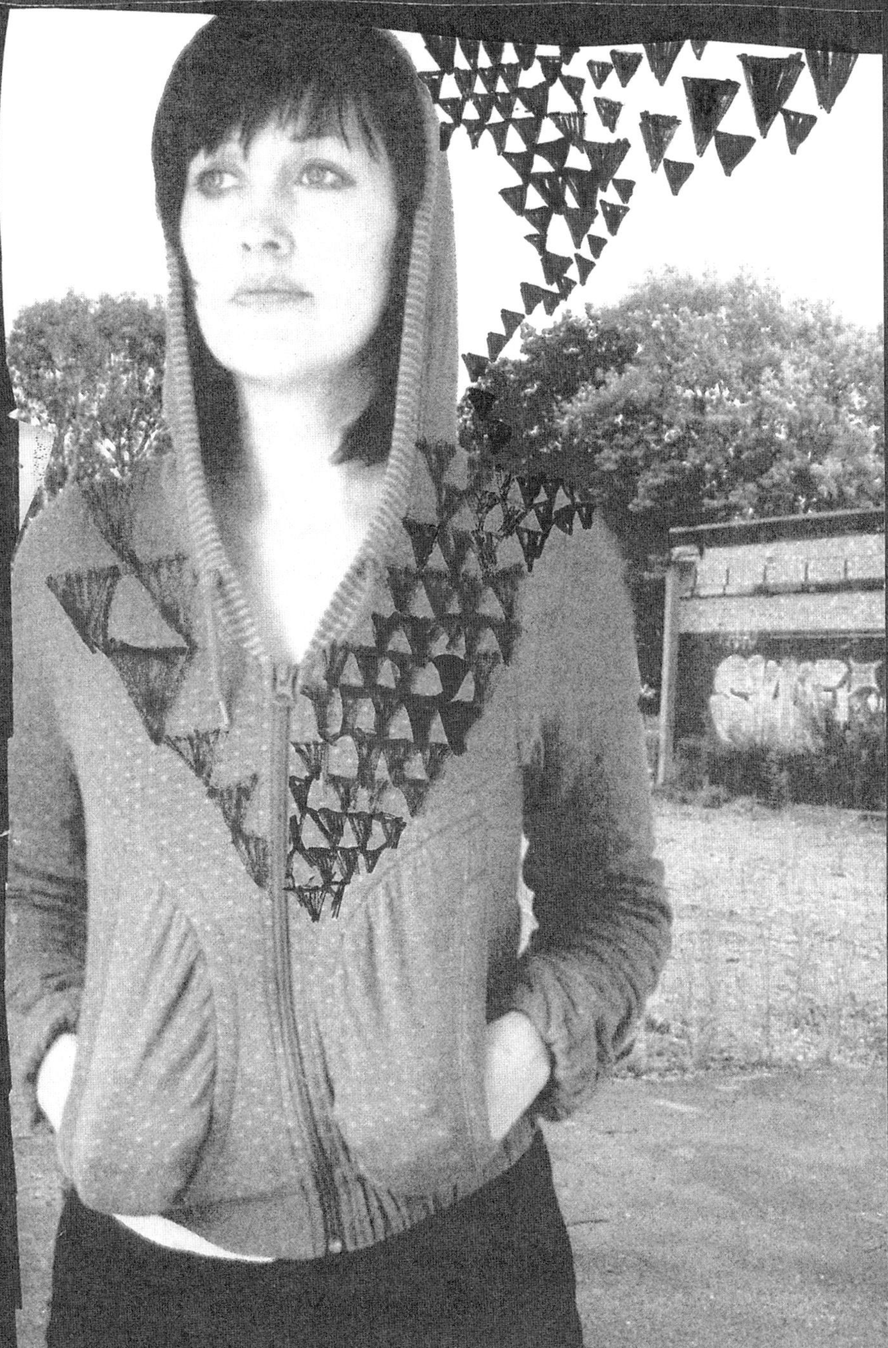

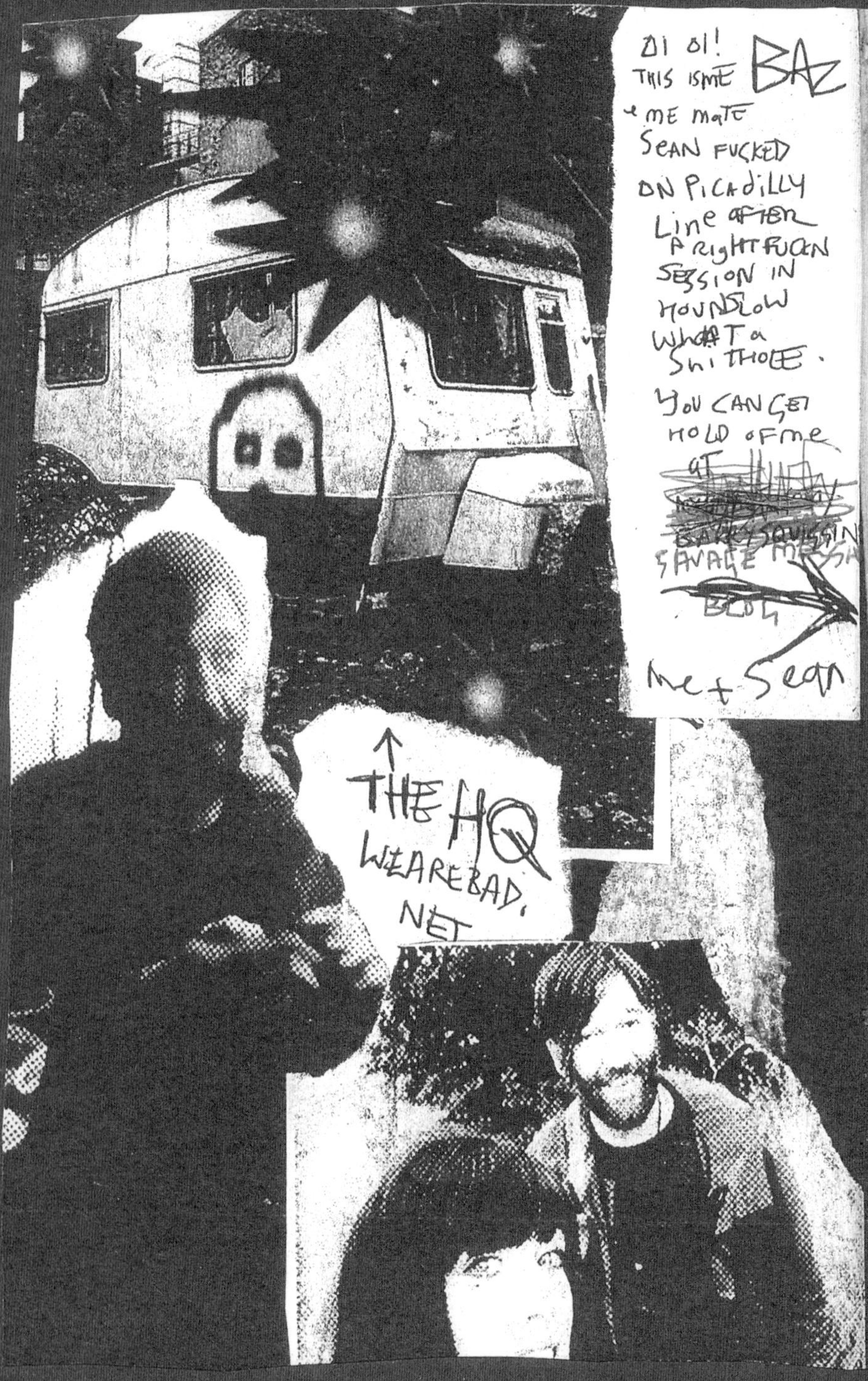
OI OI!
THIS IS ME BAZ
& ME MATE
SEAN FUCKED
ON PICADILLY
LINE AFTER
A RIGHT FUCKN
SESSION IN
HOUNSLOW
WHAT A
SHITHOLE.
YOU CAN GET
HOLD OF ME
SAVAGE
BLOG
Me + Sean
↑ THE HQ
WEAREBAD.NET

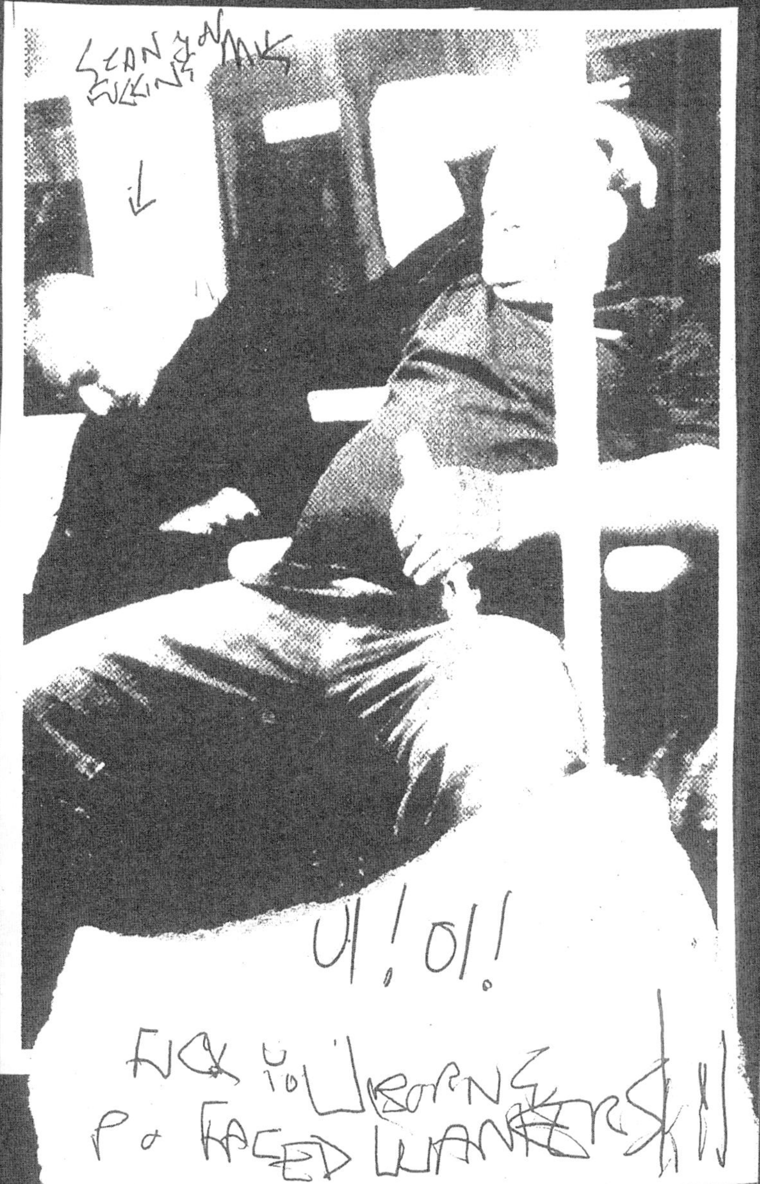
SEAN
MIK
FUCKING
OI! OI!
FUCK YOU WEBORNE
PO FACED WANKERS!!

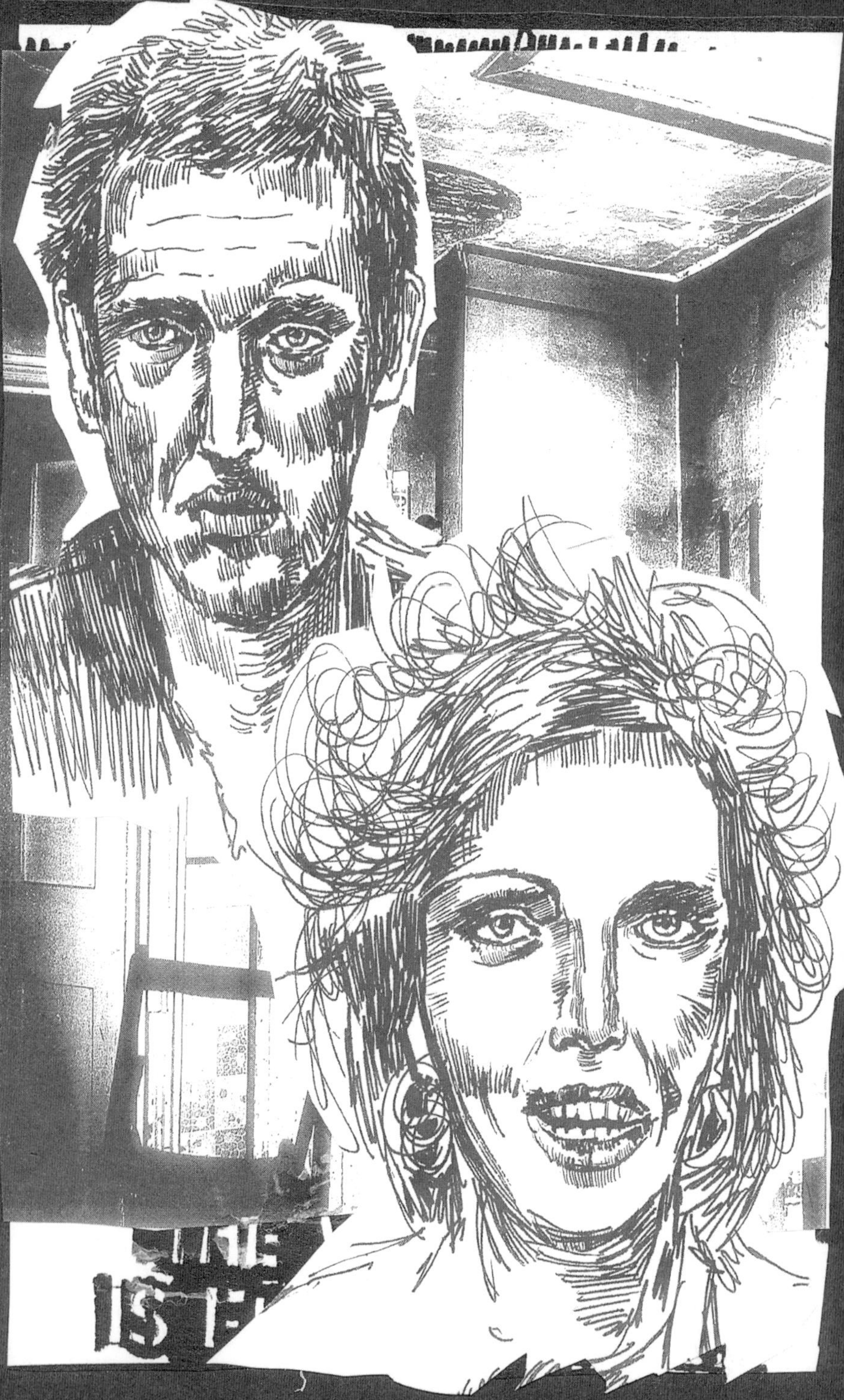

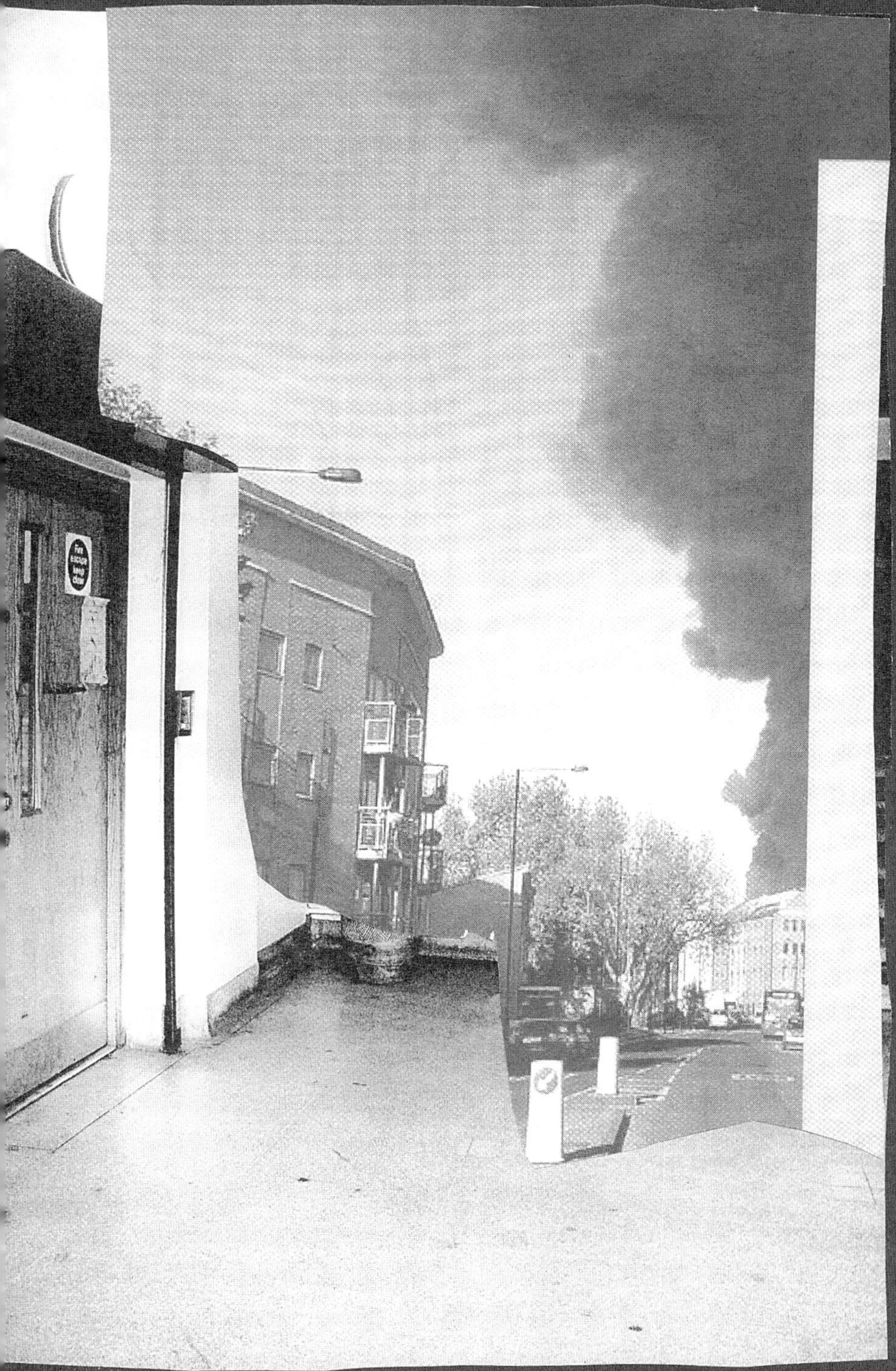
Fire escape keep clear

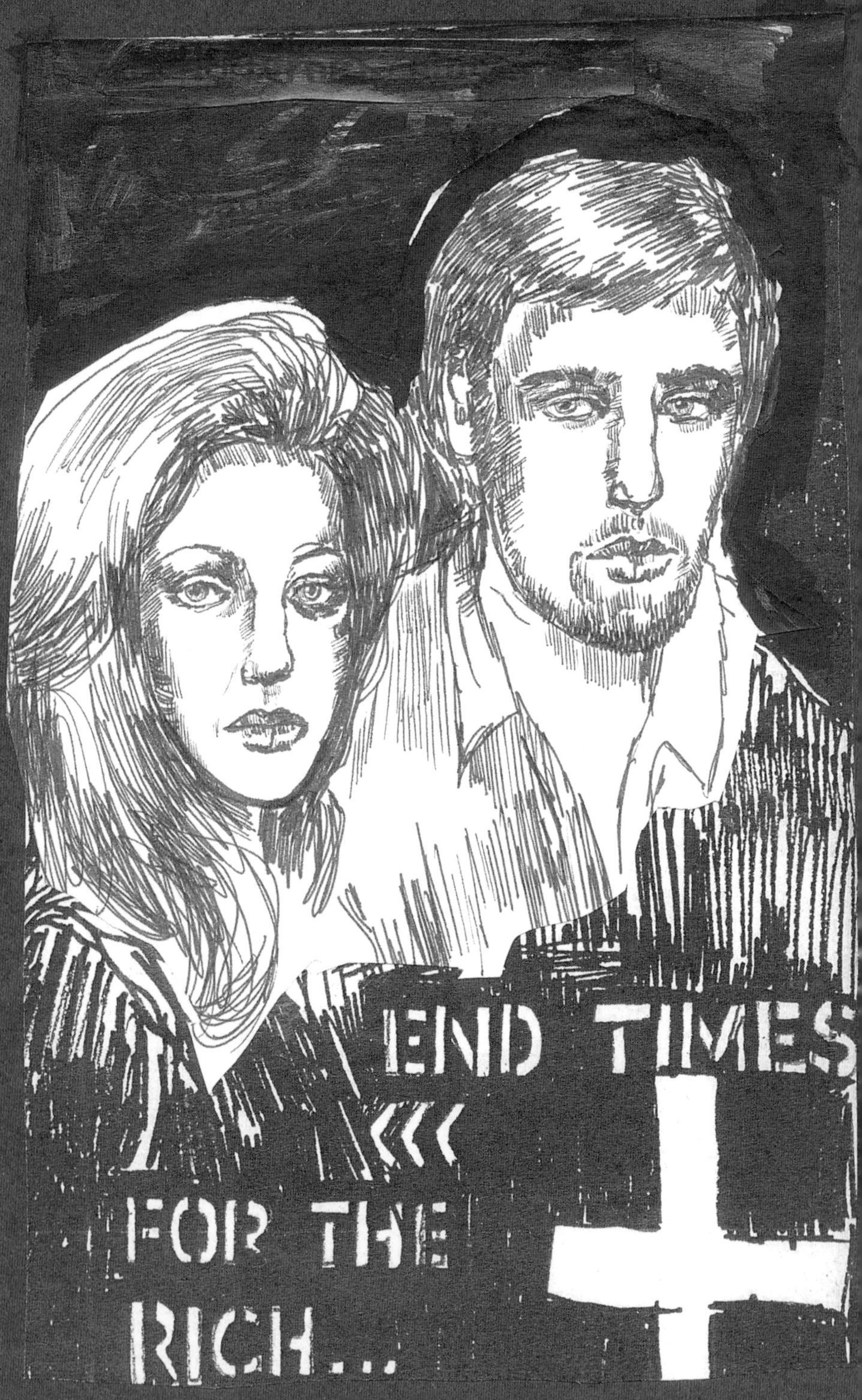
END TIMES
FOR THE
RICH...

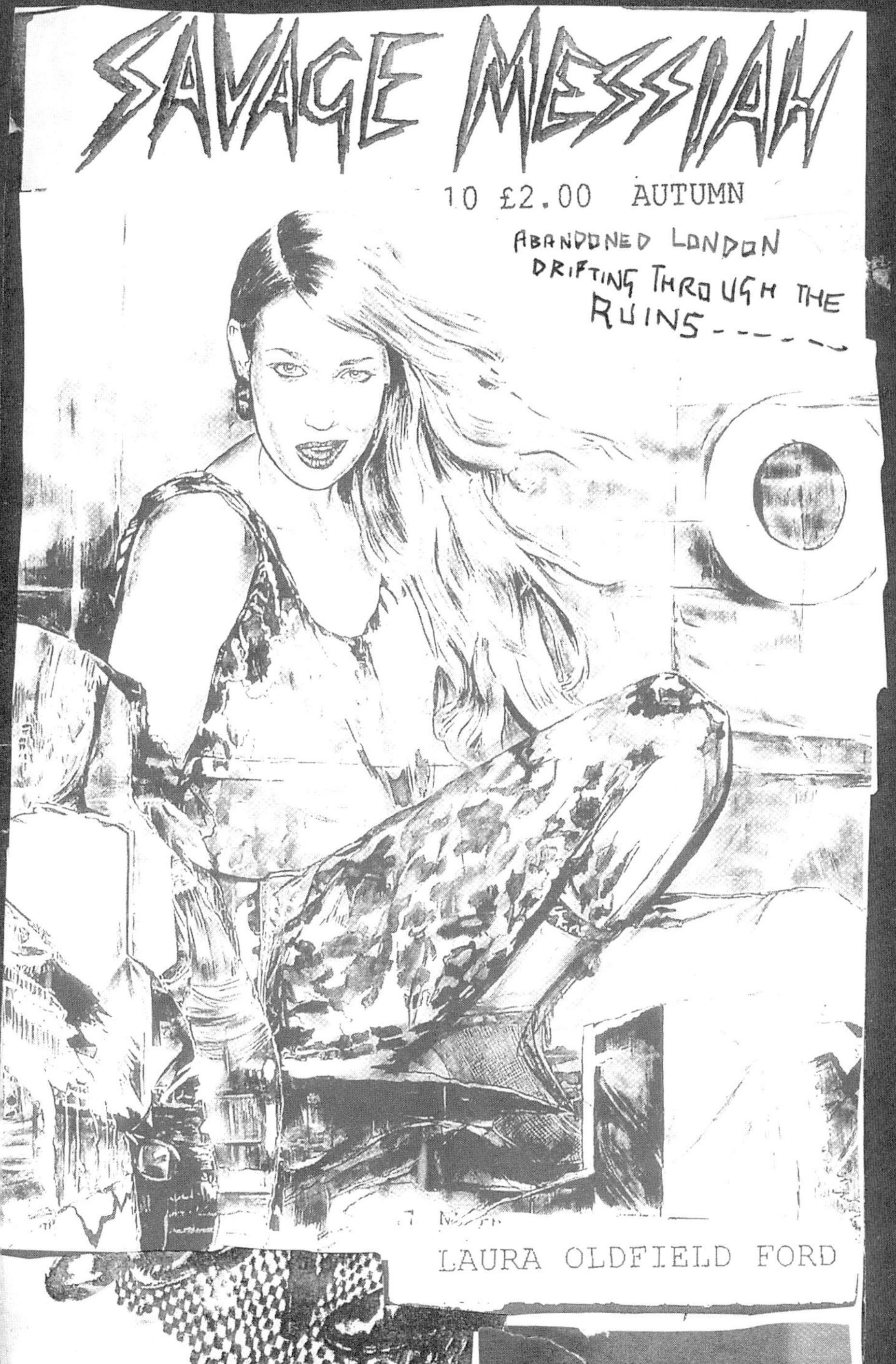
SAVAGE MESSIAH
10 £2.00 AUTUMN
ABANDONED LONDON
DRIFTING THROUGH THE
RUINS
LAURA OLDFIELD FORD

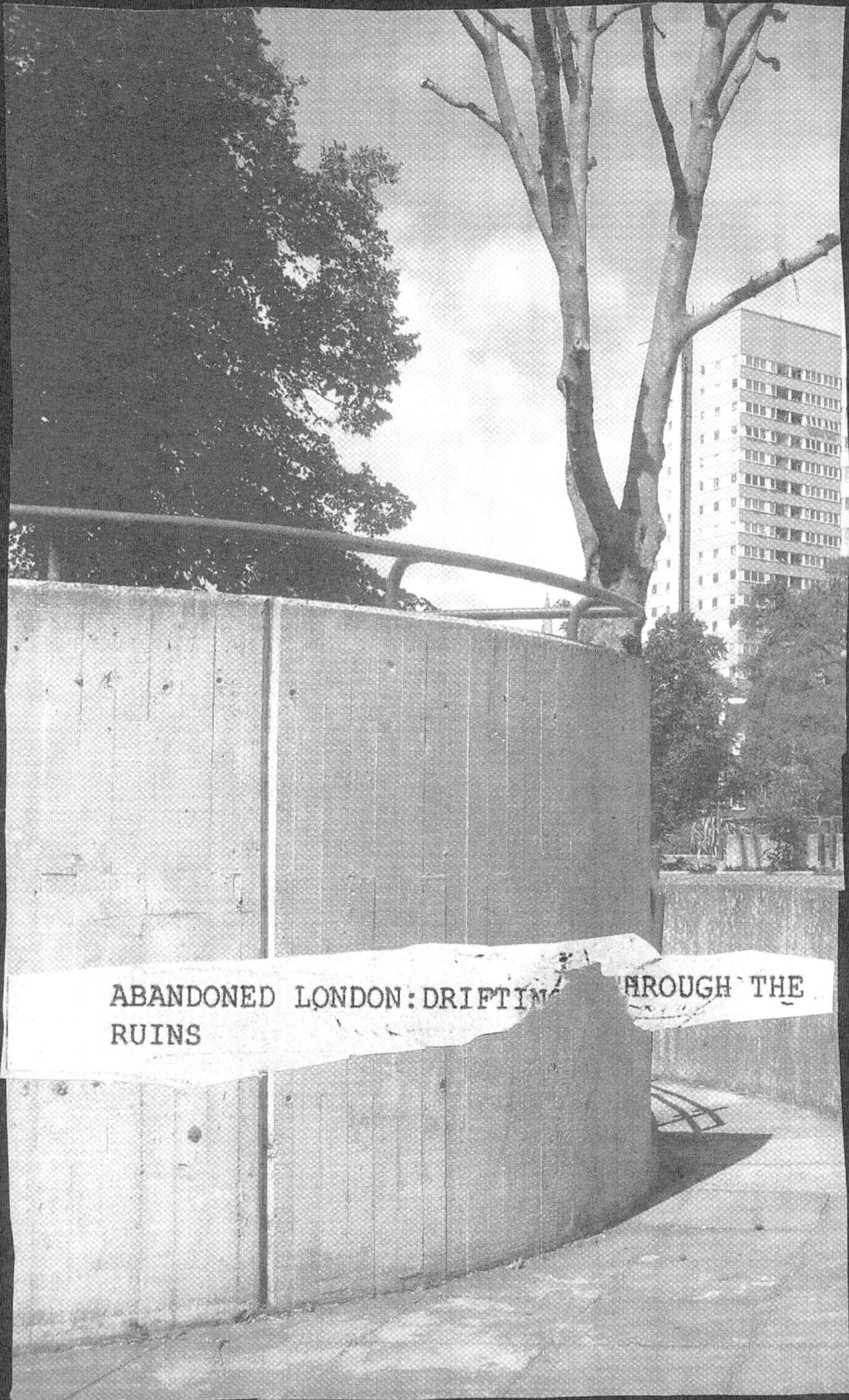
ABANDONED LONDON:DRIFTIN
HROUGH THE
RUINS

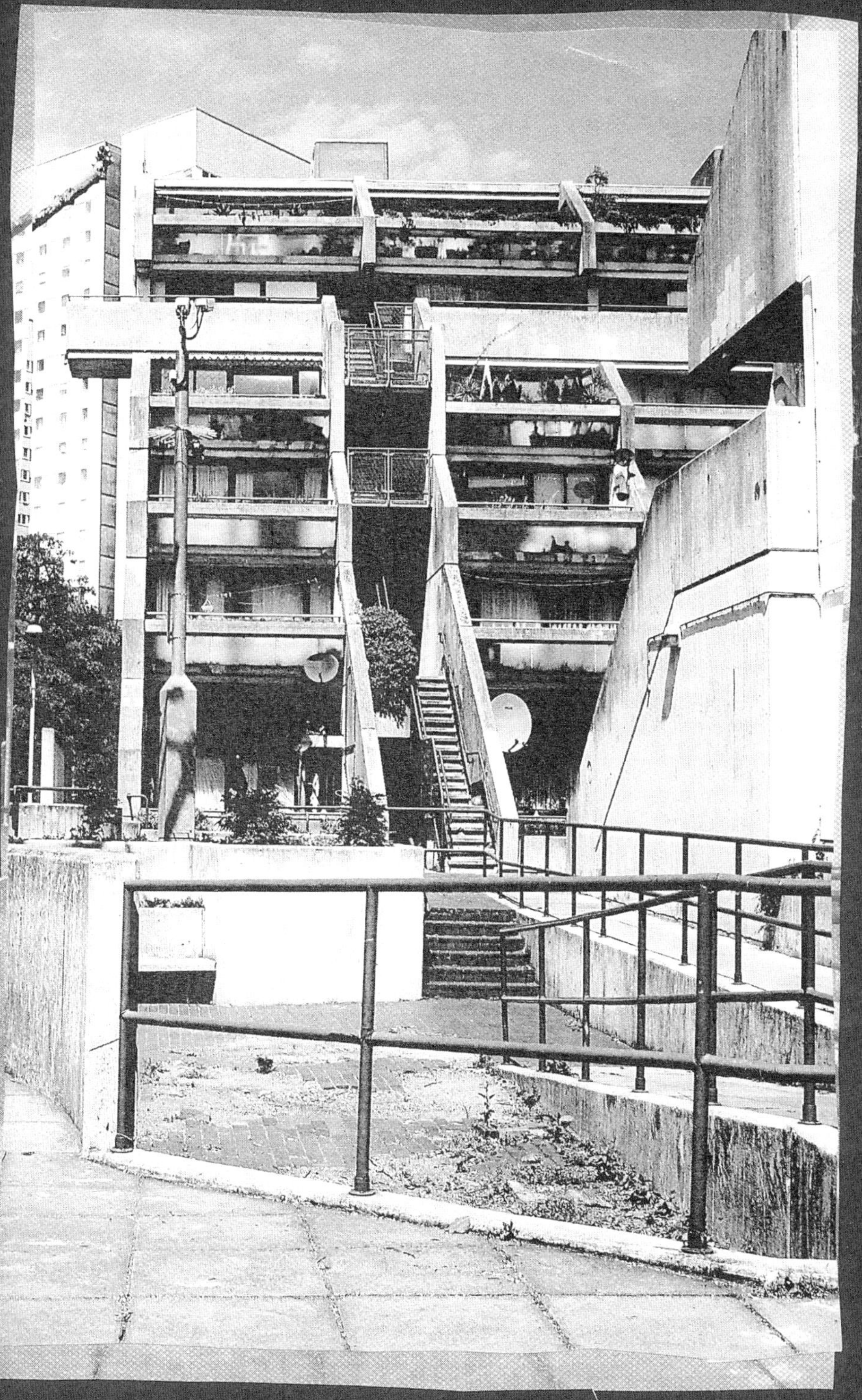

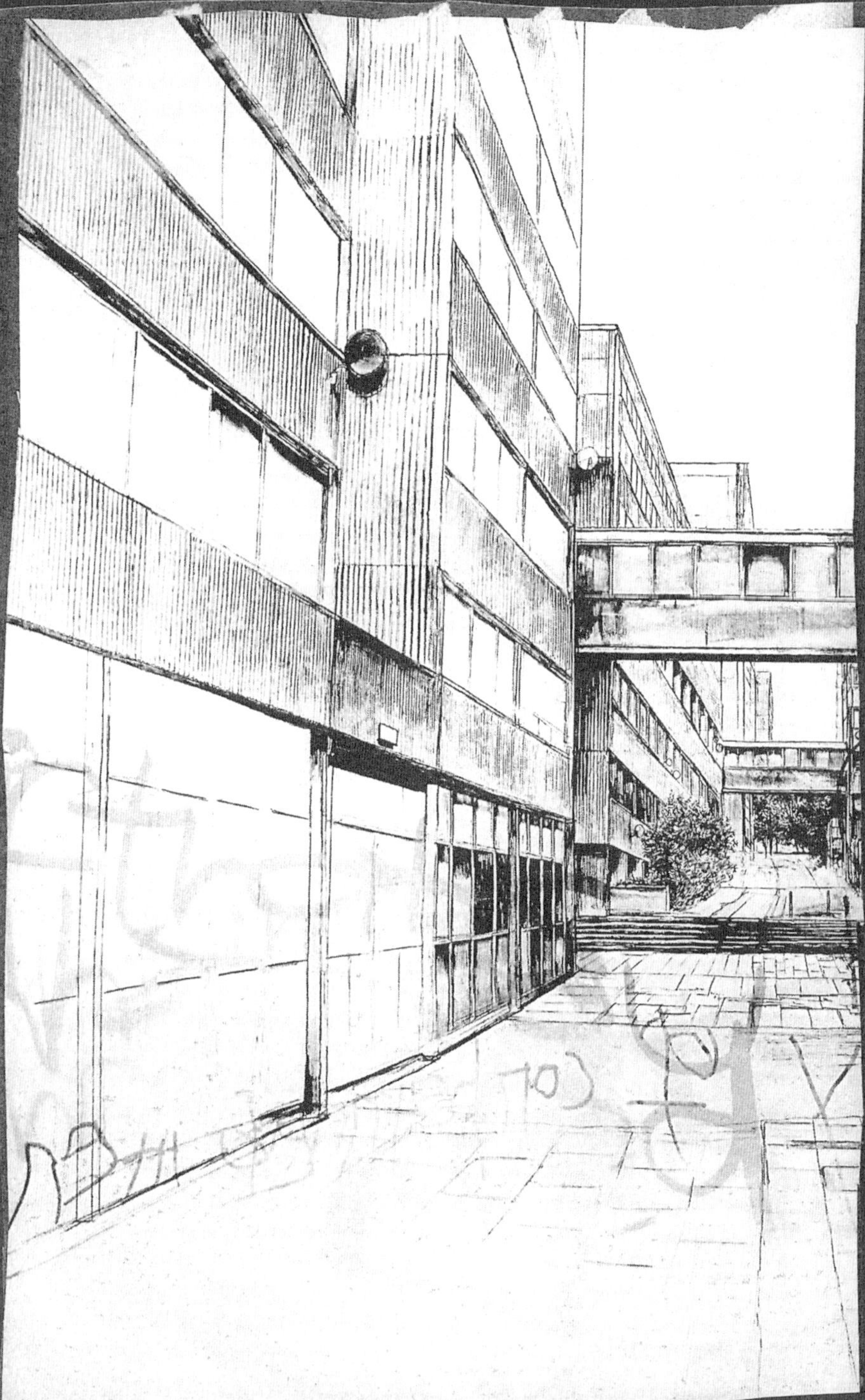

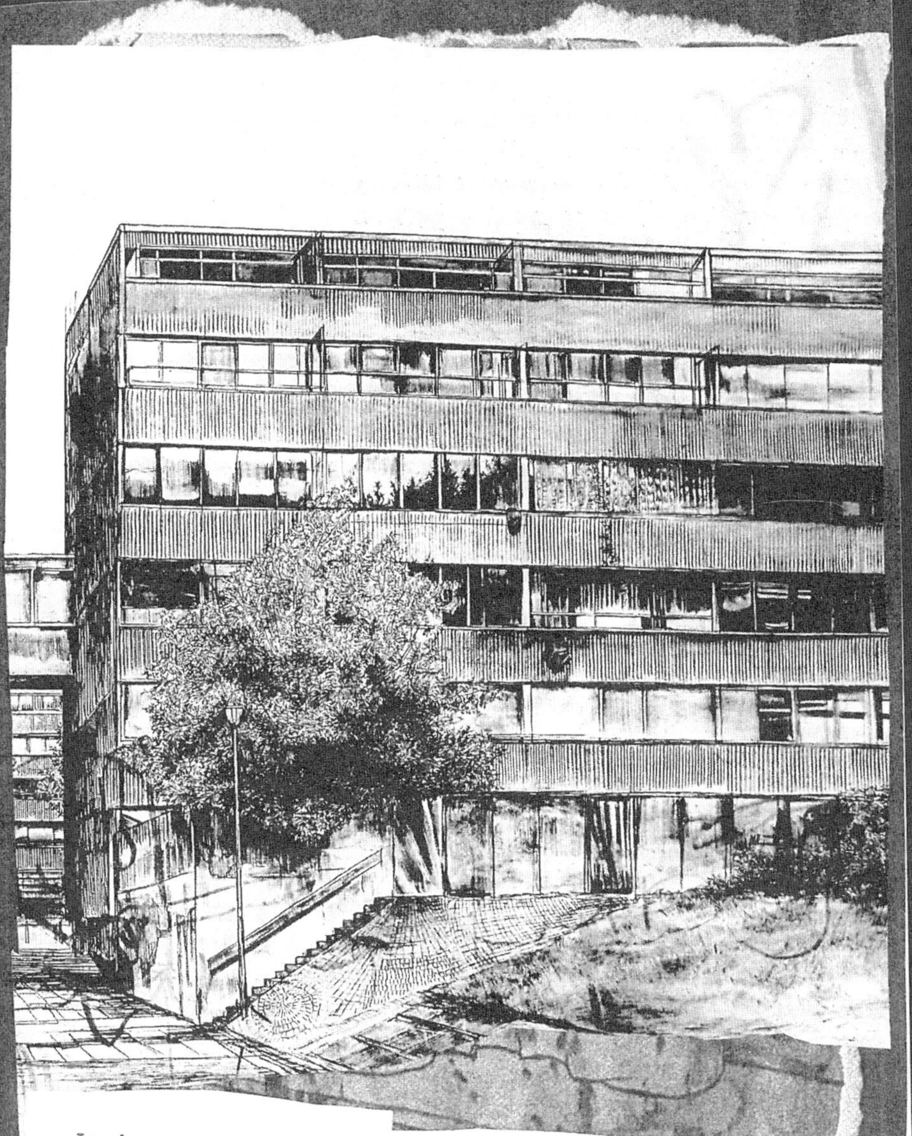

London pulsated with libidinal excess. Encounters were frequent and urgent, always taken as if for the last time. The moral codes of the past were scrambled, gone were the hypocrisies of recent decades. London was stripped of its billboards and newsagents while its people roamed the streets asserting their sexuality.

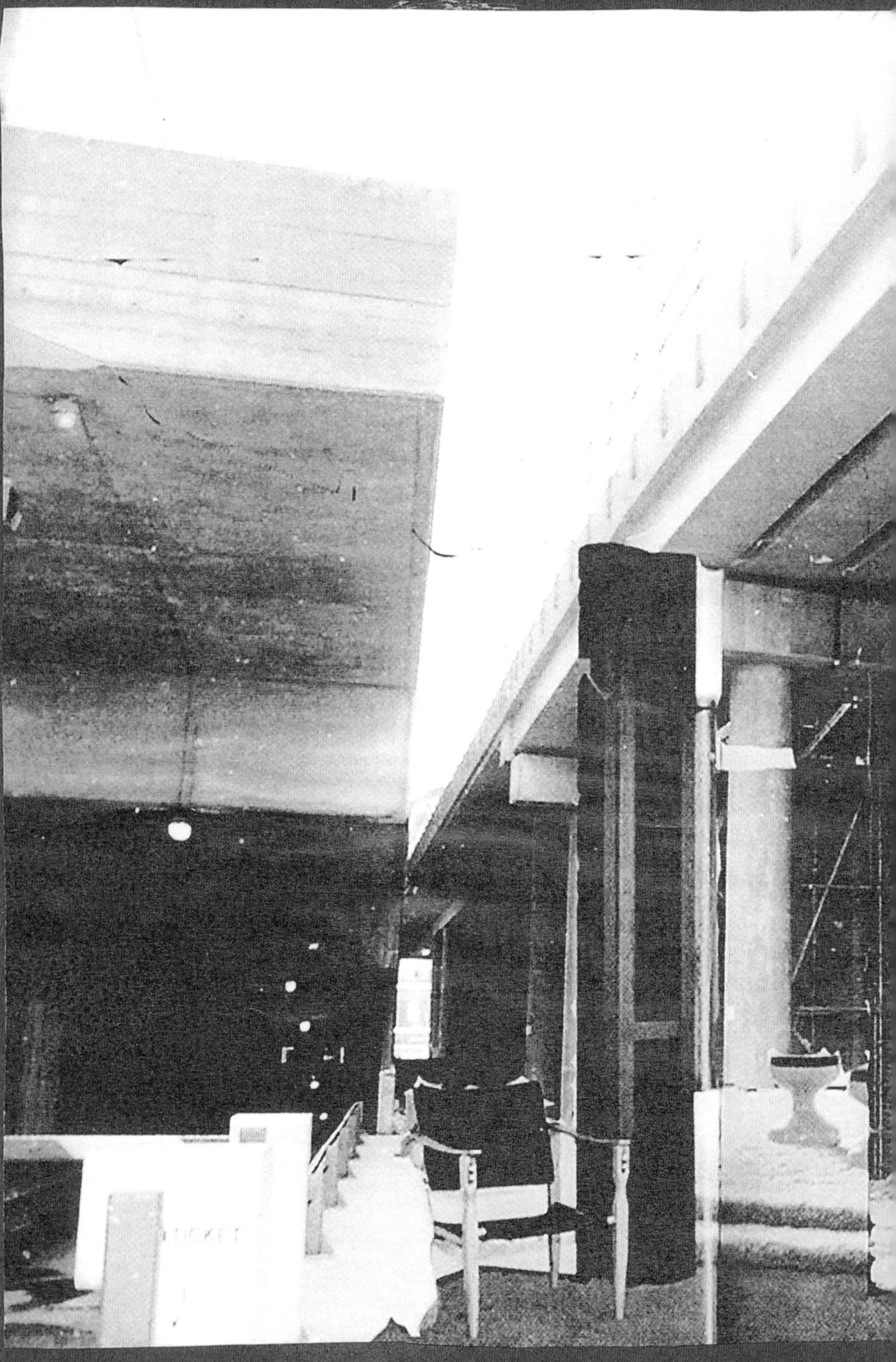

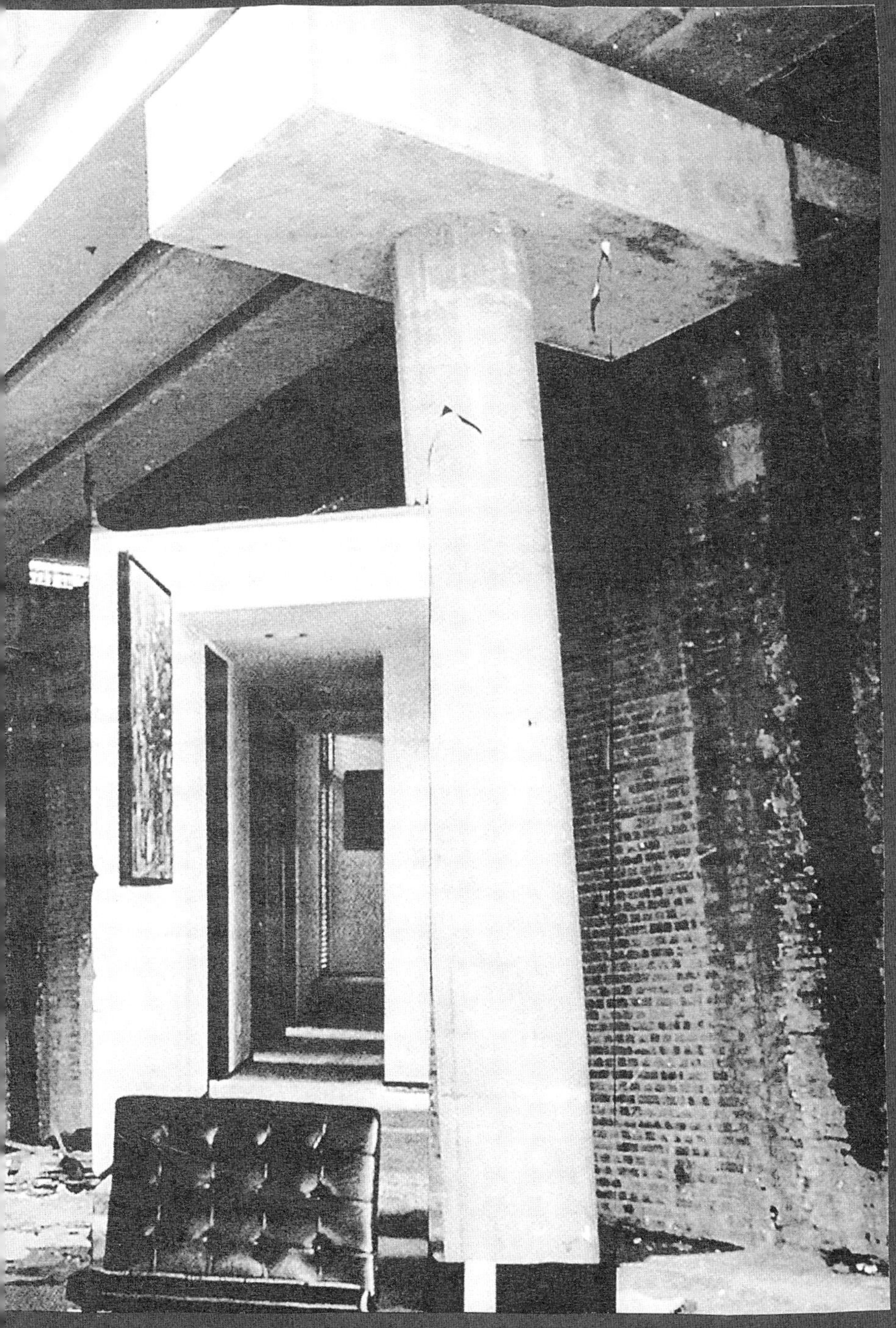

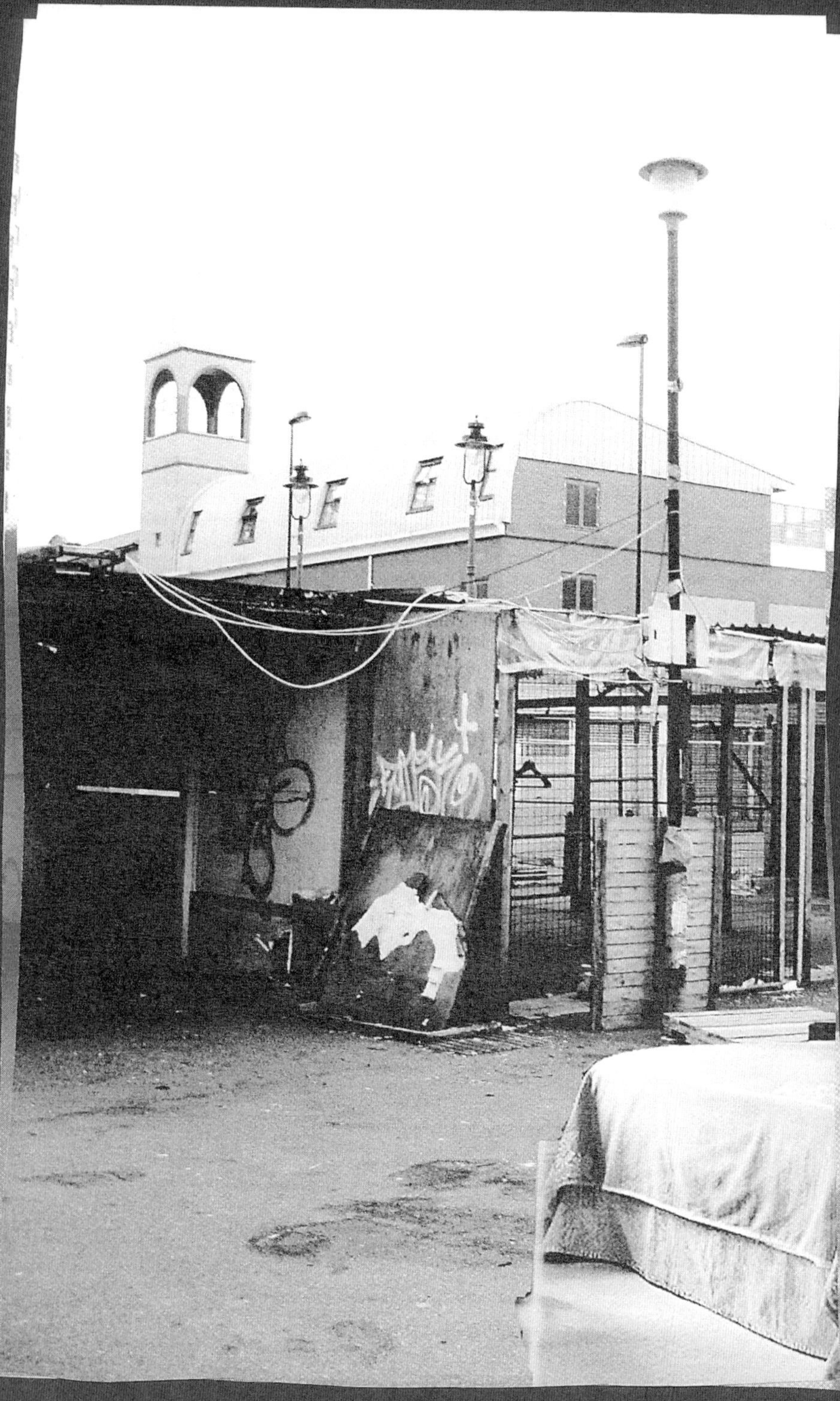

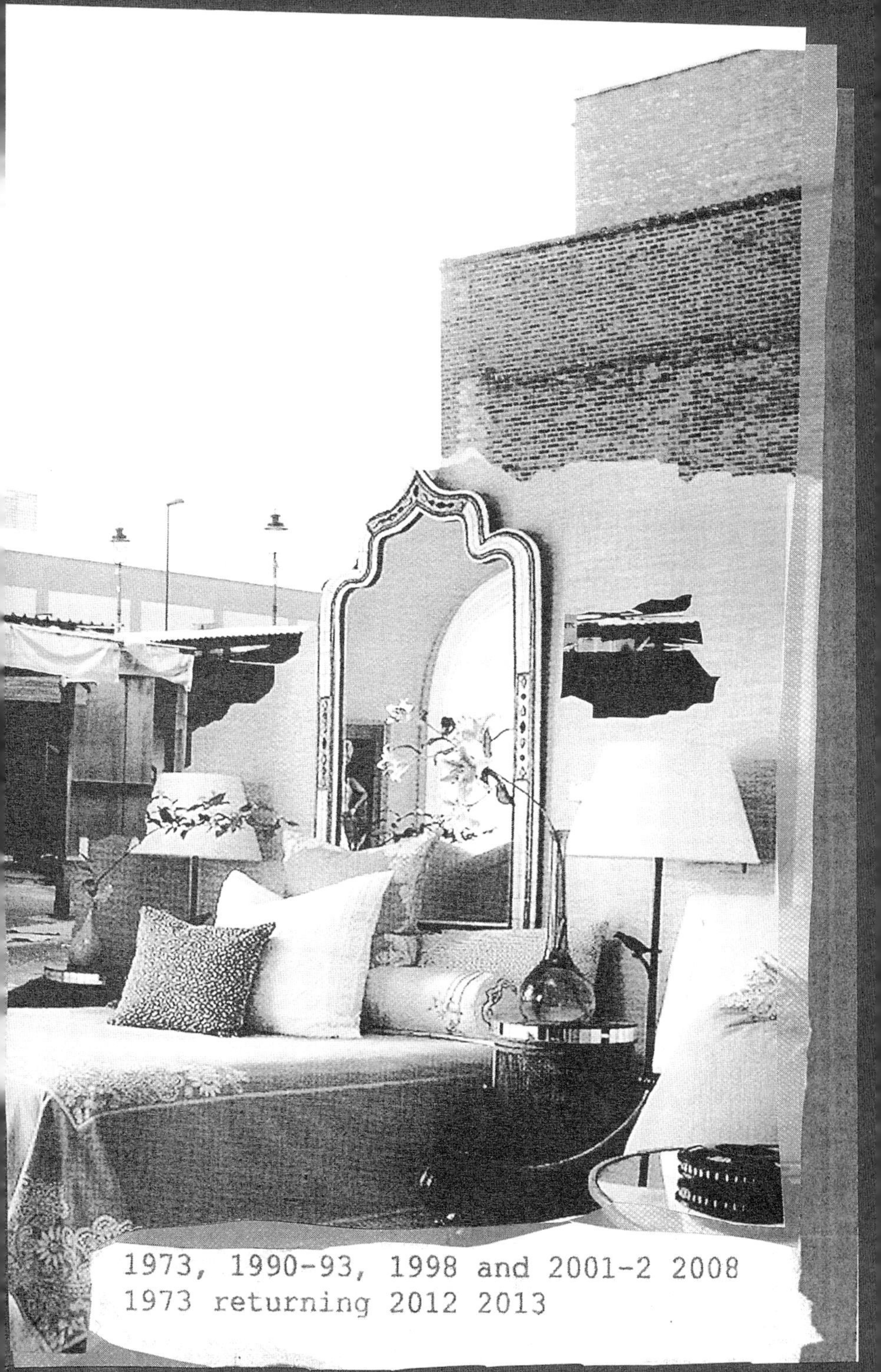
1973, 1990-93, 1998 and 2001-2 2008
1973 returning 2012 2013

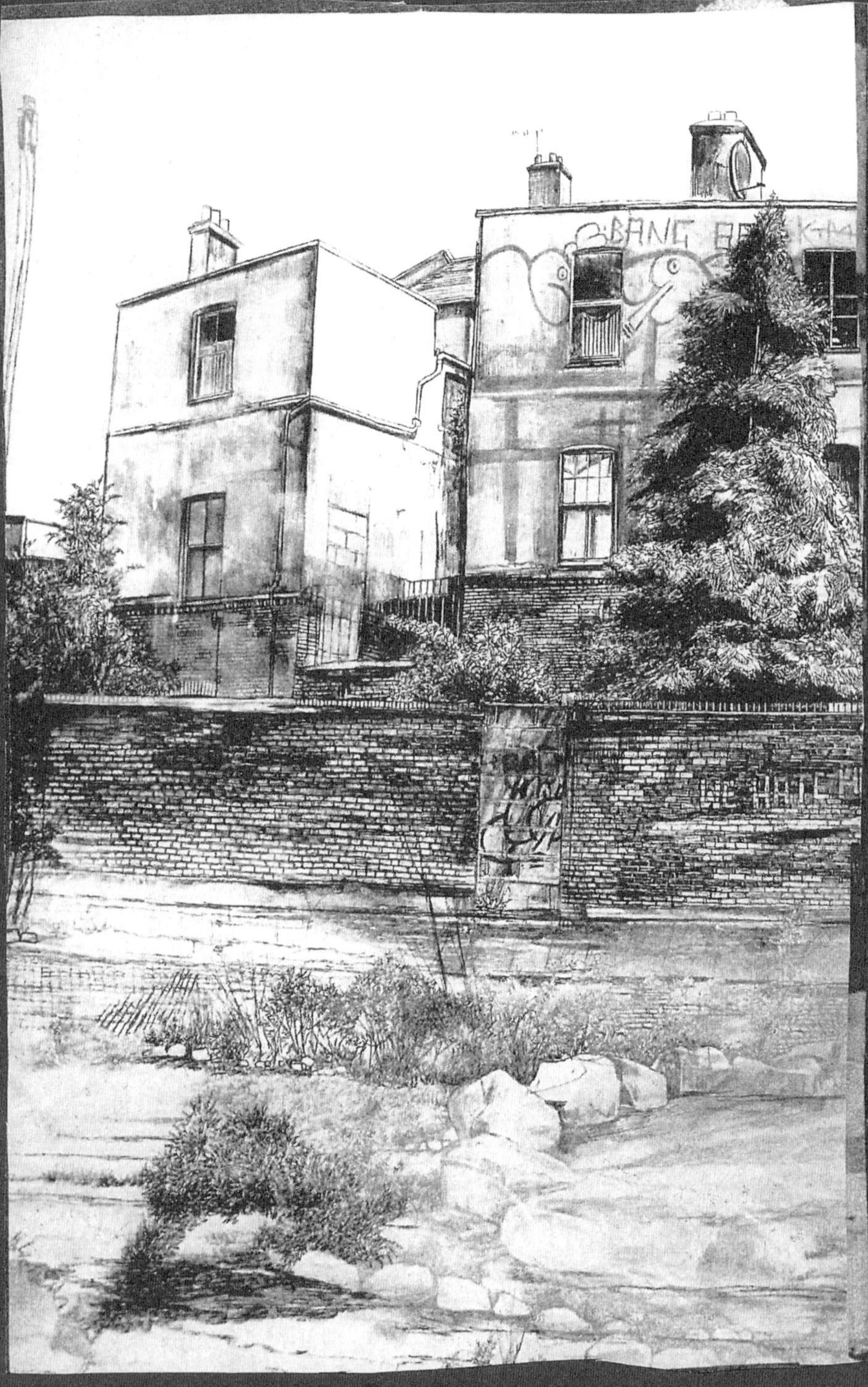
BANG

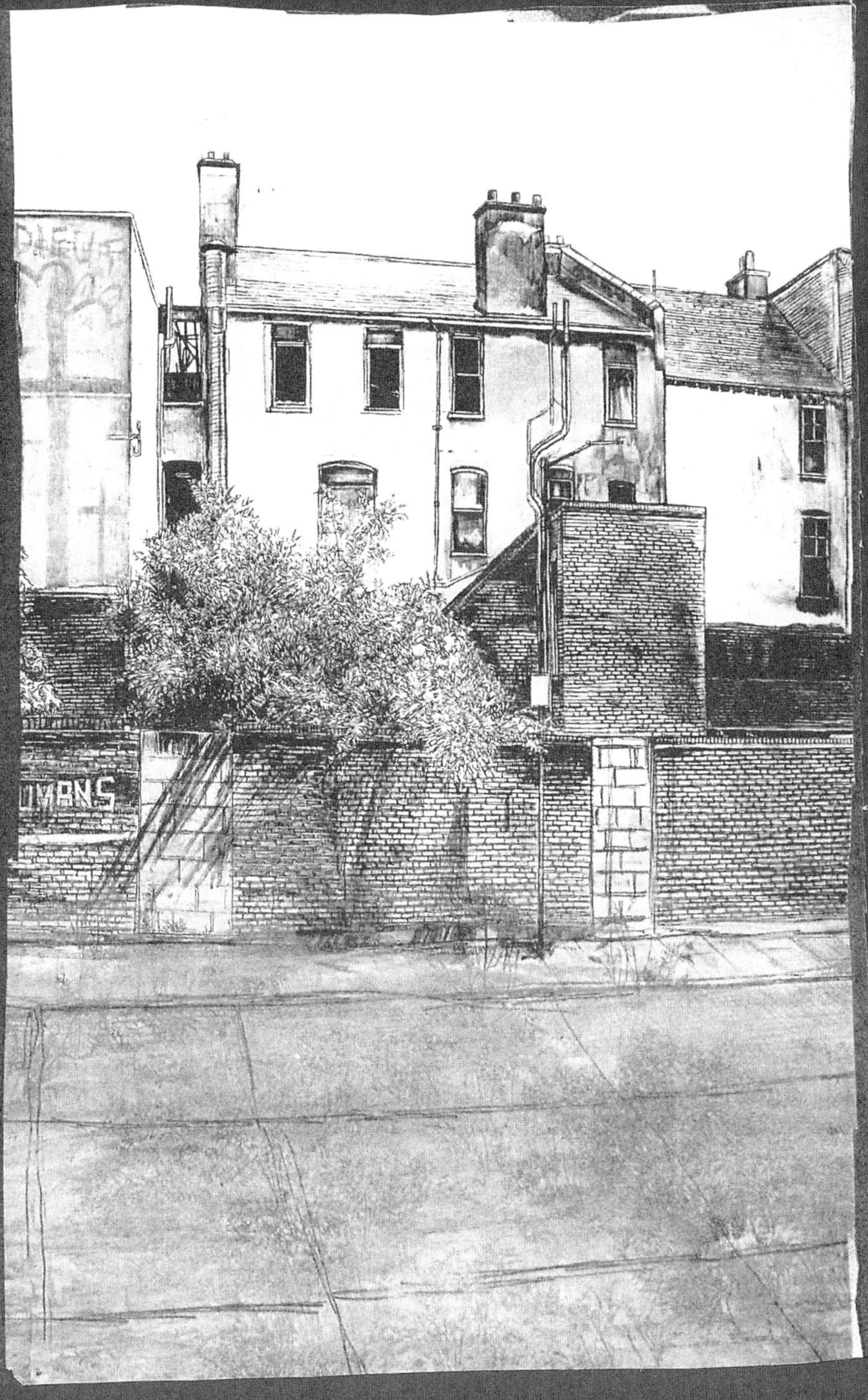

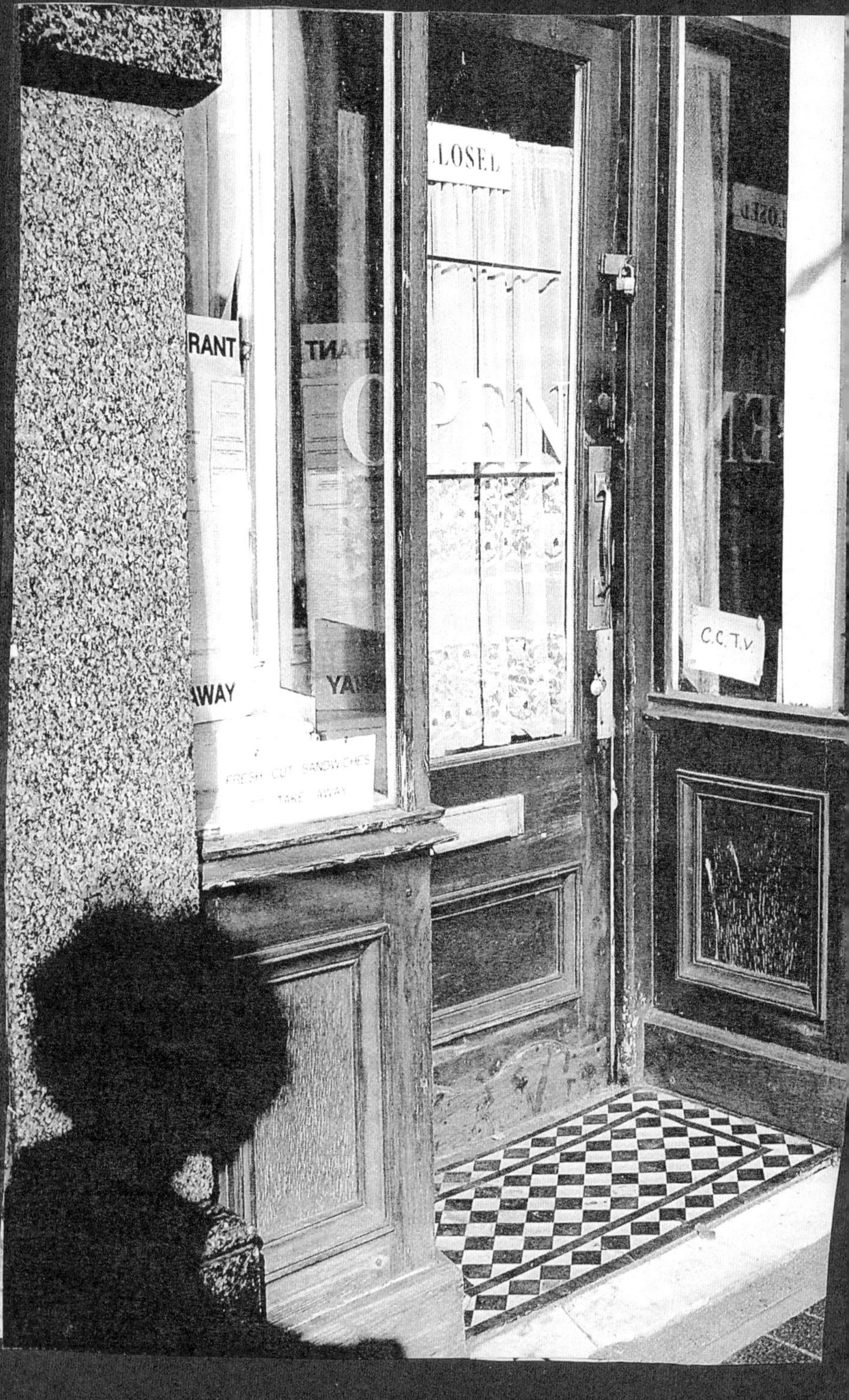
RANT
AWAY
FRESH CUT SANDWICHES
TAKE AWAY
OPEN
C.C.T.V.

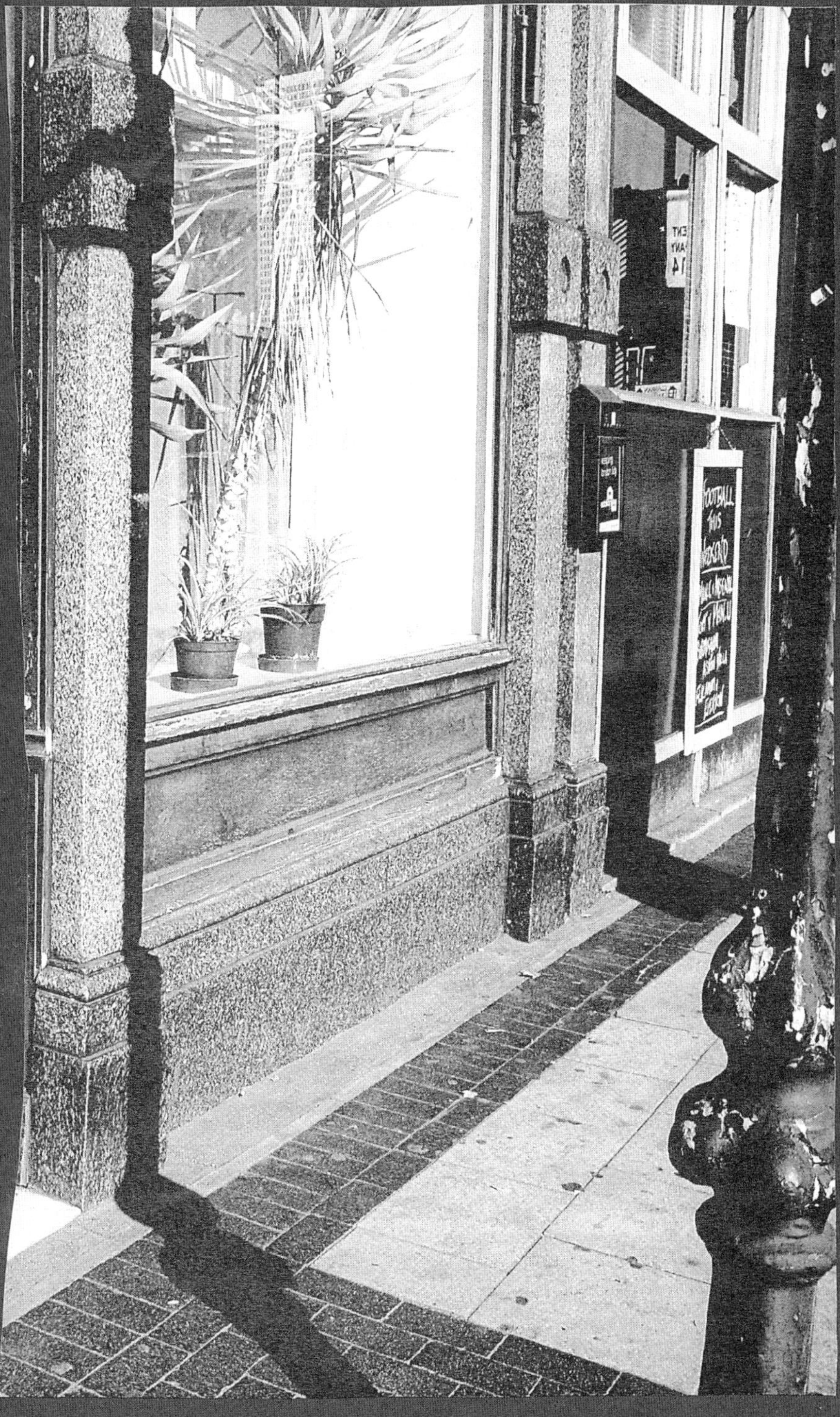
FOOTBALL
THIS
WEEKEND

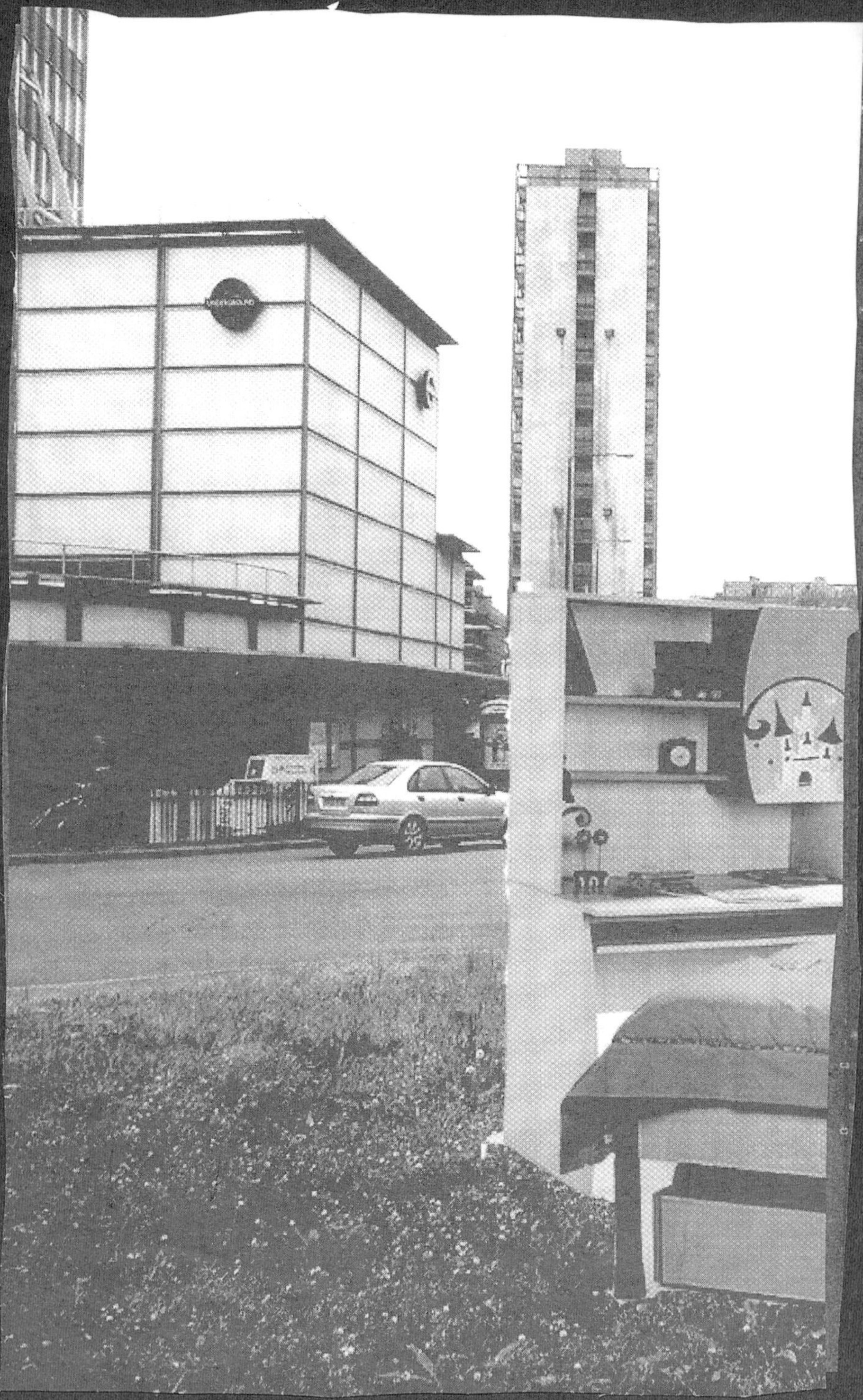

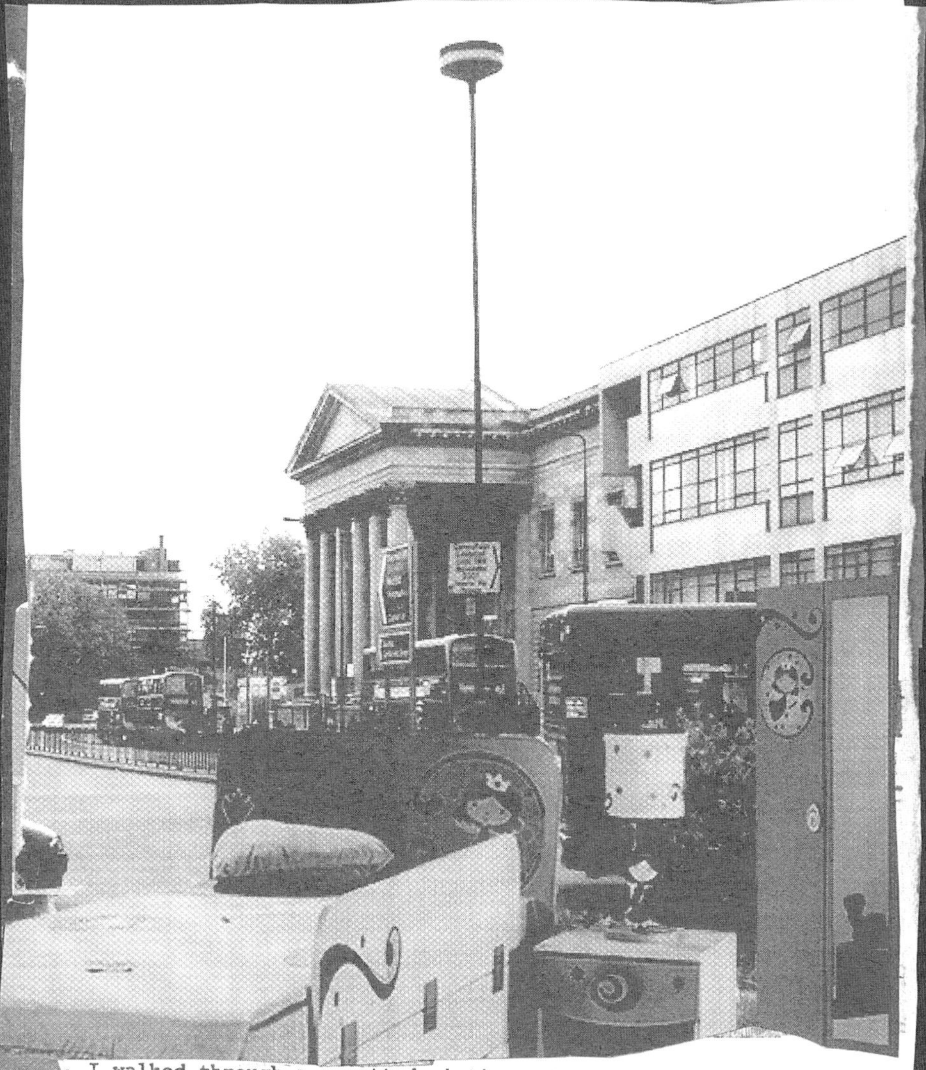

I walked through a squatted sixties estate, I think perhaps it was part of a university. There were concrete columns and tin foil squares, walls painted black and graffiti painted words in white, tribal and aggressive, *keep away, savage messiah, wrath of god upon you.* There were huge painted eyes glowering in streaks of red. Some of the windows were broken affording glimpses into sparse flats, shadowy front rooms of spider plants, mismatched furniture and blankets. I suspected that some of the old North London squatters had taken this place along with a few strays from the overcrowded hostels. I heard a sound system playing dubstep. There were fires in barrels and a few characters loitering and smoking.

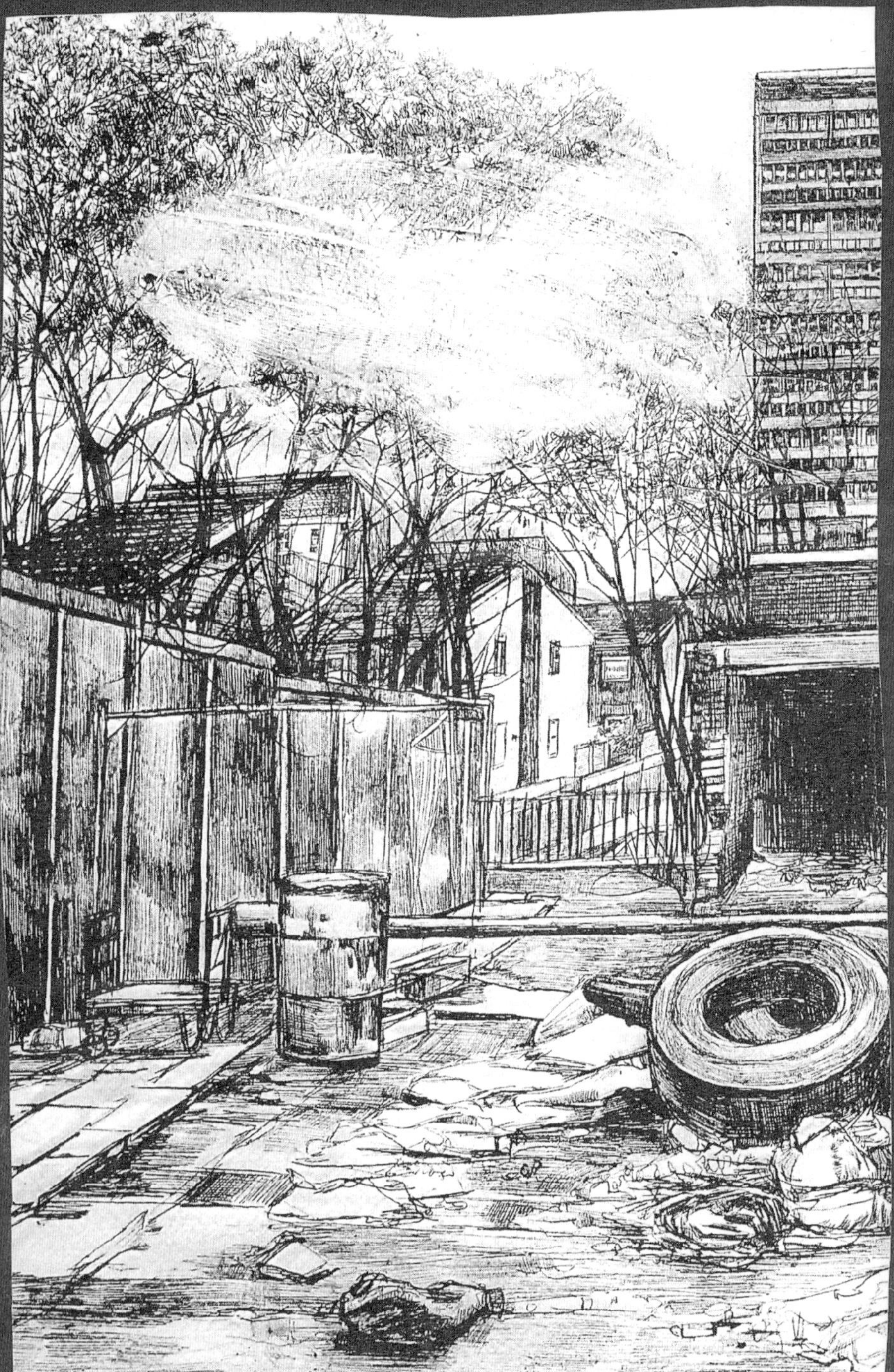

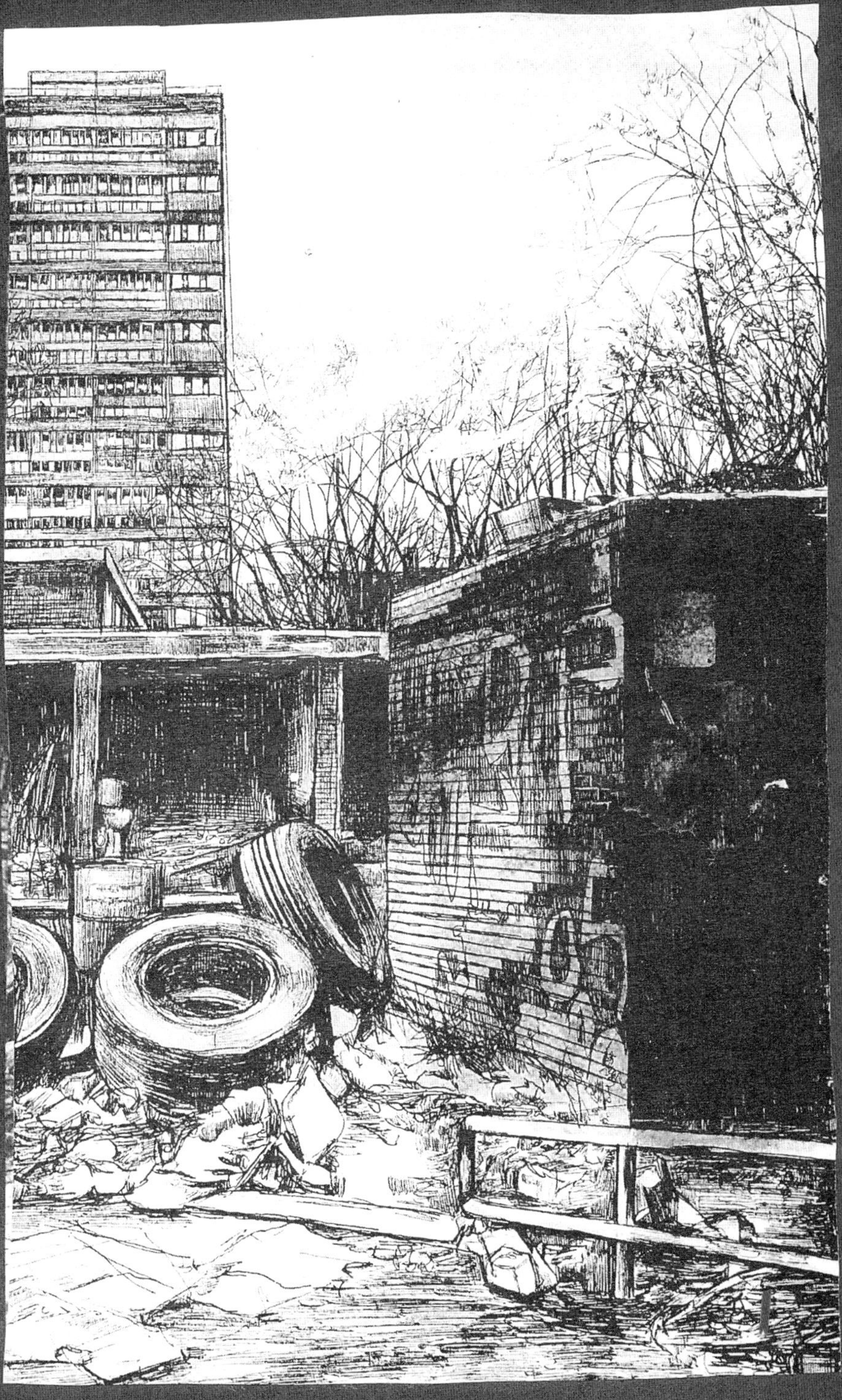

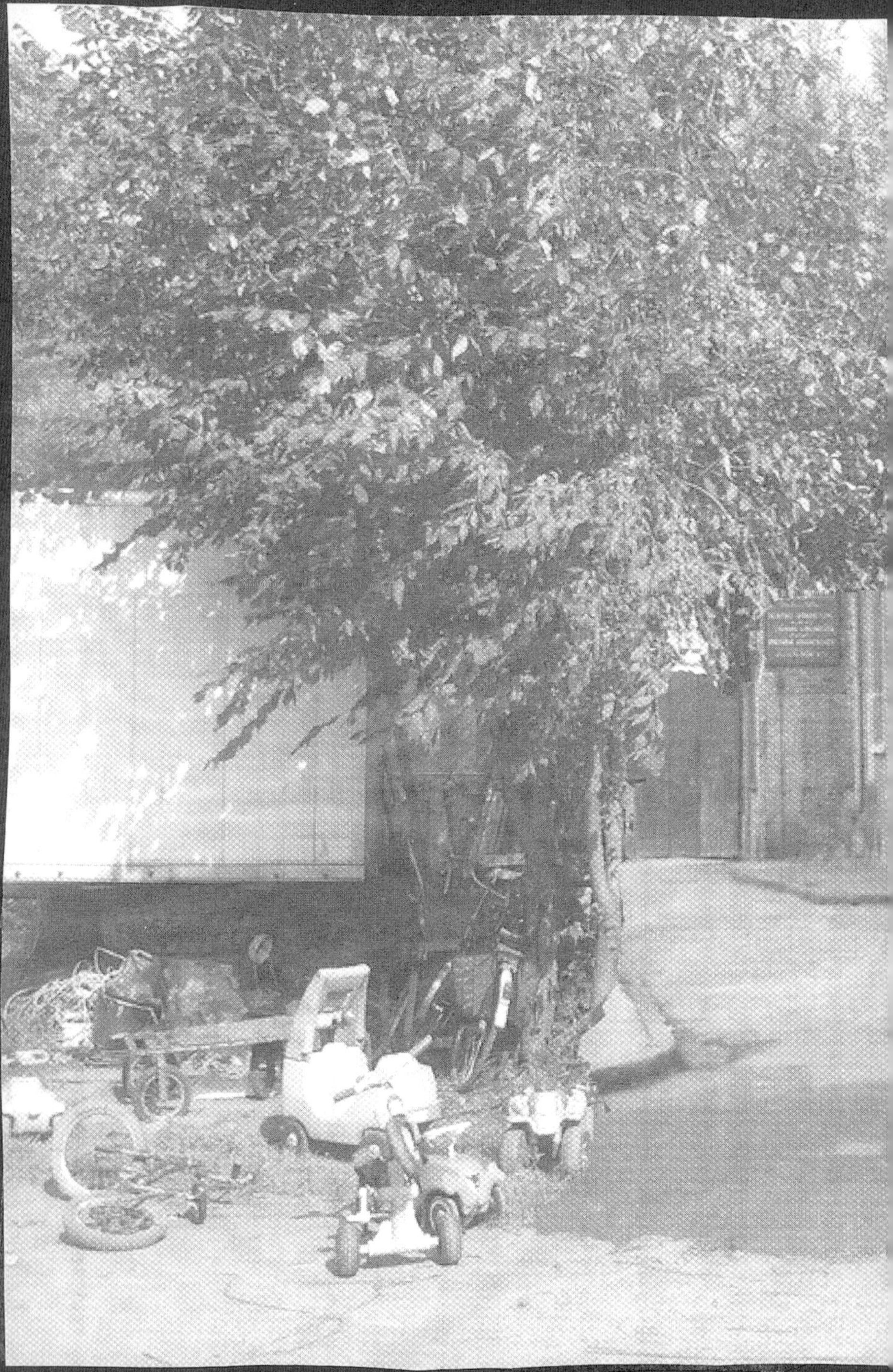

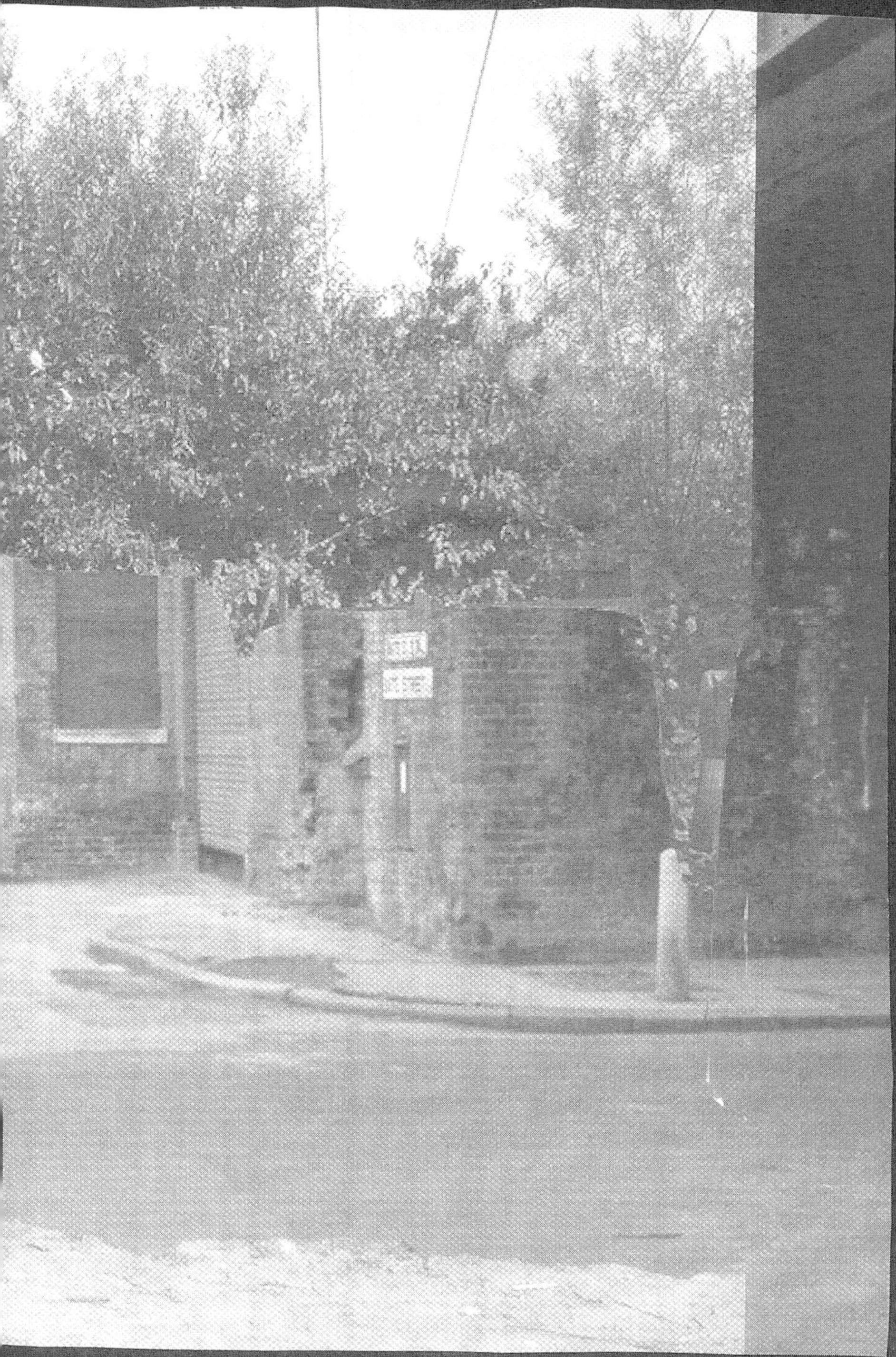

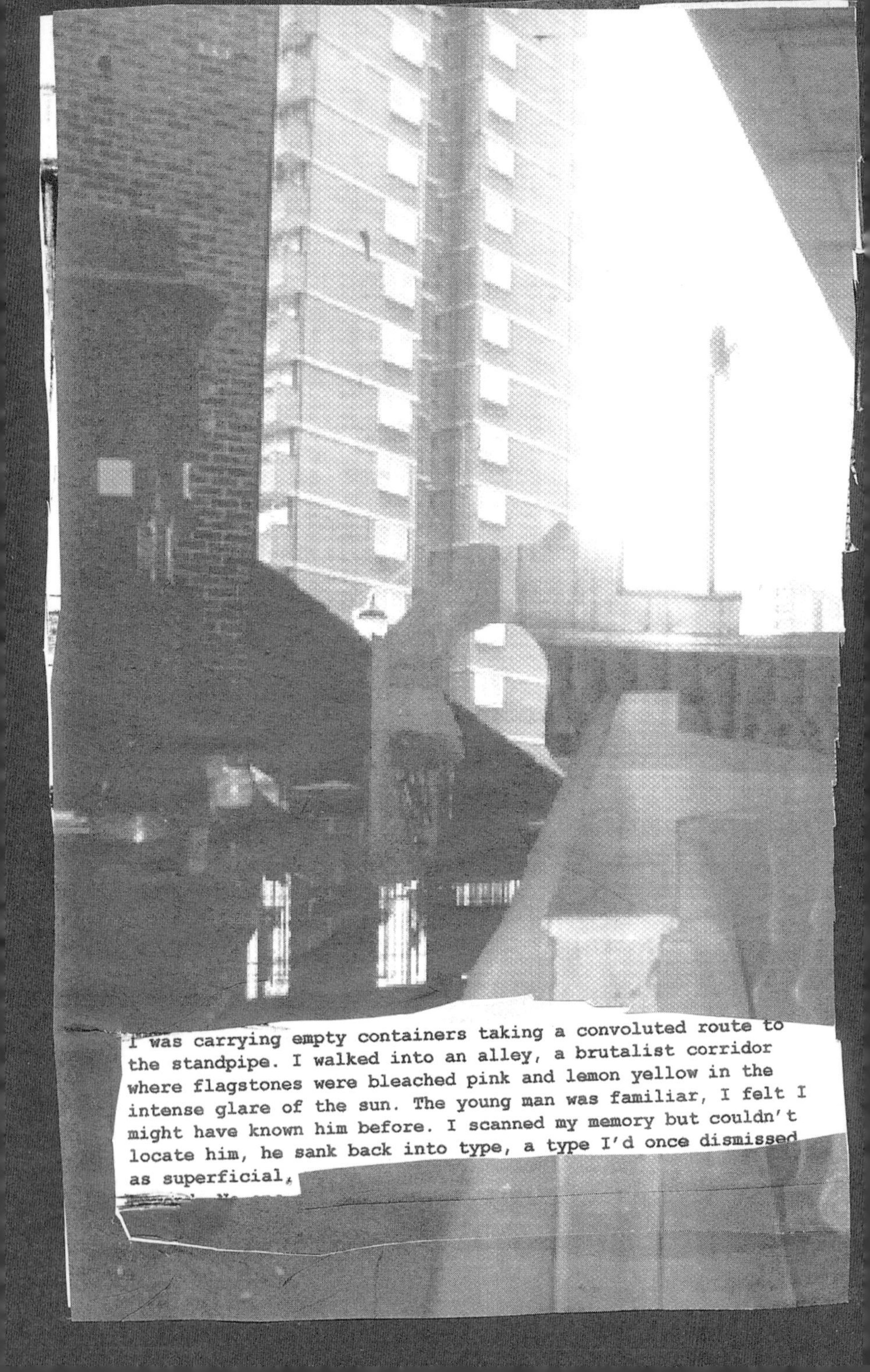

I was carrying empty containers taking a convoluted route to the standpipe. I walked into an alley, a brutalist corridor where flagstones were bleached pink and lemon yellow in the intense glare of the sun. The young man was familiar, I felt I might have known him before. I scanned my memory but couldn't locate him, he sank back into type, a type I'd once dismissed as superficial,

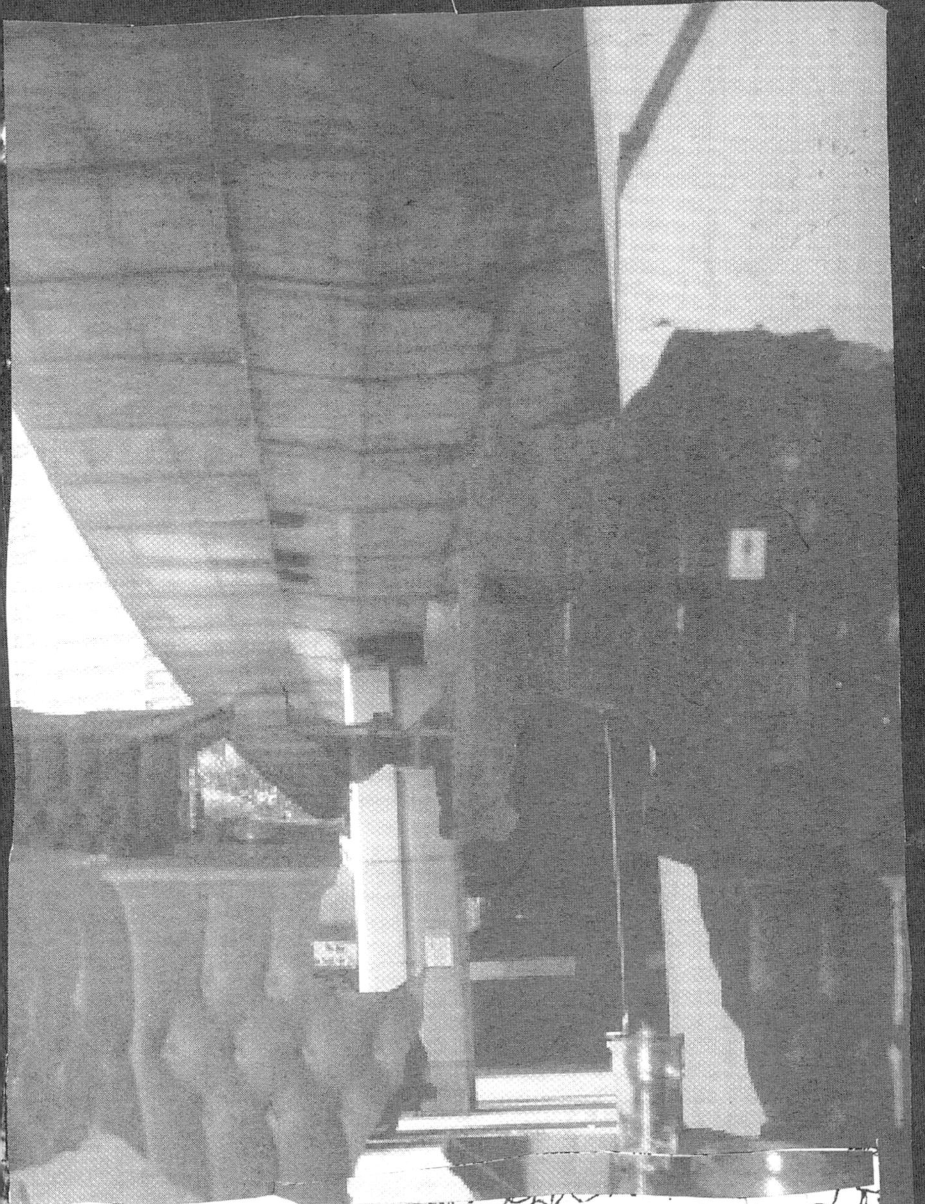

He wore mirror shades, white vest and a hat like a pilots over his long black hair. He was scorching hot, The Cult, Bradford 1981, fur and feathers, the type to loom up in dreams. And he

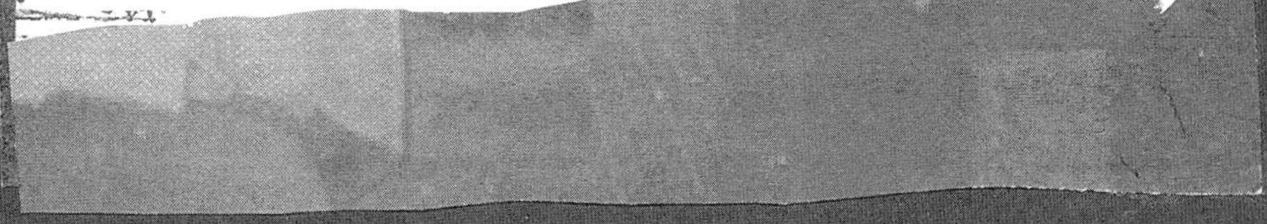

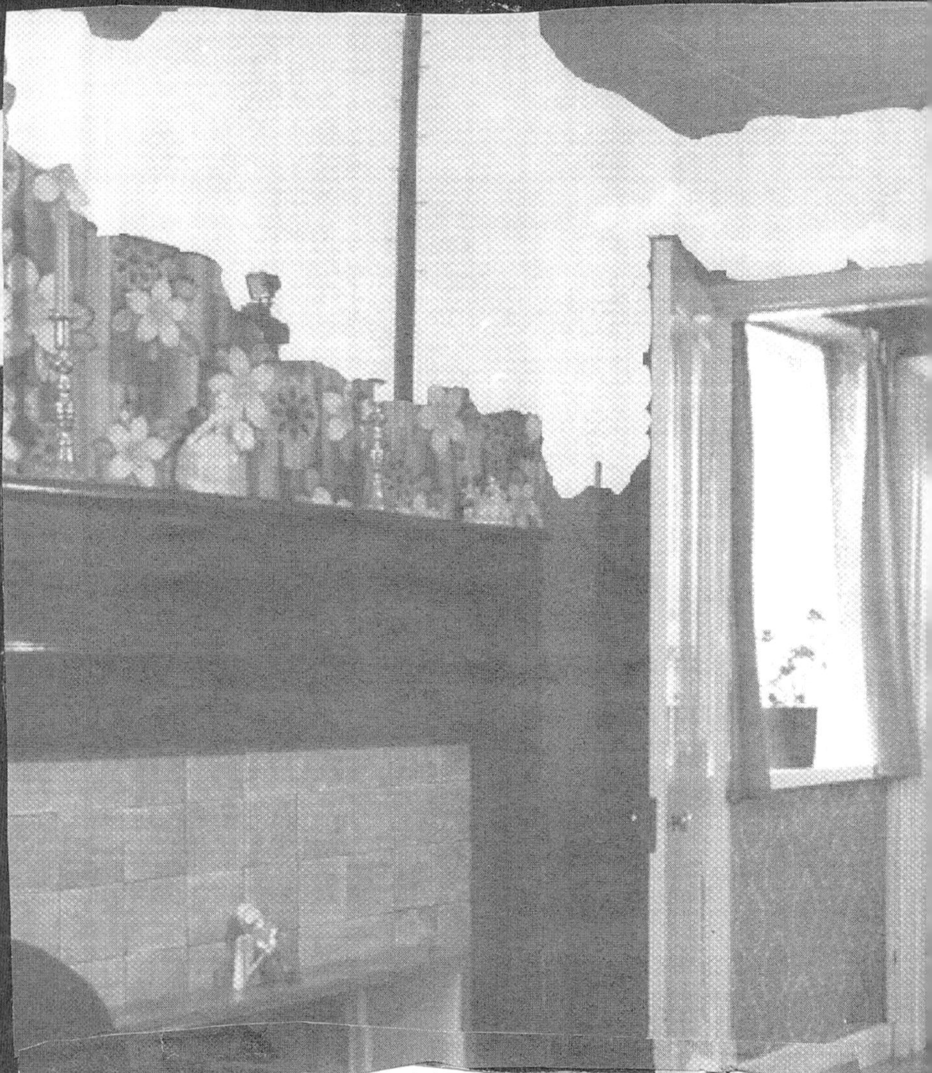

looked at me with the signalled intensity, slowing beside me, 'have you got a cigarette?' His accent was Mancunian, a shock. I'd expected something European, French or maybe the hyper chat of Spanish.
Surely he must have family up there to go to? Couldn't he get out?

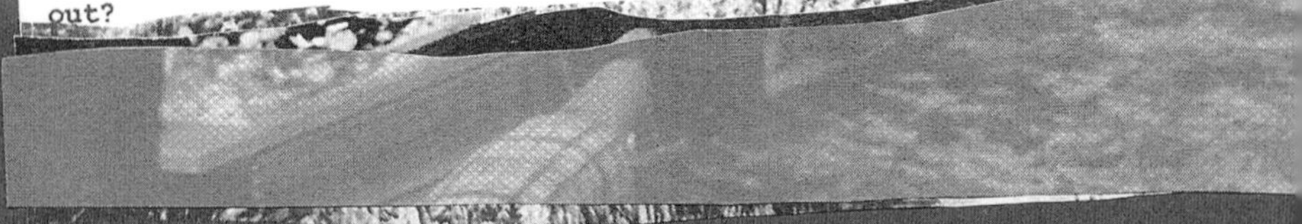

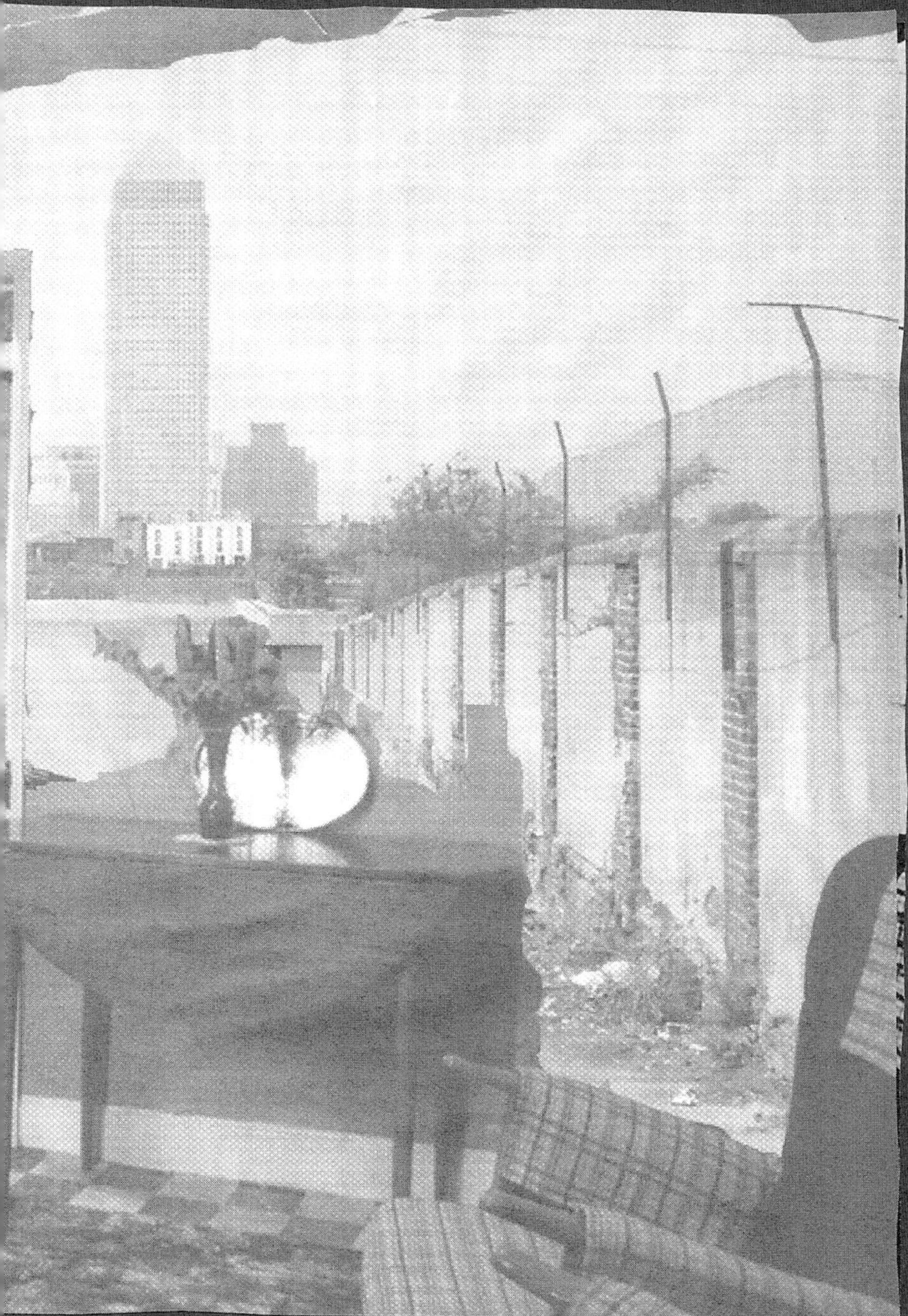

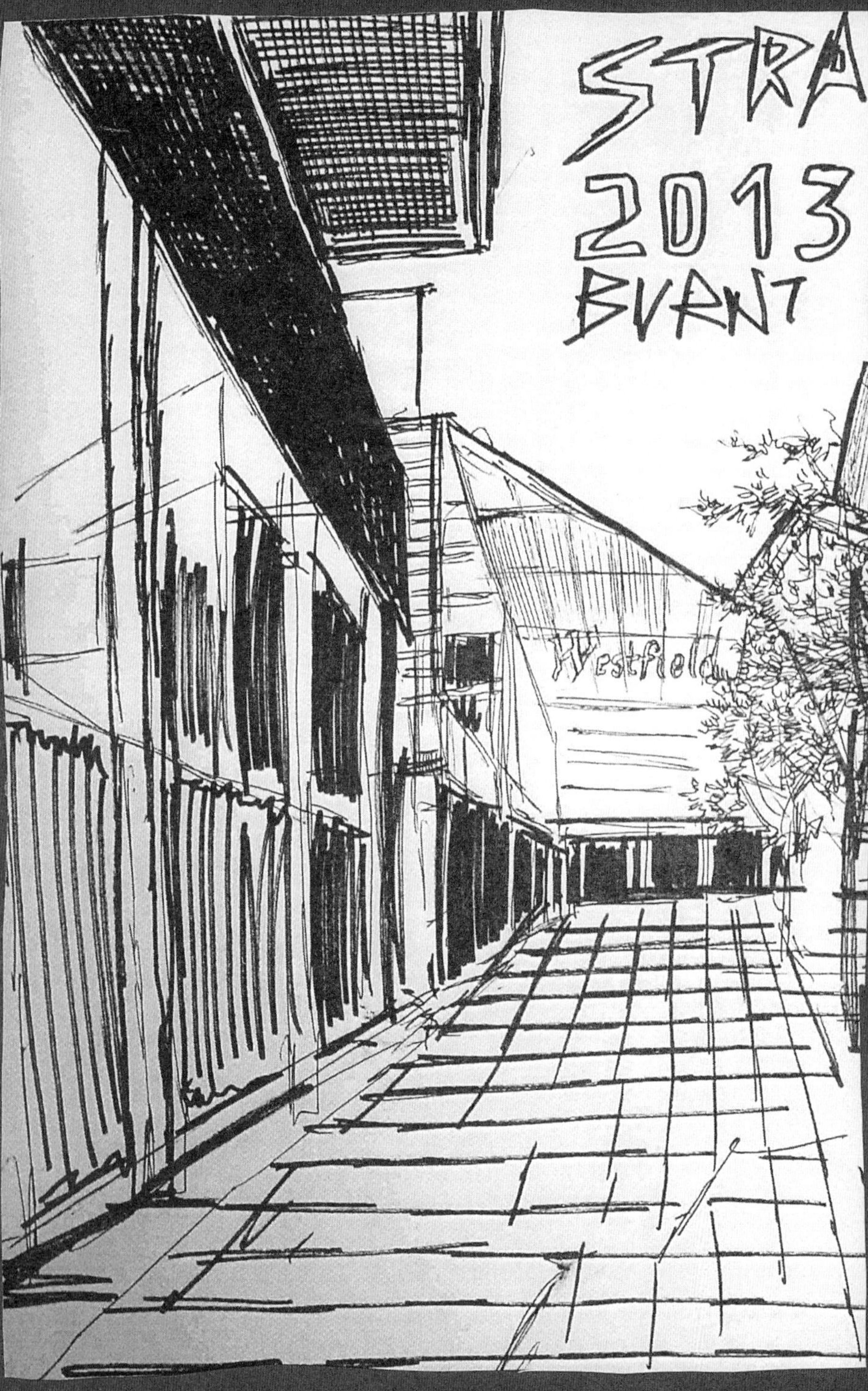
STRA
2013
BURNT
Westfield

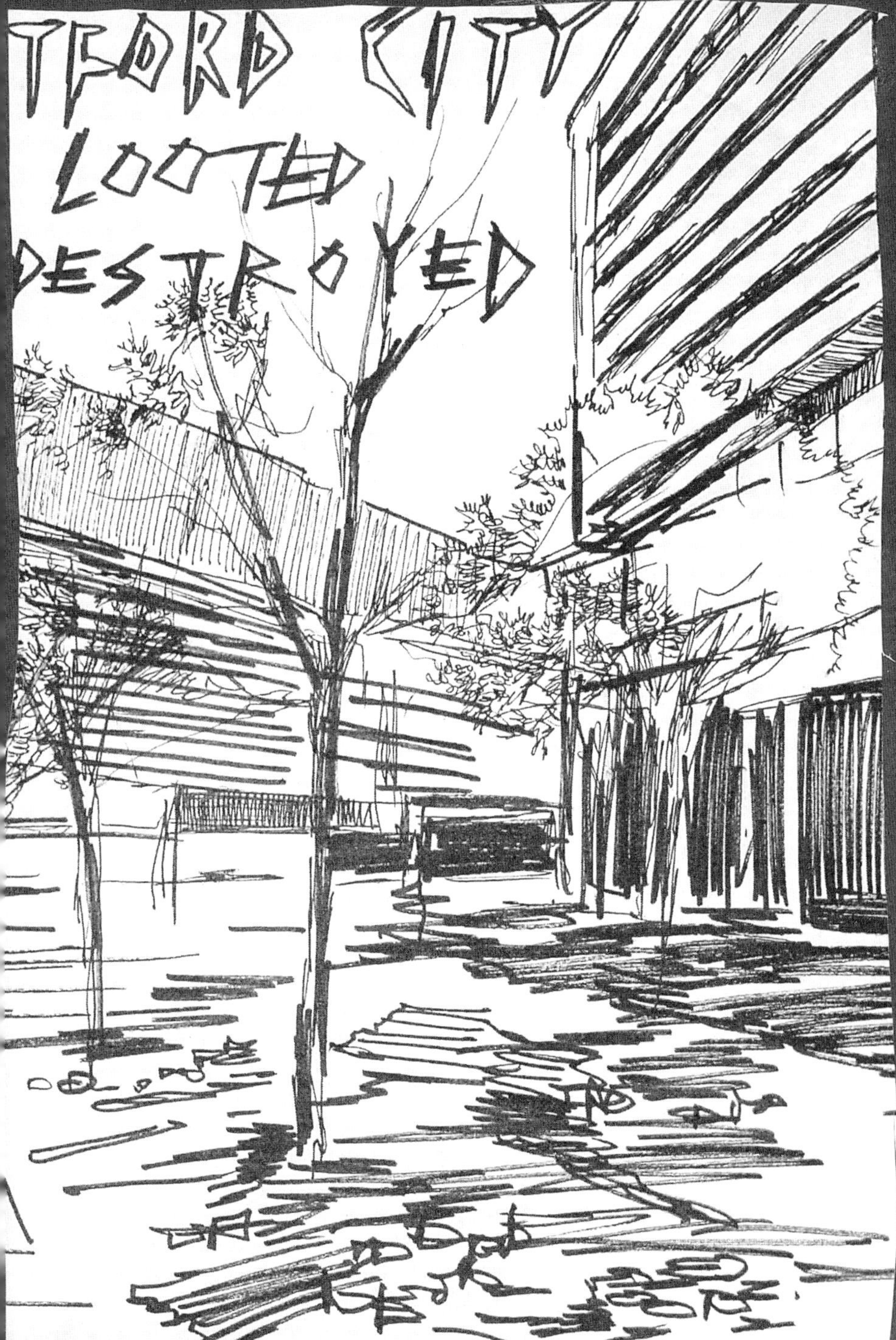
TFORD CITY
LOOTED
DESTROYED

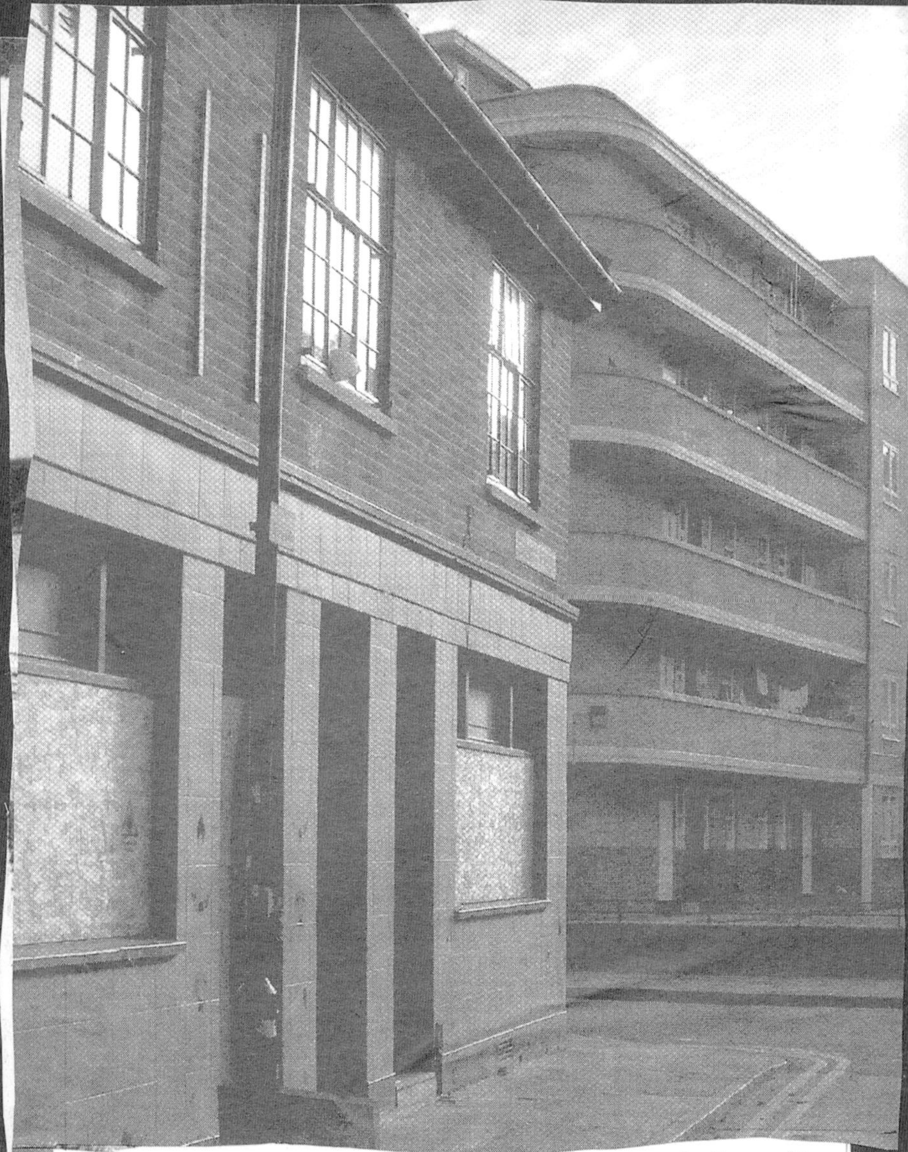

We sat on a wall in the lilac shadows of a courtyard. He smelt sexy, hot and masculine. The smoke rose in a plume, the air was still and oppressive. He kissed me with a sudden force, it had to be like this.

He pulled me through a mosaic corridor, into a small cloying room . It leapt with lozenges of violet light from a grille in the ceiling. I realised after it must be the mechanism room for the lift in the apartment block

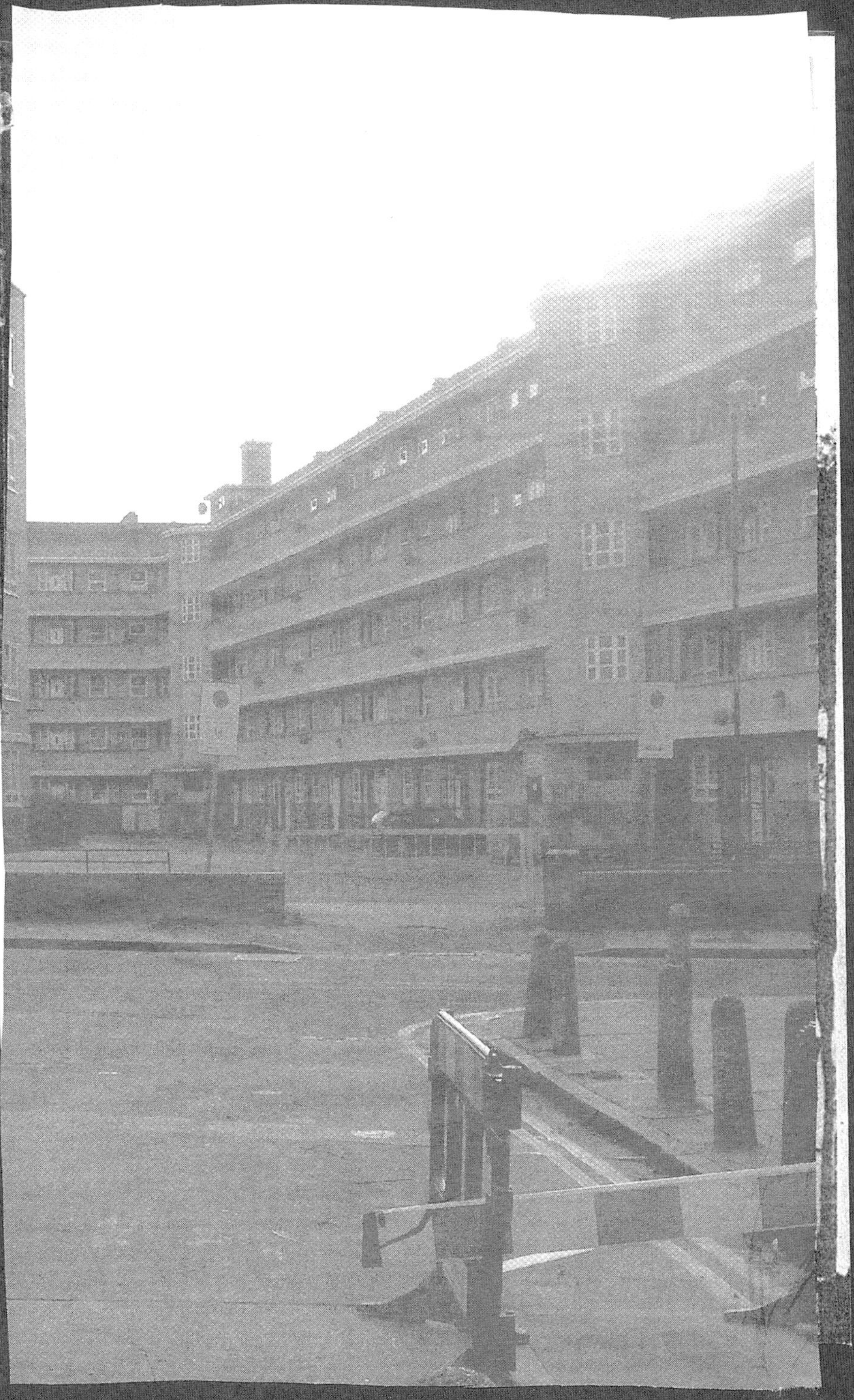

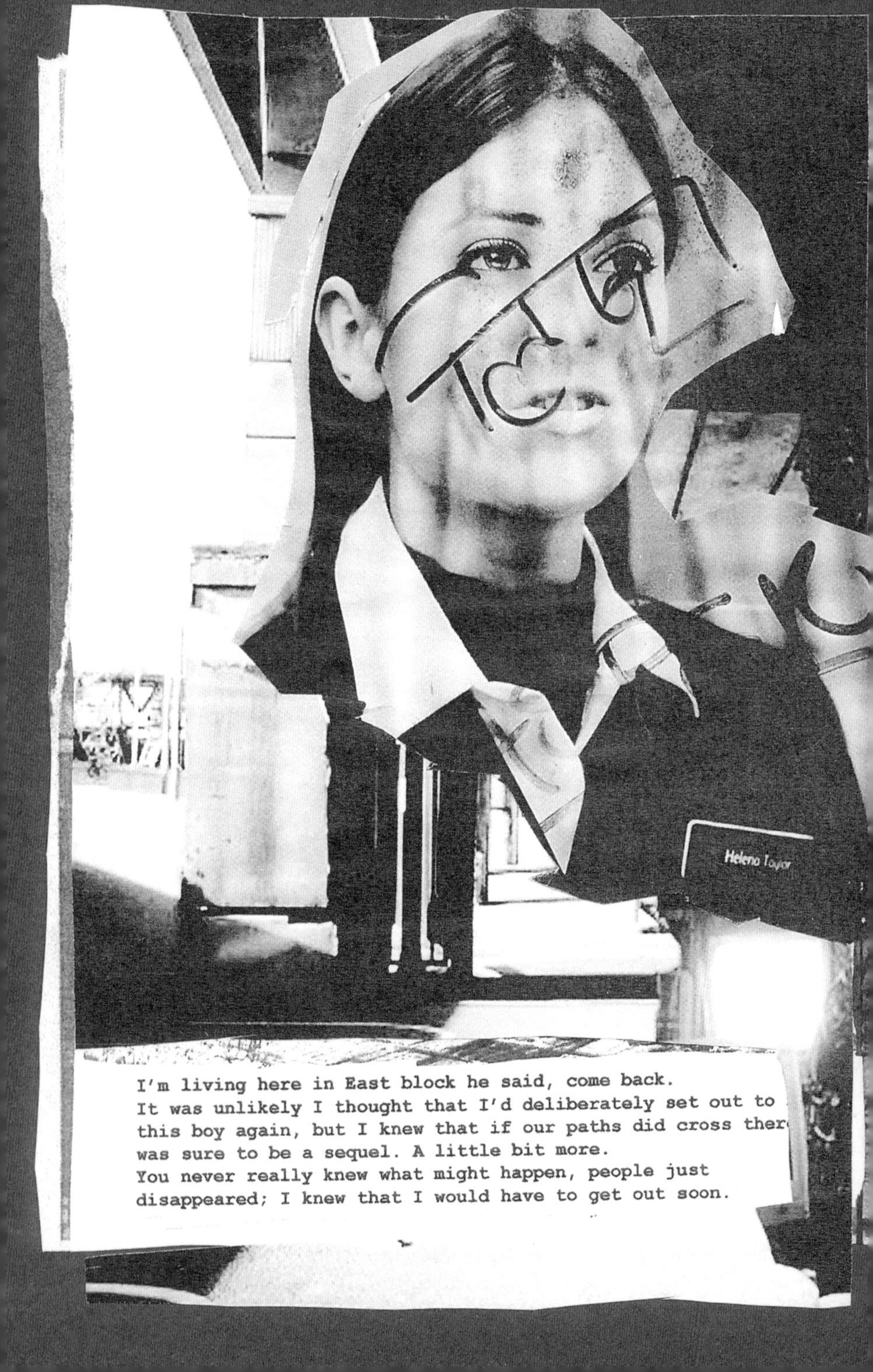
Helena Taylor

I'm living here in East block he said, come back.
It was unlikely I thought that I'd deliberately set out to
this boy again, but I knew that if our paths did cross ther
was sure to be a sequel. A little bit more.
You never really knew what might happen, people just
disappeared; I knew that I would have to get out soon.

Conversations became more intense as well.
Sometimes you might see someone and think this might be for th
last time so you told them how you really felt. I had lost so
many in this strife and walked haunted by all the goodbyes I
never said and all the feelings I had that I could have done
more to make that person know they were loved. I thought of
Arran, known later to me as Mark, it was a shock for him to go
like that. I hadn't seen what precipitated the final act.
There was a strange sense now that nothing must be wasted, not
a drop of water spilt, not a moment lost, every kiss, every
word had to have potency, it had to have meaning.

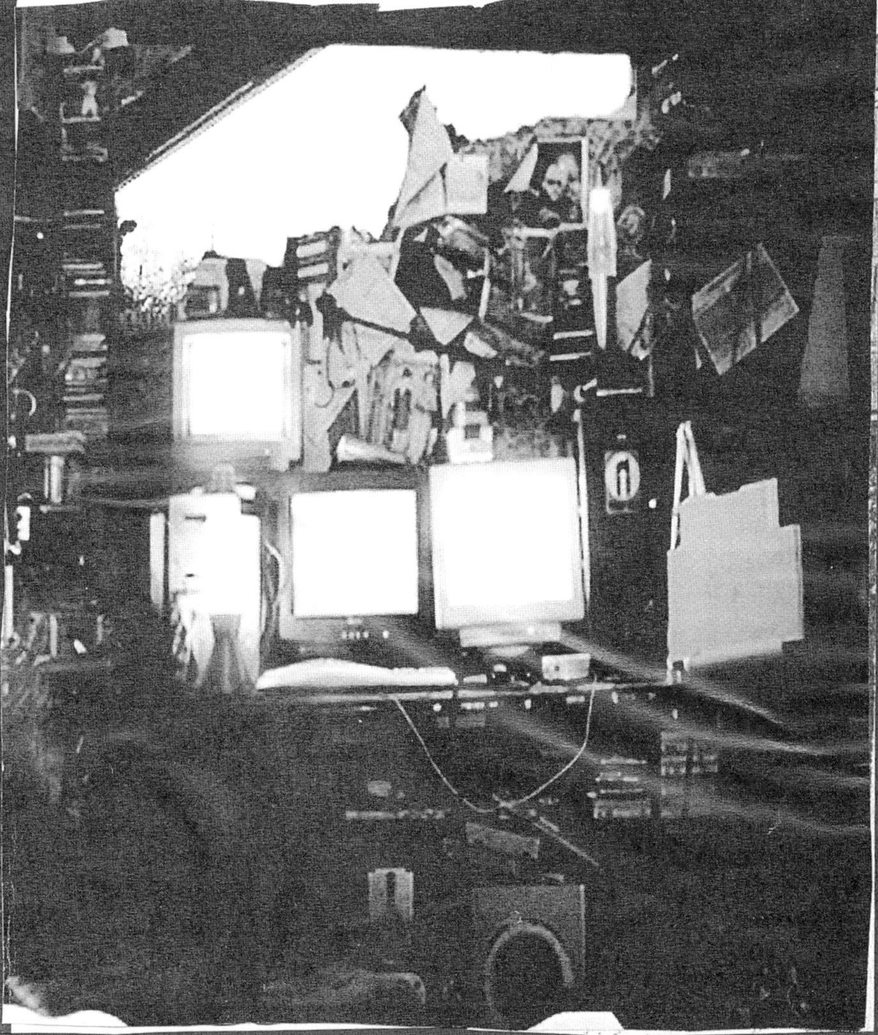

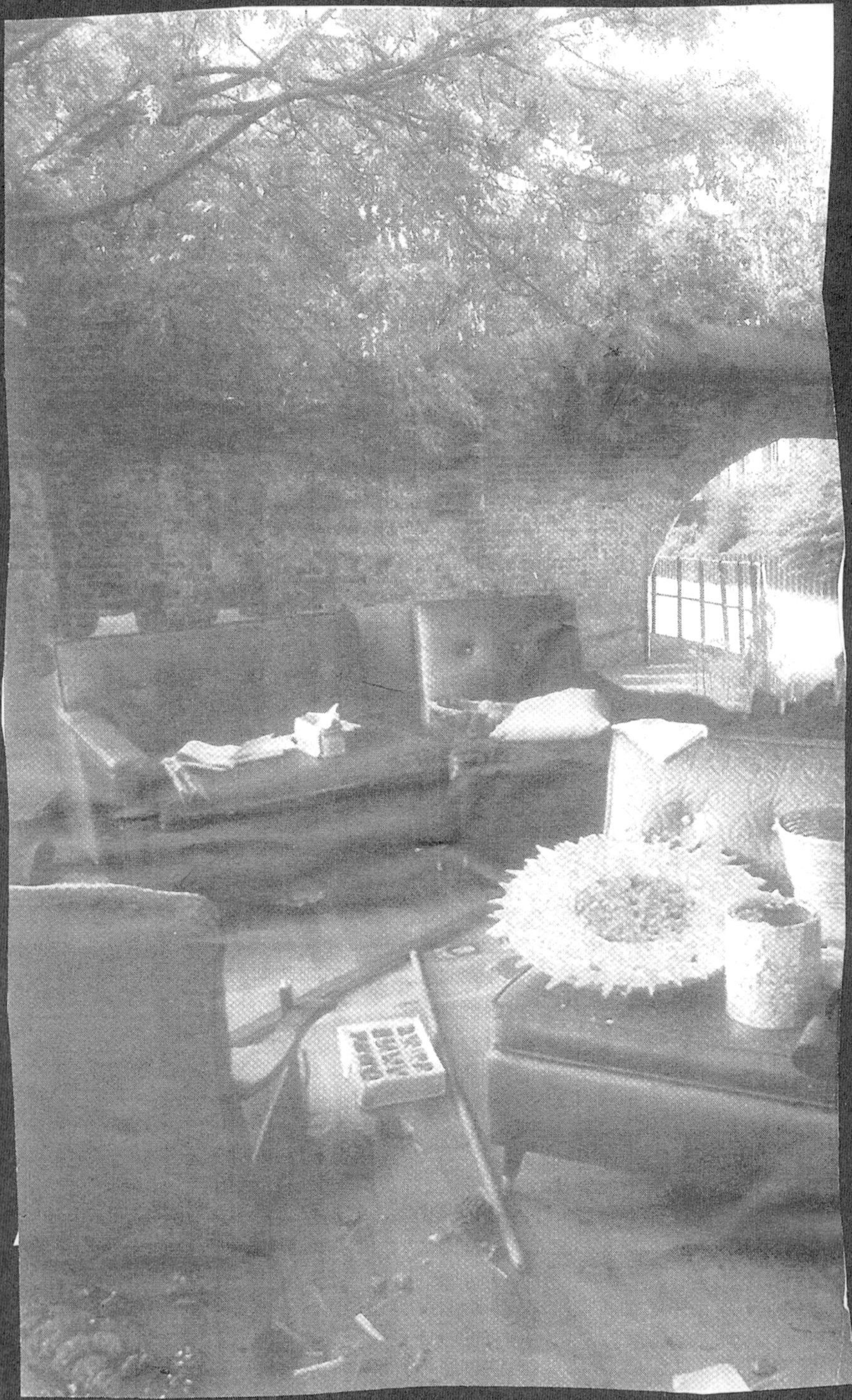

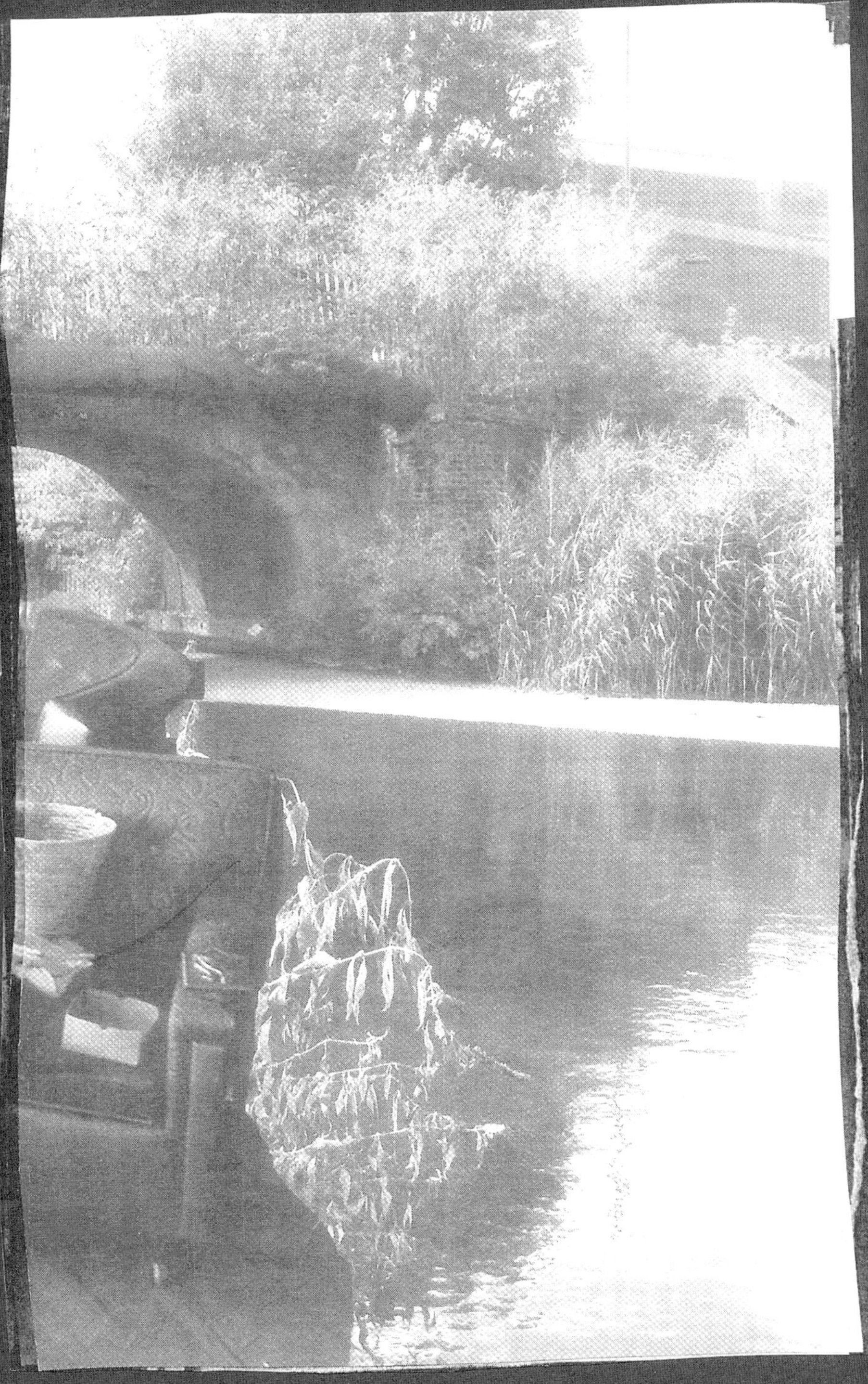

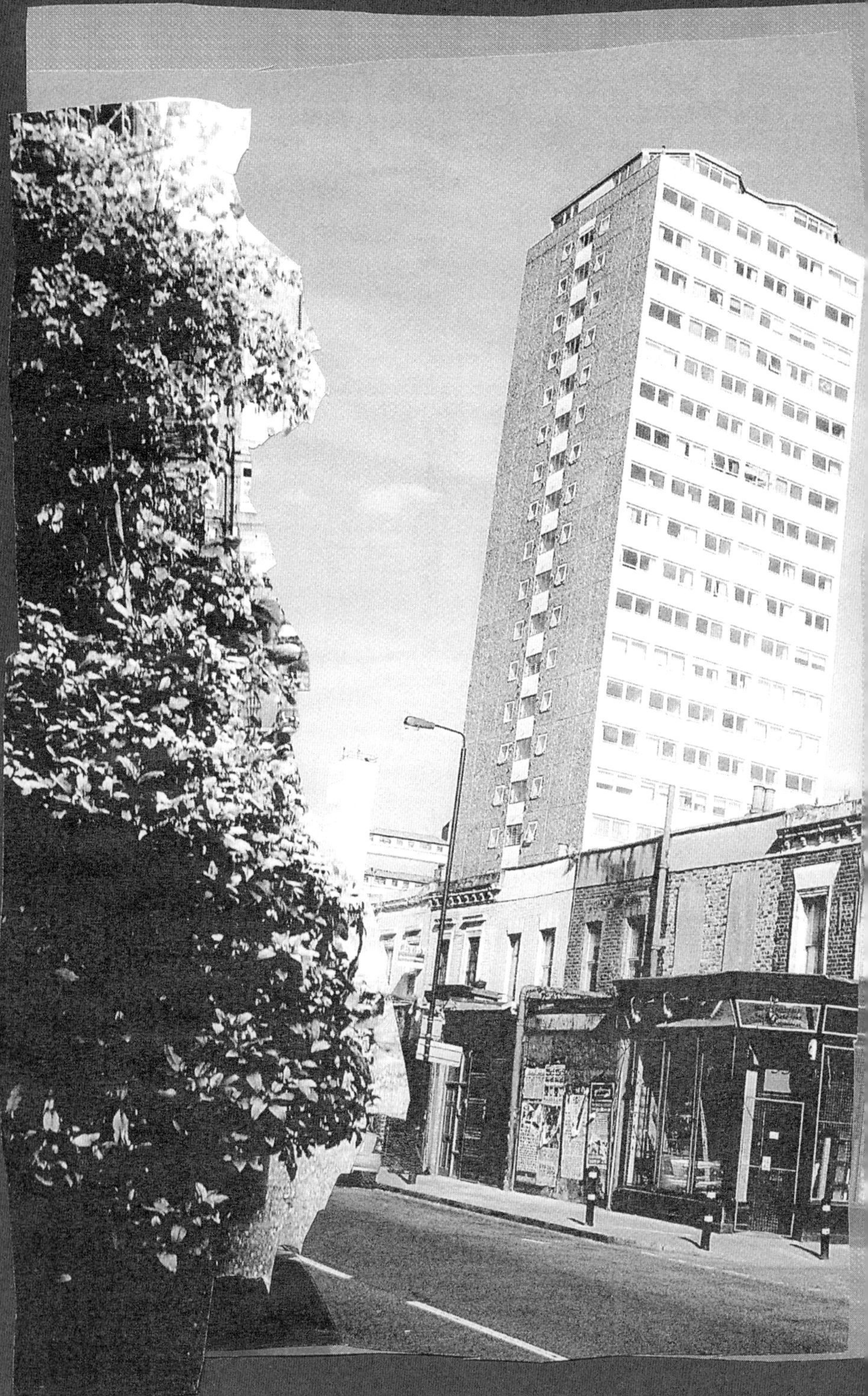

The pathways of the heath were carved from stone, little labyrinths in the dry stonewall, mosses and lichens, brooks carving out pathways on the woodland floor. Livid funghi, oranges and reds bursting through the muted carpet of grey and burnt umber.

He took my hand, he held me, we'll get through this, I promise. We wandered, for miles, in circles, lost in this magical world of hidden pathways and mist.

We made plans to get out, I knew how it would be. Scotland. The big camps north of Glasgow, he knew people up there, there was a place for us in one of the old farmhouses. It would be alright, many had made the journey easily enough, if you could get out of London you would be all right. He would sort out the documentation.

The living was quite good up there he said, they still had a water supply and services generally. There were food shortages and some restrictions on movement but it wasn't anything like London. Up there they had austerity but really the people were

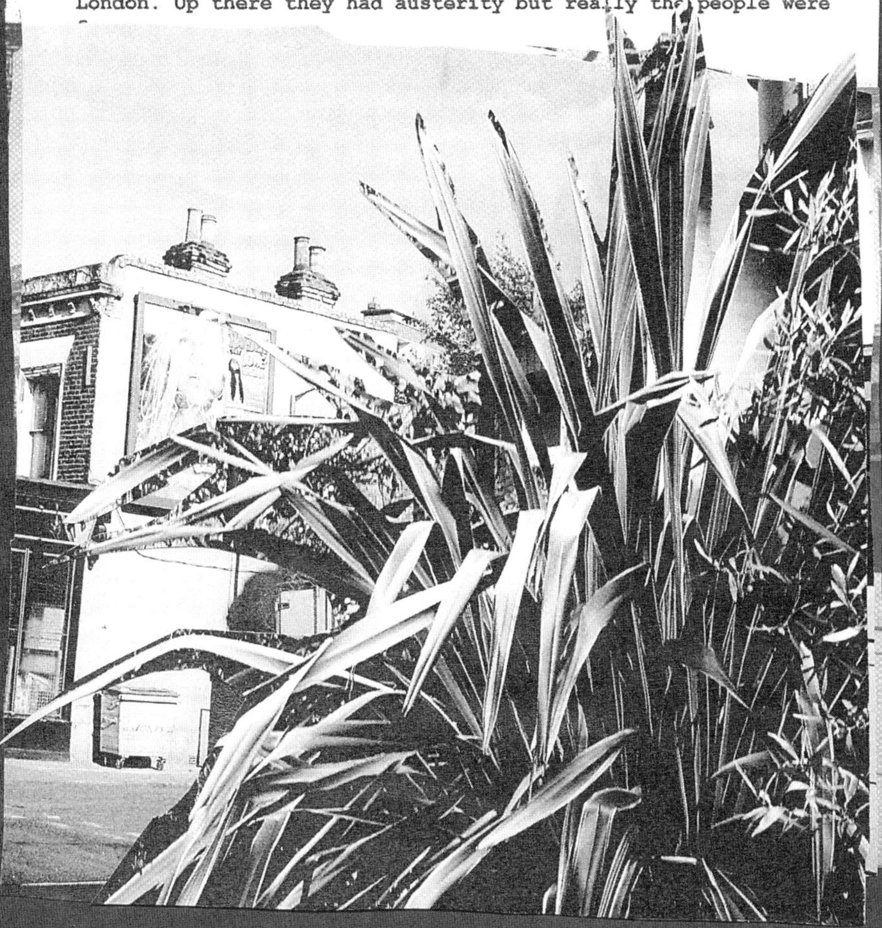

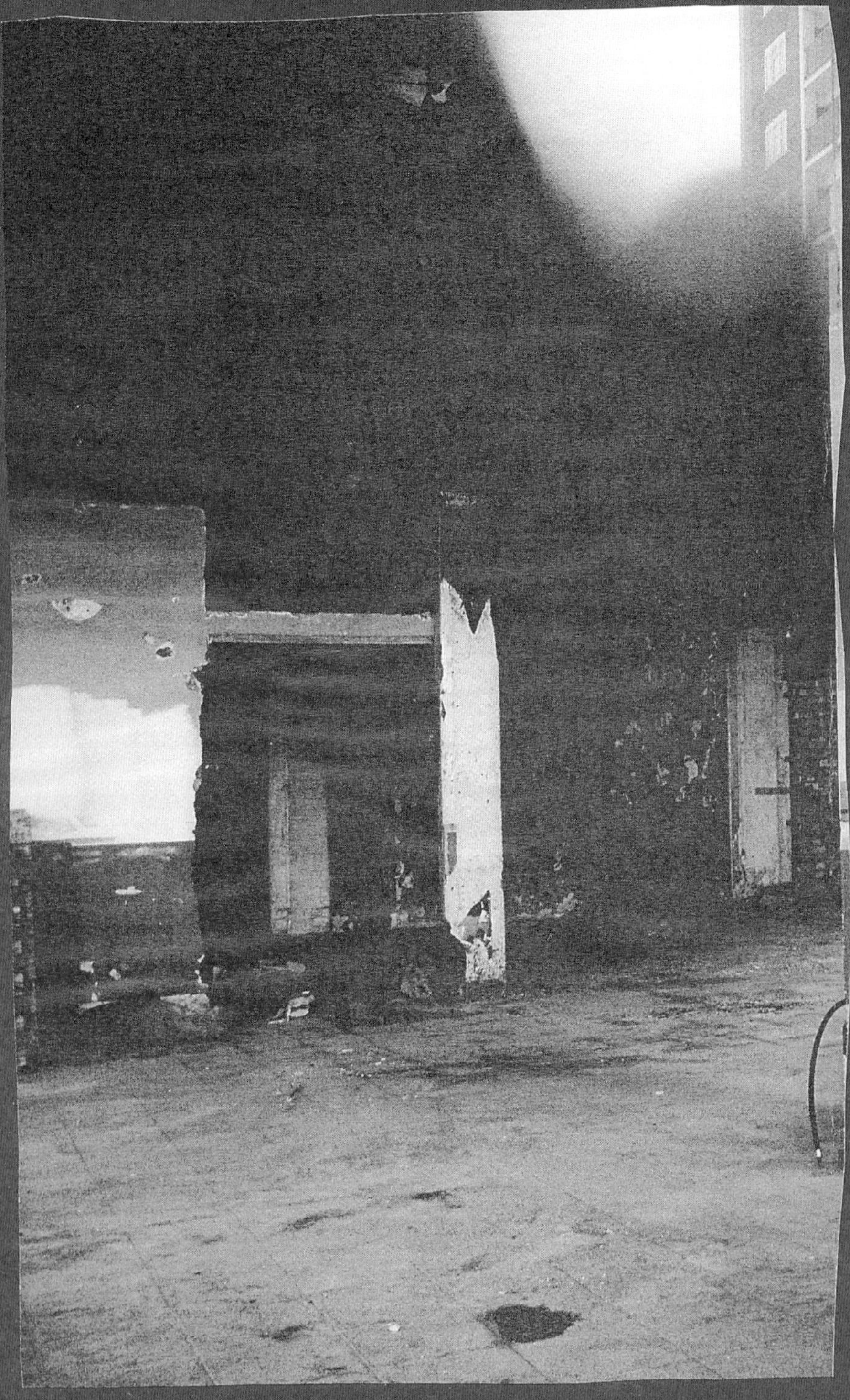

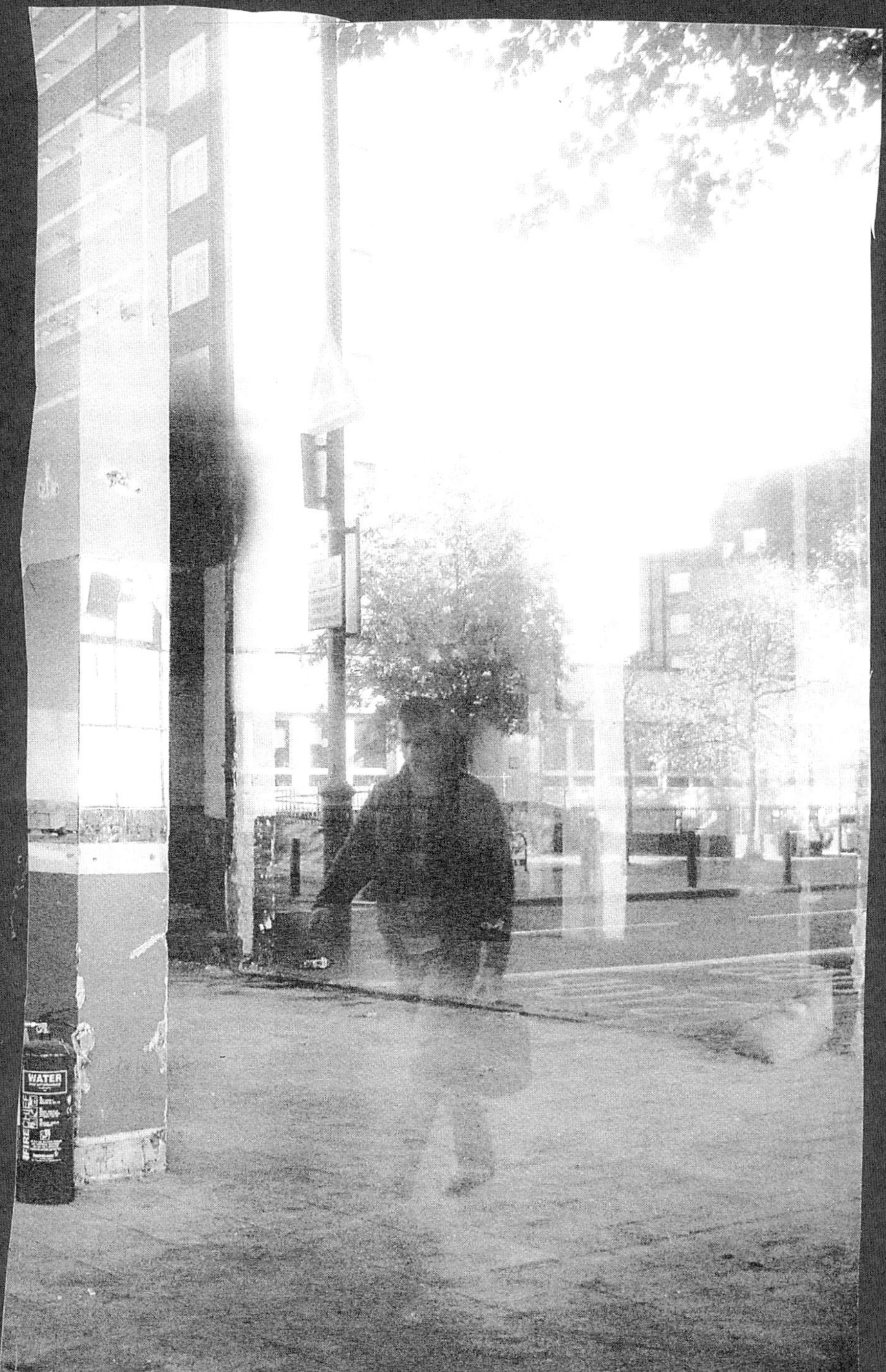
WATER
FIRECHIEF

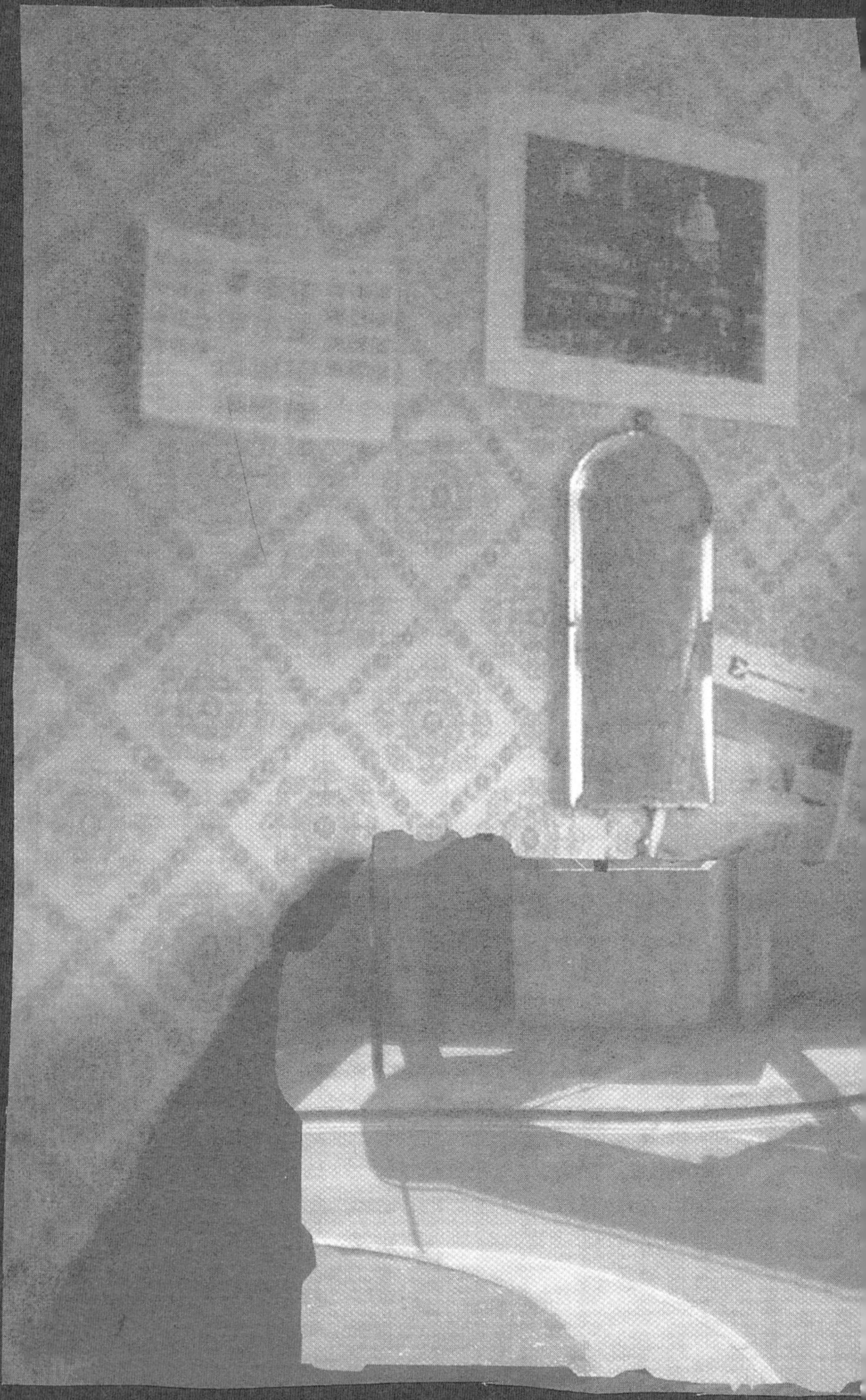

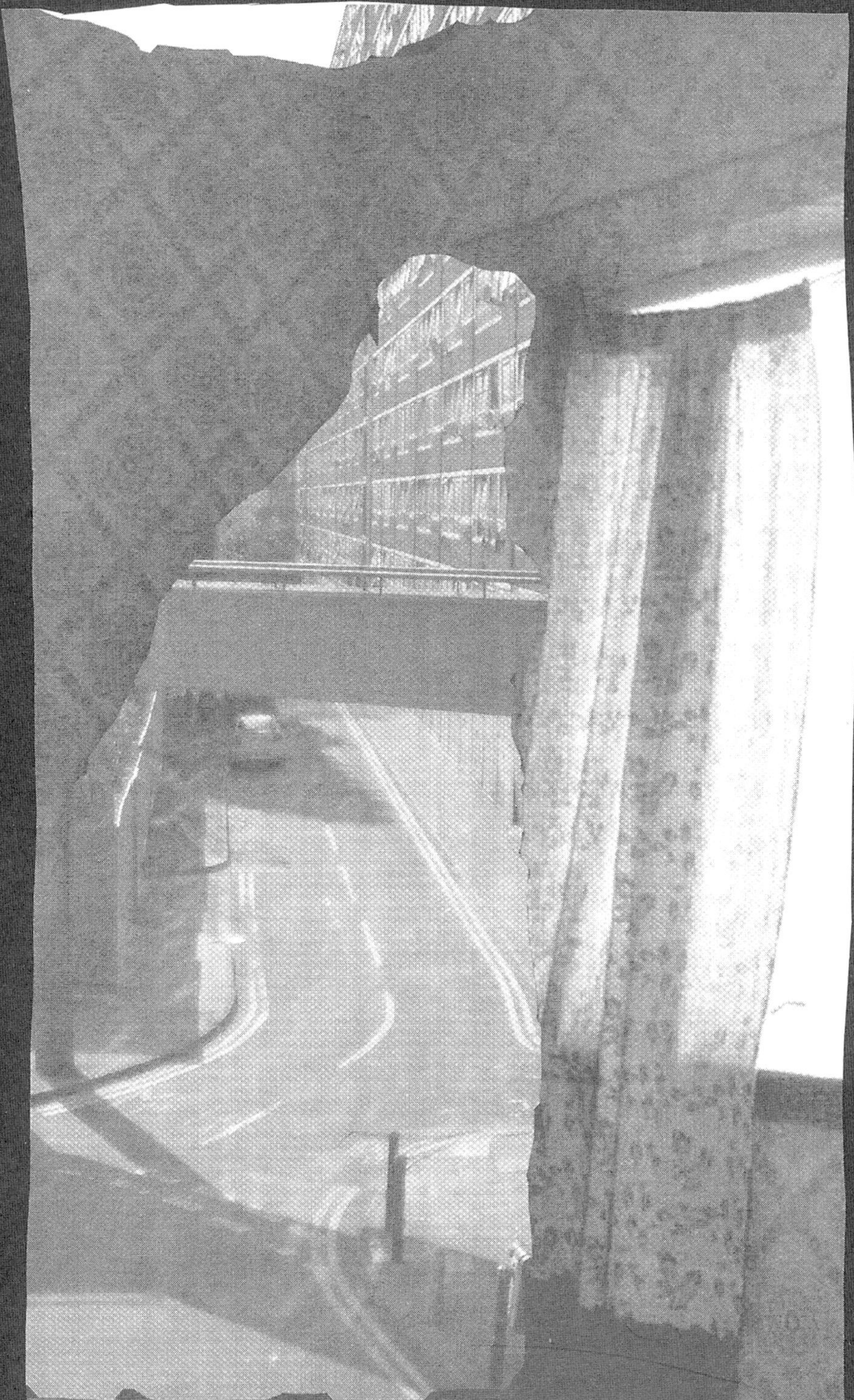

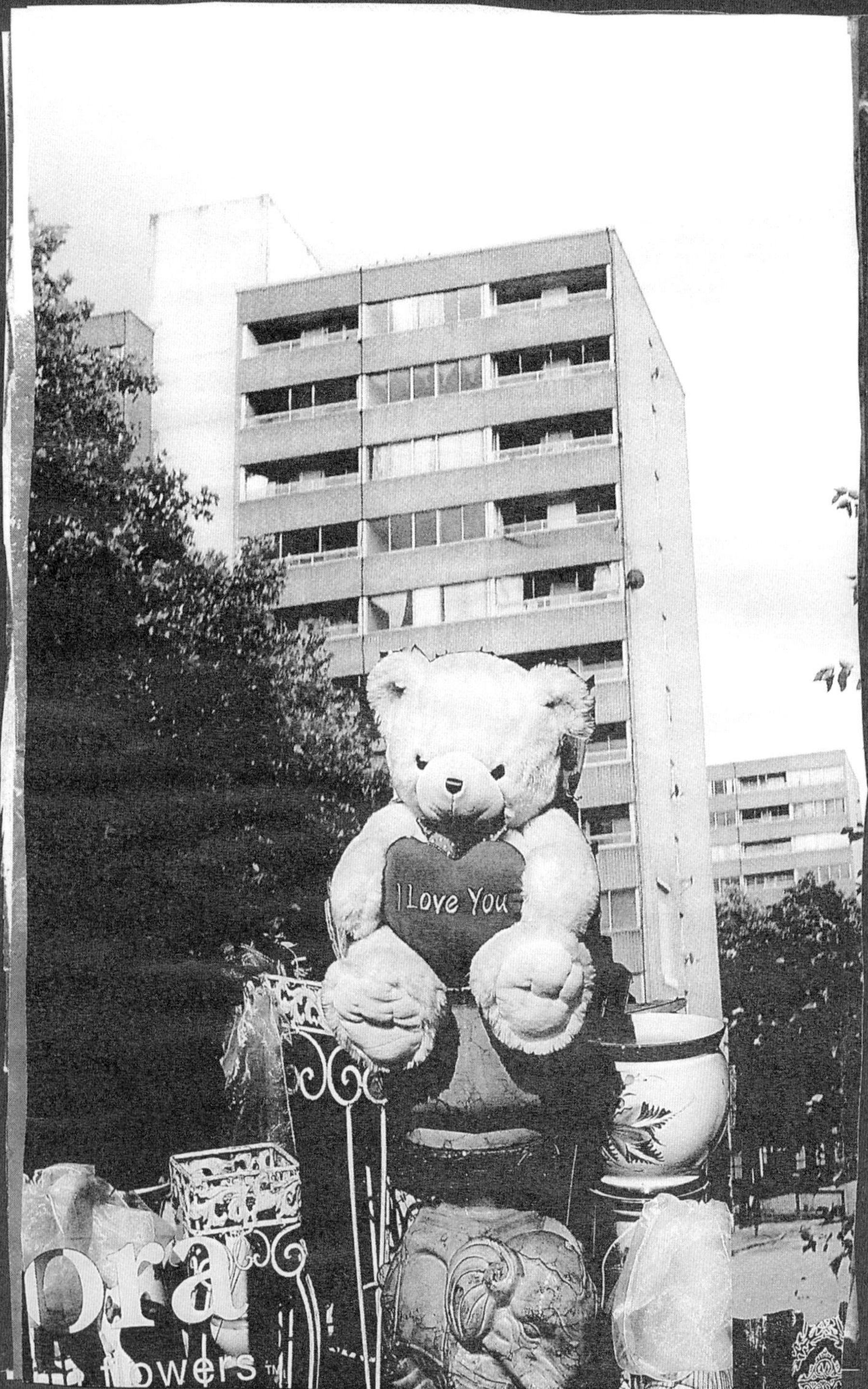
I Love You
ora
flowers™

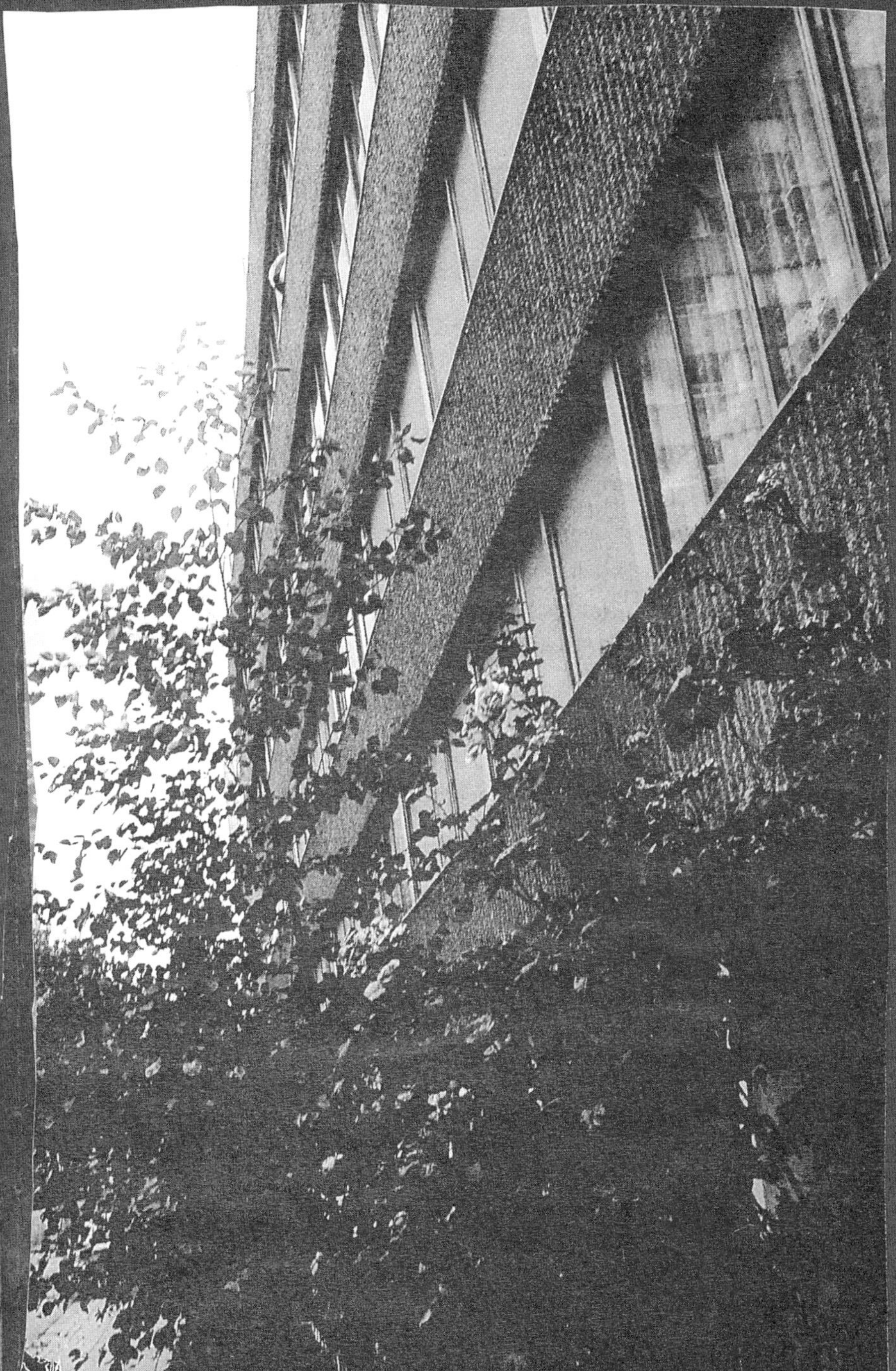

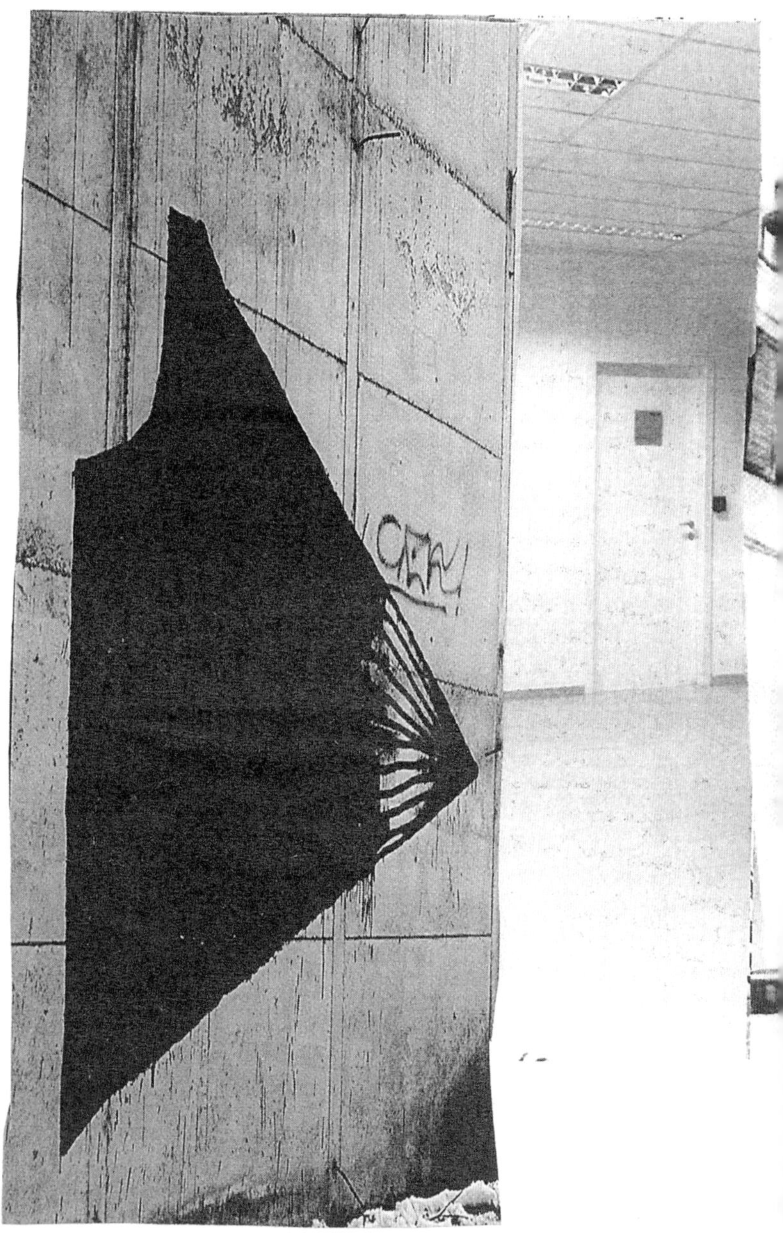

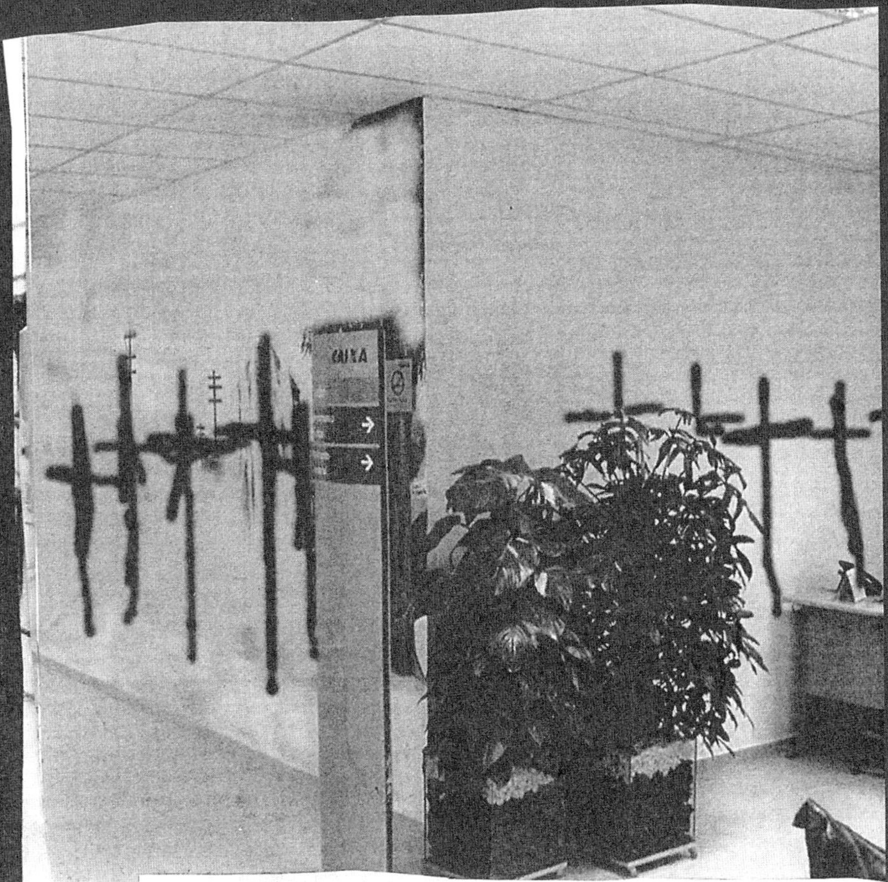

We took the path of the River Lea, it was quiet until the reservoirs where we encountered little knots of frenzied activity, the authorities were working hard to get the wat supply safe here. We knew we were facing a complete cut in supply. From up here, you could turn around and look down London, Chingford hatch, Higham, it was already shimmering the heat. There were plumes of smoke somewhere in the sout east of the city, I guessed Lewisham, that area, maybe the shopping centre there, and elsewhere flashes of fire. From you could see the cuts and gouges, the scorched swathes of London. I was stunned by the extent of the damage. You cou see from this distance that stretches miles long, particul near the Thames had just vanished into black, smouldering heaps. The smell was acrid, like a burning chemical factory There was a toxic pall over the city, but as it shimmered gleamed in the pink light I was struck by its beauty. The central London areas of the west end and the city were und heavy armed guard to stop looting and occupation, the rich imagined there would be a time when they could come back a reclaim the what was left. It seemed unlikely to us now. W felt abandoned.

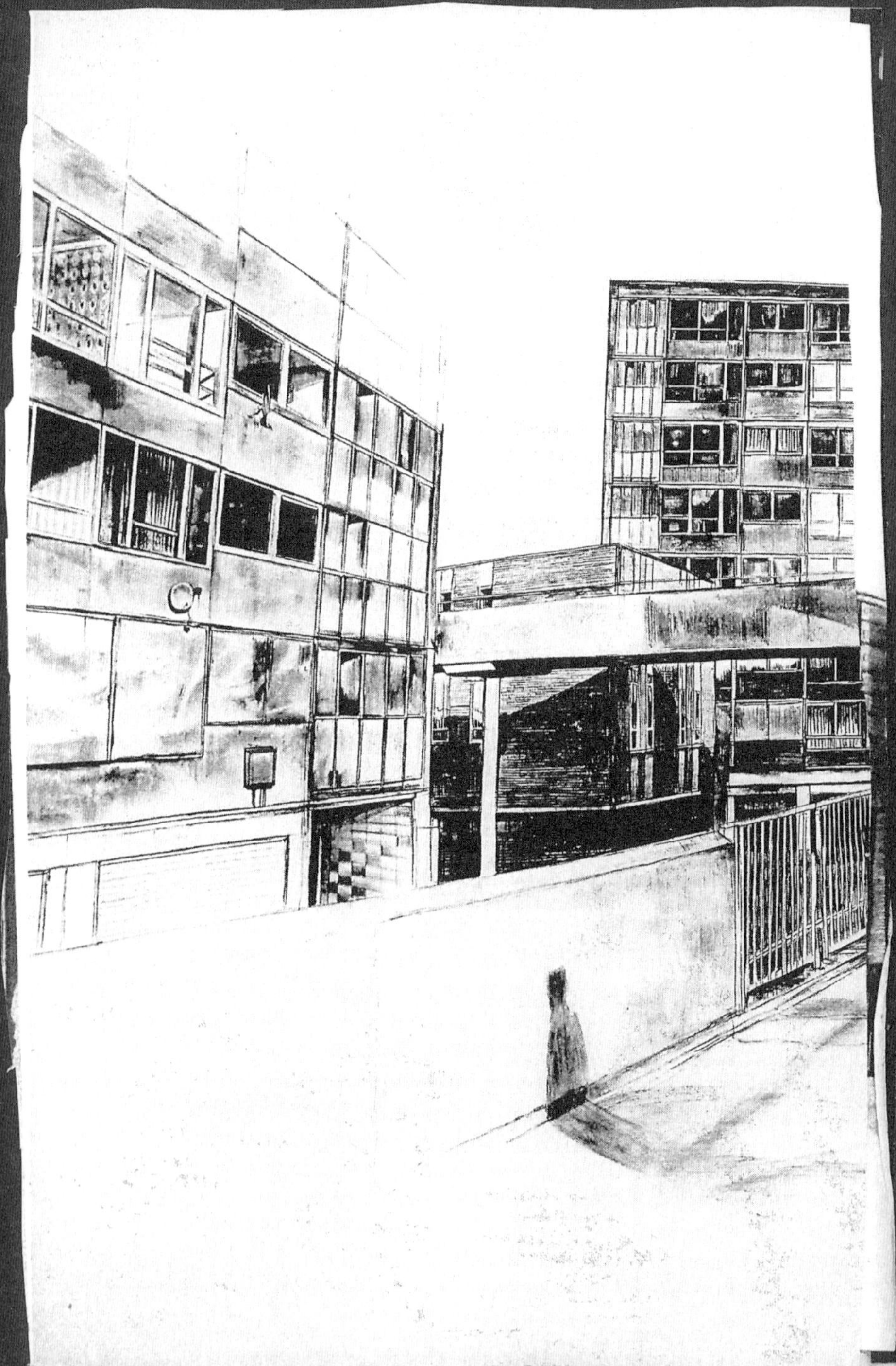

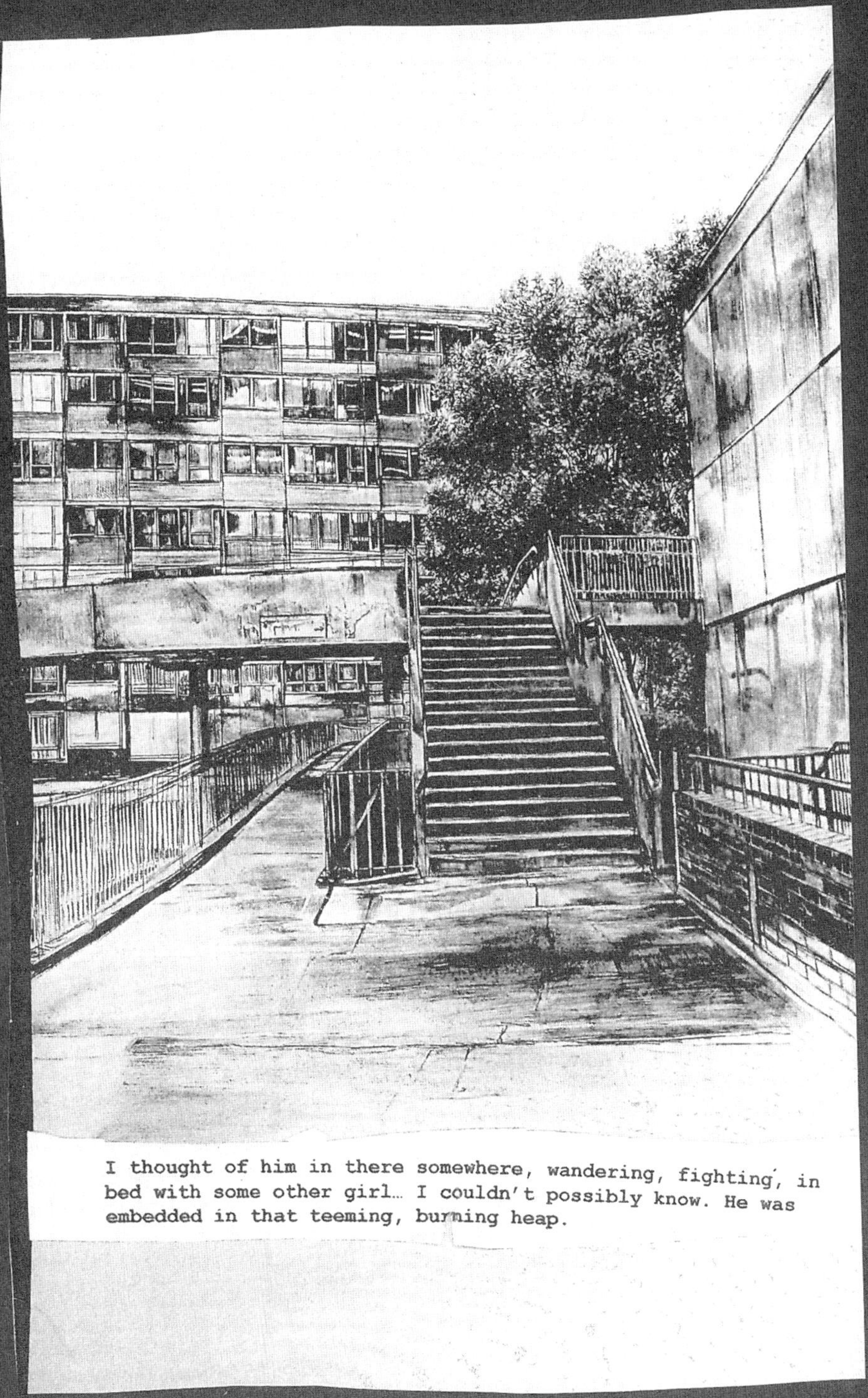
I thought of him in there somewhere, wandering, fighting, in bed with some other girl… I couldn't possibly know. He was embedded in that teeming, burning heap.

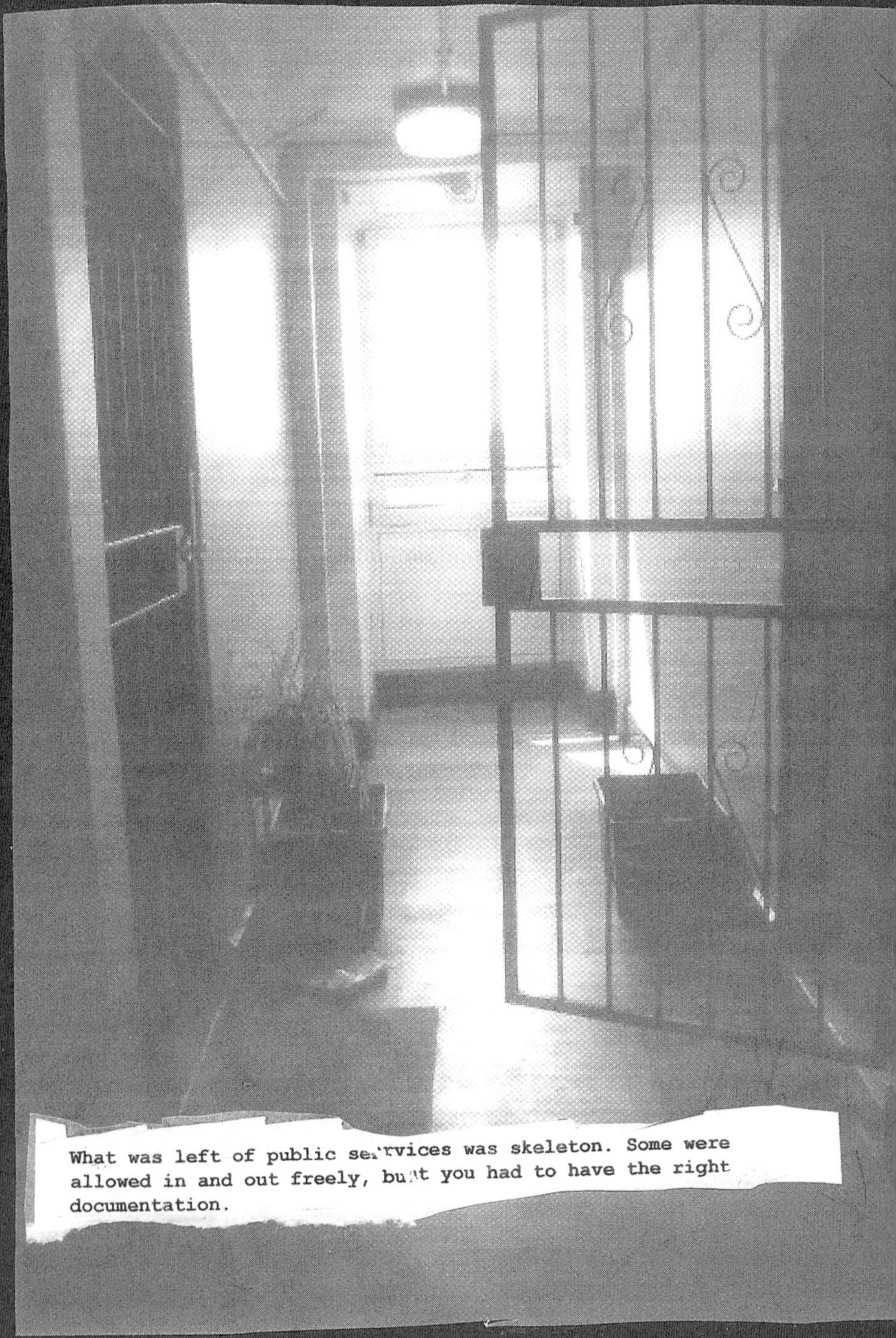
What was left of public services was skeleton. Some were allowed in and out freely, but you had to have the right documentation.

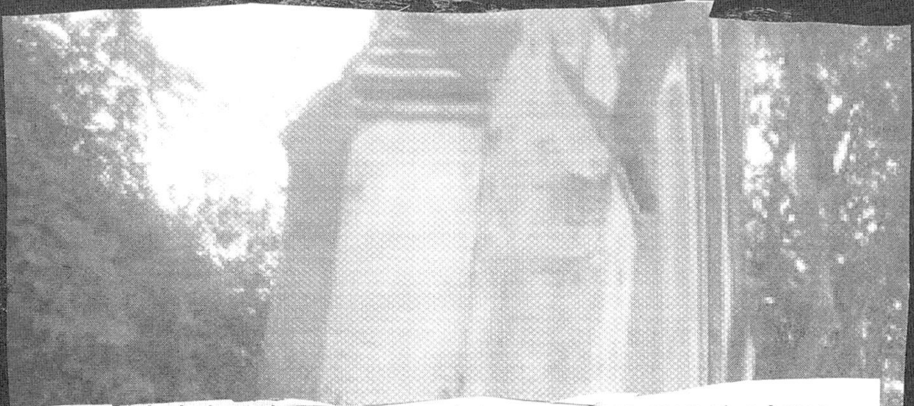

We climbed through the Barrat estates now, less executive homes more barracks. Medics and police were using these houses , we knew there was a large holding centre not far from here where the very sick were being held. It wasn't shoot to kill yet, that's what we'd heard, but you did risk being hauled off somewhere, a detention centre. Most likely we'd be interrogated and sent back, if we were unlucky they could hold us in the centres. The stories from there made your blood run cold. Someone told us they were using factories in Edmonton as holding centres for refugees. I didn't even know what our status was anymore. But I knew this was our last chance, they were struggling to find resources and men to police London, the construction of the wall was slow, we had to go now….

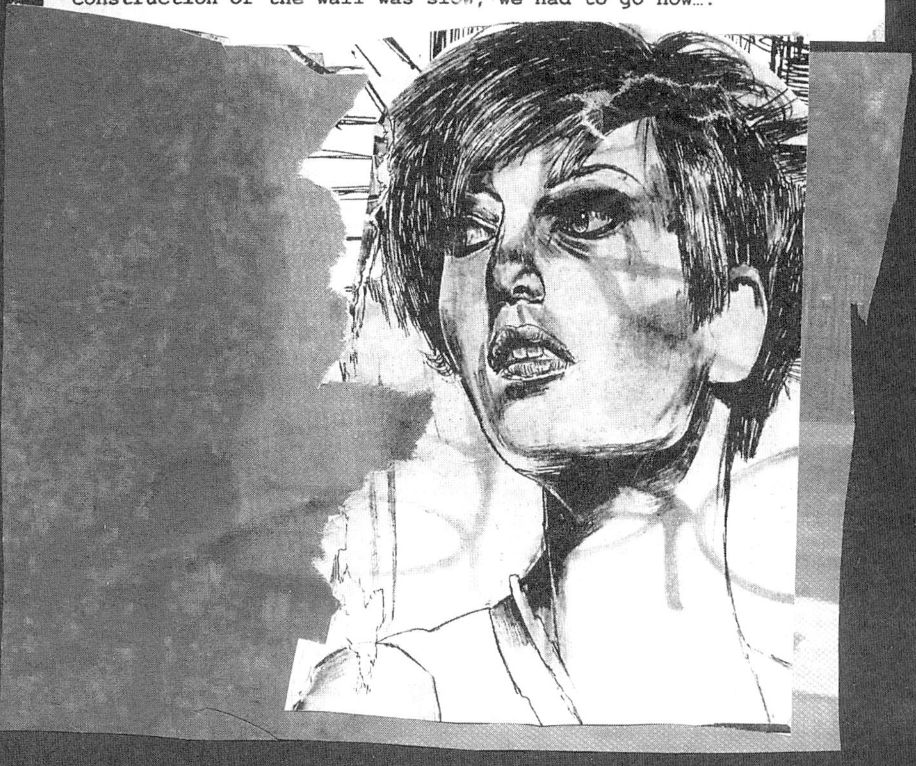

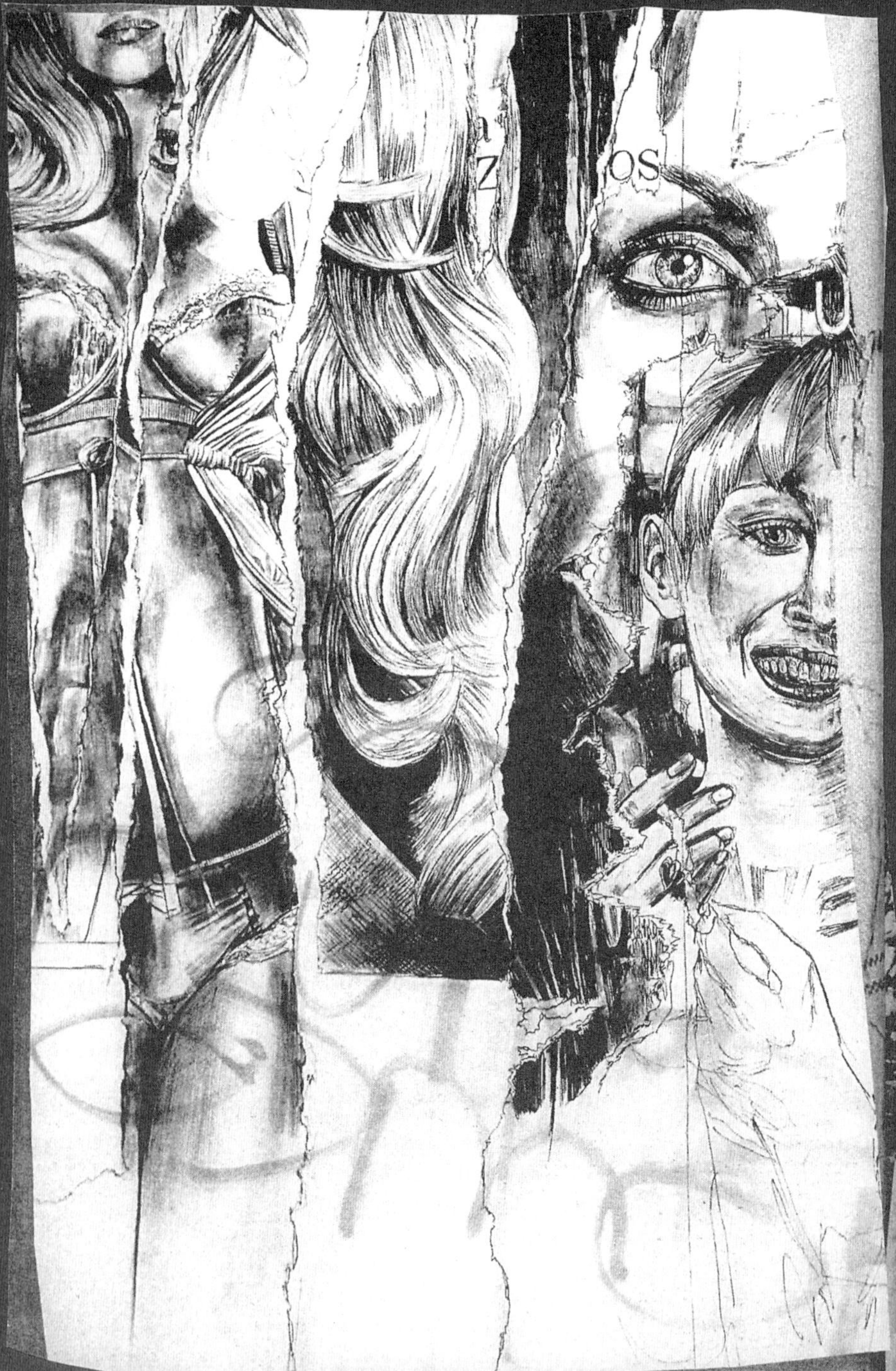

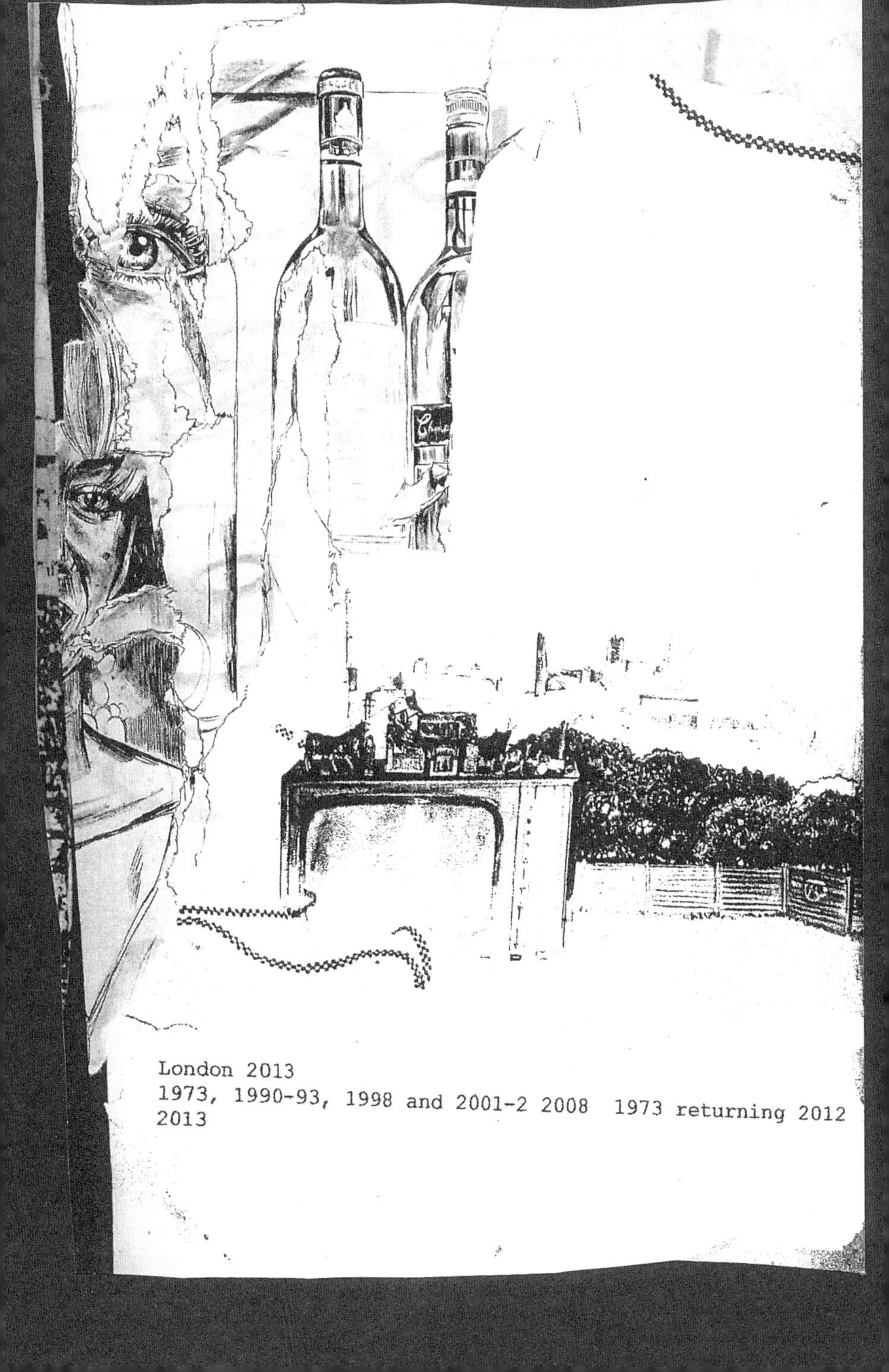

London 2013
1973, 1990-93, 1998 and 2001-2 2008 1973 returning 2012 2013

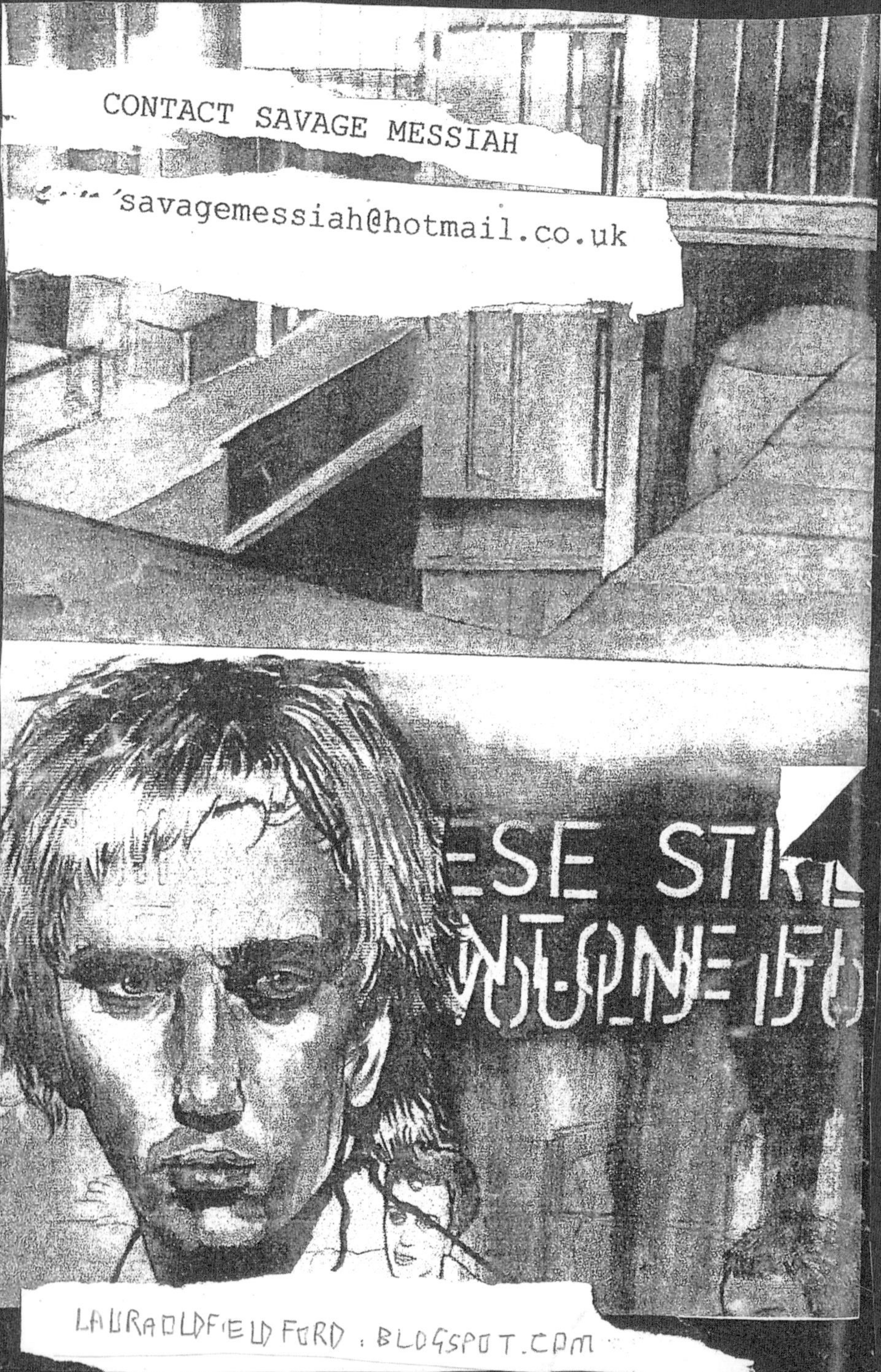
CONTACT SAVAGE MESSIAH
savagemessiah@hotmail.co.uk
LAURAOLDFIELDFORD.BLOGSPOT.COM

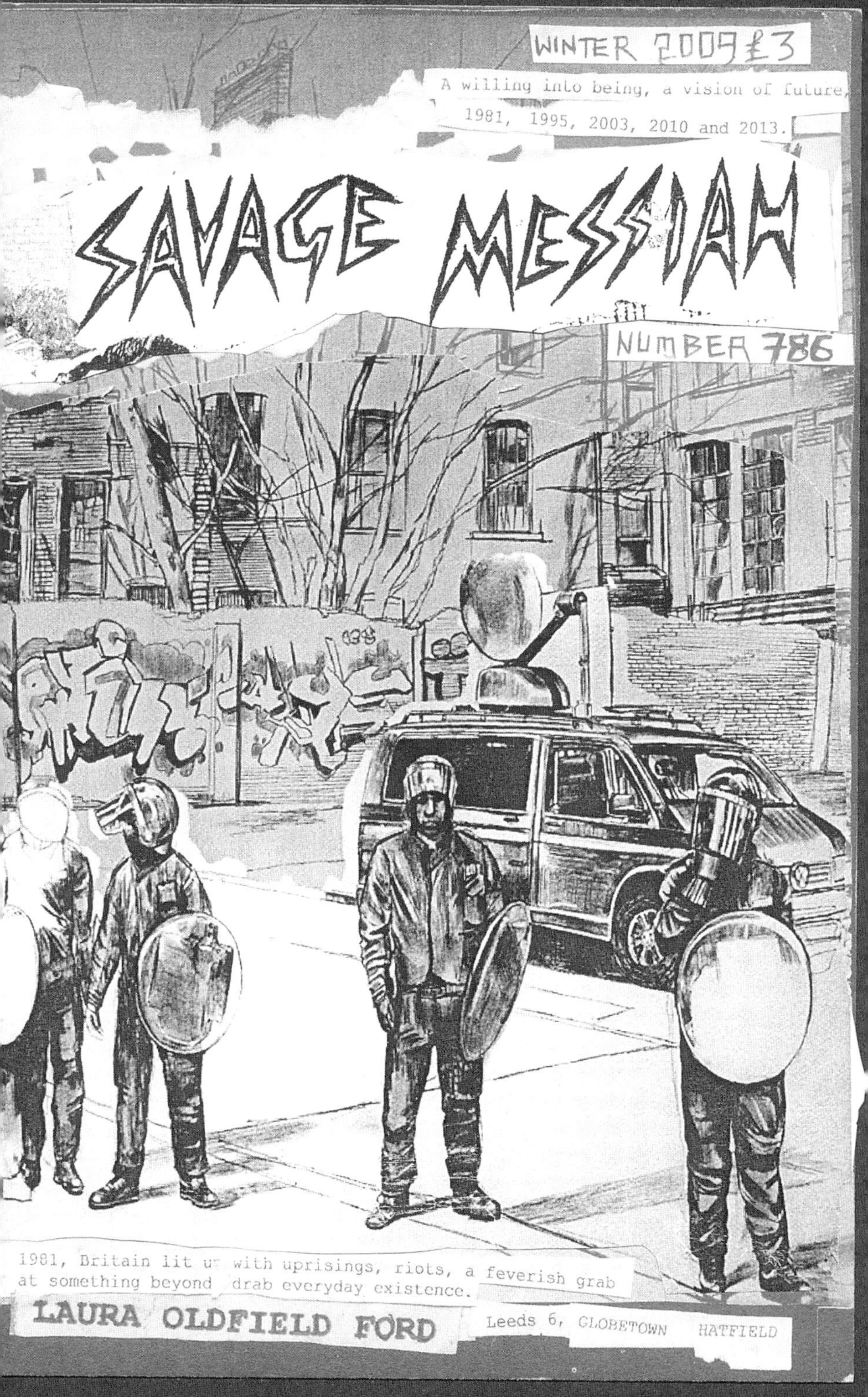
WINTER 2009 £3
A willing into being, a vision of future,
1981, 1995, 2003, 2010 and 2013.
SAVAGE MESSIAH
NUMBER 786
1981, Britain lit up with uprisings, riots, a feverish grab at something beyond drab everyday existence.
LAURA OLDFIELD FORD
Leeds 6, GLOBETOWN HATFIELD

/////FUTURE RIOTS/////

UNDERPASS HATFIELD

DESTRUCTION OF TOWER BLOCKS, DAGENHAM

Radiant Future.

1981.

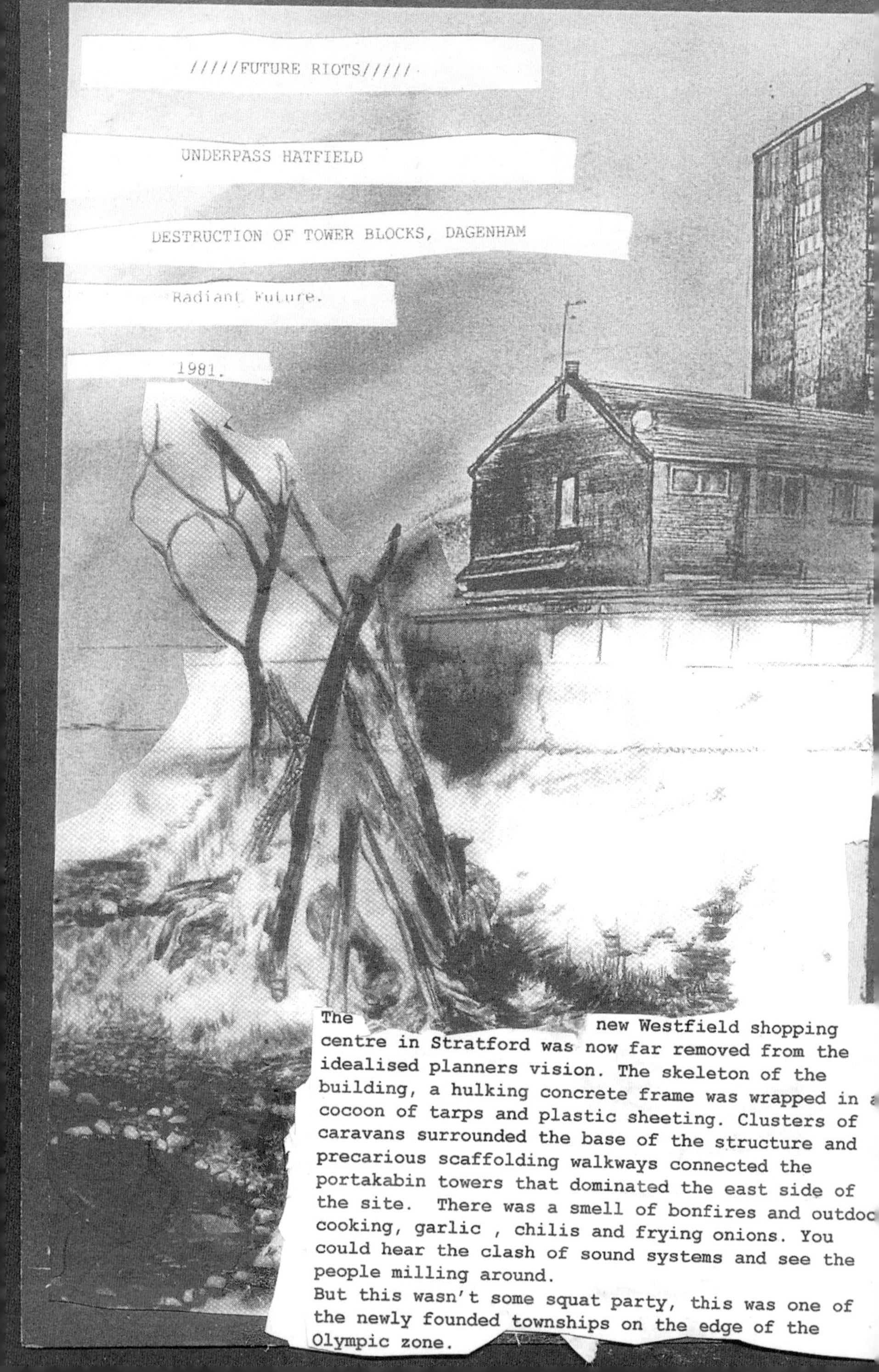

The new Westfield shopping centre in Stratford was now far removed from the idealised planners vision. The skeleton of the building, a hulking concrete frame was wrapped in a cocoon of tarps and plastic sheeting. Clusters of caravans surrounded the base of the structure and precarious scaffolding walkways connected the portakabin towers that dominated the east side of the site. There was a smell of bonfires and outdoo cooking, garlic , chilis and frying onions. You could hear the clash of sound systems and see the people milling around.

But this wasn't some squat party, this was one of the newly founded townships on the edge of the Olympic zone.

SAVAGE MESSIAH NUMBER 786, SPECIAL ISSUE TRACING THE PATHS FROM EAST END TO THE NEW TOWNS, FROM THE RIOT CITIES OF 1981 TO THE FUTURE INSURRECTIONS OF 2010-2013

TWIN FOXES PUB.

MERRION CENTRE.

HARLOW SQUARE CLUB.

MERRION CENTRE LEEDS 1993.
LIVERPOOL GARDEN FESTIVAL 1984.

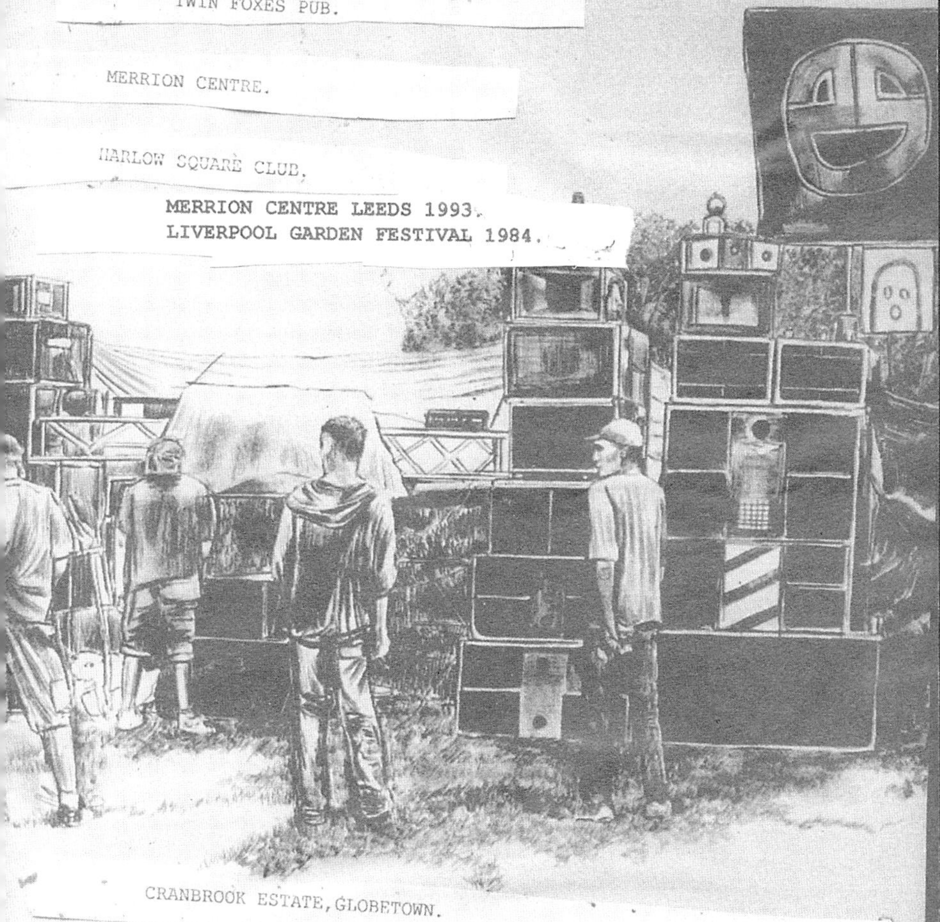

CRANBROOK ESTATE, GLOBETOWN.

THATCHER ON TV, KICKED ACROSS ROOM IN LEEDS6, 1990.

YUPPIEDROMES, NEGATIVE EQUITY GHETTOS LEEDS CITY CENTRE

SEACROFT CENTRE. Abandoned Job centre and rainbow mural stranded in rubble.

That boarded up place I grew up in, that house made my
earliest memories and haunted my dreams still. The ceramic
trinkets in the little glass cabinet, china teacups pink and
gold, the Toby jugs and horse brasses from when they ran the
pub. And the bathroom all pink, the tiles with little roses,
the smell of shampoo and the space helmet hairdryer. And in
the later years, her looking out of the window from a yellow
dreylon settee surrounded by piles of Daily Star and TV
listings magazines. I knew that house, every swirl in the
carpet, pale green and black,
the table with fruit bowl, copies of Woman's Own, remote
controls and sometimes bourbons or a plate of iced fancies.
I made tea looking out on a bare garden punctuated by rocks
and struggling roses, she would say bring that tin of
biscuits and two plates.

And now all that is gone. She is away. Not dead, but
hidden from the world, shrunk back in a diorama of memories
and fictions.
It seemed to just happen at once. But you had to keep going,
a voice came in saying it and saying it, that same voice
that always came and I was never sure if it was mine, or my
Mums or one of the ones who had gone already, that you had
to keep going because there were others who needed you,
others you had to stay for.
I had to find him.

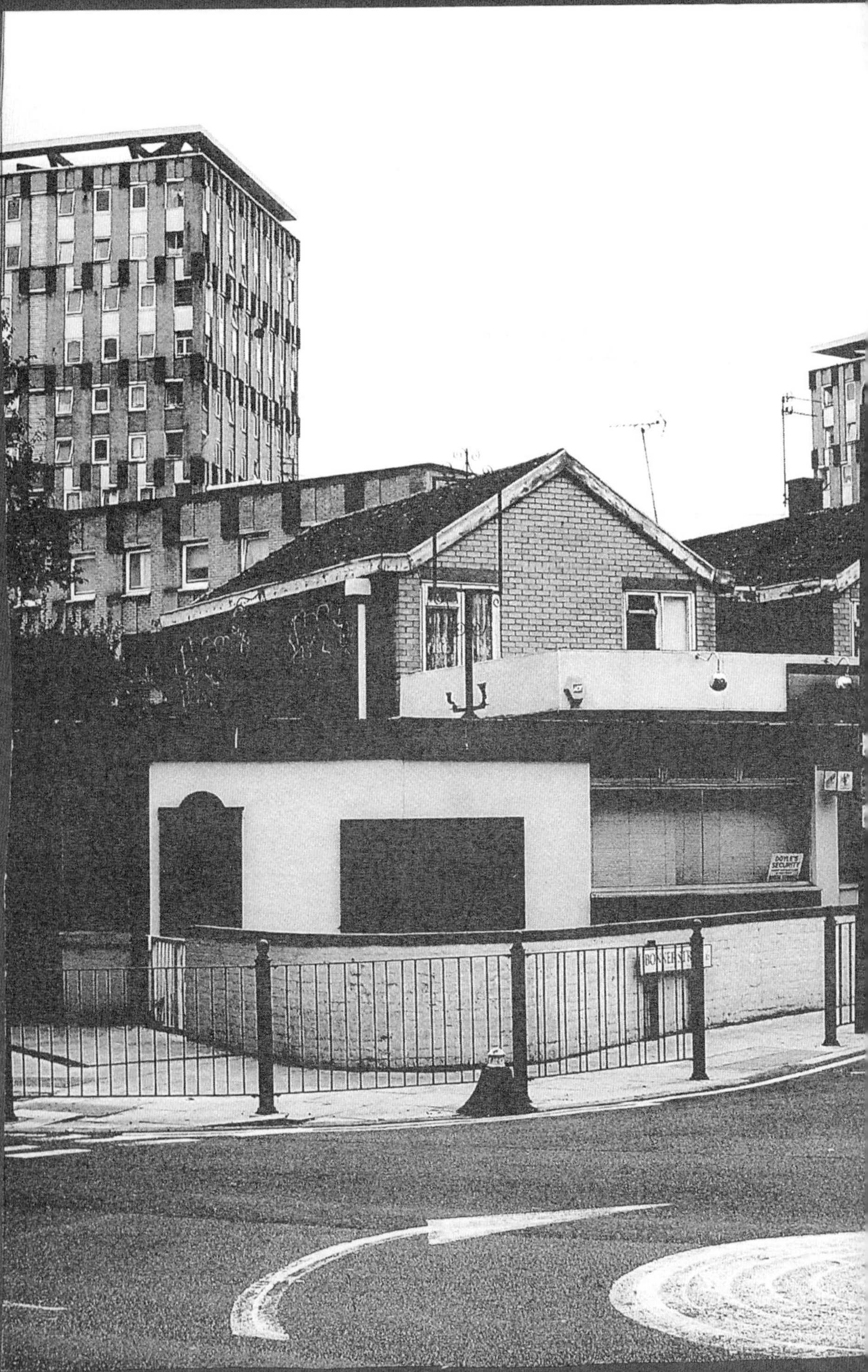
DOYLE'S
SECURITY

2013

Caffeine cuts through the dream murk.
The warm smell of sweet instant coffee. Declan on the
balcony, eyes scanning the courtyards and walkways below.

He hasn't adjusted to the height yet, the old bloke next
door been up here since the 60s and he says you never get
used to it. Its like getting a shock every time you wake up
he says, the view from your bedroom window, it just aint
right somehow.
Declan thinks that he would definitely get used to it given
time, he thinks of himself as someone who can adapt to
anything. He has the capacity, he says to the odd visitor he
takes into the 12th floor flat, to be able to deal with
whatever situation he might face, because he belongs to a
higher, more resilient species. He's thinking of extreme
weather, of drought and famine, the atomic bomb whatever….
I'm combat fit he says one day to a kid eating crisps in the
stairwell. Yeah, I'm ready.
 He has all the books, the SAS survival stuff and the ones
about serial killers on the run and fugitives and survivors
of nuclear warfare. He understands the human psyche.
He keeps the weights and dumb bells behind the door. Declan
is well built, more stocky than athletic but there's no fat
on him, it's all hardened to muscle under his punishing
regime. He takes a pride in it. And the squat up in Alzette
House, that's all part of it, surviving in extreme
situations. He'd found prising off the sitex fairly straight
forward. He'd been to see the old bloke on the landing, the
only tenant left on that floor and he'd spelt it out to him
through the gap in the door. Its security for you having me
here you understand, I'm not gonna be making no noise, you
won't get no bother from me. He showed the old bloke a bag
of power tools, there'll be a bit of racket now for about
ten minutes while I'm getting these tins off but after that
, well I'll invite you round for a cup of tea and it'll be
all nice and civilised. The old bloke, who was probably
about 80 showed no fear of Declan and opened the door to
stand on the landing with him. He wasn't going to turn down
the chance of a chat even if it was to this strange young
lad in military fatigues. At least he had a proper hair cut.
The old boy tapped the sitex with his walking stick, bloody
horrible stuff this he said, makes the estate look terrible.
Declan was glad the bloke wasn't going to go straight to the
council. Much better to take a risk and engage them first,
get them on side. Tell you what, Declan said, you could help
me out here.

2009.On the Ocean Estate there were Polish squatters being evicted by Polish baillifs. A lot of the local Sylheti community said they didn't like the squatters, they said they were a nuisance , making the whole estate look bad. My mate Joyce showed them photos of Sylheti squatters in Fieldgate street in the 1970s.

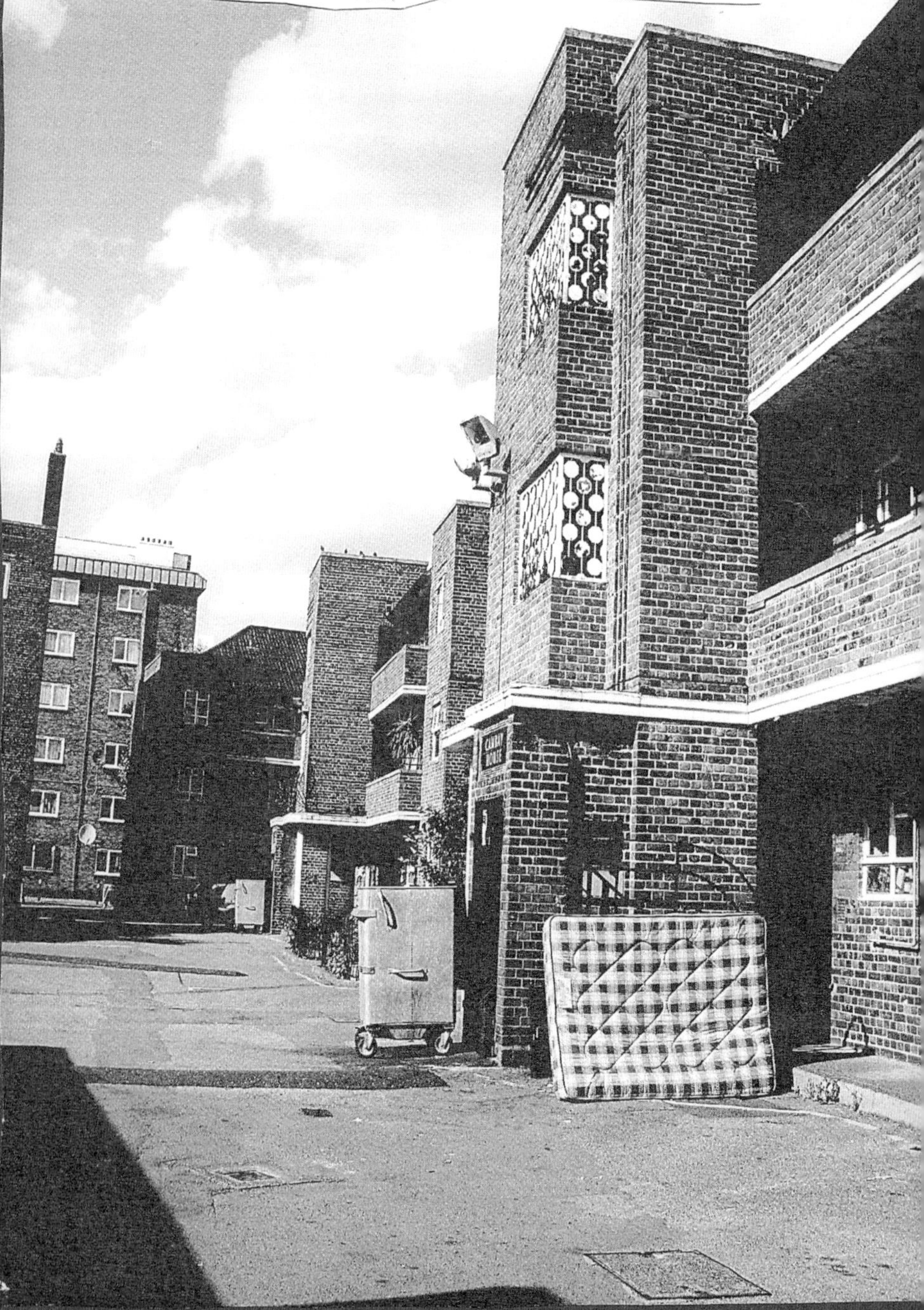

1981, Britain lit up with uprisings, riots, a feverish grab
at something beyond drab everyday existence. Time out of
joint. The summer of 1981 seized by a warped temporality,
an attenuated present.
Because suddenly in the blazing heat, out of the scorched
landscape came a sense of urgency. 1995, 2003, 2010 and
2013. I stood out , silhouetted before those blazing
bonfires, cut out of a bleached landscape. It had always
seemed dark til then, the terraces black, except for the
pink neon in the Asian video shops and the frosty spans of
red and gold through pub windows at Christmas. Always the
darkness in our towns until they blazed bright orange
against blue skies for those glorious days.

1981. 1990. 1999.
 Not old then, and nothing to lose, thinking it lost
already. The greasy flat in Leeds 6, the other bedsit in
Bradford. The mates already down South, me ready to go, sick
of Yorkshire, packed for London not knowing it was more of
the same, same shit peeling walls and cockroaches, rats
squealing in the bins. Me thinking it's all glamour and
money down there. Me not knowing the darkness going there
with me.
1981, Leeds, darkness shattered by this hot weather, a
summer of a thousand Julys. Me laughing with the rest of
them behind the fires with the houses scorched around the
edges. Me thinking I'll have the last laugh with Yorkshire
before the case in the hall gets dragged out and I leave it
forever.

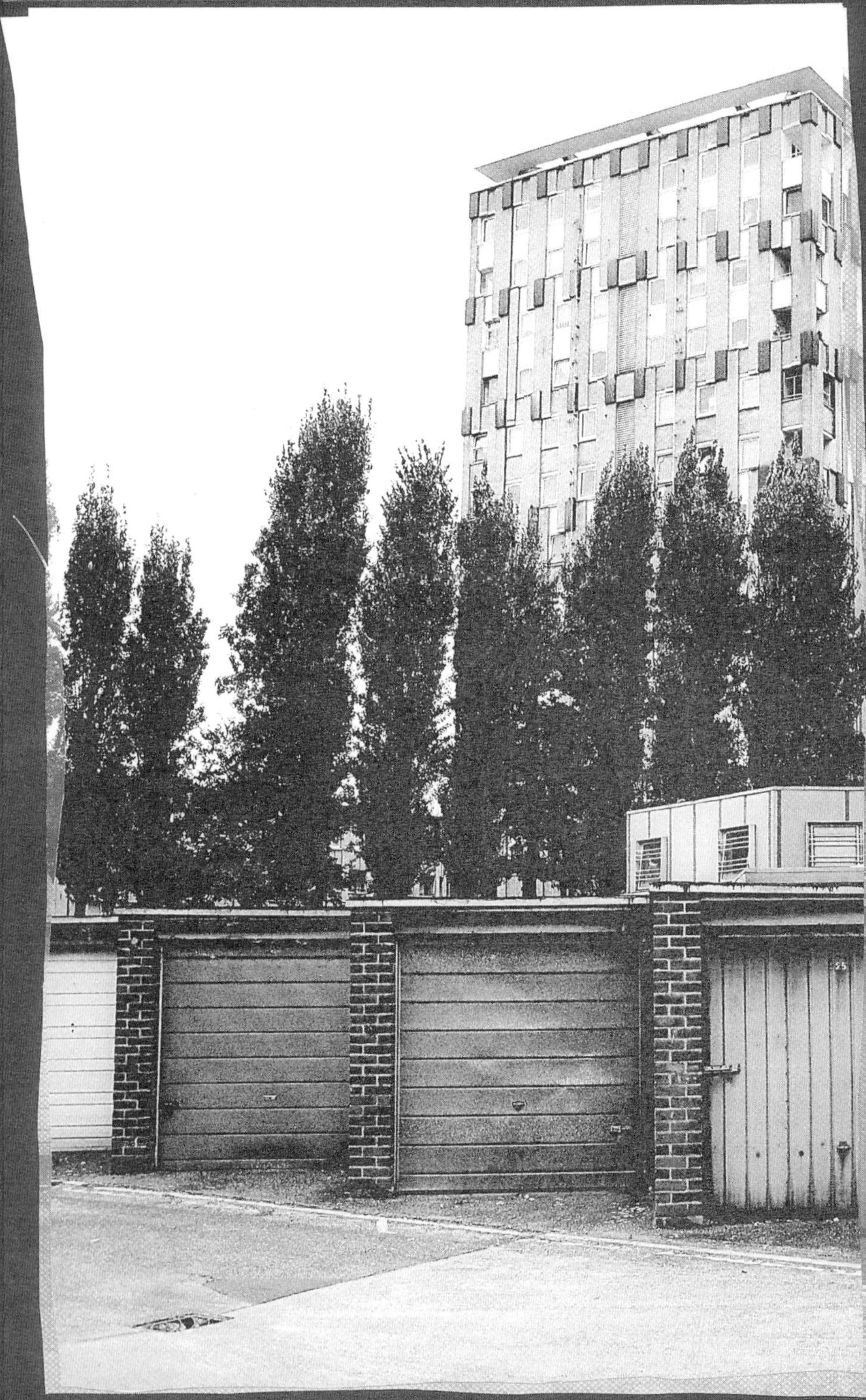

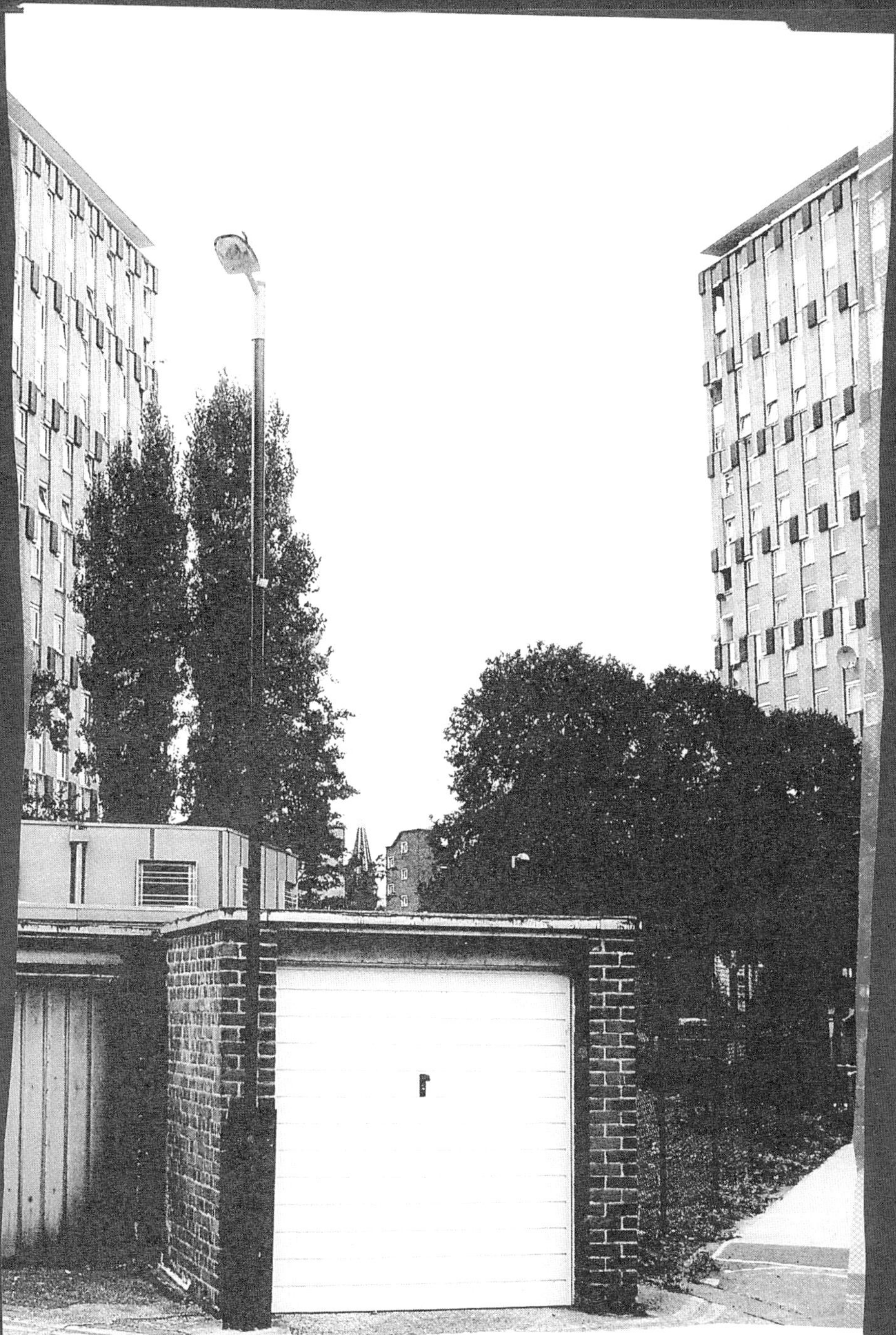

I leapt up and fled the peevish stink of the dole office . The exhilaration, the sense of unbridled freedom propelled me down Mare street, across Victoria Park and over the footbridge to Hackney Wick.

Last day of April. He remembers , some vague remnant, a
trace of the old Hatfield shopping precinct off Dog Kennel
Lane. A hidden zone, out of time and beyond the city limits,
it wasn't London. It felt like something that might have
happened after the future war. The arcades were semi
derelict, mostly boarded up. The others appeared desolate
beneath the florescent strip lights, a cloying stench of
detergent and bleach, then the luminous flare up of the last
99p shop.

Beyond it , the suburban gardens of Hatfield. Genteel
abandonment, plastic plant pots full of cobwebs, willowherb
and convolvulus. A greenhouse leaning precipitously over a
crumbling brick wall. He picked up conkers from the
chestnut tree above, to plant in pots on the balconies of
Graham Road and Kent Street. A continuation of a memento
mori, a symbolic return.
 This place shall follow me

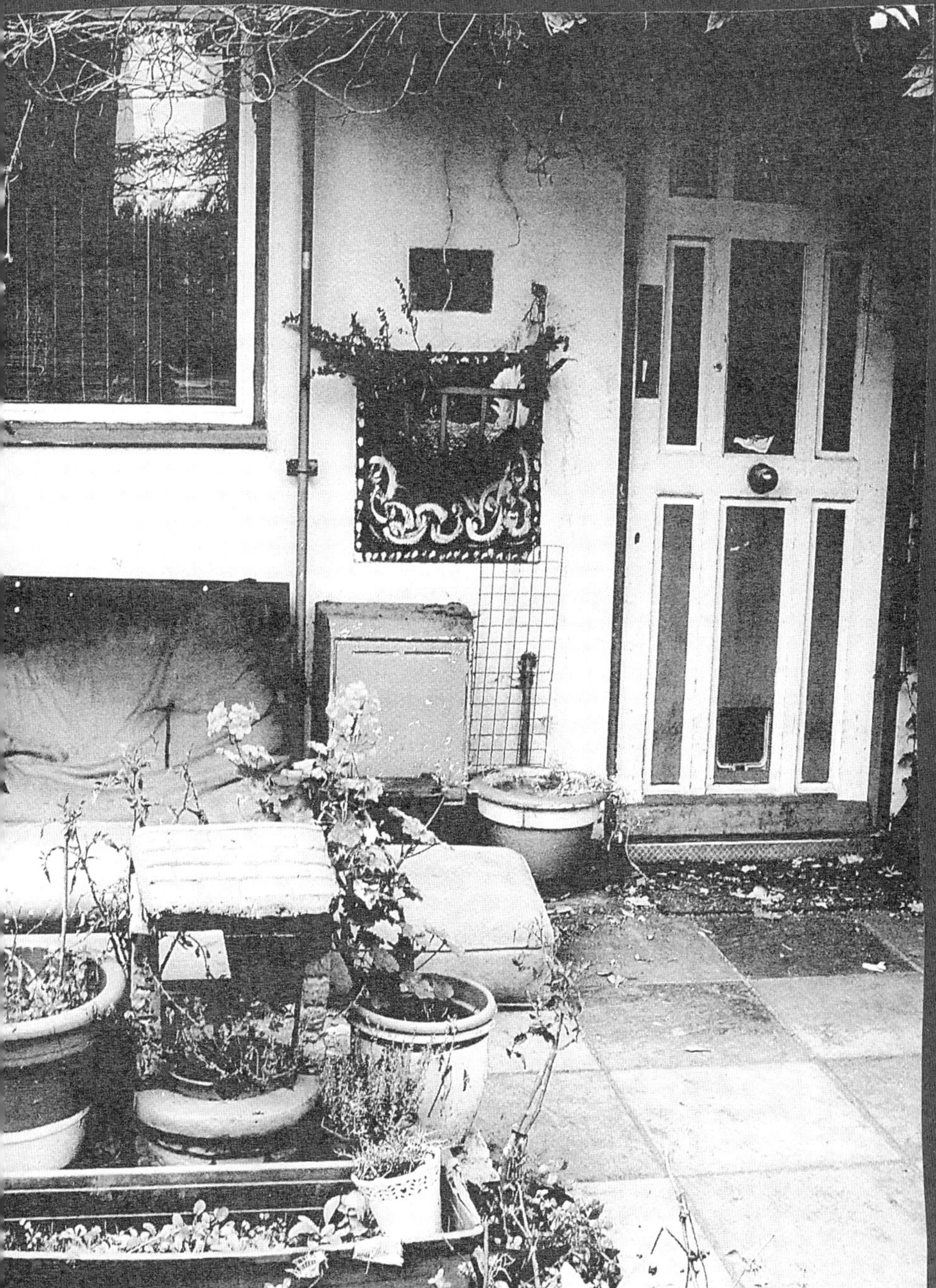

I cross the park, there's really cold wind getting up and
nowhere to call in really, lost most of me contacts on the
Cranbrook. I did know some bloke, Simon his name was, right
freak, burnt himself out of his own flat in Stubbs House to
get rehoused. They moved him up to the Ocean, one of the
punishement blocks there. Could call there maybe, on the off
chance, bit of a cold call, aint seen the cunt since, fuck
must be six years. Probably moved years back; brother went
nuts ended up in st clements the loony bin in Bow.
I get to Mile End road, swing down White Horse Lane and head
straight over to Atlantic House. I remember which one his
flat was from when I went round there for a smoke one time
with his mad brother going on about it being the number 23
writing all this psychick Tv stuff all over the door .
They'd probably got rid of all his demented daubings but I
did remember the 23.
When I get up the stairwell all the double crosses have gone
but there's little drawings in felt tip of Mickey mouse
smoking a spliff an a ganja leaf. I doubted he lived there
now. I get to the landing and there's a pink lightbulb and
coloured fairylights, more of a birds place it looks,or a
knocking shop. I knock hard through the iron security gate,
he was always a paranoid cunt and then there he is same
weird oval face, no eyelashes no fucking hair, souped up
Duncan Goodhew. He looks a bit jumpy, but that was always
his way, alright mate, long time, thought I'd drop by and
see you, see how yer getting on. He don't unlock the gate,
I aint getting in. I can hear a woman's voice.
Sorry mate, not a good time he says. I'm getting the brush
off, Good to se you though mate, he moves back to shut the
door. Can I just come in and have a glass of water then,
I've been walking miles, me medication an'all, i..
Sorry mate he says again. Can I just have a fag then, you..
The cunt shuts the door in my face.
I take that kind of shit personal. Now I don't like that,
him giving me the brush off cos he's got a bird installed
and a nice little gaff and suddenly thinks he's too good for
the rest of us, fuck that, I decided there and then I'd
bring him down if it's the last thing I do, he shouldn't
have messed with me like that, I resolved right there to get
the bastard back. I go down the stairwell shouting about
him being a liar and a devious cunt cos that's what everyone
knew he was, and I stand in the bin yard and have a slash
and look up at the pink window . I can see him chatting with
some morose looking bird with her hair stretched back in a
bun. Bony little tart. I see him scanning out briefly but he
doesn't look right down. I'll burn you out again, you mark
it! I look around the yard and find a chunk of breeze block
and go up and put his window through. I'm down the stairs
and out the other side of the estate before the wanker's
even got the fucking gate undone.

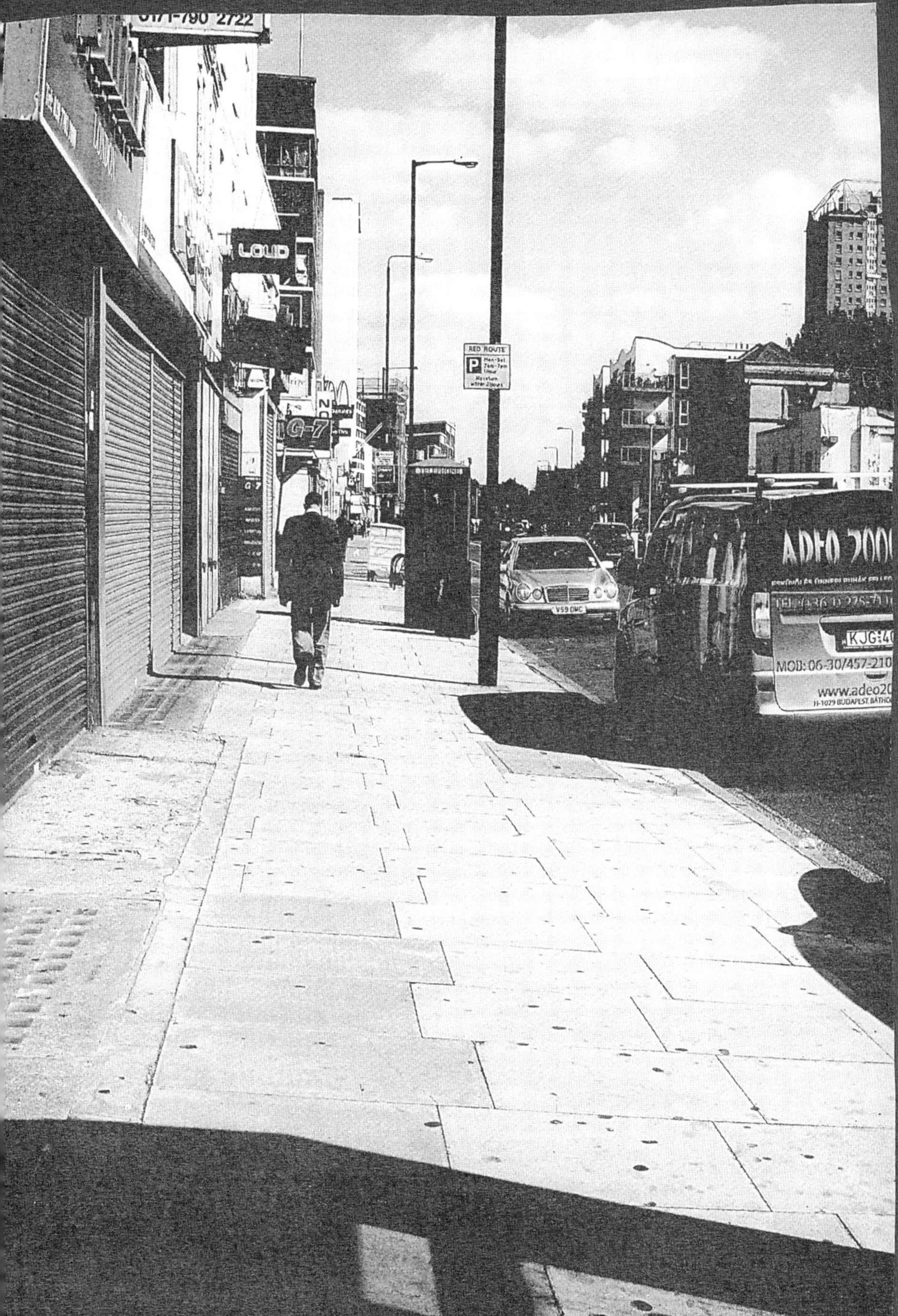
0171-790 2722
LOUD
G-7
RED ROUTE

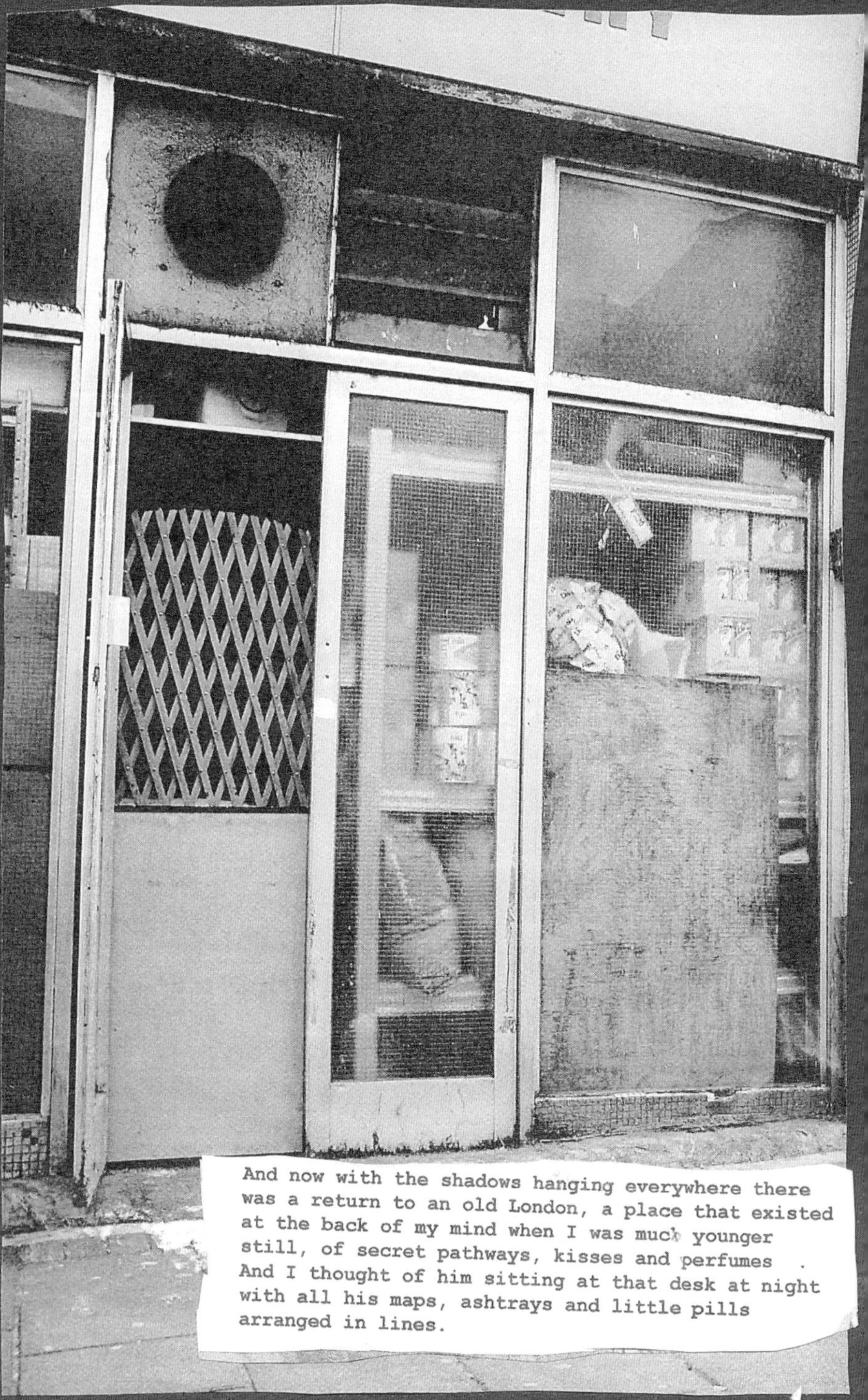
And now with the shadows hanging everywhere there was a return to an old London, a place that existed at the back of my mind when I was much younger still, of secret pathways, kisses and perfumes . And I thought of him sitting at that desk at night with all his maps, ashtrays and little pills arranged in lines.

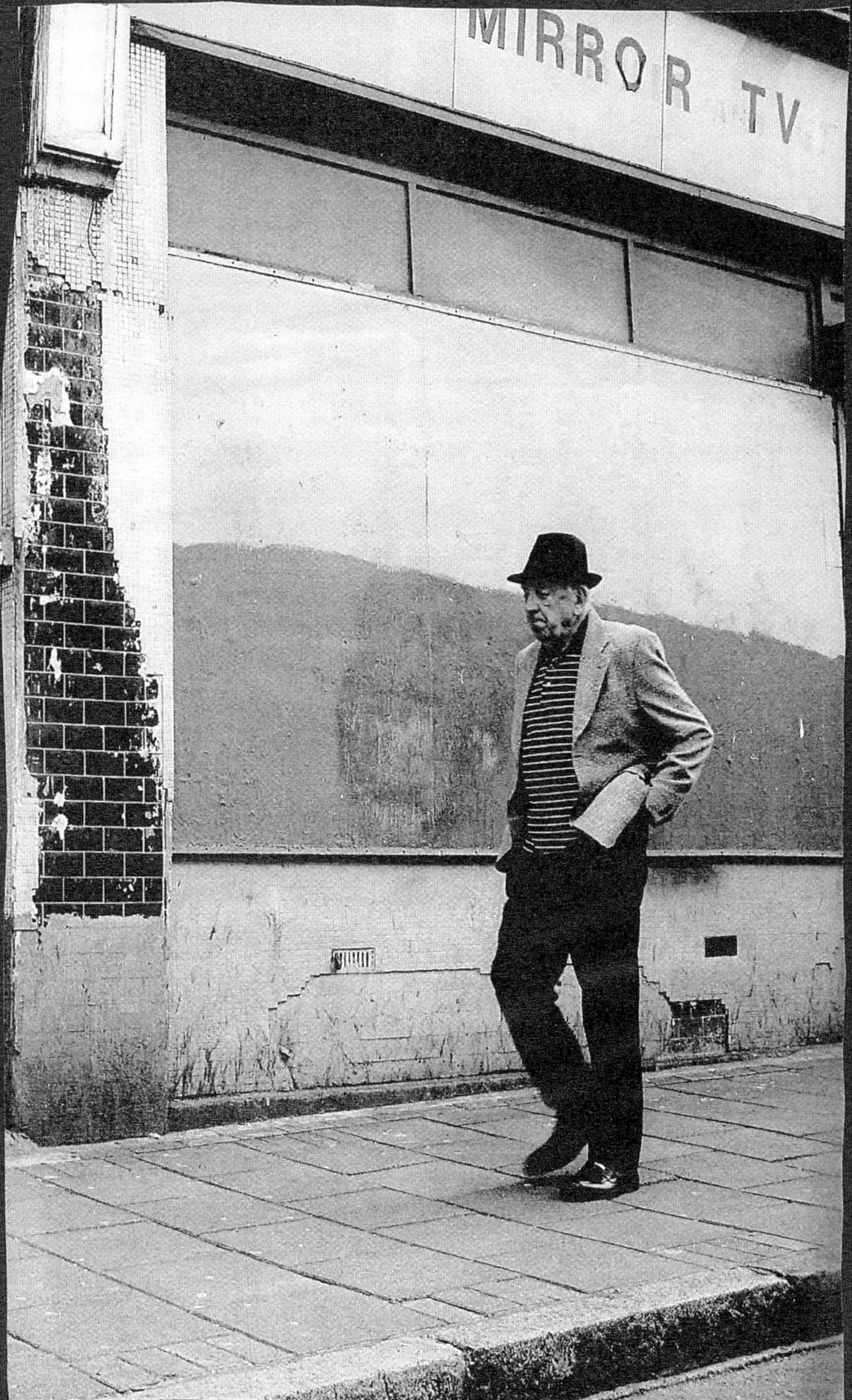
MIRROR TV

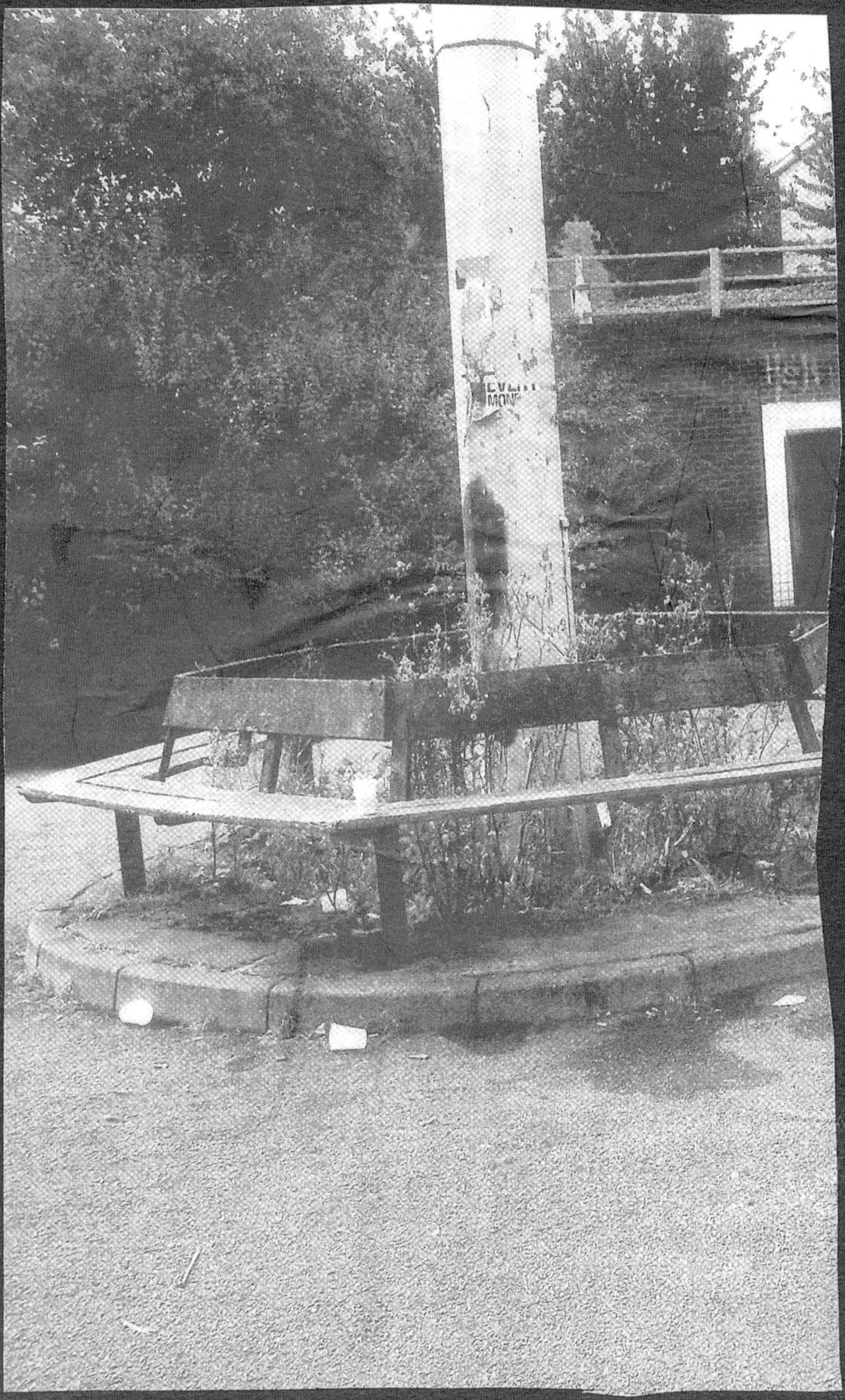

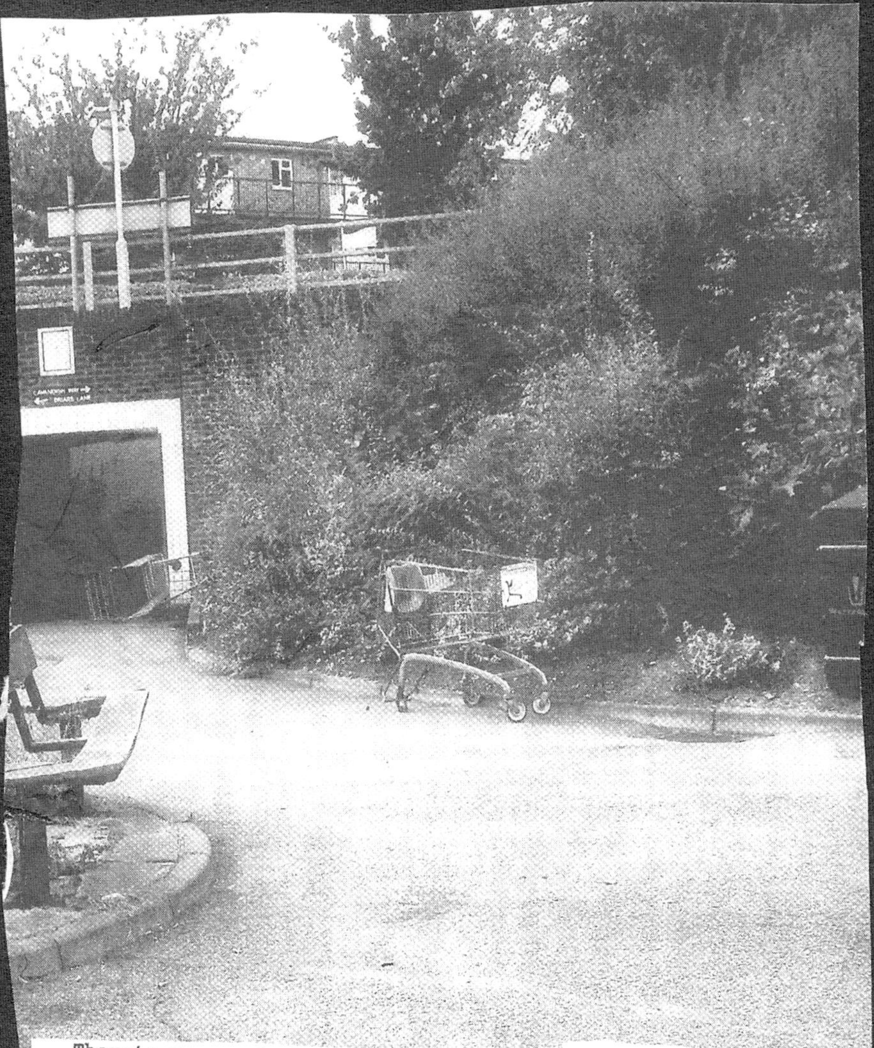

There's no angels heralding the next epoch, it's just us as the swarming underclass, the surplus people animated round fires lighting up the tawdry streets. It's coming. The next epoch.
To some it's too late.
To us just the start.
Leeds 6, dirty, violent. Attacked in phone boxes, transit vans crawling slowly up and down Quarry Street eyeing up chances to rob houses.
Leeds 7. Harehills, Chapeltown, rows of redbrick back to backs, washing spanning the streets, fires lighting up the night, milk bottles out front, sirens and plumes of black smoke.
St Pauls, Moss Side, Toxteth.

spring 1980 - *St Paul's riots.April 2, 1980,disturbance so serious that its repercussions were felt throughout the whole country.The spark which ignited the riot was a police raid on the now demolished Black and White cafe resentment black= second-class citizen/.*

Bristol St Pauls. It all going up Like Leeds, Dalston, Brixton, the whole lot, Market Harborough, Knaresborough, Kettering, erupting in flames.

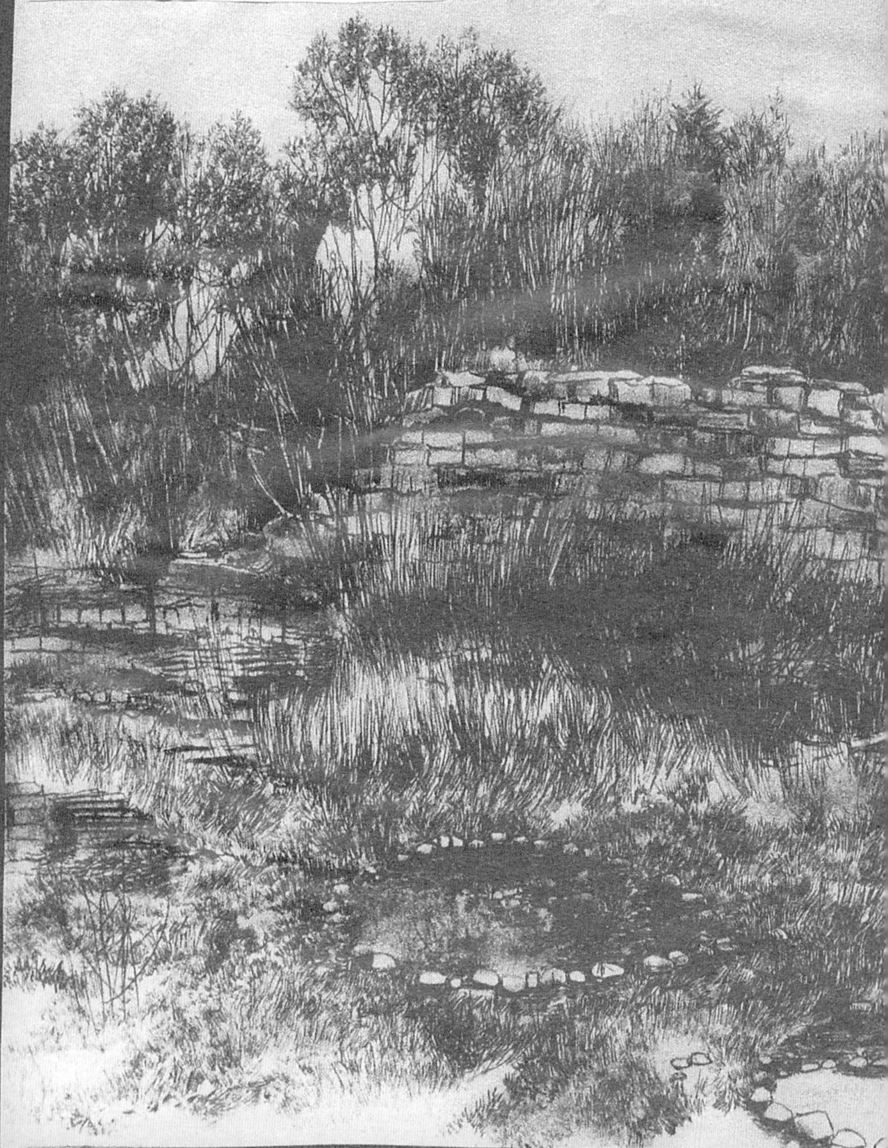

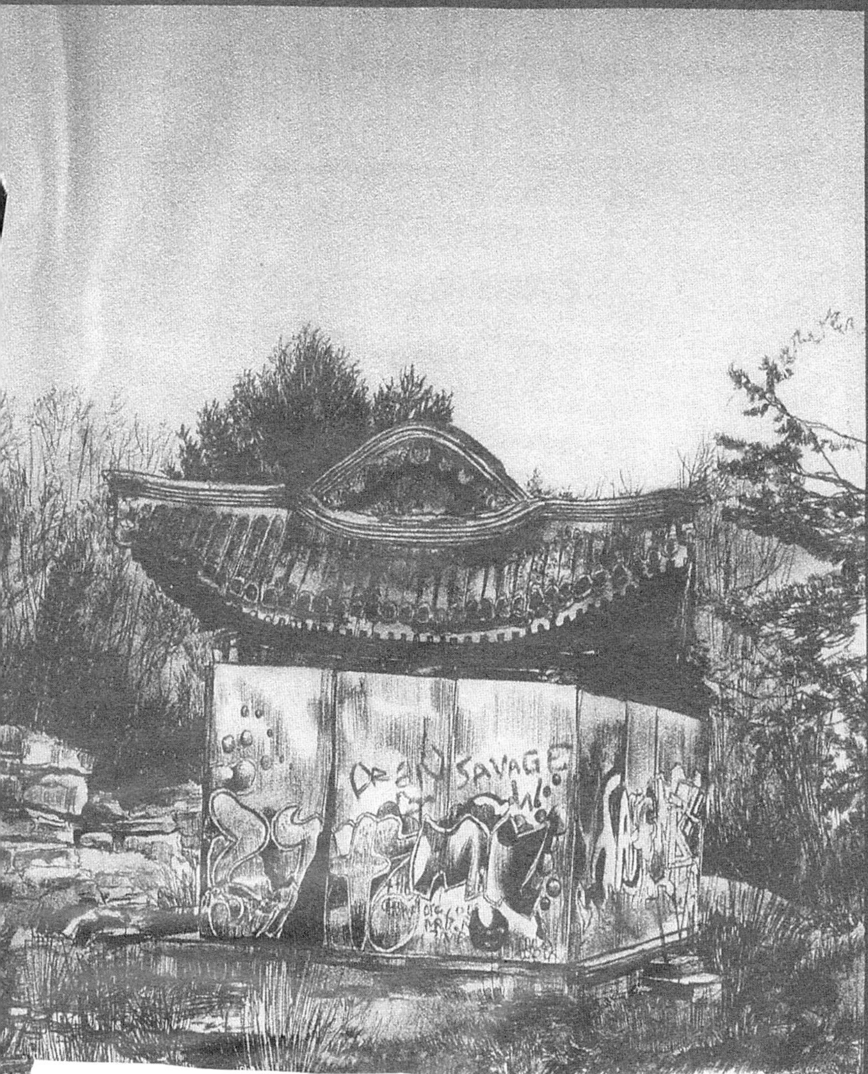

LIVERPOOL GARDEN FESTIVAL.
Many inner city areas were subjected to urban renewal schemes as a direct result of social unrest with Toxteth and the subsequent Liverpool garden festival being an obvious example. Heseltine, flak jacket and public school sneer, a forerunner of the Blairites. Second wave of pit closures 1994, HESELTINE YOU RICH TORY SCUMBAG, WE'LL GET YOU. Urban regeneration was a crude attempt to 'design out dissent.

Heseltine's patronsing, crayola box villages emerged in the rubble and detritius of the demolished slums.

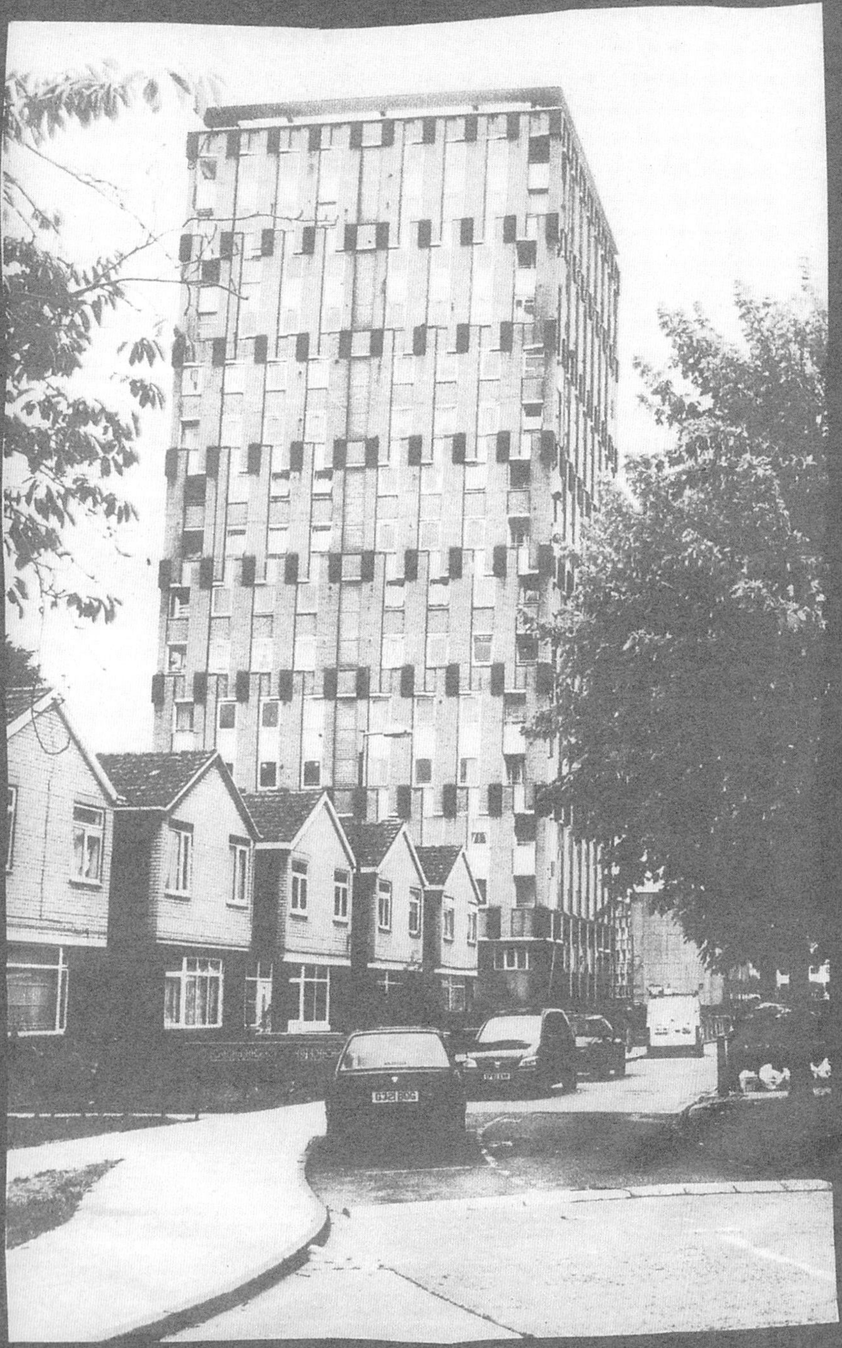

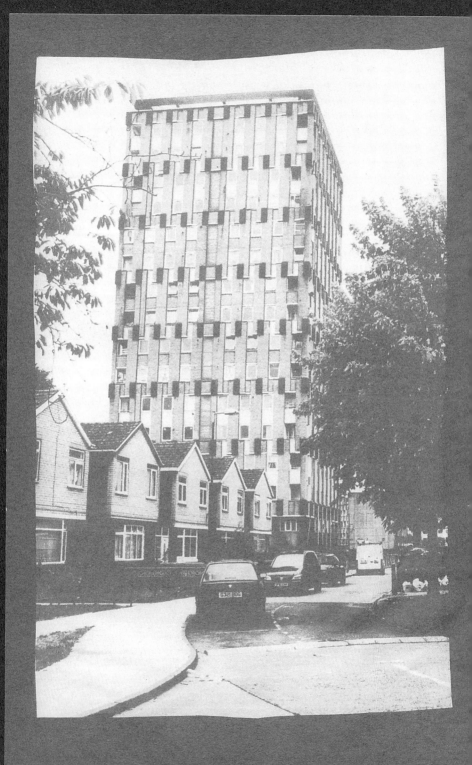

Yesterday 777 cropped up about 7 times.

May 30th 2008.
Clown Step, the interior landscape of a diseased mind. War damage//slum clearance. Screech bassline, swing beat. Horror movie aesthetics, nightmares of a five year old. Cartoons, repetition, fear, anxiety, hysteria. A venture into the darkness, unknown territories, corridors that run ceaselessly into maze like structures, inescapable and terrifying.

Cranbrooke Estate, Lubetkin showpiece unveiled in 1959, precast concrete ,abstract facades, Constructivist staircases.
As the years have elapsed it no longer seems futuristic but is imbued with memories, markings and histories. It has become part of London's past. Within the grid like structures of the large estates hidden pathways have been carved, the labyrinth has reasserted itself.

Right to Buy has filled the estate with absentee landlords cramming three families into one flat. All the pubs are closed.

Houses bombed, clearance programmes to reduce the population density . 5000 people lived in temporary housing, requisitioned properties, hutments/mobile homes,/prefabs . Old Ford and Roman roads, terraced houses, workshops and one large factory cleared…

Rookeries and slums cleared middle of 19th century to make way for the big railway stations, the poor pogrommed out of the area, displaced to the East end.

East End devastated by bomb damage. Inter-war migration Becontree Harold Hill, then the New Towns.

The East End and docks were 'Target Area A'. Between 7 September 1940 and 10 May 1941, a sustained bombing campaign, 57 nights, 'the Blitz'.
The authorities wouldn't open the London Underground for shelter, wanted to maintain an appearance of everything carrying on as normal. After sustained bombing in September East End people seized the initiative and broke into tube stations with blankets..

Maybe walk back up Hackney road, got to think about tonight, getting driven mad with that hostel, all those idiots doing my nut in. I'm thinking maybe enough time has passed to risk Denise again. She always took me in eventually, needed the hostel place though, never give up your independence, that's what I think , men and women should never live together. I had to get out last time she was doing my head in, laying down the law, giving me shit about who I was hanging round with, can't stand that in a woman, stupid bitch was on at me all the fucking time. Last straw was when Karen phoned the house, silly cow actually spoke to Denise, it all went off, Denise went fucking mad, put on a right show in the street. She's obsessed with those horrible TV programmes with hysterical morons shrieking and preaching. So here I was on the receiving end of an Americanised tongue lashing in the front of the whole fucking estate, that was quite bad but still it was down in Battersea, not my manor, I could limp away from that. The question was now, could I face going back? It's a long way to get to when your feet are fucked. I thought about it, could get the bus from Liverpool street, had enough for a fare and a couple of tins for the way, I'd be shafted if she wasn't having it though. I decided to risk it, fuck it I had more to gain than lose, it would kill a few hours whatever.

The bus crossed the river, Southwark bridge and the alleys of the Borough, down through the Elephant, past the old Park Hotel derelict now and that shithole Liam Ogs where I got barred for dealing, long time now though, six years maybe but I wouldn't bother trying to get back in.

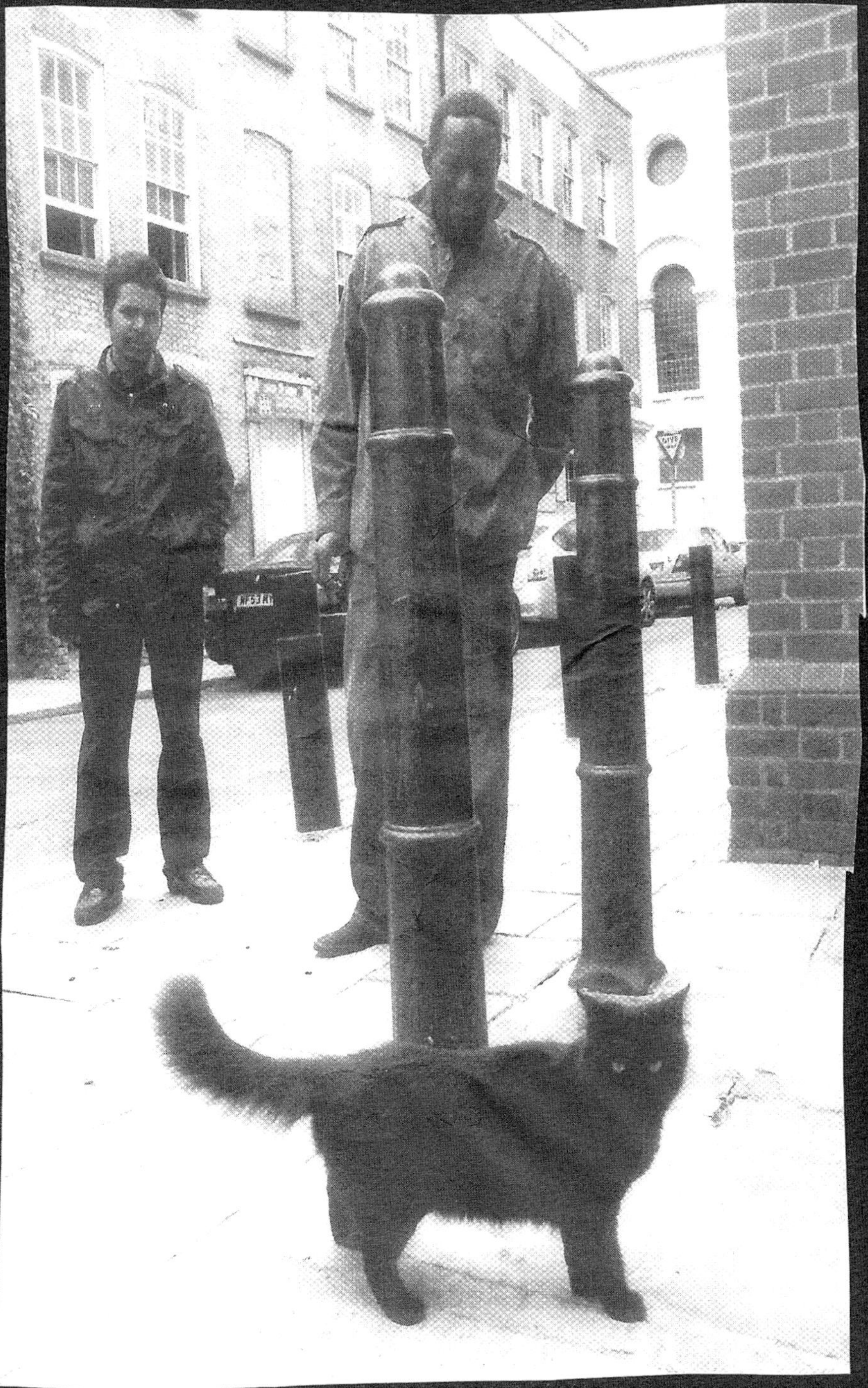

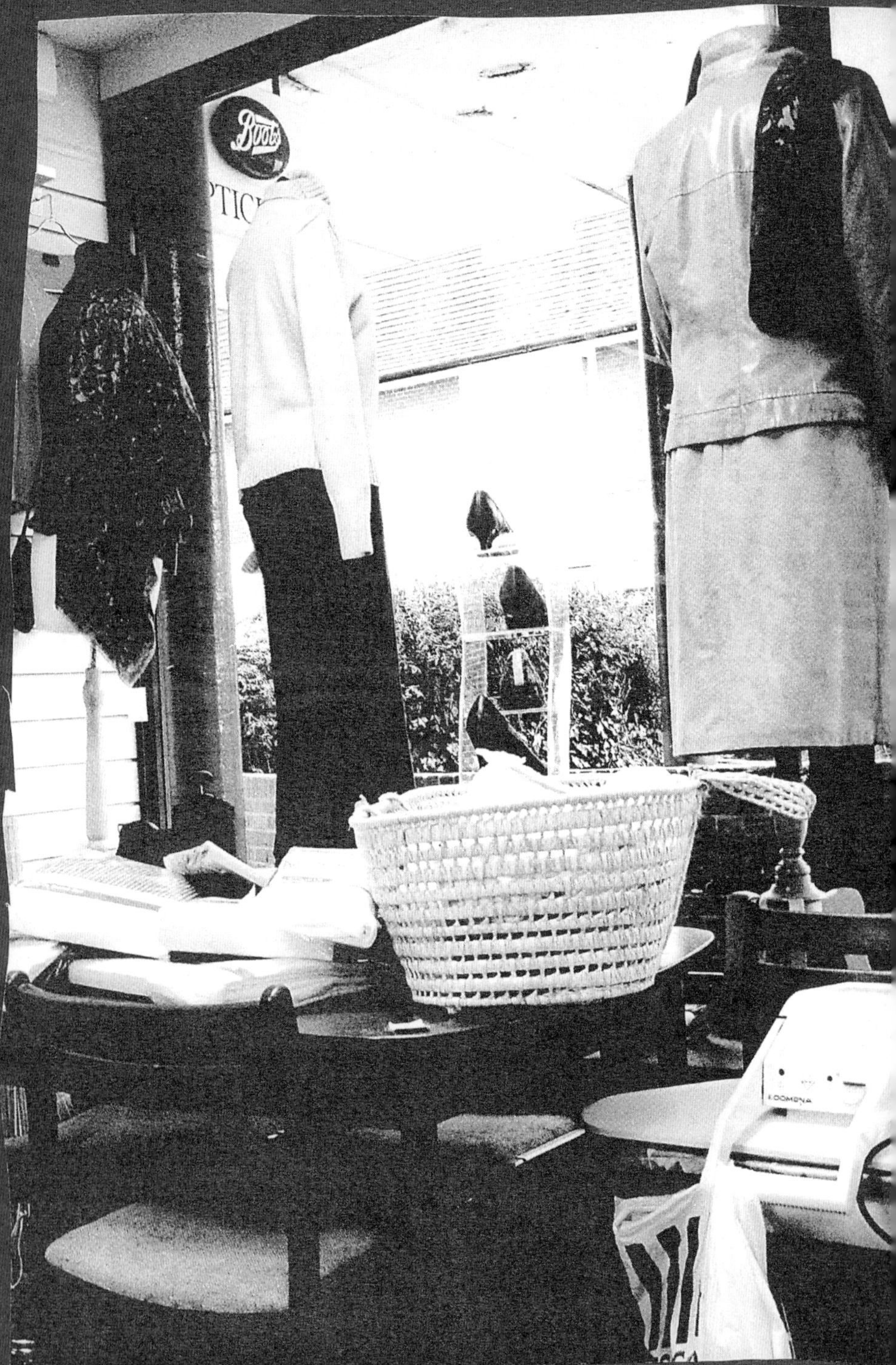
Boots

I was working in a day centre on the Roman, helping Joan
organise the clothes for next Saturdays jumble sale. We went
over to her flat in Offenbach house to collect some more
bags. I paused to look at a striking couple on the
mantelpiece, a blonde and a handsome dark haired youth.
Joan picks up the photo. Her sister and her husband just
after they got married. Passed away five years ago in a care
home in Basildon. She missed Bethnal green so much, talked
about it all the time but it might as well have been on the
other side of the world for all she got to see of it. Joan
puts the photo back and starts sifting through some black
bags. She was never suited to that move to the new town,
never lived outside Bethnal green before that and ended up
there where she didn't know a soul. The streets were eerie
quiet there not like the clatter and din round here.
She takes me in the other room, opens the wardrobe. She kept
all these, treasured them. There were beautiful dresses,
pencil skirts and a pink mohair sweater. Joan looks sad,
she used to wear that a lot.

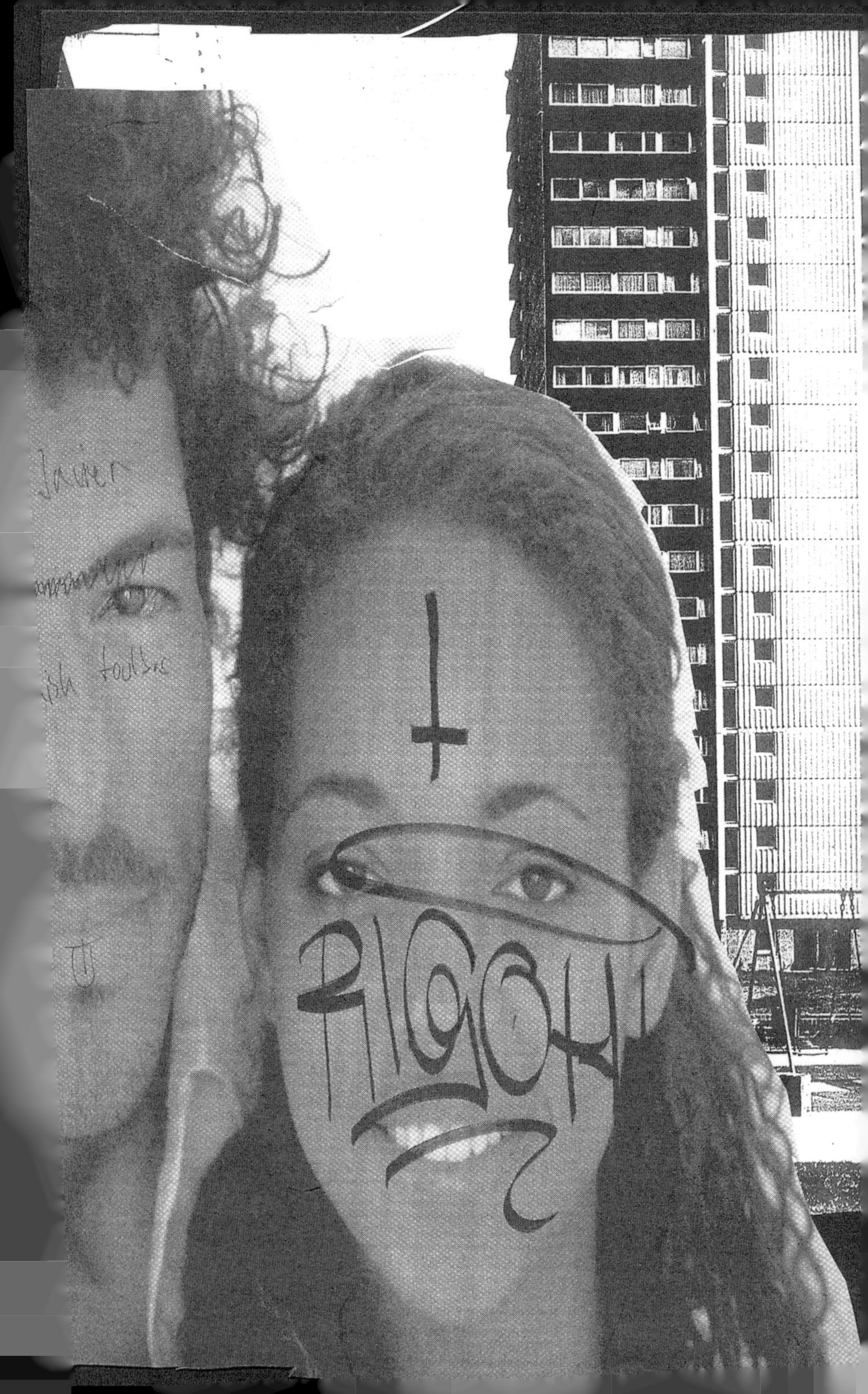

The pub on the corner of Bonner Street and Old Ford road has been left abandoned. Once it was City of Paris, then Habana's wine bar , now it's boarded up with planning application to turn it into 'Viki Park Wines'.
Soon everybody will drinking at home in front of flat screen tvs.

From the shifting communities of Tower Hamlets massive developments in the city of Sylhet are paid for by ex pats. In Bethnal Green, Whitechapel and Bow there are launderettes, shops and restaurants named as reminders. In Sylhet there are shopping malls and supermarkets called Tessco, Blue Water and London Fried Chicken.

Overcrowding in Tower hamlets. The Ocean estate. 'Squat the lot. Take it back.' That's what the graffiti said then and I'm saying it again now. I want to see whole estates squatted, like the ones near Chrisp Street market and Bow Common lane. When people are saying, I'm defaulting, I've had my housing benefit stopped, I can't pay the rent, estates should be barricaded and organised to stop the bailiffs.

2nd phase July,1981 swept entire country. Wednesday night,
rumours buzzing round it's kicking off in Dalston. Various
trouble makers, Duncan terrace, sweeping Camden in search of
people i knew. I heard the stories , went down there,
Wednesday night, met outside the Rio, there was a load of
SWP there with the paper,so I'm thinking boring Trot demo
and disappeared off to Hackney town hall where I'd heard
there might be stuff kicking off. Got there but nothing much
doing apart from a few locals hanging about looking for
something. Went back to the Rio feeling fucked off by then
but then found loads of black kids on Kingsland Road
looting a jewellery shop. They'd gone to Downs estate, to
the field at back, divided the loot, ended up surrounded by
old bill and got nicked. Friday whole country went up,
clocked off early, changed mind about Brixton and went up
Kingsland High Rd where every shop was smashed and looted.
It was late afternoon and all alarms were going off, crowds
of people everywhere, then streets empty as police came in
and cleared them. Then a riot started in Shacklewell, all
kinds of people involved, white and black, heavy, sporadic,
proper petrol bombs. Me and four others got isolated in
Shacklewell lane, whole coach of police piled out straight
into us, four of us facing 40 cops and they weren't looking
for arrests. I got my head split open .
 Went to cop shop, Stokey nick, guarded by specials with
dogs, bricks and bars at police vehicle, but I was out on
the streets next day, patched up.

 Brixton paramedic training, straight down Dalston in
 evening, this was Saturday, mate thrown through plate glass
 window by fascists.
 Black geezers looking for a load of fascists down towards
 Hoxton.
 Riots everywhere,even places like Keswick, little towns
 everywhere, hardly anything in the papers, but it was all
 buzzing round, word of mouth.

On Sunday I was meant to be going down to Brixton. The NF
were supposed to be gathering down Chapel street market.
There were rumours going round that they were going to burn
out squatters. We had an HQ in Duncan terrace. There were
things like that going on all the time around then, sporadic
things, but Friday night was the main night.

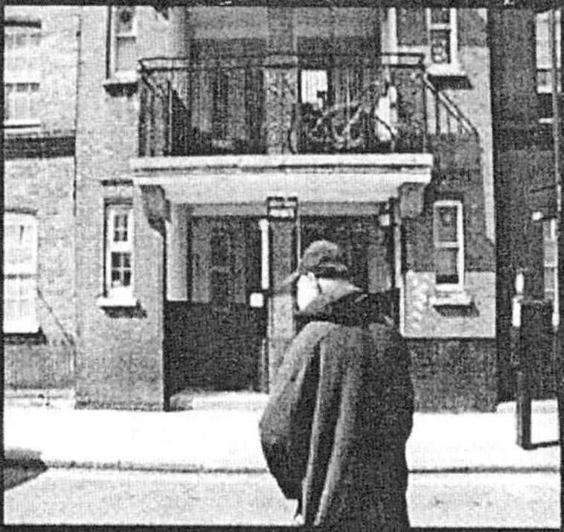
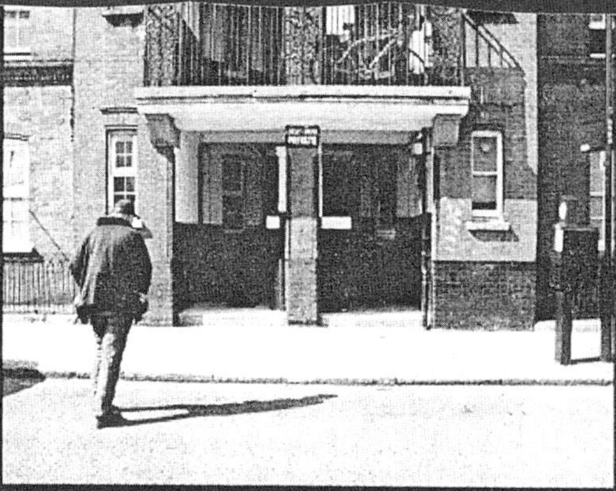
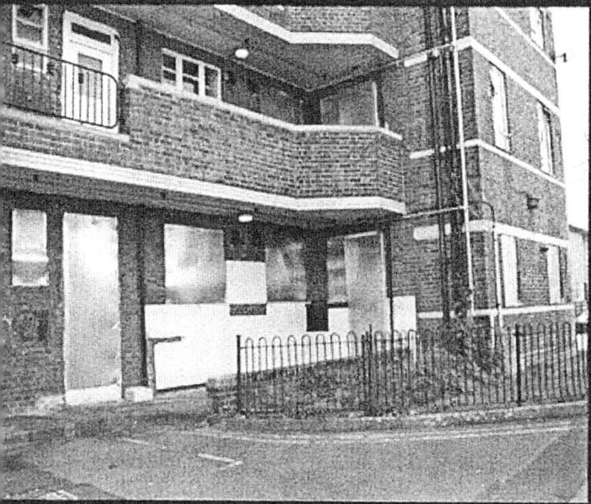
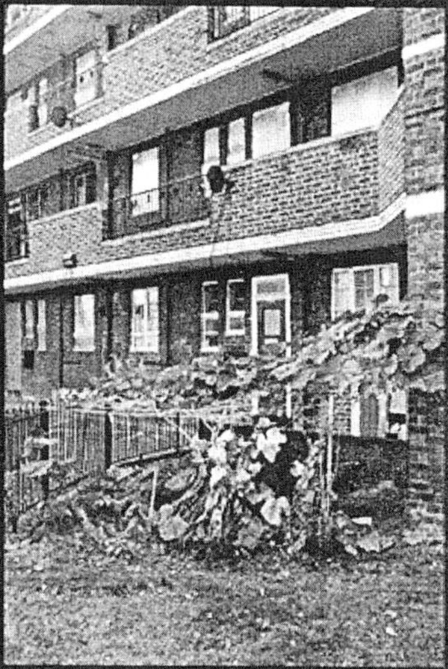
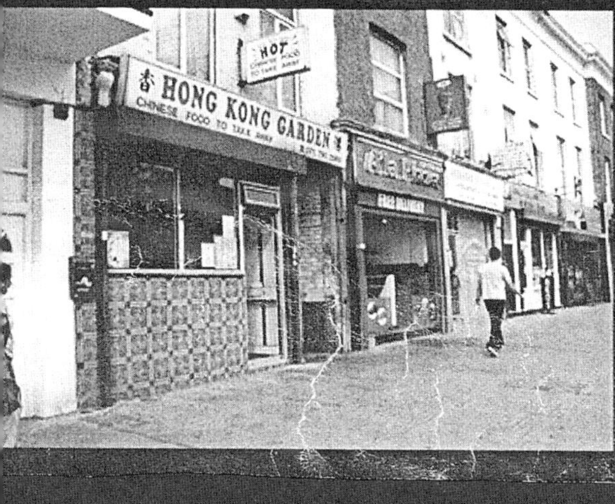
HOT
HONG KONG GARDEN
CHINESE FOOD TO TAKE AWAY
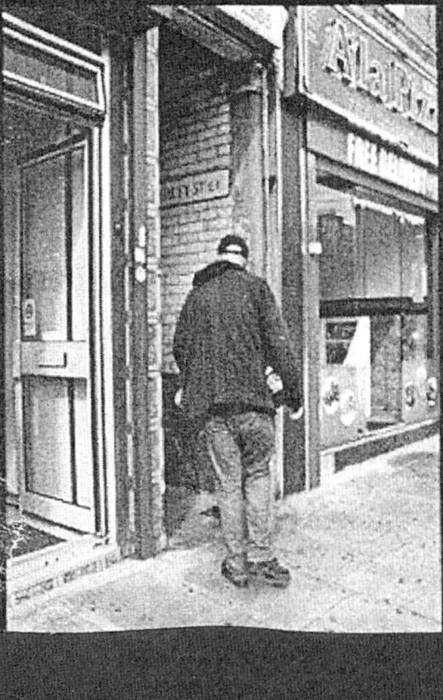

Then there was an outbreak in Wood Green, on the Tuesday
probably,some local black kids broke into camera shop and
threw them at police.
It all went off at Ducketts common, several shops on
Turnpike Lane were looted and there were shoes thrown at
coppers on Green Lanes.

Wood green shopping centre, 1984. Miners strike. Class war
intent on opening a second front in the capital, wanted to
see riots in city centres to draw old bill out of the coal
fields to emergency situations in the city.
Dragged a few cars across the street in Islington. There was
a firework display planned in Wood Green, when we got there
there were a few people hanging around but we didn't get as
many as we wanted. There was some autonomous action the same
night down in Brixton, our rivals were trying to draw people
elsewhere. We sat about for a while in the pre arranged pub,
the Old Bill knew something was going on and started
searching people coming up off tube. Nothing happened at the
fireworks so they fucked off and about twenty of us went
back to the pub opposite Wood Green station. We weren't in a
good mood, there were arguments erupting, where was the
promised mob. Then outside the pub there were about twenty
kids wanting to know where the riot was, one of them smashed
beer crate through an off licence window, then a load of
middle aged blokes started looting all the booze. Someone
shouted, here it is! Shopping centre, windows put through
with scaffolding, one end to other, smashed and looted....it
dispersed quickly after ten minutes, I walked to my mate's
house in Dalston through the back streets. The police were
left there gazing in shock, there was no mob, everyone had
gone and the place was smashed up.

Narrow way incident, 1990,, mob went up narrow way, outside
town hall, a demo against Poll Tax while they were setting
the rate inside. It wasn't a really serious disturbance, a
tv shop got looted and a police car was turned over. We
tried to drive it up towards the The Pembury Estate, hoping
the kids would want to kick it off there, , there was
sporadic looting all the way along the Narrow Way.

Millwall riot, 2004, started by banker, proper riot. Petrol
bombs the lot. Scrapyard, ,metal thrown. F-Troop/ Treatment/
WE HATE HUMANS>

There are certain historical moments where constellations of
social upheaval flare up and illuminate Britain's cities
        July 1981. 2011 2012   2013 ----

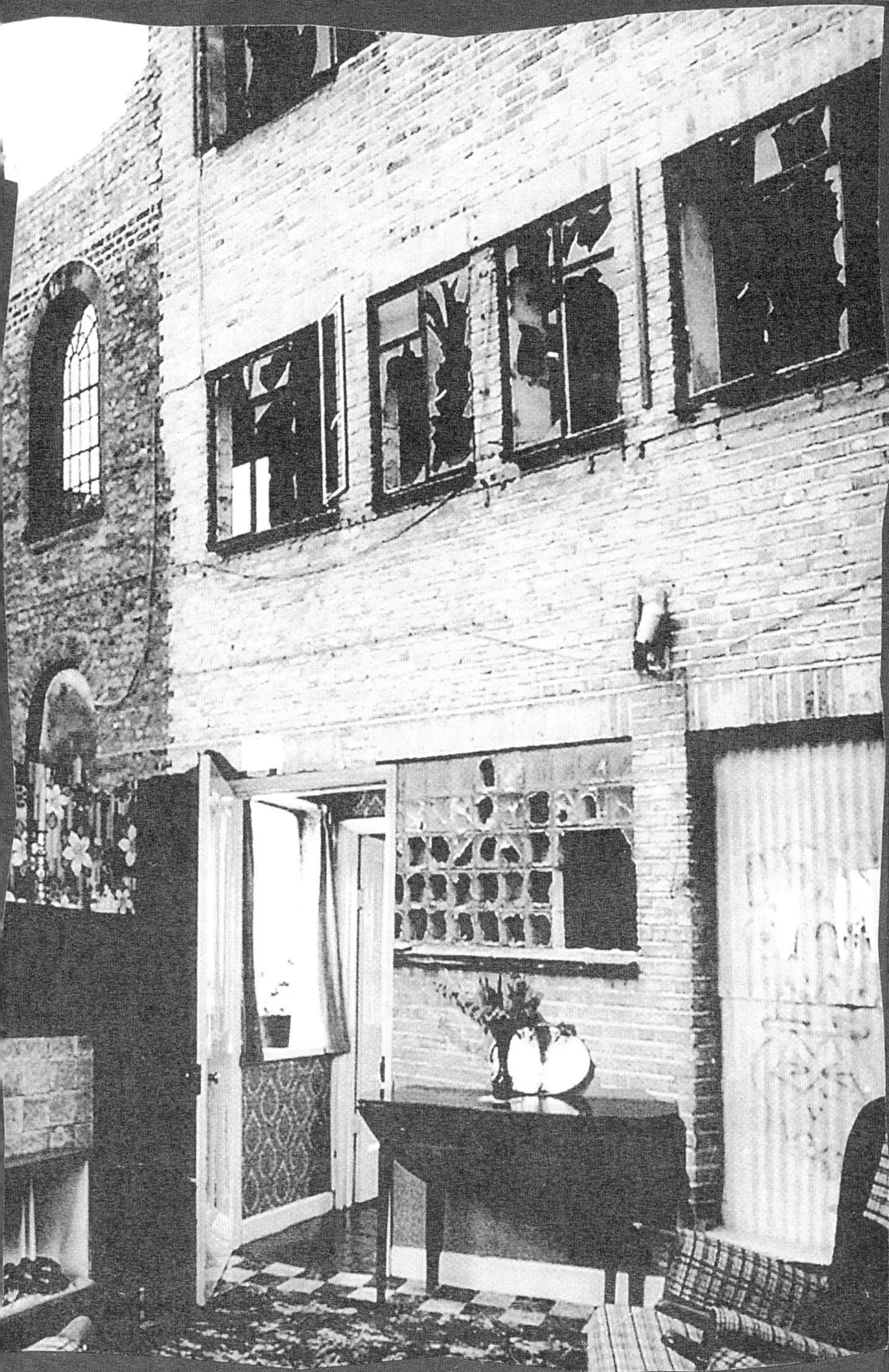

because

...k walls offer a
...ect backdrop for
...llection of black-and-
...e prints and instantly
...te a gallery feel

"...on the walls, it creates a cocoon effect"

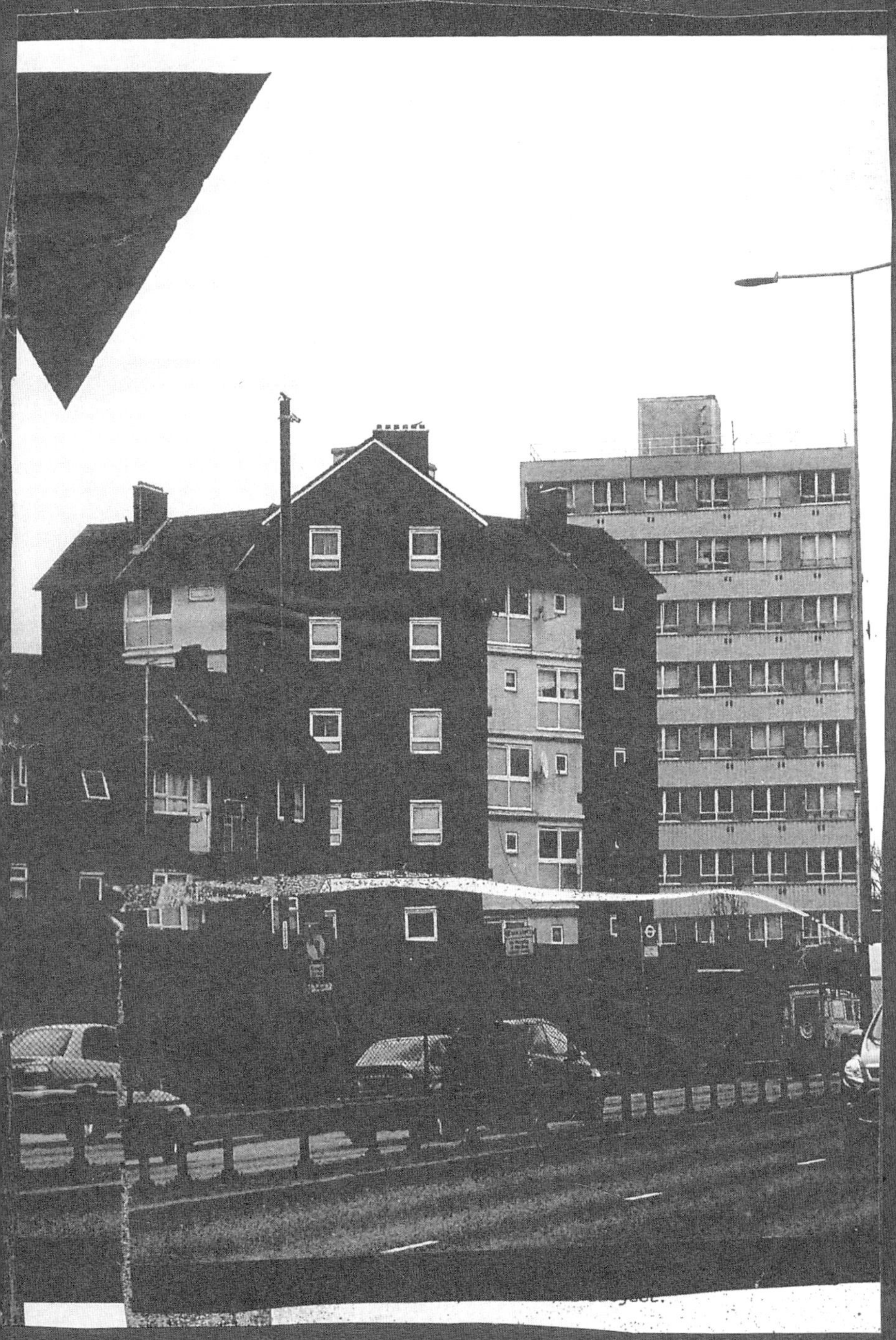

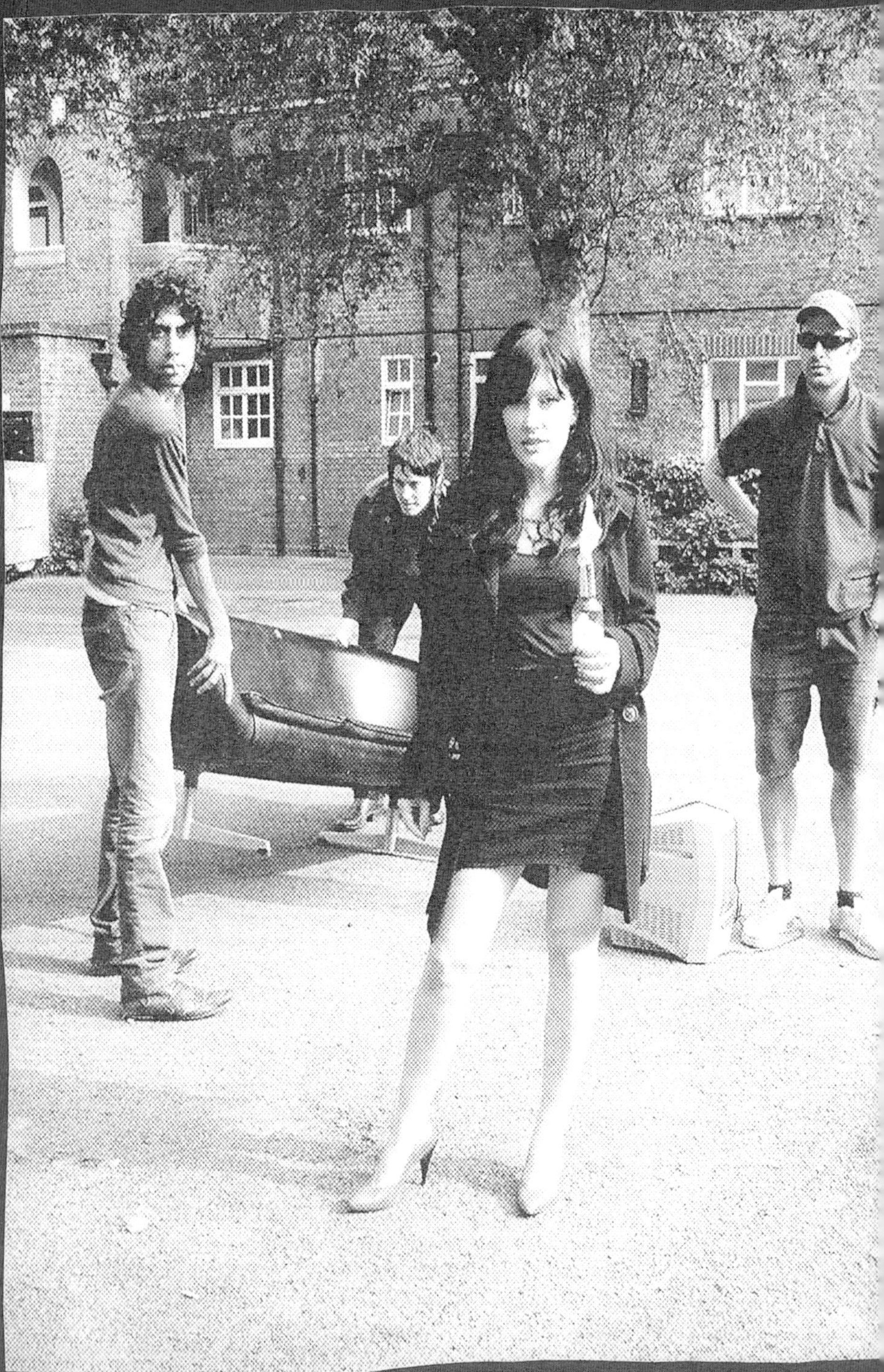

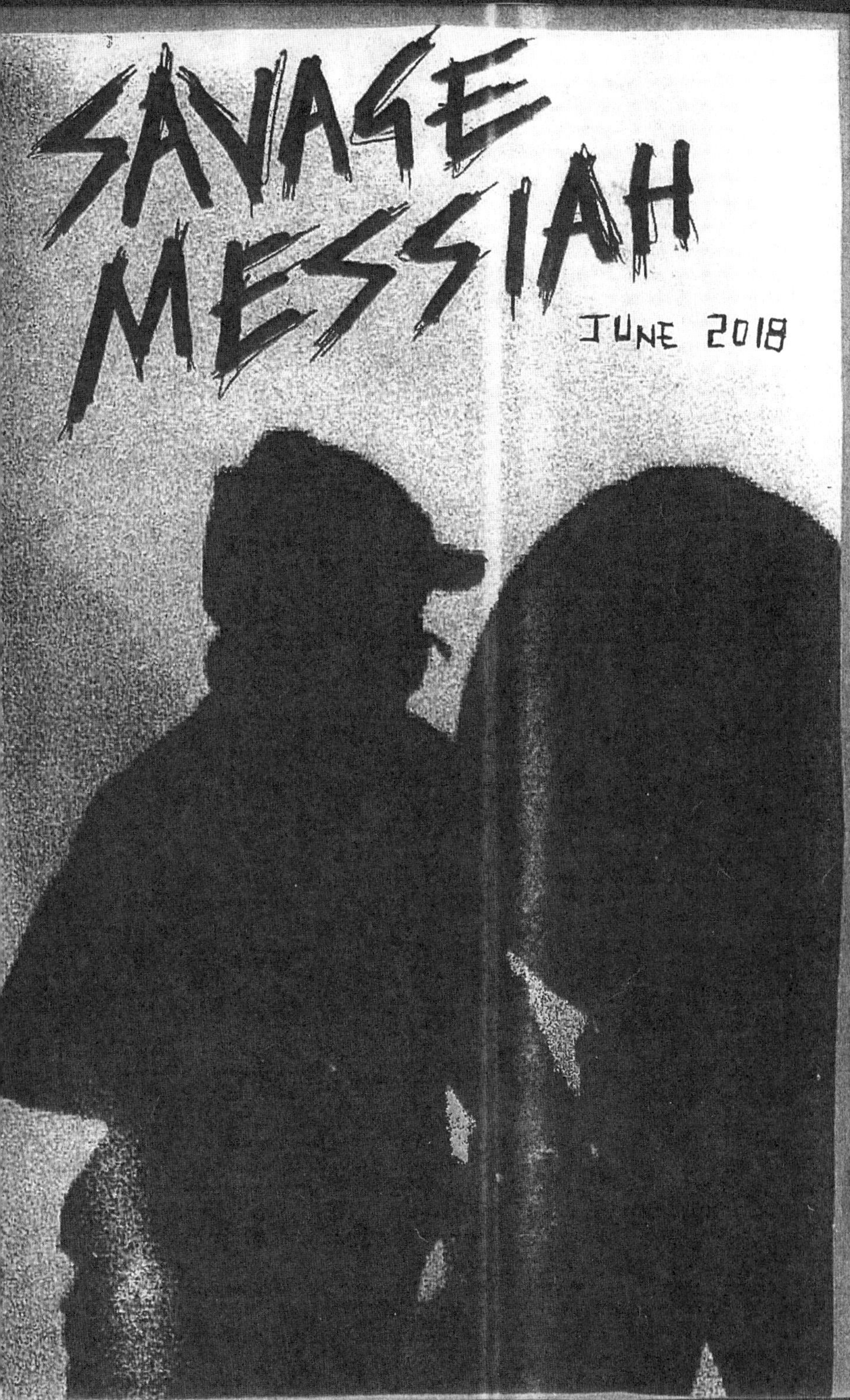
SAVAGE MESSIAH
JUNE 2018

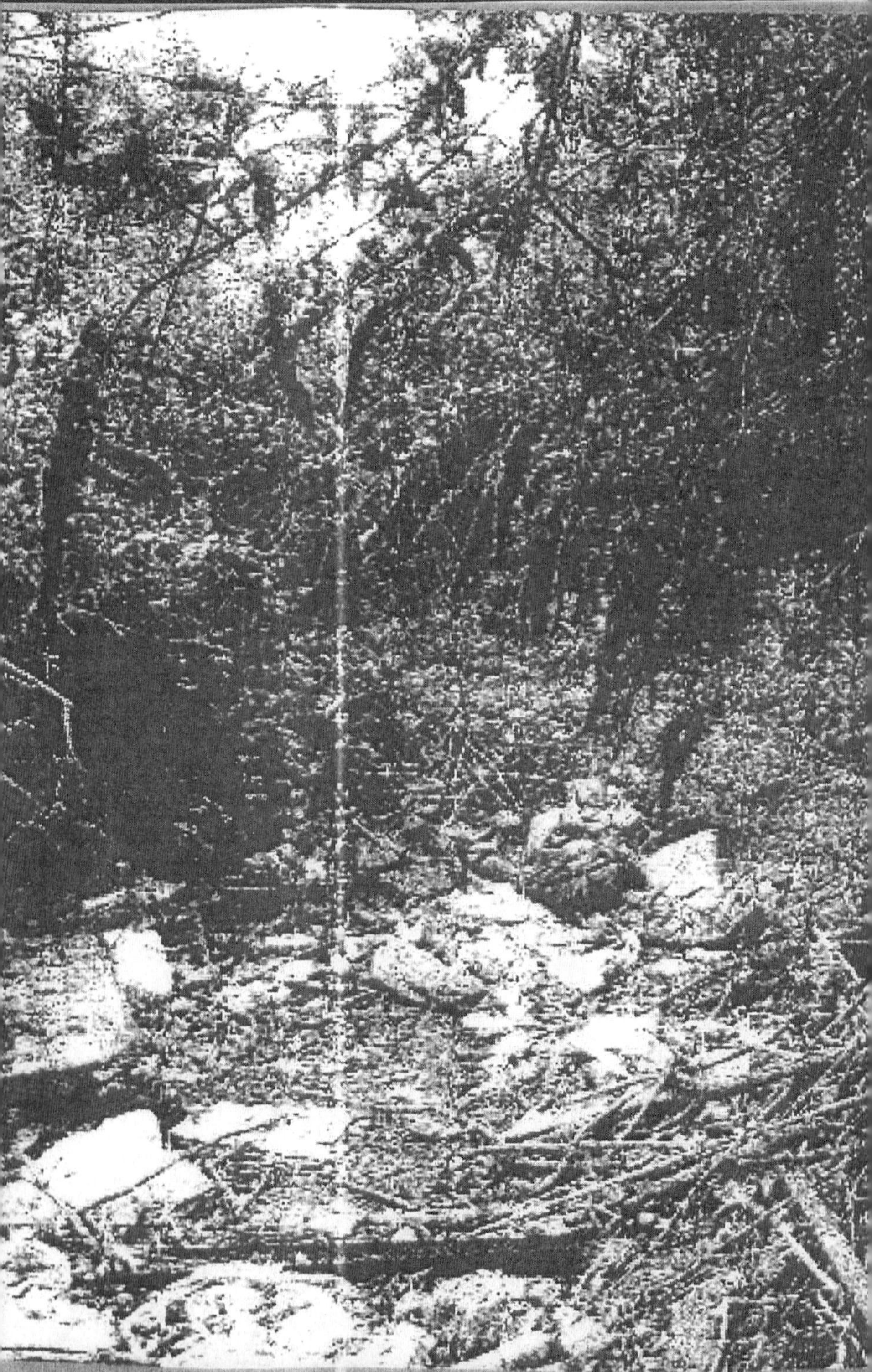

OPEN YOUR PALM, FEEL THE DUST SETTLING THERE

Wormwood Scrubs. Even the name is tangled, a
patchouli scent of undergrowth and dirt. This was
the edge of the city once, a zone of asylums and
infirmaries.
Du Cane road. I know the name , the mythology
surrounding Harry Roberts. They used to sing it at
the football, send chills through the coppers
there. I wonder where it happened, certain I can
feel the repercussions, a charge of vexed energy.
It seems a long way , the terrain is stretching,
buildings flung apart. I haven't been around here
for years.

Hammersmith Hospital. Crowded foyer, hubs of
activity, Costa, Sodexo, Subway.
I look at the instructions again. A smell of
disinfectent and rubber. The ward is upstairs, you
have to buzz in. They don't check who I am. I
think about security, the lack of it, how I could
be anyone.
I walk past three bays, three enclosures with
identical beds and grey curtains.
There are figures, shapes under blankets.
Low murmurs, Womans Own strewn across chairs.
I turn a corner and see her son and daughter,
they're both there at the foot of the bed. They
look pleased to see me. I suppose i'm a
distraction, a break in the tension.

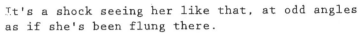

It's a shock seeing her like that, at odd angles
as if she's been flung there.
It doesn't seem right that she's here, our
conversations have always revolved around Edgware
Road where she's lived for seventy years, and
Yorkshire where she was born. Those were our co-
ordinates. I don't want her to spend her last days
here.
The ward is insulated, there are no windows facing
out, just a white glare from the strip lights, the
linoleum floors. Her face, the penetrating look
of it, is concealed, pressed beneath one I barely
recognise. Her mouth is reduced a diagonal line.
And I realise I've never seen her without a
shampoo and set, this new hair is electrical ,
tufts of it lifting from her scalp.
Her eyes are shut but she knows I'm here. I talk
to her like I always do, about the old places ,
the terrain we shared. I list them. Praed Street,
Boscobel Street, the cafe on the market. Her eyes
open, she smiles, a deep beam coming from that
continent of memories, that ocean beneath. Her
green eyes, for a second, are lamps signalling
from there.

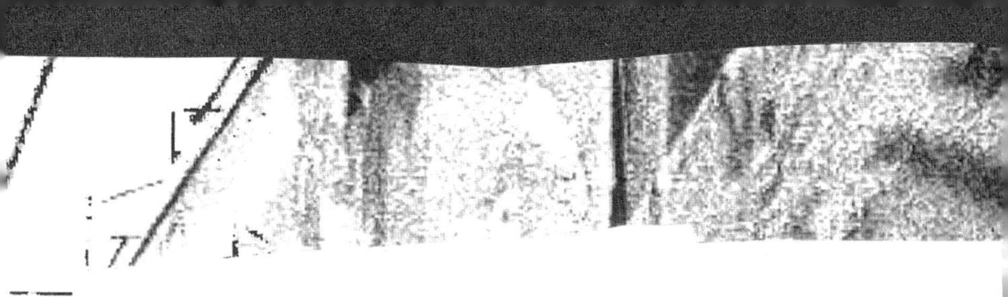

At regular intervals her daughter goes to the car park to put money in the meter, the hospital is run by Sodexo, they fine you if you don't top up, even at a time like this. And it's always a time like this for someone. The meter keeps ticking, they send their letters automatically, there's never anyone to plead with, use your charm on. Kay's my friend. We've got a connection, we'd both left Yorkshire for London, fifty years apart. Her hand feels smooth and hot as I hold it. Her face is fading, as if i'm looking at a drawing, just lines etched on to paper, nothing coloured in. But her spirit is still here, she's still fighting.

I walk through a brick arch into the car park. The prison is there transmitting Victorian darkness, brutal order. Now it's unravelling in overcrowding and squalor. Today it was on the news again, an inmate stabbed to death by four others, 90 attacks in six months.
You can hear them. Tormented shouts from deep inside the prison , the smell of weed drifting over the walls. And that other smell,stale and septic, hard to describe. Of decay, something off, something bodily, an unclean wound.

It's haunting, hearing them like that. On lockdown, calling through cell windows, waiting for answers to come back from the walls. I listen for him. You can tell so much by listening, images form in my mind, I know what they look like suddenly, I know who they are. I look up at those high brick walls and wonder if he's there behind them. I tell myself it's impossible, I would *know*, I'd have a sense of it. He's had to flee, that's the version I have to tell myself .

*

But somehow I know he's alive, the thought is resilient, unalterable. I would know if it was otherwise. The knowledge would come like an explosion, a collision wrapping me in it, it would fell me. Until then there's hope.

How many of them had been there that night, how many of them illegal, evading someone. Ever since i'd met him, all those years ago it had been fugitive like that, none of us using our names, hiding our identities, not from each other but as an allegiance, a form of protection. He'd only ever known my first name, it was all I went by, and that was all I knew of him. We found each other through bar rooms, telephone boxes, notes pushed through doors. That's how he'd find me again.
I can still smell the smoke. I know he's circling, waiting for the right moment.

*

Turning back towards White city, I see the shell of that tower, I can't avoid it. Until now I'd refused to look . I couldnt bear to see it, not even on tv. Now it's at the centre of my vision, rising over the Westway, a symbol of everything that's gone wrong. I cant let the thoughts settle, the possibilities held there; he must be out of range, on the continent maybe.
There are photos tacked to the walls, the trees. Faded now under laminte, under plastic bags, faces blotched in the rain, colours seeping as if they were drowned. I think I recognise some of them. They're missing like he's missing. The separation has been forced, riven like a gulley, a deep furrow through the centre. There can be no balance now, no equlibirium. I'm split in half like a tree in a storm.

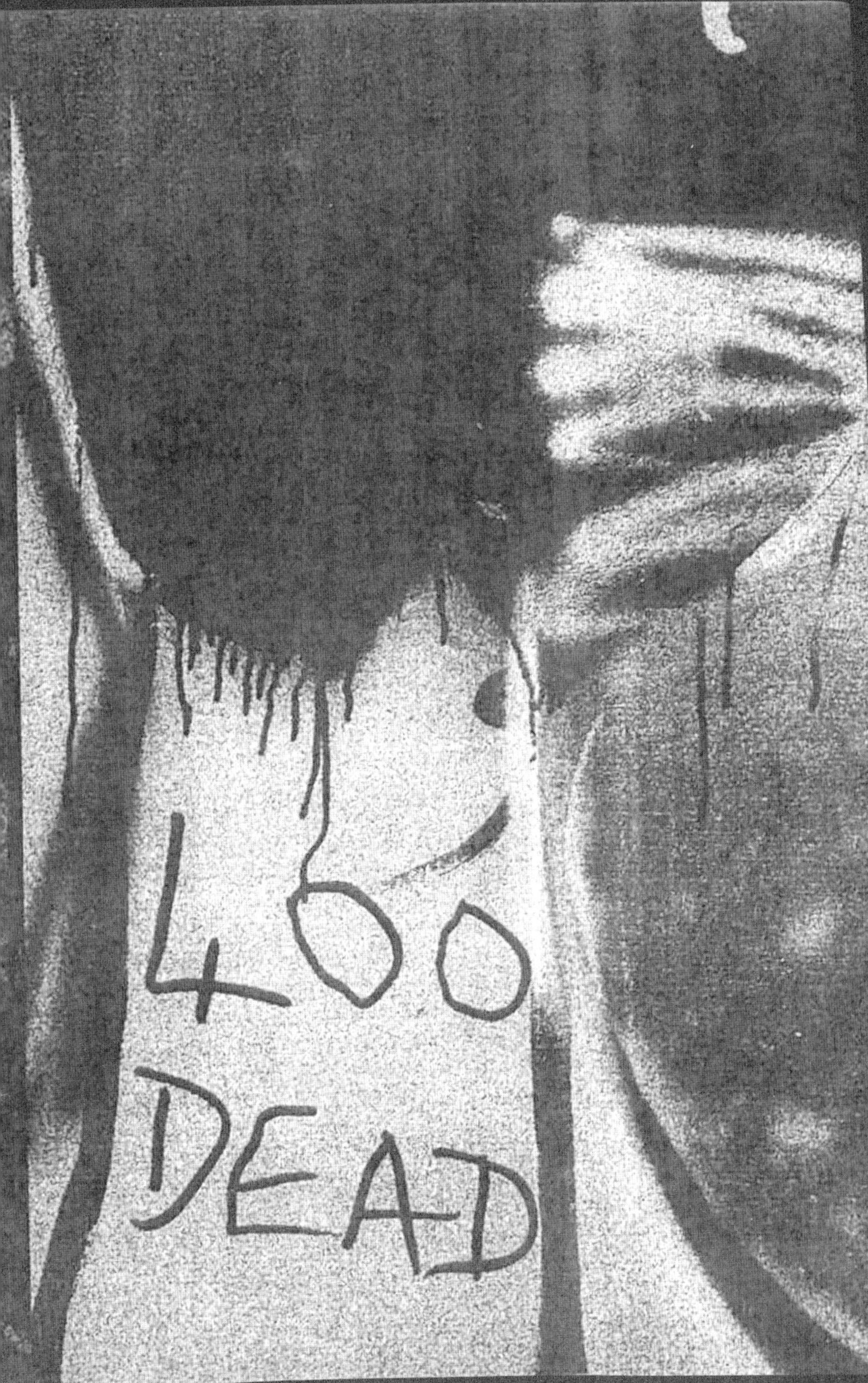
400
DEAD

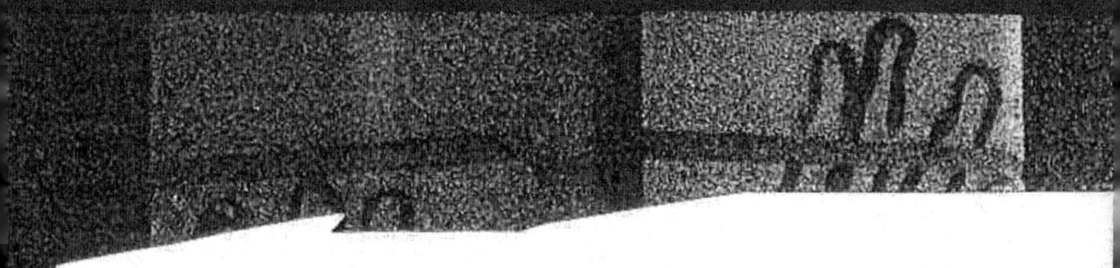

As the terrain becomes febrile, I think of him more, sense the restless searching. There are traces, . little scratches in soft brick, chalk marks on concrete stanchions.
They hadn't disappeared, not altogether. The markings are visible if you know where to look.

I retrace our steps. The cavernous Westfeld with its echoey, saccaharine pop is the frst place I go. Some of the crew had worked in here once, in kitchens and bars.

The music coalesces, crystals permaeating the space around me.. I hear this song all the time. I recognise the voice, corralling the forces, distilling it all into this moment. It guages the terrain, a conduit into the collective psyche, the euphoria of the first days spring and the anguish residing beneath. The track echoes, reverberates through bright atria.

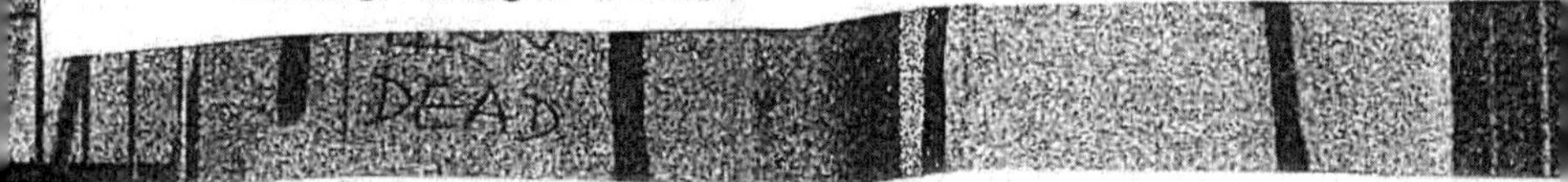
DEAD

Las Iguanas. I stop here, it's the kind of place I would go with him for an afternoon drink, that sense of exhilaration we used to get from truancy, from hiding out. He looked different every time, a new guise, a different face, that's why I can't fix an image of him now. We were careful, we didn't have smartphones, nothing that could track or capture.
It was the kind of place we mocked but secretly liked, pendant lights, luminous cocktails, happy hour. We'd have a couple then go on long rambling drifts bouyed up on rum and sugar.

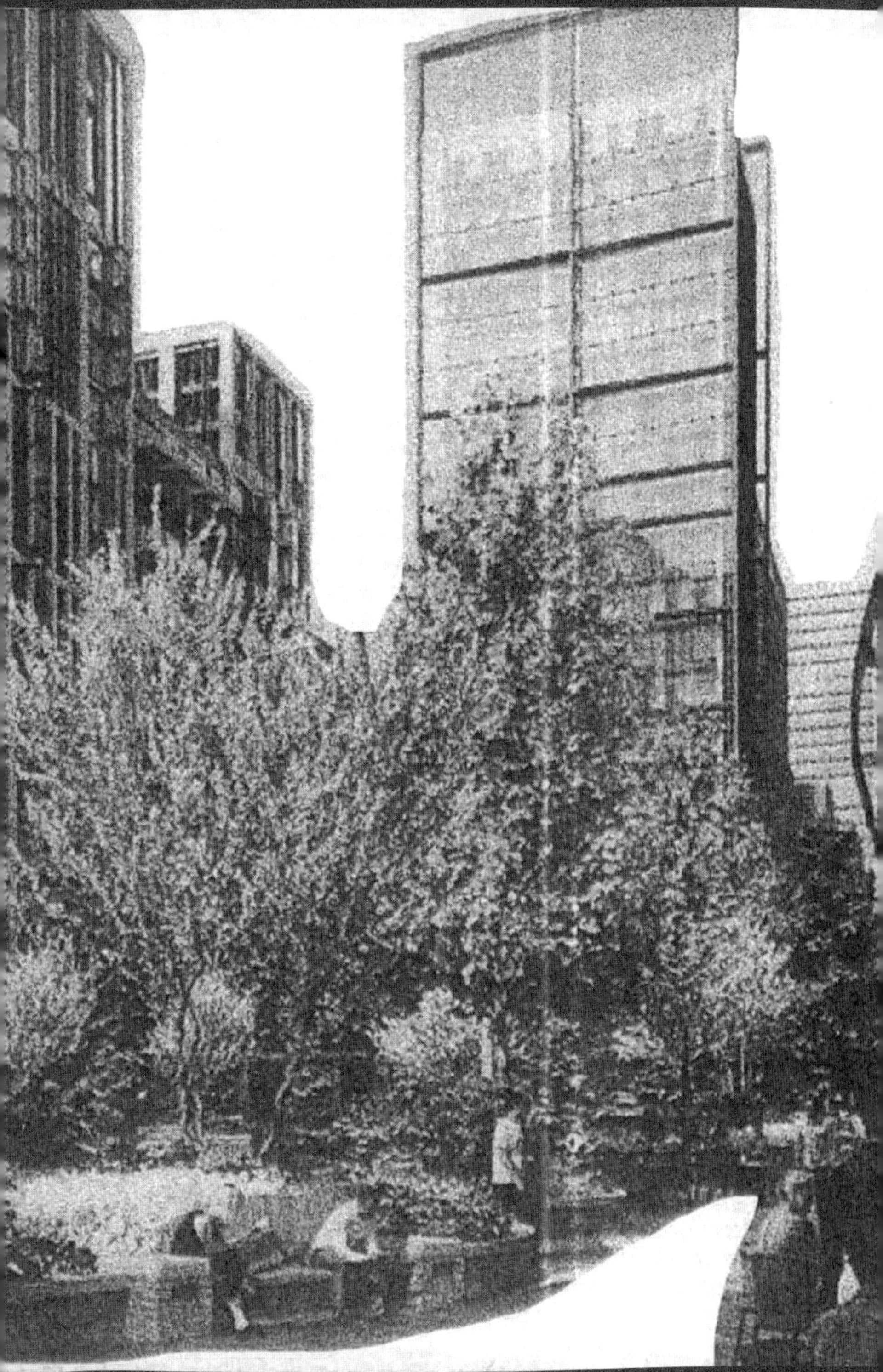

I walk back through the shopping centre to White
city, that traffic snarl round the old BBC where I
always lose my way. This was his territory not
mine, the lines of it lacerated him, connected his
nerves, his tissue. Grand Union Canal, The
Westway, Hammersmith and City. He bore the traces
on his skin like accidental tattoos.

I think of the raids, flats getting busted before
the Carnival. They were damned if they were going
to let it go up. Arrests, spurious charges, then
curfews and bans, a kind of spatial discipline.
I'd seen those strangers in meetings saying
politics was a hijack, a lack of respect. I
rememeber them telling us to stay silent.

They came to our flat, the one off Church street,
we were expecting them. Demoralised police, weak
government,they were getting skittsh.

*

Now, with my mojito, solitary in a corner with
fizzing music and bored waiters an image of his
face is gradually forming. It's from last
September, he'd just had his hair cut, I remember
his face in the neon, his eyes big and glassy, as
if he was seeing too much, as if it was spilling
out. It only lasted a few seconds.
  A security guard walks past. It's time to leave,
I thought it might yield something , a clue or a
sign, but I need to walk to find those, this place
is too sanitised, too quickly overturned. Back
there though, in the service tunnels, in the
loading bays, there could be something, someone
who might know. The way that guard looked at me
was different, not the usual absent minded
surveillance, there was a hint of recognition. Or
maybe i'm just imagining it. I imagine a lot now,
I see a lot of things.

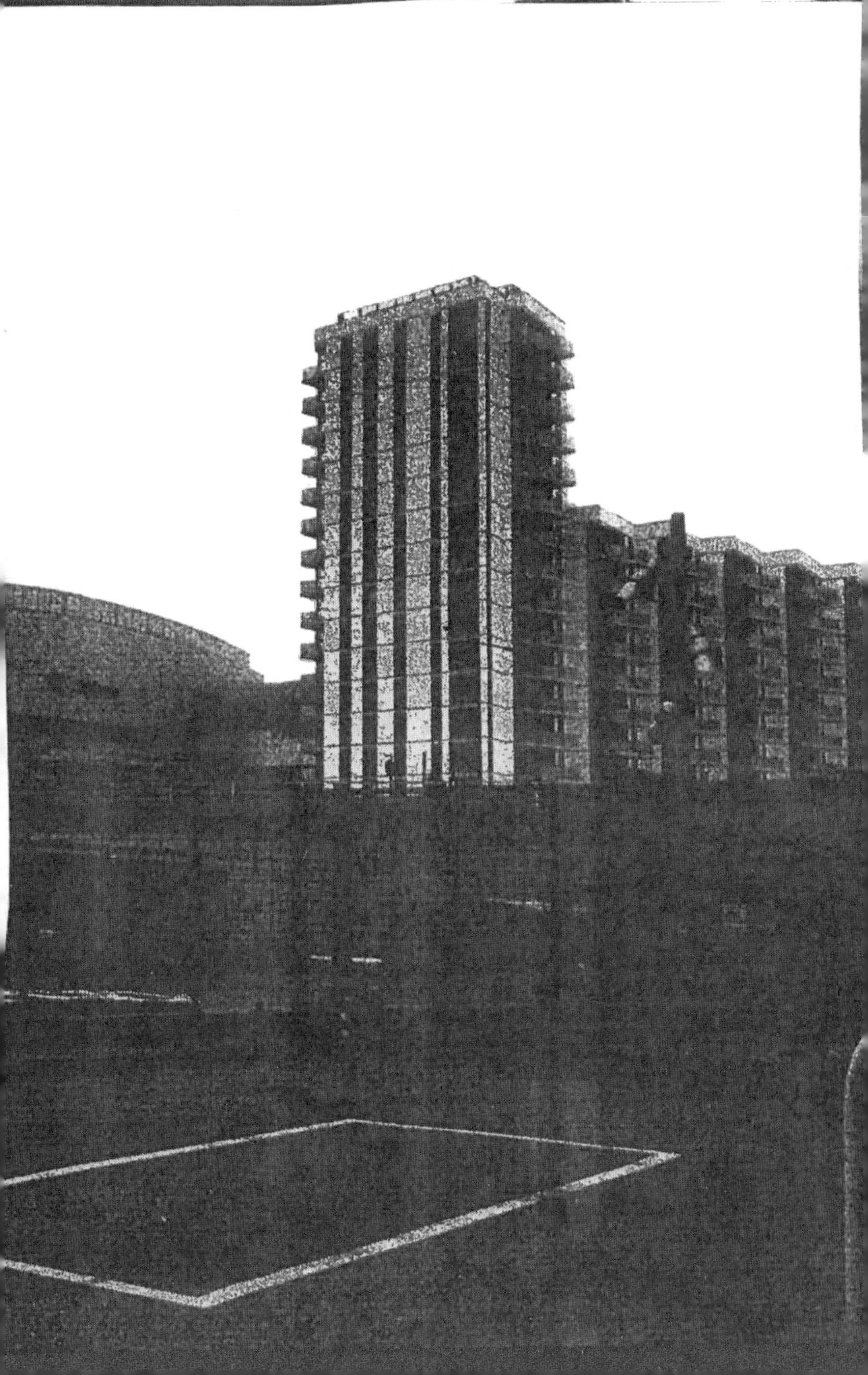

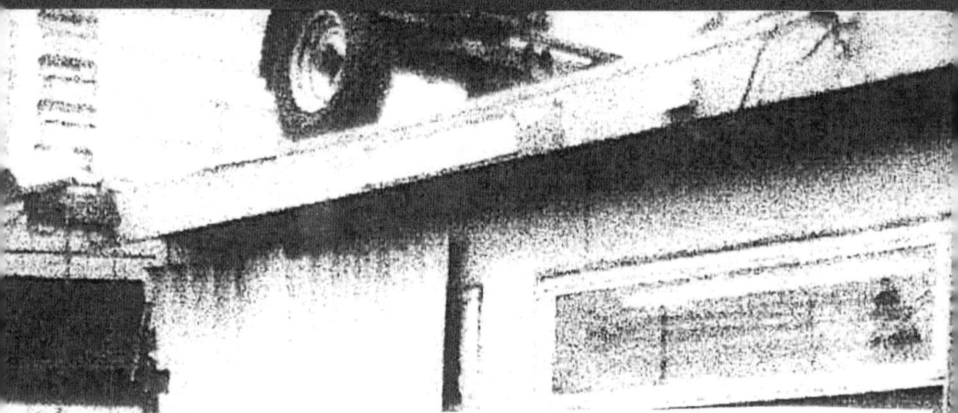

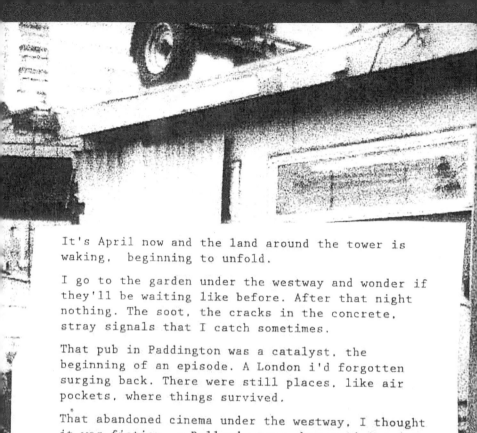

It's April now and the land around the tower is waking, beginning to unfold.

I go to the garden under the westway and wonder if they'll be waiting like before. After that night nothing. The soot, the cracks in the concrete, stray signals that I catch sometimes.

That pub in Paddington was a catalyst, the beginning of an episode. A London i'd forgotten surging back. There were still places, like air pockets, where things survived.

That abandoned cinema under the westway, I thought it was fiction, a Ballard story, but we'd found it again that night. Stepping through the threshold, the abandoned working mens club with its plywood hoardings, its peeling black emulsion, into an amber capsule.

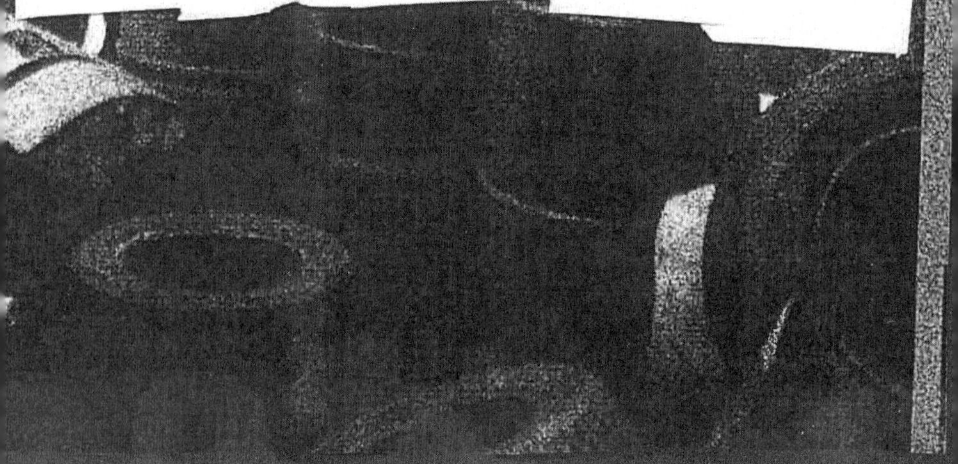

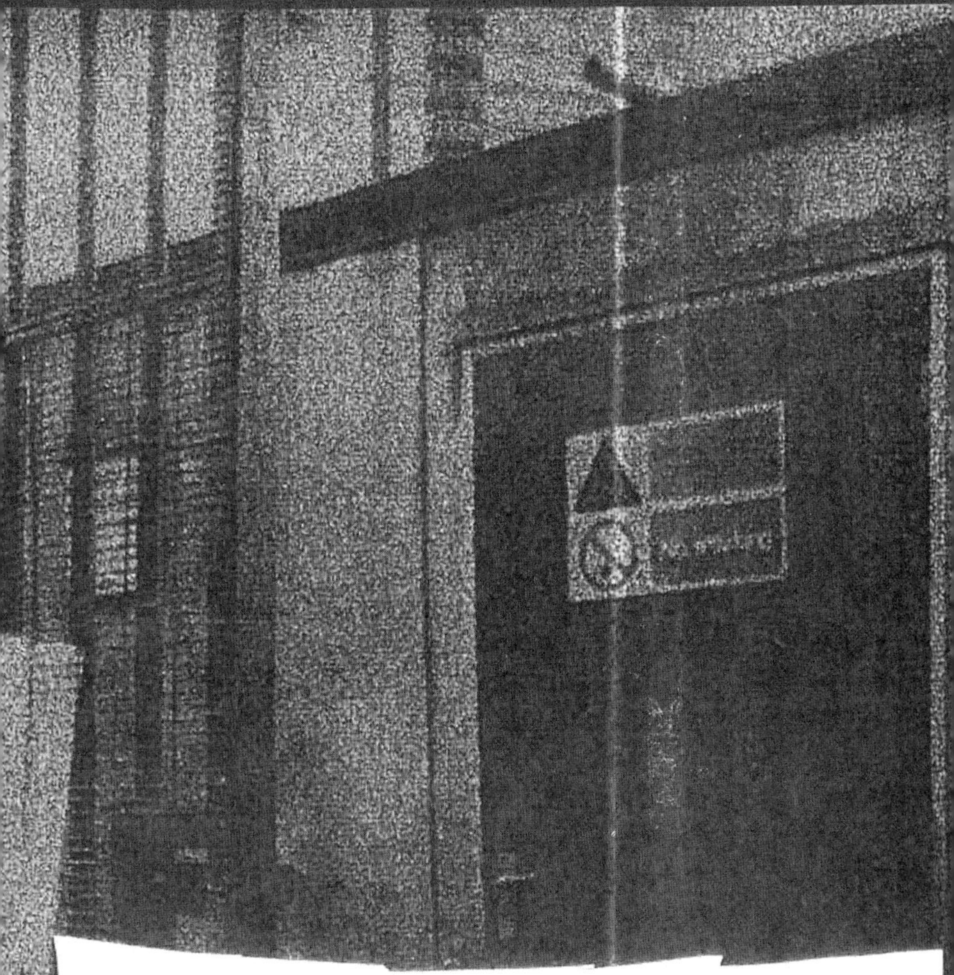

There are messages, arabic glyphs scuttling across the concrete.

Sometimes under the Westway, you still hear traces of those parties, Acid tracks pulsing in the concrete. We went deep into the foundations. concrete shells echoing with unearthly sound. You could only find them by following the reverberations, listening for the bass coming up from the ground. Those signals travelled the length of the Westway, from Paddington to North Pole Road.

I remember when I first visited Kay in that tower
block on Church street she proudly showed me the
view across the city. We looked west from Wembley
to the hazy acres of Wimbledon. You could follow
the line of the Westway as it undulated, rising at
Edgware road then swooping towards Paddington. I
looked beyond it, to the Hallfield estate where
he'd lived for a few weeks, then the tower blocks
around Latimer Road. Kay asked me something about
him once, probably on the first visit and I said
nothing, even with her I was secretive.
She was like my Grandma, being with her was a way
of making it up, compensating for lost time. With
Kay I could turn back the clock, be a friend and
companion the way I wished I'd been before.
We'd sit in a Moroccan cafe on Church street
talking, watching the comings and goings, she
never missed anything. The blokes in there looked
after her, they respected her because she was old.
She could have whatever she wanted, even if it
wasn't on the menu, someone would go out onto the
market and find it.
I thought they might know something, they might
have seen him. There were connections , covert but
perceptible. After the fire, the mood had
switched. Some of them had lived there, they still
knew people there.

I get off the tube at Latimer road. It's the first
time since the fire i've been there. I don't lift
my eyes, I stare at the the pavement. The tower is
close, its presence palpable, the smell of carbon
still there.
The sky is a brilliant mocking blue and I resent
it.
It's quiet. I ask someone the way to Hammersmith
hospital, he seems annoyed as if it marks me as a
stranger.
They're sick of gawkers I know that, chancers with
cameras circling round. I refuse to look at it,
that monument. I keep my eyes on the notices, the
photocopied faces. They should be here, pushing
prams, calling in the newsagent, stopping for a
pint of milk. Now their colours leach,
efflorescenses of bright ink.

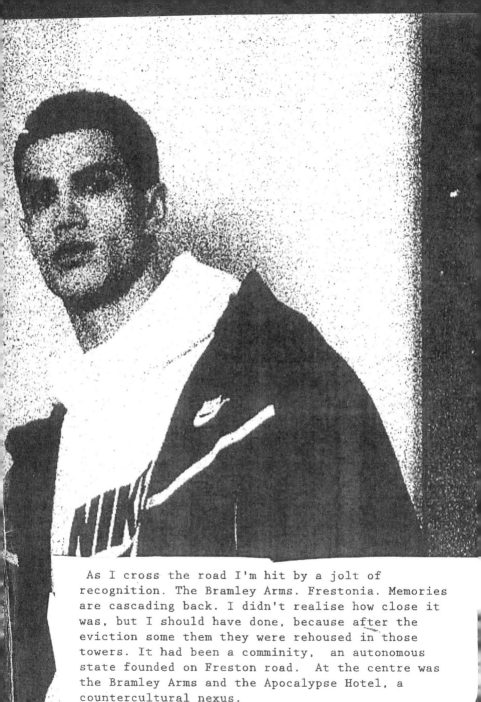

As I cross the road I'm hit by a jolt of
recognition. The Bramley Arms. Frestonia. Memories
are cascading back. I didn't realise how close it
was, but I should have done, because after the
eviction some them they were rehoused in those
towers. It had been a comminity, an autonomous
state founded on Freston road. At the centre was
the Bramley Arms and the Apocalypse Hotel, a
countercultural nexus.

A couple of years ago I walked around there with Kay, we used to get taxis sometimes, short rides around the Borough. We'd stand on her balcony and point and say let's go there, it might be a new development going up or a building she was curious about. She wanted to name every landmark, every new tower as she surveyed her realm from the 18th floor.

The cab dropped us off outside the Bramley Arms, turned it into flats by then. There was a lot of building work going on, new apartments in muted red brick. These schemes represented a heritage version of London, an unreal, sanitised city. The brutalist blocks with their collective values had to be occluded, cladded.
We were outside a new office block. I noticed the sign *Frestonia* and was shocked by the audacity. They were into this idea of placemaking, mining local archives for a micro-knowlege of the area . They were confident then that the militancy had been eradicated, that only fossils remained.

Kay stopped. I shouldn't have brought her out, it was too hot, she was looking pale. It's ok I said come in here. I pushed heavy glass doors and helped her into the large reception area, it was air conditoned, they had water coolers and soft chairs. She sat down, I went to get her a cup of water. A woman behind the desk with a helmet of blonde hair said *Can I help you?* Her face was drawn, stretched somehow, the forehead was smooth like plaster, I thought she must have had botox, a taut patch of leather above the eyebrows, like a conker, polished and smooth.
I remember the voice, the home counties sound of it. There was something disturbing about its tone, like a public announcement . She told us they'd get security guards and police to remove us from the premises. *Remove.* The way she said that, cold and flat as if we were objects, unwanted bags cluttering up space, or something worse, rats or insects, an infestation. She disappeared from view. The reception was momentarily empty. Kay

sipped the cold water. She said in a hoarse voice
we should go. It's ok I said, only when you're
able to. She sank back in the chair. I hadn't seen
her look this weak before, her strength was
dissipating, leaching like ectoplasm.

Then there were two others who looked the same, as
if the receptionist had multiplied, replicated
herself behind the scenes, three of them standing
over us, telling us to leave. They were all
wearing the same clothes, chintzy rose patterns,
linen skirts. I recognised the company HQ, a
vexed evocation of England, an England of cream
teas and cricket pavillions.

The women were brash Katie Hopkins types. I
realised, now we were face to face, how much they
despised us. The collision wouldn't have happened
before, now it happened all the time. They've
colonised this postcode, they think they own it,
demanding bye laws and legislation to keep us out.
At this time the tower hadn't been cladded, it was
brutal and raw, and they despised it, it was them
who were clamouring for the cladding, the
disguise, the melding into a nice, readable
surface.

The first one had assumed position of leader, her
voice the most strident. leading the little mob.
Now Kay was struggling to stand, and I said to the
woman don't you have any compassion, any humanity?
I didn't realise then how potent, how prescient
those words were.

I saw the flash of anger, the loss of composure
then the regaining of it, face returned to a
smooth disc, all in a split second. I'd rattled
her though, and as I supported Kay, my arm
threaded through hers I was glad, at least, of
that.

*

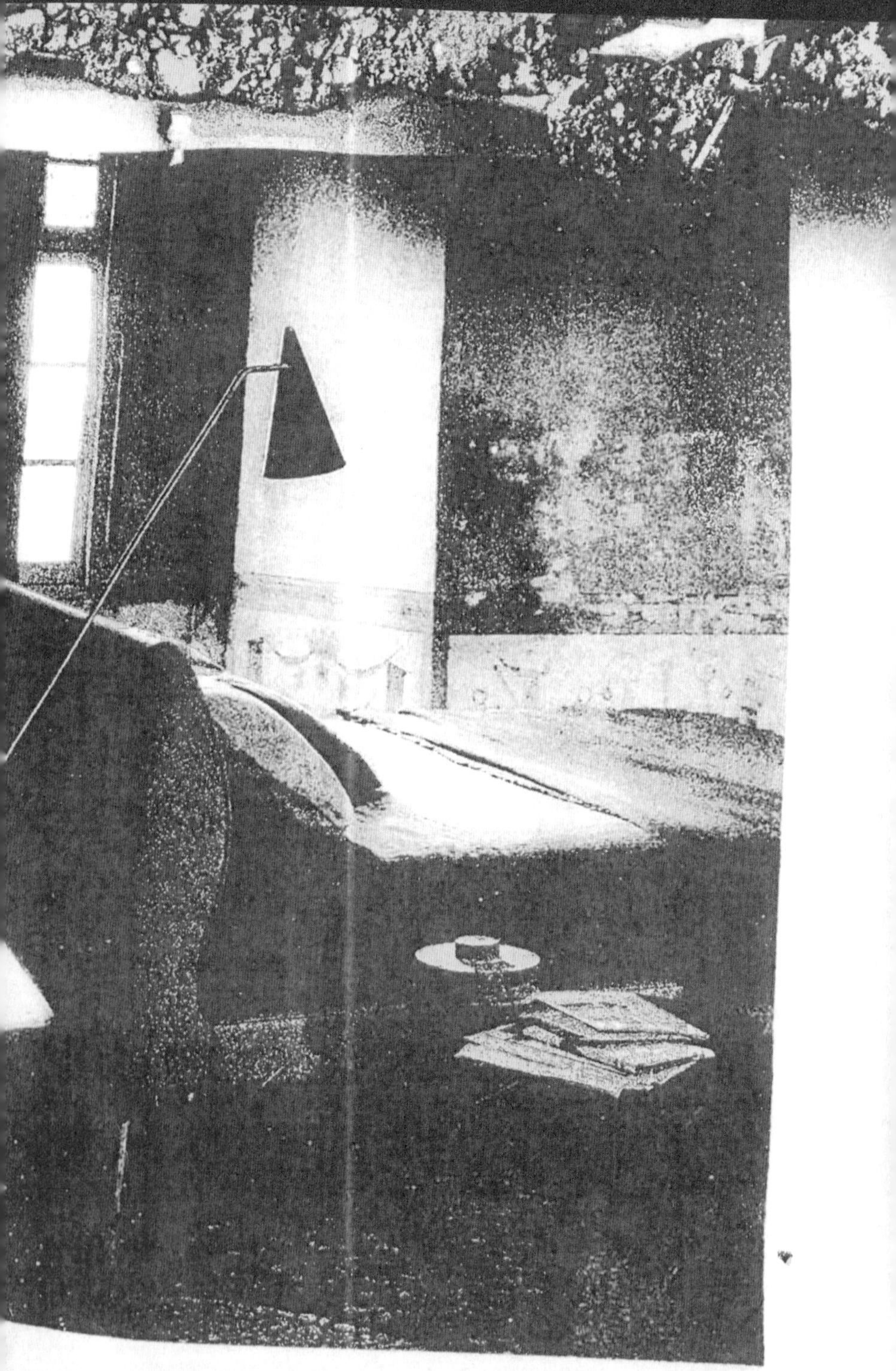

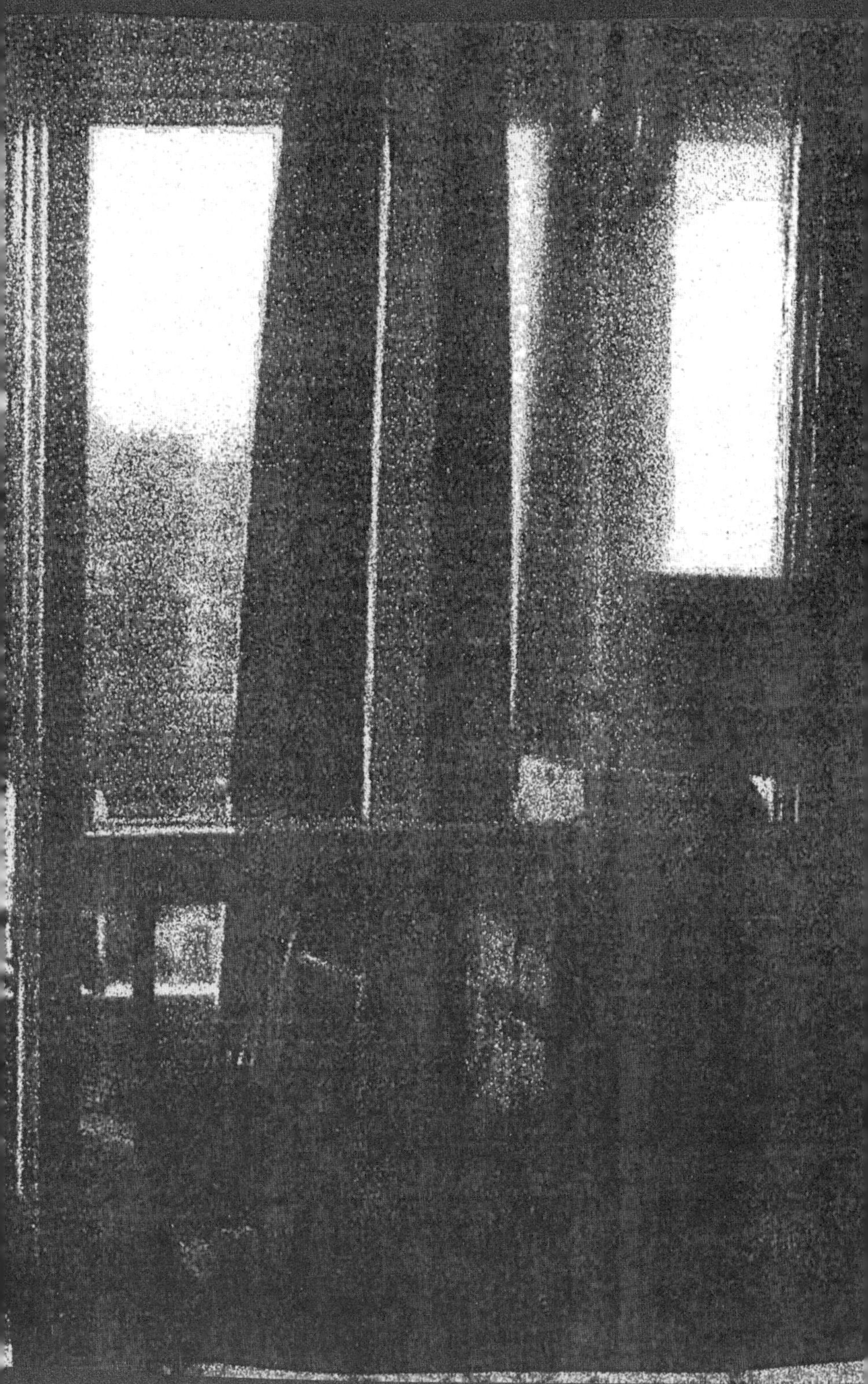

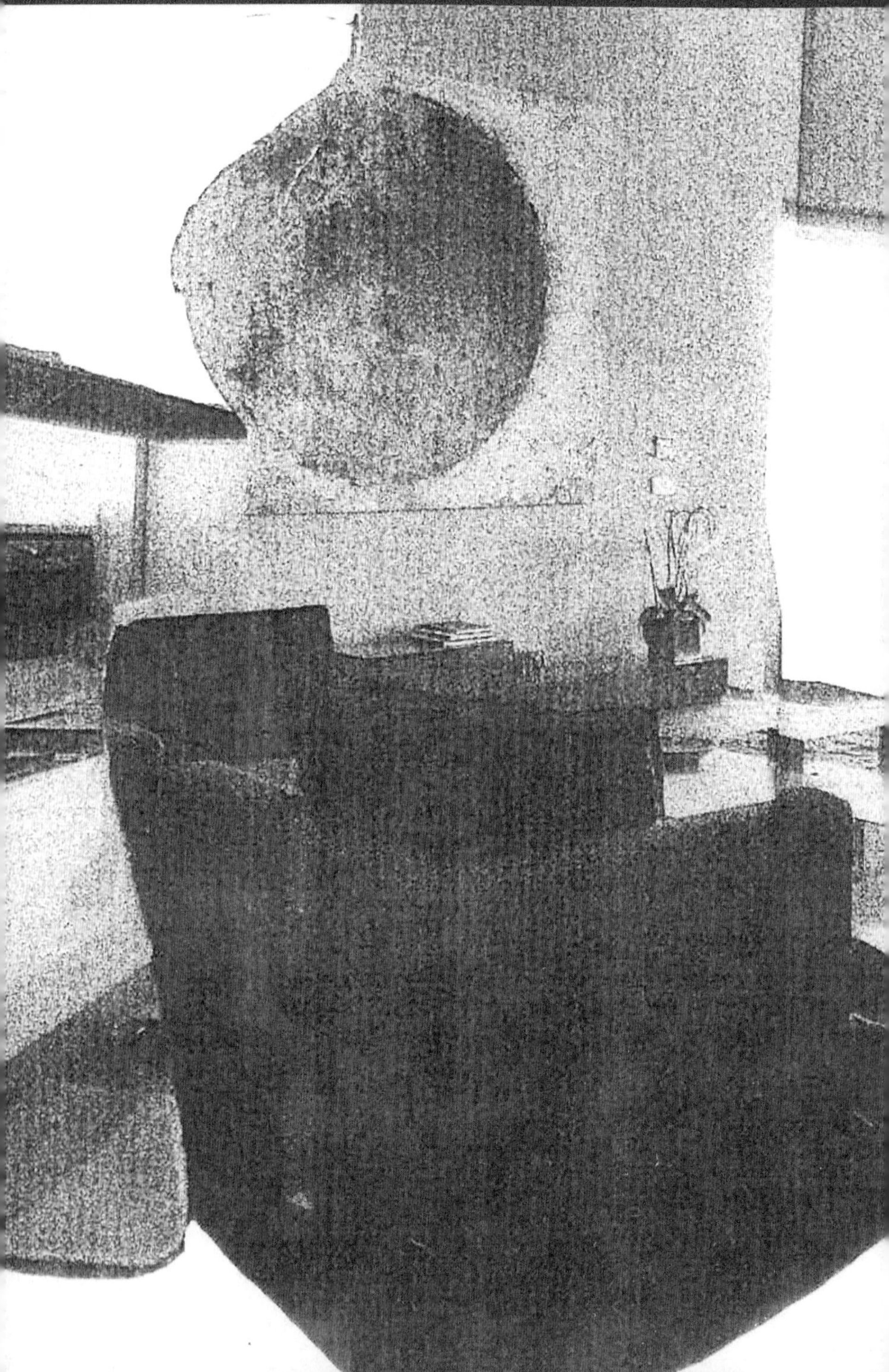

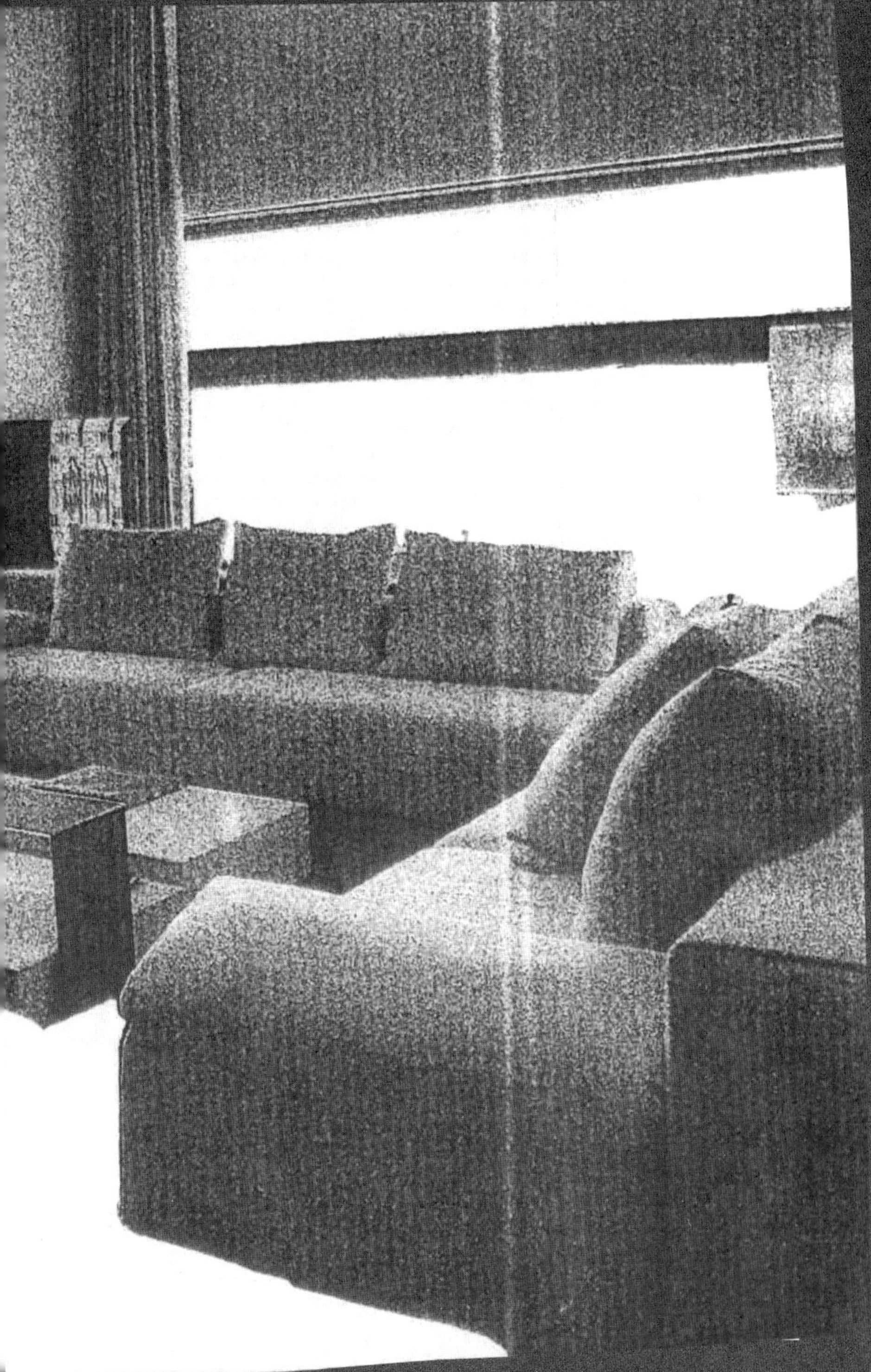

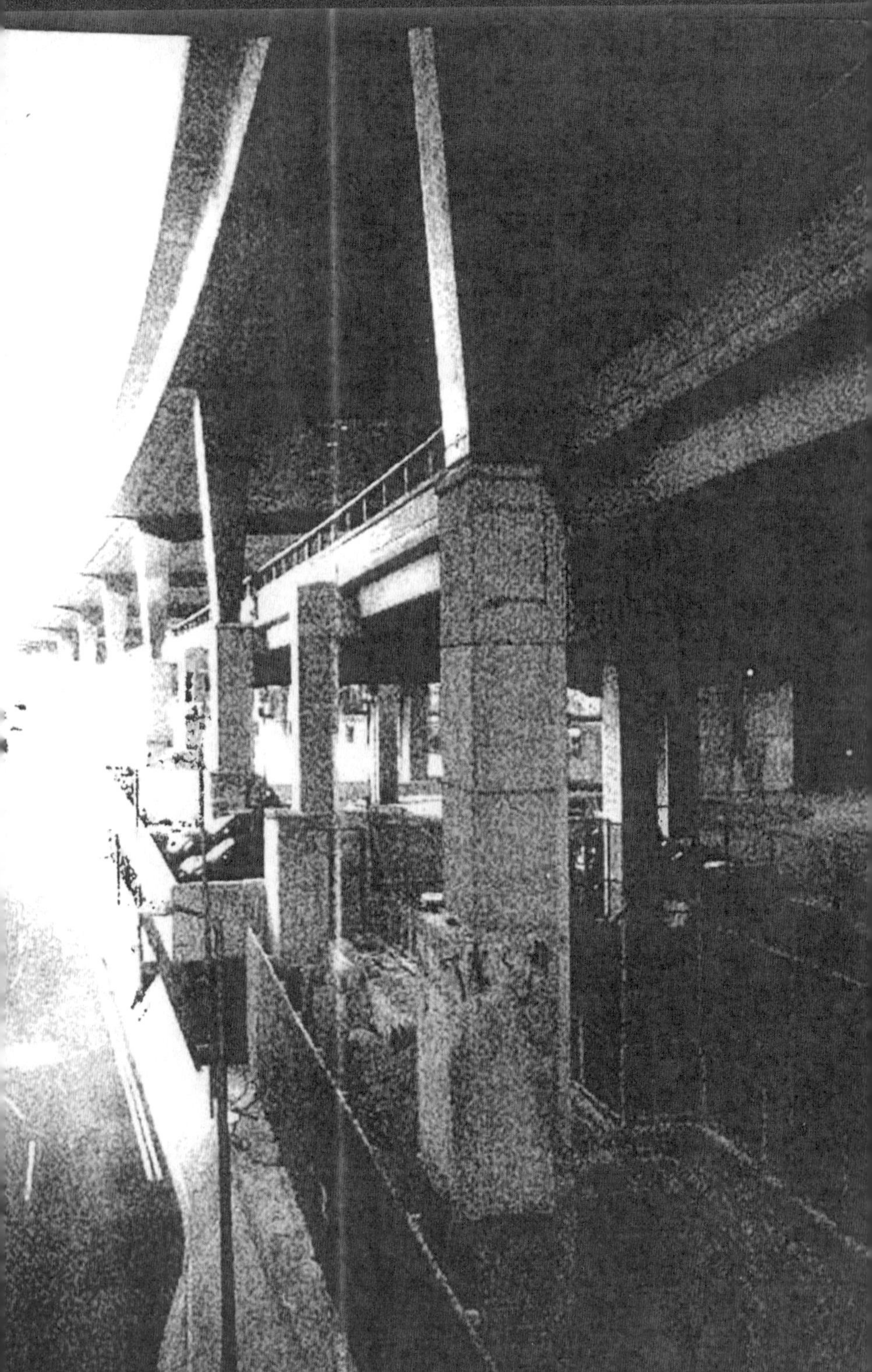

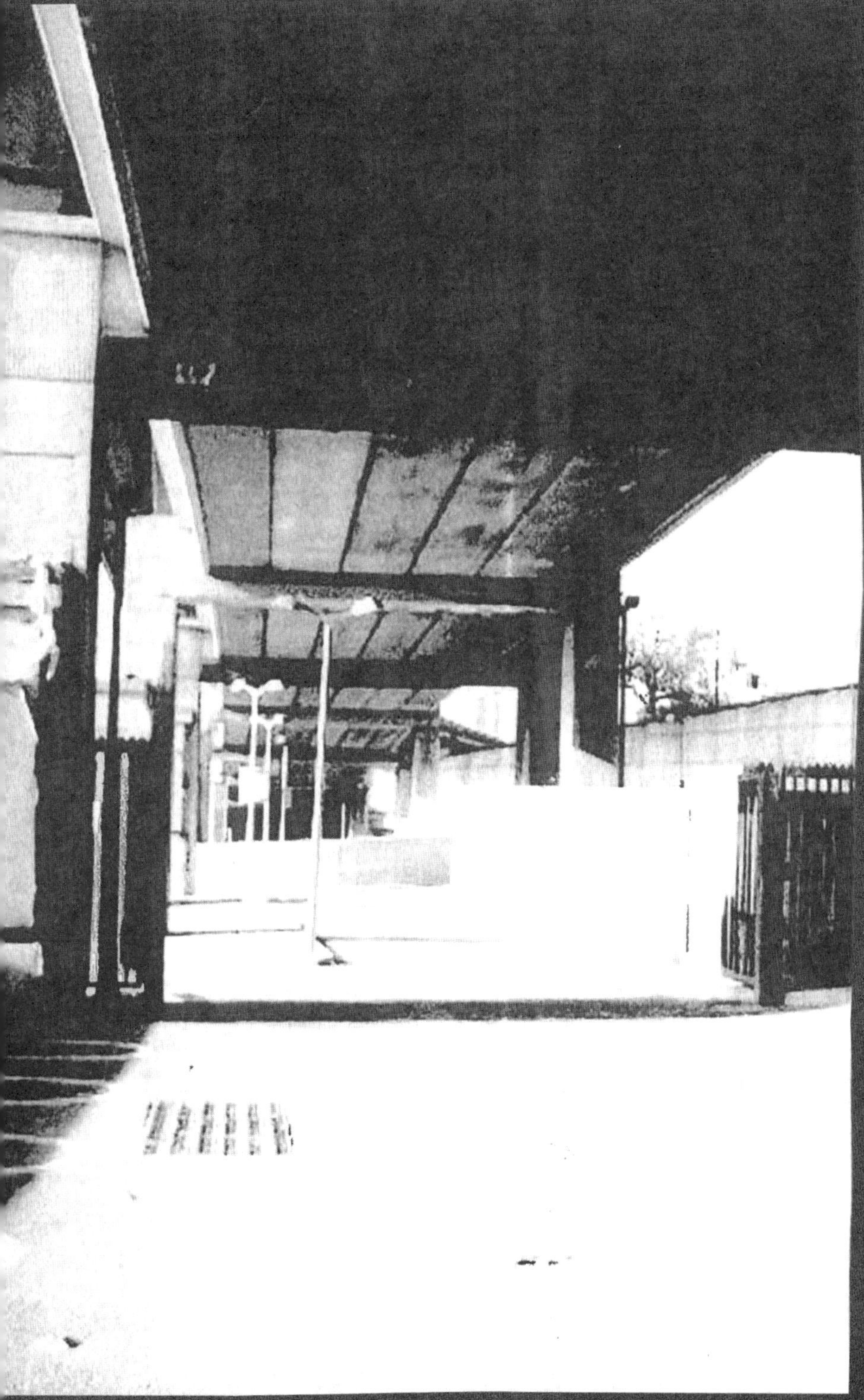

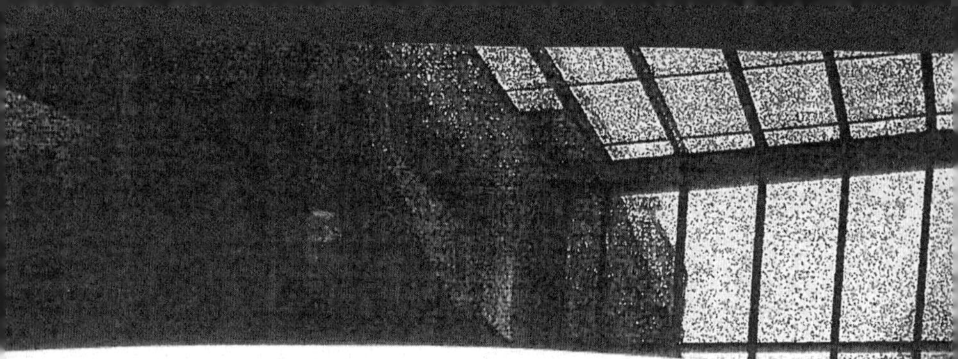

Corrugated iron seems incongruous now, a vestige
of the time before, residual and stubborn. The
fence is dinted, I push through a gap. A scent,
like nectarines, the sweet fragrance of blossom.
I don't remember it from my walks with him. He'd
have known about it, we drifted miles in search of
places like this, empty yards, abandoned
factories, wild places we could occupy. I'm
intoxicated by fragrant canopies of delicate pink.
Finding the orchard feels miraculous, I luxuriate
in the green scents of apple, the sugary notes of
plum and damson. There are little paths running
through, disrupted and overgrown but still
visible. I wonder who else knows about it, it
can't have gone unnoticed.
There's no one else around, for a second I think
I've wandered too far, that I might not be able to
get back. I know immeditely he must have felt
something like this. I've been having dreams,
vivid and persistent where he he tells me it's all
been a mistake, that he should never have crossed
over. His spirit is here, residing in the
terrain. I just have to channel it, find a way to
embody it. There are soft points, thresholds, ways
back in.

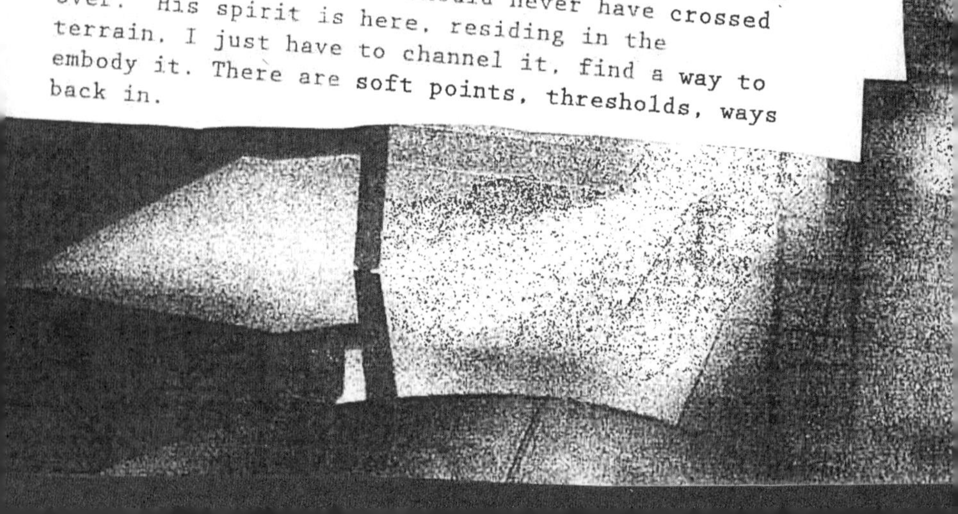

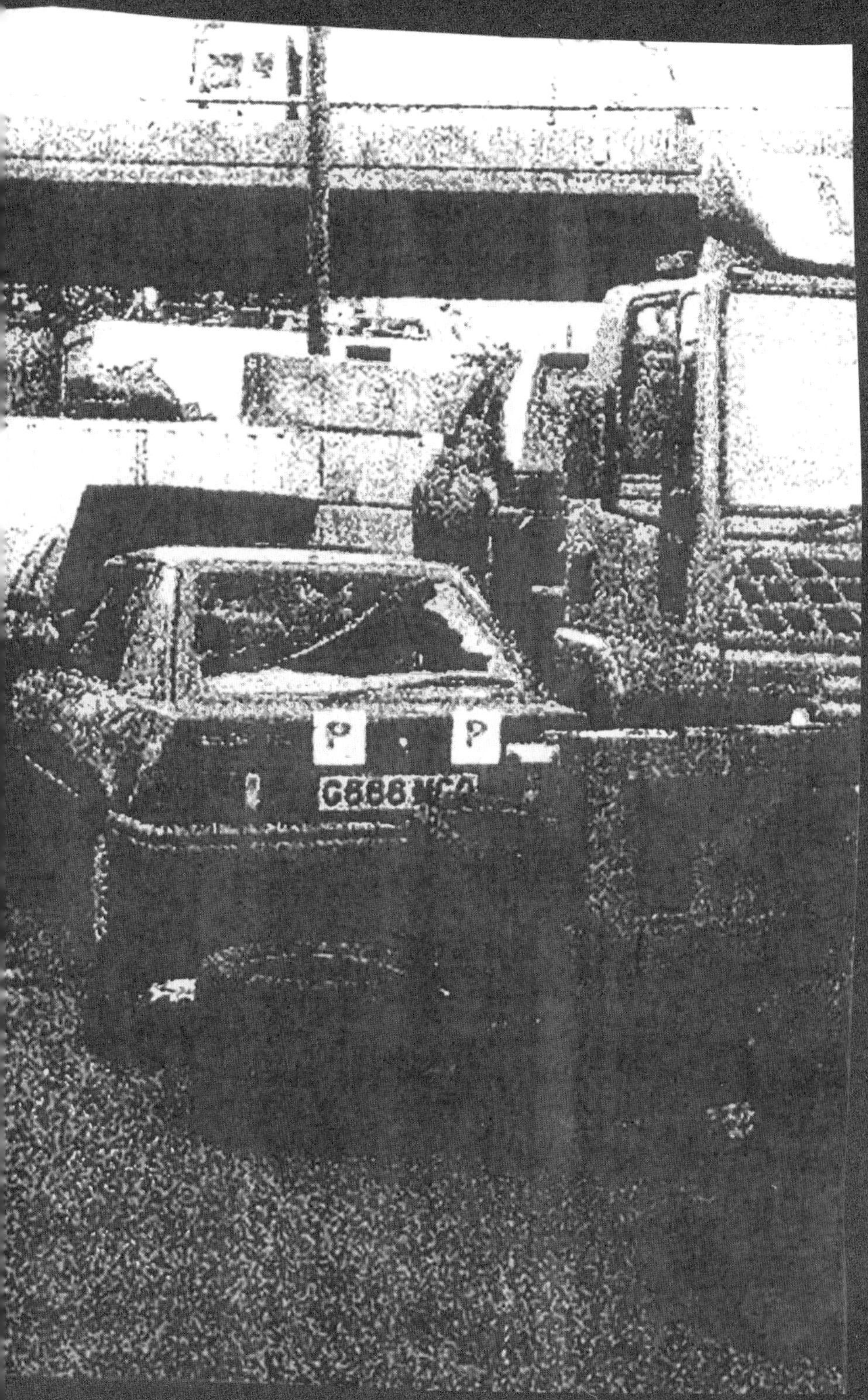
P
P

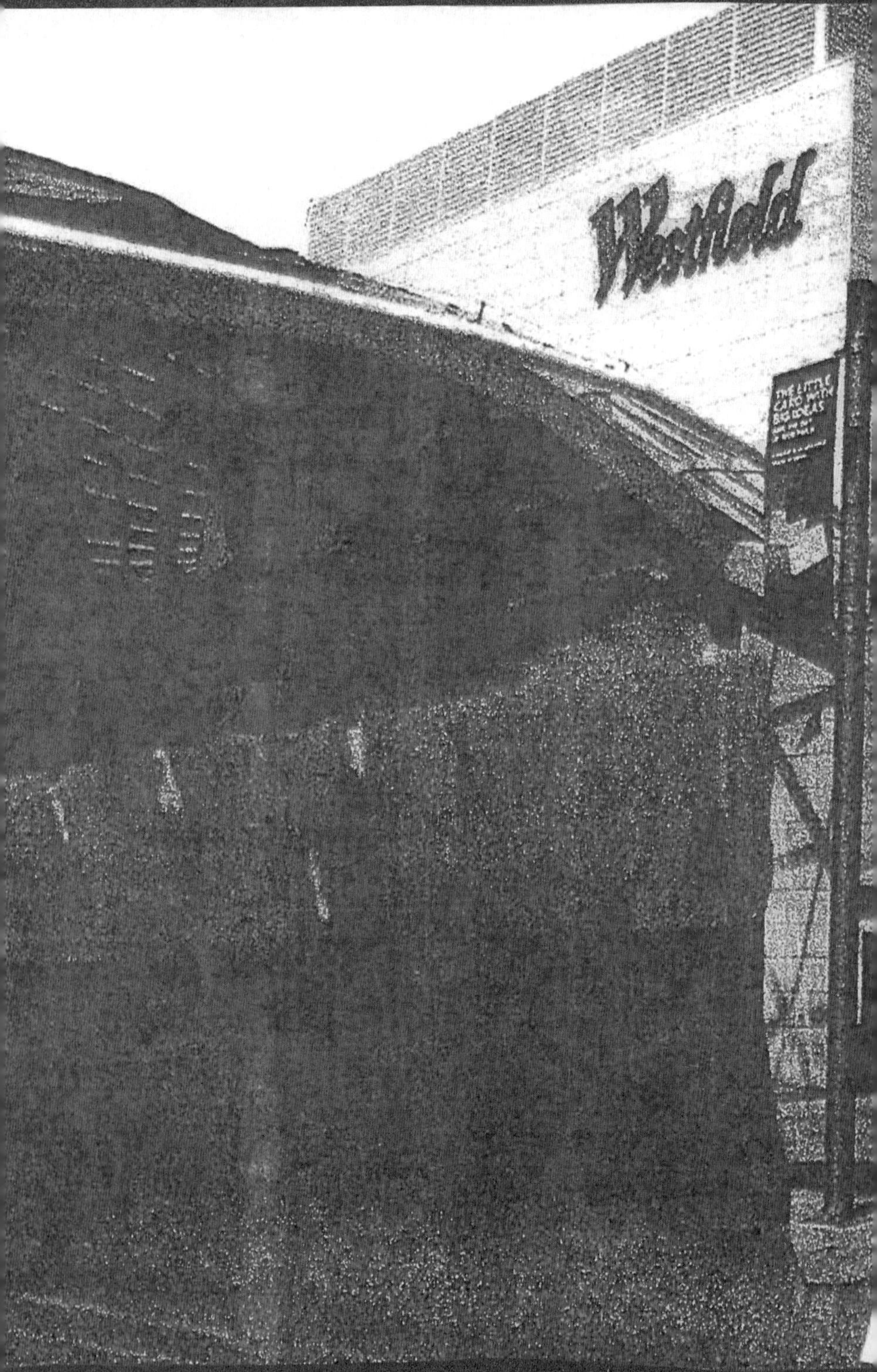
Westfield
THE LITTLE CARD WITH BIG IDEAS

I push through the tilting scrum of a collapsing
wall. A dilapidated terrace, gardens without
edges, brick enclosures growing into each other.
Fosithia and redcurrant, tangles of briars.

I realise now that the houses are occupied. There
are washing lines, clothes drying in the sun. A
bonfire, figures sitting around it. I step back,
listen hard, try to glean fragments of
conversation. There's an echo, something uncanny in
the way they mumble. They've got a cassette
player, a mix-tape, cuts and jumps between tracks.
The light feels different, metallic and searing, I
realise it's reflecting off the Westfield shopping
centre.

It's still there, the graffiti, the rusting
corrugated iron. I try to decipher the words,
traces of white paint embedded like code-

*A Class War is being waged, but only one side is
fighting. Choose your weapons, choose your sides.*

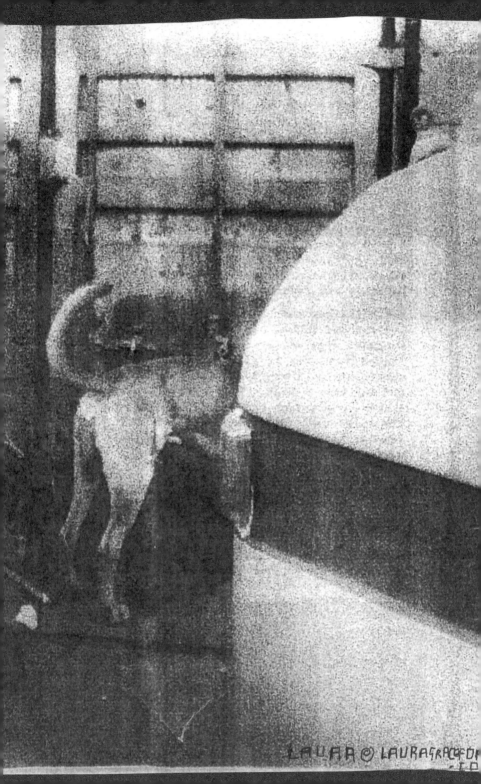

LAUAR © LAURAGRACEOR
I.D